D0872454

MISDEFENDING
THE REALM

How MI5's Incompetence Enabled Communist
Subversion of Britain's Institutions during the
Nazi-Soviet Pact

MISDEFENDING THE REALM

How MI5's Incompetence Enabled Communist Subversion of Britain's Institutions during the Nazi-Soviet Pact

by Antony Percy

The University of Buckingham Press

NEW HANOVER COUNTY
PUBLIC LIBRARY
201 CHESTNUT STREET
WILMINGTON, NC 28401

First published in Great Britain in 2017

The University of Buckingham Press
Yeomanry House
Hunter Street
Buckingham MK18 1EG

© Antony Percy

The moral right of the author has been asserted.

All rights reserved. No part of this publication may be reproduced, stored or introduced into a retrieval system or transmitted in any form or by any means without the prior permission of the publisher nor may be circulated in any form of binding or cover other than the one in which it is published and without a similar condition including this condition being imposed on the subsequent purchaser.

A CIP catalogue record for this book is available at the British Library

ISBN 978-1-908684-96-7

" Which are we, Carruthers—workers, peasants or intellectuals ? "

This work is dedicated to my parents, Freddie (1911-2006) and Mollie (1916-2011), who sadly did not survive to see me undertake the project, but who would have been its most enthusiastic supporters.

Contents

List of Illustrations

Acknowledgments i

Foreword.. iii

Preface v

Chapter 1: Historical Background 1

Chapter 2: Missing Links.. 15

Chapter 3: The Krivitsky Affair.. 48

Chapter 4: The Moscow Plot – Political Intrigue 81

Chapter 5: The Moscow Plot – Counter-Attack................................ 113

Chapter 6: Agents of Influence 136

Chapter 7: MI5 Under Stress 169

Chapter 8: Confusion – Fuchs, the Refugee 204

Chapter 9: Deception – Fuchs, the Spy... 240

Chapter 10: MI5 and the Defence of Democracy 271

Appendix: Affinity Charts 293

Biographical Index.. 296

Sources and Bibliography... 321

Index 337

List of Illustrations

Frontispiece: Osbert Lancaster: 'Which are we?' (*Daily Express* 1941)
Plate 1: Osbert Lancaster: 'Strictly neutral' (*Daily Express* 1940)
Plate 2: Osbert Lancaster: 'Suspicion' (*Daily Express* 1941)
Plate 3: Osbert Lancaster: 'Ex-service men?' (*Daily Express* 1940)
Plate 4: Osbert Lancaster: 'Anybody from MI5' (*Daily Express* 1940)
Plate 5: Osbert Lancaster: 'Careless talk' (*Daily Express* 1943)
Plate 6: Osbert Lancaster: 'MCC' (*Daily Express* 1940)
Plate 7: Osbert Lancaster: 'Pull him' (*Daily Express* 1940)
Plate 8: Osbert Lancaster: 'It's a fine state' (*Daily Express* 1949)
Plate 9: Isaiah Berlin: Cecil Beaton Archive
Plate 10: Guy Burgess: (BBC)
Plate 11: Kim Philby: (NPR)
Plate 12: Klaus Fuchs: (Christ Church Matters)
Plate 13: Rudolf Peierls
Plate 14: Ursula Beurton
Plate 15: Guy Liddell
Plate 16: Lord Rothschild
Plate 17: Dick White
Plate 18: Jane Archer
Plate 19: Lord Halifax and Maxim Litvinov
Plate 20: Walter Krivitsky
Plate 21: David Langdon: 'Secret Agent' (*Punch* November 1940)
Plate 22: L Burcaill: 'Where's your Permit?' (*Punch* December 1940)
Plate 23: Paul Crum: 'Foreign-Looking Fellow' (*Punch* April 1940)
Plate 24: Pont: 'Hush-hush' (*Punch* November 1940)
Plate 25: Anton: 'You'll have to learn German (*Punch* April 1940)
Plate 26: Anton: 'Well it's no longer hush-hush' (*Punch* March 1945)
Plate 27: Bernard Partridge: 'The Two Constrictors' (*Punch* November 1939)
End page: Osbert Lancaster: 'June 23rd' (*Daily Express* 1941)

All Punch cartoons are Copyright © Punch Limited: Punch Cartoon Library
All Osbert Lancaster cartoons are © *Daily Express*
Osbert Lancaster (1908-1986) was the pioneer of the pocket cartoon, his first example appearing in the *Daily Express* in 1939. He skillfully lampooned authority figures during World War II, but never maliciously, and his insights into the ironies and absurdities with which the war was sometimes engaged brought entertaining relief to persons in all walks of life.

For other illustrations every effort has been made to trace and acknowledge ownership.

Acknowledgments

I should like to thank my supervisor at the University of Buckingham, Professor Anthony Glees, for his constant encouragement, for the deep provocative discussions he engaged in with me, and for his insightful guidance on the underlying argument of the thesis that fostered this book. He tried to keep me focused when my natural curiosity tempted me to follow any number of attractive leads. I am also grateful to Sir Anthony Seldon and Professor Christopher Coker for their insightful remarks when acting as examiners for my thesis. I also thank my brother, Michael, for performing occasional research on my behalf at the National Archives at Kew when documents I needed to see were not available for acquisition and downloading to North Carolina.

I am very grateful to Simon Albert, Jill Bennett, Arie Dubnov, Geoffrey Elliott, Gary Kern, Nicola Lacey, Andrew Lownie, Steve Miner, Clare Mulley, Verne Newton, Nicholas Pronay, Jennifer Rees, Andrew Roberts, Arieh Saposnik, Matthew Spender, John Sutherland, Karina Urbach, Boris Volodarsky, Nigel West, Mary-Kay Wilmers, and Jim Wilson, for responding to my emailed inquiries. I am especially grateful to Henry Hardy, Isaiah Berlin's primary editor and amanuensis, for his help in identifying sources and in providing me with unpublished material on Berlin: his co-editors, Jennifer Holmes and Mark Pottle, have also provided much assistance. I shall not name the few historians and authors who declined to answer (or even acknowledge) my emailed inquiries.

The archivists at the institutions that I have been able to visit were uniformly positive and helpful, namely those responsible for the National Archives at Kew, the Isaiah Berlin Collection and the papers of Sir Joseph Ball and Sir Patrick Reilly at the Bodleian Library, Oxford, the Harold Nicolson Archive at Balliol College, Oxford, and the Cadogan Papers at Churchill College, Cambridge. I thank them, too.

My editor, Christopher Woodhead, at Buckingham University Press, has been a patient and amiable guide through the process of producing this book. We have co-operated on a challenging editing exercise, and I thank him most sincerely. Any errors in the text (or in the Biographical Index, or in the main Index, which are both my handiwork) are my responsibility. I should be grateful if readers could bring any mistakes they find to my attention, by contacting me at antonypercy@aol.com. They may also inspect related aspects of my research at www.coldspur.com.

Lastly, I should like to thank my wife, Sylvia, for her patience throughout this project. She has rightly concluded that I am not actually a spy, but merely an analyst of espionage.

i

Foreword

The research activity that spawned this book was provoked when I opened the first volume of Isaiah Berlin's *Letters*, and noticed that it was dedicated to an infamous Soviet spy, Jenifer Hart. This apparent intimacy between, on the one hand, a reputedly great defender of Western liberalism and, on the other, a subversive academic wedded to the notion of destroying the same liberalism on Stalin's behalf, led me on a wide-ranging research project. The exploration focused initially on Berlin's bizarre relationship with the Soviet spy, Guy Burgess, and their planned mission to Moscow in 1940, and then expanded to inspect the defection of Walter Krivitsky, including MI5's rather irregular policies and practices at that time, up to the Service's deplorable attempt to cover up the events leading to the trial of Klaus Fuchs.

As the book's title declares, the focus of my research has very much been on the challenge to Britain's security represented by the activities of Stalin's intelligence services in the period between the signing of the Nazi-Soviet Pact at the end of August, 1939, and the date when Nazi Germany turned against its ally and invaded the Soviet Union, on June 22, 1941. Those dates are crucial because Great Britain was during that time at war with Germany, yet the Soviet Union was a conspirator and partner of intelligence exchange with the enemy, as well as a supplier of war materiel to it. Any sympathy or commitment to the Communist cause should, I believe, have been tested with utmost stringency. And that appeared not to be the case.

I have strayed from the strict confines of that period a) to provide some historical background as to how MI5 arrived at its position at the outbreak of war, and b) to offer some insight as to how officers in MI5 tried, in 1950 and 1951, to re-write the chronicle of the atom spy's, Klaus Fuchs's, recruitment and treachery, during the time under review. It has not been my intent to second-guess the decisions made at a difficult time with the hindsight of knowledge gained after Fuchs's confession and trial. The case of Fuchs also provoked an urgent reconsideration of MI5's vetting techniques, a subject that is beyond the scope of this book.

I have tried to be strict in identifying the nations involved as [Great] Britain (not 'England', although the term should strictly be 'The United Kingdom'), the Soviet Union (not 'Russia', which has a very different connotation and significance), and the United States [of America], (although 'America' is a less contentious usage in places). Not all the sources I cite have adopted the same discipline. As for the nominal (and frequently confusing) changes in the Soviet Union's primary intelligence organisation, I have tried to adhere to the main changes that occurred (OGPU from 1934 to 1941, NKVD from 1941 to 1946, MGB from 1946 to 1954, and KGB from 1954), even though that sequence is a slight simplification and distortion of what actually occurred. I have consistently referred to the Soviet Union's military intelligence organisation as the GRU. As for the orthography of Russian and other Eastern European names (e.g. Kapitza), I have chosen the most popular spellings, and some sources may differ (e.g. Kapitsa) in some situations. I have preferred the use of SIS to MI6 to describe MI5's sister service, since the former is used by the authorised historian of MI5. Overall, I use the formulation 'Communist' to describe members and policies of the Communist Party, and 'communist' to define persons and attitudes sympathetic to the ideology without such an official affiliation, although in some passages the context may be ambiguous. Similarly, I use 'Fascist' to describe the Nazi government and its doctrines, and 'fascist' as a generic term for other statist, corporatist, nationalist creeds that shared its principles but may not have approached the barbarity of the German variety.

Preface

"In so far as an historian accepts the testimony of an authority and treats it as historical truth, he obviously forfeits the name of historian; but we have no other name by which to call him." (R. G. Collingwood)

"The good historian and the fictional detective think alike." (Fred Inglis)

"While memoirs are a valuable source of information, historians know that, in relying on them, one must keep in mind such problems as poor memory, errors about details, embellishments, self-service, sensationalism, and outright deception." (John Earl Haynes, Harvey Klehr, and Alexander Vassiliev)

This book is based on a thesis submitted for the Degree of Doctor of Philosophy to the School of Security and Intelligence Studies at the University of Buckingham in the spring of 2016. The title of the thesis is *Confronting Stalin's 'Elite Force': MI5's Handling of Communist Subversion, 1939-1941*. It was successfully defended in August 2016, and the degree was awarded the following month.

The book focuses on an enigmatic and frequently misunderstood subject in Britain's intelligence history – the conflicting challenges that MI5 faced at the beginning of the Second World War, and its apparent lethargy in countering Soviet espionage when that country was an ally of Nazi Germany. It concentrates primarily on the series of events between the announcement of the Nazi-Soviet Pact (in August 1939), which halted any attempts by the British government to form an alliance with the Soviet Union, and Operation Barbarossa, Germany's invasion of the Soviet Union (in June 1941), which immediately inspired Prime Minister Churchill to come to the aid of his previous ideological foe to wage war against Nazi Germany. It extends its attention to the arrest and trial of the Soviet spy Klaus Fuchs in 1950, since the critical events of his recruitment by the British authorities, and the initiation of his treachery, took place within the period under the microscope.

Yet, while a few historical studies have analysed aspects of the dilemmas that MI5 encountered in that critical period, as it tried to identify, assess, and counter the threats from its totalitarian adversaries, none has fully exploited the opportunity that the release of documents to the National Archives, over the past fifteen years, has offered. None has suitably set the deliberations that consumed MI5 in 1939 and 1940 in a realistic context of military strategy or contemporary politics, nor have any studies balanced the authorised histories of intelligence with a critical analysis of the wealth of personal memoir that has been published over a similar period. Historians have conventionally trusted too much the statements and memoirs of those who were actual spies (most prominently Philby, Burgess, Blunt, Spender and Cairncross), of those who abetted them (e.g. Berlin and Rothschild), and of those who were negligent in surveilling and prosecuting them (namely Liddell and White). Thus many problematic questions of security exposures during this period, such as the ability of deeply placed Soviet agents to penetrate or frustrate the British intelligence network, have been left unanswered.

This field of study is inherently very complex and opaque, because the archival record is incomplete, occasionally deceptive, and sometimes contradictory. The memoirs and testimony of participants are frequently self-serving, and thus need to be processed with equal caution. The author decided that a fresh methodological approach was required. The methodology adopted conventionally exploits the official archival material (including the latest releases of September 2015), but complements a detailed study of such records with the integration of information from a broad set of secondary sources. While this approach provides a richer historical background than traditional techniques have offered, it also sheds fresh light by subjecting existing accounts of the period to a rigorous cross-checking of sources, and reflects a highly disciplined concern for chronology.

An approach to historical analysis has been used which could be called 'Collingwoodian', namely a methodology that treats the drama as the scene of a possible crime, and attempts to go beyond the dry collection and re-statement of facts to apply some psychological testing to the evidence of the participants. The historian and philosopher R. G. Collingwood described this approach in his 1946 book, *The Idea of History*, where he distinguished sound history-writing from both the 'scissors-and-paste' style, where undue attention is paid to the memories of participants, as well as from fiction, which has its own version of truth, but not a historical one. As an illustration of this idea, he wrote: "The principles by which this evidence is interpreted change too; since the interpreting of evidence is a task to which a man must bring everything he knows: historical knowledge, knowledge of nature and man, mathematical knowledge, philosophical knowledge; and not knowledge only, but mental habits and possession of every kind; and none of these is unchanging." [1] Such a methodology requires imagination, but not invention.

The world of intelligence is a notoriously difficult domain to chart with accuracy, since secrecy and subterfuge are intrinsic characteristics of its operation. It is thus perhaps desirable to step back and consider the role that deception plays in the business of intelligence, and in its record-keeping. The assumption is made here that the practice of intelligence and counter-intelligence necessarily involves much dissimulation and distortion, while the accountability of the security services, and their internal record-keeping, should obey practised norms of democratic processes and professional integrity, so that informed historical analysis can be performed.

Given the need for clandestineness, the Official Secrets Act (OSA) is acknowledged as playing a vital role in keeping information, processes, documents, etc. confidential and protected. Espionage and undercover work require a measure of subterfuge, such as the 'legends' created by the Comintern for the illegals operating in the United Kingdom, or the dissimulation undertaken by MI5's agents to penetrate the Communist Party. In the field of international diplomacy, it may be necessary to misrepresent the truth, as, for example, did the

British government in World War II when concealing from its ally, the Soviet Union, the source of intelligence on German battle orders gained from 'Ultra' decrypts.

When it comes to procedures and communications within the security services, however, respect for honesty should be paramount. We should expect that truthfulness should be followed in internal communications between intelligence officers, and that straightforwardness and honesty should be the watchwords when the security services report to their political masters (at the time of World War II, a single minister, now to Parliament). When time-dependent moratoria on the classification of archival materials are lifted, we should expect full disclosure, as attention will otherwise be drawn to the fact that certain documents are still withheld, or that some files are heavily redacted. When intelligence officers are freed from their OSA obligations, and write their memoirs, or are interviewed by their biographers, we should expect a high degree of professionalism and integrity in such accounts, and that the OSA should be applied consistently. If such standards are not met, the public may begin to lose trust in the agencies chartered with protecting it, and speculation about the reasons for the withholding of information will justifiably arise.

Yet an analysis of the official documents, and the exploration of personal testimony when official documents are not available, frequently show up series of contradictions and anomalies that call for a fresher approach to developing hypotheses for hitherto unexplained events. Files concerning possible espionage by a suspect (Rudolf Peierls), or that may contain details about long dead colleagues of miscreants that could be judged as embarrassing to surviving relatives (in the case of Guy Burgess), are withheld long after the subject is dead, and normal expiration dates have passed. Names are redacted in official records, such as those of Victor Rothschild, scientist and intelligence officer, and of Hans Halban, an Austrian atomic scientist with Communist associates in France. Deception is shown to exist in official reports, such as in the account of Fuchs's treachery given by the post-war leader of MI5, Sir Percy Sillitoe, to Prime Minister Attlee. In the case of Soviet archives, cases of *spravki*[i] being inserted into a file to give false information are known to have occurred: the same process may also have happened in Britain.[2] In many cases, such as those the author has discovered in the voluminous archives on Klaus Fuchs, documents are posted that deliberately give a false impression of what happened, or testimony is re-written to help sanitise decisions made or not made, where only a rigorous cross-checking of events and memoranda can help identify conflicts.

Moreover, any number of personal memoirs can be shown – through a rigorous process of verification through the chronology, and cross-checking with other sources – to contain distortion or misrepresentation of the reality of events. For example, when information about lapses in security has come to the public eye, such as that concerning the absconding of Burgess and Maclean, or in the *Spycatcher* affair, many individuals with a reputation to lose have been keen to define their legacy (and in this case the offenders are almost exclusively male) in a way that cannot be easily refuted. Distortions and untruths have thus become

---

[i] From Russian *spravka*, a note.

part of the grammar of memoir. The reasons for such deception are several: the desire to protect one's own personal reputation in the light of past misjudgment; the perceived necessity of protecting the reputation of some authoritative and influential figure, or even the security institution itself; even a concern about national security, for the purpose of protecting relationships with other nations, or maintaining secrecy about practices considered vital for future counter-intelligence action.

A Collingwoodian methodology thus has to take a much broader, catholic approach to the analysis of informational conflict. In the face of contradictory information, for instance, when documentary proof may never become available, the method analyses the professional situation and probable motivations of many of the actors (e.g. the possible dissembling of Walter Krivitsky, the Soviet defector; the historical distancing of themselves, by all British diplomats, politicians and intelligence officers, from any close association with the spy Guy Burgess) in order to present a more convincing hypothesis of what actually happened. Yet it does not indulge in unjustified speculation. For example, while accepting that multiple hypotheses have been suggested about treasonable activities deep within MI5 – most notably, the existence of a 'super-mole' orchestrating treasonous activities, and the betrayal of secrets to the Soviets – the book does not look for evidence to support any individual claim, but strictly treats what evidence comes to light on its own merits. Even though this topic has been elevated by competing claims by journalists and historians about the super-mole's identity, this author is professionally cautious. He recognises that, while there may have been such a prominent spy known to Moscow Centre (in fact, military intelligence, the GRU), as 'ELLI', his or her identity may never be known. Since no solid evidence on the identity of such a person has come to light, the question, however topical and engaging, necessarily has to be bypassed. The book thus treats with circumspection all theories of the presence of such a character – and thus of the culpability for MI5's negligence ultimately resting with a lone person working for Soviet Intelligence. In contrast, it will make the case that a well-intentioned but disastrous sympathy for Communism, not directly engineered by the Comintern, that emerged in MI5 during the late 1930s was enough to destroy its effectiveness.

Key to the whole Collingwoodian notion, therefore, is the detection of untruths from archival records and from witnesses. Attempting to understand the context in which the lie, of whatever nature (omission, deception, fabrication), is made, and its probable motivation, is a critical part of the methodology.

The methodology can be summed up by the following steps:

1) Immersion in the period in question, without moving too closely to any of the actors, and thus losing objectivity;
2) Deep reading of the primary subject, but with exploration vertically (to give, for example, military and political context), and horizontally (to enhance the study of ideological dynamics through a background of contemporary arts and science);
3) The absorption of contemporary evidence (e.g. archives, diaries, letters, memoranda, news reports) for a perspective of immediacy;

4) The construction of a detailed chronology of events and actors, with sources, in order to define sequentiality, inspect conflicting versions of events, and identify possible contradictions;

5) The acquisition of knowledge of the detailed biographies of key actors, to reveal important aspects of their lives (career, associations, friendships, etc.), carefully considering timing and psychology at the time of events, as well as when memoirs are written;

6) The development of affinity charts of key actors to highlight relationships, and to identify hitherto undocumented ones;

7) The assessment of the relevance of peripheral observations from minor players (who are more likely than prominent players not to have any ulterior motives);

8) The review of testimony from major actors with a view to reliability of evidence, classifying them according to the nature of their truthfulness (should any contradictions or untruths be revealed by other evidence), and providing evidence for judgments on their reliability or lack of credibility;

9) The development of new hypotheses for unexplained events, bringing new information to the careful assessment of existing hypotheses, replacing them or enhancing them as the evidence suggests.

This book uses this methodology to present an alarming hypothesis about the corrosion of defence mechanisms against Communist subversion during the later 1930s and the first years of the war. It will not constitute the last word. The research process will continue. The hope is expressed here that other historians, with access to other sources, will pick up the threads of this argument, and extend it, improve it – even demolish parts of it – in an attempt to discern what the truth was behind the very puzzling events of 1940.

Notes

[1] R. G. Collingwood, *The Idea of History*, p 248.
[2] In *17 Carnations*, his study of King Edward VIII (later the Duke of Windsor), Andrew Morton reported that experts at the National Archives had confirmed that several forged documents concerning the Duke's alleged betrayal of military secrets to the Germans were placed in files deposited there (p 157).

Chapter 1: Historical Background

"Every time you sacrifice one of your potential allies to this pathetic desire to appease the tyrants, you merely bring nearer and make more inevitable that war which you pretend you are trying to avoid." (Josiah Wedgwood)

"The differences which . . . existed between the Nazi and the Bolshevik systems were, in fact, no greater than those which separate Woolworths from Marks and Spencer. One of them is painted red." (Harold Nicolson)

"We English hate fascism, but we loathe bolshevism as much. So, if there is somewhere where fascists and bolshevists can kill each other off, so much the better." (Stanley Baldwin)

The subject of this book – the negligence of MI5 in its handling of the menace of communist subversion at the beginning of World War II – has its roots in an event that cast a permanent shadow over the twentieth century, the Bolshevik Revolution in Russia. Marxist doctrine had been converted into action by Vladimir Lenin, the émigré firebrand and demagogue, and a devout autocracy had been quickly turned into a bloody prison-camp, with the ruthless suppression or extermination of those held to be part of the old regime. The rallying slogan calling on the proletariats of every country to unite constituted a dire warning to the elites of the western democracies, demonised in Communist propaganda as 'capitalists' and 'imperialists' who would necessarily have to be destroyed.

The 1917 Revolution had come as a severe shock for the British government. Lenin had planned to export the proletarian dictatorship internationally, and had set up the Communist International (or Comintern) to execute that strategy. The Comintern's declared mission was to destroy the stronghold of 'the bourgeoisie' and 'imperialism' that Britain's place in the world represented. Britain's ministers and civil service leaders soon identified the nation's primary security goals as protecting the Empire against the subversive influences of communist doctrine. For Britain was assuredly 'imperialist': its political leaders regarded the interests of the country and the Empire as inseparable.

Their reasoning was well-established: they regarded Britain's prosperity as being largely dependent upon protected colonial markets, and the associated control of vital resources and shipping routes. Communism, through its ideological attack on imperialism, and on the dependent status of the colonies, presented an essential threat to such arrangements. It also represented a potential menace to the British way of life, which was the cultural lifeblood of the Empire. Communism was a totalitarian system of government dominated by one ruling ideology and party, committed to extremist notions of class warfare, and deploying no division of powers. It required government control of industry and

1

the media, all accompanied by harsh punishment for dissenters subject to laws enacted by edict, or even to arbitrary sentencing without trial. If communism spread to Britain, its ruling class would be faced with the same fate that befell the tsarist system.

Although Britain's governing class did not accept the inevitability of a proletarian dictatorship, as predicted by Marx, it considered that any domestic actions to facilitate this socio-economic upheaval needed to be closely monitored and stifled. Within two years, in 1919, the British War Cabinet had set up a committee of the recently established Secret Service Bureau[i] to investigate how the country's civil intelligence should be strengthened to face this new threat of Communist subversion. The committee decided that the authority for the new Directorate of Intelligence should reside with the Special Branch of the Metropolitan Police, while MI5 (which had been created in December 1915 as an offshoot of Military Intelligence) would remain in charge of monitoring subversion in the armed forces. Nevertheless, during the next decade, the Special Branch, MI5, and the Secret Intelligence Service (SIS or MI6) had frequent disagreements about control of the intelligence machinery, and the Secret Service Committee remained in operation to oversee the three organisations.

From the perspective of the British government, the fortunes and reputation of the Soviet Union blew hot and cold after this time, but the threat of subversion remained very real. Britain's coalition government had attempted – but failed – to help strangle the emergent Soviet Union at its birth. In 1924, professing some ideological sympathy with the communist cause, the first Labour administration had decided to recognise the new state. The Labour Party was nevertheless resolutely opposed to extra-parliamentary means of implementing change, as espoused by the restive foundling on its doorstep, the Communist Party of Great Britain (CPGB). Even though the CPGB appeared to exert less direct political influence than had been feared at first, it turned out to be a corrosive factor in the unions and the armed forces, where it represented a constant threat for disruption and even mutiny. The discovery of espionage taking place under cover of the Soviet trade organisation, ARCOS, in 1927, highlighted the menace of subversion, and prompted Britain to break off diplomatic relations with the Soviet Union.

Further evidence of subversion surfaced in 1928, when a communist network was shown to have infiltrated the Special Branch of the Metropolitan Police itself. MI5 and SIS collaborated in tracking the movements of the network leader, William Ewer, who was paying his contacts with money supplied by the CPGB. Perhaps chastened by its experience of the ARCOS trial, at which testimony betrayed the fact that the Government Code and Cypher School (GC&CS) must have broken Soviet ciphers, the Attorney General decided not to prosecute the Special Branch officers who had revealed information on surveillance activity to their Communist suborners. Moreover, despite the measure of co-operation exercised during this case, both Special Branch and MI5 complained at this time about the incursions of SIS onto their mainland territory.

---

[i] The Bureau was a temporary structure set up by the Sub-Committee of Imperial Defence. See Christopher Moran's *Classified: Secrecy and the State in Modern Britain*, p 44.

The Comintern, meanwhile, had increased its pressure on British institutions, taking advantage of a deteriorating economic environment. The symptoms of the financial depression that started in 1930 turned the political spotlight anew on the ability of a market economy to sustain a high level of employment, and thus ensure a satisfied citizenry. Interest in the Soviet experiment, and the possible advantages of nationalisation of 'the means of production, distribution and exchange', [ii] increased. The voices of intellectuals and democratic socialists expressing doubts about the efficacy of private enterprise became louder. Early in 1930, MI5 reported on increased communist subversion in the armed forces, which came to a head in the Invergordon mutiny of September 1931. A more systematic approach for detecting subversion and espionage was needed. At the final meeting of the Secret Service Committee, later that year, MI5 was handed the exclusive task of managing the bolshevik threat within the United Kingdom, while SIS was directed to focus on its mission of gathering intelligence on foreign soil.

In 1929, MI5 had assigned responsibility for the surveillance of Soviet espionage to the first woman officer appointed in the organisation. The woman's name was Jane Sissmore, and her achievement represented a significant breakthrough both in British intelligence and in British professional life. (For more information on her career, see Chapter 2.) Sissmore's first significant contribution was recorded in 1935. In November of that year, she wrote a report on the Communist Party of Great Britain, stating that the department's mission should be to stay informed of 'activities, policy and mischievous potentialities of subsidiary bodies of the Comintern operating under the direction of the Communist Party of Great Britain'.[1] The spirit of the report, however, suggests that MI5, despite its alarming experience with Special Branch in 1931, had not yet internalised the threat of direct subversion of the intelligence services. Sissmore's analysis, signed off by Guy Liddell and Jasper Harker, her bosses, concentrated on members of the CPGB, and their ability to cause damage through subversion and sabotage. Yet by now, the twin arms of Soviet intelligence, the military organisation (GRU), and the state department (OGPU, which became the NKVD in 1934), had begun to apply fresh pressures, deploying new methods of subverting the Western democracies, with special attention on Britain. MI5 was unaware that the Soviet Union had recently started to recruit sympathetic high-fliers from Oxbridge, who were to be inserted into Britain's political and diplomatic ranks. The seriousness of the duel was increasing, yet the focus of MI5 was still on the Communist Party.

By the time of Sissmore's report, however, a new threat, couched in an alternative totalitarian ideology, had emerged. In 1933, Adolf Hitler had grabbed hold of power in Germany, with the objective of enforcing his ideology, and his territorial ambitions for a new German *Reich*, as set out in *Mein Kampf* (first

---

[ii] Clause IV of the Labour Party Constitution, adopted in 1918, ran as follows: "To secure for the workers by hand or by brain the full fruits of their industry and the most equitable distribution thereof that may be possible upon the basis of the common ownership of the means of production, distribution and exchange, and the best obtainable system of popular administration and control of each industry or service."

published in 1926). Now, unlike the doctrine of communism, Hitler's manichean message was not of the brotherhood of man, and of equality, but of nationalistic strength and racial superiority – with an avowed goal of expanding the Reich's borders into Eastern Europe and Russia. It was, however, equally totalitarian, and shared the same features of fully integrated control of society through government organs, and fierce repression of opponents, that were the emblems of Stalin's Russia. Thus, while the appeasing factions at the time (e.g. the majority of the Tory Party, royalty and the House of Lords, and the group known as the 'Cliveden set', which included the editor of the influential *Times* newspaper, Geoffrey Dawson) obviously did not recognise this threat, Germany also represented an existential menace to Britain. Hitler wanted to add colonial possessions, preferably re-acquiring territories conceded to Britain after World War I, and his increased warnings about uniting disparate ethnic Germans outside Germany's national borders threatened the balance of power in Europe. His claims about wanting a peaceful co-existence with the British Empire were trusted by too many: those who objected were accused of provocation – a trap into which even Stalin was later to fall. Yet what action should be taken was unclear. In the mind of those who had experienced it, the horrors of World War I resonated more strongly than the fears of German revanchism. And a specific German threat to the British Isles was not perceived by MI5 or SIS until Germany's re-occupation of the Rhineland in 1936, which caused the services to take fresh stock of their intelligence-gathering and surveillance processes.

The interplay of fascism and communism in the political and intellectual arenas of the 1930s posed considerable problems for Britain's intelligence services. Oswald Mosley founded his British Union of Fascists (BUF) in 1932, and the Home Office decided, in November 1933, that it should up its response, and that MI5's policy towards Fascists should mimic its treatment of Communists. In 1935, the Comintern developed a 'Popular Front' campaign that undermined the old class warfare slogans with a message of unison against fascism. As the thirties progressed, the traditional horror of bolshevism was reinforced in some quarters by news of Stalin's slave camps, show trials, and purges; others claimed the oppression was overstated, or even justified. In 1936, the apparent righteousness of the Republican cause in the Spanish Civil War tilted much of public opinion against the naked aggression of fascism, while Stalin's equally vicious organs were able to operate more furtively in support of the Republican government. The Nazis followed up their domestic oppression of leftists and Jews by incorporating Austria under force (in March 1938), and then by annexing the Sudetenland region of Czechoslovakia (in September). As the threat of European-wide war became more likely, countries struggled to determine who their enduring adversaries and allies were. And while Britain represented a beacon of freedom, it also became a haven for a heterogeneous set of refugees. Such visitors were initially welcomed in the cause of humanity, but they were still 'aliens', and thus inherently suspicious. In the eyes of the Home Office, they might well have been fleeing from Hitler's persecutions, but could also have been concealing their Communist sympathies from the domestic authorities. Was Britain's liberal policy of allowing asylum-seekers into the country increasing the potential success of subversion and potential insurrection, and thus making its task more difficult?

Opinion in Great Britain was sharply divided over how the country should react to these twin totalitarian threats, apparently ideologically opposed, but similar in methodology. Some of the populace regarded bolshevism as the eternal enemy, and were thus prepared to make accommodations with Hitler despite their distaste for Nazi Fascism, a point of view that dominated Chamberlain's administration, and especially the Foreign Office. Others, including most members of the Labour Party and intellectual fellow-travellers, inspired by Stalin's 'anti-fascist' clarion call, and maybe regarding the goals of communism as more healthy and honourable than those expressed in *Mein Kampf*, were ready to overlook the inherent horror of Stalin's dictatorship, believing that only communism was strong enough to fight fascism. Another set of more high-minded pacifist voices, perhaps taking their cue from Church of England clerics, remembered the carnage of WWI, and placed their hopes in the League of Nations and the idea of 'collective security' spawned at Versailles, calling for worldwide disarmament. There was also a fourth group of independent pragmatists, embodied by such as Churchill and Sir Robert Vansittart (Permanent Under-Secretary of State for Foreign Affairs), which could be said to constitute those who believed that all forms of totalitarianism had to be resisted more urgently, and looked for greater determination and muscle in re-arming the country to fight it. Such a divergence of views was the price of living in – and governing – a pluralist democracy, and politicians had to deal with the realities. While the totalitarian regimes became bolder and more oppressive, Britain's decision-making on security was characterised by further rounds of sub-committees, working-parties, memoranda, and submissions, and negotiations between different government departments. Due attention had to be paid to such topics as the constitutional role of MI5, while the Home Office's reinforcement of the principle that arrests should not be made purely on the basis of suspicion, and that popular opinion, and the morale of the workers in the factories, all had to be taken into consideration when more stringent measures against subversion and espionage were being evaluated, caused dithering and delay. Britain's peacetime values of tolerance and pluralistic debate were a liability in times of crisis.

MI5 was perhaps too complacent about the threat of Nazi subversion. Its officers may have been fed with the assertion that the Treaty of Versailles had forbidden Germany to develop an espionage service.[2] However ambiguous such a ban was, Hitler blithely chose to ignore such proscriptions, concluding, quite correctly, that 'collective security' was a paper tiger. An active Nazi organisation for propaganda and intelligence-gathering was accordingly working in Britain by the mid-1930s. The aims of German intelligence were quite straightforward. It tried to encourage the Chamberlainite policy of appeasement, to drive home to opinion-leaders the perils of bolshevism, and to bolster the native fascist movement. It sought also to determine what plans and actions Britain might be pursuing towards an alliance with Germany's eastern adversary, the Soviet Union. It exploited the disaffection with British rule of provincial groups (especially the Irish), and sought out agents in such territories. Yet its efforts betrayed no mission-critical agenda, and were blatantly obvious, such as in Hitler's wooing of

Lord Rothermere and the future King Edward VIII. As the historian Max Hastings has written: "Hitler never wished to use intelligence as a planning or policy-making tool. He recognised its utility only at a tactical level: the Nazis were strikingly incurious about Abroad."[3]

The dangers for Britain were that, if Hitler were able to keep Britain subdued, he would be free to execute his plans on his eastern borders first, gaining valuable resources for his war machine, before turning his brutal attentions to the UK, and trying to dismantle the British Empire. Elsewhere (e.g. in Czechoslovakia in 1938, and later in Poland, in 1939) Germany had been able to facilitate its invasion by use of a 'Fifth Column' of operatives in contact with military command, and to exploit the presence of native sympathisers who could assist in the takeover of political control. Despite the existence of the British Union of Fascists, it was not until after Chamberlain's demise in May 1940 that a fear of such a force appeared intensely in the United Kingdom, with the arrest in London, of the American spy working for the Nazis, Tyler Kent. The collapse of Denmark and Norway that month brought a rapid insertion of the terms 'Fifth Column' and 'quisling' unto political debate.

On the other hand, the objectives of Soviet espionage were better concealed, more strategic, more subtle. While the Soviet Union hoped to increase direct political influence through the successes of the Communist Party, and stressed the attraction of a broad leftist political front to counter Nazism, it had long-term subversive goals, such as fomenting labour unrest via penetration of the unions, initiating mutiny and sabotage in the armed forces, and influencing intellectual opinion by nurturing academics and civil servants who were favourable towards Communism. In addition, it had a very aggressive strategy for acquiring technological and military secrets to compensate for its dismal creativity back home, and for infiltrating the corridors of power to discover who might be plotting an alliance with Hitler against it. It had developed its well-crafted strategy for identifying potential members of Britain's political elite who were sympathetic to the communist cause, and gaining their commitment before they had graduated from the universities of Oxford and Cambridge. Truly, a 'Red Menace' existed on Britain's hearth. The threat of Russia's being able to undermine British society for a smoother Communist takeover was always real, and yet the Home Office responded pusillanimously. Even the success of the Woolwich Arsenal convictions in 1937 (after the detection of a Communist ring led by Percy Glading) was muted, as prosecutors displayed a desire not to upset Stalin, a behaviour of appeasement that mimicked the accommodations made to Hitler.

Moreover, MI5 seemed to have ignored some obvious signals. The 1928 lesson of Ewer and the Special Branch had apparently been forgotten. MI5 failed to consider that the Soviet Union might have been planning to infiltrate the security services themselves, and it instead concentrated its efforts on members of the Communist Party and its public sympathisers. Since 1934, however, officers of the Soviet Union's intelligence departments, such as the highly capable cosmopolitans Walter Krivitsky (in the GRU) and Alexander Orlov (in the NKVD), had been scheming to insert 'illegals' in the western democracies, and have them recruit agents who were chartered with burrowing their way deep within the establishment. Britain was singled out as the most important of such targets. Having successfully camouflaged their Communist background, these moles (with one notable exception) managed to conceal their true affiliations as they gained entry to various diplomatic and intelligence structures. The notion that effective subversives might have carefully veiled their ideological loyalties did not seem to occur to the officers in MI5. So the Security Service remained in the dark.

The authorised and official histories suggest that efforts to counter Nazi espionage were far more resolute than those against the Soviet threat.[4] Before hostilities broke out, and in the first six months of the war, however, such initiatives did not always result in decisive action. It was admittedly easier for MI5 to identify probable sources of information leaks to the Nazis, while the surveillance of Communists and their allies evolved into an interminable process of 'keeping an eye on' suspected subversives, and rarely progressed to a more penetrating stage. Reasons for such differences in execution can be suggested. Germany was geographically closer, and was the traditional adversary: Vernon Kell (who headed MI5) and Churchill (who joined Chamberlain's wartime cabinet in 1939) had vivid memories of German espionage a generation earlier. Germany's borders were more open, British visitors continued to throng there, and its menace was frequently reported on. Hitler had declared his intentions publicly (even though few British politicians had read *Mein Kampf*): his overall objectives were very clear, and his supporters and sympathisers showed their affiliations openly.

The process of closer surveillance and internment was slow to be launched, however. While the term 'fellow-traveller' was rarely applied to Nazi sympathisers[5], MI5 had, in fact, successfully identified dozens of members of the *Auslands Organisation*, and wanted it banned. (The *Auslands* (Foreign) *Organisation* consisted of expatriate members of the Nazi Party, the *Nazionalsozialistische Deutsche Arbeiterpartei*. In some countries, non-Germans were allowed to join.) Sir Robert Vansittart, Permanent Under-Secretary at the Foreign Office, was another who made an urgent appeal for action against the organisation, but who was frustrated by pro-German sympathies in government. (His repeated criticism of appeasement in fact lost him his job.) Chamberlainite lackeys continued to deliver supportive messages to the emergent enemy. So, even though the appeasers disapproved of the more rabid aspects of Hitlerism, a strange kind of double-think emerged. At the start of the war, it was as if the government considered a British form of fascism relatively harmless, and that it would be unreasonable to assume that a home-grown variant could be unpatriotic, submit to the German variety of the ideology, and provide assistance to the enemy. Mosley was not interned until May 1940, when the assumed dangers of 'fifth columns', as evidenced by Germany's successes in Norway and Denmark, were highlighted by the media, picked up by the public, and internalised by the politicians. Any potential domestic help for Hitler's plans to undermine and subjugate Britain had then to be aggressively opposed.

On the other hand, the Soviet Union was remote, less accessible and visited almost solely by those who wanted to believe in the coming Utopia. While the Russian people had suffered, and an apparently horrible but necessary experiment was under way, the apparent goals of equality and 'social justice' pursued by Communism seemed to many to be more noble and humanitarian than the creed of racial superiority espoused by Hitler. Bolshevik revolution in Britain seemed a romantic notion, only a distant possibility, and intellectuals were frequently seduced by the more pacifist aspects of its message. For example, the influential liberal thinker Isaiah Berlin, fellow of All Souls, renowned later as a fierce critic of totalitarianism, and to be recruited as a key intelligence analyst by the British Embassy in the United States a few years later, heard in April 1936 that his friend Stephen Spender had joined the CPGB. He promptly agreed with Spender's assessment that it was a 'neo-liberal' organisation. This was an extraordinary 'appeasing' opinion, which Berlin was soon to revise. A few months later, perhaps spurred by the horrors of Stalin's show trials, he urgently tried to convince his friend of his mistake.[6]

Such influential voices thus contributed to a more indulgent supervision of the broad Left. While MI5 maintained prolific files on Communists and their sympathisers, it was a gentlemanly sort of surveillance, to be converted to an arrest only if a suspect were caught red-handed. And even though many of those watched were aliens, their loyalties were not unduly questioned. Those who were not British citizens were, almost exclusively, not Soviet citizens either: the cosmopolitan flavour of Communist espionage made the identification of subversives more difficult. Nazi espionage was casual and obvious: Soviet espionage was deep and furtive. Yet Stalin's constant recalls and purges of agents set MI5 off its guard: early in 1939, Kell went so far as to make the ridiculous claim that Communist espionage was non-existent.[7] Ironically, Hitler did not take great interest in intelligence reports; Stalin devoured everything. What is certain is that, while the British did identify nearly all German spies who were engaged in short-term intelligence missions, it failed to discover the majority of Soviet agents who were focused on long-term strategic subversion.

Chamberlain continued to dither in his attitude to both totalitarian powers. While recent judgments on him have started to re-present his policy of appeasement as a gallant attempt to gain time for the country to be re-armed, detailed study of the archives still shows him to have been impressionable, ingenuous, and irresolute. His policy of appeasing Hitler, believing each time that the German leader was a reasonable man whose final demand had been made, had been shown to be a dismal failure. After the fiasco of Munich, and the rape of Czechoslovakia, when Chamberlain's trust in Hitler had been shown to be utterly misguided, he had pushed himself to make a commitment to the even more distant country of Poland that Britain would not tolerate any more Nazi incursions into sovereign states. Yet Britain's preparation was weak. Up to the outbreak of war, Chamberlain and his party whips maintained a strict control over the Tory majority in the House of Commons. Re-armament took up, more strongly than has often been suggested, but still too late. Chamberlain should be faulted not so much for a failure to recognise Britain's defensive needs, but more for overestimating Germany's power at a time when Hitler could have been forcefully countered. Appointments of ministers were uninspired. In the eyes of many, the Soviet Union was a natural potential ally against the Nazi menace. Apparently, Stalin thought so, too, since the doctrine of 'collective security' had proved to be a sham, a realisation that cost Litvinov, the Soviet Foreign Minister, his job. But it was difficult for serious negotiations between the two countries to begin. Neither party trusted the other. Chamberlain was virulently opposed to communism: Stalin had informed the CPGB, via the Comintern, that an alliance between a Chamberlain-led government and the Soviet Union would be untenable. The CPGB, in turn, characterised Chamberlain's government as 'Hitler's Fifth Column'.[8] (In truth, Chamberlain's representatives continued to try to negotiate with Germany even after the war had started.) Thus the overtures that Britain and the Soviet Union made to each other in the summer of 1939 were half-hearted, and doomed to fail. Chamberlain's envoys had instructions to extend the negotiations artificially: Marshal Voroshilov, who hosted the talks, made impossible demands over Britain's and France's ability to force Poland and Romania to agree to Soviet military access across their territories. Both countries feared communist Russia more than fascist Germany, and opposed unrequested 'guarantees' from menacing neighbours.

And then an astounding *bouleversement* occurred, which should have thrown all previous assumptions up in the air. In August 1939, Stalin and Hitler surprised the liberal democracies by signing a pact of non-aggression. This also included some secret clauses about territorial claims, which showed (when they were revealed after the war) that the Soviet Union too maintained expansionist designs. Hitler apparently wanted a complaisant Soviet Union before starting his eastbound invasions. (As late as November 1940, when Molotov visited Berlin in an attempt to resolve the conflicting interests of the two dictatorships in the Balkans, Hitler was still hoping that they might jointly be able to dismember the British Empire.) Stalin's motivations were unclear: some say he wanted to gain time after the purging of his Red Army, but, if so, he failed to make use of it. Maybe he wanted to pre-empt an alliance between Britain and Germany, the prospect of which continually perturbed him. In any case, British intelligence had not foreseen that the two totalitarian states, sworn ideological foes, would become allies. Neither of course did the Communist Party of Great Britain, which had to make some quick adjustments in its messages. Some remnants of goodwill from the Treaty of Rapallo in 1922 had been retained, despite Hitler's regular rants against bolshevism.[9]

Soon after the pact was signed, the fruits of the conspiracy by these unlikely partners were seen in the brutal carve-up of Poland and the Baltic states. In September 1939, Britain followed up on its commitment by declaring war on Germany, the latter's problematic strategic relationship with the Soviet Union remaining an irritant and a complication. Even though Britain was not at war with Russia, the risk remained that the non-aggression pact could develop into something much tighter, and more dangerous. Britain was also concerned that the Soviet Union would interfere with the economic blockade of Germany, and re-route valuable materials to the Nazi regime. The nation's home-grown supporters of the totalitarians were sparked into a response. Both the BUF (now called just the BU), and the CPGB immediately issued propaganda against the war, yet the Home Office was able to persuade the War Cabinet that no action should be taken against them, as it would in that case also have to be taken against the popular Peace Pledge Union. The fragmentation of a pluralist democracy, whereby negotiations for law and executive action continually have to test the validity of contesting viewpoints, was seen at work again, stifling any decisive response.[10] Nevertheless, MI5 and the Home Office should have paid special attention to the risk of the two totalitarian states sharing purloined secrets with each other.

Into this cauldron of frenetic espionage and counter-espionage Walter Krivitsky, the GRU officer, made his entry. Krivitsky had defected from his station in France to the USA in 1937, and had been persuaded to visit the UK at the beginning of 1940 after providing valuable information, via the British Embassy in Washington, about a Soviet spy in the Foreign Office. A singular opportunity thus presented itself to MI5, offering the chance to gain a valuable trove of information to make up for the hole in the organisation's intelligence caused by the Soviets' changing of their encipherment procedures after the ARCOS revelations. Defectors can bring a host of vital information about enemy organisations, personalities and procedures that would be impossible to gain from any other source. The urgency with which Stalin instructed his Fourth Department to track down and murder such individuals is testimony to the danger their revelations posed to the Soviets' strategies. Krivitsky's visit was an extraordinary event that merited the full attention of British intelligence.

Krivitsky had been born in Poland, as Samuel Ginzburg, in June 1899, and had eagerly embraced the goals of the Bolshevik revolution in 1917, joining military intelligence (GRU) in 1920. He then acted as a highly effective 'illegal' operative in various nations of Western Europe, becoming a high-level officer by the mid-1930s. When Stalin began his purge of old Bolsheviks and less than totally-loyal agents, Krivitsky himself had even been ordered to murder another agent, his friend Ignace Reiss (who had openly challenged Stalin). He managed to evade that responsibility. Fearing for his own life, however, when Stalin continued to kill intelligence personnel who might have been tainted by foreign ways, or by 'Trotskyism', or who simply expressed disgust with his tyranny, Krivitsky managed to avoid a recall to Moscow, and defected in 1937. He then went public with some highly provocative – but accurate – revelations about Stalin's ruthless dictatorship and police system, which must have set him more firmly in the sights of Moscow's special assassins.

In the autumn of 1939, having been helped by information originating from Krivitsky, MI5 had been able to detect, convict, and gain a term of imprisonment for John Herbert King, the spy he identified in the Foreign Office. Britain's Security Service then expressed interest in speaking to Krivitsky himself. Its officers calculated that he might be able to assist them with other suspected leaks, and he was persuaded to come to the UK. When he arrived in January 1940, Jane Sissmore was appointed as the lead interrogator, and became his key confidante. Sissmore (now Archer) was the most experienced of MI5's officers working in Soviet counter-espionage. (She had married another intelligence officer, Wing Commander John Archer, the day before war broke out). She had lived up to all the confidence expressed in her, successfully managing the Woolwich Arsenal case. She was also responsible, after Krivitsky returned to Canada in February 1940, for writing the official report on the sessions jointly held by MI5 and SIS. It is clear from the documents on file that Krivitsky, who was very cautious when the interrogations started, and overall not trusting of British intelligence personnel, gained a high degree of confidence in the sympathetic, self-assured and highly competent Jane Archer.

The information that the MI5 and SIS intelligence officers gained from Krivitsky was of exceptional value. Here was a defector who had inside knowledge of Stalin's machinations with the German government as well as insights into the Soviet Union's strategy for subversion in the UK. He named key agents working in the Soviet Embassy; he provided broad hints at the identity of Soviet spies working inside the British government and the media; he described the Soviet strategy for subverting British intelligence directly, outside the confines of the Communist Party; and he warned of the potential danger to Britain incurred by the Soviets' sharing any findings with their Nazi allies. Yet MI5 (and to a lesser extent, SIS) astonishingly failed to follow up on this unique opportunity: on the contrary, during the next twelve months, it recruited overt Communists, as well as Soviet agents who had attempted to conceal their past affiliations, into the organisation. It failed to pursue leads that might have enabled it to keep under surveillance agents acting as middlemen between traitors and the Soviet Embassy, and thus unmask such figures as the spies Philby, Cairncross, Maclean and Fuchs. It appeared to be thwarted continually by the Home Office in its attempts to intern communist activists disrupting the war effort. (It is significant that Soviet infiltration was already performing its mischief: one of the first civil servants to read the Krivitsky report was a Soviet mole, Jenifer Hart, later to become an Oxford don.)

In addition, MI5 failed to assess seriously the implications of revealing the outcomes of the interrogation to a broader audience. The slipshod dissemination of information contributed to Moscow Centre's ability to track Krivitsky's movements, with the result that a year later he was murdered in Washington by Stalin's thugs. Various excuses were later given for this negligent behaviour: shortage of staff; the vagueness of Krivitsky's information and the dubiousness of his character; confusion of leadership and the political turmoil during the 'twilight' or 'phoney' war; the demands made upon MI5 to investigate the threat of a Nazi Fifth Column; the necessity of not provoking the communistic unions and thus affecting wartime productivity in the factories. The timing was even muddied to suggest that, as the Soviets became allies, any prosecution of the leads would have been insulting and damaging to the successful prosecution of the war. But it was nevertheless an operational failure of dire proportions.

MI5 showed a total lack of effectiveness in its follow-up. Jane Archer was re-assigned as soon as she completed her analysis, and dismissed later in the year for insubordination.[11] Procedures for disseminating her report appropriately, and maintaining its security, were lax or non-existent. The report itself was well-written, and analytical, but seemingly made no recommendations. MI5 was not culturally or organisationally prepared to accept that it might have recruited subversives, and thus was not positioned to perform a strict review of its hiring practices. The voices of those who expressed concern about the possible undermining of the service by Communists were drowned out by those who regarded any threat as minimal. Government servants who had raised flags about serious information leakages to the Soviets allowed their attention to wander. After a short burst of energy provoked by Krivitsky's contribution (when even

Kell was roused into action), and suggestions were made to the Home Office about possible internment of CPGB members, observation of Communists weakened. MI5 experienced resistance from the Home Office, whose judgments leftist politicians like Ellen Wilkinson and Dennis Pritt, abetted by Harold Laski, were able to sway. MI5 failed to notice linkages between embassy staff identified by Krivitsky and incidents of previous surveillance of suspected subversives, and to follow up appropriately. Soon after, on June 10, Kell himself was dismissed by Churchill, and yet he and Jane Archer formed an extraordinary partnership in the remainder of 1940 – two discarded officers trying to track down Krivitsky again.

The preliminary conclusion might be that MI5 officers simply displayed an infirmity of purpose: they did not have a resolute and clear plan for what the result of its surveillance of communists should be, and had no mechanism for assessing and verifying what Krivitsky told them, or then pursuing such leads. This is perhaps an inevitable and enduring characteristic of a government bureau trying to maintain security in a liberal democracy. It was culturally hard for it (and the Home Office that would actually make the decisions) to arrest or banish suspects unless they were found with the proverbial bomb in their hands or with their fingers on the button of the camera taking images of secret documents. Furthermore, its instincts for security were continually thwarted by the voices of liberal society. And yet, after a proven success record against Nazi spies, it missed a number of opportunities for detecting, and acting upon, real threats from Soviet spies, and it loosened its recruitment disciplines. The visit of Krivitsky was a heaven-sent gift of unique value. Nevertheless it appears that a selective policy of turning a blind eye to communist infiltration was developed. What caused this change of course? Who made it happen? And why? Was it an open and unanimous policy? And how did the appeasers win out?

The research agenda behind this book is to answer the following primary question:

- Was MI5's apparent accommodation of communists caused by incompetence, by confusion, by lack of expertise, by higher political direction, by internal subversion or conspiracy, or by some combination of these factors?

This can be broken down into subsidiary questions:

- Why did MI5 not act upon the leads that Krivitsky provided it? Was there a reason for mistrusting Krivitsky, and defectors in general?
- How and why did MI5 start to minimise the Comintern/Communist threat?
- How did intellectual opinion and government policy influence MI5's view of communist subversion?
- Why did MI5 loosen its restrictions on hiring officers with a communist background?
- Did communist moles shape policy?
- What opportunities for catching Soviet spies did MI5 miss?
- Why did MI5 officers conceal from their superiors the decisions they made during wartime?

As a conclusion, the following question is addressed:

• What enduring lessons can be learned concerning counter-espionage tradecraft?

The book sets out to show that, even though Soviet espionage was more penetrating and more patient than has traditionally been portrayed, MI5 failed to counter it because of severe flaws in policy, organisation, tradecraft, and leadership. The Security Service's failures cannot be ascribed simply to the wiles of the Comintern, with its skills for providing deep cover for agents, and its discipline for maintaining their isolation from each other: its representatives frequently broke its own rules. Nor can they be attributed to the presence of a 'super-mole' in the ranks of the Security Service, for no traitor with significant power would have been able to exercise such influence without drawing excessive attention to his or her behaviour. MI5 stumbled along, failing to make a resolute reassessment of its mission in the turmoil of the late 1930s. It misjudged the intentions of those British citizens it regarded as 'harmless' intellectual communists, making reckless distinctions between the theory of communism and its destructive practice. It dropped its guard against the permanent Soviet threat when war with Germany was declared, even while the Soviet Union was an ally of Nazi Germany, and allowed the fact that Stalin was a temporary ally against Hitler to blind it to the dictator's permanent objectives. It failed to develop a consistent and resolute approach for dealing with potential subversives, and allowed itself to be swayed by so-called 'agents of influence', who more discreetly aided the Soviet Union's goals by softening Britain's political resistance to communism. When MI5's senior officers belatedly discovered their negligence, they adopted a strategy of cover-up and dissimulation that attempted to bury their misdemeanours, a deception that has influenced official, authorised, and independent histories of British intelligence ever since. This book offers the first comprehensive account of a highly flawed period in MI5's history.

Notes

[1] The report is titled *Investigation by SS* [the Security Service, better known as MI5] *into Activities of the CPGB and Indentification* [*sic*] *of its Members*. See KV 4/125 at the National Archives.

[2] This assertion is commonly found in histories of espionage. For example, see *British Intelligence in the Second World War, Volume 4*, by Hinsley and Simkins, p 11. Yet the only clause in the Treaty of Versailles which represents such a ban runs as follows: "Germany agrees, from the coming into force of the present Treaty, not to accredit nor to send to any foreign country any military, naval or air mission, nor to allow any such mission to leave her territory. . ." (Article 179). While this article has been interpreted as a ban on any espionage activity, it would not appear to forbid any espionage undertaken by civilians or non-military organisations.

[3] Max Hastings, *The Secret War*, p 66.

[4] See (chief editor) Hinsley's *British Intelligence in the Second World War*', Christopher Andrew's *The Defence of the Realm* and John Curry's *The Security Service 1908-1945* (written in 1946, but not published until 1999), as well as Andrew's Introduction to

Curry's work. These accounts of counter-espionage against German agents promote the notion that the process was thorough and comprehensive, with the celebrated XX Committee appearing as the most important symbol of that success. That committee did not meet for the first time, however, until January 1941, when it began its successful campaign of turning Nazi spies into agents of disinformation. And the analysts cannot be omniscient. For example, the Germans undertook, in peacetime, an illegal and clandestine enterprise to photograph the landscape of Britain, for purposes of destruction through bombing, yet the activity was undetected.

[5] Joachim Fest used the term in his memoir *Not I* (*Ich nicht: Erinnerungen an eine Kindheit und Jugend*), and the historians of the Gestapo, Dams and Stoller, referred to the term 'Mitläuferfabrik' (translated as 'Fellow Traveller Factory') in their account of denazification trials. Hitler's cinematographer, Leni Riefenstahl, was one who was judged, in 1948, to be nothing worse than a 'fellow-traveller'. (New Yorker, October 19, 2015, p 86).

[6] Berlin's rapid change of attitude is striking. In April 1936 he may merely have been acting indulgently to Spender: he much later told his biographer, Michael Ignatieff, that he had implored Spender 'on bended knee' not to join the Communist Party. The date of this event is uncertain, but presumably occurred between the Moscow show trials of July 1936 and Spender's claim that he was sent by the CPGB on a Moscow-inspired mission to Spain to track down the whereabouts of the crew of the Komsomol, which had been sunk by the Spanish, in January 1937. (See Chapter 6).

[7] Christopher Andrew recorded this in his authorised history of MI5, *The Defence of the Realm*, p 185.

[8] Ironically, it was not until Churchill came to power in May 1940 that the chances of an alliance with the Soviet Union were rekindled; Churchill, who had been the fiercest of opponents of Communism, had indicated as early as 1933 that he would enter an alliance with the Bolsheviks in order to defeat Nazism, but the Chamberlain majority of the Tory Party, and its resentment of a coalition government in which socialists gained new power each month, remained a threat to him until the summer of 1941.

[9] After the failure of the Genoa Conference in early 1922, where a dispute over inherited debts caused a breach between the Soviet Union and France, Germany and the Soviet Union turned to each other for support, and signed a commercial treaty at Rapallo on April 16 of that year.

[10] Historians frequently characterise the major ideological conflict of these decades as one of 'communism versus capitalism'. That is not so: capitalism is not a system of government. It was more accurately 'totalitarianism versus democratic pluralism'. See Chapter 10 for a fuller discussion of this matter.

[11] The career of Jane Archer was astonishing. In his Diaries, Guy Liddell wrote (November 18, 1940) that she was "sacked for insubordination", apparently for speaking up once too often about the incompetence of the head of MI5, Sir Jasper Harker. It was not Liddell's decision: "a very serious blow to us all", he added. Archer's extraordinary abilities were widely recognised: despite her sacking, she was soon hired by SIS, by her ally in the Krivitsky interrogations, Valentine Vivian, and she later worked there for Kim Philby, who testified to her strengths in his memoir, *My Silent War*. Yet she was not able to carve a path for other woman officers: no others were appointed during the war, and evidence suggests that in 1941 the new head of MI5, Sir David Petrie, issued instructions that barred women from such rank. The Diaries of Guy Liddell show that she became demoralised by the officers in SIS, however, and tried to return to MI5 in 1944.

Chapter 2: Missing Links

"One does not look twice at an offer of enrolment in an elite force." (Kim Philby)

"A Communist who's trying to infiltrate isn't going to call attention to himself." (Dr Irving Peress)

"Many of our friends had been, or had thought themselves, communists in the 1930s; and we were shocked that such persons should be debarred from public service on account of mere juvenile illusions which anyway they had now shed." (Hugh Trevor-Roper)

Great Britain's struggle with communist subversion was largely rooted in a neglect of the fact that, independent of any moves that the country might make towards a more egalitarian society, such as economic growth, lower unemployment levels, or expanded suffrage, the objectives of the pioneers of communism in the Soviet Union would still remain a potent threat. Stalin scorned democratic and parliamentary socialists even more than he loathed the aristocracy who still ran the country: the road to the workers' paradise was not to be made by incremental steps, and the security of the dictatorship of the proletariat would occur only when the campaign was successfully internationalised. It was MI5's mission to protect the realm from such assaults. This chapter shows how the Security Service dropped its guard against this permanent and durable foe, and how, in the mid-1930s, the Soviet Union's declared opposition to the new threat of Fascism confused the issue for all but the most clear-sighted and rigorous thinkers in Britain's political class. Moreover, the Comintern's successful programme of propaganda, and the dividends gained from its deep investment in undercover agents, made MI5's surveillance obligations even more difficult to execute.

By the mid-1930s, Britain had slowly begun to regain the economic benefits of its liberal democracy – an increase in business activity and employment, leading to greater prosperity. After the shock of the Great Crash, and the misery of the Depression, the National Government represented a popular aspiration for unity: revolution had been averted, insurrection had been quashed. The menace of Communism, which had hung so insidiously over the country's sense of security during the 1920s, now appeared as more distant and less troublesome. A new threat was now in the air, however – that of the Third Reich, with its message of fierce nationalism, internal revolution, and expansionary territorial demands. The role of Communism as most sinister foreign ideology had been replaced by Hitler's brand of Fascism, which seemed to present a far more urgent danger for the stability of Europe. To the British public, Hitler's evil plans at their back-door seemed more immediately dangerous than Stalin's persecutions, which were geographically remoter, and more vaguely reported in the media. The tirades of

Sir Oswald Mosley, leading his British Union of Fascists, were more strident and obnoxious than Sir Stafford Cripps's pro-communist rants from the left wing of the Labour Party. Indeed, in October 1934, the Soviet Union had responded to the growing Nazi threat by joining the League of Nations, thus executing a propaganda coup, and reinforcing the notion of 'collective security' as a valid defence against Hitlerite aggression. Such a move helped to diminish the Bolshevik bogey, and blur traditional political party stances. If a choice had to be made between National Socialism and Communism, a Conservative majority – the group of future Chamberlainite appeasers – favoured the former, but did so in the relief of seeing Communism weakened by Fascism's success. The Labour Party detached itself from its romantic affiliation for communist principles, but was split along different lines, by dint of its loathing of Fascism being tempered by strong pacifist instincts. If not yet a friend, Russia was no longer a demon. As the historian A. J. P. Taylor wrote of this time: "Labour did not plan an alliance with Soviet Russia, nor did the Conservatives plan a war against her".[1]

Such modulation of opinion was the price of a pluralist society. But what did it mean for Britain's security at a tactical level? As explained earlier, a few voices warned that both totalitarian movements still presented dangers to the nation, and that both should thus be resisted. Such opinions, however, were muted by the growing sympathy towards communism harboured by most intellectuals, who viewed Stalinism as a short-lived aberration from lofty ideals. The main menace was now Nazism, and the debate was over how to counter it. The Chiefs of Staff pressed harder than the diplomats for a more vigorous response, calling for faster re-armament to counter Hitler's military expenditures. On March 4, 1935, the British Cabinet accordingly announced it would cease to rely solely on a model of 'collective security', based on the idea of multi-national negotiations and sanctions, as a protective mechanism. In June the results of the Peace Ballot still confirmed a public preference for negotiated resolutions over military action, but showed that the number of outright pacifists had declined. While Foreign Secretary Samuel Hoare continued to promote the escapist policy of 'collective security' with enthusiasm, the Comintern in August refined its message of collective action by proposing a 'united front' with the democratic West. It thus appeared to soften the traditional Bolshevik message of hostility and 'world revolution' by suggesting that the home of Communism nurtured shared values with the Western democracies in the fight against Fascism. A propaganda battle was being waged, and Prime Minister Baldwin (who replaced MacDonald in June) sought a mandate for what was still a confused re-armament policy by dissolving Parliament on October 25, 1935. His timing was unfortunate: Italy's invasion of Ethiopia earlier that month had already begun to impose fresh strains on the League of Nations organisation as an effective arbiter for peace, and on the ability of sanctions to deter aggression.

If there was a link between these political re-assessments, and MI5's planning processes, no record exists.[2] Yet, conscious of the new political realities, as well as the indifferent results of its resource-consumptive tracking practices, the directors of MI5 chose at this time to re-inspect its strategy for countering communist subversion. In the autumn of 1935 it determined that its management of the communist threat should be sharply refocused on the Communist Party of

Great Britain (CPGB) itself, and on malicious acts that affected the armed forces and the factories, rather than on the more intangible threat of propaganda and espionage. This shift would imply a dramatic reduction in surveillance over the broader group of leftist intellectuals, writers and artists who expressed sympathy for the aims of the Communist Party, and the vaguely malevolent activities of Comintern agents *not* under the control of the CPGB. It is not clear whether higher political authority encouraged this re-assessment: John Simon (Home Secretary) and Samuel Hoare (Foreign Secretary) both had a reputation as an appeaser, and thus might have been expected to show no indulgence towards Communism. Major-General Sir Vernon Kell, the Director of MI5, may have used his own initiative to order the fresh approach. The new strategy, however, showed on the surface a pragmatic awareness of the need to harness resources to prepare for another German war, perhaps reflecting the instincts of such as Winston Churchill, and his intelligence advisor, Major Desmond Morton, who had strong ties with MI5. Thus MI5 set out on a fateful path of diminishing its expertise in, and its focus on, the danger from international Communist conspiracy.

It is educational to consider the recent history of MI5, and its organisation at this time, in order to interpret accurately the 1935 refocusing. Up until then, the need to counter the menace of Bolshevism had dominated MI5's agenda, with a watch on the British Union of Fascists being initiated only in 1933. The mission of MI5's Counter-Espionage 'B' Branch had been established in the summer of 1931, after the Home Secretary, Sir John Anderson, had convened a series of meetings to sort out tensions between the Metropolitan Police's Special Branch and a group of officers known as the 'Casuals', working under Major Morton (officially head of the Industrial Intelligence Centre of the Committee for Imperial Defence) in MI5's sister organisation, SIS. Both groups had been chartered with detecting subversive activities in the CPGB and other left-wing organisations.[3] Mutual suspicion had arisen between Maxwell Knight, working for Morton, and Colonel Carter, who had been in charge of all of Scotland Yard's Special Branch since 1928. The Secret Service Committee, which met only rarely, comprised Anderson, as well as Sir Warren Fisher (Head of the Home Civil Service), Sir Robert Vansittart and Sir Maurice Hankey[i] (Secretary to the Cabinet). After hearing all the evidence, the committee reached the Delphic conclusion that MI5 should be responsible for all "intelligence duties concerned with civil security", while SIS should restrict itself to intelligence-gathering beyond the 'three-mile limit'.[4] While the implications of this decision do not appear to have been communicated crisply to all parties concerned, and no written record of the decision has survived, the resolution was accepted gracefully and positively by all three organisations concerned, SIS, MI5, and Special Branch. Colonel Carter, of a peevish nature, did not take the transfer of responsibilities well, but Morton was happy that his team had found its right home.

As John Curry (who compiled an 'official' history of MI5 in 1946) wrote: "The functions of MI5 were thus expanded to an important extent. They became

---

[i] Hankey is wrongly identified as 'Sir Maurice Henksy' in Curry's *The Security Service 1908-1945*, p 101.

responsible for all intelligence dealing with the activities of the CPGB and therefore of the Comintern in this country." [5] Yet complete clarity in responsibilities was not immediately installed. Tracking the organisation charts of MI5 in the 1930s and 1940s is a challenging assignment: Christopher Andrew's authorised history, *The Defence of the Realm*, shows only the very high-level evolution, indicating how MI5 was split into only two Branches in 1931 – 'A' Branch responsible for Administration, and 'B' Branch for 'Defence security intelligence; Communism in GB; Russian espionage; Comintern secret agents'.[6] Andrew then jumped to 1941, where the number of branches had increased to six, with 'B' Branch now responsible for 'Counter-espionage', and 'F' Branch for 'Counter-subversion'. Curry started his pair of similar charts only with the organisation in July 1941, where the respective responsibilities are described as 'Espionage' (with Captain Liddell noted as Director) and 'Subversive Activities' (whose Director is Mr J. H. Curry himself). The Branches are now called 'Divisions': 'F' Division was created in July 1941, in Andrew's words: "to lighten 'B' Division's load", but an opportunity for further fragmentation of the effort to counter the Communist threat was thus created.[7] (The transition from 'Counter-Espionage' to 'Espionage', while bizarre, probably shows carelessness rather than any significance.) Nigel West was usefully very generous in providing lists of names of officers working for MI5, but his organisation chart is headed vaguely as "The Wartime Organisation of the Security Service", and he qualified his information with the caption: "The names shown are those of some of the leading personalities who served; but not necessarily contemporaneously".[8] Establishing precise missions and reporting paths within the Security Service for any one time is thus a cabbalistic activity.

Records from the National Archives occasionally throw up hints of organisational changes. In any case, it appears that Maxwell Knight's group of Casuals was maintained as a discrete unit, known as 'M' Section, when transferred to MI5 in 1931. (Curry indicated that this name came along later.) But since the functions of 'M' Section were, in Curry's words, "to specialise in the training and employment of agents for counter espionage purposes, i.e. to penetrate organisations such as the CPGB, known enemy Secret Service organisations, and after 1933, the British Union of Fascists", it would appear anomalous to have had this unit managed outside the mainstream counter-espionage branch. Curry's terminology is also odd, since, though it may have been astute to recognise the Comintern as 'the enemy', the country was not at war. Thus, a potential for rivalry and turf protection immediately appeared, and the fragmentation of responsibilities that seems to have been the *modus operandi* of MI5 management through this period is reflected in other documents.

The closest documented indication of MI5's structure at the time of the 1935 decision is probably demonstrated by a paper compiled a year or two later – but it clearly shows the changes that had recently been made. A wholesale reorganisation of MI5 occurred in 1937, probably as a result of the late 1935 reset. The limited documentation available shows a proliferation of departments, presumably maintained partly to protect the egos of those who headed them.[9] It also displays the new strategic emphasis, with the terms 'Fascists', 'Germany', 'Italy', 'BUF, and 'Nazi' drowning out any references to Communism or the

Comintern, the threat of which strangely appears to have been relegated to the concept of 'Civil Security'. Nevertheless, 'B' Branch still looks to have been essentially unmanageable, with the following subsections and chiefs:

B (Investigation) Harker and Liddell;
B.1 (Internal Security in HM Forces) Alexander;
B.1a (Navy) Watson;
B.2 (Germany) Cooke;
B.2a (Nazi) Curry;
B.2b (C.E. Germany) Whyte;
B.2c (BUF, Italian Fascists) Sinclair;
B.3 (Arms Traffic) Robertson;
B.4a (Civil Security - home) Sissmore and Mr Younger;
B.4b (Civil Security - foreign) Dick White;
B.5a (Spec. Enquiries) Boddington and Badham;
B.5b (M Organisation) Knight;
B.6 (Enquiries) Hunter.

This is a fascinating list which, in the context of what we know now, provokes a serious comment on structures and personalities. In January 1938 there were only 26 officers in all of MI5 (including the Director-General and his deputy), which means that the 16 managers (in 'B' Branch alone) were managing at most seven officers – assuming that 'A' Branch was led by an officer. At the end of 1938, two new branches were created: 'C' Branch, responsible for vetting, and 'D' Branch, which had the mission of supervising security in ports, arsenals, and other vital locations. These two branches contained four officers, but the total number had grown only to 30.[10] It was obviously, therefore, a very top-heavy organisation, the structure of which perhaps betrays a classical management dilemma: whether to organise teams based on speciality (e.g. by infiltration skills), or by target area (e.g. the CPGB, or pro-Nazi groups), and, if a reshuffle were to be made, what productivity would be lost because of the process itself and the inevitably bruised egos. For example, Maxwell Knight's group was inappropriately identified by a codename rather than a responsibility, as if it didn't really fit. Yet here was carried out most of the anti-Communist work – almost anonymously, as if the work needed for some reason to be concealed. Moreover, liaising and communicating with the other groups within the Branch must have been a challenge, and there must have been overlaps with the teams in 'B2'.

The names dominant at that stage also reflect something of the culture and history of MI5. The swift rise of Dick White (who would graduate to head MI5) is highly unusual. He was hired – on probation – only on January 1, 1936, and spent most of his first year abroad, in Germany, so his promotion to department head might appear to have been premature. (He was the first university graduate hired, so may thus have been considered a natural 'high flyer'.) On the other hand, MI5's traditions in countering communist subversion by maintaining its own surveillance personnel are shown by the group titled 'Special Inquiries'. It is headed by one 'Boddington', who was in fact Captain (later Major) Herbert

Boddington, the "only MI5 officer who was also an undercover member of the Communist Party" [in 1923], but who belonged to the British Fascists between 1924 and 1926, before rejoining the Communist Party. Boddington had helped uncover those responsible for the Invergordon mutiny in 1931, but 'faded out' of the CPGB in 1932. In a significant – and assuredly understated – note, Andrew remarked: "It is possible that he feared that his cover was wearing thin and that Harker believed that Knight's agents [i.e. 'M' Section] were henceforth better placed to penetrate the CPGB."[11] No doubt: Boddington's outward ideological moves were of Philbean proportions.

By this time, the group known as 'B4', identified by Andrew as "Harker's three-man Observation section", which was active in the 1920s, appears to have been dissolved, or morphed into 'B5'. Harker had recruited retired Special Branch detectives to perform the tedious but important task of following and watching suspicious characters: John Ottaway (CBE) was one such detective, and had joined MI5 in 1920 after a successful career as detective superintendent.[12] His patient efforts led him to detect the Communist agent, William Ewer, in 1928, and to unveil the spies in Special Branch who had been hindering MI5's activities, Hubertus van Ginhoven and Sergeant Charles Jane. Those two were perhaps the first 'moles' to be unearthed by MI5, showing that old-fashioned police work had driven the successful arrests. Ottaway is not mentioned in Curry's history, but, in 1941, the Director of 'B' Division (as it was then called), namely Harker, is shown to have two special staff groups reporting to him – 'B.5' ('Investigation Staff'), under a Superintendent Burt, showing constabulary origins, and 'B.6', boldly described as 'Watchers', with the name of its leader redacted. Surprisingly, Nigel West restored Ottaway's name as still active during WWII, working for the 'Watchers' again with Mr Hunter, presumably the 'Hunter' who was handling 'Enquiries' in 'B.6', in 1938.[13] Ottaway's date of birth is unknown, but, if he retired from the police force in 1920 (Andrew states he had already served 29 years with the City of London Police Force by then[14]), he would have been about 70 years old in 1940, with his powers probably waning.

The name of Captain Liddell now appears prominently in the documents. He had been part of the anti-Communist team in Special Branch: Madeira described him as "the leading Special Branch counter-subversion expert", but someone who was nevertheless not informed about the 1927 raid by the Branch on the Soviet ARCOS front, and was thus "cross not to be told about the raid by supervisors until the last moment".[15] The official history of SIS indicates that his boss in Special Branch, Colonel J. F. C. Carter ("whose political sympathies appear to have been rather more left-wing than those of either Knight or Morton"), in his evidence in 1931 considered the work that Liddell and his colleague Captain Miller had been performing as S.S.1 was "superfluous" and "could be done by Colonel Carter himself".[16] That would explain Liddell's being excluded from the ARCOS business. In any case, his pride was no doubt restored by his being appointed deputy to Brigadier Jasper Harker, head of 'B' Branch, when he transferred in 1931: it is also possible that his rapid promotion was not eagerly welcomed by the experienced officers who had been tackling Comintern subversion for some years. Notwithstanding any such resentment, by 1935 he was the officer who appeared to be spearheading the refinement of 'B' Branch's mission. In a memorandum attached to a report explaining the new focus, he wrote to his boss, on November 22, 1935, that they needed to "narrow the lines upon which we have hitherto been working, and concentrate on essentials". Three days later, Brigadier Harker indicated his approval with the note: "This is satisfactory. You now have your new charter. Carry on", and he added that Sir Vernon Kell had approved.

This important report is titled *Investigation by SS [Security Service] into Activities of the CPGB and Indentification [sic] of its members 1935*, and it was written by the officer who appears as being jointly in charge of the group 'B4a' (above), Miss Jane Sissmore.[17] Jane (born Kathleen) Sissmore was perhaps the most remarkable officer of all those listed above. As previously explained, she was the first woman officer appointed by MI5. The archives do not indicate whether this decision was an enlightened move, displaying confidence in a rising star, or was an unimaginative selection that indicated the role was of secondary importance. Sissmore's achievement nevertheless represented a significant breakthrough both in British intelligence and in British professional life. Born in 1898, she had been recruited by MI5 as a clerk in 1916, and had trained as a barrister in her spare time, being called to the Bar in 1924.[18] Few records of her activities in the first few years are available, but it would appear that she must have struck up a solid relationship with Major Vivian of SIS, the service's expert on communism and the Comintern. According to John Curry's official history of the Service, written in 1946, Vivian wrote several reports to which MI5 contributed much material. Curry highlighted two 1934 reports by Vivian where "an important part of the material . . . was obtained from Security Service sources". Vivian came to the conclusion that Communism was "an international criminal conspiracy", rather than "a political movement", and he thus helped clarify the challenges facing MI5. Sissmore was awarded the MBE in 1929.

Christopher Andrew observed that Sissmore was "responsible for Soviet intelligence" in 1929, and gave her official duties at that time: 'Defence Security Intelligence concerning Russia', 'Defence Security Service (Peace Organisation)'.[19] She clearly had much relevant experience: Quinlan reported how she with patient dedication tracked down leads, and applied pressure on her superiors to take action, as in the case of the spy William Macartney, in 1927. Her bypassing the management chain, and going directly to Kell, on that occasion, shows that her skills must have been recognised at the top. She displayed considerable shrewdness in concluding, before the ARCOS raid in 1928, that Walter Allen was in financial straits, and thus open to manipulation, and she was not afraid to voice her opinions, repeatedly, to Harker that action on the Home Office Warrant should be taken expeditiously.[20] She presented a strong argument for enticing the Communist militant Stephen Hutchings back from Moscow to stand trial after the Invergordon Mutiny in 1931, although her appeals fell on stony ground.[21]

Yet, by 1935, it would appear that her position of authority, if it ever existed, must have been diluted somewhat. It would have been tough enough, as a woman in such a male-dominated organisation, for her to command immediate respect from every officer in the club, and to fulfil her duties would have required a lot of skilful negotiation with other groups. Liddell's testimony in his account of

Sissmore's career cannot be regarded as utterly sincere, since he appears to have been the chief architect of her demise. He wrote in his diary that "she had always been in a rather privileged position as a court jester", suggesting that she used her talent for humour to help reach her professional goals. But this was said after she had been sacked, at the end of 1940: was Liddell's statement that they had "lost the services of a very valuable officer", and that "it was therefore a little short of a disaster that her services could no longer be utilised", a case of crocodile tears?[22] He did not appear to have done much to keep her in the organisation. Thus, given the timing of his endorsement, one might question Andrew's claim that Liddell was "quick to recognise Sissmore's talent".[23] Curry, extraordinarily, did not mention any of her activities before 1940, which, by omission, would appear to counter Andrew's view of the recognition by her peers. Moreover, it appears that the strategy of MI5 in countering Communist subversion had by then shifted to Maxwell Knight and his more unorthodox practices. Curry acknowledged (vaguely) that it had "always been the practice for a certain number of agents to be controlled by the officers of the sections of 'B' Branch", but added that, after 1931, "Mr Maxwell Knight specialised in the recruitment and direction of agents employed to penetrate" the CPGB.[24]

Thus Jane Sissmore's heart may not have been in the 1935 report that she was commanded to write, as she saw her influence diminished, and the real threat from Communist subversion understressed. The narrative suggests that the Security Service (not 'B' Branch specifically) had been spinning its wheels in trying to surveille too many suspected subversives, without a corresponding reward for its efforts. Thus the new mission was defined as "aim[ing] to concentrate on the essentials of 'dealing with Communism', and to keep informed of 'activities, policy and mischievous potentialities of subsidiary bodies of the Comintern operating under the direction of the Communist Party of Great Britain'". The emphasis switched from tracking every member of the CPGB to focusing on the leaders of the CPGB "and those known to engage in illegal activities and to act in this country as direct agents of the Comintern". The stress was now on subversion and sabotage ('revolutionary activity', 'mischievous activity') rather than espionage: handwritten notes on the report (which could well be Harker's) echo a concern about protecting industry and the military. Despite this reprioritisation, however, Sissmore appeared to continue to follow her own instincts and preferred targets. Indeed, the most significant victory against Communists for Britain's Security Service was gained towards the end of that decade, but a failure to prosecute, frustrations in efforts to obstruct the main subversive threat and lack of co-ordination and resolution in following up leads, showed that the Soviet Union and the Comintern were starting to win the propaganda war.

Another significant event had occurred, however. From February 1934, SIS had been passing to MI5 decrypted radio messages (known as 'MASK') that had been exchanged by a rogue Communist operator in Wimbledon and his bosses in Moscow, and had been detected by the Government Code and Cipher School's station in Grove Park, Camberwell.[25] Some of these communications indicated a revivified interest by the Comintern in spreading sedition and disruption in Britain's forces and factories. For example, a long message from Moscow of

February 16, 1934, exploiting the socialist revolt in Vienna, informed its recipients that "this is the beginning of an enormous wave of civil war in Europe", and reminded "communist parties of all countries" that "general strike and armed revolt are the only way to power".[26] Thus, the Comintern was sending an open, peaceable message to the West at the same time that it was clandestinely (as it believed) tightening the screws in the preparation for revolution.

Was MI5 taken in by this? Maybe not: the language of the 1935 Report echoed the threats suggested by recent MASK traffic. Yet the leaders of MI5 appear to have employed a more literal and one-dimensional view of Communist subversion than did the officers on the ground, such as Sissmore and Knight. It would make sense to suggest that these leaders had perhaps been influenced by an outside political agency. One writer has identified a Labour MP who had been a member of SIS as the main trigger, claiming of Rex Fletcher (later Lord Winster, in Attlee's post-war government) that "the most constructive thing he probably did was to urge the Secret Service to think more about Nazi re-armament in the 1930s, and less about its perennial Russian bogey".[27] As a source for such an assertion, Leigh cited Christopher Andrew's *Secret Service*, but the few references to Fletcher there concern his working with Vansittart in SIS.[28] Furthermore, there is no mention of Fletcher in Andrew's official history of MI5. Leigh appears to have exaggerated his claim, and may have confused Andrew's generic reference to the intelligence services with MI5's more traditional identity, the *Security Service*.

Decisive strategic intent behind the move is by no means clear, however. On the contrary, the official history of Intelligence in WWII suggests, unintentionally, some naivety. The authors wrote: " . . . MI5 believed that the threat from the CPGB was becoming greater than before because it was acquiring a cloak of respectability from its Popular Front policies and its prominence in the anti-fascist crusade".[29] (This history does not mention MASK.) The authors did not provide any memorandum to explain that conclusion, but an interpretation that claims the refocusing of 1935 was adopted because the CPGB was subtly becoming more effective owing to its general reputation is not a little bizarre, and shows a touch of retrospective justification. The conclusion might have been that it would increase the status of the Labour Party, influence the populace at the ballot-box, and incur changes through legal means rather than having to indulge in subversive activities to reach its goals. In any case, the threat of espionage, and the long-term propaganda effects of having moles installed, remained concealed. Astonishingly, Curry reported, on the MASK traffic that "the difficulties [of obscurity and context] had the unfortunate effect that a complete study and analysis of the messages was never made".[30] (Curry indicated the lack of attention was specifically by SIS, but it was really MI5's turf.) This is an extraordinary confession: that the time of intelligence officers could not be reprioritised to investigate such an extraordinary lode shows remarkable negligence. Sissmore's influence was surely waning. Her 1937 role, as being jointly in charge of 'Civil Security – Home' would not strongly reflect a reputation as the leading expert on Communist affairs that she was later praised for.

Whether Sissmore contested this decision is not known, but the policy shift represented a dismal unawareness (or forgetfulness) that the ground rules of Soviet subversion had changed since the mid-1920s. Maxwell Knight claimed to understand this, and his group was indeed successful in penetrating the Soviet spy ring, as the case of Percy Glading in 1938 demonstrated. Harker should have known this as well, as he had received, as early as May 1930, a communication from Colonel Valentine Vivian of SIS, which outlined how the NKVD had replaced its strategy of using members of the CPGB to carry out its subversion in favour of a plan that infiltrated *illegals* into the country. As Quinlan wrote: "The fallout from incidents like the ARCOS raid and the Macartney case provided an impetus for the USSR to separate itself officially from subversive and covert activity in Europe".[31] The letter from Vivian (who enjoyed a very successful and mutually beneficial relationship with Sissmore in exchanging information about Communism) is worth quoting in detail, since it is key to the entire strategy of handling communications with moles in British government institutions that MI5 failed to detect throughout the 1930s:

> "For the purpose of cover the illegal agents usually pose as business men or proceed to set up commercial companies, the business activities of which usually remain nebulous. Contact is kept up between the Embassy section and the secret section by means of more skilful agents . . . The secret agents or 'residents' of the GPU are almost invariably recruited amongst the citizens of foreign countries so that the Soviet authorities may, should any awkward incidents occur, disclaim all responsibility."[32]

Thus the focus on 'known agents of the Comintern' fails to accept the new reality of *subterfuge* – that those dedicated to subverting the democratic West would not easily be identified as such. Much has also been made of the claim that Arnold Deutsch, the illegal who arrived in Britain in April 1934, was the architect of the strategy to recruit potential high-flyers from Oxford and Cambridge Universities. Andrew made this assertion, using an authoritative-sounding statement from the Mitrokhin Archive, which purports to reflect the approval of such a decision by Moscow Centre.[33] Andrew annotated this entry with the comment: "The files noted by Mitrokhin make clear that Deutsch was the first to devise this recruitment strategy", but this may well have been an item of NKVD disinformation. Soviet intelligence would have had much to gain from pretending that the infiltration strategy was much more recent than it actually had been.

For such a strategy indeed went back at least a dozen years earlier. Madeira cited mail intercepted in 1920, in which students like Arthur Reade at Oxford, and Maurice Dobb (who tutored Philby into Communism) at Cambridge were involved. "In a letter to the YCL (Young Communist League) Chairman," wrote Madeira, "Reade wrote of creating 'a Communist nucleus among the Varsity men, who will be going out as schoolmasters, scientific workers, literary men and professional and 'intellectual' workers." [34] Madeira wisely pointed out how British intelligence should have had a clear idea of who was being targeted: perhaps the information was not embedded in corporate memory, as the warning occurred just before the head of MI5, Sir Basil Thomson, was fired. Andrew Rothstein was another Communist who worked aggressively at Cambridge

24

University, and recruited the long-time spy, Melita Sirnis (later Norwood). David Burke echoed Madeira's position that this subtle infiltration process was already underway: "When Andrew Rothstein was introduced to Melita Sirnis for the first time in 1933 her potential worth as a spy was as great as that of those spies already being cultivated in Britain's universities."[35]

The story of MI5's struggle against communism in the 1930s is thus one of repeated frustrations interrupted by the very occasional success. Special Branch consumed a vast amount of time, for instance, surveilling intellectuals who, while not holding Communist Party cards, definitely espoused communist views, and associated with more explicit adherents. The files released by the National Archives reveal how the movements and publications of dozens of famous characters, such as Auden, Orwell, and Spender, were tracked in detail. All in their different ways were foolish, or naïve: some (like Auden) abandoned their commitment for Christianity; others (like Spender and Day-Lewis) became fervent Communists on a primarily intellectual level, perhaps not realising how such impulses strongly aided Soviet propaganda, but then later saw the light, and became proper conservative Englishmen. Some took up the cause through the opportunity of the Spanish Civil War, the experiences of which either killed them, or, as in Orwell's case, made the Tory anarchist a fervent opponent of Stalinism. Most of them were patriots who naïvely did not view their romantic attachment to Stalin's version of Communism as treasonous, and would have recoiled from any involvement in bloody revolution.

The point, however, is that such surveillance did not stop with the 1935 policy remake, but continued strongly into the 1940s, with fugitives from Communist prisons, such as Arthur Koestler, joining the troops of the Watched. James Smith has written comprehensively (though making some unfortunate statements of moral equivalence concerning the fate of writers within the Soviet Union and those in a liberal democracy like the UK) of these time-consumptive obsessions. He wrote of the unproductive efforts expended in keeping all these records, with no further indication of action than that officers need to continue 'to keep an eye on' such characters. As Smith put it: "...finding no actual crimes being committed, they too often defaulted to low-level harassment, implausible security alerts, and cyclical further investigations", and the conclusions he came to are worthy of full citation:

> "It is perhaps worth reiterating that, for all the thousands of pages compiled on these left-wing artists, for all the investigations started, for all the assessments offered and all the scenarios mooted, little evidence was ever gained that provided any compelling case that they were actually imperilling the Realm (which, after all, is what MI5 was tasked to defend), or that the Comintern had achieved anything more than a tenuous and contested sway amongst the intelligentsia. Of course, Burgess and Blunt hovered at the fringes of these cultural networks, always reminding us that there were indeed Soviet agents in the fold – but the very fact they were cleared for secret work indicates the counter-productiveness of devoting so much time to intellectuals whose politics were very publicly declared."[36]

Yet the Comintern had by then achieved more than a 'tenuous sway', and the intrigues were happening under the nose of the Special Branch and MI5.

The story of the more serious efforts made to counter the Comintern's nefarious influences, and the associated failures, can be told in the accounts of three major events of the 1930s: first, the attempts to thwart the schemes of the Comintern agent Otto Katz, second, the successful prosecution of Percy Glading, ex-CPGB member and Soviet spy, in the Woolwich Arsenal case of 1938, and third, the Soviet Union's recruitment of perhaps the coolest and most committed of its spies in Britain, Kim Philby. These three figures have been selected because they each show a different but very characteristic aspect of MI5's challenges and shortcomings at this time: Katz, because the tracking and expulsion of a highly dubious and dangerous intruder were impeded by his connections with influential members of parliament; Glading, since a successful follow-up to a critical success in tradecraft was hindered by internal politics and inefficiencies; and Philby, as a reluctance to pursue a disciplined policy of vetting, despite obvious warning signals, allowed a manipulative and deceptive agent to escape the net. These profiles in total portray the unfortunate story of MI5's continual frustrations in surveillance activity, punctuated by the occasional but flawed triumph, all such events overshadowed, however, by a lack of resilience and imagination in tackling homegrown spies.

A detailed chronicle of the efforts to prevent Otto Katz from even entering the country can be found in documents released by the National Archives in 2003: the summary of his file describes his role concisely: "Katz was a significant agent of the Comintern based in Paris, a contemporary and colleague of Willi Münzenberg in Berlin. He was active in the League against Imperialism, Workers' International Relief and other Communist and Communist-controlled organisations. He visited the UK several times in the 1930s. Among other things he established a German Relief Committee in the UK in 1933 and attended the Commission of Enquiry into the Reichstag Fire, which was held in London".[37] A comprehensive, if slightly sensational, account of his life has been provided by Jonathan Miles, who diligently mined the Kew trove.[38]

Katz first arrived in Britain in March 1933, and from surveillance and intercepts of mail, MI5 and Special Branch were soon able to detect who his contacts were. However, despite repeated requests to the Home Office Aliens Branch that he should not be allowed to re-enter the country, he was able to travel between London and Paris at will. MI5 reported the following, on December 13, 1933: "Once again, Katz was nearly refused entry. Captain Liddell suggested that 'if exception was to be taken at all to visits to this country by foreign Communists, Otto Katz was about as bad a case as could be found'", but Katz was nonetheless allowed to travel unimpeded. The reason is that he had influential supporters, especially in the persons of the Labour MP (and ex-Communist) Ellen Wilkinson, and the similarly disposed lawyer and MP, Dennis Pritt. Katz several times asked Wilkinson to intervene with the Home Office on his behalf, and she successfully did so.

MI5's files on Pritt were released in 2002, where he is described as follows: "He was a member of the governing bodies of numerous organisations which the Communist Party of Great Britain (CPGB) controlled or sought strongly to influence, and played a significant part in their activities. As such he was in close contact with leading members of the CPGB".[39] As early as July 1, 1933, Sissmore wrote that Pritt was a "disgruntled man who has gone 'Bolo'[ii] for some reason", and was inciting mutiny. She characterised him as supporting the extreme left in the hope of getting a high legal appointment in a socialist government. Another significant note recorded in Pritt's file by an otherwise unidentifiable 'GMH' gives early evidence (in July 1934) of the manner in which appeasement was starting to affect intelligence policy: GMH wrote to Vivian: "by way of pacifying the Germans, it might perhaps be as well to say that in cases where people are not members of the Communist Party, we do not investigate their activities closely". A note made on February 17, 1937 states that Pritt was "impressed with the genuineness and fairness of the Moscow trials" (where he was an invited witness): it was Dick White at this stage who informed Vivian in SIS of this opinion (one might ask: why not Sissmore?[40]), and in October 1937, another note records that the election of Pritt, along with his close friend Stafford Cripps (another rich lawyer) and Harold Laski, to the Executive of the Labour Party, was "seen by CPGB as a considerable advance towards the goal of affiliation to the Labour Party". Pritt was banished from the Labour Party for supporting the Soviet invasion of Finland in 1940, and remained an unabashed supporter of Stalinism. He also assisted in gaining the family of Kuczynskis, some of them open Communists, others undercover spies, into the country.

If MI5 maintained a file on Pritt's primary partner in aiding Katz, Ellen Wilkinson, it has not been released. There are, nevertheless, indications that such a file did exist: annotations in Katz's records make overt references to it. For example, on May 2, 1935, the following note appears: "Note to copy to Wilkinson, Ellen file PF 42136. Kell [initialled by Sissmore] write to Holderness and Norton in FO informing him of Katz's approach to Wilkinson 'asking her to find some influential person whom the Home Office could not refuse' to support his application". A later entry, from June 26, 1936, consists of a letter complaining about Wilkinson's efforts on Katz's behalf, with the same file number referenced. The final paragraph of this letter recommends that the Home Office should see Wilkinson's letter, but a handwritten annotation observes that this paragraph was "expunged from the Home Office copy".

One can surmise a good reason for this coyness, for Wilkinson was almost certainly Katz's lover. The MI5 files indicate observations made when Katz stayed overnight at Wilkinson's apartment, and Miles referred to the fact that Wilkinson asked her close friend Isabel Brown (secretary to the British Committee for the Relief of the Victims of German Fascism, on which Katz, Pritt, Wilkinson and other leftists, including the spy Ivor Montagu and the publisher

---

[ii] 'Bolo': Eric Partridge's *Dictionary of Slang and Unconventional English* (1984) suggests that 'bolo', from ca. 1930, was a term used to describe generally bloody-minded or obstructive behavior, while 'bolshy' indicated more serious Bolshevik intent. (By the 1960s, the latter term had replaced the former.) In that case, Sissmore's selection of a slang term is puzzling, as it serves to diminish Pritt's real objectives by reducing what provoked him to some inexplicable character defect. The next few years would no doubt have caused her to modify her assessment.

Victor Gollancz served) to try to quash rumours that were circulating about her affair with Katz.[41] Thus a situation arose that is eerily reminiscent of the incident that contributed greatly to the downfall of Harold Macmillan's government – the Profumo Affair of 1961. In that case, John Profumo, Minister of State for War, was determined to have shared the call-girl, Christine Keeler, with Captain Yevgeny Ivanov, a Soviet naval attaché, and thus could have dramatically jeopardised state secrets.

The Wilkinson-Katz affair had some different dimensions: first of all, it was much longer-lasting and serious than Profumo's brief flirtation. On the other hand, Wilkinson was not a Minister of the Crown, and thus was not privy to similar secrets, but her life afterwards puts a very different perspective on her association. In May 1940 she became a junior minister in Churchill's coalition government, working under Herbert Morrison in the Ministry of Supply, and she later started an affair with Morrison himself, a relationship that no historian or biographer has since denied. Morrison became Home Secretary in October 1940, and stayed in that position until the end of the war. The fact that a powerful Member of Parliament had been lovers both with the Home Secretary and a key propagandist for the Comintern (though not at the same time) was undoubtedly a fact that MI5, and British government circles, would wish to keep under covers. Yet her continued activities on behalf of her old friends and lovers were well known. As late as February 1944 (Katz had absconded to the USA in March 1940), she was writing to the Ministry of Home Security to request a transit visa for him.[42][iii] And as one biographer wrote: "She was certainly still in contact with old communist friends: in March 1946 she wrote asking Morgan Phillips, the General Secretary of the Labour Party, for a 'special favour' and give help to Otto Katz, known to British Intelligence as a Soviet agent".[43]

Wilkinson's activities clearly annoyed MI5. Katz was decidedly unwelcome, but Home Office decisions repeatedly allowed his re-entry to the country. When refugees from Hitler's invasions started to apply for permission to immigrate to the UK, Wilkinson boasted to Katz, in November 1938, of "getting the 25 Communist MPs, mostly Germans, from Czech into this country", using a plane chartered by Isabel Brown.[44] Katz continued to have communications with other dangerous persons. Wilkinson wrote to Katz on February 8 enclosing a letter for the Communist agent Colonel Hans Kahle regarding the latter's visa request for London, a process Wilkinson was aiding. A note of October 14, 1939 indicates that Kahle was in contact with Katz, and in June 1940, an intercepted letter from Jürgen's cousin Hilde (a noted communist firebrand) asked him to contact Katz in order to speed up their visa applications for Mexico.

Yet MI5's guard was lifted somewhat by then, and the archive suggests that Sissmore was no longer on the case. A note of November 21, 1938 from B.4b (which would indicate Dick White rather than her) makes the following very disingenuous announcement: "The only deduction which can be fairly drawn from the letter as a whole is that Miss Wilkinson is in closer contact with Comintern circles abroad than we had previously believed. This view is borne out

---

[iii] Ironically, Katz's file notes that John Curry was effectively reprimanded for acting on the visa application.

by her reference to 'the big fellow' in paragraph 4. This is a nickname by which paid Comintern employees in Paris frequently refer to one of their Chiefs whom we have never been able to identify." Was White not fully informed of previous researches? Had he not read the relevant files? And why was he covering Comintern issues at this stage? It is quite extraordinary that White, with his very limited experience, would have been considered fit to supplant the very capable Sissmore at this stage. He had been recruited on probation at the beginning of 1936, and had spent nine months in Germany, before returning to be signed up formally (and sign the Official Secrets Act) in March 1937.[45] He was then assigned to work on contacts at the German Embassy at the beginning of 1938, on behalf of MI5 and SIS. It is entirely illogical that he should have been considered as a worthy replacement for Sissmore as the leading expert on Communism.

The deterioration of anti-communist expertise nevertheless increased. On January 16, 1940, the lack of enthusiasm, and absence of corporate memory, was shown to have moved on even further, as a memorandum, apparently from Valentine Vivian of SIS to White, questions whether Katz really was an OGPU agent, "as the description appears to depend entirely on a statement by [Laurence] Grand [of Section D]".[46] Why had Liddell suddenly depreciated Sissmore's expertise and apparently taken her out of mainstream decision-making? Why White's star had risen so quickly to the detriment of Sissmore's is inexplicable, yet by May 1940, he was promoted to Assistant Director of the whole of B Division (having spent another few months in Germany at the beginning of 1939). This was also the case with the less impressive Roger Hollis, whom he and Sissmore had recruited (against Kell's instincts) in the summer of 1938, and whom Sissmore had been training in the interim. By June 1939, Hollis was already deputising for Sissmore, and using her identification (B4A) on some memoranda. Sissmore, who in September 1939, on the day war broke out, had married Captain John Archer, (another MI5 officer),[iv] must have been astounded at the turn of events, and other officers must surely have questioned why their experience counted for so little.

In summary, the activities of Communist sympathisers in influential positions did much to stymie the efforts of MI5 to prevent Comintern subversion as represented by Katz. The fragmented organisation of MI5, complemented by the haphazard leadership at the time, was a contributing factor to the ineffectual attempts by the organisation to rein him in. His actions might have seemed relatively harmless, but he had been identified as an important member of the Comintern, whose destructive ambitions were well understood. And Katz turned out to be a useful smoke-screen for the more subtle Soviet cause. His activities resulted in a host of 'busy-work' that distracted attention from the corrosive industry of the moles in place, and no one at MI5 appeared to have the time, the knowledge and the skill to join up all the dots properly, to trace his complex associations in detail, or to take the position of leadership to make a more convincing case to the Home Office that his presence in the country should be denied.

[iv] Jane Sissmore will be identified by her married name, Archer, hereafter.

We next turn to Percy Glading and the Woolwich Arsenal Case, which was one of the few successes achieved by MI5 during this period. The successful detection and prosecution of Glading can be attributed solely to Maxwell Knight and his network of agents. Knight was a maverick, unconventional and unorthodox. Jeffery described him as "a fervent anti-Communist, mildly eccentric jazz musician and keen naturalist", and related how he had developed in the 1920s an amateur detective service in London, "consisting of about 100 individuals in all walks of life".[47] While working for the Casuals in SIS, he had not shirked at burglary of the offices of Labour and Communist Party organisations, and he brought this reputation for not quite gentlemanly codes of conduct with him to MI5. Later in the decade, Dick White was to take "an instant dislike" to him. White told his planned biographer, Andrew Boyle (whose notes Tom Bower resurrected after Boyle's death) that Knight's interest in the occult and his suspected bisexuality cast him as "a bit mad", and Bower added that White shared with Liddell his "distinctive dislike of gung-ho operators".[48] Furthermore, Knight worked from his private office, in Dolphin Square[49]: he was not well integrated with the rest of 'B' Branch, and his reputation in the group was not helped by his personal misfortunes. In his biography of Knight, Anthony Masters related how his career at MI5 was tarnished by the rumours surrounding the death of his second wife, Gwladys, who committed suicide in November 1935, and how he had benefitted financially from her demise.[50] Thus there was an obvious culture clash between, on the one hand, the more cerebral activities of counter-espionage performed by the professionals and, on the other, the buccaneering gambits of Knight and his team.

Yet Knight's tactics worked. He took the long view, recognising that he was facing a durable enemy, and was prepared to invest time in developing his spy apparatus. His belief was that the most effective way of installing an agent within an enemy organisation was for the foe to approach the agent rather than the agent appearing keen to aid the target entity: later, in 1950, he wrote a report on the Glading case that outlined his philosophy for successful infiltration.[51] Thus his most valuable agent, Olga Gray, very slowly introduced herself to the League Against Imperialism and the Anti-War Movement, until she was introduced to Harry Pollitt, the General Secretary of the CPGB.[52] When Pollitt asked her to act as a courier, she at first demurred. After eventually accepting the engagement, and working for Pollitt for a few months in 1935, she felt she needed a break from the strain, and was withdrawn from the engagement for a while. Knight persuaded her to keep in casual touch with him and such party officials as Percy Glading, and, in February 1937, Glading approached her again, asking her to lease a flat to be used for what turned out to be photographic activity supporting espionage. Knight's patience was rewarded.

In April 1937, Percy Glading brought two visitors to the flat in Holland Road that Olga Gray had leased. They wanted to meet her. Glading identified one of them as 'Mr Peters', and Gray was later able to give an accurate description of him. Moreover, she was able to learn a lot about his career history, and was able to tell Knight that, before he joined the Bolsheviks, he had worked as a chaplain to an Austrian regiment in World War I.[53] His comrade was not so loquacious, although Gray found him "bumptious", and said that Glading did not take to him so well. This encounter was one of the most significant 'near-misses' of the 1930s, for the two visitors were among the most influential illegal Soviet agents in Britain that decade, namely Teodor Maly and Arnold Deutsch, who were much later recognised (by some) as having recruited the group misleadingly characterised as the 'Cambridge Five'. It constituted a double abuse of tradecraft: the two agents should never have allowed themselves to be seen in such a compromising position, and MI5 was again disastrously negligent in not following up the leads earlier. Moreover, Deutsch may have been mendacious in describing the outcome in a written testimony to Moscow Centre: he maintained that Gray's knowledge of Maly's background came out at the ensuing trial, and observed that she must have learned it from him directly, conveniently forgetting that the rules of *conspiratsia* that he so earnestly supported had been broken by the two of them.[54] Burke, however, suggested that Gray met Deutsch and Maly on different occasions, separately introduced by Glading. It is all very murky.

Deutsch was a notoriously careless agent. One of his riskiest decisions was to take up residence in one of the Lawn Road Flats in Hampstead, alongside many other foreign Communists and domestic left-wingers, including Andrew Rothstein and four members of the Kuczynski family, all spies.[55] Maly and Melita Norwood were frequent visitors. This could well have drawn attention to his activities, and, indeed the police visited him early in September 1937 as his permit was about to expire. His studies at London University were over, and, after he started working illegally in his cousin's film company, the authorities refused to extend his permit. He gave the explanation that he was about to leave, and then quickly made arrangements to meet with Cairncross, Maclean and Burgess in Paris, and also gave instructions to Philby to meet Orlov there, too. Despite this surveillance, he was incredibly allowed back in the country in November for a few days (as a graduate student), and tidied up other loose ends before returning to Moscow.[56] Someone was falling down on the job of tracking movements of personnel to and from this open camp of subversion.

On the other hand, Masters made the claim that "in the meantime, Knight was able to identify Peters as Theodore Maly", a claim seconded in Burke's book, as well as in John Costello's *Mask of Treachery*.[57] But Costello was merely quoting Masters: Burke's comment is unsourced. Such a recognition seems highly unlikely, unless Knight had additional knowledge that he kept to himself. Gary Kern, in his book on Krivitsky, wrote that, after his defection in September 1937, Krivitsky (who knew Maly well), told the French police about him and his role in Britain, as well as his cover name of Hardt.[58] One might imagine that that information would have been passed on to British intelligence – but that would have been some months after the Holland Road encounter, and, of course, when Maly was probably already dead. (Krivitsky was selective when identifying fellow agents.) Costello asserted that Maly left Britain "a matter of days after Olga Gray reported meeting him to Max Knight", implying that he was warned by an insider about Knight's suspicions: he did not provide a source.[59] But other evidence suggests that Maly did not leave for Paris until June 1937, having received an order that month to murder the defector Ignace Reiss, in the meantime having calmly reported to his bosses on his progress with Cairncross and Maclean.[60] A report on the Glading Affair (which was almost certainly written by Sissmore/Archer, and is included as part of an Appendix in the *Crown Jewels*, since it was a significant document passed on to Moscow by Blunt) confidently states that Maly left Britain in June 1937 "in a great hurry".[61] He may have received an urgent summons from Moscow rather than receiving a warning that his cover was blown.[62] Thus it apparently took a year for MI5 to work out who 'Peters' was.

In the interim, however, came the case of Woolwich Arsenal. The most comprehensive account of the events leading up to the arrest and conviction of Glading can be found in Burke's book about Melita Norwood.[63] On January 21, 1938, Percy Glading and his contact Albert Williams, who worked in the Department of the Chief Inspector of Armaments at Woolwich Arsenal, were arrested as Williams handed Glading a package. George Whomack, who had earlier smuggled drawings out of the Arsenal, was arrested on January 29, and on March 15 all three pleaded guilty to charges brought under the Official Secrets Act. All three received a gaol sentence: a fourth defendant, Charles Munday, was acquitted. Their defence was mounted by the familiar left-wing lawyer, Dennis Pritt, who, despite his vigorous and skilled performance, informed the three that the CPGB had instructed them to plead guilty, so as to minimise any disclosures about the Party's involvement. What is more important to the story are the leads that arose from the arrests, and the identification of some of the figures behind the scenes, prominently Maly, Willy and Mary Brandes (who replaced Maly), and the spy Melita Norwood.

As for Maly, the first entry in his file at the National Archives is dated about a year later, on March 14, 1938.[64] It notes that Kell was "still asking Holderness at the HO [Home Office] to exclude the Hardts", blithely unaware that Maly had been executed by then. (Hardt and Peters were both aliases used by Maly and his wife.) Four days later, a memo – probably from Valentine Vivian of SIS – was addressed to Jane Sissmore (i.e. Archer), congratulating her "on a splendid bit of research work and a real scoop over the identification of Hardt of the Reiss case as Peters, the predecessor of Stevens alias Brandes". This message requires some explanation. First, it would appear to counter solidly the claim that Knight was able to identify Maly immediately from Gray's information in April 1937, but does suggest that Krivitsky's information to the French police was not passed on. As for the 'Reiss case', what Vivian was referring to is the fact that, on July 17 and 18, 1937, Maly was in Paris, and had been ordered to arrange the murder of the Soviet defector who openly defied Stalin, Ignace Reiss (whose real name was Poretsky). Such intelligence must have come from SIS, but the MI5 files did not record it until October 23, 1939, when Archer referred, in a memo to a link to "Walter" from a source in Holland, Walter being "administrator and cashier of Soviet espionage apparatus in Northern Europe". Archer added, ominously, that Walter was "summoned to Moscow as Trotskyist" in August 1937, but disappeared. Maly did indeed return to Moscow in July 1937 (but from his own volition), and was shot later that year. 'Walter', however, was certainly Walter Krivitsky, who was also ordered to shoot Reiss, but declined, and, after his close friend Reiss was murdered in Geneva on September 5, was able to escape in Paris after himself being ordered back to Moscow in October of that year.

The couple known as the Stephens (in fact, Brandes) were also able to escape. On August 16, 1937, Glading had announced to Gray that Peters had "gone home", and introduced Mr and Mrs Stephens, who were going to take over the photography in the flat.[65] Even though they were detected exchanging documents, they were allowed to flee to Moscow on November 2, in full view of Special Branch officers at Victoria Station. Moreover, items found in Glading's house after his arrest provided leads in the form of diary entries that, after assistance from Vivian in SIS, allowed the identification of Melita Norwood (née Sirnis), whom SIS was already tracking. Burke wrote: "For some unexplained reason they decided against taking any action against her or her husband, Hilary". But "they" were SIS; taking action would have been MI5's responsibility.

One writer has taken pains to absolve MI5 of the charges that Costello, Masters and West levelled at MI5 for being negligent in allowing Maly and the Brandeses to escape. In *A Time for Spies*, written in 1999, William E. Duff, a CIA officer, pointed out that the accounts of those three authors lack detailed sources, and tend to echo stories placed without proper attribution elsewhere.[66] "In the unlikely event that MI5 knew at once of Mr Peters's identity, mission, and residence, with what would they have charged him? No admissible evidence then existed", he wrote, next referring to the Brandes file at the National Archives to refute Costello's claim that MI5 knew of the Brandeses' illegal Canadian documentation at the time of the October 21 surveillance. But Duff may have been a bit too trusting of the MI5 files, not allowing for them to perhaps have been weeded for the sake of posterity, something hinted at in Archer's report. And tracking Maly seriously might have led to other subversive operators even if a direct charge could not have been made against Maly himself.

Despite the plaudits she received, Archer was not happy with the overall outcome. She believed that the follow-up had not been energetic enough, and that the trial had failed to identify the members of the CPGB who had been involved in the espionage. She wanted others indicted, as her later report indicated.[67] Burke attributed the weakness to the political climate: the arch-appeaser of Hitler did not want to upset Stalin. "In March 1938", he wrote, "Neville Chamberlain, the British Prime Minister, could not afford an open breach with the Soviet Union. On the day M/7 [an unnamed MI5 spy within the CPGB] had learned that Collard and Pritt were 'trying to drive a bargain with the prosecution' the Wehrmacht had marched into Austria".[68] That is a possible explanation, but it does not dovetail well with Chamberlain's noted disgust with the Bolshevik system, and the poor level of trust that existed between him and Stalin, and it would furthermore suggest a very acute and timely – but unlikely – level of decision-making between high politics and judicial execution.

Archer's report (certainly written much later, when she had left MI5) does however come to a startling conclusion that raises deep questions about the level of cooperation between B 5(b) and B 4(a). After analysing the Glading case, and then the issues surrounding such figures as John King, Ernest Oldham, and Henri Pieck, she returned to the most puzzling aspect of them all, Teodor Maly:

"There are one or two interesting facts in the file but the strangest thing is that although Hardt was recognised by everyone as an important figure in the case, no serious attempts were made to keep a close watch on him. His address was known, although it seems to me that it was only discovered after he left the country. Anyway, he could have been found at Percy Glading's home, and a watch could have been put on him. Perhaps the policy was to follow Glading, and arrest him so as to frighten the other members of the organisation into stopping operations.

After Hardt's departure, much was done to study the evidence and all the inhabitants of his block of flats were questioned thoroughly. Some of his papers and cheques were found and the people mentioned investigated, evidently without results. It is possible that Hardt was not followed systematically, perhaps out of fear that he might notice his tail thus spoiling the game. Mi5 [*sic*], as I know, is very careful about such matters and this view is confirmed by the fact that the watch on the embassy was lifted for fear that the sleuths might be recognised by people who had seen them at Party meetings. You once asked if MI5 had photographs of the people connected with this case? They have photographs of Hardt and his wife, and of Brandes and his wife, although I did not see these."

Was the leading expert on Soviet espionage not consulted on the case? Who is "everyone"? What is the distinction between an address being "known" and "discovered"? If Hardt was not followed systematically, was he in truth surveilled, but only haphazardly? If Archer knew that no efforts "were made to keep a close watch on him", then that would suggest that his identity and role were suspected, at least, so why is there no entry in the MI5 file before March 1938? (The hint described earlier that Maly was frightened off by MI5's investigating his residence would suggest that notes on file would have been made. The file could obviously have been weeded to cover up this embarrassment.) At what time did MI5 possess the photographs? Did Archer make recommendations that were not followed? Was she really completely unaware of what the "policy" regarding Glading was? Archer loyally used the passive voice in making her observations, without indicating who was at fault, but it is an astounding testimony about a failure to follow up, and hints that she was kept completely out of the loop. What is also intriguing is that the report (described as "MI5's Report", and which must have been written after Krivitsky's interrogation in early 1940, even though it does not mention him by name, describing him merely as "a reliable source") seems to be directed at her new boss ("you") in SIS, Vivian. MI5 was referred to in the third person, and it was Vivian who had been asking the questions. It must have been written in 1941, shortly after Archer was hired by SIS (having been sacked by MI5 in November 1940), and before Blunt chanced upon the document in 1942. Maybe Archer felt freer to voice her opinions only when she was no longer under the management of officers for whom she had little respect – Harker, Liddell, and even White. If this was so, it did not last long. Liddell reported, in his *Diaries* that Jane Archer came back to speak to him, in 1944, and again in 1947, about her dissatisfactions in SIS, and she began to perform analysis of the Comintern in a clandestine manner for MI5, unable to work openly so long as

Harker was still around.[69] She unmistakably appears – though identified only as "Miss X" – as an expert representative from SIS in the records of the 1948 interrogations of the spy and defector Alexander Foote.[70]

As for Maxwell Knight, his career recovered after the Glading conviction. Olga Gray was swiftly cast aside with a not-too-generous stipend, but, as Masters wrote: " . . . for Knight, the arrest and sentencing of Glading and his compatriots was a godsend, bringing him a sharp increase in respect from Kell, Harker and Liddell. The scandal surrounding the manner of Gwladys's death and the subsequent inquest was now overtaken by his successful breaking of the Woolwich Arsenal spy ring."[71] (The organisation chart for July 1941 shows "Agents", under Major Maxwell Knight, reporting as B2, directly to Liddell at the same level as White's Counter-Espionage Section, B1, and this promotion may well have contributed to White's resentment.[72]) Knight later had another success, in the Tyler Kent affair of early 1940, but his career foundered in the misjudged persecution of Benjamin Greene, a Pacifist Quaker with German connections, in the summer of 1940. He did, however, maintain a keen eye on Communist infiltration, as on the occasion when one of his agents, Tom Driberg, who had infiltrated the CPGB, was discovered by Anthony Blunt. By that time, his influence was on the wane, and Masters suggested that Knight had enemies in MI5, who were jealous of the independence of the old B5 (b) as well as his special relationship with Desmond Morton. Driberg's expulsion from the CPGB in 1941 prompted Knight to write a report titled *The Comintern Is Not Dead* to the officer then responsible for Communist counter-espionage, Roger Hollis. Hollis rejected the report, so Knight sent it to Liddell, who likewise turned it down.[73] They did not want to read about a suspicion of Soviet penetration in Britain's intelligence corps, and this mindset was soon afterwards to result in the gross misleading of the Security Executive.

Knight's claims have been supported in at least two quarters. His friend Derek Tangye (who appears in 'B' Branch organisation charts as responsible for Press Relations), wrote in his memoir *The Road To Minack*: "Soon after I joined MI5, one of the most experienced and imaginative amongst my colleagues [i.e. Knight] said to me 'The Russians are very patient. They will recruit a young man at university with Communist views, tell him to disassociate himself from the Party, watch him, and keep him on ice for years. Then one day they will come to him and say: Now we want you to do this.'" [v] This was a very prescient observation: one can imagine that Tangye was not the only other officer he had told this to.[74] And a fellow sceptic, likewise pushed gently aside by the authorities, John Curry, wrote glowingly of Knight's contributions in his official history, and referred obliquely to Knight's Comintern report[75]:

> "Major Maxwell Knight has emphasised the importance of long-term planning in dealing with the Soviet Intelligence Service which is remarkable for its thoroughness, patience and its own long-term work; and offers more serious problems than those with which the Germans

---

[v] This testimony could of course be faulty. But it is frequently sounder to rely on the statements of minor characters with no reputation to defend, or axe to grind, than on those from the Great and the Good.

have confronted us. This is a point of first-class importance for the future, with special reference to the conditions of counter-espionage work in peace-time."

This was, however, no longer a message that the directors of MI5 wanted to hear or echo.

In summary, the missteps over the Woolwich Arsenal case were self-inflicted. The leadership of MI5 had not successfully integrated the teams working within the organisation, and they let political and cultural issues affect the efficient operation of the counter-espionage machine. The voices and influence of those who recognised the starkness of the Communist threat best (Knight, Archer, Curry, and even Kell) were being drowned by those with leftist sympathies or who were too indulgent to the socialist cause, or who had their eyes on their own career advancement (Liddell), or who were simply incompetent (Harker) or inexperienced (White).

The third case-study concerns Kim Philby, demonstrating how even a rascally reputation can wrongly influence the less than rigorous historian or journalist, and contribute to the cover-up over MI5's inadequate surveillance practices. Of the Soviet agents known as the 'Cambridge Five' Philby was the most committed, the most cold-blooded, the most imperturbable. He remained loyal to the Stalinist ethos that attracted him in the 1930s, through the purges, the Nazi-Soviet Pact, the rape of the Baltic nations, the massacres, the Gulag, the oppression of the Eastern European satellite states, and the persecutions. Apart from John Cairncross, Philby was the only mole to write a comprehensive account of why he dedicated his life to the communist cause.[76] And he is the most written-about of them all. Yet the lives of spies are riddled with deception and duplicity. Despite the obviousness of this truth, and the fact that Philby's memoir was written in Moscow, indubitably under the control of his KGB masters, what he wrote – and the interviews he gave – have been taken, selectively, as a reliable version of how he was recruited by the Comintern.

Philby never worked for MI5,[vi] but his role as a key liaison officer in SIS (where he was responsible for Soviet counter-intelligence, and worked closely with MI5 at a time when the merger of the two organisations was seriously discussed[77]), his track-record as a Soviet agent, the pointers to his identity made by Krivitsky, the struggles that MI5 experienced in dealing with him, and the way his distortions of the truth have been accepted by Western journalists, all give him a substantial relevance to the story. He is a poster-child for the delusions that MI5 had about communists. Philby did not become an intelligence officer until he joined Section D in July 1940, shortly before it was absorbed into the SOE (Special Operations Executive). But his preparation for such a move was made in 1934 – if we are to believe the testimony of his avowed Communist handler; a couple of years earlier, if all the evidence is scrupulously inspected.

Part of the challenge of determining what happened is that even British intelligence officers have been taken in by his dissembling. Thus Hugh Trevor-

---

[vi] Philby worked only for SOE and SIS. Yet in his memoir, *My Silent War* (p 32), he claims that SIS "was known as MI5". Was this a secret signal that his work was ghosted?

Roper, who joined the Radio Security Service (RSS) in late 1939, and then led its successor group, the Radio Intelligence Service within SIS in April 1943, expressed a supreme confidence in being able to detect the truth in Philby's story. In an essay whose creation was encouraged by his friends in MI5, he wrote, when reviewing a series of books on Philby (including Philby's *My Silent War*): "The authors [Page, Leitch and Knightley] have certainly established the details of Philby's career with substantial accuracy – he himself has admitted that . . .", as if Philby's honesty over such an issue were unquestionable.[78] Yet he can quickly cast doubts on the testimony of E. H. Cookridge (born Edward Spiro, in Vienna, who knew Philby well in 1934) which suffers because "it is far less accurate in detail, it omits important episodes, and some of its confident assertions are hopelessly wrong." Later, Trevor-Roper added that Cookridge "claims to have met Philby" in Vienna in 1934, insinuating that this may well have been untrue, but then the learned historian confounds his own judgment by stating that the episode of Philby's "acting openly with the communists" is the best part of the book. The fact that Cookridge was a witness is a fact that is subordinate to Trevor-Roper's wisdom. The same year (1968) Trevor-Roper's acolyte, Charles Stuart, wrote of *My Silent War*, in a *Spectator* review of Philby's and Trevor-Roper's books, that ". . . it is founded on personal experience and has the authenticity that this brings."[79] That is an unjustifiable jump of logic when assessing the memoirs of spies.

One of Philby's main assertions was that he was recruited by Arnold Deutsch, known as Otto, on his return from Vienna with his new bride, Litzi Friedmann, in the summer of 1934, and only then committed himself to supporting the communist cause. That story has been distorted and misrepresented repeatedly over the years, as the following analysis shows:

- In *My Silent War* (1968), Philby elided over his recruitment, merely stating that when he left Cambridge in the summer of 1933, he was convinced his life would be dedicated to Communism.[80] (In *Deadly Illusions*, Costello and Tsarev claimed that Alexander Orlov supervised and was ultimately responsible for directing Philby as agent. Because of Soviet attempts to get Orlov back (who had defected and made a deal with Stalin), Philby was not permitted by the KGB to even hint at how he was recruited.)[81]
- In *The Third Man* (1968), Cookridge said that Philby did not return to London until the end of summer, 1934, where he was recruited by Simon Kremer at the Soviet Embassy.[82]
- In *The Philby Conspiracy* (1968), Page, Leitch and Knightley (who interviewed Philby's children in Moscow), reported that Philby told his offspring that "I was recruited in 1933, given the job of penetrating British intelligence, and told it did not matter how long I took to do the job."[83]
- In *Philby: The Long Road to Moscow* (1973), Seale and McConville reported an earlier return to London, in early April, but that Philby was not recruited for some months, and still only on probation, the first steps being "directed by intelligence officer on the staff of the Soviet Embassy".[84]
- In *The Fourth Man* (1979), Andrew Boyle indicated that Philby was already a novice agent on probation when he went to Vienna in September 1933.[85]

- In *The British Connection*, (1979), Richard Deacon suggested that Deutsch probably recruited Philby when the latter was visiting Vienna.[86] Chapman Pincher stated, in *Too Secret Too Long*, that Philby admitted to Nicholas Elliott in Beirut, just before his defection, that he had been recruited by OTTO (Deutsch) in Vienna in 1934.[87] (This claim actually makes the most sense, as will be explored later.)

- In *The Master Spy* (1988), Phillip Knightley introduced the idea of the obvious lie: "Litzi said that KP took no part in Communist activities in Vienna – a cover story that KP confirmed to Knightley that they had planned she would say". He added that the Philbys did not leave Vienna until May 1934, and stopped off in Paris on their way back to London. When he interviewed Philby in Moscow, he was told: "My work in Vienna must have caught the attention of the people who are now my colleagues in Moscow because almost immediately on my return to Britain I was approached by a man who asked me if I would like to join the Russian intelligence service. For operational reasons I don't propose to name this man, but I can say that he was not a Russian although he was working for the Russians".[88]

- John Costello, in *Mask of Treachery* (1988) observed that Philby's expressed intention to sit Civil Service exams (as he told his tutor at Cambridge) reflects Soviet determination to press moles into government, adding "that Philby would even consider a Whitehall career *after* deciding to become a Communist agent suggests that he too had come under cultivation by the Soviets before he left Cambridge".[89]

- *Deadly Illusions* (1993), by John Costello and Oleg Tsarev, gives the impression that Soviet Intelligence had successfully stirred the pot. Litzi is reported as not receiving her passport until late April, and the Philbys set off for Paris via Germany. "That Philby had approached the CPGB before his first meeting with Reif is itself confirmation that he had not, as previously believed, been recruited in Vienna. This is corroborated by NKVD archival records, and by KPO's 239-page deposition." The authors added that, in the spring of 1934, Philby went to CPGB HQ to renew [*sic*] links with the CP *before* he was approached by Reif, but received a frosty reception at CPGB headquarters. Litzi Philby invited her friend, Edith Tudor-Hart to tea, and Edith was impressed by Philby, and thus reported his candidacy to Deutsch, who consulted with Reif. Reif approved Philby's recruitment in June 1934. "My decision to go to Austria was taken before I had decided to join the Communist movement", Philby is quoted as saying.[90] But Costello and Tsarev were far too trusting of the reliability of Philby's memoir, and they attribute to "faulty memory" many of the contradictions between Moscow's and Philby's account that occur in their flawed narrative.

- *Treason in the Blood* (1994), by Anthony Cave-Brown, has the couple leaving Vienna on May 2, and spending a holiday in Paris before arriving in London in mid-May. Philby celebrated June 1 as the day he was approached by Deutsch.[91]

- The chronology shifts in *The Philby Files* (1994) by Genrikh Borovik. Philby decided to continue Party work with Litzi in England, and was back there in time to participate in the May Day parade in London. Again, Philby sought out contacts at the Soviet Embassy, but this time a man [i.e. not Edith Tudor-Hart] he met in Austria sought him out, to introduce him to Deutsch. Philby considered "it very lucky this chance happening occurred".[92]

- Yuri Modin (the handler of the 'Cambridge Five' after the war), admitted, in *My Five Cambridge Friends* (1994) to all the confusion, but clarified it all for us by saying that the NKVD was not involved, and that, "from 1934 to 1940, the Soviet secret service was the last thing on their minds". What he meant, of course, is that it was the innocent Comintern that was involved: he confirmed the meetings with Deutsch, but claimed it was another unknown NKVD officer [sic] who directed his work.[93]

- *The Crown Jewels* (1998), by Nigel West and Oleg Tsarev, has some interesting things to say about Deutsch, but merely repeats the June 1934 recruitment.[94]

- In *A Time For Spies* (1999), William E. Duff followed the Costello/Tsarev account, but pointed out the contradictions between Costello and Tsarev, indicated that Costello gave too much credit to Orlov and observed that Tsarev's original source material had not been examined.[95]

- *The Mitrokhin Archive* (1999) by Christopher Andrew and Vasili Mitrokhin suggests that the Tudor-Harts had been recruited by Deutsch in London, and given the codename STRELA. The authors cited *Deadly Illusions* as their main source for the recruitment of Philby.[96]

- Now the unpublished memoirs of Philby are revealed by his fourth wife, Rufina Philby, with Hayden Peake and Mikhail Lyubimov, in *The Private Life of Kim Philby* (2000). Here again, the Philbys were able to enjoy the May Day march in Camden Town, and then they were visited by a male friend, whom Philby had seen two or three times since returning from Vienna. This friend introduced Philby to Deutsch (i.e. there is no Edith Tudor-Hart in this variation).[97]

- Almost a decade later, Christopher Andrew changed his tune, owing to the discovery of an "untitled memorandum in Security Service archives". Thus the official history of MI5, *The Defence of the Realm* (2009), allowed Andrew to reveal 'the truth' about Philby's recruitment, deposited on the eve of his defecting to Moscow in 1963. "Lizzy came home one evening and told me that she had arranged for me to meet a 'man of decisive importance'. .... Otto spoke at great length, arguing that a person with my family background could do far more for Communism than the run-of-the-mill Party member or sympathiser."[98]

The multiple contradictions in these accounts indicate that there is a lively market in Philby mythology, and that too many reporters have deluded themselves into thinking that Philby would have no reason to deceive once he was in the safety of Moscow, and have not checked out the competing versions. Peter Shipley, who has made a detailed study of secret Soviet operations in Britain, wrote: "No fewer than twelve individuals have been identified as the recruiters, and, or, controllers of Kim Philby between 1933 and 1939".[99] The confusion is caused partly because three competing intelligence organisations, the GRU (military), the NKVD (secret police) and INO (Comintern) simultaneously deployed agents in target countries, such agents moved from one department to another, and cryptonyms were sometimes reused. And it was in the Soviet Union's interest to keep the story murky. Thus, despite the repute attributed to him, Arnold Deutsch may not have been the only or true 'OTTO' described as being responsible for the mole strategy, and the recruitment of Philby and his colleagues. It must be pointed out, however, that Deutsch and Philby were both in Vienna at the beginning of 1934, and it seems inconceivable that the Comintern would not have grasped the opportunity to recruit Philby while he was fresh, active, motivated and on neutral ground. Thus Deacon's scenario is the most probable. Many of those involved would have preferred to minimise the extent of Philby's actions in support of Communism while in Vienna – not least, of course, those like Gaitskell in politics [*see below*], and White and Liddell in MI5, who had excellent reasons for encouraging the notion that Philby was recruited out of plain sight in London later that summer.

So what about Deutsch's account of the events? A comprehensive *curriculum vitae*, which he had to supply to his Moscow bosses in December 1938, put a dramatically different perspective on events.[100] In his own words, Deutsch related that he was told that he would be sent to Britain in October 1933. But then he continued to Vienna, where he recruited STRELA and JOHN. West and Tsarev stated that STRELA had not been identified, but it is now clear that this referred to the Tudor-Harts, who were thus recruited by Deutsch in Vienna, not in London. They also stated that JOHN had not been identified, but Seale and McConville reported that, in October 1933, John Lehmann was approached three times by a Communist agent when in Vienna at that time to become a spy: he said he declined each offer. If EDITH could be Edith Tudor-Hart, there is no reason why JOHN could not be John Lehmann.

Deutsch then went on to write that, in February 1934 he went to London, where he recruited Edith, "whom I already knew in Vienna". This sounds like misinformation: if the Tudor-Harts were already signed up, there was no need to wait until London before signing up Edith separately. And he could surely have signed up Philby in Vienna as well, for Philby had shown enough of his commitment and stripes to have passed any probationary tests. If Deutsch were mixing socially with such as John Lehmann and the Tudor-Harts in Vienna, he must surely have come across Philby: the claim that the encounter in Regent's Park in the summer of 1934 was their first must be pure fiction. As noted above, this is the story that Philby told Nicholas Elliott in Beirut. Moreover, Deutsch made no mention of his recruitment of Philby in London, merely indicating that he worked there with Ignaty Reif[vii] and Orlov through 1934 and 1935. If he was ready to boast of his recruitment of the Tudor-Harts, why would he omit any mention of Philby? The Soviets had an interest in such obfuscation, as it distracts attention from the fact that Philby engaged in some real subversive mischief in Vienna.

For Philby was seriously involved with work for the Comintern in Vienna, using his British passport to perform courier services (including smuggling) between Vienna and Prague, and helping communists escape across the border,

---

[vii] Ignaty Reif is frequently confused with Ignace Reiss.

where his activities were noticed by many. Cookridge claimed he was working for the Comintern in the early summer of 1933, and given his clear mission. After an introduction to a Communist front in Paris, he mixed in Vienna with several Cambridge friends. On February 24, 1934, Philby married the very public Communist, Litzi Friedmann, thus enabling her escape with him to England. Page, Leitch and Knightley quoted Ilse Barea as saying that the sometime Marxist Hugh Gaitskell, the future leader of the Labour Party (who was in Vienna studying, ironically, under the liberal economist Friedrich Hayek) was "horrified" to hear of Philby's marriage to Litzi.[101] (Anthony Cave-Brown suggested that Gaitskell and Kollek may have attended the marriage ceremony.)[102] As one of Gaitskell's biographers, Brian Barati, confirmed, Gaitskell himself was very active in arranging escape routes, and was regularly followed by the Austrian secret police.[103] Ilsa Barea (then Kulcsar) and her husband, Leopold, were part of a Communist cell in Vienna in 1934, and headed a Leninist group called *Der Funke* (The Spark). She carried on a correspondence with Gaitskell in 1935, and when her husband died in Spain in 1938, she married Arturo Barea.[104] Naomi Mitchison also wrote in her diary that Philby was a Communist, and Lilly Jerusalem's mother sent her a cutting with a note that everyone in Vienna knew of his affiliations.[105] In *The Master Spy*, Knightley cited the future mayor of Jerusalem, Teddy Kollek, recalling Philby's moving in Communist circles in Vienna.[106] Muriel Gardiner, the lover of Stephen Spender, whose career was imaginatively glorified as Julia in Lillian Hellman's *Pentimento*, recalled Philby giving her a package of Communist literature to be delivered.[107]

What is extraordinary about Philby's escapades, and his very public abetting of Communist schemes, including his marriage to Litzi, is how dangerous they were for the concealment of his future role as a mole. One can only assume that, at this time, the Comintern was so confident about the successful spread of revolution throughout Europe (cf. the MASK traffic described earlier in this chapter) that they threw caution to the winds, applying resources to the cause without considering that the original infiltration strategy would have to be resuscitated. Thus, when the revolutionary socialist movement in Vienna was quashed, Philby had to be instructed to make a very public reversal of doctrine, and align himself with the fascists. Yet his past was unavoidable, given how visible he had been. Several writers have recorded how Teddy Kollek, then mayor of Jerusalem, was visiting the CIA in Washington in 1949, and, espying Kim Philby (who was the SIS liaison with the CIA), in a corridor, expressed amazement that such a known Communist could be working in that role.[108] And it was Flora Solomon, to whom Philby introduced Litzi, and to whom Litzi's housekeeper, Bella Meyer, explained the background in Vienna, who eventually informed Lord Rothschild of Philby's communist past.[109] What was really egregious, however, was the behavior of Hugh Gaitskell.

On May 15, 1940, Hugh Dalton was appointed Minister of Economic Warfare, and immediately appointed Gaitskell as his private assistant. Six days later, Philby reached England's shores after escaping from Paris, where he had been a journalist with the *Times* since November 1939. At the end of June, after introductions from his collaborator Guy Burgess, he had interviews with SIS, for a position in Section D. Colonel Valentine Vivian seemed convinced that

Philby's ties with Litzi Friedmann were ephemeral, and he was hired on July 17. On July 16, Dalton had been selected by Churchill to head up the new Special Operations Executive (SOE), with responsibilities for propaganda and subversion against the Nazis in Europe. On July 22, Gaitskell was given the task of organising its SO3 unit, concerned with research. On August 16, both Burgess and Philby were transferred to SOE headquarters in Baker Street. When the charter of SOE was formally set up on September 1, with more stringent recruitment practices, Philby was asked to fill out a formal application. In doing so, he lied about his marriage to Litzi. Philby's application was supported by Gaitskell, who in a forgetful testimony, characterised him as merely "an altruistic left-winger . . . eager to assist the leftwing cause without leaning quite as far as communism", rather like himself. [110] (Gaitskell's life would end suddenly, in bizarre circumstances, with hints of Soviet subterfuge.) [111] Thus Philby's Comintern-directed goal of gaining entry to Britain's intelligence services had been assured.

Philby's Communist past should undoubtedly have disqualified him from recruitment to Britain's intelligence services. (And as late as February, 1937, when Philby left London to work as a Soviet agent in Spain, he was accompanied to Portugal by Litzi, which should have raised serious red flags. [112]) The critical lesson that Philby's experiences teach, however, is that it was possible to have an *activist* communist past, yet still be accepted for an important role in security or intelligence, whether in MI5 or SIS. The outcome of this success of Comintern propaganda would appear later in the achievements of Klaus Fuchs, who could not conceal completely his subversive acts in Germany, and thus had to maintain a profile of a partially reformed but harmless communist. By summer 1940, an indulgence towards Communists (or presumed ex-Communists) had corroded MI5's defence mechanisms. Trevor-Roper, writing in 1968, typified the extraordinary woolly thinking of the intellectual of the 1930s:

> "I hasten to add that, although I myself knew of Philby's communist past, it would never have occurred to me, at that time, to hold it against him. Indeed, I was rather cheered than depressed by this unusual recruitment. My own view, like that of most of my contemporaries, was that our superiors were lunatic in their anti-communism. Many of our friends had been, or had thought themselves, communists in the 1930s; and we were shocked that such persons should be debarred from public service on account of mere juvenile illusions which anyway they had now shed: for such illusions could not survive the shattering impact of Stalin's Pact with Hitler in 1939." [113]

While Trevor-Roper was right to assume that Vivian and Cowgill in SIS had been aware of Philby's past, and had thus made a decision out of knowledge rather than ignorance, his analysis shows a dire misunderstanding of the realities of the situation: that the 'lunacy' of his superiors' anti-communism indeed represented the serious policy of the intelligence services to take an enduring subversive threat earnestly, at a time when Stalin was an ally of Hitler; that there was a distinct difference between the romantic notion of communism that Trevor-Roper's friends espoused, and the brutal repression that Lenin's and Stalin's realisation of the idea had delivered since the Bolshevik Revolution; and that any policy for excluding potential risks to the services in recruitment policies should make a distinction between juvenile affectations that expressed hopes for Equality and the Brotherhood of Man, and the serious commitments of those who had decided to work for Communist cells in foreign lands in the service of that hostile ideology.

Of course, if Trevor-Roper had considered the other totalitarian bogey, and said that his superiors were "lunatic in their anti-fascism", he would have been derided and ostracised. Yet Philby had joined the Anglo-German Fellowship, using the goodwill towards the Nazis as cover for his communism, and should presumably have been excluded from consideration by SIS on that count, too. Dick White was naturally delighted with the explanations Trevor-Roper offered in *The Philby Affair*, first published as an article in *Encounter*, as White had previously been taken in by Philby's charm, and could well have benefited from a message of exculpation.[114] In a letter to Isaiah Berlin in October 1981 Trevor-Roper wrote: 'I wrote this book (as I wrote *The Last Days of Hitler*) at the explicit suggestion of Dick White, then head of MI6 – who, however, did not see it, and did not want to see it, before publication."[115] At the time of publication, Trevor-Roper had told his friend Patrick Reilly (Ambassador to France), that "Dick White has found it [the article] so innocent that he has asked me to appear on T/V on the subject, as a corrective force, a bulwark of orthodoxy, a prop and shield of the Old Firm".[116] History and memoir rose again to the role of Public Relations: the reputation of the institution was more important than the truth.

***

MI5 in the 1930s can be described as an institution with missing links. The source documents released to the public are full of them, with redacted sections, obviously weeded files, and sterile pointers to other documents – like the defunct URLs of the World Wide Web – symptomatic of the discomfort that MI5's custodians still feel today. And there are multiple examples of failure to provide the right linkages in the operation of the institution as it tried to combat Communist subversion: the inability to recall the infiltration that occurred at the end of the previous decade, and the establishment of diehard Communists at Cambridge University; the inadequate leadership and communication from the directors of MI5 in delegating appropriately and integrating the groups within the organisation charged with detecting communist espionage and subversion; the lack of success in convincing their political masters of the seriousness and insidiousness of the actions of those who frustrated their efforts (such as Wilkinson and Pritt), and their links to Stalin's apparatus; the failure to bridge the political and cultural gaps between different sections of MI5; the laxity in following up the leads from the movements of such as Maly and Deutsch and the Kuczynskis, and the associations they made; the ineptitude with which MI5's Registry was ignored, and the multiple signals that Philby had given about his unreliability, when he was considered for recruitment as an intelligence officer. Most egregious was the sidelining of the most capable officer MI5 possessed – Jane Archer. What did work were the links of 'old school ties' and class affinity.

By the end of 1939, with White and Hollis promoted before their time, and Archer already being moved out of a leadership role, the awareness of, and attention to, the Communist threat, had been sharply diluted. As Andrew wrote of that time: "B Division (counter-espionage) was wholly occupied with enemy (chiefly German) spies".[117] MI5 was given a unique opportunity to be jolted out of its complacency when the defector Walter Krivitsky agreed to some intense discussions at the beginning of 1940. How would the institution react to his urgent and alarming message?

Notes

[1] A. J. P. Taylor, *English History 1914-1945*, p 359.

[2] MI5 appears not to have had any formal process of strategic planning in place: in October 1941, John Curry, then in charge of F Division, was moved to a new appointment as 'Research'. This was more an attempt to integrate disparate activities relating to the Germans than a focus on longer-term planning.

[3] Gill Bennett, *Churchill's Man of Mystery*, pp 127-134.

[4] John Curry, *The Security Service 1908-1945*, pp 101-103.

[5] ibid., p 101.

[6] Christopher Andrew, *The Defence of the Realm*, Appendix 1.

[7] Nigel West (*MI5*, p 351) stated that "Hollis was promoted to Assistant Director rank in 1940, after two years in 'F' Division." This is not so, as 'F' Branch (or Division) did not exist at that time. Hollis had been working in 'B' Branch since his recruitment in 1938. Hollis later replaced Curry as head of 'F' Division. Andrew made a similar mistake in suggesting that 'F' Division was active early in 1940, with a single officer (F2c) working on counter subversion in 'F' Division (p 268).

[8] West, pp 25-33.

[9] TNA, KV 4/127.

[10] Andrew, p 134.

[11] Andrew, pp 122, 123, 152, 164 and 893.

[12] See Kevin Quinlan, *The Secret War Between The Wars, MI5 in the 1920s and 1930s*, and Victor Madeira, *Britannia and the Bear*.

[13] West, p 30.

[14] Andrew, p 128.

[15] Madeira, p 174.

[16] Keith Jeffrey, *The Secret History of MI6, 1909-1949*, pp 232-235.

[17] TNA, KV 4/125.

[18] Women were allowed to become barristers only in 1922. Ivy Williams was the first to be called to the Bar, in May 1922, and Helen Normanton the first to practice, later that year.

[19] Andrew, p 887, and TNA, KV 4/127.

[20] Quinlan, pp 67-68, 74-75.

[21] Andrew, pp 163-164, and TNA, KV 2/604.

[22] The Guy Liddell Diaries, December 6, 1940.

[23] Andrew, p 131.

[24] Curry, p 392.

[25] Curry reported that MI5 started receiving the MASK information only in January 1935. Why the delay occurred is not explained, but the timing of the 1935 Report makes more sense in that scenario.

[26] Nigel West, *MASK, MI5's Penetration of the Communist Party of Great Britain*, p 119.

[27] David Leigh, *The Wilson Plot*, p 26.

[28] Christopher Andrew, *Secret Service: The Making of Britain's Intelligence Community*, pp 345, 350, 379.

[29] F. H. Hinsley and C. A. G. Simkins, *British Intelligence in the Second World War*, Volume 4, p 18.

[30] Curry, p 106.

[31] Quinlan, p 81.

[32] Quinlan, p 82, and TNA, KV 3/12.

[33] *The Defence of the Realm*, p 170; *The Sword and the Shield*, p 58; *The Mitrokhin Archive*, Volume 7, Chapter 10, para 1.

[34] Madeira, p 97.

[35] David Burke, *The Spy Who Came in from the Co-Op*, p 67.

[36] James Smith, *British Writers and MI5 Surveillance, 1930-1960*, p 154.

[37] TNA, KV 2/1382, KV 2/1383 and KV 2/1384.

[38] Jonathan Miles, *The Nine Lives of Otto Katz*.

[39] TNA, KV 2/1062, KV 2/1063, KV 1064.

[40] The timing of this note is problematic. White has been reported as leaving for a nine-month tour of Germany, in the summer of 1936, so why would he have been reporting on Pritt immediately on his return? See Note 38.

[41] Miles, p 189.

[42] TNA, KV 2/1384.

[43] Paula Bartley, *Ellen Wilkinson*, p 123.

[44] Miles, p 301.

[45] Tom Bower, *The Perfect English Spy*, pp 27-31.

[46] TNA, KV 2/1384.

[47] Jeffrey, p 233.

[48] Bower, p 26.

[49] Knight's biographer, Anthony Masters, stated that Kell decided, in 1937, that Knight should move his office out of Thames House, to Dolphin Square, primarily for reasons of secrecy. See *The Man Who Was M*, p 68. On the other hand, Knight's assistant, Joan Miller suggested that the move did not occur until October 1940, when the rest of MI5 relocated from Wormwood Scrubs to Blenheim Palace. See Joan Miller's *One Girl's War*, p 56.

[50] Anthony Masters, *The Man Who Was M*, pp 37-43.

[51] TNA, KV 4/227, *M.S. Report*.

[52] *The Defence of the Realm*, p 179.

[53] TNA KV/1022.

[54] Nigel West and Oleg Tsarev, *The Crown Jewels*, p 123.

[55] For a comprehensive account of the nest of Reds, in this complex, see David Burke's *The Lawn Road Flats*.

[56] *The Crown Jewels*, pp 109-111.

[57] Masters, p 44.

[58] Gary Kern, *A Death in Washington*, p 121.

[59] Costello, p 285.

[60] *The Lawn Road Flats*, p 103.

[61] *The Crown Jewels*, Appendix 1.

[62] In a private communication with this writer, in January 2015, Nigel West indicated that the Malys had been tipped off by their porter that MI5 had shown interest in their flat. If that were true, it could cause Knight's claim to be re-inspected, although the time-delay is still problematic

[63] David Burke, *The Spy Who Came in from the Co-Op*, pp 84-103.

[64] TNA, KV 2/1008 and KV 2/1009.

[65] Burke, pp 90-92.

[66] William E. Duff, *A Time for Spies*, pp 216-217, Note 30.

[67] The Report appears as Appendix 1 in *The Crown Jewels*. It has been able to be published only because Anthony Blunt shared it with his Moscow bosses, and it was later retrieved from the Soviet Archives.

[68] *Burke*, p 101.

[69] TNA, KV 4/195 and KV 4/196.

[70] TNA, KV 2/1615-1.

[71] Masters, p 54.

[72] Curry, Appendix II.

[73] The dates of Driberg's expulsion, and Knight's submission of his paper, do not seem to be recorded anywhere. By working back from a visit Driberg made to the USA, and when he must have left the UK, one can with reasonable confidence conclude that he was expelled in August 1941. Knight submitted his paper soon afterwards, in a very timely fashion therefore for Hollis (and Liddell) to ignore its conclusions in Hollis's report to the Security Executive, which met to discuss it on October 1. Indeed, Knight may have been invited by Liddell to write his report.

[74] In his 2015 biography of the espionage novelist John le Carré, Adam Sisman wrote, citing a *Daily Mail* article, that "it has been alleged that he [Tangye] continued to work for MI5 secretly after the war, and even that he was a Soviet agent, though the case has not been proved beyond doubt". (*John le Carré: the Biography*, p 325).

[75] Curry, p 394.

[76] Kim Philby, *My Silent War*.

[77] Much space in Guy Liddell's *Diaries* is taken up by a project known as ACE (Amalgamation of Counter-Espionage), in which he records the intense debates that carried on during the 1940s about the desirability of merging the counter-espionage departments of MI5 and SIS, and even the two services themselves. Extraordinarily, Andrew's authorised history of MI5 does not even have an entry for ACE in its Index.

[78] Hugh Trevor-Roper, *The Philby Affair*, p 21.

[79] Edward Harrison (ed.), Hugh Trevor-Roper, *The Secret World*, p 229.

[80] Philby, p 22.

[81] John Costello and Oleg Tsarev, *Deadly Illusions*, p 132.

[82] E. H. Cookridge, *The Third Man*, p 36.

[83] Bruce Page, David Leitch and Phillip Knightley, *The Philby Conspiracy*, p 61.

[84] Patrick Seale and Maureen McConville, *Philby: The Long Road to Moscow*, p 92 and p 102.

[85] Andrew Boyle, *The Fourth Man*, p 104.

[86] Richard Deacon, *The British Connection*, p 83.

[87] Chapman Pincher, *Too Secret Too Long*, pp 291-292. Pincher, for some reason, here denies that Deutsch was OTTO.

[88] Phillip Knightley, *The Master Spy*, p 44.

[89] John Costello, *Mask of Treachery*, p 228.

[90] *Deadly Illusions*, p 124, pp 131-133.

[91] Anthony Cave-Brown, *Treason in the Blood*, p 162.

[92] Genrikh Borovik, *The Philby Files*, pp 22-24.

[93] Yuri Modin, *My Five Cambridge Friends*, pp 51-52.

[94] Nigel West and Oleg Tsarev, *The Crown Jewels*, p 106 and p 272.

[95] William E. Duff, *A Time for Spies*, pp 88-89.

[96] Christopher Andrew and Vasili Mitrokhin, *The Mitrokhin Archive*, p 58.

[97] Rufina Philby, with Hayden Peake and Mikhail Lyubimov, *The Private Life of Kim Philby*, pp 219-220.

[98] *The Defence of the Realm*, p 168.

[99] Peter Shipley, *Hostile Action*, p 74. Shipley did not name these persons, but described them as follows: "These include three members of the CPGB, one Comintern agent, four GRU officers, and four members of the Soviet Embassy and trade mission."

[100] Costello and Tsarev, pp 104-106.

[101] Page, Leitch and Knightley, p 60.

[102] Cave-Brown, p 160.

[103] Brian Brivati, *Hugh Gaitskell*, pp 56-57.

[104] Cookridge's *The Third Man* and Volodarsky's *Stalin's Agent*, p 277.

[105] Naomi Mitchison, *Vienna Diary*, pp 78-79.

[106] Knightley, p 43.

[107] Muriel Gardiner, *Code-Name 'Mary'*, pp 52-53; Sheila Eisenberg, *Muriel's War*, p 87.

[108] David C. Martin, *Wilderness of Mirrors*, p 57; Morris Riley, *Philby: The Hidden Years*, p 147.

[109] Flora Solomon, *From Baku to Baker Street*, p 165.

[110] Cave-Brown, p 240.

[111] Gaitskell's political career came to a sad end, when he died, on January 18, 1963, of a mysterious disease with symptoms of immunological collapse, shortly after visiting the Soviet Embassy. The Soviet defector, Anatoli Golitsin, (who had defected to the CIA in December 1961, and had helped uncover the spy, John Vassall), later claimed that Gaitskell had been poisoned by the KGB in order to ensure that Harold Wilson would ascend to leadership of the Labour Party. This explanation was soon abandoned, but the suspicions of foul play at the Embassy were never completely dispelled. Philby fled to Moscow on January 23, 1963.

[112] Duff, p 120.

[113] *The Philby Affair*, p 29.

[114] David Leigh, *The Wilson Plot*, p 74. Leigh reported how Neill McDermott described to Peter Wright how White had introduced Philby to him: "Dick White was thrilled by Philby and thought he was wonderful. He introduced me to him. Philby was then head of section VI in MI6. Dick White asked me to come along – he told me how brilliant he was and what a pity he wasn't head of section, he was so able. Philby, I remember, had a strong personality. He was intelligent, charming."

[115] *The Secret World,* p 69; SOC.Dacre 10/44, letter of October 9, 1981.

[116] *The Secret World*, p 211, letter of March 27, 1968.

[117] *The Defence of the Realm*, p 268.

Chapter 3: The Krivitsky Affair

"Just remember. No one leaves the Soviet Union unless the NKVD can use him."
(Walter Krivitsky)

"I did not wholly trust Krivitsky. He wasn't using his real name and he wasn't a general. He hadn't mastered enough to give us a proper lead." (Dick White)

"In a way the Soviet defector was the Everyman of the twentieth century. Raised as Homo sovieticus in a totalitarian state, he evolved through conscience into a schizophrenic child of Communism and then, of a sudden, became a renegade, a deserter, a wanderer, homeless and homesick like so many others." (Gary Kern)

The Nazi-Soviet Pact, signed by Foreign Ministers Ribbentrop and Molotov, on August 23, 1939, came as a surprise to the Western democracies. Great Britain should not in truth have been astonished that its own half-hearted attempt to sign an agreement with the Soviet Union that summer had come to naught. Chamberlain and Stalin had little respect for each other, and Britain and France had sent an ineffective mission by slow boat to Leningrad, with no authority to negotiate with General Voroshilov over his urgent demands for commitment on joint military action. Nevertheless, for two sworn ideological enemies, the banner-bearers of Fascism and Communism, to act as if they had common interests, was altogether too overwhelming for Britain's intelligence services to come to grips with. Indeed, the multiple histories of this period have never really digested its implications. In his recent account of the treaty, the historian Roger Moorhouse has written in reference to such volumes: " . . . the pact remains largely unknown – passed over in a single paragraph, dismissed as a dubious anomaly, a footnote to the wider history", and he goes on to write of the paltry attention given to it in recent histories of World War II. "It is never considered to warrant a chapter and usually attracts little more than a paragraph or two and a handful of index references."[1]

The official history of British intelligence follows this remarkable trend. Professor Hinsley's team recorded, in their major volume on Strategy and Operations (published 1979), the lamentable state of intelligence on Russia's [*sic*] actions: "British intelligence about Russia's aims and policies had been no better – so that Whitehall had failed to foresee the Russo-German pact despite a flood of rumours on the subject – and this had thereafter undergone no improvement."[2] Britain's intelligence sources were not able to distinguish between hints and rumours and 'reliable and timely intelligence'. The only reference to the pact in Volume 4 of the *History*, which deals with Security and Counter-Intelligence, is in the chapter titled *Before the War*, in a footnote, where we are told: "A strong case has been made for thinking the information which reached the German embassy in London in the summer of 1939 about the progress of the Anglo-

French-Soviet negotiations was obtained from King [*a spy in the Foreign Office*] by his Soviet controller and used selectively to move the German government towards a pact with Russia."[3] Just "a pact": that is all that is said. Christopher Andrew's official history of MI5 contains one (unindexed) sentence on the pact, commenting solely on the ideological somersaults the Communist Party of Great Britain (CPGB) had to perform in response to it.[4] Keith Jeffery's history of SIS is only marginally less lapidary: it points out that, despite warnings from its own network, "Broadway was dumbfounded by the Nazi-Soviet non-aggression pact", but does not indicate that the event prompted any strategic re-assessment of intelligence needs.[5] Yet a realignment of traditional enemies – and Communism had represented a much more radical threat for much longer than Nazism – should have set off alarms in the corridors of Whitehall.

The Pact primarily concerned "non-aggression", namely a commitment not to attack each other, and not to lend support to an aggressor should the other become "the subject of belligerent action by a third power". Yet a subsidiary clause with great significance for Britain's security was to be found in Article II, which declared: "The Governments of the two High Contracting Parties shall in the future maintain continual contact with one another for the purpose of consultation in order to exchange information on problems affecting their common interests."[6] Of course, the pact concerned more than a commitment to share information: an intensive (thought not completely trustful) period of negotiation and exchange of war materiel ensued, which meant that Soviet oil and metals were soon to be used in the attacks against Britain and her allies. Moreover, an 'Additional Protocol' was signed, which essentially enabled a ruthless carving-up of the Baltic States and Poland, as well as making reference to the Soviet Union's strategic interest in the province of Bessarabia, then part of Romanian territory. The two signatories broadly succeeded in keeping the protocol concealed from the Western democracies at the time,[i] but Stalin's barbarous and cynical invasions of Finland, Estonia, Latvia and Lithuania, as well as the eastern part of Poland, immediately put the Soviet Union in the category of Moorhouse's 'Devils'. Since Britain had gone to war with Germany over the integrity of Poland's borders, she would have been morally justified – and, according to some, even obligated – to declare war on the Soviet Union as well for such territorial infringements. The intelligence threat, however, while subtle, was highly significant. The possibility that the two parties might exchange intelligence gained from espionage in countries such as Britain should have led to a serious re-assessment of security policies when war broke out a few days after the pact was signed.

Britain declared war on Germany on September 3, 1939. That same day, an American journalist who had been born in 1892 in what is now Belarus, Isaac Don Levine, secured an appointment with Lord Lothian, the British Ambassador in Washington. He came to tell him that he had knowledge of Soviet spies in

---

[i] In fact, news of the secret protocol did reach Western ears. Hans-Heinrich Herwarth von Bittenfeld, known as 'Johnnie', who was secretary to Count von der Schulenburg, the German Ambassador in Moscow, leaked details to his friend at the American Embassy, Charles E. ('Chip') Bohlen. See *The Deadly Embrace*, by Anthony Read and David Fisher, p 266.

Britain's offices of government, which, in light of recent events (namely the Nazi-Soviet pact), merited an urgent investigation. Levine believed that the presence of such spies posed "an immediate threat to Britain's military security".[7] He was acting on behalf of a Soviet defector, Walter Krivitsky, who had drawn attention to the horrors of Stalin's slave colony by having a series of articles published in the *Saturday Evening Post*, pieces that were actually ghosted by Levine. Krivitsky was not aware that Levine was about to identify a spy who had been working for one of his own agents, Hans (or Henri) Pieck: Levine acted on his own initiative, naming the spy as 'King'. After an exchange of telegrams with the Foreign Office, the latter quickly identified Captain John King, Special Branch noticed a suspicious contact during surveillance, and King was soon arrested, confessing to his crime. Gary Kern, the author of a comprehensive biography of Krivitsky, wrote: "In early October King went to prison for ten years of hard labor without a word appearing in the press."[8] British intelligence then decided that it needed to interview this valuable source. On November 15, Guy Liddell, who was deputy to the Director of the counter-espionage branch of MI5, recorded in his diary that attempts were being made to get Krivitsky to the UK.

The objective of this chapter is to explore Krivitsky's motivations in agreeing to come to Britain to be interrogated, to define what the goals of MI5 and SIS might have been in picking the defector's brains, to analyse how accurate and useful was the information that Krivitsky divulged to them, to judge how effective was the response of the intelligence services, and to analyse why MI5 was less energetic than it might have been and to review Krivitsky's overall legacy. A summary of the defector's background and the comprehensive report that Jane Archer wrote for government consumption will be given: readers can inspect the several source documents and books that provide a thorough (though occasionally unreliable) account of Krivitsky and the interviews that were undertaken.[9] It is *not* the intention here to explore all the connections among Soviet spies and their intermediaries that might have been pursued and revealed by MI5: the scholar is directed to Nigel West's *Mask*, Chapter Five, for a thorough analysis of this topic. What is distinctively displayed here is the positioning of the Krivitsky affair in the context of politics within British intelligence.

Kern's thoroughly researched volume gives a comprehensive account of Walter Krivitsky's struggle to escape Stalin's vengeance when he defected in 1937. Krivitsky had been an agent of the GRU, the Soviet military intelligence organisation, before being appointed (so he claimed) head of the NKVD operation in Western Europe in 1935, where he used the Netherlands as his base, and the role of an antiquarian bookseller as his cover. Krivitsky also described himself as "Chief of the Soviet Military Intelligence for Western Europe", as in his testimony to the US Congress on October 11, 1939. The impression he gave to his British interrogators was that there was "no distinct line of demarcation between the espionage activities of the OGPU [strictly 'NKVD', in 1937] and those of the Russian Military Intelligence Department". In his evidence to Congress, he also said that "when Stalin no longer trusted the High Command of the Red Army, he quite naturally distrusted the military intelligence as well, and placed it under control of the OGPU". He had started to become alarmed at the scope of Stalin's purges, and by the accounts of the elimination of some of his colleagues, including his close friend and associate, Ignace Reiss. In September 1937 Reiss was murdered in Switzerland, after Krivitsky had managed to extricate himself from an instruction to carry out the deed. After declining an invitation to return to Moscow, and evading two assassination attempts in France, he managed to escape, late in 1938, with his family to the USA, where he started to reveal Stalin's crimes to officials at the State Department. Krivitsky then collaborated with Levine on the articles for the *Saturday Evening Post* to publicise Stalin's purges and attempts to forge an agreement with Nazi Germany.

Krivitsky had been born Samuel Ginzburg (alternatively Ginsburg, Ginzberg), and had given this name, and his race as Jewish, when he had arrived at Ellis Island. He had experienced severe problems with the US Immigration and Naturalisation Service on his arrival, and the head of the FBI, J. Edgar Hoover, had also called for his expulsion later in 1938, as he did not take kindly to rumours being spread that the country he was protecting was riddled with Soviet agents.[10] Yet Krivitsky had allies at the State Department, who worked to extend the currency of his visa. Meanwhile, the *New York Times* took great interest in his revelations, although the publicity it gave him may have alerted Soviet agents to his movements. Stalin and Beria were keeping a close eye on him: Trotsky and he were numbers one and two on their list of targets for assassination. Konstantin Oumansky, an NKVD officer, had been appointed Ambassador to the United States in May 1939, and had presented his letters of credence on June 6. Shortly afterwards, Oumansky was recalled to Moscow, where he stayed for four months, conveniently being absent from the USA when the Nazi-Soviet pact was announced. Kern believed that this recall was initiated because Oumansky had failed to stop the publication of Krivitsky's damaging memoirs. (Since the first of these had been published in April, that would probably have been an impossible task.) On his return to the USA, early in November 1939, reporters quizzed Oumansky about the Krivitsky case, and he could only bluster in response. He even denied that he knew Krivitsky, and refused to answer questions about his own membership of OGPU. He returned to his embassy in much less favour than that in which he had left a few months before.[11]

On December 30, the *New York Times* reported that Krivitsky had left New York, without indicating his destination. His visa was about to expire, and he thus had to return to Canada. In fact, he had left Grand Central Station a few days earlier for Montreal, and, after a surprise meeting with the ex-Russian Premier, Alexander Kerensky, left St. John's, New Brunswick, on January 10, 1940, aboard the *Duchess of Richmond*, bound for Liverpool. The ship arrived on January 19, and on January 23, Lt. Col. Vivian (of SIS) and Brigadier Harker (of MI5) began to interview him. The more intense discussions were started the following day, under the supervision of Jane Archer and a civil servant, Gladwyn Jebb, who was liaison officer between the Foreign Office and MI5.

Krivitsky's rank as a 'general' was elevated by his colleague Isaac Don Levine as a way of promoting his articles in the *Saturday Evening Post*.[12] He was nevertheless a very powerful intelligence officer who had started with military intelligence in 1922, but, with the recent annexation of that organisation (the

GRU) by Yezhov's secret police, he had in fact represented the NKVD. In his articles (that were collected in a book), he continued to emphasise his role as "head of Military Intelligence in Western Europe", as if that distanced him from the purges of *Yezhovschina*.[13] His revelations about Stalin's desire to gain some sort of understanding with Hitler as early as in 1934 (the Night of the Long Knives) were astonishing to an American audience that, while highly suspicious of Communism, was beginning to view Stalin's Russia as a bulwark against Fascism. He received scathing criticism from leftist intellectuals for such claims, as well as his critique of Stalin's show trials, and his disclosures of Stalin's merciless and intense spying, not only on his own citizens, but also on his own secret police. (When Arthur Koestler read Krivitsky's compilation of his article in book form [*see Endnote 13*], several years later, he was amazed at how closely Krivitsky's accounts of confessions tallied with his own descriptions in *Darkness at Noon*.[14]) Krivitsky was, of course, vindicated when the Nazi-Soviet pact was announced in August 1939. The US Government was nevertheless a little embarrassed by him, fearful of upsetting the Soviet Union, and he was a thorn in the side of the head of the FBI, J. Edgar Hoover.

Why did Krivitsky undertake this mission to give information to British intelligence? After all, he was still a Bolshevik, and opposed to the imperialist Britons, 'bourgeois capitalists', whose Intelligence capabilities he respected, but whom he did not trust. He stated that it was because of Stalin: that Stalin had destroyed Marx's and Lenin's teachings by building a murderous dictatorship, and he felt that Stalin stood in the way of freedom. Yet he retained some sense of loyalty to his cause: he was quick to identify a mercenary spy, like King, for whom he felt little sympathy, probably deliberately vague to his hosts about communist ideologists who betrayed their own country (like Philby and Cairncross), and stubbornly silent about fellow-agents (such as Akhmerov and Cot). He really opened up only as the interviews were winding down. (If agents had already disappeared into Stalin's maw, he felt no betrayal in talking about them.) As Liddell reported: "He is quite ready to talk about representatives of the OGPU or individuals that he was up against, but he is reluctant to disclose his own 4th Dept. agents unless we can show him that we already know something about them."[15]

There was thus an aspect of revenge in his actions, since his close friend, Reiss, had been murdered by Stalin's 'Special Tasks' force. Krivitsky wanted to damage Stalin's network without putting loyal ex-colleagues in danger. Yet he knew that he, along with Trotsky, was in Stalin's sights. Soon after he defected, in an appeal for asylum in France published in December 1937, he suggested that "the GPU will stop at nothing to silence me".[16] He had drawn attention to himself in the *Saturday Evening Post* articles, and was thus hoping to seclude himself somewhere out of the limelight. His visa had expired: he had a wife and daughter to protect. With the pressure on him in the USA, and the knowledge that the US government was riddled with Soviet agents, he thought that Canada, or even Britain itself, might constitute a safer haven. He needed money: thus, like all defectors, the more he could string out his revelations, the more lucrative it would be, and he was tempted to exaggerate his stories to maintain the interest of his interrogators. The life of the defector was a constant trial: as Gary Kern wrote in a biography of another tortured defector, Victor Kravchenko: "In a way the Soviet defector was the Everyman of the twentieth century. Raised as *Homo sovieticus* in a totalitarian state, he evolved through conscience into a schizophrenic child of Communism and then, of a sudden, became a renegade, a deserter, a wanderer, homeless and homesick like so many others."[17]

MI5 and SIS were not used to dealing with defectors. They had bungled their first major exercise, with Georges Agabekov, in 1931. Agabekov had been head of OGPU's Eastern Section, working in Constantinople, when he fell in love with his English tutor, Isabel Streater. SIS and MI5 (represented by Vivian and Harker, respectively) were confused by his overtures, and suspected a provocation. Agabekov was continually on the run, separated from Isabel (now his wife), in 1936, and was murdered by the Soviet 'Special Tasks' squad in 1937. The approach of the intelligence services to the task of interrogation appears tentative: they failed to understand that an anti-Stalinist could still be a sworn Communist. A sense of allegiance to intelligence services generally no doubt inclined them to think that Krivitsky had indulged in some kind of institutional disloyalty by defecting, even though they should have judged that their own cause was just, and that of the Soviet Union and international Communism was not. They were initially nonplussed by his obvious lack of knowledge of the spy network based in Britain: even Archer herself, who had pressed so hard for Krivitsky to be brought over, in the first days of the interrogations wondered what was to be gained from the visit. After all, he had been on the run for almost three years. They must constantly have wondered whether he was some kind of plant. Their interviews were certainly not demanding, and they applied little pressure to Krivitsky – even when more persistent questioning might have revealed more useful details about the identities of agents he erringly described.

Later, MI5 officers were dismissive of the whole experience. Dick White, Assistant-Director of 'B' Division of MI5 under Guy Liddell at the time, allegedly told his biographer: "I did not wholly trust Krivitsky. He wasn't using his real name and he wasn't a general. He hadn't mastered enough to give us a proper lead."[18] There is obviously something self-serving about this statement (he attributed the same reaction to Archer, and claimed Liddell agreed with him), given at a time (1980) when White would have had to acknowledge to himself that he and Liddell had been astoundingly careless. Yet it also shows some of their naivety and inexperience, forgetting the ruthless world of deception and subterfuge with which they were involved. Krivitsky was obviously no gentleman: he used an alias, and claimed a false rank – behaviour that the English officers would have considered unthinkable. White, however, was not present at any of the interviews, and thus relied on second-hand information. Liddell, on the other hand, did get to see Krivitsky on several occasions. On his last day, Krivitsky asked for more money. Liddell's entry in his diary, describing his final meeting with Krivitsky, was frustratingly removed before the folder was released to the National Archives, but it is clear that Liddell negotiated a sum without extracting any more information from him.

Krivitsky spent several weeks under interrogation at the Langham Hotel. After initial cautiousness, his interlocutors gradually gained his confidence, and he began to speak more openly, although the utility of the information he provided has been hotly debated. Yet it is indisputable that the overall quality of his advice was of very high calibre. He strongly warned his interrogators of the intelligence cooperation that was probably happening between Germany and the Soviet Union. He provided a trove of information about the structure of Soviet intelligence, and how it operated. His allegations concerning the penetration of British intelligence may have been less than incisive – mainly because his information was so much out of date, and his ability to identify persons only sketchy – but he was providing leads that should have found an echo from a service already conscious of leaks, and presumably motivated to eradicate them. One important fact should be clarified: he did not name John King during these discussions. In this respect, some of the historians are chronologically challenged. Costello[19], working on the knowledge that MI5 was able to arrest King on information given by Krivitsky, echoed the account of Nigel West[20], and assumed that it was Krivitsky's presence in England in 1939 that led to King's arrest. It had, of course, been Krivitsky's collaborator, Levine, who provided the information on King's identity, with the result that MI5 was able to surprise – and impress – Krivitsky that King was already behind bars when Krivitsky was interviewed in February 1940.[21]

Krivitsky did, however, provide leads to other offenders. He dropped several hints about spies who were betraying British defence secrets. Although the information he gave was vague, and he appeared to merge aspects of different agents into one personality, the pointers he did provide should nevertheless have led to investigations of Maclean and Philby. Philby (even though he was early in 1940 not employed in a government department) should certainly have been investigated, because of his Communist background and record in Vienna. Krivitsky said that the NKVD in 1936 had sent a young Englishman to Spain under the cover of a newspaper correspondent, a profile that fitted Philby exactly. Moreover, Krivitsky provided MI5 with solid evidence of intelligence sharing between Soviets and Nazis in the mid-thirties, thus clarifying the subsidiary risk that leaks by Soviet infiltrators would activate.[22] Understandably, the Soviets have consistently downplayed the significance of his revelations, unwittingly providing cover for MI5's unprofessionalism. Pavel Sudoplatov, who was head of the Special Squads that hunted down defectors in the 1930s and 1940s, hardly mentioned Krivitsky at all in his memoirs[23], characterising any collaboration as disinformation from the Czech president, Beneš, calling it a "fairy-tale". Even after all this time, disinformation can be seen at work in this conflicting assessment of Krivitsky's significance.

MI5 had been made aware of a severe problem of Soviet espionage, since Sir Alexander Cadogan, Permanent Secretary at the Foreign Office, had regular meetings with Kell and Menzies on the subject. Cadogan's diaries reflect a deep concern about an ongoing exposure, to the extent that his more sensitive reflections were withheld from the published edition, "for security reasons", but partly, no doubt, because of what they show about his lack of resolve. For example, Cadogan's (unpublished) reaction to the news from Lord Lothian about Krivitsky and King ran as follows: "Very unpleasant, which seems to fix us a line on the 'leaks' of the past few years."[24] It suggests an enthusiasm about identifying and removing traitors that did not endure. It appears that Cadogan was referring primarily to the existence of a spy in the British Embassy in Rome, but he was also referring to leaks originating from domestic members of the Communist Party. Indeed, Levine again recorded the determined first reaction from the British government:

> "It was made clear to me that while King was in custody and under investigation, the British government was most anxious to get on the trail of the second Soviet spy Krivitsky had described .... Mr. Mallet [counselor at the embassy] disclosed to me that his government was deeply interested in securing Krivitsky's cooperation in ferreting out the Soviet espionage agents in Britain who, in view of the Stalin-Hitler pact, could be regarded as Nazi collaborators."[25]

This opinion was echoed in the vigorous entreaties made by Jane Archer, the Security Service's main expert. On November 20, she expressed concern that the efforts to identify spies in the Cabinet office had stalled, that day writing to her counterpart in SIS, Valentine Vivian, on November 10 that "if we wish to get to the bottom of Soviet espionage activity in this country, we must contact Krivitsky".[26] The National Archives also show that, on November 20, she implored Cadogan and Jebb to approve Krivitsky's visit. Jasper Harker, the Assistant-Director of MI5, immediately agreed: maybe it is significant that Liddell appears to have been bypassed in this planning, even as he noted the increase in Soviet espionage in his diary. In a note of January 12, Harker was insistent that he and Archer (no mention of Liddell) wanted Vivian to take on the interrogation.[27]

MI5 and SIS thus did not act in a single-minded fashion to exploit the Krivitsky opportunity. In this respect, Jane Archer's role and achievements are puzzling. She was a skilled barrister, a determined sleuth, and possessed a deep knowledge of Communist subversive practices. Yet by the time of the Krivitsky interrogations, she appears to have been falling out of favour, as if the task of handling him – alongside Vivian, with whom she had worked very effectively – had been given to her because it was *not* important, rather than because it was vital. It was she who had pressed to invite Krivitsky over, but the officer she was training, Roger Hollis, appeared to be substituting for her already in everyday tasks of surveillance, even signing memoranda with her official identity, and being seen as the leading Communist-watcher. Andrew cited Archer's interrogation of Krivitsky (as if she had been the lead, not Vivian) in glowing terms – "a model of its kind".[28] Yet, as will be shown later, Archer was removed from her post soon after she completed the report, which was an extraordinary act of timing. She had built up a rapport with Krivitsky: in a note to Vivian, dated February 9, 1940, in the middle of the interrogations, she said to him: "K is passionate to be able to communicate by some means with me after he leaves, in case he is able to remember other things of importance."[29] One might question the sincerity about his memory, but she had obviously built a relationship. (In this respect she may have forgotten her formidable skills as a barrister, and not exploited Krivitsky as effectively as she could have done.) Yet her talents were very brusquely discarded.

Archer's was the sole voice which articulated strongly the threat of Nazi-Soviet conspiracies – the danger that Levine had instantly recognised, and Mallet in the Washington Embassy had shrewdly picked up. The words she used in her Introduction to the Report are highly relevant to an understanding of her position: "Krivitsky has undoubtedly supplied the Security Service with most valuable information on which to base the work of combatting Russo-German espionage in this country." The term "Russo-German espionage" should have been a clarion call. In suggesting such a high degree of cooperation, it was perhaps overstated, but the focus was sound. And she concluded her Introduction with these chilling words:

> "Of greater importance to the contra-espionage service is the probability that the line of demarcation between the Soviet and German Intelligence Services has become equally indistinct. In view of the close co-operation which existed between Soviet and German Intelligence personnel less than a decade ago, it is only to be expected that there is now a resumption of that co-operation and that the German espionage service is taking full advantage of the existing Soviet intelligence organisation in this country."

Was this why Archer was being sidelined? That she emphasised the threat of collusion too strongly? That she failed to understand that the mutual distrust between the Nazis and the Soviets meant that they would be at each others' throats before too long? Did Mallet overstate or misrepresent the case? If she was correct, MI5 and the War Office should have reacted very promptly and energetically. If she was deemed to be wrong, it could have put the seal on her career with MI5. Paradoxically, Dick White later justified MI5's timidity on the grounds that Krivitsky's cupboard was bare from this particular commodity: "Our enemy was Germany, not Russia. Our major interest was whether Russia might help the Germans. Krivitsky provided no information on that", a statement that sheds more light on White's discomfort (and maybe naivety) than on the reality of the information Krivitsky provided. [30] The inclination to appease the Communists had already been set in train. Roger Hollis later distanced himself from Krivitsky's opinion of the Comintern's revolutionary aims in a memorandum of April 10, 1941, and ten days later, John Curry minuted nervously and evasively to Vivian, when he was preparing a version of Archer's report to send to the FBI: "It might be as well to suggest that we do not necessarily accept all the views expressed in the memorandum". [31] One can detect tensions and disagreements within the MI5 officer contingent.

It was not that this threat was negligible. As has been noted, Isaac Don Levine's primary motive in alerting the British Embassy in Washington about Krivitsky's knowledge, as he reacted sharply to the announcement of the Nazi-Soviet pact on August 23, was to prevent the Soviets from passing information to the Germans: "The thought that the Kremlin was in a position to funnel to Hitler many of the vital secrets of the free world gave me no peace, I endeavored to obtain from Krivitsky every bit of identifying information about the two British traitors." [32] Levine's concerns were due to the fact that Krivitsky had told the House Committee on UnAmerican Activities that the Nazis and Soviets exchanged secrets. Likewise, in 1939, a concern about leaks to the Soviet Union was of notable urgency in the Foreign Office, although no one appears explicitly to have come to the conclusion that the rules of the game had to change because of the pact. It is true that, in December 1939, Liddell wrote in a single diary entry that "it is almost a certainty that the information will reach both the Germans and the Russians"[33], but he was referring to independent leaks from two members of parliament with Nazi and Communist sympathies, respectively, not of secrets being passed by the Soviets to the Nazis from clandestine sources within the British government. Soviet and German subversion efforts were still seen as separate initiatives to be countered by similar means. As has been stated earlier, in Andrew's mammoth authorised history of MI5, no proper mention of the Nazi-Soviet pact is made, and thus no analysis of its implications for British intelligence appears.

A case can be made that British intelligence should have been aware of the possibility of collaboration between Nazi Germany and the Soviet Union as early as 1937. While finessing this issue in his official history, Christopher Andrew partially made this point in his earlier work, *Secret Service*, pointing out that the Northern Department of the Foreign Office dismissed the information emanating from Krivitsky's publications in the US in April 1939, as well as the opinions of the chanceries of Washington and Moscow. He quoted the Department Head, Laurence Collier, as writing: "On the whole we do not consider that these would-be hair-raising revelations of Stalin's alleged desire for a *rapprochement* with Germany are worth taking seriously." Andrew then went on to list a number of other intelligence warnings during the summer of 1939, with Vansittart (now having been kicked upstairs to a consultant post) as a lone voice in the Foreign Office, which was combatting the more pragmatic conclusions of the War Office. Thus the eventual announcement of the pact was received by Members of Parliament with scorn, demanding to know what Intelligence had been doing all this time.

The despatches sent by the British Embassy in Moscow to the Foreign Office hint at changes in attitude by Stalin to foreign threats much earlier in the cycle. For instance, a very telling memorandum was sent to Anthony Eden, the Foreign Secretary, in April, 1937:

"M. Stalin, it will be observed, makes no attempt to differentiate between the various foreign powers constituting what he describes as the 'capitalist encirclement,' though there are a few individual references to Germany and Japan; and in this respect there is, I think, some slight departure from precedent established since the adoption of the Litvinov policy. Quite possibly it is due merely to the particular circumstances in which the report was made, and a speech intended chiefly for internal party consumption it would, of course, be quite natural not to lay much stress on the question of Soviet co-operation with certain of the capitalist Powers. Nevertheless, the omission of those distinctions between Fascist and non-Fascist Powers, which have usually appeared in M. Stalin's published speeches appears to me to be of distinct interest. Outside Geneva M. Litvinov seldom enjoys, or even encourages, much publicity, but if I am not mistaken he has been even less in the limelight than usual during the last few weeks, and it is conceivable that the policy for which he stands may be losing ground in the highest quarters."[34]

And the notion of *rapprochement* referred to by Collier went back a long way. In May 1937, Ambassador Chilston was warning Eden of a possible *rapprochement* between Germany and the Soviet Union, although the rumour was at the time tainted by the association with the disgraced Tukhachevsky, who had been accused of being an agent of the West.[35] Yet that was not the only source. A similar perspective was echoed in the reports of the US Ambassador in Moscow, Joseph Davies, who even stated that Hudson, of the British Board of Trade, on his way to start negotiations with the Soviet Union in early 1939, told him that he was "startled to hear Davies's views, which he was not receiving in Embassy's reports from Moscow".[36]

Thus there were early signs that Stalin was beginning to treat Great Britain as a bigger ogre than Germany, that Litvinov's star was on the descent, and that trade negotiations between the Soviet Union and Germany had started afresh, while those with Britain struggled. Analysis and interpretation of intelligence were probably not helped by the discontinuities of Eden being replaced by Lord Halifax (in February 1938), and Lord Chilston by Sir William Seeds as Ambassador (in January 1939). While Krivitsky's US-based evidence had been largely discounted by the Foreign Office because of Levine's reputation as something of a fabulist, the latter's approach to the Washington Embassy, and the ability of MI5 and SIS to interrogate Krivitsky in person, should have triggered a fresh assessment of the security danger that had been overlooked. While a body titled the Joint Intelligence Sub-Committee operated between 1936 and the outbreak of war, it was very much dominated by military men with a prime focus on protecting overseas imperial territories, who naively believed that Poland's armament deficiencies could best be addressed by the Soviet Union's coming to its rescue.[37] It appeared to have no mechanism for taking diplomatic contributions from the embassies in Berlin and Moscow via the Foreign Office, for instance, nor from MI5 and SIS, who, with more vigorous leadership, could have alerted the War Office to diplomatic approaches being exchanged by Hitler and Stalin.[38] The Foreign Office participated from 1938 onwards, but the forum was a mechanism for co-ordinating intelligence from the relevant intelligence sections of the Navy, Air Force and Army. A notable failure to integrate and process intelligence thus occurred, that was not to be remedied until the Joint Intelligence Committee (JIC) was more formally set up shortly before Chamberlain's demise. But by then it was much too late.

By the time of summer 1940, the JIC perceived the risks of Communist spies' sharing information with the Germans as extremely high. A minute from a meeting on May 2, 1940 refers to the fear of sabotage by communists, and that "such activities will only take place as part of a pre-arranged military plan" with the invaders.[39] The transcripts of the decrypted VENONA traffic that occurred between London and Moscow show Soviet spies transmitting reports on bombing raids that could have been turned over to the Germans, to help them refine their targeting.[40] Later, on July 18, 1940, a minute reported on a possible overture to

Germany with the goal of reaching an agreement with Hitler, and news on Churchill's perilous manoeuvres at this stage were in danger of reaching the wrong hands. One Jerome Labarthe, who was working for de Gaulle, discussed talks he had with Churchill's secretary to his own secretary, Alta Lecoutre. Lecoutre was the mistress of Pierre Cot, the French Minister of Aviation, who had been one of Krivitsky's most important and influential agents in Paris, but Cot's name was not one of those divulged by Krivitsky. Liddell showed that he was waking up, a little late and very naively, to such intrigues, noting in his diary in August, 1940: "People involved in Spanish arms racket (Seymontozyk and Lecoutre) got in to the country at the time of the French debacle; now working in office of de Gaulle. We have sent a wire to Thomas [*MI5's code-name for Krivitsky*] in Canada to see if he knows these people." In the published version of Liddell's Diaries, Nigel West noted: "Seymoniczyk's wife, Alta Lecoutre, was Labarthe's secretary, and had been the mistress of Pierre Cot, the former French Minister of Air. All three were Soviet agents." [41] The danger of damaging Churchill's (and Britain's) reputation in Stalin's eyes was very real, as was the risk that the Nazis would gain highly critical information about Britain's true plans. Lastly, Leo Long, who should well be considered the sixth 'Cambridge Spy', was in 1940 installed in a War Office department called MI14, and had access to Enigma decrypts that he passed to the Communist Party of Great Britain. If Hitler had gained access to such knowledge, it would have been disastrous for the outcome of the war.

Yet further evidence of the danger of Soviet contacts' betraying information to their Nazi Allies has been well-documented. Early in 1941, Sumner Welles, Under-Secretary in the US State Department, had regularly been meeting Konstantin Oumansky, the Soviet Ambassador, trying to drive a wedge between the Soviet Union and Germany. When the US SIS (Signals Intelligence Service) in March and April intercepted Japanese messages indicating that the Germans would be attacking the Soviet Union in a couple of months, Welles proudly showed the summary report to Oumansky. Being the solid apparatchik that he was, and believing in the sincerity and strength of the Nazi-Soviet Pact, Oumansky immediately showed the report to Thomsen, the German Ambassador in Washington. Thomsen also had a spy working in Oumansky's embassy, and the Germans quickly determined that Japanese codes had been broken. Thomsen informed Berlin what had happened; they in turn informed Oshima, the Japanese Ambassador. And Oshima was suddenly cut off from any updates on Barbarossa plans.[42] Moreover, in his parallel analysis of the careers of Hitler and Stalin, the historian Alan Bullock indicated that the secrets that King betrayed to the Soviets were immediately passed on to their partners. "King not only gave the Russians access to the British hand but enabled the NKVD to pass on to the German embassy in London items elected from secret British material to play on German fears."[43] The historian David Cameron Watt reported how, as early as June 1939, the Soviets were leaking King's documents about Strang's mission to Moscow to the German Embassy.[44] Thus a serious generic threat endured beyond King's detection and sentencing.

A further concern of British intelligence should have been the fear that the pact of mutual 'non-aggression' might transform into a stronger military alliance against the Western powers. Such fears would not have been groundless: Stalin certainly treated the British Empire as his primary adversary, and considered that Hitler might have shared his opinion. The two totalitarian states had shown similar imperialist ambitions in Poland and the Baltics, and Stalin was by now an admirer of Hitler's ruthless tactics. The release of communications between the Comintern and the western Communist Parties showed that Stalin seriously considered joining the Axis Powers, and approached Hitler on such a manoeuvre in November 1940 – an approach that Hitler deftly ignored. After a meeting with Stalin and Molotov on November 25, 1940, Dimitrov, the head of the Comintern, recorded in his diary: "'If Bulgaria signed', Stalin emphasised, 'we not only have no objections to Bulgaria's joining the Tripartite Pact, but we ourselves in this event will also join that Pact. If the Bulgarians decline our offer, they will fall entirely into the clutches of the Germans and the Italians and so perish.'"[45] The authors of the analysis of the secret cables of the Comintern concluded as follows:

> "The cables offer rich evidence that for Stalin the alliance was not merely a tactical maneuver, but also the expression of a strategic vision for which he was more than willing to sacrifice his Communist comrades around the world. There is no evidence in the tone or substance of the secret cables between the Comintern and the Communist parties to support the notion that Stalin regarded the Nazi-Soviet Pact as a temporary tactical maneuver to gain time for the USSR to mobilise for war against Nazi Germany."[46]

Given the severity of the warnings, and their military implications, one could wonder whether MI5 shared the lessons learned with members of the War Office. No evidence has come to light that this occurred: Kell, as a military man most conscious of the origins of MI5, should perhaps have been the officer to exploit his contacts there. Alternatively, it should maybe have been the responsibility of SIS to channel such information via the Foreign Office. Yet the Foreign Office Northern Department was disdainful of the report: Vivian was not one to press a case vigorously. The conclusion must be that, either the warning about Nazi-Soviet collusion did not reach the right persons, or, if it did, those responsible were already conditioned not to consider it a major threat.

While MI5 was reluctant to take up Krivitsky's warnings about Nazi-Soviet cooperation on intelligence, they showed more interest in the threat to the integrity of British security represented by the presence of native moles. Here, it is difficult to conclude that Krivitsky was not being somewhat obtuse in his attempts to identify agents in place. If he had known the identity of King, who was being managed by Krivitsky's agent Henri Pieck, one might have expected him to know the names of Cairncross and Maclean and Philby, who had been handled by Maly and Deutsch. Both of the latter two met with Krivitsky in Paris, and it seems unlikely that they would refer to these key personalities in such vague terms that Krivitsky would later only be able to recall (for example) that the agent in the Imperial Council was a "young aristocrat", and that he may have been "the secretary or son of one of the chiefs of the Foreign Office". In a note sent to Vivian after Krivitsky had returned to Canada, Archer wrote:

"It was through this commission given to him in 1935 that K gained his knowledge of the efficient military and political espionage organisation operating in the UK under Theodore Maly and Paul Hardt. Hardt was not directly under Krivitsky's orders, but K had the right to know what he was doing and advise him on his work."[47]

That does not sound like the testimony of a man who was so far removed from the action that he did not know the names of the spies working for a close associate whom he advised.

Likewise, it seems highly unlikely that Krivitsky would have 'forgotten' the name of the agent, Bystrolyotov, who handled the spy Ernest Oldham, a cipher clerk in the Foreign Office. Oldham had betrayed secrets to the Soviets for money, and apparently committed suicide in 1933, as Archer's report divulges. Bystrolyotov was the most versatile and colourful of all the Soviet 'illegals' during the 1930s: Krivitsky was intimately familiar with the case, and did recite to his interrogators several characteristics of Bystrolyotov's personality and achievements, and thus would have either known his name, or not. And there is evidence that the two met. Volodarsky, for instance, pointed out that the Irishman Brian Goold-Verschoyle, Bystrolyotov's courier (who was later accused of being a 'Trotskyist', and murdered by the NKVD) visited both Krivitsky and Bystrolyotov in Paris in November 1935.[48] It is almost inconceivable to imagine that Krivitsky and Bystrolyotov did not enjoy each other's company at this time. Thus, almost certainly, Krivitsky was dropping hints, but felt that his interrogators should work hard for their rewards. And Bystrolyotov was still alive, being one of the few to survive Stalin's execution chambers and Gulag. Again, Krivitsky did not want to hurt anybody whom he admired: as early as September 3, 1939, when Mallet in the Embassy in Washington was advising MI5 about Levine and Krivitsky, Mallet wrote that Krivitsky knew the name of the Englishman who had been helping buy aeroplanes for Spain (to assist the Republican cause), but would not reveal his name because he liked him, and respected his idealism.[49]

Over the years, the accuracy of Krivitsky's testimony has been questioned, and vigorously debated, frequently in the face of persistent Soviet propaganda. Some recent research has amplified the accuracy of Krivitsky's information, especially as it applied to the Spanish Civil War. Krivitsky's accounts of Stalin's involvement in the War, such as his shipping of arms, and his fierce suppression of anti-OGPU elements in Catalonia, were for a long time challenged by leftist sympathisers. In the last few years, Gerald Howson has studied the Spanish and Soviet archives, and has concluded: "Many of the accusations that Walter Krivitsky, the Soviet defector, hurled against Stalin and all his works in 1939 have turned out to be true or nearly true, despite campaigns by Communist parties all over the world to discredit him as an imposter."[50] On the other hand, Boris Volodarsky (admittedly an ex-GRU officer) took pains to explain that Krivitsky must have invented multiple events (as did his counterpart, Alexander Orlov), since he simply was not present at the places and times claimed, and it would have been impossible for him to have known of all the occurrences that he described. Here again, the evidence is contradictory. Volodarsky himself was very ambivalent about Krivitsky; after diminishing his veracity, he then summarised the defector's contribution by writing: "To his credit, he had a good memory, was eager to help, and had learned a lot of useful details from 1935, when he joined the NKVD, until he defected in 1937."[51]

Any such dispute, however, really misses the point. Enough substance existed in Krivitsky's revelations, including the long list of Soviet agents he referred to, with such important figures as Maly and Deutsch predominant, to justify classifying his testimony as a unique opportunity. One disclosure, for example, which could have been far more useful in helping MI5 trace spies, was that of Katherine Harrison, who had been the mistress (and maybe wife) of Earl Browder, the leader of the Communist Party of the USA, and whom Krivitsky had met in Moscow in 1937. If MI5 had been able to exchange information about her with the FBI, it would have discovered that, under the not very secretive alias of Kitty Harris, she had arrived in London in May 1938, and had quickly become the courier, and then the lover, of Donald Maclean, eventually following him to Paris. The fact that MI5 knew there were leaks, and had broad hints to follow up, but in effect did very little when an opportunity was handed to them on a plate, is quite inexcusable.

Remarkably, after the energetic and successful project to catch King and force him to confess, the efforts to identify spies fizzled out, as if King had been the sole traitor. Certainly, several second-tier communist figures that Krivitsky had been able to identify, not known to the British authorities, were quietly "neutralised", in Brook-Shepherd's words, but the hunt for infiltrators already working for the government lost its steam.[52] (Kern claimed that Brook-Shepherd gained access to accessory information, not available in the released files at the National Archives, which, for example, allowed MI5 to move against as many as 61 Soviet agents active in the UK.) Krivitsky's admittedly blurry pointers to other figures were nevertheless not taken seriously enough. What happened to that "deep interest"? Why did Cadogan abandon the problem? Who convinced Liddell that it was of no consequence? What did Jebb think his role should have been? Why were War Office decisions so easily overlooked? Some of the irresolution must be attributed to the general chaos in time of war (as White claimed), and also to Churchill's desire to shake up the Security Service in May 1940, but there had been ample time to pursue matters in a more disciplined fashion in the period between Krivitsky's departure and Churchill's accession to power.

Brook-Shepherd's story is problematic. His claim was that he had access to unreleased archives, an assertion which Kern and Volodarsky have supported. Indeed, the level of detail in (for example) his account of the Krivitsky affair with which he shows himself familiar appears to point unerringly to the fact that he had somehow breached the Official Secrets Act (or had had permission to do so) when writing *The Storm Petrels*. Moreover, he had access to information that is not revealed in Archer's report. According to Brook-Shepherd (who, Volodarsky stated, was an ex-intelligence officer) Krivitsky apparently supplied his interrogators with the names of 16 British suspects who were spies, "people active in journalism and the trade unions, six in the civil service and two in journalism", of which half were not under any type of surveillance by the British authorities.[53] All these figures were reportedly 'neutralised', so they would not be able to perform any damage in the future, but they were not arrested, prosecuted or convicted. (One might argue with the unpleasant term of 'neutralised', and also question how effective the process was, if the names were not made public.) Kern wrote that Brook-Shepherd told him that he was given this information "because British intelligence was tired of Soviet propaganda touting its successes and wanted to show that Soviet defectors were victories for the West.'"[54]

This was some 'victory'. After all, Brook-Shepherd's book was published in 1977, when the treachery of Burgess, Maclean and Philby was publicly known, and that of Blunt and Long internally acknowledged by senior government and intelligence officials. It is almost as if White and Hollis judged that, by going meekly after small fry, they had fulfilled their obligations, by making a rather futile and ineffectual gesture. Futile, because no one knew about it, and ineffectual, since they abandoned the search for the really dangerous characters. MI5 could obviously not disclose then the full Krivitsky files, as they would have raised serious questions about the failures in execution. One might also suspect that even a minor initiative such as this (if the facts are true) might have encountered a backlash from the likes of the left-wingers Pritt and Wilkinson, and even from public figures less inclined to sympathise with Communists, but who felt that the Soviet Union would eventually have to come on to the Allies' side. The ambivalence reflected in this action helps, however, to explain why the excitement and earnestness expressed in the autumn of 1939 soon dissipated.

Jane Archer completed her very comprehensive report some time in March. It is in many ways an impressive document. In Nigel West's words, "Archer's final eighty-six page report proved to be a masterly analysis of Krivitsky and a skillful distillation of his exposition of tradecraft."[55] Kern himself commented on her "beautifully structured summaries".[56] Yet there is something antiseptic about it, displaying the time-honoured Civil Service skill of 'drafting', but not providing any recipe for an effective response. It is titled *Information Obtained from General Krivitsky during his Visit to this Country*, with no attempt at analysis, or considered opinion on the accuracy or value of the information. If it were a twenty-first century management consultants' report, it would have had to include some recommendations for action. Certainly, such items may have been outside the scope of what Archer was commissioned to do, and it may have been advisable not to commit any follow-up plans in writing, but the casual manner in which the report was accepted and distributed suggests an absent-mindedness and lack of seriousness that was utterly unsuitable for the situation.

Copies of the report, including summaries, were distributed, very haphazardly, to various departments, without any consideration of security (unlike minutes of the Security Executive, for example). No one seems to have reflected that, given how a pointer had been given to the confirmation of spies within government departments, the last thing that should be done would be to risk alerting them to the insights of a vital defector. By April 5, one (summary) copy of Archer's report had already been returned to her by the Home Office, signed by Jenifer Hart, although, strangely, not until April 15, did Archer send a "strictly personal and confidential" copy to Vivian in SIS. Since Vivian was the lead Communist expert in both services, and had master-minded the interrogations of Krivitsky, it is strange that he would not have received – or even pre-viewed – a copy before the Home Office set eyes on it. Archer followed up on April 29, sending Vivian an official copy, but she was also infected by the organisational negligence of confidentiality, since she wrote: "very limited no. of copies to be shown personally to a few heads of departments", and indicated "no return" was required.[57] By then, however, Hollis appeared to have taken over completely Archer's role. April memoranda from the Home Office on the Whomack case addressed him as B4a, and by May 11 it was Harker who was sending copies of her report to such as Jebb and Boyle. Harker's accompanying message (to Jebb, who had already received the report on April 1) showed, in its use of the passive voice, and its vagueness, the sheer unprofessionalism of the department: "It will no doubt be appreciated that the memorandum should have as restricted a circulation as possible."[58] The file in the National Archives includes several such messages from Harker, imploring his friends and colleagues ("my dear Gerrard") not to distribute it too liberally, and to return it after reading. By now, Archer had been taken out of the loop.

Soon afterwards, probably when the Fifth Column panic was at its height, Liddell requested Archer to set up a system of Regional Security Liaison Officers, in order to deal more efficiently with the wealth of reports coming from the public about suspicious activity, by decentralising control and communication. No doubt this was a very important role, but for the leading and most experienced anti-Communist officer to be lost from 'B' Division – when her skills could no doubt have been transferred to anti-Nazi subversion, if changed circumstances had demanded it – was a puzzling initiative. Archer applied herself very professionally, and was quickly endorsed by the group of Regional Officers. It might be understandable to conclude that Archer's extraordinary skills (even if MI5 were short of experts on Communism) might have been required in this radically different post. Indeed, when Liddell came to report on Archer's eventual dismissal for insubordination in diary entries between November 18 and 25, 1940, he took pains to express what a good job she had done, and how disappointed the RSLOs were at her departure. Andrew, however, in his authorised history, stated that the RSLO organisation was not set up until June, on Liddell's recommendation. The decision, however, had probably been taken some weeks earlier, and the announcement delayed until processes were in place. (Christopher Andrew's history of MI5 surprisingly contains only one sentence on the RSLO organisation: the term does not appear in the Index.) Curry appears to confirm the timing, stating that the scheme was adopted "early in the summer, on the suggestion of Captain Liddell and other 'B' Branch officers", and that "Mrs Archer was placed in charge of a section known as BR to develop this scheme". So what was Archer doing between the completion of her report and the June appointment?

It is hard to believe that she was given the assignment in late March, but did nothing while waiting for an official decision to be taken, which, in any case, probably arose out of the deliberations of Swinton's Security Executive and the Security Intelligence Centre (established on June 11), and was a response to the flood of inquiries coming in from the public about suspicious activities, as Hinsley and Simkins reported.[59] They referred to the RSLO organisation as "new" in August, after Swinton had brought in his legal friend, William Crocker, to sort out 'B' Division. (Crocker was in fact Joseph Ball's solicitor, and had acted for Guy Liddell in a failed custody lawsuit after the latter's wife had absconded to the USA with their children.[60]) Andrew was laconic, even sparse, about the whole affair. After crediting Archer for her interrogation, he swiftly glided on to her sacking without a mention of her role with the RSLOs, or even describing how the organisation worked. For an "authorised history" that is quite scandalous. Curry, for some reason, got the timing of Archer's disappearance from MI5, and her replacement by MacIver, wrong, giving a date of autumn 1941 instead of 1940. He gave no reason for her leaving, but that again reflects a discomfort about the whole episode that surfaces elsewhere in his history.

One central question is why MI5, under pressure from the Foreign Office to unmask Soviet spies, and benefitting from the valuable windfall of Krivitsky's testimony, would essentially break up its group with expertise on the Communists – even before the Nazi 'Fifth Column' scare was activated. On a page that has obviously been doctored for publication by someone who wished to obfuscate the truth, since it contains grammatical mistakes which make the text meaningless, Curry wrote (if it is indeed his voice), as a way of exculpating those responsible for inattention: "The few officers who had experience in cases of Soviet espionage – Brigadier Harker, Captain Liddell and Mrs Archer – were fully occupied with work directly bearing on measures for the investigation or prevention of espionage by the enemy."[61] Apart from the obvious point that the Soviets, as Krivitsky and Archer and others (including Curry himself) had observed, were no doubt leaking information to the Nazis, this statement must be challenged on several fronts. To present Harker as a Communist expert, given his clear reputation for bumbledom, and no documented evidence that he provided any insights on communist subversion, is a travesty. Liddell was second-in-command at the counter-espionage branch, but was not involved at the detailed level. Archer was the recognised expert, but was placed in limbo, apparently, for a few months, twiddling her thumbs. Moreover, Curry appears to contradict his statement on p 161 that "Mr White was supervising the work connected with the Communist Party and the Comintern" – a statement possibly negated by what Curry immediately added: ". . and the arrangements for liquidating the Nazi Party and those for dealing with the repercussions of the work of the Enemy Aliens Tribunals and the Birkett Committee", suggesting White had a full plate. Moreover, White's biographer confirmed White's lack of experience in this area:

"He had never previously debriefed or handled a rival intelligence officer, nor had he any experience of Russia and its espionage organisations. Throughout his tour in Germany, he had been barely touched by the Spanish Civil War, the raging issue which turned many British liberals into socialists and communists. Nor had he been outraged earlier by the Italian massacres in Abyssinia. While understanding the simplicities of the impending war between democracy and fascism, he was professionally unindoctrinated with knowledge of the profound ideological struggle between fascism and communism and of the NKVD's resulting ability to recruit non-Russian sympathisers as agents.

His prejudice was fed by appearances. The Russians were deemed to be sloppy people. Unlike the Wehrmacht, the Red Army was inefficient and unimpressive, and its recent invasion of Finland proved the communists' incompetence."[62]

Curry's final judgment was no doubt more correct. Such an opinion would be bolstered by Chapman Pincher, who concluded (from hearsay, mainly) that White and Hollis were close friends, and that "White was the dominant partner, to whom Hollis was likely to defer, though this soon changed as White recognised Hollis's superior expertise on Communist and Soviet affairs". [63] Liddell's evidence might support that view, as it was Hollis whom he consulted in February 1940 (see above). So why would Curry contravene Liddell by omitting Hollis and his expertise when he wrote his history in 1946, unless, on the one hand, he thought that something untoward had gone on at the time, or, on the other, that Hollis had between that time shown himself to be not as trustworthy and professional as Curry would like the record to show? For Hollis was indeed continuing his tracking of communist subversion for the period to which Curry offered his *apologia*, even if he was only a one-man band. Andrew was complimentary about Hollis's track-record during the remainder of the war, drawing the reader's attention to his perennial warnings about the threat of the Comintern, for instance, even after the 1942 British-Soviet Treaty.[64]

Further evidence of Curry's unreliability is shown when he described sections B4A and B4B as follows: "The essential function of B.4.A and B.4.B., the sections dealing with British and foreign communists respectively during the period prior to the German attack on Russia, was to obtain the widest possible range of intelligence on their subjects".[65] Given that 'B' Division's mission had by then switched to almost total focus on 'the enemy', the Nazis, this seems a strange way of representing them, but suggests that there was more manpower being directed at the Communists than Curry implied in his final summary. Andrew does not help much, either. He wrote: "Wartime Soviet counter-espionage, which was considered a much lower priority, was initially relegated to a single officer (F2C) in 'F' Division."[66] There is so much to quibble with in that bland sentence – the passive voice, the collapsing of the whole six tumultuous and roller-coaster years to a single pattern, the oversimplification of the prioritisation, the erroneous association of "initially" with a Division that did not appear until July 1941, and the vagueness and anonymity of the officers involved.

In the meantime, Archer maintained her interest in Krivitsky, with a somewhat surprising ally, Sir Vernon Kell – who was himself sacked in May 1940. Kell had expressed great interest in the case, and in Krivitsky's future, after the latter left the UK, and requested in a letter to Brigadier Wood, of the Royal Canadian Mounted Police, that that institution should take care of Krivitsky and his family. Sporadically, throughout the summer and autumn of 1940, Archer and Kell communicated about Krivitsky, trying to get hold of him so that he might help to identify people from photographs or give information on characters they were trying to track. The astonishing aspect of this exchange, however, is that both of them had been removed from their position of responsibility, with Kell in retirement, and Archer consumed with fieldwork in the RSLO. Hollis and Liddell apparently showed no involvement. In November 1940, Archer herself was sacked, for insubordination – concluding a pattern of disrespectful behaviour towards Harker (according to Liddell, anyway, who was the only witness to this episode) that had gone on for some time. Thereafter, it was Dick White who took up the reins: Felix Cowgill in SIS had approached him on December 5, 1940, asking for Archer, apparently unaware that she was no longer with MI5. Cowgill needed information about a Vera Eriksen, who had been persuaded by one Ivan Ignatieff to work for the Soviets in Paris, and wanted further information about Ignatieff.[ii] White was clearly still in contact with Archer, since he replied to Cowgill on December 19 that Archer thought Krivitsky could help, but that MI5 had lost track of him.[67]

They missed their chance. Krivitsky was killed – or forced to commit suicide – in a Washington hotel room in February 1941. He had long been on the NKVD's hit-list. During the purges, Stalin had instructed the organisation's heads, Yezhov, and then Beria, to hunt down every defector.[68] Kitty Harris had been recalled to Moscow immediately after Krivitsky's *Flight from Stalin* had been published in the *New York Times* in December 1937, and was presumably thoroughly debriefed.[69] Stalin's hands had nevertheless been somewhat tied because of adverse reaction by the French government to the abduction, and presumed death, of General Miller, head of the Military Union of Former Tsarist Officers, in September 1937. (Laqueur wrote that "Miller had to be liquidated because he was the only man who could expose the NKVD conspiracy against Tukhachevsky to the whole world".) Guilt could be directly ascribed to Moscow. The French government thus warned the Soviet Chargé d'Affaires that it would break off diplomatic relations with the Soviet Union should another such kidnapping (and assumed murder) occur.[70] Needing allies at this time, Stalin took heed. Plotting and executing murders around the world was not as easy as might have been expected, given these constraints. Krivitsky was surely saved by the French government's intervention, and the story of Trotsky's assassination is further testimony to the fact that Stalin's revenge could take years to be satisfied.

Sergey Spiegelglass had been the agent who had accosted Krivitsky when Reiss defected, even encouraging Krivitsky to kill Reiss himself. When Krivitsky demurred (not a career-enhancing decision), Spiegelglass took on the responsibility himself.[71] Later, Spiegelglass was entrusted with the task of assassinating Trotsky, but failed on the job, and was summoned back to Moscow in disgrace. He was also to fall victim to Stalin's killing machine, and was executed in January 1941, an event that Kern suspected Krivitsky heard about.[72] Furious at Spiegelglass's failure, in the spring of 1939, Stalin ordered Beria to kill Trotsky "within a year".[73] It took until August 1940 for Ramon Mercader to insinuate himself into Trotsky's encampment, and perform the bloody deed.

Krivitsky had an uneasy summer in 1940, knowing he was being watched in Montreal. Meanwhile, Sudoplatov, back in Moscow, was working through his priorities. Another unsuccessful assassination attempt, organised by Naum Eitingon (Guy Burgess's contact in Paris in 1938), was made on Trotsky on May 24, after which the directorate developed a more subtle secondary plan. During

---

[ii] Ignatieff had been head of the NKVD in Paris.

this time, Trotsky had been reading Krivitsky's book, *In Stalin's Secret Service*, which had been published in October, 1939. On August 9, he told the world that the two of them were at the top of Stalin's hit-list, and a few days later sent Krivitsky a thank-you note for his writings.[74] On August 20, Ramon Mercader attacked Trotsky with an ice-axe, resulting in his death two days later. When he heard of the assault, Krivitsky knew he was now the Number One target, and that his movements were being traced. Kern wrote that Krivitsky "had learned from a writer with ties to intelligence, William van Narvig, whose real name was William O. Lucas, that someone in the British establishment was reporting on his activities to Moscow through either the embassy in Washington or the one in Paris". His required period of absence having expired, he succeeded in leaving Canada for the United States.

Another important link in the chain was the Soviet ambassador, Konstantin Oumansky. Krivitsky had made an enemy of him by writing about an encounter they had had many years back. He had met Oumansky first in 1922, when Oumansky arrived in Moscow from Bessarabia, and worked at Tass, the Soviet News Agency. Oumansky had tried to avoid harsh military service by presenting himself to the Intelligence Department, and managing to gain a position in OGPU as a diplomatic courier. He took up residence at the Hotel Lux, where he was able to spy upon Tass reporters, and the exchanges they had with foreign Communists. Krivitsky described this process of evasion, and went on to write:

> "All of Oumansky's superiors, in every department in which he has worked, have either been removed and broken or fallen before the bullets of the purge.... Oumansky is one of the few Communists who succeeded in crossing the barbed-wire frontier that separates the Old Bolshevik Party from the new. During the purge there was only one passport across this frontier. You had to present Stalin and his OGPU with the required number of victims. Constantine Oumansky made good..."[75]

This may have been unnecessary bravado on Krivitsky's part: settling an old score only provided him with a fresh enemy, as his revelations about Oumansky could not have enhanced the latter in Stalin's eyes, and may also have contributed to the ambassador's premature demise. So it may not have been coincidence that, in May 1939, Stalin had appointed Oumansky to replace Alexander Troyanovksy as Soviet Ambassador to the United States. Oumansky was a member of the security service, not a career diplomat, nor the most tactful and engaging of men. Troyanovsky escaped Stalin's axe, and managed to outlive his boss, dying of natural causes in 1955.

Over the years, the question of whether Krivitsky's death was a lonely suicide out of desperation, a suicide stage-managed by Soviet agents, accompanied by threats to his family, or a simple murder set up to look like a suicide, has occupied the historians. The overwhelming opinion has been that it was the last option: Stalin's killers were adept at concealing their mischief. A bungled police operation destroyed some of the evidence; Krivitsky said shortly beforehand that if he were ever found shot to death, it would not be by his own hand; some of Beria's hit-men were seen in Washington and New York shortly before the event. Krivitsky himself told how the agent Basoff, whom he encountered in New York, had informed him that his wife's brothers had been executed because of their defecting, so he was under no illusions. Moreover, as Deacon reported[76], Krivitsky had told his lawyer that a messenger had recently seen a potential assassin named Bruesse, whom Krivitsky knew from his NKVD days, in New York. Kern, on the other hand, referred to an FBI report from 1955, based on an interview with a Comintern courier named Amadeo Sabatini, that identified one Joseph Katz as having been hired to carry out the assassination. Katz was later selected to assassinate the defector Elizabeth Bentley in 1945, before the operation was called off. This is not really a contradiction: Beria might well have had several agents tracking Krivitsky.

Brook-Shepherd is one who has reflected puzzlement as to how the murder squad had in fact tracked its prey from Virginia to the Washington hotel. At that time Brook-Shepherd was unaware of any secret communication between agents in Britain and their counterparts in the USA. Yet he carefully pointed out that Krivitsky was due to appear before a legislative hearing in New York the day his body was found, *not* (as others have written) before another hearing of the Dies committee in Washington, which pointed to Union Station as the obvious place to lie in wait. Sudoplatov, Philby, and Philby's collaborator, Genrikh Borovik[77], are the only writers who have suggested suicide, Borovik rather naively stating that "recent KGB reports" suggest a verdict of suicide. Of course their considerations can hardly be judged as objective. Kern's and Perry's conclusions are probably the soundest: the spy Michael Straight, who had been recruited by Anthony Blunt in Cambridge, had been informed about Krivitsky's appointment in New York, and gave the tip-off on his movements. Straight soon afterwards resigned from the State Department, his job done, and, as Perry reminded us, covered himself by suggesting he was scared that the KGB was after him.[78] Straight was one of the few Soviet agents who remained unharassed by Moscow Centre after expressing a desire to put an end to his espionage activities: his collusion in Krivitsky's death might thus have been his exit card.[79]

Another example of possibly misleading archival evidence is shown by records uncovered fifty years later. Towards the end of 1940, MI5 decided that they wanted to interview Krivitsky again, and started to make inquiries as to his whereabouts. Brook-Shepherd, who had been able to inspect the MI5 files as early as 1977, confirmed this.[80] The information may also have got back to Moscow Centre, and the urgency of his assassination might thus have become more intense. The NKVD/KGB file on him contains the remarkable *spravka* ['note'] that surveillance on him had ceased on February 11, 1939. Kern speculated that this was probably a doctoring of the record by the weeders in the Kremlin, and that the original note had indicated February 11, 1941.[81] "The KGB was active in the early 1990s selling select bits from files to foreign publishers, and sometimes it changed names, dates and details so as to maintain security or to slant the historical record in its favor", wrote Kern. So this note constitutes a disingenuous and clumsy attempt to maintain Moscow's innocence in the affair.

There is no doubt that Stalin wanted Krivitsky dead – as punishment, and as a warning to others. Krivitsky's revelations in the *Saturday Evening Post* must have made him apoplectic: Reiss wrote just one peeved letter accusing Stalin of betrayal, and was eliminated. Orlov, the other great defector of the decade, managed his survival only by blackmailing Stalin, promising to withhold information about Stalin's gold heist in Spain in order to save his life.[82] Trotsky was a bitter rival, still bleating in the Mexican wilderness and capable of inspiring anti-Stalinist thoughts; though his intelligence was out of date, he had to be eliminated first, as he constituted a figurehead for anti-Stalinist rebellion. Krivitsky was next on the list; he knew too much, and had insulted the Great Dictator. Edward Gazur was surely wrong in claiming that Krivitsky's evidence to the Dies Committee (looking into Un-American Activities) had cooked his goose, a claim similar to those made by other analysts.[83] Stalin had not changed his mind; he just needed to locate Krivitsky, and extinguish him in an untraceable manner, as the gangster-like attack that had disposed of Reiss would not work on the streets of Washington, D.C. We can safely discount the nonchalant statement of Sudoplatov, which gives new energy to the notion of *insouciance*: "There was an NKVD order issued to look for Krivitsky, but this was routine for all defectors. We were not sorry to see him go, but it was not through our efforts that he died. We believed he shot himself in despair as a result of a nervous breakdown."[84] Sudoplatov was swift to boast of his involvement with killing Trotsky, but was equally keen to keep intact the murk over the saga of Krivitsky's betrayal, the reasons for which will become apparent.

One astonishing aspect of the legacy of the Krivitsky case is how little attention, given the breakthrough nature of his revelations, has been paid to him by biographers of Stalin. The curious reader can inspect the works of Ulam, McNeal, Volkogonov, Conquest, Radzinsky and Service[85], yet find no entry for 'Krivitsky' in their respective indexes. H. Montgomery Hyde's biography contains only one very brief and insignificant reference.[86] That shrewd historian, Ronald Hingley, who skewered the hypocrisies of Soviet propaganda and misdeeds with savage irony, included a paragraph on Krivitsky's death in his biography of Stalin; he left an open verdict on whether it was suicide or murder, but used the episode in a section that clearly describes Stalin's vengeful efforts to eliminate renegades. Of *I Was Stalin's Agent*, Hingley merely recorded that it "contains much information on the dictator's life".[87] Another fierce exposer of Stalin's brutality, Robert Conquest, was even more laconic and perfunctory in his *Great Terror*: he characterised Krivitsky's book as "a useful source for the period"[88], a judgment akin to *Field and Stream*'s famous endorsement that *Lady Chatterley's Lover* contained useful tips on gamekeeping. Isaac Deutscher allowed Krivitsky a footnote[89], but his account is severely biased in Stalin's favour. Only Robert Tucker, of the mainstream biographers of Stalin (as opposed to experts in espionage and subversion), appears to have studied Krivitsky's testimony carefully, making an effort to credit him with informing the West about (for example) Stalin's parallel organisation of agents spying on OGPU itself, and the inside story on the Tukhachevsky affair.[90]

This is a sorry track-record, suggestive more of a wartime sympathy for 'Uncle Joe' than an incisive Cold War – or even *glasnost* – analysis of Stalin's machinations and cruelty. But it can probably be ascribed, certainly as far as the earlier works are concerned, to a natural scepticism, and a desire for verification from archival sources, with Krivitsky's more improbable claims occluding the more sober assertions about the Dictator. Thus his revelations appear to have been largely forgotten after the surprise of the Ribbentrop-Molotov agreement had worn off. Walter Laqueur was one of the few to make the correct historical linkage when he wrote, in 1990, of the fact (to which Krivitsky alluded) that forged documents came from Berlin alleging that General Tukhachevsky was involved with German military circles: "It was confirmed soon after the war in the Schellenberg memoirs and a book by Wilhelm Höttl, both of whom were leading members of German foreign intelligence. More recently, additional material has come to light from Czech and White Russian sources."[91]

Laqueur then went on to describe who may have planted such rumours, and concluded that they must have been engineered by Stalin, and that Volkogonov, when writing his biography, must have been prevented from seeing the NKVD files that confirmed that fact. The archives did indeed confirm Stalin's involvement.[92] This conclusion has been echoed by such as Igor Lukes, who said that Stalin's goal for the whole episode was to cover up his secret agreement with Hitler, and wrote: "All evidence points to a carefully managed plot by Stalin and Litvinov to get the Czechs to provoke Germany by rapid mobilisation." [93] Krivitsky, who was ordered by Yezhov as early as December 1936 to ease off his subversive activities in Germany, an indication of Stalin's desired rapprochement with Hitler's regime[94], in the works of Laqueur and Lukes, is finally receiving his due.

The early accounts of how the spies alluded to by Krivitsky first heard of his accusations are made purely by guesswork, but have been echoed over the years since they were first articulated. Thus Brook-Shepherd concluded that the April 1940 Report on the Krivitsky Interviews that Jane Archer compiled "would have got into Maclean's hands because of the small, cozy and confiding place the Foreign Office was".[95] Without providing any reference, he claimed that the Kremlin thus knew about Krivitsky's extensive revelations of the Soviet agent network, and that it was therefore Maclean who "signed Krivitsky's death warrant" that summer of 1940. The leap of logic that suggests that, since Maclean was the most closely described agent emerging from the interviews, he was the one who would read the evidence first, is a curious line of reasoning. Maclean was, however, in Paris at the time, and did not return to the UK until June 23, by which time Burgess was already deep in his plotting to travel to Moscow. Richard Deacon made a similar vague claim, this time assuming the report would have been sent to Paris: "Maclean was at that time working in the British Embassy in Paris and would have seen this report". Anthony Cave-Brown, another historian with a shaky understanding of the timeline, asserted that: " . . . as Philby learned from John Cairncross [late in 1939], who had replaced Maclean as the Soviet's mole in the Foreign office, a major security inquiry had developed in the Communications Department". According to Cave-Brown, the arrival of Krivitsky was designed to assist with this inquiry. The fact that Krivitsky had left Halifax "became known to Philby at some stage, as it became known to Donald Maclean".[96] No doubt, but Philby was also in France during this period, having taken up a position as the *Times* correspondent in Arras the previous November. Neither was Roland Perry very helpful, declaring, in his biography of Michael Straight:

"Maclean read the [April 1940] report, and discussed it with his control, who had already been informed about it by Blunt, as had Burgess and Rothschild (who, with Tess Mayer, was also working for Liddell in Section 'B' of MI5). The Cambridge ring was now fully alerted to the problems posed by this troublesome defector."[97]

The problem with such scenarios, involving communications with Moscow's intelligence service, is that only two of the Cambridge Spies were in the UK at the time, and they did not have a resident control for the majority of 1940. Beria closed down the NKVD residency in February 1940. Soviet intelligence sources have claimed that this was because Moscow Centre was suspicious of the spies it had recruited. It is not clear exactly when Anatoly Gorsky, the NKVD officer who had been responsible for handling the spies, was recalled. Andrew and Gordievsky have indicated that he was recalled at the end of 1939, implying that Beria may have closed it down after hearing Gorsky's report.[98] Other sources have indicated that he had been recalled to Moscow in February 1940, not to be eliminated, but simply because Beria regarded the UK networks as utterly unreliable, owing to the number of recent defections.[99] Chapman Pincher, on the other hand, suggested that Gorsky's recall took place *after* the Soviet Embassy learned of Krivitsky's visit.[100] He used this conclusion to help his case that Gorsky had been alerted to Krivitsky's presence by Roger Hollis, whom Pincher presented as the GRU spy, ELLI. Irrespective of the validity of Pincher's argument, it would seem highly unlikely that Gorsky would draw attention to himself, and to the fact that the Embassy had learned surreptitiously of Krivitsky's arrival, by making an immediate escape, whether given permission by Moscow Centre or not.

What has hitherto not been explained is what prompted Gorsky to be posted back to London at the end of 1940. Using Russian sources, the historian Jonathan Haslam has recently disclosed that the decision to send Gorsky back was taken as early as August 1940 ("common sense took hold in Moscow"), but that Gorsky was delayed by "travelling to and fro" in the intervening period.[101] If this assertion is true, the facts would neatly dovetail with the theory that the news arrived in Moscow, soon after Burgess's and Berlin's arrival in Washington and courtesy of Straight and Oumansky, that Stalin's Englishmen were safe, despite Krivitsky's revelations, and that they were still highly motivated, and needed a *rezident* contact to be re-installed.

John Cairncross was probably the primary source of the information about Krivitsky. As West and Tsarev reported[102], Cairncross had been providing a remarkable set of secrets to his Soviet handlers since being transferred from the Foreign Office to a position as an assistant to Lord Hankey, the Head of the Treasury, in April 1938. This move constituted an enormous piece of luck for the Soviets, as Cairncross's contribution in the Foreign Office had not been successful – either to his official or his unofficial masters. During the summer of 1938, however, he provided a rich set of documents to Gorsky, probably via his friend and intermediary, Guy Burgess. These secrets included plans for setting up the Ministry of Information, details of the organisation of the Secret Service, information on Colonel Grand and his sabotage and subversion activities (in

Section D, where Burgess was working), intelligence on the Government Code and Cypher School (Bletchley Park), as well as minutes of the Committee on Imperial Defence. (It was this Committee that Krivitsky had specifically alluded to: both Cairncross and Maclean had divulged the minutes of its meetings to their handler.) It is astonishing to think that the Soviets, out of mistrust, were willing to sacrifice such a bounteous resource at such a critical time. But Cairncross may have got wind of Krivitsky's actions via the communications between Washington and London, and then alerted Gorsky, considering his position was in jeopardy. Certainly his contributions did dry up in the last few months of 1939, and they could have jointly decided that it was better for him to lie low for a while, until they could determine how much Krivitsky had revealed.

Whatever really happened, Gorsky was the last operative resident in London, and a greenhorn at that, not returning to Great Britain until December of 1940, when he re-initiated contact with Anthony Blunt. Thus an alternative fiction now appeared that the NKVD did not learn of MI5's report on Krivitsky until January 1941, a story all too gullibly echoed by some of the prominent authors. Astonishingly, Nigel West and Oleg Tsarev, in *The Crown Jewels*, took their intelligence from the Soviet archives, as if the latter, unlike British records, were incapable of being doctored or weeded, suggesting that Blunt's January 1941 encounter with Gorsky was the first news the Soviets enjoyed. They wrote: "It was not until June 5 1941 that the Centre learned the full background of his [King's] betrayal by the defector Walter Krivitsky from Anthony Blunt, who supplied the relevant report to Anatoli Gorsky."[103]

In this narrative, therefore, Moscow Centre learned the full story of Krivitsky four months *after* they had murdered him. Kern accepted part of this story as well, writing that "in January 1941, Blunt handed his first package to Gorsky, a general report on what MI5 knew about Soviet espionage. It is not clear how much information there was on Krivitsky, but by this date the Center definitely knew about his debriefing", and "Krivitsky's January 1940 visit escaped the Center's notice or at least its concentrated attention for a full year".[104] Philby assisted in the disinformation: Borovik has suggested that Philby might have learned of the leaks from Krivitsky only in 1945 [*sic!*], and that agent "Johnson [= Anthony Blunt] passed testimony on Krivitsky to Moscow Centre". [105] All this disinformation serves only to minimise, in the eyes of the free world, the role of the NKVD in eliminating Krivitsky. After all, if they were not aware of his revelations, and did not know where he was, what could they have done?

Another scenario is much more likely. Cave-Brown drew attention to the tight social links that were maintained between the Cambridge Spies and their friends in Intelligence. He referred to the group that met at Chesterfield Gardens, assisting each other with employment opportunities, and listed Tomás Harris (whose house it was), Burgess, Rothschild, Liddell, Philby, Blunt, Brooman-White, Tim Milne and Peter Wilson as members of this coterie. And it was partly associations such as these that allowed information to be quickly and subtly exchanged – even if Moscow Centre did have serious concerns about the extent to which its agents knew about each other's activities, and the frequency with which they met. Moscow Centre had never been happy with such intimate relationships, as "it was a serious breach of *konspiratsia*, that required the agents be compartmentalised from each other".[106] A letter of April 25, 1938 by Maclean resides in his NKVD file: it clearly shows that, as Costello and Tsarev have pointed out, the Cambridge Spies were intimately familiar with each other's identity and role. Philby and Maclean, especially, met frequently.[107] One of them moved in high places, and had developed a rich set of powerful contacts. A letter from Burgess to Isaiah Berlin, Burgess's companion on the mission to Moscow, indicates that Berlin knew Philby well, despite Berlin's claims to the contrary when speaking to his biographer, Michael Ignatieff.[108] Nigel West stated that Burgess remained the key organiser of the Cambridge-orientated ring; he acted as courier for Blunt and Cairncross, exploiting his visits to Paris on government business, and it is his activity that set the counter-offensive in motion. Cave-Brown reported that Cairncross informed Philby of the major security inquiry that had developed in the Communications Department of the Foreign Office: the moles were in regular contact. Thus the involvement of Cairncross, with Burgess learning of Archer's report from Jenifer Hart, is a much more plausible scenario.

Britain's intelligence services missed an excellent opportunity by not following up on Krivitsky's information with due diligence. Overall, historians have been too indulgent: the analysis of the government's overall performance has rarely been severe. Cave-Brown is one who has criticised sharply the cover-up, even that of King, whose trial was not acknowledged until 1956, while Herbert Morrison, the Home Secretary at the time, was not even informed of Krivitsky's testimony. "Because MI5 could not find anyone who answered to Krivitsky's description, they tended to dismiss the allegations as being false", wrote Cave-Brown[109], which endures as an accurate summarisation of the case. Since the various profiles Krivitsky offered could not confidently be matched to any known individual, his whole testimony was abandoned. Others referred to the gestures that took place. Anthony Glees cited two unnamed sources, one former SIS officer who was amazed at the lethargy with which MI5 responded, another (more senior) officer who asserted that the department had indeed taken the warnings seriously.[110] In any case, Glees ventured the opinion that the successful pursuit of King had diverted attention from the true quest. Costello, delving further into Cadogan's unpublished diaries, wrote of the purge that did take effect, Cadogan deciding that the whole Communications Department in the Foreign Office had to be rebuilt from scratch – a process which made him feel better, no doubt, but did little to address the real problem, since King had already been removed. Costello drew attention to all known Communists (Andrew Cohen, Dennis Proctor, John Cairncross, Donald Maclean and Jenifer Fischer Williams – soon to be Jenifer Hart) who were working in various government departments at the time. He implicitly undermined the official records, quoting Liddell supporters as claiming that Krivitsky (who spoke little English) was "painfully vague", and that self-appointed 'official' historians of British intelligence operations continued to dismiss Krivitsky's significance.

As more records have been released to the National Archives, allowing a more in-depth analysis, and a measured integration of various testimonies and observations, some historians have changed their conclusions. For example, when Nigel West wrote his history of MI5 in 1983, he was highly supportive of the establishment, accepting the *apologias* of the officers involved, and underplaying the significance of the revelations and the required response from MI5[111], a position that Costello correctly criticised. By 2005, however, having inspected the files released by the Archives, West changed his tune. "Indeed, looking at Krivitsky's material today one can only gasp at the amount of knowledge MI5 accumulated in 1940, but never fully investigated or exploited. As MI5's declassified files reveal, it had within them all the pieces of the jigsaw to construct a very full picture of Soviet intelligence operations in England, and the long-suspected overlap between the CPGB and Moscow's espionage apparatus."[112]

Overall, however, instincts were to hush things up, where Cadogan himself led the way. This official line was echoed in Christopher Andrew's *Secret Service*, where he wrote that Krivitsky's reference to "a young man in the Foreign Office of good family" was too vague to have enabled MI5 to uncover Donald Maclean in 1940.[113] Andrew quoted the press release that effectively communicated the disdain felt by Laurence Collier, the head of the Northern Department of the Foreign Office. Part of it read as follows: "On the whole we do not consider that these would-be hair-raising revelations of Stalin's alleged desire for rapprochement with Germany are worth taking seriously." [114] Andrew was undeterred, twenty-three years later, when taking up his pen for the authorised history of MI5, declaiming from his pedestal:

> "With the exception of the King case, Krivitsky's information on Soviet agents still operating in Britain was too muddled to make identification possible. Claims that the Security Service should have been able to identify Maclean and/or Philby after the debriefing are ill-founded. Even if the Security Service had had the resources in 1940 to follow this up and the many other imprecise leads provided by Krivitsky, however, it is unlikely that Philby would have been unmasked."[115]

This is surely indulgence carried too far. MI5 was weakly led, and Liddell, who eventually became head of counter-espionage, struggled to deal with the phenomenon of Communism, from the tyranny and murderousness of Stalin, through the human side of Krivitsky, to the softer *marxisant* intellectual tones of the academics he hired from Oxbridge. Archer was the only officer (apart possibly from Kell himself) who grasped the reality of the threat for what it was, and was not distracted by the rival menace of Nazism. Yet her voice was already being stifled, and her career as a counter-intelligence officer in MI5 effectively came to a halt with the Krivitsky interrogations. For this was the age of the intellectual: Dick White was the first university recruit in an organisation of policemen. It appears that his was a voice for a softer approach with Communism. He helped hire and promote a figure who was in many ways an anomaly, a drop-out from Oxford, yet who had enjoyed practical exposure to Communism in China, Roger Hollis. Hollis's rise cannot be explained by natural ability or skill, but only by virtue of the fact that he had an effective sponsor.

The biggest irony was that MI5, with its roots in military intelligence, had lost track of its mission, of its connection with military strategy. Kell was the last remnant of its military heritage, but he had been there too long, and was no longer a vigorous champion for highlighting the real dangers, and had lost his allies. The evolution of MI5, as the war progressed, from robust defender of the nation's interests to an organisation dominated by academics was bitterly regretted by several experts in military intelligence. Even the Double-Cross System, run by the Twenty Committee, which successfully 'turned' German spies was criticised. Colonel Noël Wild, who headed General Eisenhower's Deception Unit for the invasion of Europe, wrote (of John Masterman, who chaired the Committee, and in 1972 published, despite British government opposition, his memoir *The Double-Cross System* in the USA), in a foreword for the memoir by his colleague, David Mure, and in tribute to the 'Master of Deception', Brigadier Dudley Clarke:

> "That a man however intellectually endowed, bereft of all military knowledge, should have been appointed Chairman of the Twenty Committee is incomprehensible and can only confirm again the absence of understanding of the place of Intelligence in a war machine by those who should have known better. So with Philby in position to misdirect the functions of SIS and the undisciplined Masterman chairing the XX Committee who can be sure that similar misguided individuals did not exist high up in MI5?"[116]

That epitaph serves as a commentary on the change in culture within MI5 that caused its eventual rottenness.

Yet recent research has thrown an even sharper beam on the reputation of MI5. Some historians have started to question the success of the Double-Cross System itself. In his 2014 revisionist study of Britain's relationship with Admiral Canaris's *Abwehr*, *Fighting to Lose*, the Canadian John Bryden claimed that MI5's amateurish efforts at deception were so transparent that the system effectively became a Triple-Cross, and that Masterman and Dick White realised this after the war. "White might have reddened when told how silly it was to have thought that the *Abwehr* was genuinely using First World War ciphers; that it would allow its spies to communicate with one another; that it did not know how to equip them properly; and so on. On the other hand, perhaps he had known. The wartime documents in which he features indicate a well-travelled, well-informed person with a keen mind."[117] Masterman's controversial book boasts of the contributions by amateurs that made the project successful, but it also poses grave questions about the apparent doltishness of the *Abwehr*, and the enigma of the Popov questionnaire that should have alerted the US Government to the Japanese interest in Pearl Harbour. Further analysis of this topic is beyond the scope of this book, but Bryden's researches might suggest that the reason that White wanted *The Double Cross System* banned was not because it had been successful, and hence might give away vital secrets, but because it had been a failure, and could thus only cause further embarrassments.

Notes

[1] Roger Moorhouse, *The Devils' Alliance: Hitler's Pact with Stalin, 1939-1941*, p xxiii.

[2] Hinsley *et al.*, *British Intelligence in the Second World War*, (Volume 1), p 430.

[3] Hinsley and Simkins, *British Intelligence in the Second World War*, (Volume 4), p 20.

[4] Christopher Andrew, *The Defence of the Realm*, p 273.

[5] Keith Jeffery, *The Secret History of SIS, 1909-1949*, p 312. Jeffery makes the alarming observation that Sidney Reilly, in 1920, "anticipated the pact" (p 181).

[6] Raymond James Sontag and James Stuart Beddie (ed.s), *Nazi-Soviet Relations, 1939-1941: Documents from the Archives of the German Foreign Office*, pp 76-78; reproduced in Moorhouse, pp 301-303.

[7] Gary Kern, *A Death in Washington*, p 235.

[8] Kern, p 240.

[9] See Kern for a very detailed, (and overall very sympathetic), account of Krivitsky's life. Krivitsky wrote a memoir, (in fact ghosted by Isaac Don Levine), titled *In Stalin's Secret Service* (USA) and *I Was Stalin's Agent* (UK). Elisabeth Poretsky, Ignace Reiss's widow, gave a more nuanced picture of Krivitsky's strengths and failings in *Our Own People*. Kern has also published, in *MI5 Debriefing and Other Documents on Soviet Intelligence*, Jane Archer's MI5 report on Krivitsky, which is available at the The National Archives, in the folders KV2/802-805. Nigel West's *Mask: MI5's Penetration of the Communist Party of Great Britain* is critical of MI5's performance after the Krivitsky interrogations. More recently (2014), Boris Volodarsky, in his revisionist biography of Alexander Orlov, *Stalin's Agent*, has identified some of the flaws in Krivitsky's testimony. Also published in 2014, Kevin Quinlan's *The Secret War Between the Wars: MI5 in the 1920s and 1930s* covers the Krivitsky interrogations in depth, but more from a perspective of tradecraft than grounding the episode firmly in a military context.

[10] Verne Newton, *The Cambridge Spies*, p 9, pp 26-27.

[11] Kern, p 243.

[12] Gordon Brook-Shepherd, *The Storm Petrels*, p 150, note 3.

[13] Krivitsky, *In Stalin's Secret Service* (1939), Introduction, p xv. Yezhov himself was executed on February 4, 1940, while Krivitsky was in London.

[14] Arthur Koestler, *The Invisible Writing* (1954), pp 484-488.

[15] Guy Liddell, *Diaries*, February 2, 1940 (KV 4/185).

[16] Walter Krivitsky, *Begstvo ot Stalina, Pis'mo v redaktsiu* [*Flight from Stalin. Letter to the Editor*] published in *Sotsialicheskii vestnik* [*Socialist Herald*], December 24, 1937, translated by Gary Kern.

[17] Gary Kern, *The Kravchenko Case: One Man's War on Stalin*, p 562.

[18] Tom Bower, *The Perfect English Spy*, p 34.

[19] Costello, pp 344-350.

[20] Nigel West, *MI5*, pp 87-91.

[21] Isaac Don Levine, *Eyewitness to History*, p 197.

[22] Kern, pp 274-275.

[23] Pavel and Anton Sudoplatov, *Special Tasks*, pp 90-91.

[24] Unpublished handwritten diary entry of September 4, 1939, (in archive at Churchill College, Cambridge), quoted in Costello's *Mask of Treachery*, p 345.

[25] Levine, p 196.

[26] Andrew, p 264.

[27] TNA, KV 2/802.

[28] Andrew, p 220.

[29] TNA, KV 2/802.

[30] Bower, p 34.

[31] TNA, KV 2/803.

[32] Levine, p 192.

[33] Guy Liddell, *Diaries*, December 11, 1939.

[34] *British Documents on Foreign Affairs, N 1909/250/38, MacKillop to Eden*, April 3, 1937.

[35] *British Documents on Foreign Affairs, N 2468/250/38, Chilston to Eden*, May 4, 1937.

[36] Joseph Davies, *Mission to Moscow*, p 436.

[37] The Joint Intelligence Sub-Committee was set up in July 1936, reporting to the Chiefs of Staff (CoS). A note placed in the National Archives, in 1969, indicates that most of the CoS minutes between 1939 and 1941 were lost, or had been destroyed. See CAB 56/7.

[38] TNA, CAB 56/1-4, Memoranda of Joint Intelligence Sub-Committee, 1936-1939.

[39] TNA, CAB 80/1043.

[40] TNA, HW 15/43.

[41] Guy Liddell, *Diaries*, August 13, 1940, from version in TNA.

[42] James Barros and Richard Gregor, *Double Deception*, pp 39-40.

[43] Alan Bullock, *Hitler and Stalin: Parallel Lives*, p 610. In a footnote, Bullock credited the "British historian Donald Watt" for uncovering these facts, but did not provide a precise reference. Watt's book *How War Came: The Immediate Origins of the Second World War, 1938-1939*, is cited in the same chapter.

[44] David Cameron Watt, *How War Came*, p 375.

[45] Firsov, Klehr and Haynes, *Secret Cables of the Comintern*, p 157.

[46] Ibid., p 248.

[47] TNA, KV 2/804, memo dated March 13, 1940.

[48] Boris Volodarsky, *Stalin's Agent*, p 245.

[49] TNA, KV 2/802.

[50] Gerald Howson, *Arms for Spain*, p 208.

[51] Volodarsky, p 432.

[52] Isaac Don Levine made the following surprising statement: "In my mind, the mystery of Krivitsky's death has always been linked with his mission to London. Louis Waldman, who made the arrangements for that mission reports: 'As a result of Krivitsky's special trip to England a few months earlier, a serious disruption of fifth column activities had resulted.' A number of agents had been uncovered with his aid". (*Eyewitness to History*, p 200). No further explanation is offered. It is not clear whether Waldman is talking about fifth column activities in the UK or the USA. He does imply, however, that Krivitsky's death resulted from the identification of such persons.

[53] Brook-Shepherd, p 166.

[54] *A Death in Washington*, p 284, describing an interview with Brook-Shepherd on September 26, 2002.

[55] Introduction to *A Death in Washington*, p xvi.

[56] *A Death in Washington*, p 280.

[57] TNA, KV 2/805.

[58] TNA, KV 2/805.

[59] Hinsley *et al.*, *British Intelligence in the Second World War*, (Volume 1), pp 66-68.

[60] West, p 198; papers of George Joseph Ball (6656) at the Bodleian Library, Special Collections.

[61] Curry, p 192. The author, Nigel West informed the author that the text of the original version of Curry's report in the National Archive is markedly different from the one published in book form. A brief inspection of the original shows that the apparent editing errors noted in this chapter were present in the version first declassified.

[62] Bower, p 34.

[63] Chapman Pincher, *Treachery*, p 66.

[64] Andrew, p 282.

[65] Curry, p 185.

[66] Andrew, p 188.

[67] TNA, KV 2/802.

[68] Costello and Tsarev, p 249.

[69] Igor Damaskin and Geoffrey Elliott, *Kitty Harris: The Spy with Seventeen Names*, p 156.

[70] Edward Gazur, *Alexander Orlov, The FBI's KGB General* (2001), p 165.

[71] Krivitsky, p 222.

[72] Kern, p 319.

[73] Kern, p 289.

[74] Kern, p 296.

[75] Krivitsky, pp 32-34.

[76] Deacon, *The British Connection*, p 147.

[77] Borovik, p 122.

[78] Perry, p 134.

[79] Brook-Shepherd, pp 165-166.

[80] As indicated earlier, Brook-Shepherd's *modus operandi*, and the claims about his access to unreleased files, are extremely problematic, given the constraints of the Official Secrets Act. Nigel West has suggested that Brook-Shepherd was given covert assistance by SIS in his literary endeavours. See Nigel West, *Fiction, Fact and Intelligence*, in *Understanding Intelligence in the Twenty-First Century: Journeys in Shadows*, L. V. Scott and P. D. Jackson (ed.s), p 123.

[81] *A Death in Washington*, p 328.

[82] Gazur, pp 164-166.

[83] Gazur, pp 292-293.

[84] Sudoplatov, p 49.

[85] Adam B. Ulam, *Stalin, the Man and his Era*; Robert McNeal, *Stalin, Man and Ruler*; Dmitri Volkogonov, *Stalin, Triumph & Tragedy*; Robert Conquest, *Stalin*; Edward Radzinsky, *Stalin*; Robert Service, *Stalin - a Biography*.

[86] H. Montgomery Hyde, *Stalin: The History of a Dictator* (1971).

[87] Ronald Hingley, *Joseph Stalin, Man and Legend*, p 269. This writer was taught by Professor Hingley, at Oxford University, in the late 1960s.

[88] Robert Conquest, *The Great Terror – a Reassessment*, p 409.

[89] Isaac Deutscher, *Stalin*.

[90] Robert C. Tucker, *Stalin in Power*, p 378, p 411, p 415.

[91] Walter Laqueur, *Stalin: The Glasnost Revelations*, p 85.

[92] ibid., p 87.

[93] Igor Lukes, *Czechoslovakia between Stalin and Hitler*, p 155.

[94] *A Death in Washington*, p 87.

[95] Brook-Shepherd, p 168.

[96] Cave-Brown, p 219.

[97] Roland Perry, *Last of the Cold War Spies*, p 119.

[98] Christopher Andrew and Oleg Gordievsky, *KGB, The Inside Story*, p 293.

[99] Nigel West and Oleg Tsarev, *The Crown Jewels*, p 144. West and Tsarev cited a message from Moscow Centre to Gorsky, dated February 7, 1940, encouraging him to meet Blunt in London rather than setting up a rendezvous with another agent in France. This would clearly indicate the recall happened later in February.

[100] Pincher, p 70.

[101] Jonathan Haslam, *Near and Distant Neighbours*, p 104.

[102] West and Tsarev, pp 209-213.

[103] *The Crown Jewels*, pp 145-146.

[104] *A Death in Washington*, p 285.

[105] Genrikh Borovik, *The Philby Files*, pp 243-244.

[106] Costello and Tsarev, p 225.

[107] Costello and Tsarev, pp 211-213.

[108] Letter of September 1934, in Berlin Archive at the Bodleian Library (244).

[109] Cave-Brown, p 219-223.

[110] Anthony Glees, *The Secrets of the Service* (1987), p 336.

[111] West, pp 85-87.

[112] Nigel West, *Mask*, p 200.

[113] Christopher Andrew, *Secret Service*, p 441.

[114] Andrew, p 423; Perry claims that this item was written by Guy Burgess (p 107).

[115] *The Defence of the Realm*, p 266.

[116] David Mure, *Master of Deception*, p 11.

[117] John Bryden, *Fighting to Lose*, p 308. This conclusion is in marked contrast to the same author's judgment of 1993, when he wrote that the Double-Cross System was "as fine a counter-intelligence accomplishment as any during the war". (John Bryden, *Best-Kept Secret*, p 82).

Chapter 4: The Moscow Plot – Political Intrigue

"The most accurate way of transmitting intelligence is by means of an orderly carrying a written message." (Manual of Instruction in Army Signalling: 1876)

"Guy Burgess is still trying to get in touch with Comintern and use them to create disorders in occupied territory." (Harold Nicolson diary entry of August 19, 1940)

"Not that I had any reason to suspect that Burgess was a Communist, still less a Soviet agent, but having met him once or twice I had formed the opinion that he was quite exceptionally dissolute and indiscreet and certainly unfitted for any kind of confidential work." (Gladwyn Jebb)

For 75 years, any official hints as to the purpose or authorisation of the bizarre – but aborted – mission to Moscow engineered by Guy Burgess and Isaiah Berlin in the summer of 1940 have lain hidden. The significance of the bewildering fact that this unlikely couple, one a radio journalist, propagandist and intelligence officer, but also an active Soviet agent, the second a prominent Oxford don and historian of ideas, conspired to visit the capital of a foreign power, which was at that time in league with a wartime enemy, has for some reason been ignored by all historians. It is as if, with the events of summer 1940 marking the mid-point of the descent of Burgess's reputation, and that of Berlin's corresponding ascent, the story is too sensitive to be told. Burgess knew too much, and the roles that were given him (in light of his later-revealed transgressions) were so inappropriate, that voices had to be hushed. Berlin quickly rose to a position of such stature, authority and wisdom that he could never be seriously questioned on the affair. Yet the October 2015 declassification of a file from 1951, after Burgess had absconded with Maclean to Moscow, has revealed that Burgess and Berlin, both working for the extra-secret subversion team, Section D, had somehow convinced the Foreign Secretary, Lord Halifax, that their connections with the Comintern gave them a good chance of convincing the Soviet Union that it should abandon its pact with Nazi Germany to join the Allies.[1]

This chapter explores the background to the mission, and suggests a sequence of events by which the improbable project was launched. Did a serious political initiative exist for creating a back-channel to the Soviets, for which Burgess was considered the most suitable candidate? What extraordinary circumstances would have convinced the Foreign Secretary that an approach by a minor diplomat could reverse a treaty by two dangerous totalitarian countries, and what were the risks? Or did Burgess, with his own ulterior motives, take advantage of a topical political situation, and his own reputation and associations, to sell an idea that allowed him to pursue a more private ambition? And how much did the Foreign

Office and the Intelligence Services know about the mission? Were they ever consulted, and why was the project aborted half-way through? How did Burgess's now open status as a colleague of the Comintern affect his own role, and the strategy of MI5 in dealing with Communist subversion?

The bulk of the evidence of the mission comes from Berlin's own testimony. In his published *Letters*, he provided his addressees with copious details of the planning and initial execution. These accounts are embellished with the conversations he had with his biographer, Michael Ignatieff, unpublished, but transcribed by the editor of Berlin's works and letters, Henry Hardy.[2] Harold Nicolson, Parliamentary Secretary in the Ministry of Information, referred in his *Diaries* to the plans of his two friends, and also pointed out when the mission appeared to be falling apart.[3] Major Bickham Sweet-Escott, who worked for the clandestine Section D of SIS, a department responsible for sabotage and subversion, in his memoir characterised Berlin's visit to Moscow as one of the most bizarre adventures that was cooked up by Colonel Laurence Grand (the head of Section D) and his affiliates.[4] Despite Berlin's claims that the venture had been approved by the Foreign Office, Government records (that have been available for some years) show how its Northern Department (responsible for dealings with the Soviet Union) later got wind of the scheme. Fitzroy Maclean, the diplomat responsible for the Russian desk, who had recently returned from that country, apparently learned of the plot only when the pair had already reached Washington – and did his best to prevent Berlin and Burgess from carrying on with the voyage.[5] Yet the recently released archives indicate that the Foreign Office heard of the plan just *before* Burgess and Berlin left the country, a note informing us that "D [*Colonel Grand*] was anxious for him to go to Moscow, where he hoped to get in touch with the Comintern and influence them against the Germans. The Foreign Office objected and he was therefore sent to New York where, he said, he had friends who would get him onward visas to Russia."[6] While this strange sequence of events raises new puzzling questions (Why the 'therefore'? Who authorised the back-up plan? Why did the FO not object to the US avenue? And to whom did Burgess explain how he would get visas there?), the hitherto cryptic note that Nicolson made in an unpublished entry for his *Diaries* ("GB comes to see me and I tell him there is no chance now of his being sent to Moscow"), which, given the pair's actual departure soon afterwards, has been interpreted as referring to Berlin, not Burgess, can now be explained by Foreign Office objections at the time that were partially overcome.[7] As will be shown, however, Halifax still endorsed the expedition to Moscow, not just to the United States, after the date of this entry. It is worth noting that, when Burgess and Maclean absconded in 1951, the US intelligence officer Robert Lamphere shrewdly made inquiries to the British Embassy as to why Burgess and Berlin had been travelling to Moscow via the USA in 1940. The Embassy replied to the effect that it had not been able to discover the precise nature of the mission. Whether anyone then thought of asking Berlin is not recorded.[8]

Was the original mission designed out of high political strategy, or from Burgess's opportunism? Both political historians and those covering intelligence matters have shown an extraordinary indolence in investigating this story. The authorised history of SIS, while pointing out the political troubles that Grand was encountering that June, and the subsumption of Section D into the new SOE department, draws a complete veil over the mission to Moscow.[9] The testimonies of the main actors, moreover, cannot really be trusted, as they each had personal (and different) ambitions in wanting to reach Moscow that they were naturally diffident to disclose. Thus it is useful to break down the motivations for the mission into three categories. First might be a secret, official charter, as presumably authorised by some senior diplomat or politician. The Soviet Union, was at this time an ally of the enemy, Nazi Germany, and any visit to the adversary's capital would obviously come under close observation by the media, especially as the communist sympathiser, Stafford Cripps, Labour Member of Parliament for Bristol South-East, had only just arrived there as British Ambassador. Second comes the ostensible role that provided cover for the primary, secret mission; and in the third category are the private goals nourished by the Soviet spy, Burgess, and his colleague in Section D, the ardent Zionist with business connections and relatives still living in the Soviet Union, Isaiah Berlin.[10]

In order to understand what possible stimuli for reaching out to the Soviets might have existed in June 1940, it is important to assess carefully the military and political situation at the time. The period in question was at one of the most frenetic and critical junctures of the war, when Churchill, new to his role of Prime Minister, was facing a rampant Nazi military machine making its advances across Europe. Churchill faced numerous challenges at this time: a House of Commons still largely loyal to his appeasing predecessor, Neville Chamberlain, and still calling for accommodation with the Germans; the ideological conflict of integrating a number of left-wingers in his Coalition government, and their demands for greater influence and control over the execution of the war effort; a struggling intelligence organisation – particularly the Security Service, MI5, which had grown exponentially during the last year, but which did not have the processes and organisation in place to operate effectively; the threat of a Nazi 'Fifth Column', the menace of which was magnified by certain portions of the Press, but which drew attention to the vast number of aliens who had reached the country in the wake of Hitler's predations in Central Europe; the only vague support given to Britain's cause from the USA, where President Roosevelt, who was seeking his third term of office that autumn, was anxious not to offend an overall isolationist electorate unwilling to intervene again in a European war; and the threat that the Soviet Union would intensify its alliance with Nazi Germany, when Churchill was deeply convinced of the fact that the war against Nazi Germany could be won only with the help of the Soviet Union and the USA.

Churchill, Stalin and Hitler were at this time engaged in an extraordinary three-way gavotte. Stalin, having decimated his officer corps in his purges of the late 1930s, needed time to rebuild his army. Suspicious of the intentions of the 'capitalists' (since he regarded both Nazi Germany and the British Empire as variants of the same species), he frequently claimed that Britain was his major adversary, because of its imperial tentacles, but he realised that Germany could pose a much more immediate aggressive threat, owing to its geographical proximity. His cynical pact with Hitler in August 1939 – which caused dismay in Communist Party headquarters around the world – gave him the time he needed, as well as the opportunity, according to the secret clauses in the agreement, to gain buffer zones around the Soviet Union (primarily the Baltic States) to push back the borders he had to defend. Yet, while concerned that the appeasers in British politics might gain the upper hand, and unite with Hitler against him, he was also suspicious of Hitler, and the latter's articulated desire for living space to his East. He had little patience for Chamberlain, and efforts in the summer of 1939 between Great Britain and the Soviet Union to forge an agreement came to nothing. As the Soviet defector and ex-officer in Army Intelligence, Walter Krivitsky revealed, Stalin had long harboured plans to build an alliance with Hitler, in the belief that the Fascist leader would be more easily controlled that way.

Whether Hitler's declarations of intent can be trusted is dubious. While his testimony in *Mein Kampf* was outspoken about his detestation of Slavs and Jews, his statements about Great Britain (frequently misrepresented as 'England') were contradictory. To those whom he considered friendly or influential, he could be very positive. For example, as early as 1925, he told the author Hugh Walpole about his admiration of England and the need for her to be allied with Germany.[11] In December, 1934, at a dinner in Berlin, Hitler expatiated at great length to Lord Rothermere on the nature of Anglo-German friendship, and how the future of the two nations lay in partnership.[12] In 1938, he told F. W. Winterbotham, the Royal Air Force officer who was working under cover for SIS, that his view of an ordered world depended upon the British Empire, the German Reich, and 'the Greater Americas' sharing the responsibility after the Germans had destroyed Communism.[13] In May, 1940, General Franz Halder, chief of the German Army staff, recorded in his diary the Nazi plans for partitioning the world with Britain. A critical aspect of the continual peace plans Hitler offered to the British government in 1940 was the offer that Britain could keep its Empire if he were allowed free rein in Europe. That summer, he told von Wiegand, an American journalist, that "it was never his aim to destroy the British Empire".[14] Yet more recent research suggests this was all a facade: in his 2016 biography of Hitler, Volker Ulrich posited that Hitler had given up on the UK as early as 1937.[15]

Historians continue to debate the sincerity of Hitler's declarations. While Hitler's failure to follow up on the chase at Dunkirk has been interpreted by some analysts as being occasioned solely by a need to refresh and reinforce his troops, others have suggested that he halted his assault in order to allow Britain to re-group and reconsider. Such a stance would have derived from a belief that communism was the real enemy, not the British, with their estimable and envied empire, and their presumed 'racial' similarities. Yet he was accustomed to express extreme frustration when British voices did not express appropriate respect for his views, and declined his negotiating advances. In December 1939 he told his Minister of Propaganda Joseph Goebbels that he wanted to beat England whatever it cost. In truth, he was as duplicitous as Stalin, and would say whatever he wanted if it furthered his goals. What concerned him most, however, was fighting on two fronts: if he could pacify Britain without actually engaging in a highly risky invasion, he would have felt empowered to attack the Soviet Union, his key target. If he had accomplished that goal successfully (a task that his advisers said would be completed in months), he would no doubt have felt energised to take on Britain with renewed vigour, and have been able to cast aside his reservations about the merits of the British Empire as an institution worth saving. His primary goal, in the summer of 1940, was thus to dispose of Britain as a military threat.

Both Churchill and his Foreign Secretary Viscount Halifax believed, in the dark days of May and June 1940, that the war was essentially unwinnable. Halifax, whose reputation as an 'appeaser' has been sharply contradicted by Andrew Roberts in his biography of the Foreign Secretary and US Ambassador[16], had in fact been one of the first in Chamberlain's Cabinet to realise the villainy and untrustworthiness of Hitler, and had recommended the principled stand that Britain should take, after the rape of Czechoslovakia, not to accept any more of Hitler's aggressive incursions. Even Churchill, of "we shall never surrender" oratory, was alarmed at the possibility that the *Luftwaffe* of Hermann Goering, the Nazi Aviation Minister, would quickly wear down Britain's hard-pressed air force and terrorise the populace through its bombing campaigns. Churchill was not alone in devoutly hoping that Germany would turn its attentions to the Soviet Union, and that the two totalitarian monsters would slug it out in the forests of Byelorussia. (The risk did exist, however, that an early winner might appear, who would then be in an even more powerful position to attack the Western democracies.) What Churchill needed was time, and the hope that Hitler, if he were unable to vanquish Britain through an air attack, could at least be held off until the seas of winter made a naval assault quite inconceivable.

Moreover, Churchill, despite his frequently articulated hatred of Bolshevism, had often expressed the view that an alliance with the Soviet Union would be necessary to defeat the greater evil of Nazism. As early as October 1933 he had told his niece, Diana Sheridan, that he would happily ally with Stalin to defeat Hitler[17], and later wrote of the time when Britain declared war on Germany: "I was still convinced of the profound, and as I believed quenchless antagonism between Russia and Germany, and I clung to the hope that the Soviets would be drawn to our side by the force of events".[18] His gesture of sending Stafford Cripps to Moscow as Ambassador in May 1940 (a move that was in fact Halifax's idea), complemented by warm letters to the Generalissimo himself, reflected an earnest, though somewhat cynical, desire to detach Stalin from a too affectionate relationship with Hitler.

It is with this backdrop that the stage was set for the curious negotiations and lobbying that led to the mission to Moscow. In the accounts of the participants, three prominent names appear as contributors to the scheme: Lord Halifax, who had turned down the opportunity to replace Chamberlain as Prime Minister when he realised that his knowledge of military affairs was vastly inferior to that of Churchill, and considered himself more capable of influencing the impulsive Prime Minister from the position of Foreign Secretary[19]; Sir Joseph Ball, a classical Tory Party fixer and crony of Guy Burgess, who, despite Churchill's misgivings (he wanted his own intelligence adviser, Desmond Morton, an ex-SIS officer, in the post), had recently been appointed as second-in-command in the new Security Executive that had taken over the management of British Intelligence, and who himself had been given special responsibility for the campaign against Fifth Columnists; and Lord Rothschild, a shadowy but influential figure who managed to keep himself out of the spotlight, but who had strong pro-Communist sympathies, was a close friend of Berlin and Burgess, and had recently joined MI5 in an anti-sabotage unit.

A glimpse of a possible explanation for the need for a confidential mission to communicate matters of importance to Stalin can be seen in an extraordinary exchange between Halifax and Churchill that took place on May 6, 1940, just before Churchill was invited to become Prime Minister.[20] It takes the form of notes passed back and forth at a Cabinet meeting[21], where Churchill had reacted strongly, and with disgust, to a suggestion by Halifax that peace feelers should be dispatched to Hitler – an initiative that Churchill considered "treasonable". Halifax claimed that Churchill had severely misunderstood what he was saying: he annotated the exchange with the comment "I had suggested that one way to gain time was to delude the Germans by Peace talk!", and Churchill graciously climbed down, with an apology. Yet, this notion of a ruse to deceive the Nazis was strangely overlooked when Roberts returned to the intense Cabinet meetings that took place at the end of the month, with Churchill now Prime Minister, and with the Nazi troops having roared into the low Countries, and apparently about to capture the British Expeditionary Force.

Most historians have likewise portrayed these sessions as representing heated arguments between Halifax and Churchill concerning the stark choices between a negotiated peace and stubborn resistance. Given the way Churchill has penetrated the public consciousness with his own account of the hostilities, historians and biographers have struggled to refine the myth of 'Churchill the Indomitable' that is almost part of British folklore. As late as 1992, Isaiah Berlin (who worked for Halifax in Washington later during the war, from 1941 to 1945, and authored the reports that were sent to Churchill under the Ambassador's name) said in an interview: "Where would we have been without him [Churchill] during the war – those marvellous speeches? We needed him, otherwise Halifax would have sought peace with Hitler, which would have lasted for a short time and then England would have been overrun."[22] In 2012, William Manchester and Paul Reid showed that they had accepted the traditional line (or had been taken in by the artfulness of the ruse) when they wrote of the events of this month: "The men of Munich were still a force, particularly in the establishment. Halifax, of course, was one."[23] Roy Jenkins, a leading Labour politician, is another biographer of Churchill who showed an accurate scorn for what Churchill claimed about the debates of the time while failing to notice the irony of the whole situation, or to recognise Halifax's sacrifice in appearing as Churchill's stooge. Commenting on Churchill's claim about the unanimity of the Cabinet over "fighting on alone", he wrote: "And Churchill, eight years later, wrote in his war memoirs, combining in almost equal parts charity (towards Halifax) and mendacity, the most breathtakingly bland piece of misinformation to appear in all those six volumes".[24] Yet, while such opinions represent the majority of conventional wisdom, other historians have hinted at a more intricate interpretation of what happened.

One such strand in the fabric has suggested that Churchill himself was an appeaser. This prompted the historian David Reynolds to write, in 1996, a provocatively titled article (*Churchill the Appeaser?*) that analysed Churchill's overall record in dealing with more powerful entities – both adversaries and allies, as the subtitle indicates (*Between Hitler, Roosevelt, and Stalin in World War Two*). [25] Surprisingly, this piece takes the traditional line of the pugnacious Churchill warding off Halifax and his Under-Secretary of State for Foreign Affairs, R. A. Butler, in the dark days of June 1940, and does not allow for any more nuanced interpretation of what happened, or whether, "even though Churchill's vision was more complex than mythology suggests", there was any more subtle and devious thinking at play than a claim that Britain would gain only worse terms from Hitler if it gave up fighting. He characterised Churchill's stubbornness as a mere "rhetorical trope", and hinted that he shared with his government the prospect of an eventual negotiated peace. But he left the "vision" unexplored: it is all very inconclusive. Reynolds then switched his attention more to the late period of the war, when Churchill is shown to be too trusting of the intentions of both Stalin and Roosevelt, and he came up with the rather tentative conclusion that "he *is* open to the label of appeaser".

John Lukacs, the Hungarian-born American historian who has made the events of this time an academic specialty, is one chronicler who in three important volumes published between 1976 and 1999 has deeply investigated the critical period under review, being one of the first to hint at a deception plan that was shared by the Prime Minister and his Foreign Secretary. [26] At the outset, he was very tentative, using an almost Halifaxian circumlocution: "Consequently, there are some indications that Churchill was not above suggesting that, under certain conditions, the British might negotiate, though not from weakness." [27] He was not much more assertive fifteen years later:

> "Now – again because he understood Hitler better than Hitler understood him – Churchill began to play for time, in more than one way. Generally speaking, he insisted on high spirits at home; he also instructed all British posts, embassies and legations abroad to show their high spirits. …. At the same time Churchill may not have been immune to the temptation to throw out some small bait to Hitler, to encourage or extend Hitler's expectations a bit longer." [28]

Lukacs was here still guarded ("may not have been immune"); by the time he came to describe the events of July, he was far more confident:

> "On 10 July Halifax again suggested to Churchill that it might be worthwhile to ascertain something about Hitler's terms. But this suggestion was different from those of late May when Halifax had been challenging Churchill's leadership and chosen course. Now their purposes were the same: to gain time for Britain. Churchill understood that – which is why, in all probability, he did not discourage a few careful and confidential attempts to throw some bait to German agents – more precisely, to pretend to listen to them. But on the larger and public level the impression of an unbreakable British resolve to fight had to be maintained." [29]

This revised assessment – that Halifax and Churchill were united in a strategy of deception – is supported by the sequence of events that ensued after the tumultuous Cabinet meetings at the end of May, but which in fact Churchill had set in train before. Part of the strategy was to claim that a 'Peace Movement' of far greater substance than actually existed, and represented by enthusiasts for Halifax (with the abdicated Duke of Windsor waiting in the wings), was a threat that could remove Churchill from office. Certainly, his position was not secure. On May 13, the ex-premier Chamberlain had received far more applause at the House of Commons than he, Churchill, had. Churchill thus had complicated messages to transmit to his conceptual ally, Roosevelt. On May 15, he wrote to him warning him of the implications for suing for peace. On May 19, he implored his US Ambassador, Lord Lothian, to impress upon Roosevelt the world threat represented by Hitler. On May 20, he again personally warned Roosevelt of this threat[30], but also stated that there was a danger of a peace movement sweeping him from office. It was imperative that Roosevelt knew how real the danger was, but that it was not so dire that it was pointless to provide any assistance, and understood that the USA would eventually be menaced, too. Roosevelt needed to know of Churchill's pugnacity and determination, and that the British leader was capable of leading a diverse Cabinet, and a nervous nation.

To what extent the whole division was staged, or from what time the two worked in close harmony, cannot precisely be ascertained. Halifax threatened resignation on May 27, frustrated by Churchill's obstinacy and hot-headedness, and Churchill made concessions. Roy Jenkins took the line of serious conflict between them. Halifax recognised he was "beaten"; by May 28, Churchill "had been able, slowly, to rout Halifax", and Jenkins treated the achievement as "one of the most important victories of his premiership".[31] On June 15, Churchill was again warning Roosevelt that Hitler could impose a "terrible peace" on the country, and by now the message was getting back to Hitler that a peace movement was challenging Churchill's leadership. On June 23, Prinz Max Hohenlohe[32] reported to his foreign ministry on the strong peace movement in London[33], and on June 28 Goebbels noted in his diary the struggles that were taking place between the militants and the pacifists in London.[34] Reynolds wrote that "the Wehrmacht started improvising military plans to make Britain seek peace in June 1940".[35] In July, Samuel Hoare (who had been recently banished by Churchill as Ambassador to Madrid) and Lothian were both making furtive approaches to their German counterparts about peace talks. As Foreign Secretary, Samuel Hoare had been the joint author of the Hoare-Laval Pact that ceded territory in Ethiopia to Italy. After losing his job because of this action, he was brought back by Baldwin, and served as Home Secretary under him and then Chamberlain until the outbreak of the war.

On June 11, 1940, Hitler recited to the commander of the German Navy, Admiral Raeder (who the same day was advising his boss that air superiority had to be gained before an invasion could be considered), new texts on offering peace to England.[36] Six days later Hitler made a new Reichstag speech, in which peace terms were freshly laid out. Around this time, the British Ambassador in Switzerland, Sir David Kelly, met Hohenlohe, and gave him the impression that Britain was playing for time, and that a strong peace movement still existed in London. On July 23, Hohenlohe's report on his meeting with Kelly reached Ribbentrop and Hitler.[37]

The strategy of exploiting Hitler's wish to believe that there was a strong 'Peace Party' in Britain was not new. SIS had been toiling diligently at it for several years. When working clandestinely for that organisation in Germany in 1934, F. W. Winterbotham detected a rift in the Nazi hierarchy similar to that which split the British political class. He had received strong signals from Hitler and Alfred Rosenberg that they eagerly sought Britain's neutrality, and he discounted the possibility that such overtures were bluff. Goering and Kesselring, however, were out for revenge, while Goebbels sat on the fence.[38] The fact that the Foreign Office and SIS had been working this particular lode during the 1930s has been reinforced by the historian Louis Kilzer, who wrote, in *Churchill's Deception*: "Unknown to the Führer, the SIS had for years manipulated his obsession about a Peace Party to influence him and divine his intentions."[39] Winterbotham had exploited Hitler's desire for negotiation by infiltrating double-agent de Ropp, who, despite serving under Winterbotham in World War I, was trusted by Hitler and Rosenberg, Hitler's chief ideologist, with information about their plans for the Luftwaffe.

The implication here is that Churchill was using the time-honoured stratagem of delicately leaking disinformation through intermediate channels. And the most dramatic of such moves was the case of R. A. Butler, and the Swedish Ambassador Bjørn Prytz. The way this sequence of events has been so carefully chronicled gives a certain disingenuousness to the whole affair. The episode has the character of the celebrated (but controversial) Double-Cross system, by which officers in MI5 turned round German spies to enable disinformation about military plans to be communicated to the enemy. The best account of what happened is provided by Richard Lamb, whose overall theme was to echo the opinion that Churchill remained aware of the 'defeatist views' of Chamberlain and Halifax, and had to take drastic action when he heard of Butler's misbehaviour:

> "He was much put out when Rab Butler, Halifax's Under-Secretary at the Foreign office and the Commons spokesman on Foreign Affairs, breached his edict. On 17 June Butler met Bjørn Prytz, the much respected Swedish Minister, in St James's Park and brought him back to his room in the Foreign Office for a chat about the probable outcome of the war. Prytz reported to the Swedish Government that Butler 'told him no opportunity would be neglected for concluding a compromise peace if the chance was offered on reasonable conditions'; further, after being called away to see Halifax, Butler returned with a message from the Foreign Secretary to Prytz that 'commonsense, not bravado, would dictate the British Government policy' and that Halifax knew that such an attitude would be welcomed by Prytz although he 'must not interpret it as peace at any price'. In his report to Stockholm, Prytz added that many MPs expected Halifax to succeed Churchill as Prime Minister. This report was discussed by the Swedish Foreign Policy Committee under obligations of strict secrecy.

At the time Sweden was desperately anxious for a peace to be arranged as it was being faced with harsh demands from Germany for transit rights for troops and materials through Swedish territory, and the report was immediately leaked to the press. The Stockholm correspondent of the *News Chronicle* informed his paper on June 20 that Butler had said Britain would only fight on if sure of victory. Ribbentrop (German Foreign Minister) immediately made enquiries through Sweden as to whether Britain wanted to negotiate, and the British Minister in Stockholm reported this approach to the Foreign Office."[40]

Lamb went on to assert that Churchill became apoplectic when he heard about this disclosure, and that Butler "was close to being sacked". Yet the episode has all the hallmarks of a carefully staged event, in which Butler was the fall-guy. Butler had to grovel, and Churchill's son, Randolph, later "assiduously fanned" the story, with the result that Butler's reputation was tarnished, becoming a factor in his failure to replace both Anthony Eden (in 1957) and Harold Macmillan (in 1963) as Prime Minister.[41] On the other hand, Lukacs revealed that Churchill, on June 25, sent Halifax a much calmer message, effectively forgiving Butler without pardoning him, suggesting he realised that Butler's words to Prytz may have been misunderstood.[42] The historian of intelligence and security matters, John Costello, in his highly detailed study of this period, accepted most of the evidence at face value, suggesting that Halifax and Butler were truly dedicated appeasers, disloyal to Churchill, but that Churchill did indeed exploit their stance to deceive Hitler. Yet Costello admitted bemusement at Churchill's failure to censure Halifax and Butler strictly. "The logical explanation is that Churchill left Halifax in office precisely so that the Germans *could* believe they were sending out peace feelers", he wrote, classifying Churchill's tactics as "Machiavellian stratagems to bluff Hitler". [43] His conclusion assuredly asserts that Halifax remained a permanent threat to Churchill: "Only if the Foreign Secretary had received such a guarantee [*from Ribbentrop*] would he have been able to challenge Churchill by resurrecting the peace issue in the War Cabinet." [44] Subterfuge on Churchill's part, bringing Halifax and Butler into his ruse, seems a much more convincing explanation.

The final element in the campaign to magnify the threat of the 'Peace Party' opposition was Churchill's repeated offer to the elder statesman David Lloyd George (who had been Prime Minister from 1916 to 1922) to join his government. Lloyd George had not just been an advocate of peace with Hitler: he was also an ardent admirer of the dictator. Andrew Roberts described him as "Britain's Pétain-in-waiting",[i] and noted that "the great liberal Lloyd George left his 1936 meeting with Hitler likening *Mein Kampf* to the Magna Carta and calling Hitler 'the Resurrection and the Way' for Germany".[45] Lloyd George did not conceal his preferences. For example, on October 3, 1939, he had recommended, in the House of Commons, that peace negotiations with Hitler be started. Yet, immediately Churchill came to power, on May 13, 1940, he made the astonishing

---

[i] Philippe Pétain was a French WWI war hero who became head of state of the Vichy government in France in July 1940, and was convicted for treason after the war.

move of offering Lloyd George the Ministry of Agriculture, which Lloyd George refused. Churchill renewed his appeal after the weekend of intense Cabinet debates, on May 28. Lloyd George again declined. This charade was repeated on June 6, when again Churchill's offer was rejected. (Lukacs reported yet another offer on June 19, but did not attempt to explain why the offers may have been made.)[46]

Perhaps Churchill expected (and hoped for) that negative response from Lloyd George, but the knowledge of the offer itself would have sent a clear message to Hitler that Churchill's position was at risk, and that he had had to make concessions to the appeasers. On the other hand, Churchill's official biographer, Martin Gilbert, represented the negotiation in a diametrically opposite light, as if Lloyd George were a militant hero who would have put the appeasers to shame. He had Churchill offering Lloyd George a seat in his War Cabinet, "seeking an extra counter to Halifax's waverings", and informs us that "the former Prime Minister, whose tenacity Churchill had so admired in the First World War, declined: 'Several of the architects of this catastrophe are still leading members of your government,' he told Churchill, 'and two of them are in the Cabinet that directs the war.'"[47] Lloyd George as romantic hero: Lloyd George as traitorous villain – posterity has to deal with both images. Official historians cannot be trusted completely.

If Churchill had indeed been responsible for a crafty campaign to deceive Hitler, and thus gain time, it was not without enormous risks. The first risk was that Hitler would see through the deception, although that was a minor impediment to action. It was not as if the dictator would automatically be prompted to more malicious deeds by being misled thus, though it might cause him to rant in the short term. Hitler's enemies – both the urbane Chamberlain and the diabolical Stalin, for example – often expressed a desire not to 'provoke' Hitler, as if he were a testy elderly relative who might ruin the Christmas celebrations. But Hitler did not need 'provocation' to initiate his mayhem (although he could be vindictive in revenge): he was quite capable of pursuing his millennial ambitions without opposition troop movements, conscription orders, or hastily drafted alliances prompting him into precipitate action. Thus any time that Churchill could have gained by deferring the air assault on Britain, and especially a naval attack until the following spring, were vital weeks.

Far more dangerous was the potential backlash on his allies, and on the morale of the people of Britain. Churchill, having invested so much in his defiant broadcasts to the nation, could not let his authority and principled stand appear to be publicly weakened. And the mental disposition of Roosevelt and Stalin was equally critical, since Churchill believed that the eventual entry into the war of the USA and the Soviet Union would be the critical factor in defeating Nazism. With Roosevelt, Churchill had a personal means of communication, although the Tyler Kent episode was fresh in his mind. (Kent, an employee of the US Embassy in London, had been passing copies of private communications between Churchill and Roosevelt to Nazi sympathisers, and had been arrested on May 20, 1940.) Churchill knew Roosevelt was sympathetic, but was struggling to carry a reluctant American public: any sign of hesitation or defeatism might have convinced his detractors and opponents that Britain was a lost cause, and thus no

91

blood or pelf should be wasted on assisting the country in its resistance to Hitler. But there was no risk of the USA's siding with Germany.

The Soviet Union presented a different challenge, primarily, of course, because it was an ally of Nazi Germany, enjoying what was notionally a pact of non-aggression and trade, but which had the potential of becoming a military alliance. If Stalin gained an inkling that Churchill might be ousted, and that Britain's new leaders would seek peace arrangements with Germany, he might well conclude that it could lead to a fresh partnership of the 'imperialists' rallying to defeat communism (Hitler's existential enemy). In that scenario, Stalin might well anticipate the move, and attempt to draw closer to Hitler in a shared project to eliminate the British Empire (Stalin's elementary foe). Thus it became essential for Churchill to let Stalin know that his resolve was unswerving, and that he was in charge of the situation, and the mood of the people. While Churchill needed to let Hitler believe that the threat from the Peace Movement was real, it was essential that Stalin understand that it was illusionary, and that Churchill had it under control. And yet, if Stalin discerned that the phenomenon was a ruse to encourage a shift in Hitler's military attentions to the Soviet Union, he would regard it as cynical, and his trust would be shattered, even though it were the mirror-image of his own strategy towards the Germans.[48] So how to communicate this delicate message? Some subtlety was required.

Stalin's Embassy in London was not a reliable medium. The Ambassador, Ivan Maisky, who had held the position since 1932, was a notorious gossip, himself both untrustworthy and mendacious. It is true that he had been suggesting that Stalin would now be amenable to approaches from Great Britain, but Maisky had a steadfast opponent in Fitzroy Maclean in the Foreign Office, one of a virulently anti-Communist cabal that included Lord Vansittart, the former Permanent Under-Secretary for Foreign Affairs until 1938, when his somewhat erratic behaviour and opinions had caused him to be sidelined into the largely symbolic office of Chief Diplomatic Adviser. As Martin Kitchen wrote: "He [Maclean] felt that Maisky had been exceptionally skilful in creating the impression that the Soviet Union and Germany were far apart and that Moscow could be won away from Germany. This myth was being disseminated by the *Daily Worker*, the *News Chronicle* and the Beaverbrook press. It was time that something was done to prepare public opinion to be more anti-Soviet, especially as we are on the verge of war."[49] Roberts reported how Chamberlain's administration learned of his earlier indiscretions and unreliable character, declaring that "the Russian Ambassador, Ivan Maisky, was an unattractive figure, whose intrigues with Lloyd George, Churchill, Hugh Dalton and other opposition figures was well known to the Government through the tap MI5 kept on his telephone."[50] Moreover he was a Menshevik, and thus implicitly not to be trusted wholeheartedly by Stalin. It was astonishing that he had survived as long as he had.

The case that Churchill and Halifax would turn to Burgess and Berlin to carry a personal message to Stalin is circumstantial, and by no means obvious at a superficial glance. Yet the actions the unlikely *compadres* undertook at this time dovetail supremely well with the actions of their political leaders, and with Halifax's little-known role in intelligence. The relationships that he and other prominent figures had with Burgess and Berlin, and the political background, point to a simpler explanation for the Moscow Plot. Yet the case has one obvious flaw: if indeed the mission had been encouraged by Churchill, it is very unlikely that he would have allowed it to be cancelled by an upstart Foreign Office. Halifax certainly approved it, but it may well have been a bottom-up idea by Burgess that took advantage of the situation, and, when Halifax faced objections from his department, he was not a strong enough character to overrule his officials. So what do the accounts tell us, and how can Burgess's motivations and actions be explained?

As Michael Ignatieff (Berlin's biographer) tells the story, on the basis almost exclusively of Berlin's conversations with him, the facts are briefly stated, though a little bizarre.[51] Early in the summer of 1940 Guy Burgess surprised Berlin by bursting into his rooms at New College, asking him to join him on a trip to the Soviet Union. Burgess, who was at the time working for Section D of SIS, was probably anxious to make contact with his spymasters after Moscow had carried out a purge of the London station.[52] He had persuaded his mentor Harold Nicolson that Berlin, a native Russian speaker, should be appointed as press officer to the newly appointed Ambassador, Stafford Cripps, at the Embassy in Moscow. Yet even the record of this conversation is problematic, and this author's recent discovery that the transcriptions of the interview, created at the time (in 1994) occasionally deviate sharply from what is detectible on the audiotapes of Berlin's conversation, highlights some near inexplicable behaviour.[53] For example, Berlin can clearly be heard describing Burgess's apology for his apparent treachery to the leftist cause by joining the Anglo-German Fellowship, out of an expressed admiration for the Nazis, as they "were doing something, there was something modern and new". Almost immediately, however, Burgess informs Berlin that he has been recruited by SIS, as if the intelligence service would not be concerned about recruiting someone who had been a blatant Nazi sympathiser, and, furthermore (although Berlin claims to know nothing of the mission) presumably divulges that he is about to engage on a voyage to meet his colleagues in the Comintern. That Berlin should not see anything amiss in such an ideological volte-face is astonishing: equally puzzling is Ignatieff's failure to ask piercing questions about such an anomalous train of events. The evidence unerringly points to the fact that Berlin must have been an accessory to Burgess's manoeuvres for some time.

In any case, Berlin was convinced that he should join his friend. Some of the necessary paperwork was arranged, and Berlin and Burgess left Liverpool for Moscow, via Montreal, the US and Vladivostok. They arrived in New York near the end of July, but never completed the journey. In Washington, Burgess received the news that he was to be recalled to London. Unlike 'recalls' to Moscow, where agents would probably be sent to the Lubianka, for no other reason than that they had been exposed to Western influences, Burgess (according to Ignatieff) was simply fired by MI6 on his return. He did, however, soon confide to Harold Nicolson that he had not abandoned his plans to make contact with the Comintern, giving as his motive his desire to "use them to create disorders in occupied territory", thus presenting the same incorrect and implausible pretext that he gave to Driberg years later.[54] Now that we know that the Foreign Office was aware of the higher strategic goal, it would appear that Nicolson was not party to the scheme, and that Burgess wanted to conceal the real purpose of the mission. Meanwhile, Cripps refused to sanction Berlin's presence in Moscow: the Foreign Office belatedly got wind of the whole scheme, and scrapped it. Berlin, apparently not a government employee like Burgess, was left to pursue his own devices, and, as noted above, eventually found an influential position working for Halifax (after the latter succeeded Lothian as Ambassador early in 1941), assisting the British propaganda effort in the USA.

Further research has shown that this account is probably a travesty of what really happened. Berlin himself has given multiple, conflicting accounts of the events of that summer, most notably in his Introduction to *Washington Despatches*[55], and in his interviews with the espionage writer Andrew Boyle.[56] To begin with, evidence provided by the spy John Cairncross and by the maverick Member of Parliament, and close friend of Burgess, Tom Driberg (not normally the most reliable of chroniclers, but in this case there seems no reason for them to lie) suggests that, despite his protestations to the contrary, Berlin had been on intimate terms with Burgess, and had mixed with him socially on frequent occasions. Secondly, Burgess's claims that his mission to Moscow was driven by an SIS need to exchange intelligence with that department's Soviet counterparts in sabotage and subversion (as he maintained to his biographer Driberg[57]) must be seen as completely spurious, given Burgess's role and experience, and the timing of the event at the height of the Nazi-Soviet pact. (Such an initiative was pursued by the Special Operations Executive after the Soviet Union entered the war, which might have given Burgess the idea.) Much more likely is that Burgess, as the ringleader and chief courier of the group of Oxbridge-educated agents of Stalin was anxious a) to inform his Soviet masters (who had withdrawn any contacts in London out of fear that their network had been compromised by recent defections) that the group was still willing, active, and committed, and b) to advise them of the recent interviews conducted by MI5 personnel of the Soviet defector, Walter Krivitsky. It is possible that Burgess wanted Berlin to accompany him as interpreter in Moscow to help him ensure that his messages to his Soviet handlers were not distorted. Krivitsky, who had been specially brought over in conditions of the highest secrecy from the USA via Canada, had come close to identifying Cairncross, Maclean and Philby to his MI5 interviewers.[58] Having conferred with his fellow-moles, Burgess seems to have been the point-man who was determined to set the NKVD on Krivitsky's trail.

Other evidence proves that Burgess and Berlin were engaged on a shared Section D mission, and that Burgess probably proposed his participation in it as a timely means of pursuing his other objectives. Stephen Dorril presented Berlin as a well-established figure in SIS (MI6). He wrote: "MI6's leading theorist was Robert Carew Hunt, who laid out his critical views on Marxism in two books – *The Theory and Practice of Communism* (1950) and *Marxism: Past and Present* (1954). These academic texts attempted to 're-examine the basic concepts of revolutionary Marxism'. Working inside the anti-communist section (R5), he developed his theories from discussions with MI6 'insiders' and 'Sovietologists', such as Isaiah Berlin, A. J. 'Freddie' Ayer and Leonard Schapiro."[59] Moreover, the notion that Berlin would have made a suitable press officer for the Embassy in

Moscow is patently absurd. The opportunities for influencing the editors of *Pravda* and *Izvestia* on the nuances of British foreign policy would have been minuscule.

Bickham Sweet-Escott was then an officer in Section D and later in SOE (Special Operations Executive), the group into which Section D was folded after Churchill reorganised the security services, and he had been appointed the personal assistant to Sir Frank Nelson, the SOE chief.[60] In his work *Baker Street Irregular*, Sweet-Escott clearly identified Berlin's mission to Moscow as one engineered by Section D, strongly suggesting that Berlin had been recruited by the same Colonel Grand for whom Burgess was chief ideas-man.[61] In his 1968 study of Kim Philby, E. H. Cookridge (born Philo, who had known Philby well in Vienna) claimed that a number of volunteers with special knowledge of Europe worked unofficially for Grand before the war, their names being maintained on a "Central Register". "This was a very secret list of men who, at one time or another, had rendered service to SIS and had agreed to join it as full-time workers in wartime."[62] Berlin's name appeared there, alongside such as George Courtauld (of the textile concern), Bill Stephenson (who was to run Britain's intelligence operation in the United States), Bickham Sweet-Escott himself, the explorer Freya Stark (with whom Berlin would later have enigmatic dealings over Zionism, in Washington), Graham and Hugh Greene, and "several university dons".

The recent release of files to the National Archives confirms that Berlin was a member of Section D, alongside Burgess, Kim Philby, Tomás Harris, and H. D. Harrison.[63] While Burgess nominally reported to Grand, he was in fact the one driving the show. Burgess was no doubt the person who came up with the scheme to influence his friends in the Soviet Union, and sold it upwards. It was a message that was listened to with sympathy: in his diaries of this time, Alexander Cadogan, the Permanent Under-Secretary at the Foreign Office, referred to opportunities for propaganda in Russia, and a possible mission there.[64] Yuri Modin, who was the spies' handler from 1948 to 1951, wrote, in his somewhat unreliable memoir, that "Valentine Vivian [in SIS] was convinced that Guy Burgess might yield spectacular results if he went to work at the British Embassy in Moscow under diplomatic cover", but there is no other evidence that SIS was involved, and Jeffery's authorised history makes no mention of the event.[65] As has been shown, Harold Nicolson claimed that both Burgess and Berlin knew *before* they left that their mission to Moscow would not take place, presumably because of the disbanding of Section D just before they were due to leave, but probably also because members of the Foreign Office were beginning to get wind of the scheme. Grand had his enemies, and they notably became more vocal in July 1940. Yet the Foreign Office did not move fast enough, or Halifax simply ignored the objections for the time being: Burgess and Berlin were nevertheless both able to embark on their ship to the United States, Burgess having successfully sold his back-up plan.

Yet there are links between Berlin and Halifax, and Burgess and Halifax, that have been hitherto overlooked. Of prime significance is the fact that Halifax and Berlin were both fellows of All Souls College, Oxford. On June 21, 1940, Berlin wrote a long and ingratiating letter to Halifax, pleading for a job in Moscow.[66] It is discursive and in many ways absurd: Berlin claimed that he was writing at the prompting of the Warden of New College (H. A. L. Fisher) and another fellow, Lionel Curtis, but his sycophancy is distasteful. Indeed, Berlin's editor, Henry Hardy, noted that "this letter appears not to have been sent in this form, but it may be a draft of a letter that was sent". One can understand why: Halifax, for all his Edwardian languor, was a busy man, and would surely have sent this missive back without giving it any great consideration. The letter should be viewed as one of the many items of evidence that Berlin left behind him that he may have thought enhanced his reputation[67], but the exaggerated style and content in fact lead the reader to other conclusions (as happens frequently with Berlin's occasionally hyperbolic assertions.) This approach by Berlin may well be interpreted as a cover for the fact that the government wanted him for the secret assignment in Section D. Moreover, Berlin was vague about the date that Burgess had approached him, suggesting perhaps that it was *after* his letter to Lothian was written, but an entry (unpublished) in Nicolson's *Diary* indicates that Berlin told him on June 17 that he wanted to go to Russia. [68] Berlin told Ignatieff that Burgess approached him in "mid-June". Hardy, in his annotations to the *Letters*, said that it occurred in "late June". This unexplained contradiction could have enormous ramifications on the motivations of the participants: for example, if the alleged meeting took place in *early* June, Berlin might have written the letter in response to a suggestion by Burgess, but, when the latter saw the expansive and obsequious text, he advised that it should not be sent. (The letter does not appear in the Halifax archive.) Another skein in the plot is the fact that Lettice Fisher, the wife of H. A. L. Fisher, also wrote to Halifax on Berlin's behalf, in a letter dated June 19.[69]

Halifax was a far more capable intriguer than his reputation frequently indicates. Roberts, who has shed much light on this side of Halifax's character, recorded that "Days after *Anschluss* [i.e. in March 1938] he [Halifax] organised with the Secret Intelligence Service 'a few preparatory steps taken in deadly secrecy by Section D to counter Nazi predominance in small countries Germany had just conquered or was plainly threatening. To this end he invited the Canadian newspaper magnate, Sir Campbell Stuart, to look into the uses of sabotage, labour unrest, inflation and propaganda".[70] Halifax also engineered the appointment of his favourite, Stewart Menzies, to head SIS when its then head, Admiral Sir Hugh Sinclair, died in November 1939, and thereby outwitted Churchill, who wanted the naval man, Commander Godfrey, to take over. Halifax was the brains behind the move to have Cripps sent as Ambassador to Moscow, and he also allied with his old Etonian friend Hugh Dalton to have Dalton take control of the emergent Special Operations Executive (including Section D), whisking it away from Menzies's supervision before the head of SIS knew it had happened. Halifax also counted Walter Monckton, an ambitious lawyer who later served briefly in Eden's government, among his closest friends; he expressed a desire to see Monckton installed at the Ministry of Information, and persuaded Chamberlain to appoint him President of the Press and Censorship Bureau in October 1939. A month later Monckton contrived to have the Bureau moved into the Ministry of Information, and by April 1940 he had succeeded in becoming Deputy Director-General.

Yet there is evidence that Halifax's propaganda efforts may have been manipulated by Monckton, who was in fact a closet subversive.[71] In one famous despatch to his friend Stafford Cripps in September 1940, Monckton wrote of ". . . showing now that we mean to get rid of the rotten parts of the established system here. . ." Cripps answered that: "What has temporarily brought Russia and Germany together is because historically they are both an attempt to get away from an effete civilisation which the countries we represent are desperately trying to cling on to and to revivify. It is indeed a revolutionary war and we are on the side of the past for the moment . . . it will be more difficult then to make any change without a revolution . . . if only we would act in time to create a new order. But why preach to the converted!"[72] By June 1941, Monckton was lobbying hard for Cripps to replace Churchill as Prime Minister. Did Halifax pull the strings? Or was he manipulated? It is difficult to tell.

In any case, Halifax maintained a close interest in the management of intelligence matters, and it was he, on July 1, 1940, who signed the Courier's Passports for Berlin and Burgess, requesting "free passage . . . proceeding to Moscow, via USA and Japan . . .". This important event occurred two days *after* Nicolson wrote in his diary that Stafford Cripps had refused to accept Berlin as his press attaché, and Nicolson gave Burgess the ambiguous news of the cancellation. Halifax was either signing critical documents absent-mindedly, or was resolutely pursuing his endeavour, unwilling to be deterred by his civil servants and diplomats in the Foreign Office. Perhaps he knew that the objective of the mission could be achieved by the participants' reaching the USA, and going no further. After all, Burgess and Berlin knew that they were going to have to rely on the offices of Konstantin Oumansky, the Soviet Ambassador in Washington, and a loyal member of Stalin's secret police, the OGPU, for their visas for entry to the Soviet Union, as Maisky was considered impotent in this regard. And as it turned out, the pair were both recalled after critical encounters in the United States.

The hint of Sir Joseph Ball's involvement comes from a brief letter by Goronwy Rees to Isaiah Berlin. Rees was a close friend of Burgess and Berlin, and also a Fellow of All Souls: in 1938 Burgess had confided in Rees that he was a Soviet agent, and he had been able to recruit Rees briefly to the cause. Many years later, in March 1956, after Burgess's defection, Rees wrote a series of anonymous articles in the *People* newspaper, unrestrainedly describing Burgess's role as a spy and depicting his behaviour as that of a blackguard.[73] Shortly afterwards, Rees was forced to reveal his identity, and was immediately excoriated (primarily by Lord Annan, who had also served as a military intelligence officer during the war) for betraying a friendship. At that time, Rees exchanged a series of letters with Berlin.[74] Berlin had obviously been distressed by the revelations (and had quickly identified their author), but wrote a "very nice letter" to Rees which Rees acknowledged on March 19, while also reinforcing how "dangerous" a man Burgess was.[75] On April 24, however, the pressure on Rees was obviously increasing. He wrote "You will remember that a long time ago you told me that when you went to America with Guy, he was supposed to be working for Sir Joseph Ball. Can you tell me whether this was true or not. It is really terribly important for me to know whether it was true; and equally if it was not." Why this was important is not clear: Rees's daughter, Jenny, who wrote a moving memoir about her father, has been unable to shed any light on the episode, or to suggest what the matter of vital importance might have been.[76]

Berlin's mood immediately changed: he was on the defensive, and had to turn to attack. His reply (the only letter in this correspondence that is available) is worth quoting in full:[77]

> "Believe me, you are mistaken. I had never seen the name of Sir Joseph Ball, as far as I know, before I came across it in your articles in the *People*, and I am therefore absolutely certain that I cannot have told you anything about whether or not Guy B. was or was not working for him at any time. I have no idea even now who he is or was.
>
> You said in your article that I was supposed to be 'recruited' by Guy into Sir J. Ball's organisation. I can assure you that I was not, and had never even heard of him, nor became a member of any organisation Guy was working for. Nor have I ever been sent on any secret mission anywhere by anyone; nor was I Guy's assistant, nor was such a telegram as the article quoted ever sent – the telegrams about Guy and me were separate. I do not know what source his came from; mine was sent by the Foreign Office, which was supposed to be employing me, and did not refer to him; nor of course so far as I know (but here I no longer speak from direct personal knowledge) did he get into any intelligence organisation as a result of the abortive American journey, but on the contrary, so far as I know, the result of it was that he was sacked from whatever office he was in, and was then put by someone into the BBC and rendered presumably less dangerous than before. However, I lost touch with him after July 1940, and this last point is based on general hearsay, I do not understand even now, and even on your premises, what the point of the story was."

This is an extraordinary reply. If Berlin had wanted the matter dropped, he could (and should) have simply written: "I am sorry, Goronwy, but I do not recall this at all. You must be mistaken." His protestations, however, while claiming a distancing from the facts of the mission as we now know them, with their scant regard for the truth, and their nervous verbal mannerisms (e.g. the superfluous insertions of "so far as I know", singularly inappropriate from a celebrated historian of philosophy) simply draw attention to Berlin's complicity, and the murky way in which the adventure was conceived. Yet an eerie parallel to Berlin's denial is found in the words of Joseph Ball himself. Andrew Lownie, in his 2015 biography of Guy Burgess, wrote that "Joseph Ball, who was named in the articles, successfully issued a writ against Rees and the *People* seeking an apology and damages, saying that he had 'never met Guy Burgess in his life and had never heard of him until he fled the country.'"[78] This must have been an enormous bluff by Ball: Lownie (not alone) stated that Ball played a significant role in Burgess's various missions, and for Ball to claim that he had not even heard his name mentioned before he absconded is simply preposterous. Ball's papers indicate quite clearly that, during the pursuit of his libel action against

Rees, he tied himself in knots on this matter, since he would have had to admit in court that he had been employed by MI5, leaving him to suggest to his solicitor (William Crocker, whom he had brought on to the Security Executive back in 1940) that the Official Secrets Act would prevent him from making such a declaration. In fact, Ball did not have to perjure himself: the matter was settled out of court, with *The People* accepting Ball's claim that he had never heard of Burgess until he escaped to Moscow, and Ball having his name cleared, and pocketing the fee paid into court.[79] Many historians, for example David Cameron Watt, have also pointed to Ball's close involvement with the radio propaganda outfit, the Joint Broadcasting Company, led by Burgess.[80] Yet this was a pattern in Ball's behaviour: in their 2016 biography of Burgess, Purvis and Hulbert showed that, also in 1956, Ball's solicitors had successfully kept Ball's name out of Tom Driberg's profile of Burgess ("A Portrait With Background"), after Ball had been mentioned in a related newspaper article.[81]

Yes, strictly speaking, Section D was not Joseph Ball's organisation, but we know now that Berlin had been formally recruited into it, and separate negotiations about the individual fates of Burgess and Berlin were exchanged. Berlin *was* sent on a secret mission; he and Burgess *did* cross the Atlantic together; Fitzroy Maclean *did* send an encrypted telegram to Lord Lothian in Washington, on July 27, that made a strong request that neither Berlin nor Burgess should proceed to Moscow; and Berlin *did* frequently meet with Burgess later in the decade. Moreover, Joseph Ball had been Director of the Conservative Research Department[82], and at the time held the highly important deputy's job in the Security Directive. Halifax would have known him well, and naturally turned to him to help organise a secret mission. Why should Berlin deny it? Only, of course, if he had been sworn to secrecy, and regretted that his loose lips had conveyed to Rees more than he should have done. Many years later, when Churchill, Rothschild, Ball, Halifax, Nicolson and Gladwyn Jebb were all dead, Berlin was quite happy to recount to his biographer his visit to the head of Section D, Colonel Laurence Grand, under the guardianship of Jebb. Jebb was then Private Secretary to Cadogan, and liaised between the Foreign Office and the intelligence services. (In 1945 he was appointed the first Secretary-General of the United Nations, and became Baron Gladwyn in 1960.) It was he who explained the mission to Berlin and handed him and Burgess their diplomatic bags to take to Moscow.[83] Berlin simply deceived his biographer about the episode, presumably under the delusion that, if official records had not been released by then, they either did not exist, or would have enjoyed a permanent embargo. The lack of transparency is astounding.

As for Lord Rothschild, Berlin hinted to Ignatieff that it was he who was actually responsible for cancelling the mission, an assertion that, if true, would place Rothschild on a more influential plane than Halifax. But the statement is probably a red herring released by Berlin to cloud the issue, and retrospectively to distance himself from Burgess. The incident involved Lord Rothschild's older sister, Miriam, and suggests that Rothschild may have put her up to the ruse, to provide a reason for Burgess's recall. As Henry Hardy recorded the event: "Miriam Rothschild, who happened to be in Washington at the time, was horrified to hear of IB's [Berlin's] plan to go on to Moscow with Guy Burgess, of whom she had long held a low opinion. At her prompting, her close friend John Foster, who shared her suspicions of Burgess, urged the Head of Chancery, Derick Hoyer Millar, to have Burgess's plans blocked. Hoyer Millar agreed to recommend accordingly".[84] There is an element of farce about this episode, as if the biologist sister of an officer in MI5, by happenstance in the vicinity of Washington, and enjoying good connections at the British Embassy, was at the time more perspicacious than her brother and the Foreign Secretary, and that she had enough clout that her intervention suddenly reminded their lordships of the frailty of their judgments, and caused the recall to be made.

Lord Rothschild was otherwise a peripheral figure in this episode. An authoritative and objective biography of him has yet to be written.[85] He had joined MI5 shortly before the Moscow Plot, and had already started to exert policies of sympathy to communists in government departments. Roland Perry claimed that he was using his position in the Commercial Espionage Unit of MI5's Section 'B' to feed his analysis of German-owned business in the UK to his Soviet spymasters. It is probably more accurate to categorise Rothschild as an 'agent of influence' who was never formally recruited by the KGB (something he was over-anxious to have disproved at the end of his life). Several commentators, including Yuri Modin, the handler of the 'Cambridge 5' from 1948 to 1951, have claimed that it was Rothschild who introduced Guy Burgess to such influential political figures as Stewart Menzies, Dick White (the intelligence officer who headed both MI5 and SIS during his career), Robert Vansittart, and Joseph Ball.[86] Rothschild's role will be analysed more closely in the following two chapters.

Burgess obviously had powerful connections, but one remaining question must be: How and why was he chosen for such a sensitive mission? With the benefit of hindsight, he appears as a disreputable and unreliable character whom the authorities would be extremely unlikely to entrust with such a confidential assignment as taking a message from Churchill to Stalin. Yet, at the time, well before he fell into disfavour, he was viewed as a figure with a reputation for handling demanding tasks. The primary source for his eventual sacking from SOE, allegedly in August 1940, is Jebb himself, who, in his memoir wrote of his close friend: "If I can claim credit for anything in this operation it was also on my recommendation that the decision was taken to terminate the appointment of Guy Burgess. Not that I had any reason to suspect that Burgess was a Communist, still less a Soviet agent, but having met him once or twice I had formed the opinion that he was quite exceptionally dissolute and indiscreet and certainly unfitted for any kind of confidential work". [87] Jebb's testimony has been picked up consistently by historians of this period, but it is highly unreliable, and indicative more of the serious distancing from Burgess that everyone of any stature, and a reputation to maintain, undertook when he was unmasked.

Jebb was not acting on his own initiative, but responding to the new head of training and planning in SOE, Brigadier (later Major-General) Colin Gubbins, a military officer with a firmly disciplined approach and a well-established disdain for the Bolsheviks, who had assumed his new post in November 1940, transferring from MI(R). As early as August, 1940, Jebb was already being undermined by Dalton himself, as well as by the ambitious Rex Leeper, who was put in charge of SO1 (propaganda), with Dalton demoting Jebb to 'Chief

Executive Adviser' on August 17.[88] Sacking Burgess (which did not take place immediately on Burgess's return from the USA, as has been suggested by many) was one of the first things Gubbins did. As Foot wrote: "One of Gubbins's first actions on joining SOE was to ensure that Burgess left it, and he refused to allow him back: not for political reasons, but because he knew that Burgess was a heavy drinker and a homosexual, and looked a dissolute rake. The man was therefore a visible security risk. Jebb concurred."[89] Thus Jebb had no choice in the matter of Burgess's sacking (although Foot's language suggests that a campaign to restore him was made with some vigour, hinting at Burgess's arrogance, and his friends in high places), which may have been occasioned by his being convicted, in September, of driving under the influence of drink.[90] Indeed, Jebb obviously knew Burgess well, and had facilitated the mission when working as Foreign Office liaison with Section D and Colonel Grand, so he may well have overlooked Burgess's questionable habits and appearance. Jebb himself would be eased out of SOE in February, 1942: M. R. D. Foot's history of SOE asserts that Lord Selborne, who had replaced Jebb's ally and friend, Dalton, in February of that year, "did not care to retain the Etonian Jebb as supervisor to [Sir Charles] Hambro, whose fag Jebb had been at school."[91] Jebb had dubious talents: In his *Diaries*, Cadogan was quite scathing about Jebb's organisational and communication skills ("G.J. is so impulsive & slap-dash & superficial. He has impulses but no plan.")[92] and Churchill was later to dub this overpromoted civil servant "jibbering-jabbering Jebb".[93] Jebb was another of the 'great and the good' whose testimony has been carelessly overrated by historians.

In the summer of 1940, Burgess was, on the contrary, a force to be reckoned with. He had acted as an intermediary between Chamberlain and Édouard Daladier, Prime Minister of France between April 1938 and March 1940. He had allies in Lord Rothschild and his close friend at the Ministry of Information, Harold Nicolson. He was a key figure in Halifax's secret organisation, Section D, and had worked there on a successful project with the Czech Prime Minister, Beneš, to drop recordings of the latter's speeches in his native land.[94] He had been a successful talks producer at the BBC, and had been a member of the clandestine Joint Broadcasting Committee (JBC). And he had also had his mysterious interview with Churchill at Chartwell on October 1, 1938. A full record of what they discussed is not available: Burgess later claimed that Maisky, the Soviet Ambassador, had urged him to see Churchill, and no doubt Burgess would have taken the opportunity to reinforce the point to Churchill that the Soviet Union needed to be an eventual ally of Great Britain, in order to defeat Nazism, a message that Churchill was not loath to hear. Burgess, moreover, was very keen to inform his masters of a possible change in British strategy. At the time of the Ribbentrop-Molotov Pact (August 1939), he had sent a report to Moscow that was chilling in its description of Chamberlain's acceptance of Germany's ambitions towards the East:

> "Several talks about our tasks that I have had with Major Grand and his assistant, Lt Col Chidson, with Footman etc gave me an impression of British policy. The principal policy is to work with Germany come what may, and, in the final analysis, against the USSR. But this policy cannot

be followed immediately – there has to be a lot of delicate manoeuvring (*'vsyacheski manevrirovat'*)…The main obstacle is the impossibility of following this policy in dialogue with Hitler and the current setup in Germany… Chidson told me directly that our aim is not to resist German expansion in the East.

In all the Government Departments and in all my talks with those who have seen the papers about the talks, the opinion is that we never thought of concluding a serious military pact. The Prime Minister's office says openly that they were counting on being able to avoid a Russian pact (the actual words of Horace Wilson)."[95]

At least Burgess was encouraged by his encounter with Churchill to send him later a paper on his ideas on what British foreign policy should be, which suggests that Churchill found the 'young man's' contributions sensible and worth attending to. [96] Information from the poet Stephen Spender confirms that Churchill concurred with Burgess's opinions, since he inscribed a copy of his memoirs: "To Guy S. Burgess, in agreement with his views."[97] Thus it is not beyond the bounds of possibility that Burgess's track record, in June 1940, if Halifax indeed was responsible for the conception of the exploit, would have resulted in his name being put forward as a suitable candidate for the mission, although he needed a native Russian speaker to accompany him, to act as interpreter. This was probably not an official Foreign Office initiative, if we can believe the shock with which Fitzroy Maclean heard of it when it was already underway. Burgess did enjoy, however, the confidence of Halifax, Churchill, Nicolson (and Nicolson's boss, Duff Cooper), Jebb, Ball and Rothschild. It all consisted of a masterful exhibition of subterfuge and deception: Burgess could move from crypto-Communist to Nazi sympathiser, and then back to friend of the Comintern in the space of a few years, without any serious eyebrows being raised. The attitude of his political masters seemed to be that one either played with a very straight bat, and thus was unimpeachable, or else displayed such arts in dissimulation that one was tailor-made for counter-intelligence. This massive failure stemmed from an inability to understand the deepset processes by which the Comintern operated.

Then why was the mission abandoned in mid-stream? One could posit three reasons, which may in truth overlap. One, its objectives had been accomplished without the need for Burgess and Berlin to travel to the Soviet Union. Two, the news that it was underway had prompted such a noise of protest among opponents of any fresh diplomatic gestures to Moscow that its champions were forced to abandon it. And three, that the original motives for the mission had been overtaken by subsequent events.

An analysis of the contacts that Burgess and Berlin made after their arrival in New York on July 21, 1940 is revealing. By July 24, they were in Washington, where Burgess had dinner with his fellow-agent Michael Straight. Michael Straight had been instructed by Anthony Blunt, when at Cambridge, to pursue a career in banking in the US, in order to infiltrate the capitalist world. He was later to provide the lead that unveiled Blunt as a Soviet agent. Moreover, Straight was not simply a Soviet spy: he was on intimate social terms with President Roosevelt and his wife. In his account of the encounter, Straight claimed that Burgess asked him simply for help in getting in touch with 'friends' (i.e. his Soviet handlers), but that he declined the request.[98] The valid reason for Burgess's approach was that the spies' handler Alexander Gromov (aka Gorsky) had been withdrawn from London in January 1940, and throughout that year the Soviet spies had no contact in Great Britain to whom they could pass information. Verne Newton reported that the visit prompted Straight to confess his espionage activities to his wife, who implored him to cease.[99]

Despite this appeal, Straight immediately re-joined the State Department, where, later that year, he was able to keep a watchful eye on Walter Krivitsky. Berlin, meanwhile, was meeting another close friend of the President, Felix Frankfurter, recently appointed Supreme Court Justice, whom Berlin had known at Oxford in the 1930s. Following up on Jebb's advice (it was he who had recommended the Soviet Ambassador as the reliable agent to provide a Soviet visa) Berlin managed an introduction to the Soviet Ambassador, Konstantin Oumansky, by Felix Frankfurter's and Joseph Alsop's friend Benjamin Cohen, from the Department of the Interior. Berlin lunched with Oumansky and Oscar Chapman, Assistant Secretary in the Department of the Interior. Oumansky authorised Berlin's visa. With these glad tidings, Berlin sent a telegram to Jebb, indicating how unexpectedly helpful the Russians had been, and how Americans (such as Felix Frankfurter) were eager to intercede, if necessary. He then awaited a formal approval of his appointment from Cripps.

What Berlin was negotiating with Oumansky is unknown. Oumansky was not a nice man – a diehard Stalinist, and OGPU professional, who had crossed swords with Krivitsky in Moscow in the 1920s, and had been Head of the Press Department of the Soviet Foreign Office in the 1930s.[100] Berlin himself found Oumansky uncongenial, and explained to a friend how he had overcome the defects in Oumansky's character, stating that "the Ambassador, who is far from nice, has been won by my discretion", although "discretion" is not normally an attribute to be associated with Berlin.[101] Malcolm Muggeridge, who represented the *Manchester Guardian* as a reporter in the Soviet Union in 1932, took such a dislike to Oumansky in that role that he was prompted to write of him, somewhat uncharitably: "He later became Soviet Ambassador in Washington, and was killed in an air crash on his way to Mexico, to the undisguised joy of pretty well everyone who had worked as a newspaper correspondent in Moscow".[102]

Moreover, it is difficult to imagine how Isaiah Berlin could have looked positively at any dealings with Oumansky in 1940. The Soviet Union had recently invaded Latvia, Berlin's country of birth. In fact, Berlin had his second meeting with Oumansky (August 6) the day after Latvia became a Soviet republic. While Berlin, the fierce critic of totalitarianism, considered himself a 'Russian Jew' rather than a Latvian, he must therefore have been under very precise instructions, or have been engaged in some highly dubious clandestine activity that reflected an appalling lack of moral judgment. These were unavoidably times of troubled consciences. Britain was then considering whether it should recognise the Soviet Union's annexation of the Baltic States as a method for seducing Stalin away from Hitler, and Roosevelt had recently instructed his Secretary of State, Sumner

Welles, to talk to Oumansky on the exact same matter.[103] Given that the war had been declared by the occasion of Hitler's rape of neighbouring Poland, this was a hypocritical submission of international ethics to cold pragmatism: one can understand the reluctance of any persons involved in such negotiations to speak frankly of what occurred.

At this stage, one could judge that the objectives of the mission (if it were purely communicating a message to trusted Stalinist aides) had been achieved. Burgess had spoken to Straight, and Berlin to Oumansky. (And both of them had developed back-channels to Roosevelt, should that have been a consideration for the exploit.) Burgess would also have discharged his private responsibility – informing his Soviet friends of Krivitsky's revelations (but also pointing out the successful activities of diminishing the threats from them, through the propagandising of MI5, and the creation of chaos within the Security Service), and re-affirming the commitment of Burgess and his cronies to their communist cause. It may be significant that, despite his avowed intentions in the UK to seek a visa for Moscow when in the USA, Burgess was not recorded as meeting Oumansky, or even visiting the Soviet Embassy. Berlin, on the other hand, still had private goals in Moscow, and thus pursued them vigorously. In any case, at this stage, Fitzroy Maclean cancelled Burgess's and Berlin's plans in a telegram to Lord Lothian (the British Ambassador). He instructed Burgess to return, while Berlin (as a non-government employee) "must do what he thinks best". On or about July 28, Burgess announced to Berlin that he was being recalled, and left for the United Kingdom on July 30. Berlin suggested that Burgess was "displeased and irritated" by the news of the recall, but that may have been an act. On the same day, in a letter to Mary Fisher (the daughter of H.A.L. and Lettice, who was working for Burgess's JBC), Berlin laconically noted: "Guy B has left for England today", as if it were no surprise to him either.[104]

Fitzroy Maclean's outrage is a little puzzling. It is true that he was a firm opponent of the Soviets, and did not trust them in the slightest. He was one of the few diplomats who had witnessed Stalin's show trial of Bukharin *et al.* in 1937, and unlike some of the "useful idiots" who were taken in by the theatre, remained a relentless critic of the Soviet regime.[105] He had written an influential paper that explained why Stalin had allied himself with Germany, in an attempt to prolong and intensify the war.[106] Yet he was not at this stage a dedicated Foreign Office civil servant, keen to enhance his career: he was eager to leave and join the military, and later had to stand as a Member of Parliament in order to gain release from the Foreign Office. Unless he was committed to causing trouble and inviting some kind of rebuke and dismissal, his behaviour in defiance of Halifax makes little sense. His claim that Stafford Cripps had no need for Isaiah Berlin in Moscow sounds a little hollow: it is not even clear that Cripps knew about the suggestion that Berlin should be his attaché, and, if such an order had come from Halifax, Cripps would presumably have had to go along with it. Perhaps Halifax set Maclean up to it – to exert the protocol, use the Cripps card, and keep Halifax and Section D out of the picture. Yet a post-mortem revealed the skulduggery: an inquiry in January 1941 showed that Berlin's passport had been issued "at the request of a Colonel J. N. Tomlinson of the Passport Control Department", the latter being the office behind which SIS practised its craft.[107]

If indeed the mission had enjoyed Halifax's enthusiastic sponsorship as a back-channel to Stalin, it is more likely that some dramatic news had prompted the need for it to be abandoned. Early in June, Hitler had started telling his generals that he was ready to take his revenge on the USSR. On June 6, 1940 Stalin's chief of military intelligence, Ivan Proskurov, sent Stalin a report indicating Hitler would attack the USSR, and explained very cogently why he believed that Germany's chances of successfully invading Britain were extremely slim.[108] This was not what Stalin wanted to hear, and Proskurov was later dismissed, and shot, but the news was out. By June 14, the Foreign Office had developed the belief that the Soviet Union had moved into the Baltic States to prepare for the inevitable conflict with Germany.[109] By the end of June, Churchill was quite eagerly using Cripps to pass on to Stalin details of the German threat – information that Stalin ignored, meanwhile requesting his Foreign Minister, Molotov, that he pass on the content of his conversations with Cripps to the Germans. On June 27, Churchill wrote to the South African Prime Minister Jan Smuts that he suspected Hitler would probably turn eastwards without attempting invasion.[110] The historian Louis Kilzer wrote, in *Churchill's Deception*, that Churchill was convinced, by July 8, that Hitler would switch his attention to the Soviet Union. This prognostication appears to be justified by Hitler's reaction to the Soviet Union's occupation of Bessarabia on June 27, since, during a conference about the campaign against Great Britain on July 18, he observed that as a result of the Russian action, "thoughtful preparations must be made", and immediately began planning for a campaign against the Soviet Union (Operation Barbarossa).[111]

Lukacs provided further evidence. On July 19, Raeder pointed out to Hitler the fatal risks of trying to invade Britain; two days later, Hitler ordered that the landing was to be undertaken if it were the only way to force the English to make peace. On July 25, Raeder instructed Hitler that the crossing of the Channel would not be possible until May 1941.[112] On July 28 (the day Burgess learned of his recall), the NKVD reported increased German troop presence near the frontier area with the Soviet Union.[113] By the end of the month, Hitler was asking his generals to prepare a five-month *blitzkrieg* against the Soviet Union, and was explaining to them why an attack against the Soviet Union took precedence over one on England.[114]

In April 1940, Bletchley Park had started to decrypt its first *Abwehr* messages relayed by the *Enigma* machines.[115] On May 22, it successfully decoded *Luftwaffe* transmissions. Certainly, by mid-July, GC&CS was picking up routine traffic, such as Hitler's current invasion plans.[116] The best coverage of *Enigma* analysis is given by F. H. Hinsley and his co-authors, who, in their official history, noted an increase in traffic at the end of June, 1940, after "a slump on the subject of invasion" following the fall of France.[117] They reported: "On 23 June the Enigma established that some GAF [German Air Force] units were resting and refitting in preparation for operations against the United Kingdom from airfields in the Low Countries and north-west France" (admittedly suggesting preparations for an invasion of Britain rather than an attack on Soviet Russia, but indicating the kind of detail that the Radio Security Service was picking up). Without a complete record of the transcripts, it is impossible to verify what other intelligence about Hitler's plans had been gained at this time, but, if the Soviet Union's Proskurov had managed to gather intelligence about the switch to the East, it is quite probable that British Intelligence had had access to the same information. And, of course, it is possible that Proskurov had obtained his insights from a Soviet spy in Britain, such as John Cairncross, who had had access to the Enigma decrypts, known as Ultra. Towards the end of 1940, even though it had at that time comprehensively cracked only the Luftwaffe *Enigma* codes, Bletchley Park picked up a considerable amount of wireless traffic indicating troop movements in the East, confirming Hitler's intentions. The first official leakage of Hitler's December 18 directive authorising Barbarossa did probably not occur until early January, 1941, from a disenchanted senior Nazi official to an American commercial attaché.[118]

Thus it is most probable that a combination of the first and third reasons contributed to the abandonment of the mission. Churchill had not only learned that his fervent wish that Hitler would attack the Soviet Union would be granted: he also felt enough confidence in the reports that he felt he needed to warn Stalin of Hitler's intentions, so that a successful *blitzkrieg* and a quick Nazi victory would not be the inevitable outcome. His approaches through Cripps made other overtures redundant. And thus one of the last major intelligence secrets of WWII would be safely deposited in the archives, with as little public record as possible – until Isaiah Berlin decided to open Pandora's Box with his reminiscences and highly revealing, though occasionally deceptive, *Letters*. For 40 years, the ignominy that Burgess had brought upon the political elite by the fact that they had been hoodwinked by him had been concealed as much as possible. Records, memoirs and diaries from those critical months in the summer of 1940 have been carefully withheld from view.[119]

Yet, if the whole Moscow Plot had been a skilful ruse by Burgess, with a half-hearted endorsement by Halifax, the conclusions are dramatically different. Burgess was recalled (or engineered his recall) from Washington immediately he had spoken to Straight: he did not meet Oumansky. Thus he had publicised his relationship with the Comintern solely to make personal contact with another agent, and deliver his message. This represented a complete volte-face of his carefully honed disguise as a right-wing sympathiser, and displayed a newly-found confidence in his real role. Whereas he had publicly renounced his Communism, and set out to prove it by joining the Anglo-German Fellowship in 1935, Burgess had in November 1937 tried to recruit Goronwy Rees, and had admitted to him he worked for the Comintern – something Rees viewed with sympathy at the time. After the announcement of the Nazi-Soviet pact (which caused intense soul-searching by Burgess, Blunt and Philby), Burgess again met with Rees, in September 1939, but this time had to pretend to his friend that he had broken his ties with the Communists, as Rees was shocked by the Soviet Union's move. Forever after, Rees was a latent threat of betrayal, to the extent that Burgess even volunteered (in June 1943, to his handler, Gorsky) to kill Rees.[120] Yet six months after the outbreak of war, Burgess, maybe energised by Churchill's much more positive attitude towards the Soviet Union than Chamberlain's, and reminded of his reassuring dialogue with the current Prime Minister back in 1938, was prepared to break his cover. If he was knowingly used as an envoy to the Soviets, he must have been accepted as a double-agent playing a dangerous game. But if the initiative was his, he had dangerously revealed an association that should have sent off alarms in the hallways of MI5 and SIS. But nothing happened. His protectors continued to protect him. Why?

It appears that MI5 knew nothing about the Moscow Plot. No suggestive blank passages, indicating redaction, appear in Liddell's *Diaries* for the period in question. Moreover, another testimony from the 1951 inquest, also released in October 2015, by default suggests that information on the mission was withheld from the Security Service. When Kim Philby was interviewed by Dick White, and asked to provide a report on what he knew about Burgess, he gave White an account of his and Burgess's activities with the training department of Section D (incorporated into SOE in the summer of 1940), but made no mention of Burgess's and Berlin's visit to the Soviet Union.[121] The gamble probably paid off (although if White knew about the mission, and detected Philby's 'oversight', it might have confirmed what suspicions he already had). If Burgess had truly been recommended as a trustworthy double agent to Guy Liddell, the latter would no doubt have been confident in recruiting him as an officer in 1941, after he was recommended by Blunt, instead of being persuaded by the hiring officer, John Curry, that Burgess was unsuitable, as Curry "was not satisfied that his claim to have abandoned Communism could be accepted at its face value".[122] If Burgess had come with a recommendation as a skilled expert in Communism, capable in subterfuge, but one whose loyalty could not be doubted, Curry himself might have reacted differently. Thus MI5 was apparently kept in the dark. This conclusion would seem to be confirmed by a later statement, made in 1956, when MI5 investigators admitted that "the reason or pretext for [this trip] had never been known."[123] Joseph Ball, number two in the Security Executive, was closely involved with the mission, but obviously did not consider it desirable or necessary to consult with the heads of MI5. The lessons to be learned from an overture to the Comintern for Soviet counter-intelligence strategy were presumably deemed to be too sensitive to be shared beyond that small group. The input of career counter-espionage officers on how to deal with the Comintern was not sought. The Joint Intelligence Committee was obviously an ineffective medium for integrating intelligence strategy (as Jeffery's *History* confirms for us). Burgess, who had recently engineered the entry of his colleagues Blunt and Rothschild into the Security Service, was clearly disdainful of MI5's role, and believed it was now in subversively good hands.

The Foreign Office's instincts were probably right. Apart from the insult of not being consulted, its officials (primarily in the person of Fitzroy Maclean, it appears) must have harboured considerable doubts about the wisdom of the mission. What were the chances of changing the Soviet Union's course, and why would the selection of the undisciplined rake Guy Burgess improve the chances of success? If it were indeed a high-level initiative to convince Stalin of Britain's true intentions, what would be the outcome should the dictator share the intelligence with Hitler, and jointly determine that now was the time to eliminate the imperialists? Why should the Soviets be trusted at all? (As has been shown, Stalin was already leaking his conversations with Cripps to the German Embassy.) Yet the fact that Burgess was allowed to make his way to the USA without his quest being openly abandoned – and that it was known to the Foreign Office that he intended to pursue his ambitions when he arrived there, and yet they waited until he had had his assignation with Straight *before* recalling him – makes no explanation readily acceptable, unless the evidence left behind is all part of an elaborate false paper-trail. Indeed, SIS was undergoing its own organisational turmoil, comparable to the struggles of MI5 and the Home Office with subversion and 'Fifth Columns' in the summer of 1940, but it is hard simply to attribute the missteps to the chaos of the new administration at the time.

The conclusion must be that Burgess's boldness paid off: he later was able to maintain his status of innocence by making the outrageous assertion that he worked for the Comintern. In doing so, he completely recast the cloak of subterfuge that he had donned when he had associated with the MP Jack Macnamara and the Anglo-German Fellowship. Yet no one appeared to wonder who the real Burgess was, or where his loyalties really lay. And it seems that, for all his boastfulness and loose talk, he, like Philby, kept the details and even the existence of the brief Moscow Plot to himself. In this, he had the connivance of the respected voices of the British Civil Service and Foreign Office, who were quite happy to pretend that Burgess's various adventures in intelligence and undercover negotiation had never happened, and, in order to bury their own involvement and compliance, dissemble to the degree that his employment by such agencies was publicly denied. What was devastating for the cause of defence against Bolshevism was that this no longer mattered. MI5 had become an irrelevance in the struggle against Communism, and had already lost its way. How Burgess and his allies managed to ensure that this trend was irreversible is the subject of the following two chapters.

Notes

[1] TNA, KV 2/4105.

[2] Tape MI7, a transcript of which was provided to the author by Henry Hardy.

[3] Harold Nicolson, *Diaries*, June 26, June 29 and July 2, 1940.

[4] Bickham Sweet-Escott, *Baker Street Irregular*, p 38.

[5] Isaiah Berlin, *Flourishing, Letters 1928-1946*, p 319 (notes by Henry Hardy).

[6] TNA, KV 2/1405.

[7] Harold Nicolson, *Diaries*, held by the Balliol College Library in Oxford; entry for June 29, 1940.

[8] TNA, KV 2/4107.

[9] Keith Jeffery, *The Secret History of MI6, 1909-1949*, p 352.

[10] In a letter to the Communist, Maire Gaster, dated January 3, 1941, Berlin told her " . . . there is no doubt that there is a job to perform & my new God Dr Weizmann is wooing me ardently into doing it".

[11] Hugh Walpole diary entry for August 1925, quoted in Rupert Hart-Davis's *Hugh Walpole*, p 264.

[12] Jim Wilson, *Nazi Princess: Hitler, Lord Rothermere and Princess Stephanie von Hohenlohe*, p 58.

[13] F. W. Winterbotham, *The Nazi Connection*, p 53.

[14] John Lukacs, *The Duel*, p 121.

[15] Volker Ullrich, *Hitler: Ascent 1889-1939*.

[16] Andrew Roberts, *The Holy Fox*.

[17] David Stafford, *Churchill and Secret Service*, p 174.

[18] W. S. Churchill, *The Gathering Storm*, p 448.

[19] Roberts, p 277.

[20] Roberts, p 245.

[21] The actual handwritten notes are reproduced in Roberts' book, in the plates following p 250 (2014 edition).

[22] Michael Johnson, *Meeting Isaiah Berlin*, at http://berlin.wolf.ox.ac.uk/writings_on_ib/johnson.htm

[23] William Manchester and Paul Reid, *The Last Lion*, (Volume 3), p 115.

[24] Roy Jenkins, *Churchill: A Biography*, p 610.

[25] David Reynolds, *Churchill the Appeaser? Between Hitler, Roosevelt and Stalin in World War Two*, Chapter 9 in *Diplomacy and World Power, Studies in British Foreign Policy, 1890-1950*, edited by Michael Dockrill and Brian McKercher.

[26] John Lukacs, *The Last European War, The Duel, Five Days in London*, May 1940.

[27] *The Last European War*, p 98.

[28] *The Duel*, p 153.

[29] ibid., p 164.

[30] Manchester and Reid, p 115.

[31] Jenkins, p 609.

[32] Prinz Hohenlohe was an intermediary living in Switzerland, who reported to Ribbentrop, the German Foreign Minister. In her 2015 book, *Go-Betweens for Hitler*, Karina Urbach analysed Hohenlohe's efforts to take advantage of Lord Rothermere as a propaganda vehicle, but she did not consider the possibility that Hohenlohe was in turn used by Halifax and Hoare at this time.

[33] *The Duel*, p 133.

[34] ibid., p 149.

[35] *Churchill the Appeaser?*, p 204.

[36] *The Duel*, p 166.

[37] ibid., p 180.

[38] Winterbotham, p 150.

[39] Louis C. Kilzer, *Churchill's Deception*, p 228.

[40] Richard Lamb, *Churchill as War Leader – Right or Wrong?*, p 75.

[41] Butler's career may not have been a sure progression. In an unpublished diary entry, Cadogan referred to him in a very unflattering manner: "Incidentally, RAB is the most baleful man. A crass pacifist, a muddle-headed appeaser and a nit-wit, he talks defeatism to Pressmen". (March 21, 1940).

[42] *Five Days in London*, p 203: This letter has only recently been made available in the Churchill Archives, indicating, perhaps, a desire that the more vigorous response attributed to Churchill was one that was historically sounder.

[43] John Costello, *Ten Days to Destiny*, p 319.

[44] ibid., p 323.

[45] Roberts, p 95 and p 269.

[46] *The Last European War*, p 98.

[47] Martin Gilbert, *Churchill: A Life, Finest Hour, 1939-1941*, p 652.

[48] Not that 'trust' was a commodity well-respected by Stalin. He would accuse Churchill of a betrayal of it later in the war, through the latter's unwillingness to open a second front, but Roosevelt (and Churchill, to a lesser extent) were far too trustful of Stalin's intentions for Eastern Europe as the war wound down.

[49] Martin Kitchen, *British Policy towards the Soviet Union during the Second World War*, p 26.

[50] Roberts, p 214.

[51] Michael Ignatieff, *Isaiah Berlin: A Life*, p 95.

[52] This is the conclusion at which Henry Hardy, the chief editor of Berlin's *Letters*, arrived.

[53] Audiotape files (of MI7) provided to the author by Henry Hardy.

[54] Harold Nicolson, unpublished diary entry of August 19, 1940.

[55] *Washington Despatches 1941-1945, Weekly Reports from the British Embassy*, edited by H. G. Nicholls.

[56] Isaiah Berlin, *Affirming, Letters,* (Volume 4), edited by Henry Hardy and Mark Pottle, p 117.

[57] Tom Driberg, *Guy Burgess: A Portrait with Background*, p 59.

[58] TNA, KV 2/805.

[59] Stephen Dorril, *MI6*, p 59.

[60] TNA, KV 2/4105.

[61] Bickham Sweet-Escott, p 38.

[62] E. H. Cookridge, *The Third Man*, p 92.

[63] TNA, KV 2/4105.

[64] Alexander Cadogan, *Diaries*, held at the Churchill College Library, in Cambridge. Unpublished entries for March 14 and May 20, 1940.

[65] Yuri Modin, *My Five Cambridge Friends*, p 83.

[66] *Flourishing*, p 302.

[67] Henry Hardy, Berlin's chief editor, has told the author that Berlin exercised no selection process over the letters, which were completely disorganised. Is Hardy perhaps a little too trusting?

[68] Harold Nicolson, unpublished diary entry.

[69] *Flourishing*, p 304.

[70] Roberts, p 131: Curiously, the reference for this claim does not appear in the *Notes* to Roberts's book. When, in December 2014, this author asked Dr. Roberts about this omission, he could not explain why it had been left out, or recall what the source was.

[71] Despite his subversive inclinations – or maybe because of them – Monckton also acted, for 20 years as personal lawyer to Edward, Prince of Wales, through the latter's kingship (as HRH Edward VIII), and after his abdication (as the Duke of Windsor).

[72] Andrew Roberts, *Eminent Churchillians*, p 241.

[73] The British Newspaper Archive (which is in partnership with the British Library) does not possess the *People* archive, but copies of the article may be found among the Joseph Ball papers in the Special Collections of the Bodleian Library.

[74] Berlin Archive at the Bodleian Library, folder 274.

[75] Berlin must have written to Rees on the publication of the first of the three articles. The latter two appear to have upset him more intensely.

[76] *Looking for Mr Nobody*, private communication between Jennifer Rees and the author.

[77] Isaiah Berlin, *Enlightening: Letters 1946-1960*, edited by Henry Hardy and Jennifer Holmes, p 526.

[78] Andrew Lownie, *Stalin's Englishman*, p 274. Lownie provided the following reference: Bodleian Library, Conservative Party Archives, Joseph Ball papers, MS England c.6656, Crocker to *People*, March 27, 1956.

[79] George Joseph Ball Papers (6656) at the Bodleian Library, Special Collections.

[80] David Cameron Watt, *How War Came*, p 397.

[81] Stewart Purvis and Jeff Hulbert, *Guy Burgess: The Spy Who Knew Everyone*, citing TNA KV 2/4117.

[82] Michael Holzman, *Revolutionary in an Old School Tie*, p 116.

[83] Ignatieff, p 96, and Tape MI7.

[84] *Flourishing*, pp 318-319.

[85] Rothschild wrote a somewhat slapdash memoir, *Meditations of a Broomstick*. In 1994, Roland Perry wrote a sensational and error-prone profile of Rothschild, *The Fifth Man*, claiming that Rothschild was the elusive person behind that *nom de guerre*, subsequently shown to be John Cairncross. Kenneth Rose's *Elusive Rothschild* (2003) is bland and sycophantic, and ignores whole sections of his subject's life, such as his Zionist activities.

[86] Yuri Modin, *My Five Cambridge Friends*, p 77.

[87] Lord Gladwyn, *The Memoirs of Lord Gladwyn*, p 101.

[88] David Garnett, *The Secret History of PWE*, p 36; William Mackenzie, *The Secret History of SOE: 1940-1945*, pp 78-79.

[89] Foot, p 202.

[90] *Stalin's Englishman*, p 113.

[91] M. R. D. Foot, *The Special Operations Executive 1940-1946*, p 40.

[92] Cadogan, *Diaries*, June 5, 1940.

[93] David Stafford, *Churchill and Secret Service*, p 376.

[94] John Costello, *Mask of Treachery*, p 376.

[95] Igor Damaskin, *Stalin I Razvedka* (*Stalin and Intelligence*) (2008), translated by Geoffrey Elliott. Elliott collaborated with Damaskin on his biography of Kitty Harris, titled, in English, *Kitty Harris: the Spy with Seventeen Names*.

[96] Martin Gilbert, *Winston S. Churchill: Companion Volume V, Part 3: The Coming of War, 1936-1939*, p 1,193 (quoted by Hugh Trevor-Roper in review of *After Long Silence*, by Michael Straight, in *The Secret World*, p 170).

[97] Anthony Glees, *The Secrets of the Service*, p 50.

[98] Michael Straight, *After Long Silence*, p 143.

[99] Verne Newton, *The Cambridge Spies*, p 21.

[100] Oumansky's cryptonym, used in Soviet intelligence radio communications, was REDAKTOR ('editor'). The Soviets were not very imaginative in their choice of code-names for their agents and officers abroad.

[101] *Flourishing*, p 338, August 22, 1940, to Shiela Grant-Duff.

[102] Malcolm Muggeridge, *Chronicles of Wasted Time: The Green Stick*, p 212.

[103] Roger Moorhouse, *The Devils' Alliance*, p 150.

[104] *Flourishing*, p 319.

[105] Fitzroy Maclean, *Eastern Approaches*, (Chapter 7).

[106] Steven Miner, *Between Churchill and Stalin*, p 38.

[107] *Flourishing*, pp 334-335.

[108] David E. Murphy, *What Stalin Knew: The Enigma of Barbarossa*, pp 239-240.

[109] Hinsley, Thomas, Ransom and Knight, *British Intelligence in the Second World War*, (Volume 1), p 430.

[110] Ibid., p 431.

[111] E. R. Hooton, *Stalin's Claws*, p 188.

[112] *The Duel*, p 155.

[113] Kilzer, p 232.

[114] Murphy, p 68; *The Duel*, p 196.

[115] In his essay on Admiral Canaris, Hugh Trevor-Roper (who worked for the Radio Security Service), wrote that "all *Abwehr* hand-cyphers were read by the British from the beginning of 1940". He was a key contributor to the decipherment of these messages. On Canaris, see Trevor-Roper's *The Secret World*, p 49.

[116] F. W. Winterbotham, *The Ultra Secret*.

[117] Hinsley *et al.*, pp 173-175.

[118] Ronald Lewin, *Ultra Goes to War*, pp 116- 120.

[119] John Lukacs, in *Five Days in London*, has written (in a note on page 57): "Chamberlain did not weed his papers and correspondence (in Birmingham University Library), or at least not much. Halifax (In the Borthwick Institute Library of the University of York) did so more considerably, as did Lady Halifax. In the Churchill Archives, Cambridge, the diaries of Sir Maurice Hankey have been culled: there is either nothing or very little for each year of the period 1939-44, though some of his correspondence is there. In the papers of David Margesson, the chief whip of the Conservatives (deposited in the Churchill Archives by his daughter), the years 1939-40 are missing. Weeded, too, are the Butler papers in Trinity College, Cambridge: the 'Guide' to these papers states, for example, 'Four items appear to be of continuing sensitivity and should not be made available until that sensitivity can be said to have evaporated."

[120] Lownie, p 78, p 103, p 133.

[121] TNA, KV 2/4102.

[122] Christopher Andrew, *Defending the Realm*, p 272.

[123] TNA, KV 2/4117, cited by Purvis and Hulbert, p 122.

Chapter 5: The Moscow Plot – Counter-Attack

"For even if he still lives, a fallen spy is but a breathing corpse." (Ladislas Farago)

"Student friends in the Party said I would be more effective by going into the Civil Service as a secret Party member." (Jenifer Hart)

"Secondly, there is no doubt that there is a job to perform & my new God Dr Weizmann is wooing me ardently into doing it." (Isaiah Berlin)

When they learned of the danger that Krivitsky's revelations might impose on them, Guy Burgess and his colleagues did not lie low and wait for the crisis to blow over. On the contrary, they went on the attack, as this chapter will show. They schemed to have Krivitsky himself neutralised. They judged that MI5's counter-communist intelligence was already so weakened that a swift body-blow might eliminate it permanently as a threat over them. Burgess himself took the lead role in ensuring that Communists and agents of influence were installed in critical positions in MI5, SIS and the Ministry of Information, in order to guarantee a more sympathetic view towards the Soviet Union, anticipating the turn of the tide that would occur when Chamberlain were replaced. In addition, they needed to inform their bosses in Moscow that the team was energised and committed. Burgess's close friend Isaiah Berlin became inextricably linked with these machinations, and his highly questionable associations with members of Soviet intelligence are also inspected.

Guy Burgess evidently engineered a cunning official project to give him the cover to talk to his Communist allies about what had happened with Krivitsky. Krivitsky had been the first major Soviet defector in ten years to make a successful escape to the West, and thus had represented a stellar opportunity for the intelligence services of the democratic countries to pick his brains. He had jeopardised his privacy and security, however, by making, in the USA, very public denunciations of Stalin, and openly communicating his knowledge of the workings of the dictator's intelligence services in a series of magazine articles, which were later published in book form. How did MI5 react to this opportunity? Did it sense the danger, and take appropriate measures? Could its officers have ever suspected that the persons they were seeking were privy to the same information? And how did the spies themselves react? When did they hear of his revelations? Did intelligence reach them that he had arrived in London for interrogations with MI5 and SIS? Were they aware of his contribution in identifying Captain King, whose trial, after all, was held in secret? Did they know of Krivitsky's precise relationship with the 'illegals' who had handled them in the late 1930s? As was suggested in Chapter 3, many commentators, frequently using a shaky timetable of events, have hazarded guesses at the method by which they (and Moscow Centre) learned of Krivitsky's disclosures: a strict analysis of the chronology is essential for developing a workable hypothesis as to what in fact happened.

Krivitsky's activities in the USA must first be recapitulated.[1] He had arrived in New York on November 10, 1938, on the *Normandie*. In January 1939, he started to reveal Stalin's crimes to the State Department. After he met Isaac Don Levine in March, the two of them cooperated on three articles, which appeared in consecutive issues of the *Saturday Evening Post* in April. He experienced visa renewal problems (FBI chief Hoover was embarrassed by the revelations), and his testimony was vigorously attacked by a group of 400 signatories in *The Nation* in August. In early September, on the outbreak of war, Levine took it upon himself to warn Lord Lothian of a spy in the Cabinet Secretariat.[2] On October 11, Krivitsky appeared before the House of Representatives Dies Committee on UnAmerican Activities to give evidence, and presented a foretaste of what he would later tell the British. In the middle of November, an exchange of telegrams between Washington and London arranged for the invitation to Krivitsky to come to Britain: the US Government insisted, from a desire not to provoke Stalin, that Krivitsky not leave for the UK from US soil. He thus went via Canada.[3] Krivitsky's articles were packaged as a book, titled *In Stalin's Secret Service*, which was simultaneously published in the USA, the UK, Sweden and Holland on November 15.[4] The *New York Times*, which had assiduously covered all the public events described above, reported on December 30 that Krivitsky had left New York that day "for an unknown destination." Anthony Cave-Brown offered the fact that one press report indicated that he was on his way to the UK (via Canada), but failed to specify what that source was.[5]

Thus any alert member of the Cambridge Spies could have picked up the fact that Krivitsky could well represent a serious threat to the continued concealment of the group. Yet, when he arrived in Britain on January 19, 1940, their situation was markedly divided. Most of them were out of the country, in France. Kim Philby, having returned from Spain at the end of July, 1939, had in September been sent by his employer, *The Times*, to join the British Expeditionary Force HQ in Arras, and from there to report on the war. As for Donald Maclean, he had taken up the position of Third Secretary at the Paris Embassy on September 28, 1938, whither his intermediary and lover Kitty Harris had followed him. Anthony Blunt, having been encouraged by Anatoli Gorsky, the NKVD resident in London, in early August 1939 to join the Intelligence Corps, had managed to wheedle his way back in after being expelled from a training course at Minley Manor at the end of the month. Again, the dates given by various chroniclers conflict, but it is certain that Blunt was reinstated by November: he was reported as passing information about the detailed structure of British intelligence to Guy Burgess on November 17.[6] Soon after that, however, Blunt was also transferred to France, and *The Crown Jewels* reports that his responsibilities for picking up purloined secrets from another spy, Leo Long, had been given to Burgess.

If any of the spies could have revealed confidential information on Krivitsky (as opposed to what the *New York Times* published), the most likely source would have been John Cairncross, who probably had access to the telegrams being exchanged between the Foreign Office and the Washington Embassy. He had been passing on minutes of the Committee of Imperial Defence during the summer, and was then appointed Private Secretary to Lord Hankey in September, 1939. At the outbreak of war, Hankey had joined Chamberlain's War Cabinet as Minister Without Portfolio, with special responsibility for intelligence. Cairncross would then have gained access to even more relevant confidential material.

Cairncross always claimed ignorance of the existence of a 'ring' of Cambridge spies. He had been recruited by James Klugmann (another Cambridge Communist, who worked for SOE during the war), not by Burgess or Blunt. Yet Cairncross was in regular touch with Burgess: while most of his contacts were directly with Gorsky, in his autobiography Cairncross's mentioned that, in July 1939, Burgess had asked him for information on Britain's plans for subterfuge in Poland.[7] In addition, after Burgess's escape to the Soviet Union in 1951, the notes made by Cairncross for this project were found in Burgess's trunk. Thus it is safe to assume that Cairncross would have informed Burgess of any startling information he found, and Burgess would have indeed passed on such news to Blunt, who was, after all, still in the country in late November.

Thus Anthony Blunt (back in military intelligence in mid-October, having benefitted from the administrations of Burgess and Proctor and dissimulated about his Communist opinions, and whose Field Security Police Unit had embarked for France on December 9) could well have passed on the latest information on Krivitsky to his colleagues already in France. Was it an advantage to be away from the main stage? If they were informed of the threat, Philby, Blunt and Maclean probably realised that theirs was a precarious existence: if they were to be unmasked, as the German Army advanced towards France, the fact that the Soviet Union was an ally of Germany would probably not have ensured that the Germans would look upon them with sympathy. If they could not return to the UK, an escape to neutral Spain would probably have been their first impulse. In any case, they must have anxiously awaited a message from Burgess indicating where they stood.

Cairncross would certainly have told Gorsky, with whom he was in constant contact. Since Cairncross was of a nervous and reserved disposition, such a discovery would have made him shy away abruptly from any further espionage activity. As Chapter 3 noted, his contribution of purloined documents diminished towards the end of 1939, which indicates that he may have suspected he was under watch. As for Gorsky, he would have asked why the source was going dry: how would he have reacted? It seems unlikely that he would have taken fright, or that his bosses in Moscow would have recalled him when he informed them of the risk. As an accredited member of the Embassy, the worst that could happen to him was that he would be expelled, and, from a Soviet intelligence viewpoint, it would surely have made better sense to leave someone in place to track what was happening, as best as possible, from close to the action. Thus Moscow Centre's decision, taken in December 1939, effectively to close down its London *rezidentura* is bizarre. The retrospective reason it gave that it believed that the cover of its agents had been blown seems premature, although West and Tsarev indicated that it happened more because Moscow Centre believed that the illegal

Aleksandr Orlov (who defected in 1938) was responsible.[8] To some extent, Sudoplatov echoed this theory: Orlov had worked for a short time in the UK, and was obviously more current in his knowledge of the spies.

The authorities in Britain, Canada, and the USA strove to keep the fact of Krivitsky's voyage to the UK, the next step in the proceedings, a well-protected secret. In this respect, the organisers in MI5 and SIS did a much more creditable job of security than they performed after he returned to Canada. As Chapter 3 explained, confidentiality considerations surrounding the distribution of Archer's report were negligible: a scrupulous and properly professional head of counter-espionage of MI5 would have immediately assessed the exposure should Krivitsky's claims about infiltration turn out to have any substance, and kept the knowledge to a very small group while his assertions were investigated further. Certainly the proceedings of the interrogations should not have been distributed so unthinkingly to other government departments. The irony is that his information was so accurate that it quickly lost its quality of secrecy. Yet even information about the visit itself could have reached the spies in time for them to plan.

On the surface, it seems unlikely that Burgess would have been able to learn about the visit until the report was written. Only one small indicator gives a hint of an alternative scenario. In December 1939, Chamberlain had chartered Lord Hankey (who had been appointed as Minister without Portfolio in Chamberlain's War Cabinet, with responsibility for Intelligence) with performing a special analysis of the effectiveness of the intelligence services, which resulted in Hankey's delivering a report to the Prime Minister on March 11, 1940. While this report has never been released to the National Archives, it has recently been published in the UK as one of a collection of documents translated from items that found their way into Soviet archives via British spies.[9] In Appendix I to his report (The Origin and Development of the Secret Intelligence Service), Hankey wrote: "There is a danger of losing sight of the fundamental truth, so well put by the NKVD general and defector Walter Krivitsky. Adequate funding is a *sine qua non* for an effective intelligence service." It is perhaps surprising that such a statement does not appear in the Archer Report (covered fully in Chapter 3), which leads one to wonder whether Lord Hankey was actually present at one of the interrogation sessions. However, while one might have expected Hankey to have chosen to extricate a more piercing insight from all the wisdom that Krivitsky vouchsafed to his interrogators, one fact is clear. Hankey had knowledge of the Krivitsky interrogations, and presumably read the source materials. What is more, this comment was registered before Archer had completed her report, which event occurred later in March. The agent who passed this document on to Gorsky (even though it would not have occurred until 1941) was almost certainly Hankey's Secretary, John Cairncross. Hankey indisputably had knowledge of Krivitsky's testimony before Archer's report was officially released, and Cairncross surely had access to it. Burgess could have been alerted to Krivitsky's presence while the latter was still in London.

Whatever Burgess knew exactly about Krivitsky's activities, he was about to be sharply enlightened by another Soviet mole in the heart of Britain's government. When Jane Archer wrote her confidential report about Krivitsky's revelations, one of the first recipients, reportedly of an 11-page summary, was the Home Office, where a civil servant named Jenifer Fischer-Williams [Hart],[i] who was secretary to the Permanent Under-Secretary in the Home Office, Sir Alexander Maxwell, was responsible for circulating it.[10] Whereas Nigel West, in his Introduction to Gary Kern's biography of Krivitsky, stated that the report was distributed to Hart on April 5, the National Archives reveal that that was the day that Hart returned it. Hart annotated that "This has been seen by the Home Secretary, Mr Peake, Sir A. Maxwell & Mr Newsam", implying that it had been circulated, and thus had probably been in her possession for a couple of weeks, in other words in a way that dovetailed with Burgess's late March plans to go to Paris. Moreover, it appears that the report was not merely a summary, as West suggested, but "Copy No. 4" of the full report, and thus Burgess would have had full access. Why would the Home Office be satisfied with a summary, one might ask?

Jenifer Hart has a vital role in the exposition of this conspiracy. Anthony Glees has written about her admission that she became a secret member of the Communist Party in 1935, and was thereafter activated by a Soviet controller as a spy for the Comintern: she even spoke on the BBC about the whole process.[11] Glees recorded that, despite her "worries" about the excesses of Stalin, particularly the show trials, she and Blunt "accepted that for a certain period they had served 'the Party' and Stalin, and they were both prepared to serve him even before 1941 when the interests of Russia and the interests of Britain were patently not the same." Thus Hart did not seek an exit-card from her espionage activities when the monstrosity of the Soviet Union's signing a pact with the Fascist enemy took place, but was quite happy to express her devotion to Stalinism by continuing to act on his behalf during 1940. She was evidently still active at this time, and it is thus fair to conclude that her first reaction on seeing the report would be to show it to her Communist friends, Burgess being the obvious choice. He does not appear in Hart's autobiography, incidentally, but that is no surprise.

Hart had been encouraged into her employment specifically for such a purpose. Andrew reported that she admitted that it was the future Labour MP, Bernard Floud, who had recruited her, encouraged her to join the Civil Service, and introduced her to Arnold Deutsch.[12] (Chapter 6 suggests that Christopher Hill mentored her after her joining.) Floud has been recognised as one of the most important members of the 'Oxford Ring' of Communist spies, having been recruited to the CPGB while at Wadham College.[13] Not so much attention has been paid to this ring (a series of suicides, including Floud's, having alarmed officers in MI5), but it was almost as malign as the Cambridge Group, and was linked by Guy Burgess to it. It was led by Arthur Wynn, and its members included Jenifer Hart, Bernard Floud, and Christopher Hill. Nigel West has added Iris Murdoch, Ian Milner, Tom Driberg, Phillip Toynbee and A. J. P. Taylor to the roster.[14]

---

[i] Fischer-Williams married the jurisprudential scholar, Herbert (H. L. A.) Hart (1907-1992), who was then working for MI5, in October 1941. This paper will refer to her as Jenifer Hart hereon, as that is her more familiar nomenclature.

If, as Glees pointed out, Hart was "ordered to infiltrate the Civil Service (in her case, the Home Office was the target)", her task would have been to deliver useful material to her Soviet handlers. She was a high-flier, to be placed in a significant position in the government bureaucracy: she had indeed astounded the examiners, her friends, and many observers, by coming third in the July 1936 Civil Service examination, an event in which John Cairncross came first. As she wrote, ". . . student friends in the Party said I would be more effective by going into the Civil Service as a secret Party member", admitting that she "would occasionally pass them useful information".[15] Berlin probably introduced Hart to Burgess: Burgess was a frequent visitor to Oxford (where he would meet Berlin), and may have assisted in setting up the rival 'Oxford Ring' of spies. Hart also claimed that she had broken off contact with Deutsch after a few meetings – an unlikely breach, given how Moscow Centre, once it had an agent in its tentacles, would not let someone go lightly. Hart's own memoir cannot be trusted: she claimed that she was essentially asked to be a 'sleeper' for ten years, but admitted she knew what would be expected of her as a secret Party member in the Civil Service: ". . . I think I supposed that I would occasionally pass them useful information." [16] Blackmail and other threats were always telling. As other witnesses have testified, once Soviet intelligence had its claws into an agent, they would not easily let that person decide that he or she wanted to retire.[17] It is much more likely that her contact with Deutsch was interrupted by Deutsch's forced departure in the autumn of 1937, thus giving Hart a convenient alibi.

When the network of illegals was erased completely by the beginning of 1938, with the role of controller reverting to Gorsky as legal *rezident*, Hart almost certainly had contact with him. Indeed, she told the authors Penrose and Freeman that she used to meet a Stalinist controller on Hampstead Heath in 1938, which timetable and profile fits Gorsky exactly, but it would have been dangerous, and she more probably used Burgess as a liaison.[18] By the time of Gorsky's recall in early 1940, she was obviously not reliant on his involvement, and she would still have been using her secret CP links to pass on information, in the same manner that Leo Long was delivering his nuggets. As far as any doubts that might have troubled her about the righteousness of the cause, it does not appear that the Nazi-Soviet Pact (she is silent about it in her memoir) disturbed her as much as did Stalin's show trials, which turned out to be a minor bump in the career of her conscience. It did not derail her Communist path. The Nazi-Soviet Pact had been the last straw for some more principled communists: Goronwy Rees had a show-down with Burgess over it, with the result that the latter wanted Rees murdered as a security risk, but, since Hart did not come in for such concerns and treatment, it can be safe to assume that she remained loyal to the movement, and was, in Burgess's opinion, safe. Whatever momentary adverse reactions they had, their conviction was that Stalin knew what he was doing, and they should loyally follow his lead.

Burgess's reaction, on learning the contents of the report, must have been mixed. On the one hand, Krivitsky had come very close to identifying two members of the Cambridge Five – Cairncross, because of his involvement with the Committee of Imperial Defence, and Philby, because of Krivitsky's hints at an English journalist sent to Spain to assassinate Franco. But Krivitsky, through muddled-headedness or ignorance, but probably out of deviousness, had muddied the waters. The pointers were fractured, and the biographies and backgrounds of the suspected agents commingled. No one had been clearly identified, and thus the spies had some breathing-space. On the other hand, Krivitsky accurately described the illegals (Maly, Deutsch and Reif) whom the spies had known intimately: he might have told more than appeared in the report. And it would have been clear that, had MI5 investigated the leads as thoroughly as they should have done, Britain's counter-espionage group would eventually have been able to home in on the probable candidates. The lack of purpose with which it followed up is in marked contrast to the doggedness that Jane Archer had already shown in pursuing Communist subversives, as for example in tracking down evidence of Maly's financial dealings. Her demise, simultaneous with the rise of the bland and irresolute behaviour of Liddell and White, symbolises all that was wrong with Section 'B' of MI5 at this time.

The defector's warnings were clear: the strategy of developing moles had been laid bare. "Krivitsky mentioned that the Fourth Department was prepared in some instances to wait for ten or fifteen years for results and in some cases paid the expense of a university education for promising young men in the hope that they might eventually obtain diplomatic posts or other key positions in the service of the country of which they were nationals."[19] Of course, Burgess was not aware at this time that the leading expert on Communist counter-espionage, Jane Archer, was on her way out, and shortly to leave Section 'B' to assume her role in coordinating the Regional Security Liaison Officers.

Thus, contrary to some of the accounts as to how the news of the Krivitsky interrogations reached the Soviets and their agents, it is clear that Guy Burgess was the point man, the sole agent close to the sources, senior to and more outgoing than John Cairncross, the last member of the Five, with a track-record as a competent fixer. He already realised that he needed to reignite the mechanism for delivering information: the secrets accessed by his colleagues Leo Long and Cairncross were being wasted without a channel to Moscow. (Leo Long deserves to be regarded as the sixth man of a putative Cambridge Six, since the secrets he had access to at this time were potentially more dangerous than any others. His story is told in Chapter 7.[20]) Burgess thus went into action. He had four major goals: first, to inform his fellow-agents in France of the danger, but to allay any fears they might have about being quickly unmasked; second, to insert a mole into MI5, in order to discover more detailed information, and to try to sabotage the process of follow-up on Krivitsky's leads; third, to alert his Moscow bosses that the ring of spies was intact, and still loyal, and needed a reliable communication medium; and fourth, to communicate to his masters the conclusions from the Krivitsky report, and to point out to them that the defector should be eliminated as soon as possible. (He would be unaware that Pavel Sudoplatov, whom Stalin in March 1939 had appointed Deputy Head of the Foreign Department of the NKVD with the express task of assassinating Trotsky, was in charge of a 'Special Tasks' department, and already devising its plan to eliminate Krivitsky.[21])

At this stage, the execution of the plot involved an intricate relationship between Burgess and his colleague and friend, Sir Isaiah Berlin. After exploiting

Hart's position in the Home Office, Burgess drew upon the services of his old friend and patron, Victor Rothschild, and then embarked upon the furtive mission with Berlin. The actions and interactions of these two are key to understanding how Burgess's plans evolved into the Moscow Plot, and why Berlin was an accomplice to it. The contribution of Berlin to this project, and his subsequent dealings with Soviet intelligence, are most remarkable and perplexing, given his stature in society between the end of the war and his death, and merits a special analysis, which occupies the conclusion to this chapter.

Guy Burgess meanwhile had been planning his visit to Paris. With Gorsky absent in the Soviet Union, he must have felt he needed to set up a meeting with Leonid (aka Naum) Eitingon, his NKVD contact at the Soviet Embassy, who had arrived in Paris in August 1938 specifically to handle Burgess, and receive information from him for transmission to Moscow. This arrangement had lasted until March 1939, when Moscow Centre decided that Gorsky, based in London, should more conveniently take control of Burgess and his comrades.[22] Burgess and his friends had not taken well to Gorsky, whom they found rather ignorant and coarse, so Burgess would have been keen to renew his association with Eitingon. Yet Eitingon had, unknown to Burgess, already moved on: as his distant relative, Mary-Kay Wilmers, recorded, he had left Paris under subterfuge in the summer of 1939, arriving in New York in September.[23] For Eitingon had been given by Sudoplatov the vitally important job – already botched by his colleague Spiegelglass – of assassinating the rebellious Trotsky in Mexico, a task he brought to a successful outcome (as far as Moscow Centre was concerned) in August 1940. Shortly before he was killed, Trotsky told an American reporter that Krivitsky was right: Stalin was set to kill them both.[24]

Late in March, 1940, Burgess thus made his trip to Paris, on the spurious pretext of having an assignment working with Paris radio. The evidence for this journey has come from his friend, the communist writer Rosamond Lehmann, who accompanied him.[25] Lehmann was another member of the extended network of communists who at this time did so much to undermine British society's defence mechanisms against Comintern subversion. She was the sister of John Lehmann, whom the writer John Costello described as cooperating, in early 1934, with the Communist underground in Vienna as a courier alongside Kim Philby.[26] John Lehmann admitted that he had been approached there by a Soviet agent, but claimed that he had declined the invitation to become a spy. As Chapter 2 outlined, Arnold Deutsch reported on his recruitment exercise in Vienna, and his recruitment of EDITH. Yet Deutsch's testimony appears somewhat unreliable: he would be unlikely to distort the truth by indicating that he had recruited the same person in two different European capitals in short order under different names. Moreover, Moscow Centre was often very unimaginative in selecting cryptonyms. If EDITH was Edith Tudor-Hart (née Suschitsky), photographer and Soviet spy, why could JOHN not be John Lehmann?

Be that as it may, Rosamond Lehmann quickly worked out what was happening in Paris. Indeed, she possessed special insights into the nefarious undertakings of her friends. She was at that time the lover of Goronwy Rees, and in late 1937 the latter had confided to her that Burgess, after admitting to him that he was a Comintern agent, had invited him to join the cause. Rees gave an evasive answer when Lehmann asked if he had been recruited as well. Much later, in 1956, after Burgess and Maclean had escaped to the Soviet Union, Anthony Blunt was to give her a hint of his involvement – a fact she suppressed until John Costello interviewed her in the mid-1980s.[27] When she and Burgess arrived at the radio station in Paris, the staff there "had no idea who she was, or why she was there, and Burgess turned up only briefly, muttered a quick apology and disappeared." He obviously had other business, no doubt linking up with Philby, Maclean and Blunt, and trying to contact Eitingon. Cairncross may also have been there: his autobiography tells that he left for a holiday in the South of France in April, but the date he gave his ghost-writer may have been in error.[28] Rothschild was probably also a party to the rendezvous, having arranged his special exploratory trip to France at that time, as may have been the scourge of Special Branch's attempts to keep unwelcome Comintern agents out of the country, Dennis Pritt, MP. After Pritt had intervened energetically that January to have the German Communists Robert and Jürgen Kuczynski released from internment, the Home Office had, in the last week of February, granted him an exit permit to go to Paris, an event that an indignant Guy Liddell thought worthy of note in his *Diary*.[29] When pursuing the second objective of his mission, however, Burgess learned that Eitingon had moved on, and that one Lev Vasilevsky was the current NKVD *resident* in Paris (in fact supervising the plot to kill Trotsky, using the cover of Consul-General).[30] Vasilevsky was not a name Burgess knew or trusted, so the group had to re-think its plans. A few months later, Burgess was to describe his fruitless attempt at contact to Michael Straight in Washington, telling him that he had been out of touch with his "friends" for several months.[31]

Several weeks passed before the climate turned more favourable for necessary action. In April, Burgess left his BBC position to work full-time for Colonel Grand's Section D, charged with establishing a training section at Brickendonbury Hall. Coincidentally, in the same month in which Burgess joined SIS, Jane Archer was officially replaced as head of anti-Soviet espionage, B4(a), by the recent recruit, Roger Hollis. In France, the spies were growing impatient. In the first week of May, in Paris, Kitty Harris was reported to have had an encounter with Kim Philby, who expressed to her his surprise that the Russians had broken contact. He told her he had valuable information to impart, and that Guy Burgess was likewise struggling in isolation.[32] On May 7, accepting the fact that the processes of intelligence-gathering and analysis were broken, Prime Minister Chamberlain agreed to General Ismay's suggestion that the Joint Intelligence Committee be set up.[33] Three days later, Chamberlain, having lost the confidence of the House of Commons, was replaced by Churchill. Burgess must then have seen an opportunity for a less antagonistic relationship between Great Britain and the Soviet Union, and grasped the opportunity to combine a political mission with a private one. He needed to take his message to his Soviet masters in person. In order to perform this successfully, however, he needed an interpreter. That man was Isaiah Berlin, the third member of the trio.

Whether fortuitous or not, Burgess's friendship with Berlin, the Oxford academic, had already paid off handsomely, for Isaiah was an intimate friend of Jenifer Hart's. Berlin had known her since 1935. His rather arch letters to her of that time can be found in the first of the four volumes of his *Letters*.[34] He was apparently completely aware of her political convictions. In a letter to Mary Fisher written later in 1940, he wrote that, in a classification of friends in American political terms "Jenifer and B.J. are both hauled up for un-American activities", a clear indication of their Communist beliefs.[35] (B.J., an abbreviation for 'Baby Junior', was Maire Lynd, a member of the Communist Party.) Later on, Berlin's relationship with Jenifer was to reach a higher level of intimacy: in the late 1940s (or so the pair declared, as it might have occurred earlier) Berlin and Hart started an affair that continued for several years, until Berlin's marriage in 1956. While this romance was recorded in Ignatieff's biography of the great historian of ideas, the identity of Berlin's *amoureuse* was only hinted at, in broad strokes that would have allowed only the *cognoscenti* to identify her. She was not named until Nicola Lacey revealed all, in 2004, in her biography of Herbert Hart.[36]

At this stage, Berlin entered centre-stage in the Moscow Plot. The inescapable fact remains that, irrespective of Burgess's invitation to join him as a government employee, Berlin assuredly harboured a serious desire to get to Moscow in 1940, as his private letters show. So to what extent was he aware of Burgess's plans? Could he really have accompanied Burgess for so long, and consorted with him so closely, without having some insight into what was happening? And if he did not realise it at the time, when might have he become aware of what Burgess was really up to? Now that archival material has been released (in late 2015) that shows Berlin was a member of Section D at the time – a status that Berlin strenuously denied - we can assume that he was intimately aware of the project that Burgess had started, and a willing conspirator. Berlin was very capable of showing a Prince Myshkin-type naivety, while simultaneously concealing a much more worldly acuity. His continued mendacity about the chronicle of events in that summer suggests he had a lot to hide. It is difficult to believe that he, who loved gossip and intrigue, never discussed politics with Burgess (who praised him for his work on Marx); it is equally hard to imagine that he shared a transatlantic crossing (but not a cabin) with Burgess without ever talking about the mission that was designed to take them along most of the circumference of the world.[37]

His untruthfulness about the whole episode is shown by the conflicting accounts he gives of the whole saga. In *Washington Despatches*, he never mentioned Burgess's role at all, presenting his appointment as a very formal offer coming from Nicolson and Jebb, one that he accepted promptly and graciously, after which he was "ordered to go to Moscow".[38] But not long before this time he was talking to Andrew Boyle. Boyle expressed his thanks to Berlin in his Prologue to *The Climate of Treason*, and in the Chapter *The Confidence Tricksters*, which included an account of the Moscow Plot, attributed some of his facts from "personal information to the author from Sir Isaiah Berlin".[ii][39] Now the story changes. Here it is Burgess's idea that Ambassador Cripps needs help: he sells it to Harold Nicolson and to Lord Perth in the Ministry of Information. Indeed, "the breathtaking cheek of the proposal... took in Harold Nicolson".

[ii] Berlin was knighted in 1957, and awarded the Order of Merit in 1971.

Furthermore, "the hardest part was to overcome the suspicions of Isaiah Berlin, a forceful personality of perception who immediately smelled a rat", and Berlin is described glowingly by Boyle as "a scholar versed in the muddy byways of politics and philosophy, and an acute student of human nature". Berlin was allowed to dwell on the proposal for a long time, but eventually overcame his slight of having been rejected by Whitehall the previous autumn. In Boyle's words, "he swallowed the bait and agreed to accompany Guy to Moscow". In neither account did Berlin appear to acknowledge reading Driberg's memoir of Burgess; or if he had, hoped that no one else would do so. Boyle's account is thus untrustworthy, and he got many key facts wrong, such as his mistakes over transport and timing, that must be attributed to Berlin. He wrote that Burgess "departed with his Oxford protégé on a VIP flight to the United States before the end of September", a colossal error of fact that draws into doubt Boyle's whole account.

And then there is the tale that Berlin wove for his biographer.[40] This time, Burgess was the instigator again, but the incident is coloured by all the murky business of dealing with Colonel Grand, Section D, and the diplomatic bags. There is no suggestion of a dignified and important role helping Cripps to convey Britain's war aims to the Kremlin, only talk of being a "press attaché", in the responsibilities of which Berlin appeared to show no interest. As the tape relates, he just goes along as the obedient poodle: "All right, I heard all this, it was all new to me, . . . I knew nothing about any of these things, and so I said, 'All right, I'll do anything you tell me,' and behaved in my usual very obedient – in that sort of situation which is true of me in general – anxiety to please."

That is hardly the "forceful personality of perception" described by Boyle. There is no mention of Burgess's plans to enter negotiations on mutual sabotage, but hints of such dark dealings assuredly loom in the encounter with Grand. Berlin was nevertheless very careful to quote Gladwyn Jebb as saying: "I forgot to add that Guy's going with you if you don't mind, he's got his own stuff to do, nothing to do with you." One might also note here Jebb's reference to "Guy", as to a familiar friend, a relationship that Jebb was quick to deny after Burgess's abscondence. So where was the suspicious-minded and rat-smelling Berlin when this little secret was vouchsafed to him? He really did not care, as he had his pretext for getting to Moscow, he had allies in the Soviet embassy who would support him, and he would be able to pursue the private business that he discussed obliquely in his letters to his parents. Later, he attempted to distance himself from Burgess, studiously avoiding him on the voyage, and suggesting they might go their separate ways. (A letter to his parents from the SS *Antonia* states: "My plans are to let my companion proceed further if he feels he is in a hurry. And stay myself until the path is clear."[41]) Yet Lord Lothian indicated that Berlin was still carrying his diplomatic bag, whose contents are unknown, and, after Burgess had been sent home, Berlin very carefully, and unnecessarily, expresses to his parents the hope that "Burgess gave you my greetings" – hinting, perhaps, that Burgess had some deeper message to convey to them about the progress of the mission.

In one key passage, however, Berlin's evasiveness gives away a lot. When Ignatieff asked Berlin whether he knew Michael Straight, Berlin replied: "I think he was new to me, no I don't think I did know till he told me about him, and not all that much. Maybe I knew there was a character like that in Cambridge, maybe I didn't, that I can't tell you, it's comparatively unimportant." This is an astonishing claim. Straight was a close friend of both Burgess and Rothschild, and mixed socially with them on regular occasions. He was also a close friend of Felix Frankfurter, whom Berlin knew very well at Oxford. And Berlin was an intimate friend of Straight's sister-in-law, Lady Daphne, who was married to Michael's brother Whitney Willard, and who was later to work with Berlin in the British Press Office in New York. She and Berlin exchanged several affectionate letters. Furthermore, Berlin admitted in a letter to Arthur Schlesinger of August 27, 1953, after Straight had published an offensive article in *The New Republic* about Berlin's controversial visit to Anna Akhmatova in Leningrad in November 1945, that "I have never liked him", which suggests an acquaintanceship going back some time. Berlin should have had nothing to hide by admitting he did know Straight: nevertheless, the memory of the incident, and Straight's involvement, clearly pained him.

Berlin revealed in several letters written during his time of inactivity in the United States that he still wanted to get to Moscow. This longing apparently preceded Guy Burgess's approach to him, and even his professed desire to help with the war effort, perhaps over-unctuously articulated in the letter to his All Souls colleague, Lord Halifax, who, he asserted, may not even have remembered him [*see Chapter 4*].[42] For example, in one of his most revealing letters, to Maire Gaster, written in January 1941, Berlin referred directly to more sinister goings-on. Maire Gaster (née Lynd), the daughter of Irish nationalists, and a member of the Communist Party, had married Jack Gaster, a lawyer and Communist, in 1938, after they met at a Communist Party meeting. Berlin described his role to her as "a courier with a bag", drawing attention to the fact that his function was to import secret material into the Soviet Union.[43] He coloured his account of the aborted trip to Moscow with the extraordinary phrase "a plot in which even Mrs Fisher [the wife of H. A. L. Fisher, Warden of New College] assisted", suggesting that there were other known accessories before the fact, while highlighting the Fisher influence. He repeated to his parents his continuing desire to get to Moscow, despite the objections of British diplomats, and, very curiously, reported that the Russians (mainly in the person of Konstantin Oumansky, the Soviet Ambassador) were still eager to see him execute his mission.[44] This is an extraordinary confession: at the time, the Soviet Union was an ally of Nazi Germany, which was perversely dedicated to a programme of oppression of Jews that was steadily evolving into mass slaughter. Yet Berlin, the ardent Zionist, seemed insensitive to what such relationships implied, or how his actions might be interpreted.

What were Berlin's secret plans? The three candidates for his mission are: family and relatives; business interests; and Zionism. Berlin's coyness over his goals, as well as his activities on a later trip to Moscow, suggest the third option. (What material he planned to transport in his diplomatic bag remains a mystery.) It is possible that Soviet Jews working in Stalin's Secret Police saw him as an ally against the threats of Nazism. Alternatively, Ambassador Oumansky might have misled Berlin about his enthusiasm for the project. He had been an NKVD officer before his ambassadorial appointment, and might have been encouraged to cultivate Berlin by facilitating his passage to Moscow, so that his brains could be picked there in a more leisurely fashion. This conclusion has recently been confirmed by items in the diaries of David Ben-Gurion, the leader of one of the Zionist labour parties in Palestine at the time, and later to become Israel's first Prime Minister.[45] Ben-Gurion recorded a meeting with Berlin in New York, just before Berlin set sail for Lisbon in October 1940, where they discussed promises of material support from the Soviets, and planned strategies for reporting back to Harold Laski in Britain. This testimony suggests that Oumansky's main role was as the primary representative of the Soviet Union in assisting the Zionist cause. Ben-Gurion spoke of Oumansky's failure to deliver "Baltic ships, Baltic money" to Jews recently under attack during the Arab Revolt in Palestine. Berlin's Latvian background might thus have been an asset here, but, instead of being able to visit the Soviet Union to make an appeal in person, he was instead tasked with reporting Oumansky's shortcomings to Harold Laski in Britain.

The peak of Berlin's enthusiasm for the Zionist cause was reached in the late 1930s, after he met Chaim Weizmann, about whom he frequently wrote in terms of idolatry in his letters. Arie M. Dubnov, whose recently published book *Isaiah Berlin, The Journey of a Jewish Liberal*, comprehensively covers Jewish identity and his activities in support of Zionism, concluded that Berlin was used by Weizmann as an "inside informer, placed in a strategic position close to the British elite's nerve system".[46] Berlin used his connections with this elite at Oxford to pass on information he gleaned about British plans for Palestine, such as the composition of the Peel Commission, announced in August 1936. During the eventful year of 1940, such concerns dominated Berlin's thinking. His move to the United States in that summer is frequently reported as an accidental by-product of his aborted trip to Moscow, but Berlin's clear desire to return to Europe to see Weizmann, and his pretence that the job offered him in the office of British Information Services was not permanent or binding, may indicate that his long-term interest was as much to help the Zionist cause as to contribute to Britain's war effort.

One other possible motivation to visit the Soviet Union was the plight of Chaim Weizmann's brother, Schmuel. Schmuel, one of two Weizmann siblings (out of fifteen) who had not escaped permanently to the West, had travelled to Palestine around 1930, and, after being charged with treason, had been sentenced to death on his return. He had been reprieved at the last moment, but had later been accused of Zionist activities, and was executed as a British spy in 1939. His family did not learn of his fate until 1955, so in 1940 Chaim Weizmann may well have sought information on the fate of his unfortunate brother.[47]

Of course, Berlin's plans were thwarted, but he later returned to the USA to begin a career with British Security Co-ordination in New York, and then as an analyst in Lord Lothian's Embassy in Washington. This chapter of his career is thus largely superfluous to the story of the communist infiltration of MI5 – except for two events, the second of which is in fact a series of possibly related incidents. The first concerns his work in the Embassy: the second involves the relationship between Berlin and Donald Maclean, and encounters between Berlin and the NKVD operators Konstantin Oumansky and Anatoly Gorsky.

As has been indicated, Berlin had been encouraging and assisting Zionist initiatives for some years. During his time in Washington, the need for his skills was one of a more general nature – broadly surveying the American political scene rather than providing a specifically Jewish perspective on it. Yet Berlin continued to pursue his private goals. His undercover work continued: he admitted to his biographer, Michael Ignatieff, that, during the summer of 1943, on hearing of a joint Anglo-American plan to issue a statement condemning "Zionist agitation", he had leaked the details of it to American Zionists, who were thus able to forestall and cancel the announcement by means of their own remonstrations.[48] Berlin had to construct an artful explanation of what happened in order to conceal his own duplicity. As Ignatieff wrote: "He had managed his conflict of interests with agility, humour and a certain amount of cunning, but when he had to choose, he had chosen his Jewish loyalties over the British ones. The episode troubled him." This was not an honourable episode in Berlin's political career, but at the time he had few qualms about deceiving his government employer.

Moreover, Berlin later had a long association with Israeli Intelligence. His distant relative by marriage, Efraim Halevy, would later pay tribute to Isaiah Berlin's contribution to the State of Israel. In the Seventh Isaiah Berlin Annual Lecture, delivered in the winter of 2009, he said: "Shaya, as we called him, was not a neutral bystander as history unfolded before our eyes. He was often a player, at times a clandestine one, as when he met me in the 1990s to hear reports of my many meetings with the late King Hussein of Jordan and his brother Crown Prince Hassan, who had been his pupil at Oxford."[49] In a letter of April 1951 to his St. Paul's schoolmate and Oxford contemporary, Walter Eytan (né Ettinghausen), who was then the first Director-General of Israel's Foreign Ministry, Berlin recorded his recent lecture to Mossad's political and intelligence department, and an unofficial source has suggested he may have been involved in training when the Israeli state was founded, three years before.[50] Berlin was a far more active negotiator on behalf of the Zionist cause than he ever admitted and his dealings with prominent Jews in Palestine, Great Britain, the US and the Soviet Union placed him in a pivotal position in the preceding years.

The second series of events that illustrate Berlin's intelligence-gathering concerns his friendship with Donald Maclean, and the latter's NKVD contact in Washington, Anatoly Gorsky. Gorsky was sent out in the summer of 1944 specifically to resume his handling of Maclean after the latter moved from London to Washington in May 1944. Gorsky had been the *rezident* in London, controlling the Cambridge spies until his recall to Moscow early in 1940, and then again after returning to the United Kingdom in December of that year. Some time after Gorsky's arrival, Berlin had an apparent public spat with Maclean, whom Berlin reputedly met for the first time that year in Washington. Maclean had introduced himself, and asked Berlin if he could, in turn, arrange for him to meet some leftist "New Dealer" types. Berlin was happy to oblige, and engineered an invitation for Maclean and his wife to a dinner hosted by Katherine Graham, whose husband, Philip, was publisher of the *Washington Post*. Incidentally, when the FBI investigated the activities of the atom spy Klaus Fuchs, it explored whether he had been responsible for the leakage of information to the

Washington Post. According to the MI5 officer Jim Skardon, the agent Lamphere "commented that the *Washington Post* seemed to be politically well informed about Anglo-American relations in 1944 and 1945". The sources were no doubt Maclean – and Berlin.[51]

The story comes to us courtesy of Graham. Further details have been added by Michael Holzman, and Ignatieff covered it in his biography.[52] The event is not accurately dated by either Graham or Berlin, but, since Graham indicated that the dinner was held during the winter, when she was living alone after her husband had been sent out to the Far East in October 1944, it probably occurred in December 1944 or January 1945. As Graham told the story (apparently using Berlin's notes and reminiscences), she considered that Maclean and Berlin were friends at the time, and she invited them to a dinner-party, at which Maclean and Edward Prichard (a protégé of Berlin's great ally Felix Frankfurter) began to tease Berlin about his right-wing social connections. Maclean, no doubt under stress, and having drunk too much, complained to Berlin that he [Berlin] "knew" people like [the Republican socialite] Alice Longworth, and continued with the following tirade:

> "One shouldn't know people like that. If I thought you knew her out of curiosity, I wouldn't mind so much, but I'm told you actually like her company. That is dreadful . . . she's fascist and right-wing . . Life is a battle. We must know which side we're on. We must stick to our side through thick and thin. I know at the last moment, the twelfth hour, you'll be on our side. But until then, you'll go about with these dreadful people."

After Berlin defended himself over the right to choose his own friends, Maclean continued the attack: "The trouble is you're a coward. You know what's right and you know what's wrong and you will not come out in time to defend the right cause. You know perfectly well what I mean." These words eerily presage what Maclean said to Goronwy Rees a few years later (if the latter's anecdote can be believed). During an encounter at the Gargoyle Club in early 1950, Maclean said to Rees: "I know all about you. You used to be one of us, but you ratted."[53] The irony of Maclean's outburst is that, while it actually does describe Berlin's chameleon-like character very well, it was hardly as if Maclean had been open at pursuing his own ideological mission, and it was the lifetime of deception that caused him such stress.

The accounts vary as to how quickly the two made up. Berlin later claimed to be very upset, and told Katherine Graham soon after that he would never speak to Maclean again. To Ignatieff, he said that Maclean wrote him a letter the next day, apologising, and they met for lunch the same week, but when they started talking about Henry Wallace, they fell out again. Berlin claimed he said that Wallace (who was then Vice-President – until January 20, 1945) "had a screw loose", a statement which appalled Maclean (as well as his wife, so he said). Maclean admonished Berlin and said he should never say such things again. Then Berlin knew that "they were no longer friends, and [I] never saw him again".

If Maclean had simply been talking about progressive new-dealerism (of which the host, Graham, was firmly in favour), it might all have been a storm in a teacup, since that is the way that fashionable, Rooseveltean Washington would have been thinking. Ignatieff suggested that Berlin never suspected that Maclean was a spy, but after the escape by Maclean and his partner in crime, Burgess, in 1951, the exchange could have been re-interpreted, in the light of the facts of Maclean's real allegiance, to indicate that there could have been another colouring to Maclean's insinuations. Would that fateful "twelfth hour" have been on the barricades, with Berlin welcoming the revolutionary zeal that he found so energising when he wrote about Marx? It seems unlikely, as Berlin may have by then come to believe in a new order that did not involve a revolution. In any case, by March 1952, Berlin had apparently changed his political convictions, and become an ally of McCarthyism, if another less-publicised anecdote by Graham can be interpreted correctly. She recounted a luncheon-party where her husband (bitterly resisting McCarthy's anti-Communist hunts through the medium of his editorials in the *Post*) had a furious argument with Berlin, the latter presumably defending the Senator's attempts to root out Stalin's useful idiots.[54] Thus Berlin had developed a different *persona* by the time of the elopements, and the Graham party may have been the first indication of his transformation.

Yet not all is as it appears. Closer inspection of Berlin's *Letters* and related material, and the development of a strict chronology, cast major doubts on the accuracy of the incident as Berlin recalled it. Berlin's account of his friendship with Maclean is unlikely, given their previous collaboration; the timing of Maclean's references to the widowhood of Cressida Ridley (who was identified by Maclean as one of their shared friends) points unerringly to the fact that their supposed encounter did not occur before the autumn of 1944 [iii]; Berlin's representation of his political affiliations is highly inaccurate; and he lied about whether he and Maclean made up by offering directly contradictory accounts of such a reconciliation to Katherine Graham and Cressida Ridley. In short, the episode has the appearance of a staged argument between Maclean and Berlin, with the goal of Berlin's distancing himself from Maclean, which may have spun out of control. The reasons for such a charade will be explored.

For the episode has more disturbing reverberations. At about the same time as the Graham dinner, Berlin was involved with a secret document titled *Casual Sources*. The historian Verne Newton has reported that the British Embassy in Moscow regularly wrote up a report of "casual sources" (contacts considered treasonous by Stalin), a report always kept under the tightest secrecy.[55] In December 1944, reference was made to it in an exchange between the Foreign Office and the Embassy in Moscow. This was noticed by John W. Russell, a press attaché who had served in Moscow and was now supervised by Maclean in Washington. Russell sent London a cable, almost certainly cleared by Maclean, asking that he and Isaiah Berlin be provided with a copy of the *Casual Sources* report. "We make this request partly out of idle curiosity, partly out of a genuine need to keep abreast of developments in the USSR", the cable pleaded. The

---

[iii] Cressida Ridley (née Bonham Carter) (1917-98), married in 1939 Jasper Ridley (1913-1943), who was killed while fighting in Italy. In his memoir of Jasper Ridley and Esmond Romilly, *Friends Apart*, Philip Toynbee wrote that the War Office did not announce Jasper Ridley's "probable death" until June 1944 (p 183).

Moscow Embassy and the Foreign Office refused because of the danger. Maclean then intervened, promising that it would not get into the hands of Americans, and the Foreign Office finally relented. The information no doubt ended up in the hands of Stalin. When questioned by Verne Newton[56], Berlin gave an evasive and unsatisfactory response, claiming he never knew of the existence of such a document.

That very same month, Berlin met Anatoly Gorsky, now the Soviet First Secretary, at the Soviet Embassy. It would have been very inappropriate for someone in Berlin's position to build friendships with known members of the NKVD, even acting under diplomatic cover. Yet, in his years in the USA he did associate with – even (in his own words) "cultivate" – a couple of Stalin's thugs.[57] He had four years before sought out Oumansky when he arrived in Washington, and found him a very encouraging ally, since the Ambassador seemed very keen on Berlin's plans to get to Moscow – far keener than "the foolish Cripps", for example, and Berlin met him several times after being introduced to him by Ben Cohen and Oscar Chapman of the Department of the Interior. Oumansky was an ally of the Zionists, and met frequently with such as the founder of the World Jewish Congress, Nahum Goldmann, an old friend and co-conspirator of Berlin's, in Mexico.[58] In a letter back to the Foreign Office, Berlin referred to Goldmann's attempts to reach the Soviet Union early in 1944, and reported how his [Berlin's] friend Jacob Landau was trying to intervene with Oumansky in Mexico to assist Goldmann's visit.[59] Oumansky was probably also involved in stage-managing Trotsky's death. He had been moved to the Ambassadorship of Mexico in 1943, and was to die in an air-crash a couple of years later. It was rumoured that it had been caused by a bomb placed by Trotskyists, but that report emanated from the Soviet Embassy, and thus cannot be trusted implicitly. Maybe he was another of Stalin's dupes who now knew too much, and it was thus time for him to be removed.

In a letter to his parents about the first encounter with Gorsky, dated December 12, 1944, Berlin justified the contact by suggesting that he was following orders. He wrote that "I am encouraged to cultivate him by the Embassy . . ." (but did not indicate by whom), and added that Gorsky "warmly pressed me to stay with him in Moscow".[60] Who was giving him instructions? Might it have been Maclean, with Berlin acting as a go-between, trying to make some reparation for disappointing Maclean a few months earlier, and using the cover of his reputation and lofty position? Did Berlin know who Gorsky was from his intimate friendship with Jenifer Hart? The relationship continued. By May 1945, Berlin was "assiduously cultivating him", as he appeared to be a fellow-Jew, and was clearly under a directive to mix with foreigners like him, who may be "useful sources of information". Did Berlin consider that meeting Gorsky's needs for information was appropriate behaviour? They could indeed have had a lot to chat about. When he met Gorsky, for at least the second time, Berlin wrote to his parents of his wondering: "Is he *ex nostris?*"[61] This arch phrase has been translated by Henry Hardy as "is he one of us?", which gives it a more shallow Thatcherite ring, suggesting a common set of political principles rather than the deep ethnic link that Berlin implied. More accurate would probably be: "Is he from our tribe?" This is a telling observation by Berlin, since it expresses his natural Jewish inclination to seek out a fellow-Jew, and want to consort with him on that characteristic alone, rather than considering the man's background and role as one of Stalin's disreputable secret police officers. Berlin appeared to have forgotten that the unfortunate Krivitsky, also once an NKVD officer, but with scruples, and now a victim, was of course '*ex nostris*', as well.

Why would Berlin want to cultivate Gorsky? Gorsky was to achieve notoriety, a few months later, by almost being caught by the FBI while he was meeting a Soviet agent who was in the process of defecting, Elizabeth Bentley. Having suggested to her the previous year that they should become lovers, he now urged his bosses that she should be assassinated, but they declined his appeal.[62] In the words of Haynes, Klehr and Vassiliev: "He thought that Bentley would be willing to meet with Joseph Katz, who could drop poison in her wine or on her makeup. Alternatively Katz could use his locksmith skills to break into her room and use 'a cold steel weapon or stage a suicide.'"[63] The echo of the "staged suicide" should be noted. Gorsky was not a nice man – even though he might invite you to stay with him on one of your occasional drop-ins to Moscow. To bring the story full circle, when deputy head of the First Directorate, back in Moscow in 1951, he was to call the meeting that determined to respond to the appeal of Burgess and Maclean, and offer them asylum.[64] Soon afterwards, however, he was himself to be ousted in a purge, following the arrests of the Rosenbergs and others in the US.[65] This may have been because he was considered part of the Jewish plot that Stalin was manufacturing: other reports say that it was because he had misrepresented his bourgeois background, and lied on his résumé.[66] He fortunately did not lose his life through it, not dying until 1980. Apparently, Berlin did not take up the invitation to visit him when he took his wife to Moscow in 1956.

The evidence is clearly circumstantial, but it is quite possible that Berlin was acting as a courier for Maclean. During his regular visits to New York in the summer of 1944 (under the guise of visiting his pregnant wife), Maclean had delivered documents to his NKVD contact, Pravdin, as the publication of the decrypted Soviet cables known as VENONA later disclosed.[67] When Gorsky arrived in Washington, Maclean now had a more convenient contact, geographically. But it would have been very dangerous for him to be seen in Gorsky's company. As his friend Robert Cecil who arrived in Washington in April 1945 as Second Secretary, wrote: "As he [Maclean] never had a 'dark room' in his house and was notably unhandy in using a camera, he must have made frequent use in Washington of *duboks*, as the NKVD termed 'dead drops', from which documents could be collected. It would have been far too risky for him to have had frequent meetings with 'Al' [Gorsky] in Washington, which at that date was still little more than an overgrown town, where evasion of FBI 'watchers' would have posed grave problems. These problems were much reduced in the teeming and cavernous city of New York, where the NKVD had its headquarters."[68] Such problems would have intensified when Maclean was promoted to First Secretary in December, 1944. Since Berlin was clearly allowed to visit Gorsky unchallenged, he would have had the perfect cover for passing on Maclean's secrets – as well as those he shared with Maclean, for example the *Casual Sources*.

The VENONA traffic was released by GCHQ in 1996, after the NSA [iv] published it in the USA in 1995. While MI5 has encouraged the notion that Maclean was not identified as HOMER (the cryptonym mentioned as a source in Soviet cables) until the end of 1950, recent analysis since then has indicated that British cryptanalysts, working on messages sent by the Soviet Embassy during 1944 and 1945, probably determined as early as 1948 that Donald Maclean was the Embassy official who was passing on secrets.[69] Some of the most revealing messages cited in various books on VENONA are to be found in a batch of cables known as the 'Washington to Moscow Maclean Cables'. All were sent in March 1945. The former US intelligence agent, C. J. Hamrick, claimed that Maclean could have been identified as the leak known as HOMER much earlier, reasoning that the cables, which consisted of highly confidential exchanges between Churchill, Halifax and the British Ambassador in Moscow, Sir Archibald Clark Kerr, about Stalin's apparent backtracking on the Yalta agreements over the setting up of the new Polish government, were seen by only a very small number of diplomats.[70] This was an extremely critical and sensitive matter: after all, Great Britain had declared war on Germany because of its invasion of Poland, and now Britain and the USA were in danger, because of Stalin's duplicity, of ceding the country to the Soviet Union instead. MI5's suggestions, as it investigated the leak, that the evidence indicated that a list of 39 suspects had to be whittled down, are thus probably spurious. Nigel West judged that MI5 "dragged its feet": there was a reason.[71]

Berlin's most intense involvement with Gorsky was between December 1944 and May 1945. Gorsky has been specifically identified, from Soviet archives, as well as from the source texts of the cablegrams, as the agent who transmitted the reports from Washington to Moscow.[72] The first volume of Berlin's *Letters* (dedicated, incidentally, to Jenifer Hart) was published in 2004. Any enterprising analyst who was aware of the Maclean story should have picked up the extraordinary revelations about Berlin's visits to the Soviet Embassy that were revealed in the letters that Berlin wrote to his parents at that time, describing the events, and should have made a linkage between the two events. Certainly the FBI would have regarded such casual contacts as suspicious, and such assignations should have been fraught with danger. As Harvey and Klehr wrote in their book on VENONA: "After Bentley defected in late 1945, the FBI opened an investigation of her Soviet supervisor at the time, Anatoly Gromov [Gorsky's real name], a KGB officer operating out of the Soviet embassy in Washington under the guise of being a Soviet diplomat. A report on the investigation in February 1946 cited several meetings between Gromov and [Lauchlin] Currie. In 1947 the FBI interviewed Currie, who stated that he had met twice with Gromov in early 1945, once at Gromov's residence and once at his, and that they had had at least two other meetings after his leaving government service in June 1945."[73] Currie, Roosevelt's chief economic advisor, was a Soviet spy. Of course, if Berlin's involvement with Burgess in 1940, and his collusion with Maclean in 1944 and

---

[iv] The National Security Agency (NSA) was established in 1952. During World War II, interception and deciphering of the communications of foreign powers was undertaken by the SSA (Signal Security Agency).

1945, were already known, that would have thus helped to provoke the cover-up. At the time, Berlin was either being very naïve, or using his prestige to good effect.

One can search the transcripts of the VENONA archive to determine whether any of Berlin's activities were recorded, and whether Berlin had at any time been given a cryptonym. A large number of names have never been identified, and one message points to a possible link. The VENONA traffic of September 17, 1945, (Moscow to London) refers to EDWARD, mentions his working in Washington from 1939 to early in 1945, and asks about his new place of work, and the politicians with whom he had been in touch.[74] Berlin had arrived in Moscow on around September 12, having been stationed in New York/Washington from 1940 until early 1945, when he was officially transferred from the Ministry of Information to the Foreign Office. Gorsky and Clark Kerr had obviously worked on Molotov to gain Berlin his visa, but it would not be surprising if an official was asked to find out more information about him. If this were ever confirmed, it would not be proof that Berlin had been conducting espionage, as the Soviets used code-names not just for agents, but for 'agents of influence' as well as leading political opponents. Yet Berlin's possession of an official cryptonym at this stage would strongly indicate that Moscow had been in contact with him for some time before.[75]

Why would Berlin undertake such a risky and treacherous activity? It was probably because it helped him gain his Soviet visa, a long-expressed desire since before the war. That is why he had courted Oumansky, and the same goal pushed him towards Gorsky. Berlin had also been in regular touch with the British Ambassador in Moscow, Clark Kerr, (he wrote to his parents about the latter's visiting him in Washington in January 1944), who was a friend and sympathiser, and would no doubt attempt to facilitate matters at the other end. In response to Clark Kerr's letter of February 20, 1944, to Molotov, the Soviet Embassy in London confirmed, on April 20, that a visa had been issued to Berlin for travel to the Soviet Union. Berlin had got his wish. Thus it is probable that the whole incident of the spat at the Graham party was a sham, a set-up to show influential people of the ideological distance between Maclean and Berlin, to demonstrate that Berlin was in truth a reactionary quite out of sympathy with the Soviets, and thus to dispel any possible suspicion about his visits to the Soviet Embassy. In his cups, Maclean may have gone over the top, and fumbled his lines, exaggerating the supposed contempt he felt for Berlin. No other explanation of the anomalies and falsehoods in the account has been suggested. Of course, if Berlin did act in this way, it would put him almost on a level with Burgess and Philby – certainly guilty of more reprehensible behaviour than the noted Stalinist, Eric Hobsbawm.

In any case, Berlin shows himself to have been an utter fabulist. The account of his friendship with Maclean sounds as if it had been invented on the spot, and he was as misleading over Maclean as he was elsewhere over Burgess (who likewise sprung unexpectedly into his room, at Oxford), Alexander Halpern (whom Berlin claimed not to have met until New York in 1941), Straight (whom he denied knowing at all), Philby (whom Burgess refers to in letters to Berlin), Joseph Ball (whom Berlin denied knowing to Rees) and probably many more. It is as if he harboured a deep-seated shame about his earlier associations with so many spies, but thought he could leave a decent legacy intact before he died by lying about the relationships, and trusting he would not be questioned, or that third-party sources would not be able to confirm his deceits. It is an unedifying pattern of behaviour, and in strict contrast to the reputation of the man as a pillar of liberal values, and a dedicated opponent of totalitarianism.

In conclusion, the major irony of these private exploits is that the pair put themselves in greater danger of being detected by British intelligence through harassing Krivitksy and making overtures to members of the Comintern and of the NKVD than if they had left the defector alone. Krivitsky was not going to say any more than he had, and the ball was in MI5's court. But by drawing attention to their Comintern links, and appearing with Philby as Section D officers, they might well have attracted a very watchful eye from a skilful and persistent counter-intelligence officer, such as a Jane Archer, or a shrewd assistant like Milicent Bagot. But the mechanisms for sharing intelligence between the Foreign Office, MI5 and SIS were severely broken. The Joint Intelligence Committee was beset by too many rivalries and lacked clear and crisp direction. MI5 did not have the determination or imagination to take Krivitsky's warnings seriously, and were kept out of the loop on the Moscow Plot, which meant they did not have the inspiration or opportunity to go back to check the files they maintained on the plotters. Burgess was right: Goronwy Rees could have been the major threat to his being unmasked, and if Rees had been a stronger character, he might have been able to stop the subversion at the beginning of the war. Burgess and his friends displayed poor tradecraft by confiding in their friends (Rees, Solomon, and, vicariously, Rosamond Lehmann) directly when they were not absolutely assured of their commitment, but the professionals at MI5 allowed them to get away with it because of poor intelligence integration, and a lack of resolution and insight.

Notes

[1] Details of Krivitsky's movements and achievements are taken primarily from Gary Kern's *A Death in Washington*.

[2] This is confirmed by Guy Liddell's diary entry of September 4. Captain King was sentenced on October 18.

[3] Verne Newton, *The Cambridge Spies*.

[4] The British title was *I Was Stalin's Agent*, published by Hamish Hamilton.

[5] Anthony Cave-Brown, *Treason in the Blood*, p 219.

[6] Nigel West and Oleg Tsarev, *The Crown Jewels*, p 144.

[7] John Cairncross, *The Enigma Spy*, p 75.

[8] ibid., p 213.

[9] *Triplex, Secrets from the Cambridge Spies*, edited by Nigel West and Oleg Tsarev, p 190.

[10] TNA, KV 2/805.

[11] Anthony Glees, *The Secrets of the Service*, pp 20-21.

[12] Andrew, pp 538-540.

[13] Nigel West, *The Historical Dictionary of British Intelligence*, (Second Edition), p 210.

[14] ibid., p 455.

[15] Glees, p 70.

[16] Jenifer Hart, *Ask Me No More*, pp 70-71.

[17] See, for example, the account of Noel Field in Kati Marton's *True Believer: Stalin's Last American Spy.*

[18] Barrie Penrose and Simon Freeman, *Conspiracy of Silence*, p 480.

[19] TNA, KV 2/804.

[20] Christopher Andrew identified Long as the spy named ELLI, a cryptonym revealed by Gouzenko, and judged to be Hollis, Liddell and yet others by various commentators. See *The Defence of the Realm*, pp 350-351.

[21] Pavel and Anatoli Sudoplatov, pp 65-67.

[22] Costello and Tsarev, p 237.

[23] Mary-Kay Wilmers, *The Eitingons*, p 298.

[24] Newton, p 22.

[25] Michael Holzman, *Revolutionary in an Old School Tie*, pp 133-34, quoting Selina Hastings's *Rosamond Lehmann*, p 207.

[26] Costello, *Mask of Treachery*, p 140.

[27] Costello, pp 29-33.

[28] Cairncross, p 82.

[29] TNA, KV/185, February 27, 1940.

[30] Boris Volodarsky, *Stalin's Agent*, p 362.

[31] Michael Straight, *After Long Silence*, pp 142-143.

[32] Damaskin, p 195.

[33] Keith Jeffery, *The Secret History of MI6, 1909-1949*, p 343.

[34] Isaiah Berlin, *Letters 1928-1946*, pp 113-114.

[35] ibid., p 338.

[36] Nicola Lacey, *A Life of H. L. A. Hart, The Nightmare and the Noble Dream*, p 177.

[37] Tape MI7.

[38] *Washington Despatches, 1941-45*, edited by H. G. Nicholas, p vii.

[39] Andrew Boyle, *The Climate of Treason*, pp 195-197.

[40] Tape MI7.

[41] *Letters, 1928-1946*, July 16, 1940, p 315.

[42] ibid., June 21, 1940, p 302.

[43] ibid., January 3, 1941, p 355.

[44] ibid., p 318, p 329.

[45] The diaries have not been published. This information has been provided to the author by Arie Dubnov in a private correspondence.

[46] Arie Dubnov, *Isaiah Berlin*, p 147.

[47] See http://wis-wander.weizmann.ac.il/family-trials#.VZ26Iq5Z148

[48] Ignatieff, p 118.

[49] See http://www.hampsteadshul.org.uk/lectures/diplomacy-and-intelligence-in-the-middle-east/ (The Seventh Annual Isaiah Berlin Lecture, delivered on November 9, 2009).

[50] Isaiah Berlin, *Letters, 1946-1960*, April 10, 1951, p 224. In his posthumous autobiography, *The Man With Two Hats*, p 84, Ya'acov Caroz, one of the founders of Israel's secret services, stated that this lecture was part of a routine Political Studies course. The 1948 occasion remains unconfirmed.

[51] TNA, KN 2/1251/1.

[52] Katherine Graham, *Personal History*, p 155: Michael Holzman, *Donald and Melinda Maclean*, pp 165-166; Ignatieff, pp 128-129.

[53] Goronwy Rees, *A Chapter of Accidents*, p 191.

[54] Graham, p 207.

[55] Verne Newton, *The Cambridge Spies*, p 68.

[56] From private correspondence between the author and Verne Newton, 2013.

[57] It may be coincidental that Berlin used the term 'cultivate' – a classic verb of tradecraft in intelligence which indicates the process of identifying and softening up a potential agent (see, for example, Edward Lucas's *Deception*, p 34).

[58] Richard Breitman, *FDR and the Jews* (2012), p 300. Berlin's interest in Oumansky (Umanskii) may be explained by this passage: "Wise also relayed to FDR that President Edvard Beneš of Czechoslovakia had learned from Stalin that if Britain and the United States approved of a Jewish commonwealth in Palestine, the Soviets would go along. In fact, high Soviet authorities had already signaled to Jewish leaders during the previous year that they favored Jewish immigration to Palestine – even from Eastern European countries – and Jewish hopes for statehood. Soviet ambassador to Mexico Konstantin Umanskii, for example, met in Mexico City with World Jewish Congress cofounder Nahum Goldmann to discuss possible Soviet solutions for a Jewish state. The ambassador even suggested that his government might endorse a joint security guarantee by the Big Three. Umanskii asked Goldmann how many Jews would want to go to Palestine; Goldmann answered as if it were established fact that the Soviets would let perhaps a quarter million Polish and Soviet Jews settle there. A Jewish Palestine would pose challenges for the British Empire, and create opportunities for the Soviets."

[59] *Letters, 1928-1946*, p 476, February 1, 1944, to Noel Malcolm of the Foreign Office.

[60] ibid., December 12, 1944, p 506.

[61] ibid., May 5, 1945, p 501.

[62] The initiation of such a relationship may have come from Bentley herself, who had had an affair with her previous handler, Jacob Golos (who died in her apartment). Bentley was highly-sexed.

[63] John Earl Haynes, Harvey Klehr and Alexander Vassiliev, *Spies*, p 520.

[64] Robert Cecil, *A Divided Self*, p 133.

[65] Pavel and Anatoli Sudoplatov, p 214.

[66] Gorsky had represented his father as a country schoolteacher, when he was in fact a Tsarist police officer. He was instantly dismissed when this fact was discovered in 1953. See Andrew and Gordievsky, *KGB: the Inside Story*, p 293.

[67] Nigel West, *Venona*, p 132.

[68] Robert Cecil, *A Divided Life*, p 77.

[69] S. J. Hamrick, *Deceiving the Deceivers*, Chapter 3.

[70] ibid., p 86.

[71] *Venona*, p 134.

[72] ibid., pp 129-131.

[73] John Earl Haynes and Harvey Klehr, *Venona: Decoding Soviet Espionage in America*, p 147; John Earl Haynes and Harvey Klehr, *In Denial: Historians, Communism & Espionage*, p 175.

[74] See https://www.nsa.gov/public_info/_files/venona/1945/17sep_eduard_igor.pdf

[75] In his compilation of documents that the Cambridge Spies passed on to Moscow ('*Triplex*'), Nigel West included a cable sent by EDWARD to Moscow on November 29, 1944 (p 233). West suggested that Cairncross (previously MOLIERE and LISZT) had been given this cryptonym when he joined SIS. This matter merits further study, as the description of EDWARD in VENONA does not comply with Cairncross's role in London.

Chapter 6: Agents of Influence

"Yes, he is obviously in sympathy with the Communists, perhaps he is even a party member. But that isn't against the law. Besides, you know our Communist intellectuals: they talk ideas, make propaganda, but they aren't militant."
(Carlson, in Helen MacInnes's 'The Venetian Affair')

"While I believe that Blunt dabbled in Communism, I still think it unlikely that he ever became a member." *(Guy Liddell)*

"I am not a member of any political party. I support Russian economic socialism because I think it is a better economic order and nearer Christianity than the capitalist economy of the West." *(Reverend Dr Hewlett Johnson)*

One of MI5's key failures had been a lack of disciplined follow-up to Krivitsky's warnings. It performed no rigorous investigation of the profiles of subversives that he had presented, nor did it pay close attention to the guidance he offered to the Comintern's well-established strategy for the recruitment of Oxbridge graduates, and installing them in government offices. MI5 failed to look deeply into the milieu and societies that might have encouraged such candidates to sign up for service to the Comintern. This was not good tradecraft, of which the spies took full advantage. This chapter explores the web of influence that encouraged and protected the agents themselves, and describes, by focusing on three representative players, how such a shadowy group of influential characters was able to contribute to MI5's struggles.

Three of the group known as the 'Cambridge Spies', namely Burgess, Philby, and Blunt, remained close friends and met frequently. Maclean was slightly less tight-knit with the circle, but still was able to exploit the relationship. All had enjoyed common social ties at Cambridge, their careers crossed, and they supported each other in times of need, such as with Blunt's challenges at Minley Manor, the shock to their confidence triggered by the announcement of the Nazi-Soviet Pact, the task of creating back-up strategies when they were abandoned after Gorsky's recall to Moscow in early 1940, the crisis that emerged when Krivitsky's revelations became known, and the news that the atom scientist Klaus Fuchs was being investigated. While such associations were good for morale, they were in fact very poor tradecraft, breaking the compartmentalisation of lives that Moscow Centre urged. Burgess's dramatic discussion with Goronwy Rees in September 1939 was an example where the ties of friendship might have betrayed the whole group.

If MI5 had taken a forensic approach to the Krivitsky testimony, drawn up a list of candidates, performed their homework properly (such as inspecting the records of the Cambridge University Socialist Club) and then surveilled their suspects in a more disciplined manner (which, after all is what 'keeping an eye on' can only mean), the Security Service would surely have picked up overtly suspicious behaviour. As it was, the fact remained that all four had a history of left-wing thought (and sometimes action), had then undergone public changes in political conviction, but later passed some test of their political commitment during an interview process. Maclean at his Civil Service Appointments Board, Philby in Vienna, and then with the Anglo-German Fellowship Society and his review by Vivian at SIS, Blunt with his reputation for communistic journalism facing obstacles at Military Intelligence, and finally Burgess's double volte-face with the same Fellowship Society before his assumed admission of familiarity with Comintern officials, and his rejection by MI5: all these events should have alerted MI5 officers to a pattern that merited closer investigation.

Yet the blurring of lines helped the spies, and misled the protectors of the realm. A recognisable continuum of left-wing thought existed, from dedicated (but secret) Communist agents through agents of influence, fellow-travellers, and open Communists to those more florid Socialists who claimed they wanted to build the proletarian paradise through parliamentary processes. Some of the latter, such as Dennis Pritt and Ellen Wilkinson, had been fairly elected as Members of Parliament before engaging in conspiratorial behaviour with Comintern agents that was highly subversive. Moreover, the fatal misconception that leading officers in MI5 harboured, namely that communism in well-educated Britons was a mere affectation of no consequence, encouraged them to ignore the warning signs and trust such characters because of their obvious intelligence and savoir-faire.

The most obvious in this category was Anthony Blunt [*see Chapter 5*], who had successfully overcome objections to his recruitment by Military Intelligence that were prompted by his authorship of Marxist articles in the *Spectator*. Liddell showed his naivety about the divisibility of Communist thinking when Blunt first came under suspicion in 1951 and 1952. Blunt was able to convince Liddell that he thought Burgess was "working for anti-fascism, not the Comintern", Liddell concluding that the art historian was not "Communist in full political sense".[1] A year later, he was echoing the same theme: "While I believe that BLUNT dabbled in Communism, I still think it unlikely that he ever became a member. He was, however, on his own admission, deeply interested in the Marxian interpretation of art, and is in fact still interested. He denies, however, that he ever believed in the Russian application of Marxian thought. He has nearly all his life been absorbed in artistic matters that it seems unlikely that he has ever really been interested in politics."[2] Here Liddell betrayed three crucial flaws in one short paragraph: the belief that only Communist Party members could do harm; the assumed separability of communist thinking on art from its political ideology; and an inability to consider that such a person under suspicion might be economical with the truth, in short, to discount the craft of subterfuge.

Another intellectual who benefitted from such misjudgment was the less illustrious but still highly influential agent James Klugmann [*see Chapter 7*], who, despite, an open commitment to Communism politically, was still considered harmless, such beliefs not being seen as any threat to the health of the Empire since they were assumed to be removed from any practical consequences. British intelligence officers seemed to adopt blinkers when they assessed the risk represented by such Englishmen who were certainly better educated than they were themselves, but nourished subversive ideas. It is as if they had learned nothing from the exploits of Stephen Spender, who had joined the Party, and in early 1937 undertaken a mission to Spain on its behalf [*see this chapter, p 21*]. MI5 had watched this exploit with amazement: how could this character, whom Cyril Connolly called "an inspired simpleton, a great big silly goose, a holy Russian idiot, large, generous, gullible, ignorant, affectionate, idealistic", ever be a dangerous Soviet spy?[3]

On the contrary, the more intelligent of the MI5 officers – those whose company Hugh Trevor-Roper appreciated, as opposed to the humdrum time-servers he believed dominated Britain's intelligence structure – found mixing socially with such men stimulating and rewarding. "There are only two classes of men in the British Secret Service – those who protect their incompetence by neurotic secrecy, and those who screen it with bombastic advertisement", he wrote, commenting on his experiences in the Radio Security Service.[4] Trevor-Roper certainly enjoyed the company of White and Liddell. For Dick White, it was a natural habit to mix with such congenial persons and discuss high art and intellectual issues. For a non-Oxbridge man like Guy Liddell, who had musical talents of his own, it was flattering to be invited to associate with such as Blunt, Burgess and Rothschild. Yet becoming absorbed into such a liberal intellectual milieu must inevitably have damaged the objectivity of these prominent counter-intelligence officers. And this milieu contained its share of characters who exercised a more subtle pressure on political events – the so-called 'agents of influence'.

The subject of 'agents of influence' has not received the attention it deserves, yet some commentators assert that such persons could be even more dangerous than 'penetration agents', spies who handed over documents. While spies provided the enemy with information that might help with policy or with negotiations (such as Soviet preparation for the Yalta conference), agents of influence could directly manipulate policy so that such manoeuvres were no longer necessary. Such agents worked in a twilight world: not members of the Communist Party, but identified by the Soviets as allies with an ability to influence domestic policy. (Such figures were frequently named in messages exchanged between the *rezidentura* and Moscow, as the VENONA decrypts show. Not all persons identified were agents of influence, but the cryptonyms of many who must have performed damage have still not been assigned to their real counterparts.) These agents were careful never to be engaged in the act of passing physical information to a Soviet handler, but might consort with Soviet diplomats in their official roles. In their study of such actors in the USA, where a large body was installed in government departments, Evans and Romerstein showed how such persons as Alger Hiss, Harry Dexter White, and Lauchlin Currie were able to assist major policy initiatives in such areas as material support to the Soviets, and negotiations over Poland and China.[5] They concluded: "But a fixation on cases in which suspects were caught passing documents to Soviet handlers excludes numerous agents, contacts, and episodes with impact on policy matters. As espionage convictions were relatively few and far between, this self-denying method drastically understates the extent of the Cold War security problem."[6] As proof of the extent of the subversion, the authors cited the infamous 'Gorsky memo' of 1948, which reported to Moscow that 60 agents of influence, all identified, had been put at risk by the revelations of Whittaker Chambers and Elizabeth Bentley. The document was disclosed by the defector Alexander Vassiliev. Anatoly Gorsky was the same *rezident* who had handled the spies in London, then Maclean in Washington, and whom Isaiah Berlin had tried to cultivate.

As far as is known, the United Kingdom was not infected to such a large degree, or so systematically. The process by which such agents gained influence had been similar, but much more discreet. In the USA, a strict ban on the recruitment of communists had been in effect before Pearl Harbor, yet not long after, it was ruled illegal even to ask candidates what their political affiliations were. By the end of the war, the Soviets were remarkably able to arrange for the dismissal of government officers who were 'unfriendly'. Loy Henderson, who had taken up Krivitsky's cause, and continued to question the USA's appeasement towards the Soviet Union, was banished to Iraq.[7] As has been shown, in the UK, agents of influence had for some years been subtly easing their way into positions where they could alter policy. The culture of militant anti-bolshevism that had prevailed in the USA simply did not exist: matters were not so black-and-white. Thus, outside the obvious strident Communist sympathisers like Laski, Cripps and Wilkinson lay a group of well-respected figures who could pull strings less obviously – people like Victor Rothschild, Walter Monckton and Rudolf Peierls. (The career and role of Peierls will be covered in depth in Chapters 8 and 9.)

In 1955, the Joint Chiefs of Staff performed a post mortem on the Burgess-Maclean affair. This was a more serious investigation than one that took place immediately after the defection, in 1951. The latter, under Foreign Office auspices, was crucially flawed in that it was chaired by Sir Alexander Cadogan, who could not really be described as objective, since he had put his signature to a document in March 1944, requesting that Burgess be transferred from the BBC to the News Department of the Foreign Office. Yet some of the evidence, which has only recently been released, is astonishing: Dick White indicated that MI5 had known about Burgess's peccadilloes, but for that reason didn't believe that he would have been capable of espionage, stating also, in very loose and imprecise terms, that the Security Service "had not regarded him as a member of the Communist Party". White went on to say that "Burgess had given the strong impression in his large circle of acquaintances that he had been a Communist at one time but severed his connection with the Communists at the time of the German-Soviet pact of 1939".[8] This convenient excuse overlooks the fact that Burgess had before then been a member of the Anglo-German Fellowship: White's uneasy testimony does not appear to have been questioned. The output of this committee was predictably feeble, the conclusion being that no serious problems existed in the recruitment practices of the Intelligence Services or the Foreign Office.

The 1955 Committee applied itself in a more disciplined fashion. Its report concluded, among other things, that "Burgess and Maclean were Soviet agents for many years prior to their defection. They were apparently protected from exposure and dismissal for a long time by other highly placed officials of the British government, particularly the Foreign Office."[9] This was a significant admission, echoing what had been reported to Sir Ivone Kirkpatrick when he became Permanent Under-Secretary of State for Foreign Affairs in 1953.[10] Later, the British government indicated that it did not want Burgess to return to the UK since it said it had no evidence it could use in court to prove that Burgess was a spy. Yet Burgess was not named in VENONA transcripts (the obvious reason for secrecy): if the government had evidence, why was it not prepared for a court-case?

The 1955 report did not identify who these abetting officials were, and did not say whether they should have been charged with negligence and incompetence, or with conspiracy. Moreover, the identification of the Foreign Office as especially responsible focused the spotlight more on Maclean and the latter years of the spies' activity, and would have deflected the attention of the curious away from some more deserving candidates, such as Joseph Ball, to less obvious figures, such as Gladwyn Jebb. What is extraordinary is that British officials claimed that Burgess had had no involvement in intelligence matters in the critical years of 1939 and 1940. When a statement had to be made to the House of Commons, Sir Patrick Reilly helped prepare the speech. Reilly, who had worked at the Ministry of Economic Warfare before being appointed Private Secretary to the head of SIS in 1942, indicated that Burgess's sole employer since leaving Cambridge had been the BBC, after which he joined the Foreign Office in 1948, as if he had never been associated with British intelligence beforehand. The Moscow Plot was conveniently concealed and forgotten, and the collapsing of Burgess's career became a fiction that was eagerly echoed elsewhere, and never challenged. Thus, while also rather arrogantly claiming that he could have changed the outcome of the Burgess/Maclean affair had he been a member of the Promotions Board in 1950, Reilly was in actuality an accessory to the wholesale cover-up that affected the security services as well as the civil service.[11]

It is overall very clear, however, that the spies were able to exploit an extended support network, which had a political, an intellectual, and a social dimension. This chapter analyses the roles of three important and representative allies who were involved with the Moscow Plot, with differing degrees of culpability and commitment: Victor Rothschild, Gladwyn Jebb, and Isaiah Berlin. It spends most time on the contribution of the last, for several reasons: because of Berlin's hitherto unblemished yet unmerited reputation, his under-publicised contribution to Marxian studies, his intimate friendship with the Communist Party operative and booster, Stephen Spender, the range of his work in intelligence (and especially his dubious contacts with NKVD agents), despite his persistent denial that he was involved at all, and, lastly, his role as a conspirator with the arch-traitor, Guy Burgess, in the Moscow Plot, and his curious relationship with Donald Maclean.

Victor, Third Baron Rothschild, appears as an enigmatic, but potentially very influential, figure in the story. He was an illustrious name, a talented scientist, and had also been a member of the Apostles at Cambridge, where he became friends with Burgess, Philby and Blunt. Burgess had acquired a position as financial adviser to Rothschild's mother in 1935, but the spy Michael Straight believed that this was a front for channelling Burgess's energies into spying on the Nazis, and that it was the Rothschilds who launched Burgess on his career in espionage (see below). Rothschild himself was meanwhile engaged in elevating his status and influence in government affairs, making useful contacts and building a reputation. According to Andrew Lownie's 2015 biography of Burgess, when Burgess's friend David Footman in 1938 introduced Burgess to Commodore Norman of SIS for a job, Norman confided in him that Rothschild was working "on a secret scientific project at Cambridge for the War Office".[12]

The first documented sign of Rothschild's involvement in intelligence matters, probably facilitated by Burgess, is his sudden appearance in the operation of MI5's counter-espionage division. On March 28, 1940, Guy Liddell, then deputy head of that division ('B'), recorded in his diary (in an entry that does not appear in the published version) that "[Lord] Rothschild is going to France under cover of MI5, on sabotage business."[13] Rothschild's work at Cambridge becomes clear. He had been working, as personal assistant to Sir Harold Hartley, on issues of sabotage and unconventional (primarily chemical) warfare for a government department called MI/R, and had engaged in occasional discussions with Liddell on such topics.[14] The first of these discussions had taken place on February 15, the day before Krivitsky left for Canada, which might suggest that Burgess was aware of Krivitsky's presence in London at the time. By April 18, Liddell was pleased to report that Rothschild had "offered his services to MI5", and three days later, he could record that his boss, Jasper Harker, had agreed to take on Rothschild part-time, "with Hankey's approval". Lord Hankey, as explained earlier, was at this time performing an analysis of the efficiency of the three intelligence services (MI5, SIS and GC&CS), and would thus have to be informed of such a move, and to bless it. Lord Rothschild moved quickly: by April 25, Liddell was proudly able to state that he was "coming in to look at our files", and that the department would gain "the benefit of his advice and assistance 3 times a week". MI5, by its own admission in a rather chaotic state at this time, was gaining some free consultative advice from a man of obvious ability, honesty and integrity. Later that summer, Rothschild was installed as head of B1(C) (Sabotage), working for Liddell, logically alongside Herbert Hart, who headed B1 (B) (Special Research), having been recommended to Guy Liddell as a recruit by his future wife, Jenifer.

Towards the end of his life, Lord Rothschild busied himself vigorously trying to get himself exonerated from insinuations that he had been a Soviet spy. The MI5 officer Peter Wright had delved deeply into the MI5 files, and had in 1968 been encouraged by the defector Anatoli Golitsin to suggest that Victor and Tess Rothschild might have been the spies indicated by the cryptonyms DAVID and ROSA in VENONA traffic, hitherto unidentified.[15] More recently, Jonathan Haslam has recorded that "several retired operatives of the KGB long insisted that he [Rothschild] was recruited as an agent": Haslam opined that it was a suspicion that Rothschild "never really shed, although the proof is lacking."[16] Andrew Lownie quoted a letter from the American spy who was also recruited at Cambridge, Michael Straight, written to the journalist and author John Costello: "The tie between the Rothschilds and the Soviet intelligence service was, in my opinion, the skeleton in the closet which drove V. R. to fund Wright, in writing a book [*Spycatcher*] in which the role of the Rothschilds would be wholly excised."[17] Of course, Straight should perhaps not be trusted unconditionally, but it was his evidence that unmasked Anthony Blunt, and, at this late stage of his life, maybe he sincerely wanted to correct the record.

Rothschild was very sensitive over any such allegations. "The Director-General of MI5 should state publicly that it has unequivocal, repeat unequivocal, evidence that I am not, and have never been a Soviet agent", Rothschild wrote in a letter to the *Daily Telegraph*, published on December 3 1986. To prove such a negative would have been an impossible task for any intelligence chief, and his lordship did perhaps protest too much. The story was amplified in Roland Perry's not highly scholarly book *The Fifth Man*, which, in a somewhat haphazard chronological context, makes the claim that it was Rothschild, not Cairncross, who was the legitimate 'Fifth Man' of the Cambridge Five.[18] This is perhaps the wrong way of making any case that Rothschild might have been a vital contributor to the Communist – and Zionist – cause. Certainly it does not diminish Cairncross's treason, but Rothschild was probably not a named agent for the Soviets in the way that the traditional members of the Cambridge Spies were. Parry nevertheless makes a reasonable case that Rothschild, while being very careful not to ever pass any secret directly on to any Soviet control himself, might well have assisted the Comintern by passing on information via his close friends, Burgess and Blunt, especially, and may have used his reputation and influence to alter the climate in which communists were viewed in government.

Ample evidence exists of Rothschild's snooping, and his belief that the Soviets, as a wartime ally, should be handed more information. Even his sycophantic biographer, Kenneth Rose, drew attention to the episode in Paris, towards the end of 1944, when Rothschild and Kim Philby vigorously argued that secret traffic derived from the Ultra decrypts should be passed on to the Russians.[19] And Guy Liddell's *Diaries* show several incidents where Rothschild used his influence to wheedle information from the all-too-trusting Liddell. In one notorious and thinly veiled extract, Rothschild asked Liddell for a list of scientists working on atomic research, so that he might pass it to a reputable unnamed friend "who worked with the team in Canada and also with Joliot-Curie", so that the friend could help identify those with "doubtful" persuasions, claiming that the friend would do a better job than the Harwell Security Officer, Arnold. Liddell duly handed over the list, and no doubt Hans Halban[i] (for the nuclear scientist who was banished from the USA because of his Franco-Communist ties was surely the contact) would soon pass the list on to the Communist Joliot-Curie.[20] Yet, allowing for the degree to which the impressionable Liddell was easily manipulated, the evidence of his journals shows Rothschild in a positive light: when, in July 1943, many officers of MI5 felt that the Director-General, Petrie, would probably soon resign, Rothschild, despite his inexperience, was one of those suggested as his replacement, by Duff Cooper and others.[21] Given Rothschild's machinations in MI5, and later reputation and protestations, this

---

[i] Halban had been the second husband of Isaiah Berlin's wife, Aline (née de Gunzbourg) (1915-2014: m. to Berlin 1956).

"We shall remain strictly neutral and defend our territorial integrity at all costs."

"Of course, at the moment it's still just a suspicion."

Britain was generally horrified about the advances [of] Communism and Fascism, but irresolute over how [to] resist them. This cartoon indicates the helplessness [of] the Baltic States as they were carved up between [Ge]rmany and the Soviet Union (see Chapter 1)

2. MI5 struggled with the notion of subterfuge, namely that subversives would disguise their identity and ideological commitments, and thus it suffered from the delusion that Stalin's agents would naturally belong to the Communist Party (see Chapter 2)

"Ex-service men? Certainly not—that's the regimental band of M.I.5."

"Anybody here from M.I.5 . . . Anybody here from M.I.5 . . ."

The defector Walter Krivitsky warned of communist [in]filtration in the corridors of British power, but his [wa]rnings were ignored. MI5 believed the communists it [rec]ruited were harmless intellectuals (see Chapter 3)

4. The existence of SIS (MI6) as a counter-espionage organisation was a state secret: Lancaster depicted foreign intelligence exploits as if staged by MI5. Burgess and Berlin set out on their mission to Moscow, although working for SIS's D Section, with the cover of diplomats (see Chapters 4 & 5)

"Heard any good careless talk lately?"

5. 'Agents of influence' were frequently more dangerous than spies who actually stole and passed on documents, as they were trusted in positions of authority,
had access to vital information, but were (mostly) careful never to get their hands dirty (see Chapter 6)

"I'm being dropped by parachute on Lord's to co-opera
with the Fifth Column of the M.C.C."

6. The 'Fifth Column' scare may have been artificiall
provoked, and it was quashed by the same man who I
helped to engineer it, Winston Churchill. In any case,
provided a useful distraction from the investigation i
communists (see Chapter 7)

"Funny. I thought we told the Home
Office to pull him in weeks ago."

7. MI5 and the Home Office were perpetually troubled
by the task of identifying threats to the war effort – especially when such figures were refugees from Hitler's
Germany. Were leftists opposed to Fascism useful
democratic allies, or representatives of the enduring
communist menace? (see Chapters 8 & 9)

'It's a fine state of ecclesiastical
affairs when the Dean of Canterbury believes everything he reads
in Pravda, and the Bishop of
Birmingham doesn't believe half
he reads in the Bible.'

1.iii.49

8. The Soviet Union's role as an ally, and the delusion by some that Stalin would help construct a new
democratic post-war order, contributed to Labour's
1945 election victory. It would take some years befor
Soviet ruthlessness in Eastern Europe struck home (se
Chapter 10)

9. Isaiah Berlin

spite his insistence that he was never involved with elligence matters, Berlin worked for SIS, and devel- :d ill-judged relationships with members of the Cam- dge Five as well as with Soviet intelligence personnel.

10. Guy Burgess

Burgess's outrageous behaviour, and his connections with both the right-wing and the Comintern, disarmed his colleagues into thinking they were attributes of his role as a fixer.

11. Harold ('Kim') Philby

ilby's activities in Vienna, his marriage to a commu- st, and the hints provided by Krivitsky should have masked him before he joined SIS.

12. Klaus Fuchs

Fuchs never concealed his communist affiliations: MI5 tried to cover up its oversights in assessing the risks of his contributing to atomic weapons research.

13. Rudolf Peierls

Peierls maintained deep connections with Soviet intelligence, and sought to recruit Fuchs to the atomic weapons project while the latter was still interned in Canada.

14. Ursula Beurton (SONIA)

Ursula Beurton, née Kuczynski, achieved a remarkab escape from Switzerland under SIS's eyes, and then proceeded to work brazenly as Fuchs's intermediary.

15. Guy Liddell

As head of MI5's counter-espionage B Division, Liddell was clever and curious, but never prepared the organisation to deal with the reality of Soviet subversion.

16. Lord Rothschild

Rothschild was a classic communist 'agent of influenc who used his position and reputation subtly to und mine British institutions on behalf of the Soviet cause

17. **Dick White**

18. **Kathleen ('Jane') Archer (née Sissmore)**

e first Oxbridge graduate to be hired by the Intelli-
nce Services, Dick White was the only man to head
em both, but his decency blinded him to the tactic of
bterfuge.

MI5's leading expert on Communist espionage, Archer
was roughly dispensed with as soon as she completed
the interrogation of Krivitsky.

19. **Lord Halifax & Maxim Litvinov**

20. **Walter Krivitsky**

ord Halifax, a cannier politician than he appeared,
otted with Churchill to deceive Hitler. The dismissal
f Maxim Litvinov, a Jew and Anglophile, as Foreign
ommissar, signalled the solidifying of Soviet-German
egotiations in 1939.

Krivitsky felt betrayed by Stalin, but remained a staunch
communist until his assassination by Stalin's goons. MI5
did not understand defectors like him.

"WHERE'S YOUR PERMIT FOR THAT FIREARM?"

" Who was that foreign-looking fellow who insisted on seeing the plans? "

"What I said was, 'My husband is leaving on a frantically hush-hush mission to Belgrade on Tuesday!'"

"Now, if we're going to put this over properly, you'll have to learn German."

"You remember my telling you all about my job last month? Well, it's no longer hush-hush."

THE TWO CONSTRICTORS

"I don't know about helping you, Adolf, but I *do* understand your point of view!"

scenario is perhaps the closest credible circumstance for having a 'mole' installed at the head of Britain's Security Service.

Later, Rothschild would use his influence and charm to distract attention from himself. After Burgess and Maclean absconded in May 1951, a serious investigation into the friends and associates of the pair was initiated, and Guy Liddell started to reflect on who else may have contaminated the intelligence services. While Blunt expressed his astonishment at the whole affair when the Press picked up on his friendship and collaboration with Burgess, and Philby gave vent to his disgust with Burgess's behaviour, Rothschild sprang into action to help direct the investigation. He and his second wife Tess[ii] had dinner with Liddell in mid-June, Liddell's diary entry for June 12 running: "They were as confused about Burgess as we were. Tess, however, thought that it would be worth our while to keep an eye on James Klugmann, who was at one time a fairly close friend of Burgess and the moving spirit of his group at Cambridge."[22] Liddell may not have been completely taken in, as the investigations appeared not to exclude any of the associates of the two spies. Records recently released to the National Archives indicate that Rothschild had clumsily attempted to distance himself from Burgess, claiming, in 1956, that he had told Liddell at the time of Burgess's "unsuitability to go to Russia". This is especially ironic given his sister's insertion into the drama, and Purvis and Hilbert pointed out that MI5 for some reason did not follow up this insight with Liddell, who was still alive when Rothschild made his claim.[23]

When Rothschild was looked into, it seems that clumsy efforts were made to protect him. In the file on W. H. Auden in the National Archives, the former Special Branch interrogator, William Skardon, who had joined MI5 in 1940 (and who was credited with eliciting a confession from the atom spy, Klaus Fuchs: see Chapter 9) is recorded as interviewing Burgess's lover Peter Pollock, on June 12, 1952, during an exercise to find out who might have known more about Burgess (and thus, presumably, to determine where mistakes were made). The text runs as follows: "Goronwy Rees he thought to be a more recent friend and Isaiah Berlin he [Burgess] admired and knew fairly well. Pollock spoke of the Bentinck Street ménage, consisting of Burgess, [*name redacted*], Tess Mayer and Pat Rawdon-Smith. He had been at Tom Wylie's parties at the War Office, but even now was unable to give a positive appreciation of Guy Burgess's politics."[24] The redacted name can clearly be distinguished as Rothschild's: moreover, the name of his future wife appears next to his. Rothschild indeed had influence and clout, and carried the prestige of his peerage. Much later on, Rothschild was to disarm the inquisitive and suspicious MI5 officer, Peter Wright, who came to idolise his noble acquaintance, partly because he deigned to be so patient with an uneducated 'technician' such as him. "I doubt if I have ever met a man who impressed me as much as Victor Rothschild", he wrote.[25]

What is strange is that there appears to be no public or academic storm of protest at Roland Perry's allegations – just mild objections, as if either the unpleasant odour would go away if it were ignored, or that there was so much that

---

[ii] Having divorced Barbara (née Hutchinson) (1911-1989), Rothschild married his MI5 assistant, Tess Mayer (1915-1996), a Cambridge friend, in 1946.

appeared close to probable truth that his assertions could not really be countered. Certainly Rothschild had helped Burgess earlier in his career, most notably in 1935, when Burgess was being courted by the Soviet illegal Arnold Deutsch, and being required to abandon his attempt to gain a fellowship through writing a Marxist thesis, and needed money. Rothschild gave him that position as a 'financial consultant', when in fact the job was to aid "with a Rothschild-backed publication of surveys on economic and political matters being run by a German Communist émigré named Rudolph Katz."[26] Rothschild was known to operate occasionally in an erratic manner: Rose wrote about his "shadowy" role in introducing the author Chapman Pincher to Peter Wright as "the ghost-writer of Pincher's *Their Trade is Treachery*".[27] A solid and straightforward biography of him remains to be written. Kenneth Rose's offering is a very restrained and cautious affair, in which Rothschild's many and varied energetic contributions to the Zionist cause and the development of atomic power by the Israeli government are conspicuously overlooked. What is certain, however, is that Rothschild was quickly installed within MI5, where his authority and reputation enabled him to perform serious damage control on behalf of Stalin's Englishmen and Englishwomen.

Thus Rothschild's stature and influence enabled him to provide an excellent cover of respectability for Burgess, yet avoid having to explain himself over his apparent connivance at Burgess's misdeeds. Overall, Burgess's friends (apart from Goronwy Rees) were very careful to indicate that they knew nothing about his treachery, or even his political affiliations. Berlin told Ignatieff (with a bizarre reversal of ideas): "I never knew he was a Communist, not even an agent."[28] Jebb similarly defended himself, as previously reported: "Not that I had any reason to suspect that Burgess was a Communist, still less a Soviet agent". Dick White bizarrely claimed he only met Burgess once, but also vouchsafed the following observation to his biographer, Tom Bower: "he [Burgess] behaved so badly that no one could have thought for a moment that he was a spy", as if the group of intellectuals who gathered together during the war were on the lookout for betrayals of espionage activity from their friends.[29] And yet a recent insight from the son of Isaiah Berlin's closest friend, Stephen Spender, belies all this, indicating that Burgess used an outrageous ploy to make his possible role as a spy appear ludicrous.

When, in 1951, MI5 and the Special Branch engaged in that series of interviews with anybody of importance who had known Burgess, in order to determine why his treacherous activities had gone unnoticed, Berlin was one of those interviewed (but Rothschild apparently was too elevated to be interrogated). And according to Spender's son, Matthew, his father was also questioned – although the poet's MI5 file denies it. As Matthew, in his recent memoir[30], explained it, William Skardon, the afore-mentioned MI5 interrogator, arranged to interview Spender on July 9, 1951 in Oxford, but they missed each other, and MI5 decided not to reschedule the meeting. As the file says: "At one time it was thought that it might be worthwhile interviewing Spender but after further consideration the idea was dropped as it was thought he could produce no further information."[31]

Yet Matthew Spender says he knows otherwise. As he wrote: "This is what Spender's MI5 file says, but I don't believe it. My father told me that in fact he <u>had</u> been interrogated. He was asked if he was aware that Guy Burgess was a Communist agent. And he'd said: Yes. 'Whenever Guy got drunk, which was almost every night, he'd tell us he was a Russian spy.' Why had he not reported this information to the appropriate authorities? 'I thought that if we all knew, you must know, too'."[32] Matthew Spender drew the obvious conclusion that, if that assertion were true, a whole host of Burgess's friends, including Liddell, Dick White, and Rothschild of MI5, and all those who socialised at Rothschild's Bentinck Street flat during the war, would have heard the same drunken admission.[33] Thus a vital cover-up occurred, concealing this damning evidence. At the time, his too-generous friends probably rolled their eyes, agreeing: 'There goes Guy being absurd again!', until the horrific news of his defection informed them that what he had been saying was absolutely true. Burgess's cover was describing his role unflinchingly, knowing he would not be taken seriously. When he later absconded to the Soviet Union, and then gave a press conference, in February, 1956, his statement ran: "Neither in the BBC nor in the Foreign Office, nor during the period that he [Burgess] was associated with the Secret Service and also MI5 itself, did he make any secret from his friends or colleagues either of his views or the fact that he had been a Communist." And then Burgess threw his mask right back in the faces of his ex-colleagues and friends: "His attitude in the positions was completely incompatible with the allegation that he was a Soviet agent."[34] As the ex-SIS officer Malcolm Muggeridge slyly wrote: "But for his unfortunate withdrawal to Moscow, he [Burgess] would almost certainly have thriven at MI6. His temperament was exactly right – flamboyant, untruthful, deceitful and energetic. Intelligence Services are unfortunate in that, the more suitable a person is for recruitment to them, the more disastrous he is like to prove."[35]

Burgess was in a powerful position. Like his fellow-spy Anthony Blunt, he had knowledge of a highly secret mission on which he had been personally engaged. Revelations of it would have been extremely embarrassing for the British government. He was thus allowed to get away with outrageous behaviour for years. Burgess did probably not tell Churchill or Halifax that he was a Soviet spy, as they surely did not see him in his cups, but it was almost certain that he did not hold back in disclosing his sympathies for the Soviets. That admission led to one of the most bizarre, puzzling, and shocking intelligence episodes of WWII, the Moscow Plot – one with which, even 75 years later, the British intelligence organisations still struggle to come to terms. We are still waiting (as Lukacs has reminded us) for that sensitivity to evaporate. And we are left with Isaiah Berlin's provocative epitaph on the whole affair of the Plot, that it was Rothschild who had engineered Burgess's recall from Washington in 1940, on the grounds of Burgess's unreliability[36] – a scenario so unlikely, given what we know of the chronology, but one that might give a hint that Rothschild's overall knowledge of the mission and its objectives meant that he was the architect behind it.

To shed further light on the contradictions and dilemmas of the Moscow Plot, and the possible cover-up from the Foreign Office, we turn to a civil servant who was closely involved with these events of 1940, someone who should thus presumably have been objective and unprejudiced about the whole affair, Gladwyn Jebb. Jebb – later Lord Gladwyn – turns up, Zelig-like, at all phases of the adventure. He is critical for the story since, as liaison between the Foreign Office and MI5, he was involved in all phases of the Krivitsky interrogations as well as the mission to Moscow, and should presumably have been able to give a complete and balanced account of the events. Given the comments of the Chiefs of Staff about Burgess's protectors in the Foreign Office, and the fact that there are few prominent persons who were witnesses to the key events of the Moscow Plot, Jebb's role merits special attention. He was Cadogan's Private Secretary at the time of the Krivitsky affair, and was present at some of the interviews that Liddell stage-managed. He was Hankey's right-hand man in guiding the official analysis of the intelligence services: part of his expertise derived from the fact that he had worked for SIS in Italy before the war.[37] He saw the final MI5 reports on Krivitsky[38], and it was he who in 1986 advised Christopher Andrew that Krivitsky's reference to "a young man in the Foreign Office of good family" (omitting other clues, such as his previous bohemian habits, his Scottish background, and his custom of wearing a cape) was too vague to have enabled MI5 to uncover Maclean in 1940.[39]

Jebb was later to repeat this particular claim to Verne Newton, this time actually distorting Krivitsky's evidence, stating, in a letter to Newton, that he had little information, apart from the following item: ". . . there was a man of a 'good family' in the Foreign Office who was giving away information to the Russians, but as he could go no further in describing this person – who it turned out later was clearly [*sic*] Donald Maclean – we were unable to pursue our investigation very far."[40] Newton adds, in a footnote, that Jebb asserted that his interview with Krivitsky appeared in his Memoirs ". . . which is not so. It might be that he did include it originally, but that it may have been subsequently excised by the Foreign Office." In any event, Jebb appears here to take some responsibility for the half-hearted investigation that took place at the time. Costello, on the other hand, stated that Jebb was "carefully vague about why Krivitsky was so valuable an informant" when he interviewed him in 1982.[41] As a permanent civil servant with special responsibilities between the Foreign office and MI5, Jebb did not appear to take them seriously enough. If information was being given away, the leakages were not going to be stopped under his watch.

Later in 1940, in July, Jebb was seconded to Hugh Dalton as Chief Executive of the Special Operations Executive (a position he did not hold for long). As Chapter 4 explained, Cadogan may not have been upset to see him go. Jebb was also a close friend of Harold Nicolson, and supported him after Churchill appointed Nicolson to the Ministry of Information. It was at this stage, in June 1940, that Nicolson introduced Isaiah Berlin to Jebb after Berlin was offered his apparent 'invitation' to become a press attaché in Moscow. Jebb in turn introduced Berlin to the colourful Laurence Grand, who headed Section D, responsible for sabotage and subversion, which was later to be folded into SOE. As one of Jebb's roles was liaison between the Foreign Office and MI5, while Burgess fulfilled the same role between the Ministry of Information and MI6, they must have been closely familiar with each other. Moreover, Jebb occasionally betrayed his sympathies for the Communists. An Anglo-American intelligence reassessment of the post-war threat of the Soviet Union began in the months before D-Day, and Stephen Dorril wrote of Jebb in his history of SIS as follows: "In August 1943, they [the Chiefs of Staff] had established a Post-Hostilities Planning Sub-Committee (PHP) chaired by Gladwyn Jebb, who was in immediate conflict with the chiefs insistent on the identification of the Soviet Union as the only potential enemy after the defeat of Germany. Jebb described PHP members as 'would-be drinkers of Russian blood'."[42]

Jebb had also showed poor judgment when, in reviewing plans to send an SOE mission to Moscow, he expressed enthusiasm for encouraging Soviet agents to be inserted into the British Empire. As Michael Smith wrote: "The Foreign Office pointed out the rather obvious dangers of helping Soviet agents infiltrate the cornerstones of the Empire, but Gladwyn Jebb, then executive head of SOE, defended the proposal. In a remarkably naïve assessment of the organisation that would soon change its name to the KGB, Jebb said: 'These agents will not be Comintern men but agents of the Russian National State Police. I really do not think therefore that there need be any apprehensions.' Both the Foreign Office and MI6 rightly rejected the suggestion as suicidal."[43] Cradock echoed this view of Jebb's judgment, although Cradock is rather more flattering about Jebb's qualities than either Cadogan or Churchill was, describing him as "one of the Foreign Office's brightest stars", who was "highly intelligent and self-confident".[44] Yet Jebb reflected the current Rooseveltean philosophy (influenced by Anthony Eden) of the Foreign Office at the time, which was to treat Stalin and his henchmen as men of good will, who harboured pacifist ambitions close to its own.

Berlin was quite open about Jebb's role. In his Introduction to *Washington Despatches*, Berlin explained that Harold Nicolson invited him to go to Moscow as press attaché, and that it was put to him by "Mr Gladwyn Jebb of the Foreign office, who was concerned with such appointments, that, with my knowledge of Russian and interest in Russian culture, I could be of use at the Embassy in Moscow".[45] Berlin went into further detail in his conversations with Ignatieff, explaining, since Foreign Office approval was required (Nicolson being in the Ministry of Information), that Nicolson said: "So would you mind going to see a rather good looking young man, handsome young man called Gladwyn Jebb, he is the Private Secretary of the Permanent Under Secretary, Harry [*sic!*] Cadogan and talk to him about it."[46]

Jebb turned out to be very enthusiastic about the mission. He expressed his hope to Berlin that he would not mind being accompanied by Burgess, who was on work of a different sort, explained that they would both be taking diplomatic bags, recommended that Berlin obtain his visa in Washington from the Soviet Ambassador there, Oumansky, who had apparently more clout than Maisky in London,[iii] and then took Berlin to see Colonel Grand. What is crucial about this dialogue is that Berlin wanted to make sure that his audience recognised that Burgess's mission was quite distinct from his own. We have no statement from Jebb about the scene, so it may have been partially invented. (Jebb did not die

---

[iii] How Jebb knew this is not clear. We are, however, relying on Berlin's possibly unreliable account of the episode.

until 1996, but may not have read Berlin's *Letters*.) Jebb was very cagey about his involvement with Burgess, trying to set a clear distance between them. He also claimed responsibility – probably erroneously – for firing him, writing in his *Memoirs*:

> "If I can claim credit for anything in this operation it was also on my recommendation that the decision was taken to terminate the appointment of Guy Burgess. Not that I had any reason to suspect that Burgess was a Communist, still less a Soviet agent, but having met him once or twice, I had formed the opinion that he was quite exceptionally dissolute and indiscreet and certainly unfitted for any kind of confidential work."[47]

While this language intriguingly echoes Berlin's opinion of Burgess, this was indeed a hasty judgment to make about any character's professional fitness, if he truly saw him that little. (The comments by M. R. D. Foot suggesting that Burgess was sacked from SOE only after a struggle may indeed indicate that Jebb was one of Burgess's defenders: see Chapter 4). From the episode of the Moscow Plot, however, it sounds as if Jebb in fact knew Burgess much more familiarly, and, in retrospect, was trying to distance himself from the traitor. According to Cave-Brown and others Burgess was not 'dismissed' until November, and Jebb must have encountered him several times by then. After the defections, Jebb similarly tried to give the impression that the employment of Burgess would not have occurred on his watch, in June 1951 telling his boss, Sir William Strang, that "I always regarded Mr B as about the most unreliable man I ever met."[48]

Another telling episode suggests that Burgess and Jebb were somewhat closer than Jebb claimed. It is explained by Driberg, occurring in 1950, and there seems no reason that Burgess made it up: "I used to go to New York for the week-ends", Guy told me, and Gladwyn and I used to cry on each other's shoulders about the American attitude to the Far East."[49] At that time, Donald Maclean's brother, Alan, worked as Private Secretary to Jebb in New York, when Jebb was the British representative to the United Nations. Alan knew about Donald's espionage activities from the latter's revelations in Paris: on December 1938, having met the American Melinda Marling, Maclean confessed to her, his future wife – and Alan - that he worked for Soviet intelligence. This news may have travelled further. Robert Cecil wrote that the Foreign Office moved fast to control embarrassing leaks after Maclean and Burgess absconded on May 25, 1951: "On 30th May Donald's younger brother, Alan, who was working for Sir Gladwyn Jebb (Lord Gladwyn) at the United Nations, had been summoned back from New York and sworn to silence."[50] In any case, Burgess used his friendship with Alan Maclean as a pretext for taking messages from Philby in Washington to his Soviet contact, Makayev, and Jebb became so accustomed to the visits that he concluded the two "shared a flat".[51] Just before he left the United States for good, at the end of April 1951, Burgess spent a "few days in New York, in a state of semi-permanent intoxication, staying with Alan Maclean".[52] Gladwyn Jebb was not telling the whole truth about the level of his acquaintance with Burgess and Maclean.

Jebb was also less than straightforward when he tried to minimise the damage that Maclean had done when both were participants in the (supposedly) highly secret planning meetings for NATO in March of 1948. The meetings, held at the Pentagon, were unusual in that no note-taking was allowed, and minutes had to be reconstructed from memory. At the same time that Jebb was compiling them for Whitehall, Maclean was preparing his account for the Kremlin. Jebb rather astonishingly voiced the opinion that Maclean's passing of information "may well have exercised restraint on any Russian 'hawks'". [53] Robert Cecil was generous to the then Lord Gladwyn when he wrote the following:

> "Lord Gladwyn's views naturally merit respect: one may doubt, however, whether he would have expressed them at any time during the year that elapsed before – in April 1949 – NATO came into being. He could scarcely have wanted the Kremlin to know how anxiously we debated the constitutional restrictions requiring the US government to consult the Senate before engaging in hostilities…"

The pattern is clear: Jebb came far too close to most of the Cambridge Spies in his career. He either did not have the antennae to detect what was happening or, if he did, quickly realised after Burgess's and Maclean's defection that he had better keep his lips sealed. He thus dissimulated in order to protect his reputation. His actions and silences about the whole affair are representative of the clampdown on any acknowledgment by the Foreign Office, and Britain's Intelligence organisations, of the embarrassing irregularities that went on with Guy Burgess and his colleagues. Costello and Tsarev characterised Jebb as one of Guy Burgess's protectors at the Foreign Office, alongside Hector McNeil and Bill Dening, and Burgess acknowledged that his influential friends in high places were able to salvage his career. [54] Both Jebb and Berlin were nevertheless apparently able to muse loftily (and a little cynically) about Burgess's fate, and conveniently distance themselves from him, as Jebb related in his autobiography:

> "The essential mistake was to give Burgess any responsibility at all, for he was a totally irresponsible character. I remember subsequently wondering with Isaiah Berlin what work the unfortunate Russians could suitably confide to Burgess in Moscow; more especially since it was believed that they regarded homosexuality as a criminal offence. We decided that he would either be shot (a possibility which incidentally is solemnly discussed in Tom Driberg's rather oleaginous biography) or, more probably, die of boredom. The second suggestion turned out to be correct." [55]

Jebb and Berlin both played a role in the process of deceit and camouflage that took place after the events of 1940. Jebb was more a naïf and a 'useful idiot' than an agent of influence like Rothschild, but he should be held as morally and professionally responsible for the lapses that allowed the treachery of Burgess and Maclean to endure.

The third abetter of the spies' activities was Isaiah Berlin. As has been shown, Berlin played centre-stage in the Moscow Plot. Yet there is another aspect of his contribution to the story of subterfuge and subversion that merits deep analysis.

Apart from his disturbing involvement in dubious political warfare, Berlin acted as an intellectual mentor for the misguided ideologies of the Cambridge spies. His role is thus a pivotal one in the story of how British intelligence was gradually inoculated against the threat of Communist subversion, and yet it goes completely against the grain of educated perceptions of Berlin's status in political and academic life. Berlin has today an almost unassailable reputation as a foe of totalitarian systems, as a defender of liberty and of pluralism. As the website dedicated to his memory asserts: "His defence of freedom and diversity against control and uniformity is widely endorsed. His distinction between the monist hedgehog and the pluralist fox, and his celebration of 'the crooked timber of humanity', have entered the vocabulary of modern culture, together with his widely influential elaboration of the concepts of 'positive' and 'negative' liberty."[56] Berlin was a person of stature and influence, the first Jewish Fellow at All Souls, who mixed with powerful politicians and influential academics. Later in life he developed a career as a pre-eminent historian of ideas, building the reputation that still endures, and which his Literary Trustees assiduously protect. In 1971 he was awarded the prestigious and exclusive Order of Merit for his services to culture. Yet he was a much more complex individual than the hagiographic website would indicate, and this chapter explores several aspects of that personality.

The analysis must start with his attitude towards Communism. During the 1930s, Berlin harboured an interest in the doctrine that went beyond the familiar enthusiasm that touched so many intellectuals of the time. Many of his friends were open Communists, and Berlin himself frequently gave the impression of sympathising with them. The objective observer has to analyse carefully the circumstances of Berlin's affiliations, in the fashion that the departments of the British government, had they owned a rigorous recruitment process, should have reviewed any indications of Communist leanings in potential candidates for sensitive posts. Which traits and actions were exploratory moves, the indiscretions and enthusiasms of youth, and which were serious commitments later concealed by subterfuge? Could such interests be purely intellectual, with no practical implications, and thus posing no threat to security? The British Labour Party minister Dennis Healey was member of the CPGB from 1937 to 1940. Maclean slyly told his Civil Service examining board that he hadn't completely thrown off his leftist ideas, and was rewarded by his apparent honesty. Blunt managed to portray his communist notions as mere intellectual attitudes. The Civil Service never asked Jenifer Hart about her Communist past (although her husband later regretted not telling her employers about it). Philby's brazen activities in Vienna should have disqualified him automatically.

Thus Berlin's complex associations with Communism need to be examined closely. It was as a student of Marx that he made his first entry into publishing, his *Karl Marx: His Life and Environment* appearing in the autumn of 1939. He had started it in 1933, at the urging of H. A. L. Fisher, the Warden of New College. (Harold Laski, Frank Pakenham (later Lord Longford), and G. D. H. Cole were among many who declined the assignment.[57]) His letters from the 1930s show a constant fascination with Marx's ideas, as well as a rich set of associations with persons who would unabashedly describe themselves as communists (whether with a capital 'C', denoting membership of the CPGB, or simply as adherents, with a lower-case 'c'). Yet Berlin's letters are notoriously unreliable as a guide to his true thinking: he had an unconfident habit of presenting events in a way that would please the current recipient of his correspondence, only to contradict himself to another contact soon after. True, the writer Virginia Woolf, on meeting him, described him in 1933 as "a communist, I think, a fire-eater", but he may have been playing a role of trying to impress her, admitting to being a bit overwhelmed by the occasion.[58] Far more revealing are his interactions with the person he considered his closest friend, the poet Stephen Spender.[iv]

The relationships between Spender, Berlin, and Burgess display all the conflicts of divided loyalties between ideas and friendships that led to such deceit (both self-delusion and distortion of truths for others) in the decades afterwards. Spender's affair with the Communist Party in the 1930s is also emblematic of the mental struggles that opponents of Fascism had when faced with the cruelties of Stalin's Soviet Union. Spender's sympathies for communism, and actions in support of it, went back many years. As early as September, 1931, Harold Nicolson was writing that "Stephen is going bolshy like most of my young friends". In 1934 (or maybe earlier), Spender became the lover of Muriel Gardiner, the model for Lillian Hellman's Julia, who encountered Philby in the cells assisting communists to escape in Vienna.[v] [59] The following year, Spender wrote to Christopher Isherwood from London, on November 14, that "Tony Hyndman [his boyfriend] is joining the Communist Party next week", and his further correspondence with Isherwood suggests that CP affairs were dominating Hyndman's time – as well as his own.[60] Thus, in October 5, 1936, back in London after a voyage to Greece and Austria, he wrote that Hyndman was busy working for the *Left Review*, adding: "The other half of the week he works for me; there is also the C[ommunist] P[arty] work, so he is rather busy." And a few weeks later, on October 30, a similar message came through. "The C[ommunist] P[arty] are amazingly exacting, but I dare say that is a good thing." Spender was also writing poetry reviews for *The Daily Worker* at this time, so was fully absorbed with Communist-related activity. In January 1937, after the Comintern had requested help from the CPGB to investigate the fate of the crew of the Soviet ship, the *Komsomol*, which had been sunk by the Italians in the Mediterranean, he was somewhat improbably chosen, with Cuthbert Worsley, for the task.

A significant event was Spender's writing of a book to promote the Communist ideal. He had been commissioned by the Left Book Club to write a work, originally titled *An Approach to Communism*, which appeared on January 11, 1937 as *Forward from Liberalism*. That was followed by some controversy that has not been clearly described. Soon after the book came out, in a letter to Elizabeth Bowen (March 3, 1937), Berlin wrote that he was "frightfully upset

---

[iv] After Spender's death in 1995, Berlin wrote to his widow, Natasha: "I have never loved any friend more – nor respected, nor been happier to be his friend."

[v] Lillian Hellman was a member of the US Communist Party. Her book *Pentimento* was made into a film titled *Julia* (1977).

about Stephen's public renunciation of his book & joining of the Com. Party, partly out of pique, because of my wasted eloquence . . .".[61] In a note, Berlin's chief editor, Henry Hardy, explained this "renunciation" as follows: "Spender had argued that the show trials and execution (in August 1936) of Zinoviev and other Trotskyists indicated a need for liberalism in the USSR in the form of a democratic constitution allowing criticism of the Soviet government. Soon afterwards Harry Pollitt, the head of the CP in Britain, persuaded him that those executed had been plotting against the State. Spender joined the CP on 16 February and on 19 February the *Daily Worker* published his retraction of the liberal views expressed in his book." But this assessment surely misrepresents what actually happened.

From a detailed examination of records, including John Sutherland's biography of Spender, and Spender's own accounts in his *Letters* to Christopher Isherwood, the historian must come to the conclusion that Spender's article in the *Daily Worker* was not a "retraction" of his views, but a *confirmation* of them. The tone of *Forward from Liberalism*, despite Randall Swingler's scathing critique in *Left Review*, was a definite pro-Communist, pro-Soviet stance.[62] Sutherland presented Spender's actions and opinions more accurately, noting that *Forward from Liberalism* was completed in late July 1936, but that Spender made a late change to his text in the final proofs that cast some doubt on the justification of the recent show trials. This was the only sniff of "liberalism" to appear in the work. Sutherland stated that the main point of the book was to praise the new Soviet constitution, not to declare that it needed an improved one. "The book concludes with a eulogy on the Soviet Union's new constitution", he wrote, and quoted Spender: "In the new constitution the Soviet has removed the main barrier to real liberty of thought and discussion: terror". Sutherland added that "with the appointment of Nikolai Ezhov [*Yezhov*] as head of the NKVD in September 1936 Stalinist terror would, in fact, reach unprecedented peaks." Sutherland then quoted Spender's late amendment to the text: "Since I wrote these [immediately preceding] pages, the execution of Zinoviev and his fellow-Trotskyists has taken place. This trial emphasises the fact that unless the democratic constitution is quickly introduced, there must be many more such trials." Sutherland commented: "What Spender demands is that the USSR should go backward to Liberalism. As likely (in January 1937) as water flowing uphill."[63] Apparently Gollancz, Laski, and Strachey had not seen Spender's late insertion, and they were not pleased. After a lecture from Harry Pollitt, the head of the CPGB, Spender had to retract his reservation. The outcome was the *Daily Worker* piece, published on February 19, 1937, in which Spender sophistically claimed: "Some time before my book had appeared I had read the rest of the evidence and I became convinced that there undoubtedly had been a gigantic plot against the Soviet Government and that the evidence was true. However it was too late for me to alter my book."[64]

Spender's accounts of his involvement, including the mission to Spain, are evasive and mendacious, as Sutherland reported. Later, Spender also misrepresented the dates of his membership of the Communist Party (partly in order to obtain an entry visa to the United States), and attempted to minimise his involvement with the organisation. He also tried to erase all references to Burgess from his papers after Burgess's escape to Moscow.[65] Berlin too gave some hints to Spender's deceptive behaviour, while revealing his own benevolent attitude to the Party. In a letter to Spender (April 25, 1936), Berlin wrote to him: "News (via Grigson) that you have joined the CP seems to me to alter nothing", adding later that "in England, the CP is, as you say, neo-liberal". Spender replied to Berlin, in a letter dated May 6, 1936, denying that he had joined the Party, and he was scathing about Grigson. He wrote: "No, I have not joined the CP. I agree with what you say about them, & I am writing my book in order to say much the same thing. But if one joined the party, one would not be able to speak quite so frankly, I imagine. Also, any good I do, is through writing and I can do that best from outside. If I were not a writer, perhaps I would join. Grigson is a donkey and a gossip and worse." Thus Spender trivialised his propaganda efforts on behalf of the CPGB through the Left Book Club, and tried to reinforce the notion that his acolyte, Tony Hyndman, would have joined the Party whereas he did not. If he were, indeed, independent of the Party, why would he have obeyed a summons by Pollitt? A little later, in another encouraging letter to Spender of June, 1936, Berlin was to express his sympathies for Spender's mission, and his confidence in Marxism's becoming more serious: "I am convinced . . . that now unlike previous years, we are going to get some intelligent and sensitive Marxists", suggesting that such an influx of new intellectuals was what was required to restore Marxism's poor reputation.[66]

What is important, however, in Berlin's ideological development is the fact that, whereas in the summer of 1936 he had considered the CP a neo-liberal organisation (and appeared to approve of Spender's joining it), nine months later he implored his friend not to sign up (or so he claimed). Hardy reported, from one of the transcripts of the discussions between Berlin and his biographer that Berlin's "wasted eloquence" had probably been displayed on the occasion when he begged Spender "on bended knee" not to join the CP, at a luncheon attended by Bowen as well.[67] The timing of this encounter (if it actually took place) is not given. It does not sound as if this event could have occurred in February 1937, when, in *World within World*, Spender described his recruitment as an impulsive and swift affair, where he was given his party card by Pollitt after the latter's invitation to his office. Berlin would not have had the opportunity to intervene at that stage. The evidence might suggest that, between May 1936 and January 1937, Berlin had an intense meeting with Spender (where Bowen was present), at which, having read a draft of *An Approach to Communism* (as it was then titled), and hearing about Spender's plans to join the Party, he tried to talk his friend out of it, but failed. Maybe his warnings were intensified by Stalin's show trials of Kamenev and Zinoviev, which started on August 19 that year, and that is what caused his volte-face on the status and reputation of the Communist Party of Great Britain (that 'neo-liberal' institution). The enduring ideological challenge of Stalin's trials was reinforced by the fact that the trial of Radek and Pyatakov (both to be sentenced to death) started on January 23, 1937, the day after Spender and Worsley returned to the UK from their Comintern mission. On the other hand, the luncheon with Bowen and Spender may never have happened, and it could have been introduced to indicate a recognition that open endorsement of Communism in 1936 needed to be countered.

In fact, Berlin's comments at that time about *Forward from Liberalism* give the impression that he had not even read the book, since he interpreted Spender's public renunciation as going back on an overall enlightened message, when in fact Spender was only succumbing from pressure from Pollitt to accept the justice of the show trials, and take back the postscript he inserted at the last minute. Can Berlin really not have been *au fait* with what the Left Book Club was up to, and what his intimate friend was doing? After Spender's death, his comments on the work reflect more sentimentality and a sense of friendship than pure critical analysis. Thus his change of opinion must been prompted by a realisation that either Spender's book was dangerously subversive, or a very sudden belief that the show trials meant that the CPGB should be ostracised, or possibly a conviction that any membership of the Party had to remain secret.

Of course, Berlin's intimate friend and later lover Jenifer Hart was a secret member of the CPGB. Whether or not Berlin knew in the late 1930s of Hart's entanglement with the Comintern cannot be proven either way. She joined the Party in the summer of 1935, directly after coming down from Oxford. In her autobiography, Hart claimed that she did nothing as a member of the Party, adding: "The only specific task assigned to me was Christopher Hill's suggestion that I should recruit Isaiah Berlin as a member, but I knew him well enough to realise that this would be impossible although he was friendly with several Party members e.g. Norman O. Brown and Bill Davies."[68] The statement is startling and revealing, nevertheless, since, while it correctly reflects Berlin's probable antipathy for belonging to such a doctrinaire organisation as the Communist Party, it says a lot about his political convictions and sympathies at the time: otherwise Christopher Hill would not have risked making the suggestion. While Berlin's joining the CPGB as a public member would have been a morale-booster for the organisation, and given it intellectual heft, it would have been a disastrous and unnecessary career-move for the Oxford philosopher. In this context, it is worthwhile recording that Berlin wrote an effusive Foreword to Hart's memoir, which includes the following defence of Hart's political stance:

> "Certainly those who supported the Republic in Spain (myself, for example) had no notion then of the sinister part played in that war by Soviet agents and Spanish communists. If I had not myself spent some years of my childhood in the Soviet Union, I think I too might have drifted in that direction – that was the world I was surrounded by. But those few tears, even at the age of eight or nine, had inoculated me against illusions about Soviet reality – I remained passionately anti-Stalinist, and indeed, anti-Leninist, for the rest of my life; but my words fell on deaf ears: my contemporaries thought that there was something curiously perverse in my failure to understand who were the sheep and who were the goats in the political world. There is no doubt that Soviet propaganda remains the most successful hoax ever perpetrated on the human race. The Soviet trials made some impact, and the Soviet-Nazi treaty of 1939 opened a good many eyes – and yet, not enough. My liberal friends – the world in which Jenifer moved – at that time believed that although no doubt mistakes, even crimes, might have been

perpetrated in the Soviet Union, yet despite that they were moving in the right direction – they were in a sense on 'our', the decent, social-justice-seeking, side – and much could be forgiven to so backward and impoverished a land. It took a great deal of revealed monstrosities to lift this particular veil."[69]

Berlin went on to praise the sincerity and selflessness of the woman who was an agent for a foreign power – a power that would have ruthlessly expunged the freedoms that Hart and Berlin enjoyed. Hart was no principled opponent of capitalist, democratic society: she hypocritically took advantage of the benefits it offered her. And Berlin was to an extent taken in. It is a revealing piece, over-the-top and unnecessarily laudatory, in that it reflects a naïve sympathy for those Communists and communist fellow-travellers whom Berlin knew and associated with so well, and their utopian beliefs, even though it is accompanied by a strident claim that Berlin saw through all that nonsense. It is also a subtly deceptive account: the Soviet Union was not established until 1922, when the Berlins were already safely installed in Hampstead, a misrepresentation that undermines Berlin's personal claims about "Soviet reality". He disavowed Leninism and Stalinism, but not specifically Communism or Marxism. The piece was written shortly before he died, and is not a convincing testimony from the reputed champion of liberalism.

Lastly, as far as Berlin's documented opinions on Communism are concerned, there exists the testimony in Berlin's book on Marx. It is a work of interpretation and explanation, rather than of critical analysis. It is sparkling and erudite, but not really scholarly. (This may not be wholly surprising: Berlin once confided to Henry Hardy: "As to my bits and pieces – I'm not at all surprised that my footnotes are inaccurate. I am wildly unscholarly . . ."[70]) The Marx opus is strong on philosophy, mediocre on sociology, and weak on political economy, showing little understanding of how industrial enterprise under capitalism actually works. It fails to distinguish between, on the one hand, the mechanism of capitalism as a means for allocating investments to industrial enterprises, and, on the other, the phenomenon of democratic political constitutions, which may vary from country to country, and whose enabled governments may or may not be unduly influenced by the owners of capital. Such an approach accepts the rhetoric of the Marxists instead of challenging and questioning the dogmatic Communist notion of monolithic power-blocs that oppress the proletariat.

In his method and style, Berlin echoes much of Marx's verbosity, and displays an unexpected lack of precision in his references to such concepts as 'civilisation', 'class', 'nation', 'race', 'community', 'people', 'group', 'culture', 'age', 'epoch', 'milieu', 'country', 'generation', 'ideology', 'social order', and 'outlook', which terms all run off the page without being clearly defined or differentiated. (In a note to the First Edition, Berlin thanked his colleague, the philosopher A. J. Ayer, for his advice on the text, which probably says more about Ayer's view of Marxism than it does about the relevance of logical-positivist verification of questionable assertions.) Thus Berlin never inspected closely the basic tenets of Marx's class-based, materialistic, deterministic, brutal view of history: for someone avowedly so adverse to violence, Berlin's apparent acceptance of the murderous dogma at the heart of Marx's creed is astonishing. In a letter to A. D. Lindsay, Master of Balliol, who had criticised the balance shown in Berlin's book between the empirical and the prophetic side of Marx, Berlin replied that, for Marx, "Ends were good or bad, behaviour moral or immoral entirely according to whether they were or were not being forwarded by the cosmic process. I agree with all of this – & if I seemed to disagree it can only be because I had not expressed it clearly and forcibly enough in my book."[71] Such an opinion is in stark opposition to the liberalism of the older Berlin. Maybe, as a young man over-anxious to please, he also did not want to upset any of his Communist friends. In any case, Guy Burgess liked the book, writing: "I thought it was clear, selective, humane, intelligent, intuitive, objective and lofty".[72] This was not a surprising assessment, as one close friend suggested that Berlin had "imbibed the principles of economic interpretations of history from Burgess himself." [73] Berlin was happy to conclude that "the true father of modern economic history, and, indeed of modern sociology, in so far as any one man may claim that title, is Karl Marx."[74] Offering an endorsement of that nature, Isaiah Berlin should (in 1939) have been classified as a Marxist. In summary, Berlin exercised a serious intellectual influence on contemporary opinion about the validity of Marxist theory, the theory that drove the ideology of the traditional threat to Britain's security, the Soviet Union.

Did this interpretation of Marx affect Berlin's stance on the Soviet Union? We must recall that Berlin's main role in Moscow was almost certainly to be confidant and interpreter for Burgess in communicating to Burgess's masters the details of the Krivitsky affair, which Burgess must surely have explained to Berlin in detail. Yet Berlin's track-record of pronouncements against the Soviet regime might suggest that he would have felt very uncomfortable over such a mission. What were his true feelings about the Soviet Union? How did his assessment of the Communist vision for mankind, and his enthusiasm for Marxism, evolve?

In fact, Berlin witnessed the gestation of the Soviet regime at first hand. He always considered himself a 'Russian Jew', although he was born in Latvia, and his affiliations were always with the greater expanse of Russia than with that outlying colony. In 1916, his family had moved to Petrograd [now St. Petersburg, formerly Leningrad], where they were present at the February Social-Democrat Revolution. Berlin used an incident he saw at that time, a policeman being dragged away by a mob, to explain a life-long aversion to political violence (see above). As his biographer put it, retelling the story that Berlin related in his Foreword to Jenifer Hart's memoir: "Much later, in the 1930s, when contemporaries were intoxicated with revolutionary Marxism, the memory of 1917 continued to work with Berlin, strengthening his horror of physical violence and his suspicion of political experiment, and deepening his lifelong preference for all the temporizing compromises that keep a political order safely this side of terror".[75] After surviving the Bolshevik Revolution, the Berlin family moved back to Riga in 1920, and thence to London in 1921.

The sceptical observer might find this claim of well-established hatred of Soviet tyranny somewhat overdone. Berlin was only eight years old at the time of the incident, and he did not actually see the policeman being killed. To claim that such an episode - an instance of mob violence, rather than police brutality, it should be pointed out - somehow gave him a life-time resistance to Stalinism and Leninism (when both tyrants had yet to make their mark), is at best precocious and bogus, and at worst, mendacious. One might have expected Berlin to have been exposed to yet darker cruelty in the first two years of the Revolution, and for his view to have matured with the passage of time. Would such events have inoculated him against the general idea of violence in pursuit of political ends (or simply the horror of anarchic mob activity), or might they perhaps have suggested to him that it was implicit in the doctrines of communist dogma, and inevitable in a process of revolution, to murder members of the 'bourgeoisie' and the aristocracy in order to cleanse the world? Berlin tended to melodramatise and embroider such accounts. Ignatieff repeated another anecdote, offered by Berlin concerning his Uncle Lev, who was accused by the KGB of belonging to a British spy ring. "He was held in prison for over a year and released in February 1954, after Stalin's death. He was walking in the streets of Moscow, still weak and undernourished, when he saw one of his torturers cross the road in front of him. He suffered a heart attack and died alone in the snowy streets."[76] If he was alone, how could anyone have known what occasioned his heart attack?

Berlin's writings rely on a familiarity with the literary climate of the Soviet Union that could be gained only by exchanges with members of the intelligentsia in that country, which suggests he had some private – or clandestine – means of gaining information. Yet he did not travel there frequently: after his abortive effort in 1940, he visited for a few months in 1945, ostensibly for government-sponsored research that did not turn out as planned, and more briefly in 1956. On these occasions, he incurred the wrath of Stalin and (after Stalin's death) the KGB by making unauthorised visits to literary figures (such as Akhmatova and Pasternak), as well as to relatives. In 1956, he was accompanied in Moscow by his distant relative Efraim Halevy (who was later to become head of Israel's Secret Service organisation, Mossad), where they made a furtive visit to Berlin's Aunt Zelma. Berlin and Halevy had not informed the KGB of their plans, which was a serious offence, and could have brought grief to Aunt Zelma and her kin.[77]

In addition, the KGB had reasons to keep a special eye on him. His father, Mendel, had been accused of spying (Stalin treated all such foreign representatives as spies, and unauthorised contact with members of the Soviet citizenry was illegal) during an enigmatic visit to Moscow in 1935. Mendel, whose British naturalisation documents describe him as a timber-exporter, was reported to be in Moscow with a timber delegation, but escaped his minders to visit his brother Lev.[78] (One might wonder exactly what a timber delegation could hope to accomplish in Moscow. The OGPU managed the timber industry, which was supplied almost exclusively by slave labour. This was a contentious issue back in the House of Commons at the time. It is unlikely the delegation was able to make any successful demands for improved employee safety standards.) The unfortunate Lev was later arrested and tortured, accused of being complicit in the so-called 'Doctors' Plot' against Stalin in 1952. The brothers were charged at this time of being links in a chain, passing information illegally to Isaiah Berlin. A recent study of Soviet archives suggests how Stalin contrived the existence of this chain of spies when "in December 1945 L. B. Berlin had met his brother

Mendel's son, Isaí, who had moved to Moscow as Second Secretary of the British Embassy, thus enabling regular delivery of classified information abroad". [79] Whether any information was passed is not clear: Berlin's uncle was tortured until he finally confessed to working for British intelligence from 1926 until 1952. Only Stalin's death saved him.

It is difficult to interpret what was going on here. If Stalin had been extorting information from Mendel and Isaiah Berlin by threatening to harm their relatives, he may have turned against them in frustration if they let him down, or Isaiah had behaved in too provocative a fashion in his approaches to members of the literary intelligentsia who were out of Stalin's favour. Berlin was aware that his overtures might harm his relatives, although he displayed a lack of political acumen over such matters. Later in the 1940s, he went openly to great pains to make a show of protecting his sources, even writing to the *New York Times* to complain about its coverage of a speech he made at Mount Holyoke College, which might have betrayed his contacts in the Soviet Union. [80] The wisdom of drawing attention to such a process through the medium of a celebrated international newspaper must be strongly questioned. He was either extremely ingenuous, or else must have concluded that it simply didn't matter.

The evidence of Berlin's involvement with intelligence-gathering is patchy, and the calendar has to be moved backwards and forwards from the pivotal year of 1940, for four or five years each time, in order to flesh out the exposition. One relevant article is an extraordinary letter, not yet published in the printed works, which appears on the Berlin website maintained by Henry Hardy. [81] It is written by Isaiah Berlin to his father, with a presumed date of Autumn 1935, and appears to respond to a number of questions from Mendel about Britain's probable response to European events, specifically about threats from Mussolini, and England's guarantees to France. The letter from Mendel that this item responds to has apparently not survived: but why Mendel should have developed a sudden interest in the broader political climate in Europe immediately after his return from Moscow, and why such a request was made in writing, as opposed to being offered in a friendly domestic chat, remains puzzling. In 1940, Walter Krivitsky informed his interrogators from MI5 that all visitors from trade delegations (especially those with relatives still in the Soviet Union, whose safety could be threatened), as well as all visitors from Communist parties abroad (such as Harry Pollitt and Willie Gallacher), were firmly pumped for information when in the Soviet Union. [82] Stalin considered his country on a war footing from 1935 onwards: Mendel Berlin would have been an excellent pipeline via his son to All Souls College, where the British intelligentsia mingled with the country's leading politicians. It is possible that the NKVD applied pressure on Mendel to provide intelligence on British preparations and intentions concerning the impending conflict, and his son became inextricably involved in this channel of information.

The conclusion from such episodes is that Berlin had a highly ambiguous relationship with the Soviet Union, a relationship that may help to shed light on the contacts he pursued during the attempt to reach Moscow in the summer of 1940. He remains a puzzling figure. Apart from broad generalities, he was notoriously reluctant – or unable – to articulate his private political views succinctly. As Noel Annan wrote of him: "He did not pronounce on public issues.

No one could say what his views were on trade union reform, the balance of payments, university entrance or the poverty trap. He remained marginal to the central issues of any region of national life."[83] For a period in the 1930s, however, Berlin certainly had communist sympathies, and mixed with a varied group of acquaintances who were even more entranced with the communist vision than he was. He was a close friend of the most disreputable of all Stalin's Englishmen (Burgess), and was approved by high political authority to embark on a secret mission to Moscow with that man. He had some disturbing relationships with the Soviet regime, which reflected poorly on his judgment, but which may indicate that he was under psychological pressure because of the safety of relatives he had left behind. As Chapter 5 described, he became engaged in a rich career in intelligence in New York and Washington (though later denying it all), but at least once betrayed his allegiance to the British government for the sake of Zionist ambitions. The evidence points to a cover-up on his part of a role as collaborator in Maclean's treachery.

Isaiah Berlin thus presents a permanent enigma, with paradoxes and contradictions that cannot be explained away purely by the fact of his evolving ideas with the passage of time. He was undoubtedly a man of the Left, but was not confident enough of any political stance to draw a clear line between democratic socialism and the illiberal attractions of Communism. He enjoyed the company of communists, and gave publicity to the ideas of Marx, while claiming that he was fiercely antipathetic to any totalitarian impulses. He engaged in dubious activities with members of the Soviet intelligence services, without appearing to understand that such behaviour was highly inappropriate. He mingled with Stalin's English spies, but claimed to know nothing of their affiliations, even though one of his closest intimates, Burgess, was known to boast of his loyalties to Communist Russia. He misrepresented the past, with naivety and occasional deceptiveness, a behaviour that now appears shocking. He denied his wartime role in intelligence, as if it was beneath him as an intellectual.[84] A more generous assessment might conclude that Berlin's reticence arose out of a respect for the Official Secrets Act – ignoring his activities on behalf of the Zionists, for instance. However, with the passage of time, and so many other reminiscences in the public eye, such a defence appears unlikely. Moreover, Berlin, rather than concealing his activities overall, misrepresented them, and was over-keen to protest his intelligence innocence voluntarily, under no pressure, which behaviour rather over-egged the pudding.

And yet his reputation suffered not at all. It was as if this brilliantly erudite man, who spoke so eloquently and authoritatively about the history of ideas, was somehow an exception, an exotic transplant, whose endearing qualities meant that he had to be accepted utterly on his own erratic terms, and that to challenge him would only show one's ignorance. In a recent memoir, the Oxford don R. W. Johnson has reinforced this notion of Berlin's inviolability, remarking that "Isaiah was indeed an institution and so widely regarded as such that he could get away with things that others couldn't."[85] Nevertheless, in the final analysis, it seems that Berlin privately regretted much of what had happened, and thus felt he needed to control the enduring version of the events of his life, leaving a rich oral testimony in the hands of his biographer so that a dignified legacy would be created. At the same time, he left minor hints around (such as in his released letters) that seemed to invite the fresh observer to investigate, and test, and challenge, the received story-line in order to detect what really happened.

His most lasting, yet subtle, influence may be in his book on Marx, released in 1939, and revised and reissued several times since. By somehow appearing to make Marx part of the European liberal – and even pluralist – tradition, and by minimising the frightfulness of the call to bloodthirsty revolution, Berlin made Marx more broadly palatable. He made Marx respectable. As Terrell Carver wrote in his Afterword to the 2013 edition of the book: " . . . while rooted in the values of European liberal democracy and national liberation, he *includes* [author's italics] Marx in this heritage, despite his occasional comments on Marx's relentless single-mindedness and inability to tolerate dissenters with any grace," adding "After Berlin it was not only respectable to work on Marx as an important intellectual in a broad sense . . . , it was also valid to approach Marx through his own texts, on his own terms . . ."[86] Yet the failure of Berlin (and others) to discern that a commitment to Marx's ideas would lead directly to the tyranny and cruelty of Lenin's and Stalin's regimes meant that they became part of the roster of "useful idiots" who helped to undermine British democracy, playing directly into the hands of the Comintern, helping crypto-communists like Stafford Cripps and Dennis Pritt, and softening the defences of Britain's security services. That, indeed, was the pattern that started to rot Britain's Intelligence Services – when those with persuasions that had recently been the prime target of MI5's surveillance activities started to be welcomed into the organisation with open arms.

Yet the illusion that communists might operate purely on an intellectual level, with no concern for revolutionary action, has a long history. In his study titled *The Young Kim Philby*, Edward Harrison cited the biographer of King George V, recording how His Majesty inquired of Lord Balfour, the Chancellor of Cambridge University why the Marxist, Maurice Dobb, was allowed to indoctrinate undergraduates. "Balfour carried out enquiries and replied that Dobb's influence was only academic", wrote Kenneth Rose.[87] Liddell was taken in by Blunt's claim that his Marxism had no practical application. The official historian of intelligence, F. H. Hinsley, apparently endorsed MI5's sophistical distinction that there existed a tribe of "sophisticated Communists", who realised "that the British Empire was the greatest obstacle to the victory of the Communist International, were prepared to see Hitler defeat the British at the expense of the temporary set-back of their own ideals". Yet Barbarossa diminished this threat: "Their overt propaganda ceased to be disturbing and it was sufficient to oppose their new tactics with discreet obstruction".[88] Thus Discretion became the better part of Defending the Realm.

In summary, Berlin and Burgess both exercised serious negative influences on Britain's security, but were, in their different ways, untouchable. In 1940, Berlin was on the ascent: Burgess had started his decline. Berlin had encouraged the acceptance of communism through his indulgence towards Marxism, and connived at Burgess's nefarious undertakings with Moscow. For reasons that no one has satisfactorily explained, Burgess was moved on to important Foreign Office postings even after his peremptory firing from SOE. Berlin rapidly acquired a reputation for inscrutability and wisdom that meant he was never seriously questioned about the bizarre goings-on in the summer of 1940. And his intellectual influence had been a factor in encouraging the sympathies to the Soviet Union that permeated the minds of the leading thinkers and officers in MI5. Rothschild, Jebb and Berlin thus formed an extraordinary trio: mostly regarded as pillars of society, they in their different ways helped their friends in the scheme to demolish the foundations of that same structure.

Yet is there another explanation as to why MI5 displayed such pusillanimity towards the spies and agents of influence in their midst? Is it possible that a directive came down from high that encouraged it to take a more indulgent attitude towards Communists, in order to maintain the goodwill of Stalin and the Comintern, and to anticipate and accelerate the entry of the Soviet Union into the war on the side of the Allies? That the Section D initiative to reach out to the Comintern was part of a broader strategy that involved Britain's Intelligence Services in a more concrete plan? Were the 'agents of influence' deliberately planted, perhaps? There is little evidence of such, either in the minutes of the Joint Intelligence Committee, or the Diaries of Guy Liddell (of which the redacted parts supply a form of insight via their dates and size), or the memoirs of the participants. It is true that a more positive attitude towards the Soviet Union at premiership-level occurred when Churchill replaced Chamberlain, but Churchill's respect was not unlimited. It is also true that he met Ambassador Maisky regularly, and tried to cultivate him, for instance telling him that the differences between Britain and the Soviet Union were "a ghastly misunderstanding", and that the interests of the two nations "did not collide anywhere". Maisky's version of events, however, must necessarily be taken carefully.[89] Moreover, Churchill's admiration was not unlimited: in March 1940 he was still willing to risk Stalin's wrath by using the potential bombing of the Baku oilfields as a bargaining-counter with Stalin. His pro-Soviet advances were also fiercely opposed by officials in the Foreign Office, notably Vansittart and Fitzroy Maclean, who resisted any appeasement towards Communism, and they were backed up in the military in the person of General Ismay.[90] Besides, in the summer of 1940 Churchill still faced a Chamberlainite majority of Tories in the House of Commons.

One intriguing piece of the puzzle is the contribution of the ex-intelligence officer David Mure, who made a veiled assertion that MI5's recruitment of Communists had taken place in response to an edict on high. It must at least be considered, before being rejected out of hand, because of the form in which it was made, as an apparent blatant flouting of the Official Secrets Act. Mure had worked for SIS in the Middle East (SIME). He wrote a rather coarse account of his activities in 1977, *Practise to Deceive*, and followed it with a very scathing attack on MI5 and its recruitment of intellectuals, and the culture of allowing the "Philbys and Blunts" to thrive in MI5 and SIS, in *Master of Deception* (1980), a paean to his mentor, Brigadier Dudley Clarke. Typical of his judgments found in the latter book is the following: "A man under service discipline is forced to maintain a high standard of conduct as he is liable, rightly, to be sternly disciplined for the slightest misdemeanour. One immediately thinks of homosexuality, then a criminal offence, perpetual drunkenness, drugtaking, black market operations. People like Blunt, Philby and Tommy Harris would not have survived six weeks in the Middle East Intelligence Services." [91] Thus it was astonishing that Mure brought out, in 1984, a work titled *The Last Temptation*, written as a whimsical *faux* memoir of Guy Liddell, recalling his life as he journeys through limbo. Apart from an imaginative but rather arch use of characters from Charles Dodgson's (Lewis Carroll's) works, [vi] the book is remarkable because it obviously was written with the benefit of Liddell's *Diaries* at hand, as a passage boldly declares. [92]

The serious historian would not normally consider a volume such as this (described as "a novel of treason" on the cover) as part of the documentary archive, but its essence, its provenance, and some reactions to it all conspire to suggest, in a world where information fights an eternal struggle against disinformation, that it needs to be inspected. What makes the book noteworthy, indeed unique, is a generous display of facts from Liddell's *Diaries*, which are instantly recognisable by anyone familiar with the latter work. (Two volumes of the *Diaries*, for the years 1939-1945 – a small proportion of the total work, which is available on-line at the National Archives – were published in 2005. The diaries were declassified in 2002.) Yet the truth and reliability of such a chronicle would have been lost on almost everyone at the time. That Liddell had written an almost-daily diary throughout the war, and after, was a highly protected secret. The author who brought the journals to print, Nigel West, initially claimed to this writer that Mure could not have known even of the existence of the *Diaries* (let alone their content) until Peter Wright referred to it in 1986, in *Spycatcher*. West wrote in his Introduction to Liddell's *Diaries*: "Liddell's own diaries were never intended for publication, and were read only by selected MI5 officers as a training aid to give an idea of how the Security Service had risen to the challenge of a world war with the Axis powers", and ". . .they were considered so sensitive that they were codenamed WALLFLOWER and retained in the Director-General's personal safe." [93] Apparently, Mure did not discuss his access to them with West, and West was unaware of the revelations. When West was advised of the chronology, he expressed bewilderment: this anecdote is even more extraordinary since West said he knew Mure socially in the 1980s, and yet he makes no reference to Mure's work in the Introduction. Yet Mure's work is the fullest account of Liddell's life – both factual and possibly fictional aspects – that we can enjoy in any source.

Mure's copious and unmistakable citations from the diaries thus give his book a large dose of verisimilitude – but only to a post-2002 readership. That fact alone explains why *The Last Temptation* now appears a forgotten book. Yet, at the time, Mure must have believed he had a serious purpose, and a sensible strategy for achieving it. His main objective appears to be to exculpate MI5 of its negligence in not detecting the Communist agents in its midst, strongly indicating that its hiring of the spies and agents of influence had been decreed to it. For example, he wrote: "Next, the task – not only for me [*i.e. Liddell*] but for all concerned – had been to get bloody Redland [*the Soviet Union*] into the war and, having got her there, to keep her there. To do that, I had to recruit into my Service

---

[vi] Liddell was related to Alice Liddell, who was the model for *Alice in Wonderland*.

able young men who were not only acceptable to Redland but who readily accepted the alliance with her."[94] Moreover, the fictional Liddell very skilfully puts all the blame for inappropriate vetting of such candidates on Maxwell Knight, which is not only a travesty of how MI5 was organised, but also promotes the philosophy that it was possible to distinguish between harmless intellectual communists (who might have enjoyed Stalin's sympathy) with truly dangerous subversives (who might have been in Stalin's pay). Mure also created such alarming incidents as a confession to Liddell by Blunt, in 1944, that he was a Comintern agent – otherwise unverifiable, but not totally absurd, given what we know of Liddell's doubts, and the implications of the Leo Long incident that is covered in the next chapter.

To maintain that MI5 could single-handedly ensure the allegiance of the Soviet Union, helping to bring it into the war, and keep it there, is manifestly absurd. If any department should have been charged with that assignment, it would have been SIS, given how hostile the Foreign Office was to the Soviet Union at that time. Moreover, MI5's weakening of its defences against communist subversion had started well earlier, and there is no other evidence of such a programme. Liddell's diaries were reportedly written with no intent of publication, and they maintain a naivety and honesty that both belie any such external influence in strategy, while consistently showing how much the counter-espionage officer was manipulated. And it is difficult to imagine how a critical and opinionated officer like Mure could so rapidly change his views so suddenly, in a fashion that reminds one of Burgess's jump from member of the Anglo-German Fellowship to Friend of the Comintern. So is the whole exploit just a whimsical fantasy? If so, how did Mure get his hands on the diaries, locked away in the Director-General's safe?

An inescapable conclusion must be that the publication was a case of public relations on the part of the Security Service, probably engineered by Dick White. In what must surely have been a breach of the Official Secrets Act, he probably arranged for a showing of the diaries to Mure. How would this have worked? Mure claimed he had a photographic memory ("However I am lucky in having a photographic memory and even after more than thirty years I can remember almost word for word those passages in the traffic which intrigued me at the time . . ."[95]). Ten years after his retirement in 1972, White's record was still under pressure from mole-hunts, and accusations of cover-ups. In 1979, Margaret Thatcher had cancelled the publication of Volume Four of the *History of British Intelligence in the Second World War* (which would have showed MI5 in a positive light, White claimed), and White in his annoyance had thus encouraged Nigel West to write his own history of the service, a puzzling move by one who had criticised Masterman's breaking the rules with *The Double-Cross System* in 1972. In March 1981, Thatcher admitted that Hollis had been investigated as a Soviet spy. White was uncomfortable, and under fire. "The new generation of Cabinet Office mandarins were unimpressed. Detached from the investigation and the era, they blamed White for a mess."[96]

With such demands from Whitehall, and under the pressure of the *Spycatcher* affair, and the revelations of Joan Miller [*see Chapter 7*], White probably conceived the idea of engaging the help of an old intelligence colleague, formerly antagonistic to what Liddell and White had done, and convinced him that, in the interests of the Service, an effort should be made to present an alternative view of history that might deflect the searching investigations into culpability that were clearly going to arrive in the coming years. This Mure did, but it appears his work was ignored, failing even to catch the attention of Nigel West. The conceit of basing the narrative on the fact that Liddell was a dedicated diary-writer would certainly have been lost on the reading public if intelligence officers themselves were not aware of the activity. Whom did Mure and his accomplice think they would be influencing?

Yet some historians thought his work worth mentioning. In his study of SOE (incidentally published in the same year as Mure's work), M. R. D. Foot stated, when commenting on Burgess's recruitment by the Foreign Office after Gubbins's sacking of him in the autumn of 1940: "How Burgess got himself accepted by the Foreign Office is another story", adding the annotation: " . . . for an informed guess, see David Mure's *The Last Temptation,* pp 134-137, pp 200-202."[97] And Andrew Lownie claimed that John Costello (who made a vigorous case in *Mask of Treachery* that Liddell himself was "the grandfather mole") was greatly influenced by *The Last Temptation.* Since the work was designed to deflect accusations away from Liddell, however, it must have been other revelations that excited Costello.[98] For example, Costello wrote (in 1988):

> "Then, too, other sources told me about Liddell's premarital love-affair in the early twenties with a London University student (believed to still be alive), whose Marxism and links to the Communist party were well known to her contemporaries. This lead has so far proved impossible to corroborate, but if true, it could explain how one of the ranking officers in Special Branch might have become an early victim of a Soviet 'honeytrap'."[99]

Mure did indeed make an affair with an attractive left-wing student at Cambridge a central part of his story,[vii] but, if Costello had been able to read the *Diaries* themselves, it is unlikely that he would have come to the same novelettish conclusion. Strangely, he made no reference to Mure or *The Last Temptation* in *Mask of Treachery.* The background to these events may never be known: some who were close to them obviously believe that there is much truth in Mure's story, but it may be impossible to determine where fact stops and fiction starts, and all is clouded by Mure's inventive but rather irritating practice of identifying all the participants by names from the works of Charles Dodgson, whose creativity was

---

[vii] The lady in question is called "Alice" by Mure, and she marries "Hector", a Lord Mayor of London. If Mure's facts are correct, Hector would be Sir Dennis Lowson, and Alice would be Ann Patricia Macpherson. Further research offers another hypothesis. In his 1982 memoir *With My Little Eye,* Richard Deacon wrote: "In the early 1920s, when Liddell was working at Scotland Yard, supposed to be keeping a watch on communists, his mistress was Miss Joyce Wallace Whyte of Trinity College, Cambridge, and at that time one of the first women members of the Cambridge Communist Party. In 1927 she married Sir Cuthbert Ackroyd, who later became Lord Mayor of London. Whyte, born in 1892, was the daughter of Robert Whyte, JP, of Chislehurst, Kent."

inspired by Liddell's second cousin Alice. Mure missed the mark by treating his material with too much whimsy, and thus making his 'novel' neither fish nor fowl.

Thus, contemplating the written record from mendacious spies, secretive bureaucrats, deceptive memoirists, misleading intelligence officers, and an archive that is never complete and frequently redacted, all garnished with the speculations of the conspiracy-seeking and supermole-hunting espionage journalists, the analyst has to come to an assessment of the culpability of MI5's counter-intelligence officers, and Liddell in particular, in dealing with an increasing set of influential actors displaying pro-Soviet sentiments. The influence of the spies and their informal network of supporters was indeed furtive, not approved. It is more likely that Liddell was neither the "grandfather Soviet mole" (as claimed by Costello) nor "an exceptional intelligence officer in every way" (West), but something more prosaic. He was indecisive, naïve, impressionable, and too cerebral, learning as he went along, not bringing conviction or authority to his mission. His job was admittedly difficult. The agents he should have been investigating were smart, and well versed in subterfuge, and they were helped by a variety of well-intentioned but ingenuous acquaintances as well as some more dangerous miscreants, the 'agents of influence'. In 1940, after the revelations of Krivitsky should have moved MI5 into a heightened sense of security, the challenges of counter-subversion were however, made even more intense by the arrival in Britain of thousands of Europeans escaping from Hitler's oppression.

Notes

[1] The Guy Liddell *Diaries*, July 10, 1951; TNA KV 4/473.

[2] ibid., July 7, 1952; TNA KV 4/474.

[3] Cyril Connolly, in review of Spender's *World within World*, reprinted in *The Evening Colonnade*, p 360.

[4] Hugh Trevor-Roper, *Wartime Journals*, June 1942.

[5] M. Stanton Evans and Herbert Romerstein, *Stalin's Secret Agents: the Subversion of Roosevelt's Government*.

[6] ibid., p 252.

[7] ibid., p 226.

[8] Stewart Purvis and Jeff Hulbert, *Guy Burgess: the Spy Who Knew Everyone*; TNA KV 2/4117.

[9] TNA, RG/218; see also Andrew Lownie, *Stalin's Englishman*, p 319.

[10] TNA, FCO 128/26.

[11] Sir Anthony Reilly Papers (6920), at the Bodleian Library, Special Collections.

[12] Lownie, p 88.

[13] TNA, KV 4/186.

[14] Kenneth Rose, *Elusive Rothschild*, p 65.

[15] Peter Wright, *Spycatcher*, p 317.

[16] Jonathan Haslam, *Near and Distant Neighbours*, pp 102-103.

[17] Lownie, p 60; letter of October 25, 1988.

[18] Roland Perry, *The Fifth Man*.

[19] Rose, p 85.

[20] TNA, KV 4/472, November 17, 1950; KV/4/473, January 27, 1951.

[21] TNA, KV 4/192.

[22] TNA, KV 4/473.

[23] TNA, KV 2/4115; Stewart Purvis and Jeff Hulbert, *Guy Burgess: the Spy Who Knew Everyone*, p 123.

[24] TNA, KV 2/2588.

[25] Wright, p 117.

[26] John Costello and Oleg Tsarev, *Deadly Illusions*, p 229.

[27] Rose, p 262.

[28] Tape MI7.

[29] Tom Bower, *The Perfect English Spy*, p 47.

[30] Matthew Spender, *A House in St John's Wood: In Search of My Parents*, pp 117-118.

[31] TNA, KV2/3216, document 55.

[32] Communication between Matthew Spender and the author, June 2014.

[33] Lownie provided, in *Stalin's Englishman*, several examples of witnesses who admitted that Burgess told them he was working for the Russians, including the Reverend Eric Fenn (p 125), Osbert Lancaster (p 146), Robin Maugham and his sister (p 167), and Harold Nicolson (p 328).

[34] Driberg, Appendix, p 123.

[35] Malcolm Muggeridge, *Public thoughts on a secret service*, published in *Tread Softly for You Tread on My Jokes*.

[36] Tape MI7; see also Michael Ignatieff, *Isaiah Berlin: A Life*, p 98.

[37] Helen Fry, *Spymaster: the Secret Life of Kendrick*, p 92.

[38] Costello, p 348.

[39] Andrew, *Secret Service*, p 441.

[40] Newton, pp 16-17; Lord Gladwyn's letter to Verne Newton, February 18, 1986.

[41] Costello, p 347.

[42] Stephen Dorril, *MI6*, p 13.

[43] Michael Smith, *The Spying Game*, p 183.

[44] Percy Cradock, *Know Your Enemy*, pp 30-33.

[45] Washington Despatches, p vii.

[46] Tape MI7.

[47] Lord Gladwyn, *Memoirs*, p 101.

[48] TNA, FCO 158/3.

[49] Driberg, p 84.

[50] Robert Cecil, *A Divided Life*, p 149.

[51] Mitrokhin Archive, p 157; Newton, pp 281-282.

[52] Lownie, pp 222-223.

[53] Cecil, p 86; *Sunday Times* interview with Jebb, November 11, 1979.

[54] Costello and Tsarev, p 183.

[55] Lord Gladwyn, p 205.

[56] http://berlin.wolf.ox.ac.uk/

[57] Isaiah Berlin, *Flourishing: Letters*, 1928-1946, p 67.

[58] Ignatieff, p 40; Ignatieff cited Virginia Woolf, *Letters*, V, 255.

[59] Muriel Gardiner, *Code Name 'Mary'*, p 51.

[60] The quotations in this paragraph all come from Stephen Spender's *Letters to Christopher*, edited by Lee Bartlett.

[61] *Flourishing*, March 3, 1937.

[62] John Sutherland, *Stephen Spender, A Literary Life*, p 207; *Letters to Christopher*, p 102.

[63] Sutherland, p 207.

[64] *Spanish Front: Writers on the Civil War*, edited by Valentine Cunningham, p 8.

[65] Holzman, p 135.

[66] *Letters 1928-1946*, June 20, 1936, pp 173-174.

[67] *Letters 1928-1946*, March 3, 1937, pp 230-231 (and editorial notes); Tape MI9.

[68] Jenifer Hart, *Ask Me No More*, p 70.

[69] ibid., p xiii.

[70] Letter of November 13, 1975, from Isaiah Berlin's *Affirming: Letters 1975-1997*, p 13.

[71] *Flourishing*, October 31, 1939, pp 296-297.

[72] Bodleian Library, Berlin Archive, 107.

[73] Goronwy Rees, *A Chapter of Accidents*, p 131. In the published version of this work (1972), Rees referred solely to "a clever young English historian", but the writer Andrew Lownie has pointed out to this author that Berlin was specifically identified in the original version of the book.

[74] Isaiah Berlin, *Karl Marx*, p 147.

[75] Ignatieff, p 24.

[76] Ignatieff, p 169, "based on Berlin's notes on Russian edition of Kostyrchenko, 21.3.96."

[77] Isaiah Berlin, *Enlightening: Letters 1946-1960*, p 540, with annotations by Henry Hardy.

[78] Ignatieff, p 139.

[79] Gennadi Kostyrchenko, *Out of the Red Shadows*, p 282.

[80] *Letters 1946-1960*, June 30, 1949, p 99.

[81] http://berlin.wolf.ox.ac.uk/published_works/f/l1supp.pdf *Supplementary Letters, 1928-1946*, p 14.

[82] TNA KV 2/805, Security Service File on Krivitsky.

[83] Noel Annan, *Our Age*, p 275.

[84] Berlin made this claim several times; see, for example, http://berlin.wolf.ox.ac.uk/searchresults.html?cx=016211802011731888823%3Asspybdmovrs&cof=FORID%3A11&q=nothing+intelligence+&sa=Search&siteurl=http%3A%2F%2Fberlin.wolf.ox.ac.uk%2F

[85] R. W. Johnson, *Look Back in Laughter, Oxford's Postwar Golden Age*, p 134.

[86] *Karl Marx*, p 287 and p 289.

[87] Edward Harrison, *The Young Kim Philby*, p 20, quoting Kenneth Rose's *King George V*, p 369.

[88] F. H. Hinsley and C. A. G. Simkins, *British Intelligence in the Second World War*, (Volume 4), p 83.

[89] Maisky's *Memoirs*, p 204, and Maisky's *Diaries*, p 232. The phrase "melancholy misunderstanding" does not appear in *Diaries* published in 2015.

[90] Martin Kitchen, *British Policy towards the Soviet Union during the Second World War*, pp 6, 16, 21.

[91] David Mure, *Master of Deception*, p 267.

[92] David Mure, *The Last Temptation*, p 150.

[93] *The Guy Liddell Diaries, Volume 1: 1939-1942*, edited by Nigel West, p 7.

[94] *The Last Temptation*, p 210.

[95] David Mure, *Practise to Deceive*, p 15.

[96] Bower, pp 379-382.

[97] M. R. D. Foot, *SOE: The Special Operations Executive 1940-1946*, p 202, and Note 33.

[98] Lownie wrote that *The Last Temptation* suggests "Guy Liddell was a spy" (*Stalin's Englishman*, p 332). This writer disagrees with that conclusion, believing that it shows that Liddell was naïve, and initiated a cover-up to protect himself and the Service. This is the conclusion on Liddell's behaviour that Nigel West has reached.

[99] John Costello, *Mask of Treachery*, p 721, Note 41.

Chapter 7: MI5 Under Stress

"Since the end of the last war MI5 has been constantly aware that in this country it is by no means impossible for men in positions of trust and authority to become enamoured of Communist doctrine to the point where they will spy on behalf of the Russians and feel no shame in doing so." (Percy Sillitoe)

"The ideology of the Communist involves, at the least, a divided loyalty, which might in certain contingencies become active disloyalty." (Government memo of 1947)

"It was common for people to be very left-wing. If you talk about communists you have to ask yourself: could we have proved someone was actually a member of the party?" (Dick White)

MI5's attitude towards Communists, in the period from 1935 to 1945, evolved from a policy of disciplined opposition to a position of reluctant tolerance, which in turn developed into a stance of ambiguous endorsement, and finally a state of strategic confusion. This path was not an even one, broken into clear phases, and guided by strategic insight. It was subject to waxing and waning political influences, and punctuated by asymmetrical events such as Stalin's persecution of his own agents, the influx of refugees from Hitler's persecutions, the Nazi-Soviet Pact, the enigmatic testimony of Krivitsky, the rise of Churchill and his ascent to the Premiership, the fears of Fifth Columns, and, lastly, Hitler's invasion of the Soviet Union. That last event caused the latter to become an ally of Great Britain, and changed the groundrules for ideological battles, at least until the end of the war.

MI5 would have preferred the Communist threat to have come exclusively from the domestic Party, the CPGB, and for long periods of time it assumed that no bolshevik subversion could possibly arise unless it had close contacts with the Party itself, and that the main threat would come from open Party members. The Security Service continually struggled with the challenge of detecting, among the thousands of immigrants and visitors who appeared to find the cultural climate in Britain stimulating and liberating, those whose goals were actually to destroy it. It perpetually had trouble in dealing with the notion of subterfuge – the practice by which persons with nefarious purposes would go to great lengths to conceal their intentions, or even their identity.

During the first phase of disciplined opposition, MI5 struggled to identify an essentially shadowy target, since one of the critical components of the Soviet Union's espionage apparatus in the 1930s was the system of clandestine 'illegals'. Later, Walter Krivitsky was able to educate his British interrogators about such structures, which had been originally created by the Fourth Department of Military Intelligence. Krivitsky's emphasis was on Military Intelligence structures, although Archer's report shows that he represented OGPU as using the same techniques. And, as Krivitsky told MI5, OGPU began to control Military Intelligence in 1935, thus blurring the organisational distinctions between the two departments. These groups of infiltrators were not called 'illegal' because they were necessarily in the targeted country under false pretences, although, as it happened, in nearly every case their members would enter on a forged passport, or a visa acquired by illicit means. As illegals, they were contrasted to the *legal* organisation of spies found in the Soviet embassy, where the resident NKVD or GRU officer would carry out his tasks under cover of a diplomatic title. Thus the members of the legal structure had all the protections afforded to diplomatic personnel, and were able to exploit reliable and secure communication facilities at the Embassy, but were under consistent watch because of their official status. The illegals, on the other hand, enjoyed much more freedom of movement, but had to be more imaginative in delivering their espionage results, and could be left high and dry should their actions be detected.

As with much of Soviet tradecraft, the origins of the strategy of illegal subversion are not precise and indisputable. Boris Volodarsky set the initiation as far back as August 1925, when, after the unmasking of espionage efforts involving local Communist Party members, the Politburo banned their use as agents, and a joint meeting between the heads of the Comintern, Military Intelligence and OGPU resolved to sort out the problem. "It was during this meeting that Iosif Pyatnitsky, the head of the [Comintern] OMS, Berzin [GRU], and Trilliser [OGPU] decided to shift the main responsibility for intelligence collection from 'legal' to 'illegal' networks and to use local Communist parties and their members but only after getting permission from the Comintern's leadership." [1] Volodarsky went on to cite Berthold Ilk, in Germany, with pioneering the practice, Ilk acquiring by the end of 1929 ten major sources and 30 sub-agents. Yet this exercise was flawed, and Moscow Centre did not entirely trust the agents hired by Ilk, some of whom were later revealed to be relatives, others non-existent. [2] In 1930, Trillisser was replaced by Artur Artuzov as head of INO, OGPU's Foreign Intelligence service, who started to demand greater discipline in recruitment, training, and the creation of suitable 'legends' to make the biographies of such persons seem authentic. In 1932 Artuzov selected Leonid (aka Naum) Eitingon (a name that crops up frequently in the events of the Moscow Plot) "to coordinate the operation and training of illegals". [3] One of his first recruits was Teodor Maly, who played a significant role in Great Britain.

Soviet citizens would not have made good illegals. Artuzov and Eitingon realised that, in order to mix in smoothly in Western democracies, candidates would require some exposure to the ways of a liberal, merchant economy. Thus agents tended to come from the fringes of the Soviet Empire, and Central Europe, from territories with a history of changing boundaries, and varied ethnicities, where they could have picked up habits of modest entrepreneurialism, and where too demanding questions about birthdates, education and weddings could justifiably come to fail. They were cosmopolitan, and multilingual, yet had to believe in the Communist vision. Many were Jews, and took up occupations which lent themselves to excuses for regular postal transmission of goods and frequent travel, such as antique bookdealers. Krivitsky broke down the types of illegal into three – the chief, the assistant, and the *spekulant*, or speculator, an opportunist who enjoyed a precarious interdependent relationship with the Fourth Department because he was effectively stateless, and was open to blackmail, yet possessed skills that the Soviet organs vitally needed.[4]

During the 1930s, as Chapter 2 showed, MI5 struggled to deal with a variety of foreign intruders with apparently dubious motives. Were they engaged in dangerous subversion, or were they merely collaborating with members of the CPGB, which was, after all, legal? Tracking the movements and associations of someone like Otto Katz, who openly consorted with Communist sympathisers, and made his support for the anti-Fascist ferment obvious, took up a lot of time, yet the efforts of intelligence and Special Branch simply to keep him out of the country were thwarted by the energies of Pritt, Wilkinson, and Laski. On the other hand, while MI5 did not have a clear idea of the methods and structure of the illegal organisation until Krivitsky explained it, it was alert enough to try to track the most important illegal agents, namely Teodor Maly, Aleksandr Orlov, Arnold Deutsch, and Ignaty Reif (not to be confused with Krivitsky's close friend, Ignace Reiss, the illegal based in France who was murdered in 1937), who mostly took evasive action when making their appointments with their contacts. Obviously, Pritt and his colleagues could not help them if they got into trouble with the authorities. Yet, while the gradual disappearance of the illegals was largely self-inflicted, some paradoxes remain, since MI5 has withheld information on them in a puzzling and provocative manner. Ignaty Reif is the main enigma.

Reif arrived in Britain on April 15, 1934, to run the NKVD *rezidentura*, and had thus not been the illegal *rezident* "from 1931-1934", as Krivitsky claimed to his interrogators. (It is noteworthy that Reif and Deutsch both arrived in April, from Vienna, just as Philby did. This coincidence appears not to have been studied in the literature of espionage, where Philby's claims that he had not been recruited in Vienna have been accepted on faith too readily.) Reif is given the credit for recruiting Maclean, and guiding him into the Foreign Office. After requesting Philby to set up a meeting between him and Maclean in October 1934, Reif successfully cultivated Maclean, and signed him up. However, he was summoned to the Home Office shortly after, in January 1935, as his visa had expired, and he was told to leave the country.[5] What is extraordinary is that the Soviet archives suggest that the reason for his recall was the discovery by the Austrian police of a set of forged passports that had been used by Maly and Reif, and which had caused Maly to leave Paris in a panic. Yet the British authorities did not yet seem aware of Reif's forgery, and presumably wanted him out of the country for other reasons. As Costello and Tsarev related the event: "But, much to his relief, after a round of questioning by an official at the Home Office, Reif was not charged with passport fraud, but simply advised to arrange for his prompt departure from England by March 15 1935. As Reif reported it to Orlov, on the desk of the Home Office examiner he had observed a 'bulging file' stamped 'Wolisch', suggesting that his alias had been the focus of a considerable investigation by British authorities."[6]

This episode raises several questions. If there was indeed a "bulging file" on him, why has it not been released into the National Archives? (No indexed entry for 'Reif' or 'Wolisch' exists.) If Reif had indeed caught the eye of MI5 so conspicuously, in what activities had they detected his involvement? (He was heavily dedicated to nurturing Maclean during those few months.) And since MI5 apparently did not know that the real name of the person they had expelled was 'Reif', why would they not inspect their files for synchronicity of events after Krivitsky gave them such a good lead, and perhaps even show Krivitsky photographs in order to resolve the matter of Wolisch's identity? Had there in fact been another cover-up along the lines of the one that Archer suggested had occurred with Maly, in her report to Vivian in SIS [*see Chapter 2*]? By the time Krivitsky spoke about him to MI5, Reif was dead. After heading the NKVD British desk in Moscow, he was arrested on July 29, 1938, and shot a month later.[7]

As for Orlov, in October of that year, he claimed he had the bad luck to encounter in the street someone who had known him in Vienna, and he also had to make a hasty exit from the country. Early the next year, Maly was in turn appointed to head the illegal London network, and was able to supervise the recruitment of Cairncross in April 1937. But by then, the Great Terror had taken hold; Stalin had become frustrated with the Comintern's inability to foment revolution, and had grown feverishly suspicious of old-Bolshevik non-Soviet cosmopolitans like Maly. Maly had also spoken up rebelliously, questioning the order for Philby to assassinate Franco. He was summoned to Moscow in June 1937, and sentenced to death on September 20, 1938.[8]

Lastly, Arnold Deutsch, reputedly the most highly-regarded of all by his agents, behaved in a rather amateurish manner. In June 1934, he had moved into the Lawn Road Flats in Hampstead, a nest of Communists that should have caused Special Branch to give it close attention. In October 1935, he took over the handling of Maclean from Orlov, in the next couple of years having a strange set of relationships with other illegals, sometimes working for Maly, sometimes for himself. Burgess introduced him to Cairncross and Footman. In the spring of 1937, his identity was carelessly exposed by Percy Glading to the MI5 agent Olga Gray. And then, in June 1937, a potential disaster occurred: he lost a folder with contacts and monetary receipts, and left the country for Paris (where he met Krivitsky) to report it. Just as he was about to be withdrawn, the intermediary between Deutsch and his agents, Edith Tudor-Hart, found the folder in her sofa. Three months later, however, the police visited him in his flat, to check on his intentions to leave. He arranged for Philby to be introduced to Orlov, in Paris, and somehow succeeded in re-entering Britain in November (on the pretext of becoming a graduate student) "to conserve the network". Later that month, he returned to Moscow, but escaped the purge, only to be killed during a Nazi U-Boat attack a few years later. His last task in London had been to introduce Cairncross to the new legal *rezident*, Gorsky. MI5 did not know it at the time, but the Age of the Great Illegals was over. Yet the strategy of using such groups would endure for another 50 years, and MI5 needed to stay alive to it.

What that period showed was how difficult it was for MI5 to determine the true actions and objectives of nomadic Middle-Europeans with dubious contacts, and to decide what preventive measures they could take until such persons were caught red-handed in some illicit activity. The number of known illegals also points to a potentially far greater problem: Nigel West, for example, has surmised that, to justify themselves, they must have been handling a much larger quota of spies who have never been identified.[9] Yet MI5's efforts in this domain were rapidly frustrated, and their problems intensified, for other reasons. By 1937, the capabilities and capacities of the organisation were being stretched by a new challenge – the entry into Britain of thousands of escapees from Hitler's oppression, first from Germany, then from Austria, and finally from Czechoslovakia. The matter was first raised in Cabinet on April 5, 1933. In recent research, the struggles and the awkward manoeuvrings of British government departments in trying to develop a sensible policy in regard to this influx have been exhaustively explained by the historians Brinson and Dove, and from Louise London.[10] Brinson and Dove reported that "by the end of 1933, 600,000 refugees had left Germany, of whom only 2,000 came to Britain. . . At the end of 1937, only 5,500 [ex 155,000] had sought sanctuary in Britain".[11] Thus, compared with other countries, the problem was minor. Yet it was still an extremely complex one. To begin with, the only aspect the refugees had in common was their opposition to National Socialism. They included persecuted Jews deprived of their livelihood, as well as Communists driven underground, Catholics, pacifists and Social Democrats. Only later did the Jewish exodus dominate the matter of refugee policy.

To a twenty-first century pluralist sensibility that treats racial divisions as all very arbitrary, the pusillanimity of government officials during this period now appears difficult to explain away. Attitudes were apparently very much driven by the overall strategy of appeasement (in the sense of not ruffling diplomatic feathers, and avoiding war) that dominated the offices of state. There were few politicians or diplomats who would speak up to claim that the problem was really a German problem, not a Jewish one. A high priority was not upsetting Germany, and a regrettable trend arose of concluding that the 'Jewish problem' was one shared by the rest of Europe. Many bureaucrats and well-wishers wound themselves into contortions over the status of Jews, and the question of whether assimilated persons of Jewish origin who had become Christians were really nationals, with sophistical discussions about Jewish agnostics, non-Aryans not of the Mosaic faith, and, maybe saddest of all, the status of those who are "racially 100% Jewish but are not accepted by the Jewish communities as co-religionists", and had thus forfeited their claims to Jewish charity.[12] In any case, the failure of Britain and the other democracies to resist the Nazi strategy of expulsion only encouraged further oppression: as London wrote: "Indeed, as late as 1938 it was generally believed that the Nazis' expulsion of Jews from Germany and Austria created a manageable problem solvable by orderly emigration. The international community was generally resigned to the Jews' permanent expulsion."[13][i]

Thus the British government faced a multi-headed problem. It knew of official Nazi sympathisers already established in the country. It was aware of

---

i It is doubtful that the phrase 'the international community' was in broad use at this time, although it has been attributed to Adolf Hitler (in 1933) and Alexander Kerensky (in 1917). Nowadays, it is heavily overused, a shorthand for 'all other countries except the one who is misbehaving in this instance'.

Comintern agents encouraging subversion. And it was faced with the humanitarian challenge of absorbing a vast influx of refugees that might contain in its numbers concealed German spies, as well as genuine refugees from Hitler who in turn could be dangerous Communists or harmless social democrats. Above all, it lacked firm leadership to deal with the challenge. Brinson and Dove asserted that MI5's primary concern was still the threat of communism "at least up to 1935, and arguably until early 1939".[14] Yet, overall, MI5 was ahead of the government in its awareness of the Fascist threat. Its head, Vernon Kell, had been reluctant to investigate the Nazi mechanism for rallying nationals overseas, the *Auslands Organisation*, but had been persuaded, early in 1934, to do so by 'B' Branch and by Vansittart in the Foreign Office, someone who consistently opposed both totalitarian regimes.[15] Thus, by 1938, MI5 was at least realistic enough to see a double threat from the increase in refugees, namely a probable surge in Nazi espionage as well as in Communist subversion. It was unaware at this time that Germany harboured no deep penetration plans at this stage (unlike the Soviets), being content enough with its strong associations for nationals, and ideological allies in government, to further its political goals.

Moscow and the Comintern took advantage of all this confusion. Exiled members of the German Communist Party were able to enter the UK freely, with the active support of the familiar triad of Pritt, Wilkinson and Laski. By July 1936, the newly established German Communist Party (KPD) had between 30 and 40 members: that year, for instance, the economist Jürgen Kuczynski entered the country and joined his parents in London, claiming persecution and an inability to perform his research back in Germany. MI5 knew he was a Communist, and opened a file on him. In November 1938, after the invasion of Czechoslovakia, Ellen Wilkinson successfully appealed to the Home Office to grant immediate visas for as many as 32 Communists, some of whom had been refused entry several years before.[16]

While the arrival of a swarm of open Communists entering the country was alarming, both as a propaganda engine, and for the threat of espionage and subversion, the entry of Communists who concealed their affiliations (or pretended that they had abandoned them) was potentially even more damaging. One of the more deeply and darkly committed was Klaus Fuchs, who gained entry into Britain, largely owing to the help of his Quaker associations (an affiliation that has since turned out to be bogus) as early as November 1933. Despite the fact of his KPD membership being known by MI5, Fuchs rapidly advanced his career as a scientist, and was recommended to a position with Max Born in Edinburgh. The ownership of scientific skills was a strong card to play; the Communist Engelbert Broda was another, arriving from Austria in the summer of 1938, and successfully being employed at the Cavendish Laboratory, and later the Tube Alloys project, in 1941. Brinson and Dove observed: "The fact that his [Broda's] activities remained undetected, or at any rate unproven, within his own lifetime, was partly a matter of luck on his part – had he been apprehended he would almost certainly have served a lengthy prison sentence. But it was also to a large extent the result of serious misjudgment and inaction on the part of the British Security Service."[17] Another was the Czech communist, and crony of Kim Philby, Peter Smolka, who changed his name to Smollett, befriended Churchill's right-hand man, Brendan Bracken, and succeeded in entering the Ministry of Information at the beginning of the war, before rising to be head of pro-Soviet propaganda. MI5's reputed inaction was not so much listlessness, as a lack of communicating the threat with enough clarity and vigour, and thus being easily overruled. And it allowed its concern about the threat of 'German aliens' to subdue its enduring fear of Communist infiltration.

As the threat of war became real, in the summer of 1939, the focus changed to a generic concern about 'aliens', namely enemy nationals who had gained entry to Great Britain. Yet the definition of 'alien' was immediately problematic, and provoked a more humane but ultimately impracticable response. Indeed, the primary cause of the admitted chaos in MI5 at the end of 1939, and in the first few months of 1940, was the need to evaluate 'aliens' individually, by testing their background and beliefs, for the purposes of determining whether they should be interned. The Emergency Powers (Defence) Act had been passed on August 24, 1939, and consisted of a broad set of measures to intern enemy aliens, control exit from the country, and to apply postal and telegraph censorship. It was the interpretation of the alien measures, and the different perspectives concerning individual rights (represented by the Home Office) and more energetic concerns about national security (in the opinions of MI5) which caused the political clashes and confusion.[ii] Of course, there was a problem in considering any refugee from Germany or Austria a naturally hostile alien, as the person in question was probably opposed to Hitler's regime, but the fear that dangerous agents might have been clandestinely inserted into the ranks of such led the more pragmatic and hardnosed officers to prefer to err on the side of blanket internment at the risk of punishing any innocents. (In his history of MI5, John Curry frequently used the term 'Fifth Column' to describe the possible group of agents infiltrated at the time, but this terminology really consisted of some retrospective rewriting of history, as the Fifth Column phenomenon did not surface until May 1940.) In order to defer the prospect of universal internment, however, the Home Secretary had set up three classes for tribunals to consider. As Hinsley and Simkins reported:

> . . enemy aliens on the arrest lists would be interned, but tribunals would be set up to review the cases of all other enemy aliens aged 16 and over and determine whether they should be interned (Category A) or be subject to the restrictions prescribed in the amended Aliens Order (Category B) or be subject only to the rules applicable to all aliens and allowed to take employment (Category C). MI5 expressed general agreement with this policy, and orders to the Police to detain enemy aliens and British subjects on the arrest list were issued on 1 and 2 September."[18]

Yet, during October and November 1939, the Home Office issued guidelines to the tribunals to be far more lenient in their interpretation, and many candidates were moved from the B Category to the C Category. MI5 was not happy, and had obviously hardened its anti-German sentiments. The conflict between nationality

---

[ii] Of course, this debate continues, and is as relevant in 2017 as it was in 1940.

and ethnicity resurfaced. "MI5 was dismayed: in its world view, all Germans were *ipso facto* potential spies. Although some 90 per cent of German and Austrian refugees in Britain were Jews, MI5 considered them no less German for being Jewish", wrote Brinson and Dove.[19] Apart from the workload caused by internment cases, MI5 was flooded with requests for general vetting, the volumes increasing from a weekly average of 2,300 in January 1939 to 6,800 in September of that year, and rising to over 8,000 by June 1940. At the same time, it received complaints from a suspicious public that not enough attention was being paid to genuine subversive activities. Its officers were seriously overworked, and its complex (and of course completely paper-driven and ponderously-indexed) Registry system, where files were constantly being checked out and hence unavailable for anyone else, was under severe stress.

This climate contributed to a more indulgent view of Communists, despite the Nazi-Soviet pact, and the CPGB's vigorous opposition to the war effort. MI5's attitude towards Communists gradually shifted from disciplined opposition to reluctant tolerance. No resolute strategic direction could have been set by the Security Service, which very much had to attune itself to parliamentary, and popular, opinion; advocates for weaker and tougher approaches existed in all government organisations; the reality of a pluralist democracy consisted in the fact that issues were coloured with infinite variety, and a divergence of opinion was the norm. In addition, the period of the 'phoney' war was a confusing time. The war was being waged by a reluctant Prime Minister, who was temperamentally unsuited for the hard-headed single-mindedness required. The public was confused, as the *casus belli* of Poland appeared quixotic, with no suitable military response available, and the war aims were vague. Both MI5 and SIS (as well as the Foreign Office) appeared to be excluded from the deliberations of the Joint Intelligence Sub-Committee, which was dominated by Empire-oriented military men. The first few months of the war were thus characterised by paradoxical events that betrayed such confusion in all quarters.

For example, while Churchill, as First Lord of the Admiralty in Chamberlain's War Cabinet, started to make speeches supportive of the Soviet Union, General Ironside, "a furious opponent of the USSR", was appointed Chief of the General Staff on September 7. That appointment would appear to have countered Liddell's observation, made on September 5, that Communists would be allowed into the army rank and file, but not have access to confidential information. The reason for Liddell's confusion is clear. The CPGB had initially announced qualified support for the war effort, information that Hollis had passed on to Liddell on September 2, but, after Stalin's intervention with the Comintern, and the public shaming of Pollitt on September 18, when he published a pamphlet on winning the war, the *Daily Worker* articulated a volte-face, and the CPGB urged non-cooperation with the war effort for its members.[20] That could have spelled disaster for the factories and provoked rebel-rousing in the military. On the other hand public and private Communists were increasing their influence. On September 3, the crypto-communist Walter Monckton, the crony of Stafford Cripps, had been appointed Director-General of the Press and Censorship Bureau in the Ministry of Information: Cripps, meanwhile, after writing an article for *Tribune* justifying the Soviets' conquest of eastern Poland, then negotiated with the appeaser Halifax to venture on a mission to Moscow. Already, the substance of the Nazi-Soviet Pact was being seen to be ignored in the interests of defeating Hitler, and leftist leaders were starting to exert more influence. Chamberlain's administration was at a loss as to how to respond to Communist elements.

The diaries of a man central to the whole matter of countering harmful Communist influences can be seen as a reliable barometer to the political climate within MI5. An early entry of Liddell's perhaps symbolises how the growing intensity of the paramount need to defeat Hitler, and the battle between those consumed with anti-fascism, and those strongly opposed to both dictatorships, was evolving. On October 20, 1939, Liddell referred to the dilemma of holding tribunals on admitted Communists: "Kendal doesn't think he can put Broda before a tribunal as, despite working for the Comintern, he would say that he had the same objective as the Chairman, i.e. the defeat of the Nazis."[21] Yet this statement was made the very same day that the Chiefs of Staff warned about the Soviet dangers arising from the Nazi-Soviet pact, and two days after the CPGB had changed its tune to align itself with the Comintern's line that the war was an anti-imperialist war against the Chamberlains and Churchills of the world.[22] Ironically, the Chiefs of Staff were voicing their concerns about a matter that would very soon resonate forcefully – via Krivitsky's testimony - with MI5. Nevertheless, even though the Nazi-Soviet pact was fresh and the Soviet Union was starting to take a predatory interest in the Baltic States (Latvia, Lithuania, and Estonia), the mood was changing.

One major reason, as indicated above, was Churchill himself. At the beginning of October, he made a speech in which he cited the "community of interests" between Great Britain and the Soviet Union, and Ambassador Maisky noted Churchill's observation that he supported the country's moves to defend itself. A few days later, on October 6, Maisky reported that Churchill had told him that the differences between the two countries represented a "melancholy misunderstanding".[23] Similar moves were being made in Moscow: Maisky informed Cripps, who then told Halifax, that the Russians wanted to open trade negotiations.[24] And Sudoplatov of the NKVD hinted at more furtive manoeuvrings to influence opinion and policy in Britain. In the Soviet build-up to pre-empt the Nazis for control of the Baltic States, he wrote after a meeting with Beria in October 1939: "Now, with Europe at war, intelligence priorities had greatly changed, Beria said. He quoted Stalin, who demanded active involvement of intelligence operatives in political manipulations and exploitation of conflicts in ruling circles of foreign powers . . . We must play on the conflicts of British and Swedish interests in this area . . . [*the Baltic states*]."[25] This somewhat opaque description of exploiting well-placed allies within the fabric of the democracies reflects the little-publicised mechanism of deploying 'agents of influence', namely trusted persons of stature, sympathetic to the Soviet Union's mission, to say positive things about its goals. Elsewhere, Sudoplatov described the tactic in these words:

"The line between valuable connections and acquaintances, and confidential relations is very shaky. In traditional Russian espionage terminology, there is a special term, *agenturnaya razvedka*, which means that the material is received through a network of agents or case officers working under cover. Occasionally the most valuable information comes from a contact who is not an agent in the true sense – that is, working for and paid by us – but who is still regarded in the archives as an agent source of information."[26]

Sudoplatov did not identify who was helping the Soviet cause in Great Britain at this time, but he did use that precise term in referring to how the Soviet Union employed Prince Janusz Radziwill of Poland to negotiate with Goering.

The political climate was thus continuing to change, through internal pragmatism and by externally initiated propaganda, to express a higher degree of accommodation of Communists and their allies. As Penrose and Freeman wrote in their biography of Anthony Blunt: "At the outbreak of the war in 1939 there were hundreds of Marxists who were, in theory at least, security risks. Most scientists ignored the Communist Party's instruction to have nothing to do with the war. When the Home Secretary, Sir John Anderson, was told that it might not be wise to recruit J. D. Bernal as a scientific adviser, Anderson said: "I don't care if he's as red as the fires of hell. He's bright and he's committed to winning the war.""[27] As a recent example showed, MI5 did not think very imaginatively in those days. When, in 1938, MI5 had asked the vice-consul in Hong Kong, Derek Bryan, about the actions of the open Communist, James Klugmann, Bryan (who was admittedly a sympathiser) responded "that Klugmann may be a communist [but] he did not think either he or [Bernard] Floud are likely to be engaged in activities damaging to the British Empire'."[28] If that answer satisfied MI5, the service showed a woeful misunderstanding of what the mission of Communists was. Klugmann, who played a significant role in the Special Operations Executive rallying support for Tito in Yugoslavia, was both influential agent and spy. In August 1945, MI5 overheard Klugmann admit to Bob Stewart of the CPGB that he had passed on secrets to the Soviets.[29] Similarly, the Ministry of Information appeared not to have been briefed adequately by MI5, reflecting a very passive stance instead of a vigorous propaganda role. "At a meeting of the Cabinet's Home Policy Committee in November Lord Macmillan brought up the question of public meetings and observed that as the Conservative and Liberal supporters had 'gone off on war service the field had been left open to the Pacifist and Communist elements.'"[30] Such elements filled the vacuum. And the defiance by known Communists of direct orders from the CPGB *not* to support the war effort immediately put a heroic gloss on such initiatives, and made them acceptable.

Intriguingly, one of the first significant and symbolic examples of this development involved Anthony Blunt, *before* he was recruited by MI5. Having been rejected, late in 1938, by the Territorial Army when he applied to join the Officers' Emergency Reserve, a unit his brother Christopher belonged to, Blunt re-applied to the War Office shortly before war broke out.[31] He then received two letters – one of rejection (which he tore up), and one of acceptance, which ordered him to report to Minley Manor, the depot of the Corps of Military Police. Here was an example of the split personality of the Army: on the one hand, it needed smart linguists to defeat Hitler; on the other, it was highly suspicious of communists. Blunt was not a CPGB member, but he was an example of the 'disobedient' communist trying to assist the war effort, and his initiative could thus be seen in a favourable light. Early in October, he started a five-week course in military intelligence (along with such notables as Enoch Powell and Malcolm Muggeridge), only to be withdrawn after five days: on September 29, MI5 had submitted a report recommending that it would be "inadvisable to employ him on intelligence duties".[32] His fellow-officers were told that the reason was Blunt's communism. As Blunt's biographer, Miranda Carter, recorded, Blunt's first reaction was to panic, and invoke the help of Gorsky and Burgess. The latter intervened by contacting Dennis Proctor, who knew Major Kevin Martin, the Deputy Director of Military Intelligence based in London, and who was able to persuade the Major that Blunt's leftism was quite normal and harmless.[33] Blunt was thus able to convince Martin that he was well-connected, that his visit to Moscow in 1935 had been in some distinguished company, and that he should be reinstated. Martin ordered his return to Minley Manor. Blunt would later try to repay Burgess's favour in an attempt to have MI5 recruit him.

This episode is remarkable for several reasons. First, it was the War Office, and real Military Intelligence (as opposed to MI5, which bore a vestigial trace of that capability in its name) that rescinded its own policy of not hiring known communists. Second, MI5 was overruled – not by the Home Office (to whose opposition it was accustomed) – but by a supposedly more rigorous War Office, an event that must have influenced MI5's leaders. Third, it was a major indication that the policy towards Communists/communists had not been well deliberated, clarified, or communicated, and it was a gross lapse that it was left to an individual officer to make an impromptu distinction between intellectual marxism and practical communism, as if being an academic of *marxisant* leanings implied no security risk, no threat to the realm. Fourth, the volte-face was made very public, in that the attendees at the course would have interpreted the decision as an indication that communist principles were no longer an inhibition to military or intelligence service, and talked openly about it. However much the more vigorous opponents of Communism in various government departments would try to stand on principle in the next couple of years, the case of Anthony Blunt would have been readily cited as a reason for a more open-handed approach to harnessing communists in the fight against Hitler. 'Tolerance' of communists was now official.

And the pressure was on for MI5 to hire quickly. Liddell claimed that, in December 1939, four-fifths of MI5's time was spent trying to sort out the influx of refugees. Whereas MI5 had only 36 officers in July 1939, the number had risen to 102 by January 1940. Hiring was haphazard and reporting structures were non-existent. Curry admitted that "the organisation was in a state of confusion which at times amounted to chaos".[34] Vernon Kell had lost control. The battle between the Home Office and MI5 over the issue of selective or general internment continued. MI5 was forced to change its policy under the stress of the huge increase in workload caused by vetting individuals, and controlling departures from the country. As Hinsley and Simkins wrote: "MI5, on the other hand, which before the outbreak of war had attached far less importance to general internment than to the arrest of dangerous individuals, insisted from early in September that the deferment of general internment was not only dangerous but was being forced on it in contravention of the policy agreed before the war."[35] Such an attitude would later be echoed in a report by Nevile Bland (who claimed to have insider knowledge of the capture of The Hague, because of his previous role as His Majesty's Ambassador to the Netherlands) to the Home Secretary, at the height of the 'Fifth Column' crisis. He wrote: "It is better that one innocent man should be killed by mistake by the police than that dozens should be killed deliberately by a German with whom the police have no adequate means of dealing."[36]

The debates and ideological clashes continued throughout the winter. In October, the War Cabinet considered taking action against the anti-war propagandists of the British Union (BU) and the CPGB, but was talked out of it by the Home Office, which was sensitive to public opinion and the Peace Pledge Union (PPU).[37] Chamberlain continued to negotiate secretly with German generals who, he believed, were ready to stage a coup. Liddell and Cadogan noted increased Soviet espionage activity, and Liddell made representations to the Ministry of Information that it should not hire the communist John Lehmann. On December 1, Cripps published an article defending the Soviet Union's attack on Finland, and, a few days later, Ambassador Seeds in Moscow reported that the Soviet Union "has settled down into an undeclared war against Britain": he was soon afterwards encouraged to resign. The *Daily Sketch* warned on December 22 that Stalinism was "a kind of Hitlerism, to be defeated", while intellectuals like George Bernard Shaw and the Webbs issued a pro-Soviet press release.[38] By January 1940, CPGB membership has risen to 20,000, yet Hinsley and Simkins reported that public frustration at the lack of action against pacifist organisations had become widespread. Typical of MI5's concern was Communist infiltration of the Czech Refugee organisation, represented by those dozens of refugees whom Ellen Wilkinson had urged the Home Office to accept back in November 1938. MI5 still had the resources to write a long memorandum on this issue on January 15, 1940.[39] No overriding voice of leadership brought clarity to the picture.

Walter Krivitsky arrived in Liverpool on January 19, 1940. His testimony over the next four weeks should have provided a wake-up call to MI5 and the War Office – a renewed warning about Nazi-Soviet cooperation on intelligence, some deep insights on the long-established Soviet strategy for inserting moles into the halls of British government, and the structure of the illegal apparatus, some pointers as to the sources of recent leaks, and a reminder of the Soviet Union's enduring hostility to the interests of the British Empire. Indeed, the official history of Intelligence even claims that, for a while, MI5's awareness was raised. Hinsley and Simkins suggested that the attitude of MI5 concerning the Communist threat did in fact "harden" after the interrogation of Krivitsky, but offered as evidence only a memorandum of April 12 concerning refugees promoting Communist propaganda under the shelter of the Czech Refugee Trust Fund.[40] That was not a new issue, however, and the claim is hollow. Vernon Kell did, it is true, write to the Home Office, on January 30, with Krivitsky's testimony clearly fresh in his mind, claiming to have "very recent and extremely reliable information to show that the German Intelligence Service has been, for a long time past, collaborating with Soviet Intelligence", but there is no evidence that he energetically took up with his contacts in the War Office the lessons that should have been learned. On March 13, Dick White also wrote to Valentine Vivian of SIS of the "serious Communist problem" caused by the scores of refugees who had been allowed to enter.[41] Why he was addressing Vivian, however, is not clear: Vivian could not do anything about it. Curry in turn wrote that Jane Archer started to engage in "a long inquiry" into Soviet espionage after Krivitsky's return, but that was largely wish-fulfilment. At the same time he noted that Dick White was now supervising surveillance of the CP and the Comintern.[42]

What needs to be established, therefore, is why Krivitksy's warnings did not enjoy greater airing beyond the confines of MI5 and SIS. Certainly, no competent integration of intelligence inputs took place in the early months of 1940. During the phoney war, Chamberlain displayed a somewhat disdainful neglect of intelligence matters, as if he held espionage and counter-espionage to be rather sordid and ungentlemanly affairs. Stung by criticism from Churchill, however, who on October 31 had persuaded the War Cabinet to investigate leakages, Chamberlain had asked Lord Hankey to investigate the effectiveness of the services, first SIS, and then, early in March 1940, MI5.[43] Astonishingly, the text of Hankey's report has never been released to the National Archives by MI5: one immediately suspects the existence of embarrassing revelations that might have betrayed dire secrets. Did Hankey spell out gross mismanagement of the threats to the nation? Since he appears to have been exposed directly to Krivitsky's testimony, did he sound the alarm? What do the historians tell us of this period?

The accounts of MI5's role and mission in the months of the war when Chamberlain was in charge are very uneven. The official historian, Christopher Andrew, largely ignored what went on, neglecting even to mention the Hankey report in his coverage of this period.[44] John Curry's internal history, with its rather convoluted arguments, is honest about MI5's lack of preparation, and rapid descent into chaos, as it tried to handle the workload exerted by the need to intern aliens. He was outwardly very critical of the Home Office, led by a weak Home Secretary, John Anderson, who was very quick to shift his moral positions in the House of Commons under pressure from boisterous MPs. Implicitly, Curry criticised the leadership of MI5 for not engaging energetically in better strategic planning, failing to sell ideas upwards and thus not obtaining greater representation of security needs at cabinet level, and not demanding additional funding for MI5, to allow hiring of more officers and urgently required administrative help with the vital Registry. He was scathing about Lord Hankey's inability to understand what MI5's true mission was, and for failing to detect how broken the system was.[45] Hinsley and Simkins were a little more restrained: they provided good detail on the bureaucracy surrounding the bills passed in August and September 1939 to control aliens, and were more generous about Hankey's report (which arrived too late to help Chamberlain, as it was not submitted until the day Chamberlain resigned.)[46]

In fact, in 2009 Hankey's report was at last published – not by the government, but in translations of documents retrieved from the Soviet archives, courtesy of John Cairncross's purloining of secret material [*see Chapter 5*].[47] Yet no obvious scandals came to light that might have justified its withholding. Hankey's report is mostly pedestrian and superficial: he did not spend much time beyond briefly interviewing MI5 officers and representatives of those departments who depended on its services. He was a dedicated civil servant whose major impulse on detecting inefficiency was to recommend the creation of more committees. Some subtle references, however – the import of which Hankey may not have imagined – do stand out. He emphasised MI5's service role ("MI5 is essentially an inter-ministerial, advisory and non-executive body"), and was explicitly critical of its timidity in promoting its case ("I do not find MI5 to be as powerless to present its views properly as its representatives tend to assert"), although Hankey's instinct was for the well-drafted memo rather than building personal relationships ("For example, if the Director of MI5 feels that Home Office policies or decisions are insufficient to ensure adequate CI [counter-intelligence] efforts, he has the right to make representations to the Home Office and send copies to the Service organisations"). [48] He made the surprising revelation that it was the Foreign Office "that is responsible for MI5 and disburses its funds", but it "is not the department primarily interested in its organisation, efficiency and work methods", thus hinting at dysfunction. His knowledge of the Krivitsky interrogations has been shown earlier: he echoed the awareness that the CP was "working actively in the interests of the enemy". But why was the Committee of Imperial Defence (of which he was the chairman, and to which the Joint Intelligence Sub-Committee reported) not working successfully? He stated that the Deputy Director Sir Eric Holt-Wilson represented "MI5 at government and inter-departmental meetings, including the Committee of Imperial Defence". But Holt-Wilson, an old-school Christian imperialist whose nickname was 'Holy Willy', was almost as old as Kell, and does not appear to have been privy to the complications of Nazi-Soviet plots. [49] He would not have been an effective ambassador for MI5 at meetings of the Joint Intelligence Sub-Committee (JISC).

Since Hankey saw MI5 as too divorced from policy issues, he recommended the creation of a new committee "to meet regularly (at least once a month) to discuss issues of interest to all departments principally concerned with CI". At this forum would be invited the directors of naval, military and air intelligence, with the chairman an independent voice, probably from the Foreign Office. Maybe that notion became the germ of Churchill's Security Executive, but the mechanism was already in place – the JISC, which clearly needed more vigorous and committed participation. Hankey's conclusion is thus bizarre. In any case, his report appeared to fall by the wayside. Under a Prime Minster who believed in the value of intelligence, the JISC was given new energy and elevated to new full committee level (i.e. the JIC). Yet with the dismissal of Kell and Holt-Wilson, the rise of the intellectuals in MI5, and the Fifth Column panic, the warnings of Krivitsky still remained subdued and ignored.

Meanwhile, the forces of subversion and propaganda moved rapidly to work. Liddell's defences must have been detectably lowered by the time he encountered Victor Rothschild at the beginning of 1940. The first mention that Rothschild receives in Liddell's *Diaries* is that, apparently after a request from Admiral John Godfrey (Director of Naval Intelligence), Liddell dined with Rothschild, who "is doing sabotage work for MI/R". Rothschild suggested that the research he was undertaking for offensive purposes might be useful for MI5, in guiding factory owners in how to detect sabotage. (This dinner took place on February 15, the day before Krivitsky left for Canada.) The next time they met was March 6, when Rothschild was explicitly quite critical of MI5, claiming to represent the opinion of the Committee of Imperial Defence that MI5 was being negligent in not preparing to counter Nazi sabotage energetically enough, an issue about which Rothschild was "quite ruthless". In an unpublished entry for March 15, Liddell reported that Rothschild had essentially been taken under MI5's wing, as he was going to Paris on some business of sabotage research "under cover of MI5", to discover how the French address the problem: it is probable that Rothschild might not have been able to justify his mission to meet with his conspirators without such a cover. Liddell noted Rothschild's return on April 15, entering in his diary the same day that the 20 Regional Security Offices were being set up, to deal with sabotage (the organisation of which Jane Archer was to be put in charge). On April 18, Rothschild offered his services to MI5, and three days later, Liddell noted that Kell had given his approval for bringing Rothschild in as a part-time member of staff. On the 25th, Rothschild's support had been esteemed so greatly that Liddell happily reported that he would be coming into the office three times a week to look through their files, and give them the wisdom of his advice. Liddell did not define where this assistance may have lain, but Rothschild was no doubt able to gain a better fix on the state of Krivitsky's revelations, and any actions arising from them. Shortly after (the date appears not to be recorded anywhere), Rothschild became a full-time officer for MI5, heading a one-man counter-sabotage department, B1c.

From this period on, Liddell, an essentially decent but vulnerable and impressionable individual, became increasingly split between his professional instincts and his attraction towards colleagues and friends of a distinctly free-spirited, even bohemian, disposition. He became more strongly influenced by Rothschild, and was introduced to the latter's artistic friends. Most significant of all was Rothschild's introduction to Liddell of Anthony Blunt. Whereas Blunt's biographers have stated that Blunt was not recruited to MI5 until August 1940, after appealing to Rothschild for help, Liddell's testimony reveals that that timetable is suspect.[50] He wroteites as early as June 7 that his organisation is "taking on Anthony Blunt". Blunt had made a perilously late escape from France via Boulogne on May 25, showing a reluctance to leave that may have indicated nervousness about his reception back home.[51] But thanks to Rothschild's rapid infiltration of MI5, he landed quickly on his feet. Decades later, Dick White, reminiscing and trying to cover his tracks in conversations with the journalists Penrose and Freeman, attempted to present such an event as inevitable, suggesting that "there was little anyone could have done to prevent men such as Blunt from joining MI5":

"Remember the climate of the time. There was nothing resembling positive vetting. It was common for people to be very left-wing. If you talk about communists you have to ask yourself: could we have proved someone was actually a member of the party? Very few of them were card-carrying members of the party. Remember the size of the intake that came into MI5. We would have needed something positive to go on. And even if we had wanted to do that we would have been discouraged by the government. The feeling was that anyone who was against the Germans in the war was on the right side."[52]

This is sophistry of the first order. First of all, it was not an issue of card-carrying members of the party. Blunt had shown communist sympathies, MI5 had given the War Office firm advice that he should not be hired, but had then folded into irresponsibility itself by hiring the unreformed Blunt. White and Liddell were in positions of authority to make such decisions, but chose not to do so, with White cloaking everything in a vague, romantic nostalgia for generic leftism (was he one of those "people"?), at a time when the Soviet Union was not an ally, and Communism was a defined threat. Margaret Thatcher also partially exculpated MI5 after Blunt was exposed, saying to the House of Commons on November 16, 1979: "It might seem extraordinary that an avowed Marxist should have been able to join the security service. But it was all very well to say that with hindsight: it had to be remembered that the intelligence services were under enormous pressure and had neither the time nor the manpower to vet every recruit".[53] But she was wrong. He had been vetted, and the answer was negative.

Thereafter, the problem intensified, although Liddell was not helped by the incompetence of his boss, Jasper Harker, another phenomenon that reinforces the fact that MI5 was poorly led. Jenifer Hart (then still Jenifer Fischer-Williams), who had already infiltrated the Home Office, was approached by Harker in June 1940 and asked whether she knew any suitable candidates for recruitment. (Almost certainly, it was Rothschild who put Liddell and Harker up to this.) Her intimate friend Herbert Hart, having been recommended by her on June 17, signed the Official Secrets Act on July 3, and began working for Liddell soon after. As Herbert Hart's biographer, Nicola Lacey, described it, the incident had a touch of farce, and merits citation in full:

> "He apparently started work before a formal recruitment check was completed: a few weeks later, Harker again came to see Jenifer to tell her that MI5 'liked Herbert and thought him very able' but wondered if he was 'all right'? Later in the day, MI5 had discovered that his home address was subject to a warrant authorising the Post Office to intercept foreign mail directed there. The suspect turned out to be Douglas Jay, then a journalist on the *Daily Herald*, who had been reported to MI5 as having 'sinister foreign contacts'. Herbert was duly cleared and his formal appointment to MI5 confirmed. Confident of Douglas's loyalty, he was able to reassure MI5 and, ultimately, to have Douglas's file destroyed, though the imputation delayed for at least a year Douglas's recruitment by the Ministry of Labour and Supply, despite his presence on the national register of those keen to do war work. In the meantime Jenifer, her communist past not far behind her, had a nasty fright. In the course of her conversation with Harker about Herbert, the name of one of her Communist Party friends had come up, and Harker had asked her, 'You weren't a communist, were you?' 'Oh, we were all red in our youth,' Jenifer replied, with a *sang froid* which belied her deep alarm."[54]

Such was the rigorous process of vetting possible Reds. Hart herself echoed the episode in her own conversations with Penrose and Freeman, though making out the process to be more straightforward than it actually was: "I saw a lot of the MI5 people and got on very well with them. One day the head or deputy head of MI5 said – and I think this was May 1940 – that they were desperately short of people and did I know of any bright young men? I recommended someone who got in at once. They were very pleased with him. I could have easily recommended someone who either was or had been a communist."[55]

Blunt even tried to infiltrate Guy Burgess into MI5 – much later in 1940, after the Moscow Plot had unravelled, and Burgess had been 'fired' from the ashes of Section D that had been absorbed into SOE. The account comes from Christopher Andrew's official history, which explained that Blunt appeared to have convinced Liddell that Burgess's track record in successfully running agents, and his knowledge of the Communist Party, justified his consideration as a Service officer. Blunt had an opening: he had encountered Guy's sister-in-law, Constance Burgess, at Wormwood Scrubs, whither MI5 had been moved on the eve of the war, and Constance had managed to have her husband Nigel Burgess recruited by MI5, and eventually installed under D. K. Clarke in F2 (a), a subsection of the new 'F' Division's F2 (Communism and Left-Wing Movements), which was led in 1941 by Roger Hollis under John Curry.[56] Despite Liddell's recommendation (and admission that Guy Burgess had been a Communist, but had "completely abandoned" his commitment), Curry, to his credit, rejected Burgess, since he did not trust his claim about having outgrown Communism.[57] Liddell would later congratulate Curry on his judgment, but Curry was shortly to be moved out of his mainstream position and replaced by Hollis.

Meanwhile, Liddell's schizophrenic approach to Communists was further evidenced in his dealings with other departments. In the middle of March, 1940, he noted that Roger Hollis's plan for dealing with the Communist Party was complete, and being sent to the Home Office: "It envisages internment under 18b for organisers and other important people and a number of searches." At this time, the Government was very concerned about subversive efforts by the CPGB to undermine the war effort, either by mutiny in the armed forces, or by sabotage in the factories. Three days later, Liddell insisted to Newsam in the Home Office (who on January 15 had taken over responsibility for all matters involving MI5, as the Home Secretary was too passive) that "every communist must be regarded as an enemy agent" and he recorded (with Krivitsky's warnings clearly fresh in his mind) that he told Newsam: "The liaison between the two Intelligence Services [Russian and German] had existed since 1923 although it had perhaps been somewhat thin from 1935-39. The link nevertheless remained and we must therefore assume even in the absence of confirmatory information that anything that went to the communists ultimately reached the Germans if it was likely to be of any use to them." On April 4, in a discussion with White and Hollis, he reiterated his determination to tighten the screws against Communists: "We recommend internment of certain aliens now, internment of selected members of the CPGB in the event of war with Russia, close control of other alien communists and restriction of their movements, restriction of the movements of British communists wishing to proceed abroad or to Ireland and control of export of communist literature." Noteworthy is the reference to the possibility of war with "Russia": also the revealing statement about "alien" communists, as if those who were not British nationals were untrustworthy, while British Communists had only Britain's (imperial) interests at heart. [58] Brinson and Dove called attention to this delusionary sentiment: "It is striking that some of the few successful spies within the German-speaking refugee community, like 'Sonya', Edith Tudor-Hart and Margaret Mynatt, were able to establish themselves in Britain more smoothly than most, thanks to a significant technicality – British nationality."[59] That attitude would set the tone for the next ten years.

A touch of self-delusion was starting to appear, as if the reluctant and far too sentimental Home Office were the barrier to B Section's ability to protect the country from malevolent alien influences. The Home Office "interferes" in surveillance of subversive elements (April 26); Maxwell (Hart's boss) gave unsatisfactory responses about internment (May 8); the reluctance of the Home Office to act came from "old-fashioned liberalism" (May 25). Yet the face Liddell showed externally was very different from the one he displayed with more influential persons whom he respected. For example, Rothschild's influence is again shown in a remarkable entry for June 29, where Liddell described a meeting he had with Rothschild and Sir George Gaytor, who was Permanent Under-Secretary to the Ministry of Supply. "He was evidently worried that we had turned down certain people who were of communist tendencies. I explained to him that this work had of necessity to be done by rule of thumb, that we were not all Blimps, that we would be glad to review any case with which he was not in agreement. 'It was up to somebody else to say whether the risk should be taken in the interest of urgency of production'." Resolute action against possible Communist subversion was now caricatured as "Blimpishness", and Liddell had effectively abdicated his responsibility. The new phase of 'ambiguous endorsement' of Communists had been reached.

Perhaps surprisingly, given Churchill's strong support for intelligence, MI5's morale was adversely affected by his accession to the premiership after Chamberlain was ousted on May 10, and any opportunity for tightening up its strategy disappeared. Churchill immediately put his personal stamp on matters, promptly firing Vernon Kell, and introducing a new Security Executive to oversee intelligence matters, under his trusted associate, Lord Swinton, to whom Kell's deputy, the ineffectual Jasper Harker, had to report. The precise reasons for Kell's dismissal are not clear. He may have been made a scapegoat for the disastrous Norwegian campaign: other accounts suggest that Churchill was infuriated by an episode of sabotage in his constituency, at Waltham Abbey. Kell was relatively old (66 when he was fired), but only a year older than Churchill. Yet the manner of his dismissal was curt, and the transition to new leadership clumsy. Andrew has given a good account of the confused months of that summer, when morale in MI5 fell precipitately because of uneducated interference on the part of Swinton and his business efficiency experts.[60] Yet a more subtle influence was at work: Churchill's government was, of necessity for national unity, a coalition into which significant Labour/Socialist politicians had been brought, which introduced a whole new complexion about war strategy, and a completely new dimension to official attitudes towards the Left. For example, the crypto-

Communist Stafford Cripps (who had been the bane of MI5 in the 1930s, promoting revolution, and thus being expelled from the Labour Party, and praising Soviet excursions in the Baltic) was appointed Ambassador to the Soviet Union at the end of May. Later in the year, in October, Ellen Wilkinson, another thorn in MI5's side, would become Parliamentary Private Secretary to the newly appointed Home Secretary Herbert Morrison. Thus in a matter of months, individuals previously characterised by the Security Service as threats to the nation were now its political masters.

The change in mood can be seen in the proceedings of the Security Executive. The committee was instantly caught up in the fever of the hunt for 'Fifth Columnists', a cause to which Swinton brought instant energy, as Churchill himself had been alarmed at the reports coming from Poland, Norway and the Low Countries, of subversive actions instigated by spies and sympathisers who were in communication with the invading army. Yet the matter quickly morphed into a generic concern about opposition to the war rather than a hunt for Nazi intruders and sympathisers. Swinton began to soft-pedal the issue, referring to the "delicacy of whole question of taking action against communists", with Ernest Bevin, the Minister of Labour and National Service, expressing, on May 29, his firm opposition to any action against Communists.[61] Such a policy was reinforced at a meeting on July 10, where it was conceded that "repressive force might alienate factories and left-wing sympathy, as well as provoke hostile reaction from the Soviet Union". Here, already, was evidence of appeasement – of Stalin, not Hitler, this time, although the two were allies – but also a subtle indication, carefully nourished by Churchill, that a real need to keep Stalin's goodwill was necessary in order to prosecute the anti-Hitler war successfully. Stalin would, of course, have scorned such pusillanimity and lack of conviction, yet this essential cowardice was to last. On January 28, 1941, Swinton continued to draw Talmudic distinctions between Communist 'bad men' and their better colleagues who might be weaned away by suitable publicity.

The irony of the whole scare was that a true 'Fifth Column', the notion of which originated in the Spanish Civil War, when ethnically undistinguishable civilians who were ideologically opposed to the government in control of the territory in which they lived, and were controlled by an enemy military power, was a rare phenomenon. It had been a factor in Poland, where ethnic Germans lived within the boundaries, and to a lesser extent in other Northern European countries: for example, there were 100,000 Germans living in Holland, when it was invaded. A few spies had no doubt been landed in the UK, but they were poorly organised. Rumours were allowed to thrive, and insignificant episodes granted too much importance. One government minute of June 25, 1940, reported that "the possibility of the Germans letting loose prisoners, lunatics and wild animals" appeared to have started with Dennis Wheatley's *The Invasion and Conquest of Great Britain*, but gave it credibility simply by recording it.[62] Another report indicated that all sorts of trivial exploits, such as inattention to black-out restrictions, and minor sabotage at work in order for the miscreant to get dismissed, were being reported to the authorities as 'Fifth Column' activity.[63] On the other hand, the US diplomat Madeline Albright recorded in her memoirs that "One summer morning announcers [*from the New British Broadcasting*

Station in Germany, delivered by William Joyce] spread an alarm that during the night 'German parachutists wearing civilian clothes were dropped in the vicinity of Birmingham, Manchester and Glasgow. They carry capsules to produce fog and to avoid capture. Some are equipped with an electromagnetic death ray.' Many listeners, having been warned for so long about the terrors of war, were quick to believe the worst." [64] Irresponsible British journalists were thus complemented by effective German propaganda.

In that way the Ministries were carried away from a focus on a real danger to an all-encompassing campaign about opposition to the war. A memorandum from the Ministry of Information issued on April 27, 1940 declared: "The Fifth Column is the title now applied to all those elements in this country which oppose the National war effort. . . Fifth Column adherents may be divided for convenience into four groups: Communists, Fascists, Pacifists, Aliens."[65] John Anderson, the Home Secretary, tried to bring some sanity to the debate on May 17: "There are among the Czech refugees Communists who, like the British Communists, are opposed to the war, but there is no information to suggest that these persons would be likely to assist the enemy", and "Although the policy of the British Union of Fascists is to oppose the war and to condemn the Government, there is no evidence that they would be likely to assist the enemy. Their public propaganda strikes a patriotic note." [66] Nevertheless, Churchill remained very excited and suspicious for a while, wanting to intern all aliens, which resulted in a flurry of internment and deportation activity. As Andrew reported, "between May and July 1940 about 22,000 Germans and Austrians and about 4,000 Italians were interned".[67]

Yet a German Fifth Column in Britain was almost certainly non-existent. This has been the studied conclusion of most histories of the period: that no armed organisation *in communication with the Wehrmacht* (which, technically, is how a German Fifth Column would have been described) was operating in Britain. Yet the verdict is not undebatable. After Sir Oswald Mosley, the leader of the British Union (formerly the British Union of Fascists) was interned in May 1940, a large cache of arms was found at his residence. Despite Mosley's claims of patriotism, the question has to be asked: in what situation, and against whom, might the British Union have used such weapons? This question has not satisfactorily been resolved.

At the time, however, the threat of a Nazi-controlled, or Nazi-inspired, military force was felt to have passed. Liddell, bitterly annoyed by all the phantom reports coming in from well-intentioned citizens, expressed his frustrations in his diary on July 3, 1940, characterising the "Fifth Column neurosis" as "one of the greatest threats with which we have to contend at the moment."[68] The establishment of the 12 Regional Security Liaison Officers in late June took much of the load away from MI5 centrally, thus easing some of the strain. But the sinking on July 2 of the *Arandora Star*, carrying over a thousand internees to Canada, with great loss of life, put the spotlight back on the inhumanity of the programme. The government accepted that too many innocent persons had been detained. The cause was dropped. As Andrew wrote of its demise: "Later in the month [August], Churchill told the Commons, with what one historian has called 'an impressive display of amnesia', that he had always thought the fifth column danger exaggerated."[69] There is no evidence that Guy Burgess engineered the whole fiasco, but he would have been delighted with the way that government energies were distracted from the warnings that Krivitsky had given to the chasing of illusionary menaces.

What had happened in the meantime was that a notionally dangerous Nazi 'Fifth Column' had been replaced by the establishment of a long-term strategic threat – the nest of Communist agents and sympathisers in all sections of government. The goal of this gang was not to provide immediate military help to an invader, but to help rot the fabric of society so that it would eventually be subjected to the Communist revolution that its leaders believed in. MI5 had reached the stage of confusion and self-delusion. It could no longer take a stance against the Communist threat, as it had brought such ideologues into its ranks, and no longer had the authority to prevent their acceptance elsewhere in government. It made spurious distinctions between patriotic English communists, and untrustworthy aliens of the species. It convinced itself that it was merely acting in tune with the tide of public opinion, and the desire for national unity, failing to distinguish between democratic socialism and totalitarian communism. It failed to realise (and warn) that the Soviet Union was only a temporary ally, and that, as soon as the war were over, it would revert to its traditional position of ideological foe and existential threat.

It is true that the occasional voice would remind authorities of the permanent danger. In October 1940, Roger Hollis would voice his amazement at the Ministry of Information's indulgence towards communism, and would make a similar plaint in November of that year. [70] But since he had approved the Ministry's employment of 'Red Cecil', the communist poet Day-Lewis, in April of 1940, his reaction was hypocritical, and his disgust can by no account be justified. On August 6, Liddell again showed similar ambivalence (having just hired Blunt) in a diary entry: "Roger has put up a memo advocating that communists should not be allowed to remain in key positions either in Govt. departments or in industry. He is going to submit the proposal to Leggett before we put it forward to the HO. I think the moment has come when they will have to put their cards on the table. It is quite obvious when a man is removed that he is removed on account of his political views and I think we may as well say so in suitable form namely that as he owes allegiance to a foreign government, he is not a suitable person to be in position of trust where confidential information is available." [71] Liddell's 'cognitive dissonance', the ability to hold two contradictory ideas in his head at the same time, is remarkable. But the cause was essentially lost. By December, Churchill was convinced that Hitler would turn East, and invade the Soviet Union, and it would not be long (June 1941) before the monster Stalin would begin his metamorphosis into the more accessible and lovable 'Uncle Joe'. Occasionally a voice would declare that the Soviets should not be trusted simply because they had become the country's (temporary) allies, and Swinton and the Security Executive would still warn that "the Communist Party was not loyal to this country", but the messages increasingly fell on stony ground.[72]

MI5's attitude towards Communists was however to take yet one more turn during the war. The story of one major Soviet agent of this period proves that

MI5 could no longer be described simply as struggling to find pride in a policy that had lost its way: it indeed had to try to cover up for some irresponsible and highly negligent actions in failing to prosecute an identified spy. His name was Leo Long, and the story of his remarkable escape from prosecution shows how MI5 and Section 'B' moved from ambiguous endorsement to strategic confusion.

The Case of Leo Long

When the media and historians have written about Soviet espionage, they have concentrated almost exclusively on the concept of the 'Cambridge Five', echoing the irritating propaganda of their Soviet handlers. This misguided flattery extended even to the pen of the future authorised historian of MI5, Christopher Andrew, who wrote of the 'Magnificent Five', which might be characterised as an unnecessarily respectful method of classifying some of the most dangerous traitors this country saw in the twentieth century.[73] The deliberate attention given to the pentad, which aims to subtract from the importance of spies excluded from the group, obscures the fact that there were other significant players at work.[74] The above-mentioned Leo Long certainly deserves to co-reside in this pantheon of renegades, especially as far as the risks and exposures of 1939 to 1941 are concerned. If there were a 'Sixth Man', Long would be that person. Long, like Blunt, a member of the Apostles at Cambridge University, had been recruited by Blunt in 1937, and had successfully managed to be installed in a War Office Department, MI14, in 1940. He was eventually revealed by Blunt as one of the latter's sources, but also gained immunity from prosecution, his identity not being revealed until 1981.

A much overlooked account of Long's activities appeared in a book that MI5 tried to ban. Shortly before she died, in Malta, in 1984, Joan Miller completed her memoir of the Second World War. Miller had been an agent working for Maxwell Knight, the head of MI5's B5(b) unit, and had early in 1940 infiltrated the Right Club, and thus assisted in the successful prosecution of Tyler Kent, the American who was leaking secrets of the Churchill-Roosevelt exchanges to the Germans, and of his fellow-conspirator, Anna Wolkoff, a Russian émigrée who was the club's secretary. Another personal account of exploits fighting Hitler 40 years before might not have been expected to cause much of a ripple: was there much new that could be revealed? Yet, *One Girl's War*, subtitled *Personal Exploits in MI5's Most Secret Station* was no ordinary memoir: the writer was subject to the Official Secrets Act, as, after her involvement with MI5, Miller worked for the War Office, in a unit concerned with gathering information on German activities, MI14. Miller struggled to get the book published. It eventually appeared in 1986, but had to be published by Brandon Books, in Dublin, outside British jurisdiction. As its back-cover proclaims: "This is the book the British Attorney General tried to stop in the High Court in Dublin, saying that its publication would do irreparable damage to the British Security Service, MI5." Yet historians of intelligence have strangely diminished its importance: in his Introduction to Guy Liddell's *Diaries*, Nigel West described *One Girl's War* as "an innocuous memoir", failing to discern why the British government would seek injunctions to its being published in the UK. In his biography of Tom Driberg Francis Wheen similarly dismissed it. "Absurdly, the British government prevented this charmingly innocent book of wartime memoirs from being published in the United Kingdom."[75] Are these critics perhaps missing something? Why would the British government have tried so strenuously to ban the book?

What is crucial about this episode is its timing. It came at a very awkward period for the British government, which was attempting to stop the ex-MI5 officer, Peter Wright, from publishing his memoirs, in what became known as the *Spycatcher* trial, held in New South Wales's Supreme Court, in November 1986. When an enterprising journalist on the *Observer*, David Leigh, noting that a book about to be published by rival journalists, *A Conspiracy of Silence*, quoted the statements of numerous ex-MI5 and SIS officers by name, he drew the attention of the Treasury Solicitor, John Bailey, to the work, suggesting that it was rank hypocrisy to persecute Wright when other officers were being allowed to break their own confidentiality agreements with impunity. As the authors, Barrie Penrose and Simon Freeman, reported, the Treasury had to back down – not out of principle, since it was clear that the officers were at fault, but out of pragmatism, as it did not want another battle on its hands. Instead, it showed a token force by throwing the book at Joan Miller:

> "To show that they meant business Whitehall's guardians of the secret society decided to stop publication in England of the biography of the late Joan Miller, who had worked for Maxwell Knight of MI5 during the war. Miller's book seemed harmless. She had no secrets to reveal; she was just a butterfly-minded old lady reminiscing about what it had been like to be a very young, pretty little thing in MI5. It was not even the first time she had spoken about her work with Knight. Her book was just an extended version, padded out by a ghost-writer with background information, of an interview which she had given to Barrie Penrose in the early 1980s and which had been published in the *Sunday Times Magazine*. But the government was determined to stop the book; it had a point to make. No one who worked for British intelligence, even old ladies with nothing much to say, would be allowed to write their memoirs."[76]

This seems a very clumsy and hypocritical action, if indeed Miller's book had nothing to reveal. Yet Penrose and Freeman, like everyone else since, missed the important reason why the government wanted to ban Miller's memoir. In his account of the Hess peace initiative, the historian John Costello claimed that Tyler Kent and Anna Wolkoff had been "stitched up" by MI5 in a ruse to discredit the US Ambassador Joseph Kennedy, and for that reason the British government prevented the publication of Miller's work.[77] This seems an unlikely explanation: Miller gave no indication that her role was anything but an effort to uncover genuine subversive activity, or that the pilfering of documents by Kent never happened. Moreover, if MI5 had indeed "stitched up" Kent in order to rid itself of the unpleasant and dangerous Kennedy, it would have been an achievement to be proud of.

MI5, on the other hand, tried to make it appear that it wanted the story of the homosexuality of Miller's boss, Maxwell Knight, covered up. Yet this was a revelation that could have hardly excited the British public in the mid-1980s. The over-emotional response on the homosexuality issue was designed to cloud an even more damaging revelation. Joan Miller never identified by name the character involved, but, after she fell out with Knight, in February 1944 she was given a job in MI14, where she worked alongside "an ex-bank manager and a Major". "To this office came all the top-secret cables, already decoded; our job was to read each one and send it on to the correct destination . . .".[78] This "Major" irritated Miller by his intense questions about her remuneration, and she became perplexed about him when she noticed that he displayed a constant habit of writing down the substance of cables coming from the Middle East on a separate piece of paper. Saying nothing, she instead contacted her old mentor, Knight, who expressed much interest in the matter: he discovered that references to those particular cables had been picked up on the telephone lines from the CPGB headquarters in King Street, as well as in the reports of his agents. Knight arranged for the Major to be arrested outside Bush House (where MI14 was located) by two Special Branch officers.

Miller gave a later hint to the identity of the Major when she wrote: "Much later, after VE day, the Major turned up in Germany in the Control Commission."[79] Now this combination of clues points unerringly to Leo Long, whose cryptonym at Moscow Centre was RALPH.[iii] An independent verification of Long's career in MI14 has been provided by the distinguished academic, Noel Annan, author of the very influential *Our Age*. In his memoir about his wartime and post-war activities, *Changing Enemies*, Annan wrote of his encounters with Long. Early in 1941, he had found Captain Long (the "Major" was a slight distortion) already installed in a unit dedicated to discovering facts about "the operations of the German secret services, the Abwehr, Gestapo and Sicherheitsdienst". "Its head was a theatrical character, Brian Melland, and he was aided by Leo Long, an efficient young officer who was to be shamed years later when he was identified as one of the Cambridge spies."[80] Annan also offered evidence for the type of information that fell into Long's hands, presumably destined to be passed via Anthony Blunt to Bob Stewart at the CPGB, when he described the efforts of the supreme code-breaker at GCHQ at Bletchley Park: "Dilly Knox broke hand-cyphers, which the Abwehr used. These were invaluable to Melland and Long in MI14 (d)."[81] Annan provided further confirmation of Miller's description by explaining that Long worked alongside him in the Control Commission in Germany in 1945 and 1946.[82] The Mitrokhin Archive reports Long as being Deputy Director of Military Intelligence there.[83]

The implication from Annan – and everyone else who has written about Long – is that his espionage activities did not come to light until 1981, when Blunt, under interrogation, revealed his complicity in 1964, and explained that he had recruited Long in 1937. This is the account that the Prime Minister, Margaret Thatcher, provided in a response to a question tabled by Mr Canavan in the House of Commons, on November 9 of that year.[84] Thus even the most current

---

[iii] Leo Long is normally identified as RALPH. Some writers have also given him the codename ELLI, who was a spy in MI5, but Long never worked for MI5. See also Endnote 18 to Chapter 5.

research echoes the accounts of Peter Wright, and his interrogations of Long, as given in *Spycatcher*. For example, in his 2014 biography of one of Stalin's key agents, Alexander Orlov, Boris Volodarsky simply repeated Wright's account that Long, during his time with MI14, handed over "any intelligence he could lay his hands on" to the man who had recruited him in 1937, Anthony Blunt.[85] What everyone has overlooked is the fact that, according to Miller, Long was detected, apprehended – and then set free. Soon after Long's release, she questioned Knight about the handling of the case, but her ex-boss behaved very casually about the whole incident. The Major had escaped prosecution. "He [Knight] told me the Major had been posted to a dreary job miles away from London where he could do no harm."[86] Moreover, Peter Wright boldly reported (in 1987) that "throughout the war he [Long] met clandestinely with Blunt and handed over any intelligence he could lay hands on", adding the detail that, after the war, Long moved to the British Control Commission.[87] Nothing could have provided a firmer confirmation that the man whom Joan Miller had seen arrested was Leo Long. But Wright had clearly not read *One Girl's War*, and no one not in the know made the connection.

No independent verification of Long's arrest has come to light, and thus one has to progress with some caution about the reliability of Miller's testimony. Yet what could her motives have been for lying about the incident? There seems no strong reason to doubt her account: it is presented as an incidental observation about the bizarre policies of MI14, where she believed she acted in a professional manner by alerting Knight, but found that her concerns were apparently no longer relevant. If one considers the timing, perhaps Miller considered Prime Minister Thatcher's statement about Long inadequate and deceptive – which it indeed was, relying too much on Long's confession being honest. For example, one of Thatcher's observations ran as follows: "He has all along said that he did not pass information to the Russians during this period" (i.e. 1945-1952), as if the claim of a traitor could be accepted at face value, and the questions of members of parliament could be assuaged by such assertions. Moreover, Blunt had died in 1983: Miller's book came out in 1984. Having kept quiet about the incident for four decades, she presumably became troubled by the lack of openness in government statements about espionage during the war, and felt she had nothing to lose by providing such insights near her deathbed to help set the record straight. Miller had had original evidence of Long's treachery, and Blunt's abetting of it. She may well have resented Blunt's expiring without the truth coming out, and it clearly troubled her that MI5 had done nothing about the discovery of a Soviet spy in its midst.

So is Miller's story trustworthy? Even though Long's career as a spy is now public and well-known, hers is the sole account of the witnessing of his pilfering of secrets. There is no record of Long's 1944 malfeasance and 'arrest' (if it were such) in the National Archives. Yet the implications are astounding. If Long had been "taken away by a couple of Special Branch officers" (as Miller wrote) there would surely have to be a record of an arrest warrant. If there is no record of such, either he was not arrested, or the record has been destroyed. Of course, such an event would not have been unique. After Commander Crabb, naval frogman and SIS agent, went missing during an exploratory reconnaissance dive on a Soviet cruiser in 1956, SIS officers tore out the relevant pages from the hotel register where he stayed. Records are sometimes tampered with. Thus one is left with the following conclusions: either Miller fabricated the whole affair, a reason for which it is difficult to conceive, and the British government in truth tried to ban this "charmingly innocent" and "innocuous" memoir for as yet undiscovered reasons; or, the anecdote is true, which means that Liddell and White engaged in a cover-up of a monumentally irresponsible proportion, an embarrassment so deep that one can understand why MI5 would wish to suppress it over 40 years later. But by attempting to ban it, the Security Service merely drew attention to it.

One remarkable aspect of this event is the testimony of Chapman Pincher, who was apparently advised by Miller of the conduct of the 'Major', but never managed to link his identity with that of Leo Long, despite all the obvious clues, and Pincher's track-record as a sleuth. When Pincher published *Too Secret Too Long* in 1984, he recounted an anecdote that Miller had told him, when she was "working in another secret department in Bush House in the Strand", which exactly corresponds to her description of Long. Pincher's focus was on Hollis: he wrote that "while compiling a book in the late 1970s about her experiences, Miss Miller claims that she concluded that he [Hollis] must have been a Soviet agent". [88] Elsewhere in the book, Pincher related how the news of Long's treachery was received by Arthur Martin of MI5 "with a low groan", as if a familiar truth had now leaked out, and he later chastised Hollis ("supported by some of his senior colleagues") for granting Long unofficial immunity. [89] Of course, Long had the knowledge up his sleeve that he had been found out, and let off, so was no doubt able to negotiate a deal that preserved his silence. Yet Pincher recorded that Long worked both for MI14 during the war, and also for the Control Commission in Germany. He repeated the whole story in *Treachery* (2009), again failing to make the linkage between Miller's account and the facts as Long had then confessed to. [90] It was a rare miss of a scoop, no doubt occasioned by Pincher's relentless and single-minded pursuit of Hollis.

If a spy had been discovered in 1944 within the War Office, it must have come to the attention of Liddell and others at MI5. The only rational explanation for his being let off is that, at that time of the war, with the Soviet Union now a valuable ally, and Hitler's Germany being slowly crushed, someone in authority was of the opinion that sharing secret information with the Soviets, however unauthorised the manner of its delivery, could somehow be overlooked or forgiven. Maybe it was forgotten that the Soviet Union's role as an ally did not mean that individuals could take it upon themselves to set policy: the Official Secrets Act specified that secrets should not be disclosed to "any foreign power". That argument was, of course, the way that the Cambridge Spies justified their own actions to themselves, deeming that the Soviet Union, as an ally, merited access to any intelligence maintained by the UK and the USA, blithely ignoring the fact that the control of the transmission of information to the Soviet ally was no doubt being managed capably by some other agency. An astonishing hint to the possible insouciance of the authorities is however offered by the availability of a report that Kim Philby gave to his Soviet controllers after a briefing by his boss, Valentine Vivian, on May 10, 1943. (The report was retrieved from the KGB archive in the late 1990s.) In Philby's words:

"Vivian said that the Russians had known about Operation TORCH in advance, repeating what he had already told me – namely, that the Russians had had accurate intelligence on the codes, beaches, medical supplies, etc., for the operation long before it was launched. In other words, senior officers involved had gone straight from their desks at the War Office to clandestine rendezvous with Communists. Frank Foley then asked where those officers were now. Vivian replied that they were still in their jobs. 'We did not want to make a big thing of it', he added. This reply of course leads one to assume that the authorities know who these officers are, although I cannot vouch for the accuracy of what Vivian said."[91]

Vivian's casualness is breathtaking, and his willingness to explain the indulgence suggests that this was an accepted policy, agreed to on high. In the absence of any other documentation, it is difficult to imagine how such a policy could have been arrived at, especially so late in the war, when sharper intelligence officers were already starting to question the sincerity of Soviet strategies, and their possible long-term harmfulness. It presumably must have had MI5's approval as well. In such circumstances, it is surprising that Leo Long was even reprimanded, but the statements would have returned to haunt the intelligence services, had they come to light a few decades earlier.

Such a policy, however, did overlook the vital fact that Long had been employed by MI14 since the beginning of the war, and that he had probably, therefore, been passing on information illegally to the Soviets from a time when the Soviet Union was enjoying its non-aggression pact with Germany (and possibly, even earlier), and had therefore represented a distinct threat to Britain's security. Thatcher's 1981 statement strongly implied that Long had been passing information to Blunt between 1940 and 1945. Andrew and Gordievsky confirmed that Long "had full access to the Ultra intelligence derived from the success of Bletchley Park in breaking the Luftwaffe variant of the Enigma machine cipher in May 1940".[92] Indeed, if the Soviets had chosen to share such information with its ally (as its pact allowed), the fact that the German codes had been cracked by Knox and his associates could well have reached the enemy, with devastating results.

Moreover, MI5 and the Foreign Office were keenly aware of increased Soviet espionage activity in 1939 and 1940, as the diaries of Guy Liddell (at that time the head of 'B' Division, responsible for counter-espionage) and of Alexander Cadogan (Permanent Secretary at the Foreign Office) show. In addition, the interrogation of Walter Krivitsky in the early weeks of 1940 crisply alerted MI5 officers to the dangers of moles within the Security Service. Liddell's behaviour over the threat of communist subversion is bewildering: he must have been responsible for the laxity in recruiting standards even before the Nazi invasion of the Soviet Union (in June 1941), yet could write in his Diary as late as October 27, 1942: "There is no doubt that the Russians are far better in the matter of espionage than any country in the world. I am perfectly certain that they are well-bedded down here and that we should be making more active enquiries. They will be a great source of trouble for us when the war is over."[93] The responsibility – and blame – for later mayhem lies firmly at Liddell's door.

It was surely scandalous that Long, having been discovered transporting secret information to the Soviets, should ever have been re-hired in a government position. By 1946, the war was over, and the Soviet Union was the new threat, with the security of atom bomb research of primary importance. On September 5, 1945, the cipher clerk Igor Gouzenko had defected from the Soviet Embassy in Ottawa, which prompted an immediate review by MI5. In fact, this meeting accelerated an existing concern, as Calder Walton has informed us: "In August 1945 he [Sir David Petrie, Director-General of MI5 from 1942 to 1946] held a high-level meeting with the Chief of SIS, Sir Stewart Menzies, about the problem of crypto-communists employed in secret work – on which Philby in SIS would certainly have been briefed – and on September 5 he, Hollis and other 'F'-Division officers discussed at length, the 'leakage of information through members of the Communist Party.'"[94] Somehow communications broke down over Long's crime and status, or else a wilful and criminal high-level decision was made that it was in the country's interests to re-install him in a sensitive position.

The last implication is that a serious investigation into Long's *curriculum vitae* would surely have led to the Apostles at Cambridge, including Anthony Blunt, who, as described earlier, after being rejected for a position in intelligence because of his communist past, had managed to weasel his way back in. The Apostles was (and is) a secret society of intellectuals at Cambridge University. It has a track-record of encouraging extreme left-wing thought: Burgess, Blunt, Cairncross and Long were all members of the group. Thus a solid lead was overlooked. Blunt was Long's contact, but had been temporarily replaced as such by Guy Burgess when he was posted to France in November 1939. As was explained earlier in this chapter, Blunt had escaped from France via Boulogne in May 1940, and had then succeeded in entering MI5 after an introduction to Liddell by Lord Rothschild, and by July he was installed as Personal Assistant to Liddell himself. From there he was to exert a baneful but subtle influence. Miller herself told how Blunt exercised his charm on Knight: "I am sure M never suspected Blunt, which is rather odd really, as he had had several protégés at Cambridge before the war, and certainly knew all about the Apostles." Knight seemed unwilling to pursue any investigation. Later, Blunt was to continue his mischief, even trying to get Long into MI5. Chapman Pincher wrote that Blunt serviced Long in Germany after the war, and that the KGB was applying pressure to get Long into MI5.[95] He added that the selection board "turned him down by a narrow margin": it would be interesting to know how many on that board knew about his past. But, of course, Blunt must have had a high degree of confidence that Long had been forgiven, and that he himself was not at risk of being unveiled, for him to be as aggressive as he was in putting Long's name forward. Long must surely have had to explain to Blunt why he had been arrested.

In fact, there is evidence of Blunt's approaching MI5 on Long's behalf before the war was over. Guy Liddell recorded in his *Diary* entry for May 11, 1945, that he lunched with Anthony Blunt and Leo Long – the latter presumably soon restored to respectability after the penance of his dreary job in the countryside.[96]

Liddell made no reference to recruitment, but the inclusion of, and introduction from, Blunt suggests that this was an attempt at bringing Long in. Liddell no doubt was suffering pangs of conscience. Peter Wright (the ex-MI5 officer of *Spycatcher* fame) confirmed the 1946 attempt at recruitment, venturing the opinion that Long's non-hiring could be attributed to a bias of Liddell's. "Luckily for MI5, Guy Liddell had a marked prejudice against uniformed military officers, and blackballed him at the Board", he wrote, adding, quite astonishingly, "even though Dick White supported him, much to his later embarrassment." [97] That claim would suggest that White knew nothing about the arrest of 1944, or, being aware of it, thought it no longer mattered – or would never come out in public. What is also remarkable is that, at this stage of the war, and with Leo Long apparently restored to respectfulness, Blunt might himself have become more open about his sympathies. In 1984, Chapman Pincher wrote the following, based on a conversation he had with T. A. R. Robertson: "Blunt ceased to work full time for MI5 in November 1945. At which point he remarked to a colleague, Colonel T. A. Robertson, 'Well it's given me great pleasure to pass on the names of every MI5 officer to the Russians.' Robertson, who knew that Blunt made no secret of being a communist, passed the information on to those who should have reacted to it, but nothing was entered on Blunt's file." [98]

In fact, when White was interviewed by Penrose and Freeman in 1985, he showed an artless deceitfulness about the whole affair: "Yes, Blunt tried to get Long in. Long struck me in Germany as an able man with a good grasp of things. The sort of chap one wanted to have on one's side. I advised him to get back to university. I didn't think we wanted these chaps hanging around the service. I don't think I had any suspicions of Long at that stage. Indeed, when it was discovered that he had been helping Blunt I was rather appalled." [99] Given that Long had been detected red-handed in giving secrets to the Soviets, White must have been desperately trying to define his legacy, and the reputation of the service, before he died. One cannot really believe that he was of such leftish persuasions that he wanted Soviet spies "on his side". It was one thing for White to be indulgent about Long in 1944, when Stalin was an ally, and his goodwill needed to help conclude the war against the Nazis, but quite another for him to pretend, when the Cold War was on, and Burgess and Maclean had shown their true colours, and he suspected Philby of being the 'Third Man', and the cryptonyms of JOHNSON and HICKS in the VENONA transcripts pointed alarmingly to a nest of Soviet spies in the fabric of British government, that the whole episode had never happened. Indeed, his irresponsibility is even more striking since, a few months before Burgess and Maclean defected, White had received a public rebuke from Sir Percy Sillitoe, the head of MI5, for not following up recommendations made in 1945 by a 'B' Division officer, Michael Suppell [*sic*][iv] that the atom spy Klaus Fuchs should have been investigated at the time. Sillitoe was persuaded to lie about the cover-up to Prime Minister Attlee. White had shown unacceptable naivety in the face of Fuchs's life-history, while the banished

---

[iv] 'Suppell' is an incorrect transcription of oral testimony, as provided to Tom Bower and Nigel West. The officer's correct name is 'Serpell', as the National Archives confirm. For more on Serpell, see Chapters 8 and 9.

Jane Archer had reportedly written: "Fuchs is more likely to betray secrets to Russians than the enemy."[100v]

If Liddell were sincere in his observation about 'embarrassment', that would on the other hand indicate that White in fact knew nothing of the arrest, which in turn suggests a degree of secrecy about the whole investigation of Long in 1944 that is breathtakingly unlikely. After all, if Knight knew the outcome, one would have expected White (who was Deputy-Director to Liddell in 'B' Division at the time) to know, too. As for Liddell, the thought that he, after discovering that Long was a Soviet spy, did not immediately perform a detailed background check to ascertain who the offender's associates and connections were, defies belief. Rothschild and Blunt must have worked some peculiar magic on him.

One additional factoid that may have some bearing on the case is the extraordinary book, *The Last Temptation,* published in 1984 (two years before Miller's delayed book appeared) by the ex-intelligence officer David Mure [*see Chapter 6*]. What is noteworthy is that the work represents a kind of apologia for Liddell and MI5 in general over the Communist spy crisis, and is a dramatic volte-face from Mure's work of 1980, *Master of Deception,* which is very scathing about MI5 and in particular the Double-Cross System. One of the major claims of *The Last Temptation* is that MI5 was directed to hire Communists in order to secure the Soviet Union's entry into the war, and keep it there.[101] One could thus easily assess the book as an item of White-inspired disinformation to counter the brewing challenges from the *Spycatcher* affair and even Miller's publication. Part of the narrative involves Blunt's confession to Liddell that he had been a Soviet agent since he joined the service (p 182), a statement that Liddell accepted with little shock. Blunt opened his heart to Liddell in 1944, after he had been appointed as liaison between MI5 and SHAEF (the Supreme Headquarters Allied Expeditionary Force): whether this anecdote came from the unredacted diaries, from insider knowledge, or had been completely fabricated, is impossible to tell.

And what about Knight? After all, he had a reputation for being one of the most diligent pursuers of communists, and of constantly reminding his superiors of the Communist threat. It would have been unlike him to stand idly by as Long escaped from justice. But by then, his reputation was crumbling. He had disgraced himself with the affair of Benjamin Greene [*see Chapter 2*], and he would no doubt have been reminded of his security obligations at the time of the Long disclosures. His methods fell out of favour with the new head of MI5, Percy Sillitoe, who replaced David Petrie in April, 1946, and his allies Jasper Harker and Desmond Morton also retired. Joan Miller came to the conclusion that Knight was being subjected to blackmail in the later years of his life, and the threat of exposure might well have been an added pressure applied to him as he tried to establish a new civilian career. She concluded that one risk he may have taken in his private life may have caught up with him: she no doubt did not recognise the threat that his involvement in the unmasking of Long represented to the established heads of MI5.[102]

---

[v] This statement was in fact made by Jane Archer's husband, John, as is explained in Chapter 9.

What exactly transpired will presumably never be known, but the whole episode reeks of a woeful dereliction of duty. The attitude to Communists in government was highly indulgent at that time – and even later, when the Cambridge Spies were unmasked. Annan himself played lightly on the theme, as if treacherous espionage were a naughty, schoolboyish pursuit, when he wrote of Long, after the latter had congratulated him on his OBE in 1946: "Whether he was still passing information to the Russians I do not know, but my activities in Berlin against the KPD, of which he can hardly have approved, did not affect our relations."[103] The sense of moral equivalence from the chronicler of *Our Age* is astounding in its naivety, but Annan clearly had more sensible afterthoughts in his later years: in his own conversations with Penrose and Freeman (1985), he said:

> "There were ways in which material from Bletchley was passed to the Russians. But, of course, the Russians weren't told. No doubt they guessed but it was essential, the whole security for the invasion of Europe depended on it, that Ultra was kept secret. It could easily have been captured from the Russians in a German offensive. It was monstrous to communicate this material to the Russians. I have no sympathy with the argument that the Russians should have been told. None at all. That was the job of the British government. But then Long had the same sort of arrogance which Blunt had. The two were very alike in temperament. Long was very dismissive about anything which didn't coincide with his views."[104]

Thus, when the true treachery of Long and his associates came out in the succeeding decades, certain officers in MI5, and members of government, must have realised that, in their not pursuing Long seriously, they had committed an enormous error of judgment, and they accordingly determined that the British public had to remain uninformed about the secret so long as MI5 existed. By drawing attention to Joan Miller's memoir, they unwittingly pointed out that within it lurked a revelation of highly damaging potential. For almost 30 years, the Security Service managed to elude close inspection because of Knight's erratic and inappropriate lifestyle. Now, in 2017, the organisation has to face the facts anew, and have the wraps once again removed from its dismal history of failing to uncover Soviet penetration, and claiming that the institution behaved completely honourably during its 'time of troubles'.

Notes

[1] Boris Volodarsky, *Stalin's Agent*, p 31.

[2] Christopher Andrew and Vasili Mitrokhin, *The Mitrokhin Archive*, p 38.

[3] William E. Duff, *A Time for Spies*, p 54.

[4] TNA, KV2/805-52x.

[5] Volodarsky, pp 85-88; Duff, p 77.

[6] John Costello and Oleg Tsarev, *Deadly Illusions*, p 144.

[7] Volodarsky, p 105 and p 546. The chronology surrounding Reif's movements is very complex. On page 83, Volodarsky suggested that Reif arrived in Vienna on August 29,

1933, and stayed there a couple of weeks, before going to Geneva to receive his instructions from Zarubin, whence he left for Copenhagen before entering Britain in April 1934. But, on page 546, Volodarsky added, in a note, that "in reality [*sic*], Reif was sent to Britain in August 1933, travelling via Vienna and arriving in London in mid-September". *Deadly Illusions* is sloppy about dates: Costello and Tsarev had Reif writing his report "after his return to Moscow in 1939" (p 188), and suggested that Reif "for nearly a year had been running the NKVD *rezidentura* in London" at the time Orlov first arrived in Britain on July 15, 1934, even though they stated that Reif arrived there for the first time on April 15 (pp 114-115).

In a private communication, Volodarsky told this author that neither Costello/Tsarev nor Duff can be trusted, as their works are riddled with errors. But Volodarsky is inconsistent, too: his chronology for September 1933 does not work, and his notes contradict a portion of his main text. He provided no sources for his claim that Reif was in London as early as September 1933. He also asserted to this author that MI5 had no file on Reif, "since Christopher Andrew found none there", ignoring the fact that it may have been destroyed. Volodarsky indicated that the anecdote about the 'Wolisch' file appeared first in *Deadly Illusions*, but was unsourced, and that neither the Home Office nor MI5 had ever released files on Reif/Wolisch. Of course, that does not necessarily mean that they never existed. He also claimed that the whole issue of dubious passports was invented by Orlov to facilitate his permanent departure from a country he was not comfortable in. Lastly, Volodarsky appears to have been a little too trusting about the degree of attention of Soviet agents to principles of tradecraft, asserting that Krivitsky, when he met Bystrolyotov, would never have heard him referred to by his real name, but only by his alias, Gallieni. But Krivitsky knew the real name of Commander King. Admittedly, Burgess and Blunt (especially) consistently broke tradecraft rules, to the despair of their handlers, while Maclean and the American agent Golos both had 'illegal' affairs with their couriers (Kitty Harris and Elizabeth Bentley, respectively).

[8] Duff, p 183.

[9] Nigel West, *The Illegals*, p 139.

[10] Charmian Brinson and Richard Dove, *A Matter of Intelligence (MI5 and the Surveillance of Anti-Nazi Refugees 1933-50)*; Louise London, *Whitehall and the Jews 1933-1948: British Immigration Policy, Jewish Refugees and the Holocaust.*

[11] Brinson and Dove, p 22.

[12] London, p 126 and p 128.

[13] ibid., p 281.

[14] ibid., p 79.

[15] Brinson and Dove, p 46.

[16] TNA, KV 2/2798.

[17] Brinson and Dove, p 219.

[18] Hinsley and Simkins, *British Intelligence in the Second World War*, (Volume 4), p 21.

[19] Brinson and Dove, p 103.

[20] Liddell, KV 4/185, Hinsley and Simkins, pp 305-307.

[21] Liddell, *op. cit.*

[22] Geoffrey Moorhouse, *The Devils' Alliance*, p 104.

[23] Martin Kitchen, *British Policy towards the Soviet Union in the Second World War*, p 2; Ivan Maisky, *Memoirs of a Soviet Ambassador*, p 33.

[24] Gabriel Gorodetsky, *Grand Delusion*, p 16.

[25] Sudoplatov, *Special Tasks*, p 100.

[26] ibid., p 195.

[27] Simon Penrose and Roger Freeman, *Conspiracy of Silence*, p 140.

[28] Geoff Andrews, *The Shadow Man*, p 93; TNA KV 2/788.

[29] *The Shadow Man*, pp 102-104.

[30] Ian Maclaine, *Ministry of Morale*, p 47.

[28] *Conspiracy of Silence*, pp 229-231.

[32] Christopher Andrew, *In Defence of the Realm*, p 269.

[33] Miranda Carter, *Anthony Blunt: His Lives*, p 244.

[34] Andrew, p 222; John Curry, *The Security Service, 1908-1945*, p 145.

[35] Hinsley and Simkins, p 32.

[36] TNA, CAB 79/4/74.

[37] Hinsley and Simkins, pp 36-38.

[38] Moorhouse, p 75.

[39] Brinson and Dove, pp 144-145.

[40] Hinsley and Simkins, p 38.

[41] Brinsley and Dove, p 144: TNA KV2/2715/34.

[42] Curry, p 161.

[43] Hinsley and Simkins, pp 39-40.

[44] Andrew, pp 222-223.

[45] Curry, pp 145-161.

[46] Hinsley and Simkins, pp 22-40.

[47] Nigel West, *Triplex*, (Part III, Document 31).

[48] ibid., p 213.

[49] Andrew, p 42, p 227.

[50] Penrose and Freeman, p 252.

[51] Penrose and Freeman, p 235: evidence from George Curry.

[52] Penrose and Freeman, p 265.

[53] ibid., p 554.

[54] Lacey, *A Life of H. L. A. Hart*, pp 84-85.

[55] Penrose and Freeman, p 480.

[56] Penrose and Freeman, pp 256-257. Nigel Burgess does not appear in any of the organisation charts offered by West or Curry, although West confirmed his role as a "career MI5 officer", and Costello confirmed that Burgess worked next to Kemball-Johnston. Otherwise, Nigel Burgess appears to have suffered some Soviet-style airbrushing out of history, although Guy Liddell did briefly refer to him in a diary entry for April 11, 1941, alongside Roger Fulford, a crony of Guy Burgess whom Hollis had brought into MI5. (The National Archives: KV 4/187). Nigel Burgess was one of many ex-intelligence officers who were named in a House of Commons Debate on National Security (Prosecutions), on November 20, 1986, where the Attorney-General was asked what steps he proposed to take against those suspected of leaking information on matters relating to national security to "Mr Rupert Allason, alias Nigel West". (See http://hansard.millbanksystems.com/written_answers/1986/nov/20/national-security-prosecutions).

[57] Andrew, pp 270-272.

[58] TNA, KV 4/186.

[59] Brinson and Dove, p 235.

[60] Andrew, pp 227-230.

[61] TNA, CAB 21/3498.

[62] TNA, CAB 120/468.

[63] TNA, INF 1/336.

[64] Madeline Albright, *Prague Winter*, p 166.

[65] TNA, CAB 75/7.

[66] TNA CAB 67/6/31.

[67] Andrew, p 227.

[68] TNA, KV 4/186.

[69] Andrew, p 230; David Stafford, *Churchill and Secret Service*, pp 280-281.

[70] Maclaine, p 187.

[71] Liddell, KV 4/186.

[72] Hinsley and Simkins, p 82.

[73] Andrew, *The Hunt for the 'Magnificent Five'*, (Section D, Chapter 6).

[74] Cairncross stated that Michael Straight, not he, was really the 'Fifth Man'. Roland Perry's book on Rothschild was titled *The Fifth Man*. Moscow's emphasis on the 'Cambridge Five' helped shift attention from the others.

[75] Nigel West (ed.), Introduction to the *Guy Liddell Diaries, Volume 1: 1939-1942*, p 9; Francis Wheen, *Tom Driberg: His Life and Indiscretions*, (Chapter 7, Note 12).

[76] Penrose and Freeman, p 600.

[77] John Costello, *Ten Days to Destiny*, p 119.

[78] Joan Miller, *One Girl's War*, p 131.

[79] ibid., p 133.

[80] Noel Annan, *Changing Enemies: The Defeat and Regeneration of Germany*, p 3.

[81] Annan, p 14.

[82] Annan, p 214.

[83] Christopher Andrew and Vasily Mitrokhin, *The Sword and the Shield*, p 140.

[84] See http://hansard.millbanksystems.com/written_answers/1981/nov/09/mr-leo-long-1

[85] Volodarsky, p 118.

[86] Miller, p 133.

[87] Peter Wright, *Spycatcher*, p 221.

[88] Chapman Pincher, *Too Secret Too Long*, p 80.

[89] ibid., p 361, pp 377-378.

[90] Chapman Pincher, *Treachery*, p 144.

[91] Nigel West and Oleg Tsarev, (ed.s), *Triplex: Secrets from the Cambridge Spies*, p 106.

[92] Christopher Andrew and Oleg Gordievsky, *KGB: The Inside Story*, p 300.

[93] Guy Liddell Diaries, TNA, KV/4 190, October 27, 1942. This entry does not appear in the published version of the Diaries (*The Guy Liddell Diaries Vol. II: 1942-1945*), which, for that day, records only a conversation with Roger Hollis that claims that "we appear to be very well informed about their [the Communists'] activities".

[94] Calder Walton, *Empire of Secrets*, p 71.

[95] Pincher, *Treachery*, p 522 (Pincher's assertions are unsourced).

[96] Nigel West (ed.), *The Guy Liddell Diaries Vol. II: 1942-1945*, p 291.

[97] Wright, pp 221-222.

[98] Pincher, *Too Secret Too Long*, p 351.

[99] Penrose and Freeman, p 324.

[100] Tom Bower, *The Perfect English Spy*, pp 92-100.

[101] Ibid,, p 132.

[102] Miller, p 154.

[103] Annan, p 214.
[104] Penrose and Freeman, p 303.

Chapter 8: Confusion – Fuchs, the Refugee

"Traitors typically salve their consciences with the idea that they are playing a great role in geopolitics." (Edward Lucas)

"Any man of progress had two homelands, his own and the Soviet Union." (Jacques Duclos)

"The essence of security is to make up one's mind without the evidence because if one waits for the evidence it is too late." (R. H. S. Crossman)

By the summer of 1940, MI5's state of strategic confusion over Communists was well-established. Victor Rothschild and Anthony Blunt were now officers, and able to spread their influence both within and outside the service, endorsing 'good communists' who would help the fight against fascism. Jane Archer, the organisation's expert in countering communist espionage, had been safely removed to the management of the Regional Security Liaison Officers. Churchill's coalition government included left-wing politicians who were better disposed towards the Soviet Union, and the Ministry of Information started talking about 'peace aims' in terms of socialist goals. The anxiety over 'Fifth Columnists' (which group included Communists and pacifists as well as supposed supporters of the Nazi war machine) had subsided. As the threats of invasion grew, the focus turned even more sharply on Hitler's Germany: the Soviet Union's brutal June invasion of the Baltic States was downplayed, with the Cabinet in August seriously considering the recognition of Stalin's annexation of Estonia, Latvia and Lithuania.

At this time, a saga of deep Soviet espionage and incompetent counter-espionage unfolded, involving the betrayal of nuclear secrets by the German Communist Klaus Fuchs. At the outbreak of the war, Britain had been leading other nations in research into atomic energy and weaponry, admittedly largely helped by scientists who had escaped from the growing Nazi empire. As the official historian, Margaret Gowing, related, in 1939 scientists (apart from Professor Chadwick) were sceptical of the possibility of any atomic weapon becoming effective for many years. [1] They consequently withheld research findings from the government, considering that Hitler would likewise be unable to exploit the technology in what was nevertheless perceived as a multi-year war. This scenario changed sharply after the production of a paper, in March 1940, by Professors Peierls and Frisch at Birmingham University, which radically redrew the practicalities of constructing and detonating a highly powerful bomb. The necessity for advancing the research rapidly, and for ensuring that the information did not reach the hands of the Nazis, intensified. Moreover, because of the Nazi-Soviet pact, it was equally essential that the secrets did not find their way to the Communists, since a high risk of their being shared existed, and it was not impossible that Stalin and Hitler would collaborate further to attack the British Empire. At this time, MI5 should have been on heightened alert because of Krivitsky's revelations, and the reality of the pact.

Klaus Fuchs was the primary agent who betrayed atomic secrets to the Soviets. This chapter explains the depth of the Soviet Union's plans for penetration, and tells how MI5, throughout the period from the first move to recruit Fuchs to the British uranium project (shown to be as early as late summer 1940) to MI5's eventual guarded approval in November 1941, displayed a reckless disregard for national security by ignoring, or condoning, his blatant political allegiances, and failed to pick up multiple indications that his loyalties were to a foreign power, and that he was thus a security risk. (Chapter 9 will analyse MI5's performance after he began his espionage activities.) Yet MI5, probably out of embarrassment at its own negligence, then acted cravenly and deceitfully in the belief that its own lax execution would not be uncovered. When Fuchs was eventually detected, made a confession, and then was tried and convicted in early 1950, MI5 took several steps to conceal its part in letting his employment go through. While on the one hand doctoring the archival record, in order to conceal its inept performance, it decided also to blur its own culpability by supporting Fuchs's claim that he had started spying only in 1942, long after Germany's invasion of the Soviet Union in June 1941, when the Soviet Union joined the side of the Allies. Through their emphasis on the alliance between the communist Soviet Union and liberal-democratic Great Britain, MI5 thus gave credence to the opinion (held by many communist sympathisers) that Fuchs was somehow justified in sharing confidential information.

The British government was so anxious to secure a conviction for Fuchs, and to keep the sources of its evidence of Fuchs's treachery (the VENONA cable traffic) secret, that it behaved in a very indulgent manner when extracting his confession. The claim made by Fuchs that he did not reveal any secrets about research into atomic weaponry until 1942 suited the Soviet Union, the British government, as well as Fuchs himself, and was not contested.[2] The officers of MI5 were thus able (temporarily) to bury all the uncomfortable details of his recruitment and the organisation's failure to prevent his treachery. Yet the fact of the alliance with the Soviet Union was irrelevant: the Official Secrets Act forbade the revelation of confidential information to *any* foreign power, and it was MI5's responsibility to represent steadfastly the risks of subversion and espionage by any such power. The motif that the Soviet Union was after June 1941 an ally was nevertheless encouraged by MI5, and has been constantly adopted by historians of the Fuchs case to minimise the crime he committed, to provide an extenuating circumstance, and to mitigate MI5's culpability in not detecting him. This perspective has coloured assessments of Fuchs's crime for decades since.

An integrated analysis of the various testimonies and memoirs, and of documents released by the National Archives, suggests that Soviet plans for infiltrating British scientific research antedated Fuchs's recruitment to the Maud Committee's project. (The Maud Committee, a name taken from a misunderstood telegram from the physicist Lisa Meitner to her nephew Otto Frisch after the invasion of Denmark by the Nazis, was the preliminary committee set up in April 1940 to investigate the possibility of atomic weapons. It evolved later in 1941 into the Tube Alloys project, the alias for the firm set up to develop atomic weaponry.) Such an analysis would point to the fact that Fuchs was well prepared for his mission by the time he joined Rudolf Peierls in Birmingham in May 1941. Previous accounts of the Fuchs case have overlooked the pattern and detailed chronology of activities initiated by Fuchs and his allies, namely Hans Kahle, the Kuczynski family, Rudolf Peierls, and their allies in the crypto-Communist sector of British politics, as well as MI5's track-record in not executing a disciplined approach to vetting Fuchs, and ignoring signals.[3]

The bare bones of Fuchs's career can be told as follows: Klaus Fuchs was a Communist German physicist who escaped from Hitler's harassments in 1933, and came to England in September of that year, where he was welcomed by communist contacts in Bristol, Ronald and Jessie Gunn. Neville Mott, a professor in theoretical physics at Bristol University, accepted Fuchs as a research student in October 1934, and supervised him for his Ph.D., whereafter Fuchs moved to Edinburgh University to perform research under Max Born. Fuchs applied for British naturalisation in July 1939, but was classified as an enemy alien. Initially, he escaped internment (November 1939), but in the intensification of detention in May 1940, when the 'Fifth Column' scare was at its peak, he was confined to the Isle of Man, and then sent to Canada in early July. He was released on December 17, 1940, "because of his high qualifications as a mathematician and a physicist"[4], and returned to the UK, where he continued his research in Edinburgh. In May 1941, another German émigré scientist, Rudolf Peierls, who was contributing to the British programme on atomic weapons research, then offered Fuchs (according to Peierls's own testimony) a job as an assistant. Although the Ministry of Supply, advised by MI5, at some stage expressed some concerns about his hiring, Fuchs was able to join Peierls at Birmingham University at the end of May. Some time afterwards he signed the Official Secrets Act, and the following year applied for British citizenship, taking the oath of allegiance in August 1942. In August 1943, he applied, with Peierls, for a visa to travel to the USA, to work more closely on the Manhattan Project (the USA's codename for nuclear weapons research). The pair left in November 1943, and, after successful activity at Los Alamos, returned to the UK in June 1946, where Fuchs went to work at the AERE (Atomic Energy Research Establishment) at Harwell, as Head of the Theoretical Physics Division. Investigation in the USA of espionage and leakages of atomic secrets to the Soviet Union, assisted by decryption of Soviet cable traffic in the VENONA programme, helped, in August 1949, in the confident identification of Fuchs as the scientist responsible. After a few months of surveillance, when he apparently failed to contact any Soviet agents, he was interviewed in December 1949, arrested in January 1950, and sentenced, on the basis of his confession, to fourteen years' imprisonment on March 1 of that year.[5]

Where did MI5 go wrong here? It is educational to start with Fuchs's confession, transcribed and signed from Fuchs's dictation by Jim Skardon at the War Office on January 27, 1950.[6] In this initial statement, Fuchs gave no exact date as to when he decided to reveal secrets to the Soviets, indicating vaguely that it was when he learned the true goals of the project he was working on. Yet in an earlier interview (January 24), he had told Skardon that he "was engaged in espionage from mid-1942". In his oral confession soon afterwards to Michael

Perrin, who had been Assistant Director of the Tube Alloys project, he was reported by Perrin as saying that his first contact with the Soviets was "early 1942".[7] As will be shown, these statements contain several lies. He was aware of the nature of the work when he was hired by Peierls in May 1941; he had encounters with an NKVD officer before he joined Peierls at Birmingham, and he in fact conveyed atomic secrets to his masters in Moscow during the summer of 1941, even before the partial approval of his employment came through; and it is highly probable that he had plotted such conspiracy with other members of the Communist Party as early as the period of his internment in Canada. MI5's failure to trap and exclude Fuchs from the time of his internment in May 1940 represents a colossal failure in execution.

Given the inaccuracy of Fuchs's confession, and thus the overall unreliability of his testimony, as well as MI5's reluctance to shed any light on the sequence of events, can it be established precisely when and how Fuchs was recruited to the atomic weaponry project by the British, and how the Soviets exploited this opportunity? How do the contributions of other participants either confirm or negate parts of his story? The primary persons who need to be investigated are the professor who hired him in Birmingham, Rudolf Peierls, the strident and open Communist with whom he associated in Canada, Hans Kahle, his friend and equally vocal KPD officer in London, Jürgen Kuczynski, and the latter's sister, Ursula, who became Fuchs's contact and courier some time in 1941 or 1942, and who had previously deceived the authorities in order to gain entry to Britain at the same time that Fuchs re-entered the country from Canada. Tracing this chronology is important in identifying the opportunities that MI5 missed – or deliberately overlooked – during the critical period of Fuchs's recruitment.

One remarkable aspect of Fuchs's treachery is that he did not have to insinuate himself furtively into Britain's secret research structure: he was open about his beliefs, and was sponsored by sympathetic friends who exploited their status to wield influence. It is thus necessary to step back from Fuchs himself, and, in the first place, to inspect closely the career and situation of his prime mentor and scientific partner, Rudolf Peierls, who played a very significant role in the affair. Owing to his personal profile, and the close cooperation and parallel careers of Peierls and Fuchs on the Manhattan Project, Peierls underwent exactly the same kind of surveillance that was exacted on Fuchs, both in 1947 and in 1949, when MI5 requested Home Office Warrants to open their mail and record their telephone conversations. This fact is recorded in Peierls's files at the National Archives.[i8]

Ironically, Peierls was able to benefit financially from this process. In 1979, in the mistaken belief that Peierls was dead, and thus not able to sue for libel, the ex-Naval Intelligence officer Richard Deacon (whose real name was Donald McCormick) wrote: "When indications reached the British government that there had been leakages of information to the Russians by scientists working on these various projects, Peierls was one of the first to be suspected."[9] Peierls sprang into action, in his 1985 autobiography characterising Deacon's inherently harmless –

---

[i] The National Archives list a still-classified file with the beguiling title "Espionage by Fuchs & Peierls" (HO 532/3). It is described as "not available: held by Home Office".

and utterly true – language as "some extremely damning and quite unjustified statements about me".[10] "Because of this," he added, "I was able to take legal action very early, and a writ was served on the publishers and the author a few days after publication. The matter was settled out of court very promptly; the distribution of the book was stopped at once, so that the few copies that were sold are now collector's items. I received a 'substantial sum' by way of damages." Deacon was absolutely correct in what he wrote, but could not reveal his source because of the Official Secrets Act. As a coda to this episode, Christoph Laucht, in his 2012 study of Peierls and Fuchs, reported that Deacon "unleashed a barrage of accusations against him [Peierls]", directly echoing, and referring to, Peierls's claim from his autobiography, but failing to identify a detailed reference to Deacon's work. Such an omission suggests perhaps that Laucht had not even read what Deacon wrote.[ii] [11] Deacon's reasonable assertion was clearly no "barrage of accusations", but Peierls's reputation was still such that he gained the immediate sympathy of a contemporary historian.

In fact one might conclude that MI5 would have shown great dereliction of duty if it had *not* investigated Peierls, given that his profile was similar to that of Fuchs, that they collaborated closely in both the United Kingdom and in the United States, and that Fuchs turned out to be guilty. In fact, a short series of memoranda at the National Archives expresses strong suspicions (in October and November 1946) that Fuchs and Peierls were spies, indicating that suspicions had been latent for some time.[12] [*See Chapter 9 for a detailed discussion of this matter.*] If Deacon had pointed out that Peierls had been completely exonerated (even if MI5 still had doubts about him), his book might well have been allowed to be published as it was – with a minor *corrigendum* to indicate that Peierls was still alive. Peierls obviously over-reacted: he should not have been surprised that suspicion would have fallen on him, and should have realised by that time – with a CBE in 1945, and a knighthood in 1968 – that his reputation was probably safe. However, in the hyperactive manner of someone who probably has a guilty secret to hide (compare Isaiah Berlin and Lord Rothschild), Peierls's first instinct was to protest too much.

Nevertheless, suspicions did not go away, and were resuscitated by the FBI, which had posed further questions about him in 1951. According to Nigel West, the FBI reinvestigated Peierls and his wife several years later, in March 1956, when Peierls applied to join the Brookhaven National Laboratory, thus echoing an earlier report that he was not all that he seemed. The FBI further asserted "that he had even joined a Communist Party front in Switzerland and that his wife had been a member of the Kommunistische Partei Deutschlands (KPD). [13] Furthermore, West reported that the FBI's investigations into Peierls's membership of the Council of the Association of Atomic Scientists (a body with a policy of appeasing Soviet desires to have access to the atom bomb), and other pro-Communist activities, including an appeal made to reduce the prison sentence of another atom spy, Alan Nunn May, prompted a permanent removal of Peierls's security clearance in 1957, after which he resigned his consultancy post at Harwell. This change of status did not impede his award of a knighthood, in the

---

[ii] Dr Laucht has failed to respond to the author's inquiry on this point.

next decade. Further evidence of their conspiracy with Fuchs has appeared: Eugenia Peierls organised a trip to Switzerland for her, her husband and Fuchs in September 1946, so that they might all meet Fuchs's Communist brother, Gerhard.[14] Furthermore, based on an authorised telephone tap, when the Peierls learned of Fuchs's arrest in January 1950, Eugenia immediately warned her husband that he was "in the same danger as Fuchs".[15] Their first reaction was to ensure that Fuchs said nothing that might point the finger of suspicion at his friends, and they gained a swift opportunity to speak to Fuchs confidentially in prison.

Other troubling aspects of Peierls's professional career exist. His autobiography is shallow and evasive, finessing the awkward details of his connections with the Soviet authorities, and his involvement in pro-Soviet front activities after the war. He was born in 1907 in Berlin, but was performing research in Cambridge when Hitler came to power, and was allowed to stay in the UK. In 1930, on a visit to a scientific conference in Odessa, he had met the Leningrad-based physicist Eugenia Kannegieser, and the two were married in 1931. As West wrote: " . . . to their surprise no obstacles were placed on her emigration abroad nor on her acquisition of German citizenship. This was unusual, considering the sensitive nature of her work. ."[16] Peierls does in fact describe several delays and bureaucratic mishaps in getting Eugenia's papers approved, and he even returned to Berlin without her for a while. It would have been very unusual if the Soviet Government had neither recruited Eugenia to work for OGPU at the time, nor at least applied considerable pressure on her and her husband to provide information during her time abroad, by holding the safety of her relatives as hostage.

Indeed, Peierls later hinted vaguely at such troubles, when he wrote that, while in England, towards the end of 1934, he and Eugenia received a telephone call from Moscow (the caller is not identified) informing them that Eugenia's parents and her sister had been sent into exile. So concerned about their fate was Eugenia that in 1937 she declined to accompany Rudolf to a nuclear physics conference in Moscow, as they were "warned that her presence might prove an embarrassment to her friends and relatives".[17] That sounds unconvincing: Soviet citizens living under Stalin's terror had little time to fret about being 'embarrassed'. Eugenia might well have feared that, like her eminent predecessor at Cambridge, Pyotry Kapitza (*or Kapitsa, see below*), she would not have been allowed out of the Soviet Union again. Later, Peierls was to address such a threat less obliquely when he talked about his Russian-born colleague at Harwell, Boris Davison: "But in 1953 the authorities became worried about having a Russian-born man in the highly secret Harwell laboratory – a man whose parents were still in the Soviet Union. Perhaps the worry was that he might be blackmailed into disclosing secrets by threats to his parents, but more realistically it was fear of adverse publicity if his position became known." Indeed, Peierls did not learn until 1956 about the deaths of his parents-in-law, after they went through "very hard times".[18]

As has been shown with Isaiah Berlin's father, Mendel, threatening exiles with harm to relatives still living in the Soviet Union was a favoured tactic of Stalin's secret police (*see Chapter 6*). Pavel Sudoplatov, who was Deputy

Director of Foreign Intelligence in the Soviet Union from 1939 until 1942, was in 1941 appointed Director of Special Tasks (assassination squads), and then led the Intelligence Bureau on Atomic Problems from 1944 to 1946, described how another physicist, George Gamow, suffered the same treatment because of his concern for relatives left behind. "Using implied threats against Gamow's relatives in Moscow, Elizaveta Zarubina pressured him into cooperating with us. In exchange for safety and material support for his relatives, Gamow provided the names of left-wing scientists who might be recruited to supply secret information."[19] It is highly probable that one of the scientists recruited by Gamow was the Briton Wilfrid Mann, who, in his memoir, attempted to refute the allegations of espionage that Andrew Boyle had vaguely thrown at him in *The Climate of Treason.* (Evidence of Mann's guilt has recently been provided through an unpublished memoir by Sir Patrick Reilly.[20]) Mann admitted that he knew Gamow, and described a bizarre encounter with Burgess at a party in Washington that helps seal the connection the trio must have enjoyed.[21] Like Peierls's wife, Eugenia, George Gamow had started his scientific career in Leningrad: he was also a friend of Peierls, who credited Gamow's explanation of alpha decay as "one of the earliest successes of quantum mechanics".[22] Max Born explained that Gamow made several unsuccessful attempts to escape to the West from the Soviet Union, but eventually gained a permit in 1932 after several distinguished physicists, including Einstein and Bohr, had guaranteed his return. When Gamow decided to settle in the United States, Stalin was so furious at his refusal to return that he took his frustration out on Pyotr Kapitza.[23]

That was another strong reason for the fear expressed by Rudolf and Eugenia Peierls. Peierls's appointment to the Mond Laboratory in Cambridge, in the spring of 1935 [24], had been occasioned by the fact that the same Kapitza, a Soviet physicist who had spent ten years in Cambridge working with Ernest Rutherford at the Cavendish Laboratory, had returned to the Soviet Union to visit his parents, and had not been allowed to return. Stalin, annoyed by Soviet scientists expressing less than absolute loyalty, evidently realised that Kapitza was too precious an asset to leave overseas. Moreover, the money to fund the fellowship created for Peierls, who had been a great enthusiast for Kapitza, derived from Kapitza's unused salary.[25] A connection thus arose between the two foreign physicists. Peierls also appears to have made a subtle error in writing about Kapitza's departure: he recorded that it happened in 1935, when other sources more reliably have stated it was in 1934. For example, George Gamow recorded in his memoirs that he worked under Kapitza in 1932 and 1933 in Leningrad, and that Kapitza was "detained" in 1934.[26] Gamow's account is overall hardly plausible, but there appears no reason to question the detail about Kapitza.[27] If the detention had occurred in 1935, Peierls would not have had time to secure the position approved after Kapitza failed to return from Moscow. Yet, if it did occur in 1934, the year Peierls made his visit to the Soviet Union, he could also have met with Kapitza in Leningrad, a possibility Peierls might well have wanted to overlook when he recorded his account of the times. Indeed, in a statement on file, Peierls misrepresented his 1934 visit to the Soviet Union, describing it as a "holiday trip to the Caucasus", while his autobiography shows clearly that he and

Eugenia visited her parents in Leningrad.[28] Moreover, as Andrew recorded, MI5 had had good reason to be suspicious of Kapitza:

> "Its surveillance of ARCOS, whose activities provided cover for Soviet espionage, revealed that Kapitsa was in contact with it; SIS reported that ARCOS had provided funds for research. An informant in Trinity College also revealed that Kapitsa was in contact with the leading Cambridge Communist Maurice Dobb, later the Trinity undergraduate Kim Philby's economic supervisor and important influence on him."[29]

Andrew related other episodes where MI5 had indications that Kapitza was a spy, including the occasion when the Communist Andrew Rothstein was detailed to acquire information from him, and several visits by Ambassador Maisky to Cambridge to meet the scientist.

In April 1938, Peierls was also evasive and arrogant to British customs officials when, on arriving from Esbjerg, Denmark, he was asked what business had earlier taken him to the Soviet Union, as a report from the Port of Harwich to the Special Branch indicates: "During the examination of his passport it was noticed that it contained a Soviet visa and Russian control-stamps for 1937, but the alien, when questioned beyond confirming that he had in fact visited the USSR last year, did not appear to be willing to give any reason for his visit to that country, and, in view of his substantial position as a professor, Peierls was not further questioned on the subject."[30] Almost certainly, Peierls had travelled to Denmark to see the physicist Niels Bohr, with whom he was collaborating at this time. His colleague Otto Frisch was also working for Bohr (in Britain) when war broke out, and was unable to return. An alien with a secret and a sense of entitlement – that was an inappropriate and dangerous stance for Peierls to take.

The role of Kapitza was reinforced in the official history of Britain's exploits with atomic energy, showing that any diffidence that the scientist may have initially felt about his detention in the Soviet Union had disappeared. At the time when Fuchs's espionage activity was at its height, in the USA in 1943 and 1944, the scientist Niels Bohr (with whom Peierls had collaborated) was negotiating with the US government in the belief that "the atomic bomb was so big that it could be a means of promoting confidence and co-operation between nations", and that "it would be disastrous if Russia should learn on her own about the bomb".[31] Unaware that the Soviets had already deeply penetrated the Anglo-American infrastructure, Bohr returned to London in April 1944 to find an invitation from Kapitza that had been sent several months before. As Margaret Gowing wrote:

> "Kapitza reputedly stood high in Stalin's favour and at the end of October 1943, when he had heard of Bohr's escape to Sweden, he wrote inviting Bohr and his whole family to settle in Russia, where he would be given all the help he wanted for carrying on his scientific work in association with the Russian physicists. Bohr had a strong impression when he collected the letter from the Soviet Embassy, six months after it was written, that the Russians were aware of the American project. He

sent back a warm but innocuous reply to Kapitza's invitation and showed both to the British authorities."[32]

To summarise, a pattern of sympathy for the Soviet Union is thus detectable in the actions of Bohr, Peierls and Born, all linked to Kapitza in a similar fashion. And there is no doubt about Kapitza's leading role in orchestrating the Soviet Union's purloining of atomic secrets from the UK and the USA.

So how did Fuchs become involved with this conspiracy? The documents at the National Archives show discrepancies surrounding Fuchs's recruitment to the work of the Maud committee. Ironically, when war broke out, Peierls, as an 'enemy alien', had been disqualified from being involved with highly secret work on radar, and had been encouraged to work on what was considered a much less strategic technology, atomic weaponry. In March 1940, Peierls collaborated with Otto Frisch at Birmingham University on research to show how a nuclear chain reaction based on the Uranium-235 isotope could occur, a finding which proved that an atomic bomb was a possibility. They succeeded in having the paper that explained their findings (known famously as the 'Frisch-Peierls Memorandum') sent to Sir Henry Tizard, the chief British military scientist. The clarity of the breakthroughs expressed in the paper prompted the Chamberlain government to set up a new committee under George Thomson in April 1940, which soon took on the Maud appellation.[33] After some hesitation about their membership of the full committee (which consisted of native British citizens only), Peierls and Frisch were invited to join its Technical Sub-Committee in September of that year, but only after Peierls wrote a strong letter promoting his cause.

When the Soviet Government learned about this initiative is hazy. Nigel West's *Mortal Crimes* is the most detailed account of the negotiations, and the role of spies in passing on information, but his explanation has gaps. West pointed out that the Maud committee submitted a lengthy report in October 1940 to Lord Hankey, whose Private Secretary was the spy John Cairncross.[34] By implication, he suggested that this report found its way to the Soviets, but does not explain how. Since Gorsky, Cairncross's NKVD contact at the Soviet Embassy, was out of the country for most of 1940, Cairncross would probably have turned elsewhere to find a means of dispatching it to Moscow. Guy Burgess would have been a suitable choice, as he and Cairncross had been collaborators for some years, Burgess having introduced Cairncross to Deutsch, who in turn used James Klugmann as a go-between to recruit him in Paris. Cairncross had passed on information to Burgess beforehand. Nigel West did record that when the Chiefs of Staff in September 1941 decided to accept the Maud Committee's recommendations to manufacture an atomic bomb in England, and set up the Tube Alloys front, the NKVD received a copy of the report from Gorsky, courtesy of Cairncross.[35] This account was echoed by Pavel Fitin, who was head of NKVD foreign intelligence at the time. In 1945 Fitin reported: "Extremely valuable information on the scientific developments of *Enormoz* reaches us from the London *rezidentura*.[iii] The first material on *Enormoz* was received at the end of 1941 from John Cairncross."[36] Yet Fitin's claim does not negate the fact that

---

[iii] *Enormoz* was the Soviet code-word (coined by Fitin) for the atomic weapons project.

the rival organisation, the GRU, might have received information earlier. If Cairncross did use Burgess as an intermediary, Burgess had links to the GRU. Simon Kremer, the GRU *rezident*, was still active in London, and could have served as the channel. This phase of the story is worth investigating more deeply, as Cairncross cleverly succeeded in minimising his role, a deception that has been all too broadly accepted by historians.

A close inspection of Cairncross's autobiography (*The Enigma Spy*) highlights some disturbing contradictions, and confirms even more strongly the conclusion that Cairncross played a leading role in the purloining of atomic secrets. In his memoir, Cairncross wrote about his dealings with Burgess in the summer of 1940, reporting that, in July 1939, Burgess had contacted him for some information he needed about British plans for Poland, to be given (so Burgess claimed) to a group of anti-Nazi Germans with whom Burgess was in touch.[37] He [Cairncross] provided it in note form, notes which were later found in Burgess's flat after he had absconded to Moscow. Cairncross also indicated that he believed Burgess and Blunt had been behind his own recruitment as a spy, and had stage-managed, in May 1937, approaches by James Klugmann from behind the scenes. He also described meeting Burgess socially, which would all suggest a close familiarity with him. Finally, Cairncross casually dropped the fact that, when his Soviet handler, Gorsky, returned from Moscow, he told him about the incident with Burgess, and Gorsky rebuked him, telling Cairncross to avoid Burgess in the future. Overall, Cairncross minimised his espionage activity, and differentiated himself from the 'Cambridge Five' (of which he did not regard himself as a member) by virtue of his patriotism. This account has been accepted into the lore of Cairncross's being a less substantial spy than his other Cambridge colleagues.

What is happening here? Why is Cairncross volunteering this information? Nigel West has subsequently revealed that Cairncross's account of his espionage is not to be trusted: West discovered from the KGB archives that his spying activities were more extensive and more enduring than Cairncross claimed. This writer asked West (since it was he in *Mortal Crimes* who pointed out Cairncross's access to atomic secrets) about the possibility of Cairncross's passing on the secrets to Burgess, as a courier. West's reply was surprising. He stated that Cairncross did not know that Burgess was a fellow-spy until 1951, after the defections of Burgess and Maclean. The reason he gave for such knowledge was that Cairncross was interrogated by MI5 in 1951 (because of the notes in his handwriting discovered in Burgess's flat), and told his MI5 interrogator that he had believed Burgess was authorised to receive the information he had requested in July 1939, and had never suspected that Burgess was a Soviet agent. (Cairncross described this episode in his book: it echoes Berlin's similar claim.) West rather oddly attributed (relatively) innocent motives to the contact: "Burgess asked many people for information, and offered different reasons", as if this were normal behaviour. What is extraordinary is that Guy Liddell, the head of 'B' Division of MI5, responsible for Counter-Espionage, at the time, was shrewd enough to see through Cairncross's deception. In a *Diary* entry for April 3, 1952, he wrote of Cairncross: "He was extremely perturbed when confronted with the document in his own handwriting which had been found amongst the papers of

BURGESS. His statement is somewhat contradictory: on the one hand he says that he gave BURGESS the information because he thought that he was working for some Government organisation and that it would be in his, CAIRNCROSS's, interests to keep in with him. On the other hand, he says that he was extremely nervous when he tried to get his notes back and was told by BURGESS that he had either lost or destroyed them."[38]

Now Nigel West, in view of Cairncross's mendacity, privately expressed to this writer uncertainty about such a conclusion, but the question certainly needs to be asked publicly: why would anyone trust Cairncross's statements to MI5, when he was under a serious investigation, and needed to extricate himself quickly? In fact, one would *expect* him to minimise his associations with the other members of the Cambridge Five when being interrogated. One would expect him to have then used the same claim that he was not a Communist, and had only Britain's interests at heart, as a useful argument in 1951. On closer inspection, however, Cairncross's account of his activities throughout the period of the Nazi-Soviet pact turns out to be utterly unreliable, simply because he got so much of the chronology, and of Gorsky's whereabouts at the time, completely wrong. He presented Gorsky's return to Moscow (for training) as occurring in about December 1938, and his coming back to London in January 1940. From this time up until the German invasion of the Soviet Union, Cairncross claimed to have had occasional meetings with Gorsky, at which he passed on little information – because of the sensitivity of the political situation. Thus Cairncross built a fiction that had Gorsky unavailable at a most critical time (during the whole of 1939), whereafter, on Gorsky's return, the Nazi-Soviet pact interfered with his desire to pass on secrets, until the latter part of 1941, when Cairncross believed his espionage could be more easily justified, from a moral standpoint.[39]

The whole alibi is false. As Soviet archives have shown, Gorsky was in London for the whole of 1939 (handling Blunt, Burgess, Philby, Tudor-Hart and Cairncross himself, according to other sources such as West's and Tsarev's *The Crown Jewels,* as well as accounts from such as Blunt), but was recalled at the beginning of 1940, not returning to London until December 1940.[40] Whole years of Gorsky's interactions with Cairncross have been misrepresented. Gorsky was thus in London when Burgess approached Cairncross. The key questions now have to be re-posed in the light of this fresh evidence: Why would Burgess have approached Cairncross for information unless he knew that Cairncross was already a Soviet agent? Why would Cairncross reveal such information to Burgess unless he knew that he could trust Burgess not to reveal his source, and betray him? And why would Cairncross insert, in his memoir, the gratuitous information that he informed Gorsky of Burgess's approach "when he returned from Moscow", when Gorsky was actually in London and in regular contact with him at the time?

We have to consider Cairncross in 1995 (the year he died), and the younger man, very afraid, in 1951. In 1995, Cairncross was a survivor. All his allies and all his accusers were dead (Burgess long gone in 1963, Blunt and Maclean in 1983, Philby in 1985, his MI5 interrogator from 1964, Jim Skardon, in 1987, Dick White more recently, in 1993). No revealing documents had been released by the government. He believed he had a chance to define his legacy in a positive way. But he knew that his interrogation by MI5 in 1951, his subsequent resignation, his further confession to MI5 in 1964 after a lead from Blunt, followed by a partial deal of immunity from prosecution, were all well-known facts. Cairncross had been infuriated by Chapman Pincher's publication in 1981 of *Their Trade Is Treachery*, but, living abroad, and thus protected from extradition, had withheld taking any legal action. (Pincher's allegations about Cairncross, provided by the retired MI5 officer Peter Wright, were in fact accurate. And Pincher was still alive.) John Costello brought out his *Mask of Treachery* in 1988, and Costello and Tsarev cooperated on *Deadly Illusions*, exploiting Soviet archives, in 1993. (West's and Tsarev's *The Crown Jewels*, likewise using the KGB archives, with a sharper focus on spies in Britain, would not appear until 1998.) Cairncross had been provoked to write his memoir mainly by a book on the KGB by Christopher Andrew and Oleg Gordievsky, published in 1990, in which Cairncross had been named as the 'Fifth Man', and as the "probable" source of atomic secrets leaked to the Soviets in October 1940.[41] Thus his autobiography of 1995 is a forlorn attempt to help his tarnished reputation, especially in the eyes of his much younger wife, in the belief that no one would be able to provide any evidence to counter it. He offered a concoction of misleading information, peppered with a few verifiable facts to give his story verisimilitude.

And what were his motives for lying in 1951? To save his skin: he had to acknowledge his "flirtation with Communism", he decided. The evidence of his handwriting was incontestable. It was not going to be 'damaging' enough to out him as a spy, but because Burgess was careless enough to leave the original notes undestroyed in his flat when he absconded with Maclean, it could have threatened his career. He admitted a minor offence ("passing confidential notes to the Russians", according to Andrew and Gordievsky) to avoid prosecution. If not for that discovery, Cairncross would never have mentioned Burgess at all: he had to do so, however, when faced with the evidence, and tried to make out it was a casual contact completely unconnected with Soviet espionage, but dealing with fading negotiations with the German opposition. With hindsight, one can make the obvious point that Cairncross would not have volunteered such information to Gorsky unless he knew that Burgess was a fellow-spy, but one can be sure that Cairncross did not provide that information at the time.

Unfortunately, we do not know exactly what Cairncross said to his interrogators in 1951 and 1964. A file is identified at the National Archives titled *Espionage Activity by Individuals: John Cairncross*, but a note indicates that it is still retained by the Home Office.[42] What is extraordinary, however, is that MI5 did not check the chronology in 1964, when Cairncross made his confession. If Cairncross admitted to espionage (which he did), he must have had a controller, and may even have identified that person to his interrogators, as part of the agreement. If he had lied to his interrogators about chronology in the same way as he presented his espionage activity in his autobiography, they should have been able to perform some additional checks to determine whether his story were true. Certainly, they would not have had access to KGB archives, but a simple search of Soviet Embassy arrivals and departures would have allowed them to plot Gorsky's movements, and challenge Cairncross on some of his assertions.

By 1995, however, Cairncross felt much more confident about describing his relationship with Burgess, since the latter was a known villain, and Cairncross could present himself as being manipulated. Hence the references to Burgess working behind the scenes, and the mention of parties and other social occasions when they met. Yet this tone must be balanced by even more astonishing statements that appeared soon after Cairncross died. *The Crown Jewels* tells of Burgess's nurturing of Cairncross in October 1938, and records how Max Eitingon, Burgess's controller in Paris, requested that same month permission from Moscow Centre for "contact between Burgess and Cairncross so that documents could be received from him". Whereas Cairncross's main deliveries were via James Klugmann (who actually recruited him), the book goes on to say that, in September 1938, Burgess passed on information received from Cairncross about "an important British agent" within the NKVD. The evidence looks cast-iron that Burgess and Cairncross knew of each other's role, and collaborated.

So why would the same Nigel West, who had worked vigorously to uncover the truth behind the deceptions of Stalin's men and women in Britain, in 2015 be so uninformative about Cairncross's dealings with Burgess, and appear to accept Cairncross's version of the truth? The main reason is that, even though he received no mention or attribution in the book, Nigel West was the ghost-writer of Cairncross's 'autobiography', and conducted extensive interviews with the spy. One can perhaps understand his reluctance to take up his pen and correct the story. Meanwhile, the same author's 2014 reference book on British Intelligence laconically recorded that Cairncross died "after he had completed his memoirs", while simply stating that his NKVD dossier shows how Cairncross's claims about not having betrayed atomic secrets were false.[43] Moreover, in the mid-1990s, West should perhaps have attempted to verify Gorsky's movements himself, and thus been able to demolish Cairncross's flimsy infrastructure, an oversight that provides a lesson on the critical role that a detailed chronology has to play in historical analysis, and the importance of a historian's maintaining his distance and objectivity. When this writer pointed out to West, in July 2015, the litany of contradictions inherent in Cairncross's story, the author replied: "I agree with your observations".

Cairncross's testimony is thus a whole farrago of lies. One is left with the startling hypothesis that Cairncross probably passed, in the summer of 1940, atomic secrets to Burgess, who then made plans to get them to Moscow, which would add a brand new dimension to the Moscow Plot. To reinforce this possible scenario of conspiracy, Cairncross revealed in his memoir that he was a close friend of the professor in German Studies at Birmingham University, Roy Pascal, and his wife, whom Rudolf Peierls, the prime mover in atomic research in the spring of 1940, and whose important report passed by Cairncross's desk, so accurately described as close friends. Mrs Pascal was a diehard Communist, and had been friends with Peierls in Berlin in the 1920s. Cairncross underlined that relationship by telling how Roy Pascal ("a prominent Communist") visited him at the Foreign Office after he joined in 1937, making overt gestures of wanting to introduce Cairncross to a friend of his for "intelligence-gathering" purposes.[44] And from the standpoint of personal psychology, if Cairncross had been left stranded, but had come into possession of vital material, he would have looked for an ally to help him in his cause, just as Burgess took over the handling of Leo Long and his purloined secrets when Anthony Blunt was sent abroad to France (*see Chapter 5*).

One might also surmise that Peierls himself may have passed a copy of the Frisch-Peierls Memorandum to his Communist friends. It is significant that the creation of that report happened in March 1940, just after the time that the communist MP, John Strachey helped activate Peierls's surprise approval of naturalisation (which application had been suspended when war broke out), as well as the release from internment of the GRU agent, Jürgen Kuczynski. In his later study of the VENONA transcripts, West was to make a solid case that the agent given the cryptonym VOGEL (BIRD), and then PERS, was in fact Rudolf Peierls.[45]

Peierls's account of what happened next is deceptive. In his autobiography he claimed that, several months after Fuchs's release, when thinking about technical help he himself needed in the spring of 1941, he thought of Fuchs. "I knew and liked his papers, and I had met him", he wrote, dismissing the relationship as fairly remote.[46] Yet he had never written about Fuchs beforehand, and he does not describe the circumstances in which he had met him. His autobiographical contribution is undermined, however, by what he had told MI5. When he was interviewed by Commander Burt in February, 1950, shortly before Fuchs's trial, he said that he had first met Fuchs "in about 1934, probably at some scientific conference", but also stated that "he did not know him very well until Born recommended him". Fuchs was later to confirm that he had met Peierls at a scientific conference "immediately before the war".[47] An MI5 report of November 23, 1949, states that "Peierls had met Fuchs at a Physics Conference in Bristol, when Peierls had first suggested that Fuchs should work under him at Birmingham".[48] That occasion was clearly before the war: Peierls and Fuchs had achieved more than merely discuss issues of joint interest, and Peierls clearly misrepresented the closeness of their relationship when speaking to Burt.

Without explaining how he had learned that Fuchs had been released from internment, and had returned to Edinburgh, Peierls stated that he wrote to Fuchs.[iv] asking him whether he wanted to work with him, even before he (Peierls) had gained permission to do so. He next asked for official clearance, but was instructed "to tell him as little as possible". "In due course he [Fuchs] got a full clearance, and he started work in May 1941." One might conclude that the impression Peierls wanted to give is that it was a fortuitous accident that Fuchs's availability, and his own need, coincided: he conveniently forgot the previous job offer. Moreover, the "and" in Peierls's account is troublesome, suggesting a sequence of events that did not in fact happen that way. Fuchs had not received 'full clearance' by that time: in another item of correspondence, Peierls admitted that he had to wait. The process was to drag on for several months, and some MI5 personnel were later to express horror that the relevant government ministries had proceeded so carelessly in advancing Fuchs's career without concluding the formal checks. For example, in June 1940, Peierls had taken Fuchs with him to Cambridge to meet the Austrian expert in heavy water, Dr. Hans Halban, who

---

[iv] Edwards gives the date of the letter as May 10.

was a member of the exclusive five-man Tube Alloys Technical Committee: Fuchs's training was assuredly not being held back.[49]

Moreover, Peierls's account does not correspond with other records. It is clear from his file at the National Archives that Fuchs was recommended for release from internment in Canada as early as October 14, 1940 (i.e. shortly after the meeting of the Maud Technical Sub-Committee), and that the termination of his internment (to return to Edinburgh) was officially approved a few weeks later. This followed an inquiry by the Royal Society as early as July 1940, since an MI5 memorandum states that "the Royal Society included Fuchs on list of scientists they wanted urgently released soon after Fuchs sailed on *Ettrick* on July 3, 1940." An 'exceptional case' was made on October 17, and the Home Office gave Fuchs's name to the High Commissioner for Canada.[50] These requests would later appear very provocative, as a defined role for Fuchs appeared to have been described very early in the cycle. Yet, after his arrival in Liverpool in January 1941, the Immigration Officer specified very clearly to the Superintendent of the Register of Aliens that Fuchs would not be able to "engage in any kind of employment without the consent of the Ministry of Labour".[51]

It would at first glance be quite reasonable to suppose that Peierls had initiated this action, especially given the curious testimony of Fuchs's supervisor at Edinburgh, Max Born. In a letter dated May 29, 1940, Born had written (to whom is not clear) that, despite Fuchs's being "in the small top group of theoretical physicists in this country", he and the others should not be freed from internment. Furthermore, Born wrote that "there are strict regulations that prohibit any liberated internees to return to the 'protected area' where they live". "Even if they would be released they could not join my department again", he added.[52] Either this was a deliberate deception by Born, to provide a cover-story, or he had a quick change of heart, or he was sincere, but was overruled, the British government wishing to maintain the fiction that everything happened later than supposed. The third alternative can probably be discounted, as Born soon after began writing to influential persons, trying to gain Fuchs's release, immediately after his arrest, and himself vigorously tried to find Fuchs remunerative employment as soon as he learned about Fuchs's release from internment.[53] In any case, the earlier statement represented an unnecessarily severe judgment, made just over two weeks after Fuchs's interrogation and arrest, and its only purpose can have been to smooth the path of Fuchs's employment *elsewhere* after his eventual release.[54]

A further dimension to this change of heart is reflected, however, in the rapidly evolving policy of internment. On March 18, 1940, when Churchill (not yet Prime Minister) had demanded of the Home Secretary, John Anderson, that a large number of 'Fifth Columnists' be detained (and gained the approval of the War Cabinet for such action), he had in mind both Fascists *and* Communists.[55] While he had been impressed by the report from Sir Nevile Bland on so-called fifth-column activity in the Netherlands (the details of which were mostly invention), he was also alive to advice received from the Ministry of Information, who, for example, had submitted a couple of weeks earlier the news that "This latest *[CP political Bureau]* manifesto tallies with the new line given to the German Communists by Herr Ulbricht (now in Moscow); authoritative orders are given to German Communists to co-operate with the Nazis and to inform against any German workers, Catholics, Austrians or Czechs who remain the tools of British Imperialism, i.e. oppose the Nazis' efforts in the war."[56] Anderson resisted for a while, as the blanket term of 'fifth columnists' was becoming meaningless, and the task too onerous. But he had to change his approach when Churchill became Prime Minister in May 1940, and immediately tightened the screws.

The irony is that, while some observers have interpreted the 'Fifth Column' repression that followed as an opportunity for Churchill to clamp down on Nazi sympathisers who recommended negotiations with Hitler (and also to embarrass Ambassador Kennedy via the timing of the Tyler Kent arrest), the final wording chosen authorised the Home Secretary "to deal with any person known to be an active member of an Organisation having hostile associations or subject to foreign control", or to sympathise with such.[57] "'Sympathise' was the catch-all word that permitted the government to detain without trial, indefinitely, members not only of Fascist organisations but of any group that the Home Secretary judged sympathetic to the Germans – including those who advocated negotiations with Hitler", commented John Costello.[58] A more fitting description of CP members and current Communist policy could not have been crafted.

In this context, Born's letter can be seen as echoing the concern about communists undermining the war effort, but, when Churchill backtracked on the whole 'Fifth Column' panic a few weeks later, the previously recognised threat of Communist assistance to the Nazis was broadly forgotten. The notion that the activities of Communists might impede the war effort, or simply remain as an enduring menace, in practice disappeared when the notion of a Fifth Column was shown to be bankrupt. This trend was no doubt encouraged by MI5's hiring of Lord Rothschild on April 25, and Anthony Blunt on June 7, as chapters 6 and 7 showed. It is quite certain that, when native Communists were viewed as reliable elements worthy of working for the government in joining the fight against Fascism, foreign Communists benefitted from the change of policy. On June 27, the Home Office, showing its more indulgent instincts, came out in defence of Communists, pointing out the "great sympathy" which had been elicited by "the communists' advocacy of social reform", and that they were therefore "not to be singled out for special treatment simply because they professed a certain political creed".[59] Equating revolutionary objectives with 'social reform' was a policy of abject appeasement, derived from notably weak analysis, but it reflected the changing tide of opinion at the time. In any case, by the late autumn, when most of the 'alien' internees were being released, the fact that some of them may have belonged to a second dangerous species was overlooked – except by the staunchest of the MI5 officers, and many in the military establishment. It is astonishing, 75 years later, to consider how the realities of the Nazi-Soviet pact were so easily overlooked, and the revolutionary goals of the Comintern simply forgotten.

Max Born appears to have been very conflicted about Fuchs. He knew that Fuchs was a communist ("he never concealed that he was a convinced communist"), and complained about Mott's guiding the German émigré towards Edinburgh, implying that he deemed Mott wanted to rid himself and the university of the turbulent subversive (when Born probably knew that Mott was a communist himself). Fuchs came to Edinburgh with a reputation: a colleague of Professor Born's, a Professor Edward Corson, informed the police on March 15, 1950, of Fuchs's activities. The MI5 report states: "Professor Born informed Fuchs, on his arrival in Edinburgh, that any lecturing on Communism to the students of Edinburgh University, similar to the lectures he had given to students at Bristol University, would not be tolerated. He [Corson] alleges that Fuchs, far from hiding his Communism at that time, advertised it by leaving suitable literature on the subject in convenient places, for the benefit of Professor Mott and others."[60] Corson said that this information came to him directly from Professor Born.

In fact, Born also revealed that Mott must have known that he, Born, had no funds for Fuchs's position, for Mott responded that "he would take care of the financial side of the matter", which suggests a very serious motive, and probably some external funding – maybe from the Soviets.[61] One could conclude as well that Born's position itself was a feint, and one could also point out that his attitude towards communism was somewhat dubious. Elsewhere, in giving a reference for Fuchs at the Aliens Tribunal hearing in November 1939, Born not only praised his scientific merits, but also described him as a "man of excellent character, deeply devoted not only to his science, but to all human ideals and humanitarian activities."[62] To classify a dedicated Communist as a humanist and humanitarian reflects a warped judgment worthy of the first Soviet secret police head, Felix Dzerzhinsky himself.[v] But Born may have had political motives in distancing himself from the nuclear efforts: he was an enthusiastic supporter of Fuchs's skills, but absolved himself from any contribution to atomic research as he [Born] "never learned nuclear physics properly and could not take part in its development", and, as a result, "did not become involved in nuclear fission and its application to the atomic bomb."[63] In the second memoir written shortly before he died, Born was to write about Fuchs in a vague and almost nostalgic manner, introducing him with the phrase "later so well known through the spy affair in which he was involved", as if the traitor had merely been lingering on the sidelines of some society scandal. The statement condemns Born more than it judges Fuchs.

In fact, correspondence between Peierls and the pacifist-minded Born suggests that the two collaborated to find Fuchs employment very soon after his release from internment was approved. It appears the two scientists knew each other well. In the summer of 1936, Born (whose position at Cambridge had come to an end) had received an invitation from Kapitza to work for him in Moscow.[64] The fact that Kapitza appeared then to be an unreformed Stalinist, writing in his letter of invitation: "Now, Born, is the time to make your decision whether you will be on the right or the wrong side in the coming political struggle", did not deter Born.[65] He considered it so seriously that he started taking Russian lessons from Peierls's wife, Eugenia, but instead assumed the chair of Natural Philosophy

---

[v] In his book *The Russian Secret Police*, Ronald Hingley wrote: "On 19 December 1967 the same newspaper [*Izvestiya*] published an article *Hello, Comrade Philby*, quoting the veteran master-spy in praise of Dzerzhinsky as a 'great humanist' – the formula commonly applied in Soviet parlance to successful sponsors of mass killings." (p 249).

at Edinburgh University in October 1936. Laucht's study of Frisch and Peierls refers to letters exchanged between Peierls and Born in November, 1940, where they explored opportunities for placing Fuchs successfully.[66] This correspondence continued during the spring of 1941, with Peierls expressing extreme dedication towards bringing Fuchs into his camp. "Although it looked initially as if Fuchs would not make the move to the University of Birmingham, Peierls remained tireless in his effort to find a job for the talented physicist at his university. In the end, he succeeded and offered Fuchs a temporary position," wrote Laucht. Thus Peierls's version of the recruitment process can be interpreted as another self-serving memoir attempting to distance the author from a traitor. All this was known by MI5: they had gained Home Office Warrants to read the correspondence.

Max Born, moreover, was far from innocent in helping Fuchs on his mission. In his two items of autobiography, he relentlessly reminds his readers that he had no competence in nuclear physics, a convenient pretence for his attitude of non-participation and pacifism. Yet in his later, more comprehensive volume he related the episode of a visit to Cambridge in the summer of 1939, where he met the nuclear physicist Leo Szilard, and how, on his return, he shared with Fuchs Szilard's conviction that an atom bomb could be made. He was then unequivocal that Fuchs knew that the nature of the work he would have to be engaged in was nuclear weapons research, with the goal of defeating Hitler, as he claimed he tried to talk Fuchs out of it.[67] Just as Peierls did in his own memoir, Born concealed the fact of the correspondence between the two exiled scientists at the end of 1940, supporting the lie that it was Peierls's sudden request for Fuchs in May of 1941 that occasioned the latter's transfer from Edinburgh to Birmingham.

What should also be pointed out is that Birmingham University was known as an especial focus of Soviet Military Intelligence (the GRU), because of its reputation for leading-edge scientific research. John Costello showed his incredulity that MI5 should not have been aware of the pool of Communists who gathered there. "The faculty and student body at Birmingham hosted a strong Communist organisation and even before the war had become the refuge for many of the Cambridge Communist activists, including Professor Derwent Thompson, Blunt's friend Roy Pascal and his militant Marxist wife, Fanya", he wrote.[68] Peierls had known Fanya Polyanovskaya (as she then was) and her sister when they were students in Berlin, and they remained close friends.[69] Fuchs was a member of Birmingham's 70 Club, which consisted largely of refugee German and East European Communists. MI5 had Czech informers there, but did not follow up on any leads.[70]

Other evidence confirms longer-term recruitment approaches to émigrés that were made by leading scientists. A letter from the Home Office dated December 5, 1940, confirming the release of Fuchs (and several other scientists) points out that the move was being made "in connection with Professor Chadwick's mathematicians and physicists", suggesting that a high-level initiative had provoked the end of internment for such needed experts.[71] In a report written as late as September 1949, when Fuchs was under surveillance at Harwell, J. C. Robertson of MI5 wrote: "In January 1941, because of his high qualifications as a mathematician and physicist, he was released from internment and brought back to this country", again suggesting that Fuchs's expertise was identified and required *while he was still in Canada*. Robertson reinforced this message the same day by stating that Fuchs "was released in 1941 for important research work at Birmingham University", thus giving a very broad indication that Peierls had been behind the request, and that his place had been determined *before* release.[72] Yet reports written *after* Fuchs's conviction on March 1, 1950 frequently distorted the facts. The same officer Robertson's Top Secret Report of March 2, 1950 (designed for digestion by British Embassies around the world, as well as the FBI) expressed a patently erroneous explanation: "In response to a recommendation from his University [i.e. Edinburgh], he was released. A mid-1941 application was made for him to join a research team at Birmingham University on work connected with the Atomic Energy project. After careful consideration of his security record, he was allowed to join this team."[73] Even though this account is not true, as will be shown later, history was being rewritten to minimise the culpability of MI5 in letting Fuchs through the net, and the connivance of British scientists in breaking the rules.

The conventional wisdom runs that MI5 had apparently objected to the request from the Ministry of Aircraft Production for taking Fuchs on. One dominant account, by Edwards, claims that Roger Hollis, who had been a critic of indulgence towards communists, had not been promoted to head B4 until February 1941, and thus, fresh to the job, was in the forefront of challenging the Ministry. Other accounts differ. According to Nigel West's history of MI5, Hollis was promoted to head of B4 in April 1940, replacing Jane Archer, and had thus been involved in policy much earlier, as Chapter 4 indicated. Hollis's attitude towards communists was indeed paradoxical, especially since he had been subject to a long series of accusations from Chapman Pincher that he was a Soviet super-mole (ELLI). At times, Hollis was the most outspoken of MI5 officers against the danger of communists in government, but at others, he displayed a relative indolence and carelessness that indicated his heart was not really in the job. When Hollis reviewed Fuchs's file with Michael Perrin, the Assistant to the Director of the Tube Alloys project, it was, according to Edwards, "only on Peierls's insistence" that the application for Fuchs was allowed to proceed, with the proviso that Fuchs be given only "miminum disclosure", suggesting that Hollis was easily overruled.[74] Yet this information shows again the unreliability of sources, especially the memories of those engaged in controversial matters. Perrin is the sole origin of the exchange, and provided the information during a conversation he had with Edwards as late as 1985. In the light of the documents analysed in the succeeding paragraphs, the testimony is highly questionable. Perrin might have been eager to shift the responsibility to Hollis and Peierls, since there is no indication in the official records of such a meeting, or even of an application made by the Ministry on Fuchs's behalf as early as that, when the name of the entity to be known as Tube Alloys had not even been conceived.[75]

If the account of the decision were true, it would be an astonishing revelation. Peierls had become a British citizen only a year beforehand, in February 1940. Moreover, his application for citizenship had been surprisingly resuscitated and approved (at a time when all such requests had been put on hold), but only after the intervention of the communist John Strachey, MP, abetted by Harold Laski and Stafford Cripps, as the FBI discovered from MI5 sources.[76] Thus, when the Nazi-Soviet pact was at its peak, a German citizen, who had only recently been granted British naturalisation under dubious circumstances, who had connections through his wife with the Soviet authorities, and had visited that country on more than one occasion, was allowed to make overriding decisions about recruiting a German Communist to a highly secret and strategic weapons project. Why Peierls would have been allowed such influence is a mystery, especially since, as has been shown, at the beginning of the war he had been disqualified from working on highly secret radar work, and, in the early days of the Maud committee, had been prevented from joining the committee because he had only recently become naturalised. It was not as if questions had not been asked. Moreover, Peierls had in fact been evasive about his desire to become a British citizen when he was interviewed for his position at the ICI Mond Laboratory. The conclusion would have to be that Peierls did not take the concerns of MI5 very seriously, treated the organisation with much less respect than he would have shown the NKVD or the Gestapo, and was allowed to behave that way by the Ministry of Aircraft Production (MAP).

However, as stated earlier, these testimonies have to be examined closely. For example, Peierls was wrong about Fuchs's 'clearance'. Fuchs was not given 'full clearance' at that time, as Peierls claimed. Gowing stated that Fuchs was "engaged on Maud work" at the end of May (thus indicating that he very well knew the project he was working on), and reported that he was given his 'minimum disclosure' rating in June by the Ministry of Aircraft Production, and then was required to sign the OSA.[77] In her role as official historian she reported the events as follows:

> "The Ministry of Aircraft Production security people granted the necessary clearance and in June Fuchs signed the Official Secrets Act. It was realised that the work was secret, but, like the other refugees on atomic work, Fuchs was to be told no more about it than was necessary for the performance of his duties. . . .
>
> However, later in 1941 someone in refugee circles said that Fuchs was well known in Communist circles, though it was not known whether he was a party member. The security people informed the Ministry of Aircraft Production, pointing out that while it was impossible to assess the leakage of information, any leakage would be more likely to lead to Russia than to Germany."[78]

Gowing (who, following the practice of official histories, when government records have not been made public, omitted references to such sources) appears to have been heavily reliant on Alan Moorehead's very unscholarly account of the Fuchs case [*see below*], as she openly admitted in the section *References* in her volume. The extract above implies that MI5's objection to Fuchs's recruitment occurred some time *after* his application from the MAP had been approved, because of the communication of some casual contact. Moreover, Moorehead was the *sole* source of the claim that Fuchs signed the OSA in June, and, as shall be explained shortly, Moorehead's account of the whole cycle is a complete distortion. Gowing's disorientation is reinforced by her citation of the MI5 officer who warned of a possible leakage to the Soviets, since it points unerringly to John Archer, the officer who signed off on Fuchs's work permit only in October 1941.

Thus Gowing appears to have been confused over the chronology, or else is suggesting that the Ministry believed it had the power to grant the 'minimum disclosure' rating *before* realising that it had to check with MI5. As explained earlier, policy dictated that Fuchs could not be employed without the consent of the Ministry of Labour. Yet a letter in Fuchs's personal files, sent to him by the Ministry of Aircraft Production in June, "completes the formalities of employment at Birmingham", as if such could be accomplished without the issuance of an Aliens War Service (AWS) permit.[79] Was MAP breaking the rules? In June 1941 Fuchs's work on developing Uranium 235 as an explosive began, so it suited officials to claim in retrospect that Fuchs had by then signed the Official Secrets Act. But it was not until October 1941 that he received 'full clearance' (yet still with precise provisos) from the Ministry then responsible, the Department of Scientific and Industrial Research (DSIR), and by then he had already been in touch with his Soviet contacts, and betrayed his first secrets. Thus the first time that Fuchs was officially given permission to work (and the participation of the Ministry of Labour is not evident in this decision) was granted *five months* after Peierls had accepted him in his laboratory in Birmingham.

It was, admittedly, a turbulent summer on many fronts, but especially for MI5. During that time, Hollis (whether he had been consulted or not) had been moved on from his position in 'B' Division working for Dick White as Jane Archer's replacement. David Petrie (who had taken over as Director-General of MI5 in March 1941 after conducting a review of the organisation) had in August put his stamp on the Security Service by splitting 'B' Division into three, creating newly formed 'B', 'E' and 'F' Divisions, with 'B' Division relieved of the responsibility for aliens control and subversive movements.[80] As part of this restructuring, Hollis had been transferred from 'B' Division, along with Aikin-Sneath (in charge of Fascists), to work under Curry in Division 'F' (Subversive Activities, which included those by Communists and Fascists).[81] Yet Curry reported that the responsibility for dealing with internment and release of enemy aliens did not move with Hollis: Division 'E', under Turner, now had as its charter 'Aliens Control', while Hollis had been put in charge of 'F.2', (officially, Communism and Left-Wing Movements).

Thus, when the application from the Ministry of Aircraft Production arrived in August 1941, i.e. later than the date Gowing claimed, but with the disingenuous implication that it was *considering* Fuchs for employment ("The Ministry have applied for an AWS . . . with a view to employing him on important work ..."), no one appeared to know exactly what to do. Who was responsible for alien subversives, especially when their identity as Communists or Fascists, or some other breed, might be unknown? MAP's request must have been directed to 'E' Division, apparently not highly experienced in such matters, but nominally responsible.[82] On August 6, Cochran, 'E.4.(2)' , wrote for help to Miss Bagot, not an officer, but previously Hollis's assistant, identified as 'F.4b(2)'. ('F.4' is described by Curry as 'Pacifist Movements, Peace Pledge Union, New Politico-Social and Revolutionary Movements', under Roger Fulford, a crony of both Burgess and Hollis). On August 9, Bagot wrote a letter – under Director-General Petrie's name – to the Chief Constable of Birmingham – reminding him of Fuchs's Communist past, and asking whether the officer knew of any fresh political activity. (This was obviously a pointless request, as Fuchs had at that time been in Birmingham for only a couple of months.) The same day she sought information on Fuchs from Robson Scott ('E.1.a'), responsible for Nationals of Western Europe (although Curry's list does not include 'Germans' in his ambit): now, however, Bagot identified herself as 'F.2.b', a separate unit which Curry described as "Comintern Activities generally; Communist Refugees"), although Bagot is not named in his August 1941 chart, as she was not an officer. At least the correct department had been located, even though the authority of the person responsible would appear to have been sub-optimal.

Swift progress was not made. Admittedly, on August 11, the Birmingham Chief Constable replied promptly and thoroughly to Petrie, confirming that Fuchs had resided in Birmingham since May 28, and had apparently behaved himself since. (As it happened, The Chief Constable of Birmingham had written to his counterpart in Edinburgh on May 27, asking for information on Fuchs, to judge whether "the alien should be brought before the Regional Advisory Committee for Review". A statement that was positive about Fuchs was sent on June 9, all of which shows that the Chief Constables were being more diligent than MI5.)[83] On August 16, Cochran informed Miss Griffith ('F.4.b') that the Ministry was pressing for a response: by August 29, Bagot had still not heard from Robson Scott, so she sent him a reminder. Nothing appeared to happen, so 'E.4' referred the request to Group Captain J. O. Archer on October 9, who took the initiative in calling up the Ministry. Archer then recorded a note to file on October 10, identifying himself as 'D.3', i.e. in his traditional role as head of liaison with the Air Ministry and Ministry of Aircraft Production. It is at this stage that he made his famous remark that "it was impossible to assess the risk, but such information was more likely to go to the Russians than to the Germans"; he also noted that it was the view of the Ministry that Fuchs was irreplaceable on this particular work. Stephens of the Ministry followed up the same day, addressing Archer as 'A.I.1(d)' (suggesting Archer was seconded to Administration and Registry, or had been presenting himself as such to the outside world), with a memorandum to him that reinforced the message that Fuchs "will have knowledge only of such part of the work as is necessary for the performance of his duties", and committed to reminding the authorities at Birmingham University "the necessity for minimum disclosure to Fuchs". It should thus be carefully noted that there was still no 'full clearance' given at this time. Stephens asked "for the necessary formalities to be expedited", and the case was completed when Archer signed off (as 'D.3'), with "no objection" to the Permit on October 18.[84]

It is not clear why Group Captain John Archer was the decisive element on the case.[85] In any event, MI5 had been shown to be massively dysfunctional. Through the misfortune of the timing of Petrie's reorganisation, but also owing to some surprising lack of internal communication and initiative across the divisions, none of the experts in communist counter-espionage appears to have been involved in the application made on behalf of Fuchs. These symptoms of systemic breakdown must have been apparent to the Ministries who had to deal with MI5: yet there was turmoil among them, as well. By this time, ICI had lost control of the bomb project, and in October 1941 the Department of Scientific and Industrial Research (DSIR) took over from MAP the responsibility of what was now known as the Tube Alloys project. This change was for two primary reasons: first, the project, as Gowing reported, "embraced power as well as bombs", and 'Aircraft Production' had too narrow a focus; second, the Americans, who were starting to become involved, did not want the project to be managed by a competitive private enterprise with post-war commercial ambitions. (The fact that ICI executives continued to manage the project would later cause problems with the Americans.) Therefore, through that process Fuchs became a civil servant. Gowing wrote that Sir Edward Appleton, the DSIR Secretary, considered Fuchs so important that the security risk should be taken, and all restrictions on Fuchs were thus lifted.[86] But what nature of risk would have caused Appleton to change his mind? Had Fuchs been shown to be an active member of the CPGB, would Appleton have cancelled his recruitment, five months after he started work? Had the inefficiencies of MI5 led the Ministries to believe they should just press on, regardless? Or had they been deliberately dilatory?

The whole account, as it can be discerned from inspection of the Fuchs files, presents three major problems for the historian. The first concerns the application by the Ministry of Aircraft Production for the Aliens' War Service permit. If one assumes that the latter was a necessary part of Fuchs's recruitment process, one might assume that the Ministry would apply for it as soon as it knew that Peierls had made the offer (May 10, 1941), and Fuchs had in principle accepted it. As Gowing reported, Fuchs started work on Maud activity at Birmingham on May 28. Yet the AWS application was not sent until early August, and the Ministry showed no sign that haste was required. Fuchs was not granted 'partial clearance' until the middle of October, a decision that Stephens of the Ministry appeared to be comfortable with. Yet, by this time, Fuchs had proved his indispensability to the project, and also begun his traitorous behaviour: his first reports on his work arrived in Moscow on September 22 and 30.[87] One could easily conclude that, once the decision to release Fuchs from internment was made at some high level, the AWS application was not taken very seriously – or that it was somewhat reluctantly pursued, and delayed until a time when a) MI5 was undergoing some organisational turmoil, and b) the Soviet Union had been invaded by the Nazis, and was now an ally in the war.

The second problem concerns the process within MI5. As has been shown, while the AWS was sent to the department nominally responsible ('E.4' – 'AWS Permits'), it would appear that this new department had historically processed far less critical applications, and that it might have been a mistake cutting it adrift from 'B' Division. According to Curry's chart, Colonel Ryder reported to Mr Mitchell (in charge of 'E.4', 'E.5' and 'E.6'), who himself answered to Major Younger (Assistant Director) and then Mr Turner (Deputy Director). Thus the chains of command were well removed from those of Soviet counter-espionage: it doesn't even appear that 'B.4.A' ('Espionage in UK', under Whyte, who reported to White), or Hollis's unit, 'F.2' (Communism and Left Wing Movements in 'F' Division, responsible for 'Subversive Activities'), were ever involved. Curry, who in his new position as head of 'F' Division was trying to prevent the hiring of Communists in government[88], not surprisingly made no mention of Fuchs in his history, and Curry's name never appears in the Fuchs files. Moreover, it is Bagot's name that is prominent, and yet she, known to have a keen eye for detail, bizarrely wrote what appears as a fruitless letter: surely she would have known to write to Edinburgh or Bristol rather than Birmingham? (And maybe she did so, but the letters were never declassified.)

The role of Bagot is perplexing. It appears almost as if she were on a private assignment to Petrie, bypassing the normal chain of command. As indicated above, her name appears on the letter drafted for Petrie to the Chief Constable of Birmingham: equally intriguing is the fact that her reminder to Robson Scott of 29 August is signed off as 'F.2.b./DG'. The 'DG' can only mean 'Director-General', which was surely introduced to indicate some weight behind the request. As the following chapter shows, Bagot was a very observant and meticulous employee, with a fine memory and a special nose for the bogus. Curry noted her extraordinary capabilities in his history, when he referred to her "exceptional knowledge of the subject and her ability to connect traces from our records even when names had not been carded in the Central Registry." Curry also lamented the inability of MI5 or SIS to maintain adequate records about the Comintern after April 1941 (although he did not indicate what made that date significant), adding: "The only palliative to this situation was that 'F.2.b' was in the hands of Miss Bagot whose expert knowledge of the whole subject enabled her to find and make available a large variety of detailed information based on the records of the past."[89]

Thus the choice of Bagot as the apparent project manager, and her being assigned to work with Petrie directly, is very surprising and irregular. One also has to question why Petrie suddenly became involved with such a low level procedure – unless he was in contact with authorities at the Ministry, and pretended to set the correct wheels in motion. Is the whole paper-trail an elaborate attempt to disguise what really happened, and instead show some apparent seriousness of purpose, as a ruse to absolve the leadership from blame? It is very taxing to believe that MI5 could put on such an incompetent front over such an important matter, and, in retrospect, the records chosen to be released to the archives display a large amount of naivety. In any case, Curry did not come out of this period well. In the very same month that the AWS for Fuchs was signed off, he was moved aside to work on 'Research', and Hollis continued his remarkable ascent by replacing him as head of 'F' Division.

Another scenario would suggest that the reputation and influence of Milicent Bagot were much higher than conventional organisation charts would indicate. In his 2015 biography of the intelligence officer and novelist John le Carré, Alan Sisman wrote:

"Nor were there many women in senior positions: one of the few was the fiercely loyal and hard-working Milicent Bagot, the Service's expert on international Communism, who had been with MI5 since 1931, the first woman within the Service to reach the rank of Assistant Director. Bagot was also one of the first to raise doubts about Kim Philby. Younger officers were wary of her as a stickler for meticulous office procedure;

moreover she was a difficult colleague, whose robust opinions were expressed with passionate conviction. But her memory for facts was so extraordinary as to have passed into Service folklore."[90]

Sisman may have promoted Bagot too far with this assessment: Christopher Andrew noted that Bagot in 1949 was "promoted from administrative assistant to the rank of officer, in recognition of her extraordinary memory for facts and files on international Communism . .".[91] She had joined MI5 from Special Branch in 1931, and thus maintained a high degree of corporate memory and operational expertise, in a poignant way eclipsing that other star female expert in Communism who had paved the way, Jane Archer. The record of Bagot's dogged observations and accurate instincts, as shown in this chapter, indicates perhaps that she was given much more authority than her rank merited, and that Petrie's prejudices against women officers (exemplified in his 1941 regulations making it impossible for women to be promoted to officer rank) may have been somewhat overcome by Bagot's contribution, and that it was natural for him to want to have her working directly for him.

Irrespective of the regularity of this arrangement, a third problem arises – the fact that MI5 promoted an account of the process that is entirely at variance with the official record. When Alan Moorehead's book, *The Traitors*, came out, with MI5's help and approval, in 1952 (*see Chapter 9*), it described a brief and very efficient – though not entirely satisfactory – vetting process that all occurred in May 1941. A summary of what Moorehead wrote runs as follows: Peierls interviewed Fuchs, and offered him a job, which he accepted. Peierls moved to get the appointment approved (suggesting it was in his power to recruit Fuchs); the security services were consulted, at which point MI5 said that Fuchs was "more likely to give information to the Russians". The decision was however the Ministry's, and since "MAP was producing aircraft to fight the Battle of Britain, anyone willing to help win the war should be pressed into service". Fuchs was thus employed and had to be told what work he was engaged in. He was given access to classified material, and began work in May 1941, when he signed the OSA.[92] Moorehead later added an appropriate amount of sanctimony and equivocation by writing: "The authorities would have had no right whatever to refuse Fuchs employment in 1941 on the grounds that he had been a Communist eight years before, even if they had known this."[93] One should note, also, that this account is abetted by Perrin's 1985 testimony, which likewise suggested that an efficient and business-like meeting was held between the Ministry (Perrin) and Hollis in May 1941.

As is now very clear, this account is a travesty. Perrin is the sole source of the anecdote about Hollis, who, according to archival records as released, never played no role at all. The archive, as well as Fuchs's personal file of letters, suggests that the first written confirmation of the OSA did not come up until October 11. (Fuchs appeared to be an obsessive hoarder of correspondence. This item is the only reference to the OSA in his correspondence boxes.)[94] The statement by Archer about the Russians likewise did not occur until October. The Battle of Britain is generally considered to have concluded at the end of September 1940, thus Moorehead's reference to it is irrelevant. Fuchs was given only partial clearance, but not until October 1941, and thus certainly would not have been authorised to have access to classified material beyond the scope of his work. The chronology of Moorehead's statement suggests all the vetting and negotiation occurred before Fuchs *even started work*, which was utterly impossible and is negated by the evidence. (Fuchs was still communicating about "completion of formalities" with MAP in June 1941, and his private papers show that he was still exchanging letters with the Ministry of Labour over prospects for employment up until August.)[95] What it all suggests is that Dick White (who hand-held Moorehead through his 'research') wanted to publicise a version of events that suggested that MI5 reacted efficiently to the Ministry's request, but was regrettably overruled. And the statement by Perrin, 45 years after the event, suggests that he and White conspired to concoct this story.

One has to conclude that the whole exercise was a charade, and that a false paper-trail was created. If the Ministry had determined, with guidance at a very high level, purely on the basis of Peierls's and Born's references, that Fuchs was an indispensable asset for critical war work, was it going to follow the rules, or be in any way deterred by what MI5 said? At a time when the climate had changed to such a degree that pressure had been successfully applied to hiring communists in other ministries in the fight against fascism, it would have taken remarkable resolve for MI5 to insist that his background made him an unacceptable risk, especially when the organisation had by then accepted a known communist (Blunt) in its own ranks. Moreover (even though it is not explicitly stated in the memoranda), the Nazi invasion of the Soviet Union in June must have encouraged the Ministry to believe that the cause of trusting Communists could assume new life, and that Fuchs's clearance could safely be taken on to the next level. In addition, at that time, the Soviet Union initiated a massive propaganda campaign for scientists to unite in creating atomic weapons to beat Fascism, a programme that reached the British press, as Gowing reported.[96] [vi] MI5 had simply not prepared the ground well enough to be able to articulate a policy that declared that, despite the alliance with the Soviet Union against the Nazis, Communism remained an existential threat, and that engaging known Communists on sensitive war-work was simply beyond the bounds of sensible practice.

As with Peierls, the pressure next intensified for Fuchs to become naturalised. In May 1942 he again applied for British citizenship, using the same documentation, and the same references, from 1939, and it was granted three months later. Thus had logic been overturned: instead of disqualifying a known risk from secret and important work, because of his track-record as a Communist,

---

[vi] "Fascism is a mortal menace to culture and science. In his attempt to conquer nature the scientist has been moved primarily by the desire to benefit culture and humanity whereas Fascism has employed science for devastation and destruction. On us scientists rests the duty of finding means to resist the Fascists. We Soviet scientists are employing all our knowledge and all our endeavour to secure the early defeat of Hitler's hordes. But we know that this can be secured only by the concerned struggle of the peace-loving nations, all the progressive people of the world. The scientists of the world must devote all their energies and all their knowledge to the fight against the most horrible tyranny history has ever known, against Hitlerism." (Quoted in *Daily Telegraph*, October 13, 1941)

a candidate was approved and granted citizenship because the confidential work required statements of loyalty, and the word of another suspected risk was used as a testimonial to abet the process. The idea that deception and subterfuge may have been used was beyond the compass of the British authorities. They did not understand that a dedicated spy would sign the OSA without a qualm of conscience, nor did it realise that forcing a man with a chequered past to sign such a document because of protocol would not magically convert him into a loyal civil servant.

Did Born and Peierls know about Fuchs's ideological attitudes, and, if they did, did it deter them? Again, the evidence is outwardly ambiguous. In his 1968 memoir, Born had only one sentence about Fuchs, in which he reported that he was "a highly gifted man who never concealed the fact that he was a communist".[97] Peierls gave the impression that he knew Fuchs was indeed very left-wing, indicating that, when he "looked around for a suitable person" (testimony now seen to be false), and thought of Fuchs, he recalled him "as a student had been politically active as a member of a socialist student group (which was essentially communist) and had to flee for his life from the Nazis."[98] On the other hand, Norman Moss, whose account of Fuchs's recruitment was based on interviews he had with Peierls, gave a more nuanced account, where Peierls clearly wanted to leave the impression that Fuchs's communism was not blatant: "He [Fuchs] talked a little about university days in Germany, and his activities with the student Socialists. He never said that he was a Communist, although Peierls would not have been deterred from hiring him, and would not have thought less of him, if he had. People talked politics and talked about the war. Fuchs rarely expressed political opinions; he left a vague impression that he was a democratic Socialist and blended in, as he had in Bristol, with the moderate left-wing background." [99] That was not how Born had seen it. In his later autobiography (1978), Born asserted that Nevill Mott, Fuchs's supervisor at Bristol, had sent Fuchs to Edinburgh because "he spread communist propaganda among the undergraduates", an allegation which, according to Laucht, Mott "forcefully rejected".[100][vii] Laucht presented Mott's judgment that any 'anyone who was against the Nazis' would have been acceptable at the time, and suggested that this was a prevalent attitude of many Britons at the time, inconveniently forgetting that these events occurred during the time of the Nazi-Soviet pact, an arrangement that finds no mention in Laucht's book.

Fuchs's activities as a Communist were known to MI5 at the time. Williams, citing Nigel West's history of MI5, and a letter from an MI5 officer, stated that SIS had opened a file on him in 1932, with a report on his Communist Party membership offered by an SIS agent in Kiel. SIS passed Fuchs's file on to MI5 when he arrived in the UK.[101] One frequently mentioned datum is the refusal of

---

[vii] The footnote by Mott (who provided the Introduction to Born's autobiography) reads, in part: "I do not remember believing that Fuchs spread communist propaganda among the students, and at a time when Hitler was the enemy I would not have worried unduly if he had." This is a naïve presentation of the Comintern-inspired message that 'only Communism can beat Fascism', and shows Mott's true colours. Would Mott have worried if Hitler had *not* been the enemy? Surely not.

the German consulate in Bristol to renew Fuchs's passport in 1934, a decision that is frequently described as an irrational act by a government committed to making life difficult for all its ideological enemies, whether democratic socialists or communists. (In fact, an MI5 note from September 22, 1949, reporting on the Ministry of Aircraft Production's application for Fuchs's AWS permit, claims that this item from 1934 was the only information available on Fuchs.)[102] The German consul, Mr C. Hartley-Hodder, may not have been totally honourable in his intentions, but he wrote, on October 11, 1934, as follows: "The student Klaus FUCHS, born 29.12.11 at Russelheim was as . . . presented here and dated 31.8.32 member of the Social-Democratic Party. Here he was excluded 1932. FUCHS joined then the Communist Party and worked for this Party as orator in the election campaigns. FUCHS was leader of the Nazi Commission of the Sea-District, the task of which it was, to break up the National-Socialist Party. On the 1.3.33 at FUCHS house an inspection was made and different leaflets and books of the Communist Party were found."[103] A month later, the consul followed up, saying that Fuchs was a "notorious communist". This should have been strong enough evidence of Fuchs's ideological beliefs. Yet Laucht claimed that MI5 did not expose Fuchs as a Soviet agent earlier because his work as a communist was "inconspicuous". Laucht nevertheless admitted that Fuchs worked on a committee to help Republican forces in the Spanish Civil War, and that he organised the shipment of propaganda leaflets to Germany on behalf of the KPD while he was in Edinburgh. The National Archives are dotted with claims that Fuchs's Communist sympathies were well known by anyone who got to know him.[104]

Moreover, Fuchs maintained links with known Communists. In the early days of their investigation into Fuchs in September 1949, MI5 officers recalled a report from 1942 that Fuchs had associated closely with one Hans Kahle in the internment camp in Canada. That information had been given to them by a source identified as KASPAR (a Dr Schreiber), who had an informant, a Dr Ernst, in Canada: MI5 even concluded that Kahle may have recruited Fuchs to the Communist Party.[105] Brinson and Dove said that Fuchs left from Liverpool on July 3, 1940, on the *SS Ettrick* alongside Hinze and Kahle, countering the oft-repeated claim that Kahle and Fuchs met for the first time in Canada, and they also mentioned that an MI5 agent, probably Claud Sykes, reported that the "notorious" Colonel Kahle had caused a lot of trouble at the Isle of Man internment camp where he and Fuchs had been held before their deportation.[106] A confirming perspective is provided by another witness: in his 1980 memoir of the passage to Canada, and internment there, Eric Koch wrote: "To what extent Kahle and Fuchs were friends is hard to determine. There is some evidence that Fuchs was already a communist agent by the time he was interned. According to one theory, it was Kahle who during the summer and fall of 1940 inducted him into the Soviet intelligence system. A few of us are certain that Fuchs was a member of Kahle's 'cell' in the camp."[107]

Kahle was a well-known Communist, a Spanish Civil War veteran who had helped Jürgen Kuczynski organise the KPD in the UK in the late 1930s, and was probably responsible for introducing Fuchs to Kuczynski on their return from Canada. Kahle's release had been engineered by Professor Haldane (Soviet cryptonym INTELLIGENTSIA), an expert in Air Raid Precaution, and also chairman of the *Daily Worker*, who had invited Kahle to work with him in the spring of 1940.[108] As West reported, Haldane was next involved in highly secret work with the Air Intelligence Branch, 'AI-4', which liaised with Bletchley Park. Ursula Kuczynski reported Kahle as working as a military correspondent for *Time* and *Fortune* magazines at the time she was introduced to him late in 1941. Thus, despite his "notorious" track-record, surveillance of Kahle was low: he must no longer have been seen as a threat, and he was allowed to associate unhindered with Haldane and the Kuczynskis. No surer indication of MI5's inattention could be given.

More evidence of Fuchs's open Communism during internment was provided by Asik Radomysler, who volunteered information to MI5 after Fuchs's trial – one of many who were amazed that Fuchs could have been hired for secret weapons work, given his obvious allegiances. Radomysler, a teacher at the London School of Economics, who had known communists in Germany, was interviewed by the MI5 officer, Serpell on March 23, 1950. While interned in Canada in the autumn of 1940, he had been shrewd enough to detect from Fuchs's discomfort over the fact of the Nazi-Soviet pact that Fuchs, along with other members of the Communist party, were very reluctant to criticise the Party in any way, and found it difficult to find common ground with the more critical views of Leftists not shackled by party dogma. Radomysler said nothing to camp authorities at the time, as the actions of the ten or so Communists were so obvious. Nor did he speak up when he learned with incredulity that Fuchs was at Harwell, some time after the war, when he discussed Fuchs with a friend: they both believed MI5 must be on top of the case.[109]

Fuchs, at this stage – even when he had just been released from internment – was apparently still declaring his Soviet colours. As Nigel West wrote, describing Fuchs's confession to Len Burt of Scotland Yard soon after his arrest: "Relations between MI5 and the FBI deteriorated even further when Fuchs mentioned that in 1941, following his return to England from internment in Canada, he had emphasised his anti-Nazi credentials by declaring, at his hearing before the Aliens Review Board, that he was a Communist."[110] While this statement turns out to be highly controversial for many reasons, and demands special analysis, Fuchs (and his handlers) must have known that he could not conceal his Communist past completely, and to attempt to do so would arouse suspicion. Moreover, the Philby experience had shown that, so long as he had committed nothing untoward recently, his past actions would not disqualify him from a sensitive post. Yet he ran a great risk (or should have done so) – especially before Hitler's invasion of the Soviet Union in June 1941 – when articulating his opposition to Fascism a little too boldly.

The source of this report on Fuchs's open admission to Communism in 1941 appears to be testimony provided by the FBI. MI5 had been understandably obstructive in providing FBI agents access to Fuchs after his trial, but the organisation persisted, and eventually gained an interview. Robert Lamphere was one of the most senior of the FBI's agents engaged in counter-intelligence against the Soviets, but someone who was also careless over dates, as he ascribes MI5's lack of concern over Communists as due to the "wartime alliance with Russia". In 1986 Lamphere wrote as follows: "Fuchs told me, for instance, that while interned in Canada he had been classed as a German Communist: he told an aliens hearing board in Britain in 1941 that he was a Communist in order to convince the board of his anti-Nazi sentiments so that he could get a job in war-related research." [111] Either Fuchs was being exceedingly naïve, or misremembered the date, or he at this time sincerely believed, based on advice he must have received, that espousing Communism was no barrier to engaging on secret war work for the imperialist enemy. But there is no record of an "Aliens Review Board" hearing for Fuchs in 1941, and no suitable date when it would have made sense for him to present such a case.

If the hearing *had* occurred, the event could perhaps constitute the most damning evidence of all against the pusillanimity and deceitfulness of MI5. The case is very murky, however, and has bizarre consequences. For it appears that MI5 learned of this interview from an article by Rebecca West in the *New York Times* of March 4, 1951. Here, West wrote:

> "When war broke out between Great Britain and Germany the Aliens Tribunal, before which he appeared to show cause why he should not be interned, accepted his membership in the Communist Party as proof that he was anti-Nazi. . . . In 1942 [*sic*], he was allowed to return to Great Britain, where a position was waiting for him at Glasgow [*sic*] University. Soon afterward he was asked by Professor Peierls, a very eminent German-born refugee physicist, to come to Birmingham University to help him in some war work."[112]

Despite the mistakes made by West (Fuchs returned to Great Britain early in 1941, and resumed his position at Edinburgh, not Glasgow), MI5 became markedly perturbed at this report. Stung by the criticism that it had ignored such a blatant declaration, the organisation went to great lengths to try to track down the records of the Aliens Tribunal, interviewing the persons who officiated, and attempting to uncover the written records of the proceedings, as if the demonstration of proof that Fuchs never said such things would absolve them of all negligence. Was it naivety or cunning that made MI5 concentrate its energies on the records of the Aliens Tribunal, when the focus should have been on the far more critical vetting process for Fuchs's work permit? But it was all in vain. MI5 never found the records. During the months of March, April and May 1951, MI5 officers diligently interviewed and delved: the National Archives reveal that "the Detective Officer who was Clerk to the Tribunal assures that there was no mention of the CP when Fuchs was before his Tribunal". Sillitoe himself, in a memorandum of June 5, wrote: "Indeed, it hardly seems believable that Fuchs would gratuitously have drawn attention to his Communist past at a time when the position of Russia in the war was by no means clear – in November 1939 she had recently signed a non-aggression pact with Germany and it was the eve of her attack on Finland."[113] MI5 could, however, not disprove West's claim. That news must have reached West, for, by the time (1966) when she issued the updated version of her 1945 book of treason, she wrote as follows: "It is not possible to know in what terms his statement was made, for by an administrative act of incredible folly all or most records of the proceedings before the Aliens Tribunal were destroyed after the war."[114]

If West received her information from Lamphere, however, she had made a careless error. Lamphere's account clearly points to a hearing in 1941, *after* Fuchs's internment, and his statement carries a different authenticity, as he says that Fuchs made his claim in the context of trying to gain employment, which suggests that his statement was made at a second, separate hearing, at some time *after* his return to Edinburgh in January 1941, and probably *before* he received the formal offer from Peierls in May. Nigel West, when echoing this story, has introduced the entity of an "Aliens Review Board", but no other reference acknowledges the activities of such a structure in 1941, all of which leaves the question of Fuchs's reliability up in the air.[viii] Did Fuchs invent such an episode? Why did he claim to be "seeking employment" when Peierls had offered him a job before the war, and he was lined up now to assume it? Did his claim perhaps appear in one of his letters to the Home Office of that period (*see page 21*)? Did Lamphere mishear the message from Fuchs? Did Lamphere read West's article, and consider contacting West to correct her, or was he, like her, chronologically challenged? Why did MI5 not follow up more closely with Rebecca West?[115] The most plausible explanation is that Fuchs muddied the waters with Lamphere, Lamphere faithfully recording 1941 in his notes as he was not familiar with the chronology of Fuchs's internment, and then West implicitly corrected the year (in fact she left it out) in the awareness of how the Tribunal worked. But was she perhaps relying on another source? It is astonishing that MI5 did not question her about it, nor draw attention to the blatant chronological errors in her essay as a means of discrediting her.

To pile on the pressure, Rebecca West published another uncomfortable article about MI5's mis-steps in the *Evening News* of June 4, 1951: its officers had another opportunity and cause for interviewing her to determine her sources. Had they been able to verify that the FBI (as opposed to leaked Home Office files) had provided the information, and to show that no such hearing occurred after Fuchs's release from internment, they would have been able to demolish the accusations of West, as well as the reputation of Fuchs in the latter's attempts to vindicate himself in the eyes of the FBI. Given his previous activities, and his very public association with Kahle and other Communists in Canada, Fuchs might well have believed that his affiliations were well known, and there was nothing to be lost by reinforcing his anti-Nazi beliefs in his mission to join what would shortly be known as the Tube Alloys project. Moreover, at this stage of the war, Hitler's plans to invade the Soviet Union were known to British intelligence, and the attitude towards communists had markedly changed since 1939. And why would Fuchs lie to the FBI in 1950? After all, he was just starting a 14-year gaol sentence.

As it was, the popular story dominated that MI5 had kept a traditional eye on Fuchs, but apparently ignored the signals. Yet, had Parliament, the press, and the public been aware of other attitudes towards Fuchs a few years earlier, they would have been amazed at MI5's misplaced zeal in trying to discredit Rebecca West. For far more damaging evidence must have come to light five years

---

[viii] Nigel West has not been able to shed any light on the source of his reference to an "Aliens Review Board" of 1941.

beforehand. *At some stage Fuchs had transitioned from a possible communist who might be a security risk to a candidate suspected of specific acts of espionage.* Hints of this crucial change in status are provided by a remarkable set of terse statements in Fuchs's files. This stage coincided with Fuchs's return to the UK. In November 1943, he had left, with Peierls, to work on what was now a US-dominated atomic weapons project. Fuchs returned from the USA to the UK in the summer of 1946, and assumed his post at AERE Harwell on August 1. For some reason (a sad echo of its discomfiture in the summer of 1941), MI5 did not hear about this appointment until October 9, when the Harwell Security Officer, Arnold, informed them that Fuchs would be attending a meeting of the Physics Club of the Royal Society. This discovery prompted a sudden flurry of commentary and suspicion. The next major stage of the cover-up over Fuchs occurs.

In summary, the period of Fuchs's recruitment to the Tube Alloys project during 1940 and 1941 was the most significant for the study of MI5's role in vetting and detecting him – much more so than the much discussed naturalisation processes that took place in 1939 and 1942. From the point of view of tradecraft, this was a most critical stage. It was far easier – and safer – to disqualify a person for reasons of perceived risk than it was to approve someone reluctantly, and then have to spend the rest of that person's career surveilling him, waiting for a mistake to be made, and living with a suspicion that would either constantly defer the inevitable, or force a probable spy to be let loose before he revealed his contacts. But the system failed. At that time, MI5's informal vetting procedure was too haphazard, too *ad hoc*, too reliant on whoever happened to be in the relevant seat at the time, and thus dependent upon that person's judgment and connections. What is apparent is that senior officers in MI5 never believed, when they sanitised and doctored the whole story about the Aliens War Service permit, that a policy 60 years later would open up an array of documents that would undermine utterly the story they wanted the world to know. And yet, a careful analysis of the Fuchs files that have been released points to yet another account – an account which suggests that some lofty powers were manipulating the whole system to allow Fuchs to proceed unhindered. Such unknown figures may have been acting out of sincere motives, and having to make risky decisions in the heat of war, but MI5 was no longer providing the muscle to help government institutions avoid such disastrous mistakes. With Fuchs now installed on a highly confidential and strategic project, MI5's tradecraft of surveillance would be sorely tested.

Notes

[1] Margaret Gowing, *Britain and Atomic Energy 1939-1945*, pp 36-39.
[2] In his 2012 study of Fuchs and Peierls, *Elemental Germans: Klaus Fuchs, Rudolf Peierls and the Making of British Nuclear Culture, 1939-1959*, Christoph Laucht asserted that Fuchs's espionage started in 1940 (p 82).
[3] Notably Robert Chadwell Williams's *Klaus Fuchs: Atom Spy*, Norman Moss's *Klaus Fuchs, The Man Who Stole the Atom Bomb*, and Chapman Pincher's *Treachery*. Pincher's account is the most broad, but is devoid of verifiable references, and is marred by its

obsession with attempting to prove that Roger Hollis was a super-mole. In 2014, Mike Rossiter published *The Spy Who Changed the World*, which has some fresh insights, derived (he claimed) from Russian and German archives. His work lists an impressive set of sources, but the text unfortunately lacks specific references to them.

[4] TNA, KV 1246/2.

[5] An interesting twist to Fuchs's arrest is provided in Costello's and Tsarev's *Crown Jewels*. Philby, about to move to Washington in September 1949, learned about the identification of CHARLES as Fuchs, and, as his last rendezvous with his Soviet handler had already taken place, asked Burgess to pass the news on. Through various acts of incompetence, neither Blunt nor Burgess was able to provide Modin with the information until after Fuchs's arrest in February, 1950, so Fuchs was not able to be spirited out of the country, or be trained on how to handle his interrogator (pp 180-181).

[6] Early works had to use a copy of the confession owned by the FBI. It was not until Fuchs's papers were released to the National Archives in 2003 that it has been available for inspection in the UK. See KV 1250/2.

[7] Williams, Appendix B.

[8] TNA, KV 2/1658/2.

[9] Richard Deacon, *The British Connection*, p 134.

[10] Rudolf Peierls, *Bird of Passage*, p 325.

[11] Laucht, p 123.

[12] TNA, KV 2/1245/1.

[13] Nigel West, *Mortal Crimes,* p 171.

[14] TNA KV 2/1252/2.

[15] TNA KV 2/1251/1.

[16] West, p 169.

[17] Peierls, p 113.

[18] Peierls, p 267.

[19] Pavel Sudoplatov, *Special Tasks*, p 192.

[20] Andrew Lownie, *Stalin's Englishman*, p 213, and Note 7 on p 369.

[21] Wilfrid Mann, *Was There a Fifth Man?*, p 70, pp 79-80.

[22] West, p 207.

[23] Max Born, *My Life*, p 279.

[24] Two letters to the Home Office from Lord Rutherford, accessible in Peierls' file at the National Archives, confirm Peierls' appointment. The second states that he took up his appointment on October 1, 1935: TNA, KV 2/1658.

[25] ibid., p 114.

[26] George Gamow, *My World Line*, p 81 and p 130.

[27] Gamow claimed to have made a miraculous escape (with his wife) from the Soviet Union, to attend a scientific conference in Brussels in October 1933, by appealing to Molotov's sense of humour, but only after they had made an abortive attempt to escape to Turkey by kayak. Gamow appears in a bizarre episode involving Kim Philby, Basil Mann, and Guy Burgess in Mann's *Was There a Fifth Man*? Gamow's testimony might suggest that the whole saga of Kapitza's 'detention' was an elaborate charade organised by the Soviet Intelligence Service. Moreover, some subtle inconsistencies appear in Gamow's and Peierls's account of their relationship. In *Bird of Passage*, Peierls offered a very warm profile of Gamow, recounting his jovial side, and how they went on a hiking-tour together in Switzerland in 1930. Gamow, on the other hand, in *My World Line*, was very restrained about Peierls. He did present, however, a fetching photograph (p 49) of an alluring young

lady sprawled on his lap in a "private room at a restaurant" in Leningrad. The lady in question was Yevgenia Kanegiesser, who was to become Rudolf Peierls's wife. But Gamow merely noted, coolly that Yevgenia "eventually married a German theoretical physicist, Rudolf Peierls, and left Russia", as if he really didn't know Peierls at all, saying nothing about their friendship or hiking-tour. The conclusion must be that neither Gamow nor Peierls is a trustworthy witness. For further information see http://www.coldspur.com/mann-overboard/

[28] TNA, KV 2/1658/2.

[29] Christopher Andrew, *The Defence of the Realm*, p 167.

[30] TNA, KV 2/1268/2.

[31] Gowing, p 349.

[32] ibid., p 350.

[33] Laucht, p 41.

[34] West, p 10.

[35] ibid., p 11.

[36] Michael Smith, *The Spying Game*, p 210.

[37] John Cairncross, *The Enigma Spy*, p 75.

[38] TNA, KV 4/474.

[39] Cairncross, pp 80, 90, 91, 102.

[40] Nigel West and Oleg Tsarev, *The Crown Jewels*, pp 103-104.

[41] Christopher Andrew and Oleg Gordievsky, *KGB: The Inside Story,* p 311, p 400.

[42] TNA, HO 523/4.

[43] Nigel West, *Historical Dictionary of British Intelligence*, p 104.

[44] Cairncross, pp 41, 54.

[45] Nigel West, *Venona, the Greatest Secret of the Cold War*, p 174.

[46] Peierls, p 163.

[47] TNA KV 2/1249/1.

[48] TNA KV 2/1251/2; KV 2/1248/1.

[49] Rossiter, p 86.

[50] TNA, KV 2/1245/1.

[51] TNA, KV 2/1259/2.

[52] TNA, KV 2/1426/2.

[53] Williams, p 32; TNA, AB/172.

[54] The 1940 correspondence between Born and Peierls, held at the National Archives (AB 1/572), is not very revealing. It represents an exchange between Peierls and Born in the period November 1940 to May 1941, and could be interpreted as intended to give the impression that Fuchs' release from internment had come as a surprise to them both. For instance, in November 1940, Peierls told Born that he had heard from Mott that Fuchs had been released, but Born did not reply, and Peierls had to remind him again in March 1941. A false paper-trail seems the likeliest explanation for this correspondence, as well as for the discouraging message in May.

[55] TNA, CAB 65/7.

[56] John Costello, *Ten Days to Destiny*, p 83, 93; TNA, CAB 75/7.

[57] TNA, CAB 65/7/28.

[58] Costello, p 158.

[59] Ian McLaine, *Ministry of Morale*, p 57.

[60] TNA KV 2/1254.

[61] Max Born, *My Life*, p 284.

[62] Laucht, pp 25-26.

[63] Max Born, *My Life and My Views*, p 6.

[64] ibid., p 40.

[65] Born, *My Life*, p 280.

[66] Laucht, p 21; TNA, AB 1/572.

[67] Born, *My Life*, p 287.

[68] John Costello, *Mask of Treachery*, p 529.

[69] Peierls, p 22, p 124.

[70] TNA, KV 2/1252/1.

[71] TNA, KV 2/1250/2.

[72] TNA, KV 2/1426/1.

[73] TNA, KV 2/1253/1.

[74] Edwards, p 143.

[75] It is not clear exactly when the term 'Tube Alloys' was established as the cover name for the project managed up until then by ICI. Gowing suggested that the name was determined in October 1941, and that the first committee meeting of Tube Alloys took place in early November. Certainly, Perrin could never have discussed Fuchs's application with Hollis when he (Perrin) was a Tube Alloys officer.

[76] *Mortal Crimes*, p 170.

[77] Gowing, pp 53-54.

[78] Gowing, *Britain and Atomic Energy 1945-1952,* (Volume 2), p 146.

[79] TNA, KV/1252/2.

[80] Hinsley, p 70. Curry stated, in his history (*The Security Service, 1908-1945*), that 'F' Division had been constituted as early as April 1941, with himself as leader (Deputy Director). He implied that Hollis and Aikin-Sneath were transferred at that time, but maintained their 'B' identity until Petrie's formal announcement on July 15, 1941. Curry's tenure did not last long: he was made Research Officer in October 1941, and Hollis was promoted to Assistant Director in charge of the whole Division. (Curry, pp 349-350).

[81] Curry, p 202.

[82] Nigel West's *Historical Dictionary of British Intelligence* recorded, under "E Division", "E4, headed by Colonel Ryder, responsible for dealing with Aliens War Service permits". (p 193).

[83] TNA, KV 2/1259/2.

[84] TNA, KV 1245/1.

[85] From the Fuchs files at the National Archives, Archer is clearly designated at this time as 'AI1(d)'. Yet Curry's organisation chart has Archer heading up 'D3' in August 1941, and shows him still in that position in April 1943.

[86] Gowing, p 146.

[87] *Mortal Crimes*, p 59.

[88] Peter Hennessy, *The Secret State*, p 79.

[89] Curry, *The Security Service, 1908-1945*, p 358 and p 351.

[90] Alan Sisman, *John Le Carré; The Biography*, pp 190-191.

[91] Andrew, p 332.

[92] Alan Moorehead, *The Traitors*, pp 81-82.

[93] ibid., p 202.

[94] TNA, KV 2/1252.

[95] TNA, KV 2/1252/2.

[96] Gowing, p 88, Note 1.

[97] Born, *My Life and My Views*, p 40.

[98] Peierls, p 163.

[99] Moss, p 35.

[100] Born, *My Life*, p 284; Laucht, p 94.

[101] Williams, p 144.

[102] TNA, KV 2/1426/2.

[103] ibid.

[104] TNA, KV 2/1251/1.

[105] KASPAR had been used earlier. When MI5 was considering the MAP's application in October 1941, KASPAR reported that he was "uncertain whether Fuchs was a Party member". TNA, KV 2/1245/1.

[106] Brinson and Dove, p 120.

[107] Eric Koch, *Deemed Suspect: a Wartime Blunder*, pp 84-85. Koch claimed that Kahle was a close friend of Ernest Hemingway, who modelled 'General Hans' in *For Whom the Bell Tolls* on Kahle, and that it was Hemingway who secured Kahle's release (*Deemed Suspect*, p 85).

[108] *Venona*, pp 84-85.

[109] TNA, KV 2/1270; Koch, p 86.

[110] *Mortal Crimes*, p 133.

[111] Robert Lamphere, *The FBI-KGB War: A Special Agent's Story*, p 155.

[112] TNA, KV 2/1257/1.

[113] ibid.

[114] Rebecca West, *The New Meaning of Treason*, p 178.

[115] Roger Hollis did in fact suggest doing so, on April 10, 1951, but it appears his advice was not followed up: TNA, KV 2/1257/2.

Chapter 9: Deception – Fuchs, the Spy

"Secrecy may be essential, but confidence must be restored." (Hugh Gaitskell)

"Secrecy is maintained less to secure the safety of the state than to protect those who rule it from the scrutiny of the rules, and helps perpetuate the hierarchical structure of British society in the age of democracy." (David Stafford)

"British security is symbolised by a very fine veneer on top and utter departmental confusion underneath." (Klaus Fuchs)

After Fuchs's qualified clearance to work on Tube Alloys, granted in November 1941, he worked industriously, and spied without detection, until he relocated to the USA in November, 1943. Relations between the USA and Great Britain over the sharing of nuclear secrets had not been smooth: the USA mistrusted Britain's post-war commercial plans, and disapproved of the treaty of June 1942 by which the Soviet Union and Britain committed to exchange scientific information. Only the personal intervention by Churchill to Roosevelt was enough to overcome suspicions, and Britain was again invited to participate in what was now called the Manhattan Project. After the Quebec Agreement was signed on August 19, 1943, the project's leader, General Groves, met with Peierls, and it was quickly decided that Fuchs was needed to work on gaseous diffusion. While Fuchs's movements were restricted in the USA, he successfully made contact with his new courier, and in August 1944, moved to Los Alamos in New Mexico. He continued passing on secrets to his controller, and visited his sister in Boston. A successful test of the bomb was carried out in July 1945, and Fuchs left the USA to return to Britain in late June, 1946.

The news that Fuchs had been back in the country for some months came as a surprise to the officers of MI5 when they received the incidental report from Arnold, the Security Officer at AERE Harwell in October 1946. Yet something provoked a sudden flurry of observations: on October 15, 1946, T. A. Robertson (the officer responsible for the operation of the Double-Cross System, by which German spies were 'turned' to provide misinformation) wrote that he "suspects Fuchs may be passing information to the Russians"; on November 13, Serpell (who would later join Skardon in interviewing Ursula Kuczynski) reminded his readers of Fuchs's communist background, and relationship with Kahle, and offered a warning about him, as well as about Peierls, "who may be even more important". On November 19, Hollis wanted to warn Arnold about Fuchs and Peierls, while eight days later, J. O. Archer (the husband of Jane, who had hinted at the risk inherent in Fuchs's recruitment back in 1941), joined the chorus in asserting that Fuchs "is a probable Russian agent", and recommended that ties with him and Peierls be severed at once. Archer went on to say: "unless my knowledge of Lord Portal [the controller of atomic energy] is at fault he will not

240

allow these men to continue working on atomic energy. To do so may compromise the future of atomic energy security, which is a great deal more important than the fact that such secrecy must be considered compromised up to date."[1]

What had caused these alarming concerns – especially as there are no documents in the archives that suggest these were issues that had gained previous attention? Three scenarios present themselves. First, Fuchs could have been observed behaving in a highly suspicious manner, possibly passing on information to Soviet handlers or their intermediaries. Second, a general programme of detecting espionage had prompted a reassessment of known security risks. Third, confirmed reports of secret information appearing in the wrong hands had led MI5 officers to consider that Fuchs's position and opportunities made him a possible suspect. There appears to be no clear archival evidence of the first scenario. The second, the possibility of widespread Soviet espionage, might have been provoked by the recent revelations of the defector, Igor Gouzenko, with MI5 sensibly concluding that other British subjects could also have been involved. Gouzenko, a cipher-clerk at the Soviet Embassy in Toronto, had defected in 1945 with information that led to the arrest of another British atomic spy, Alan Nunn May, among others. The third scenario sounds very much like VENONA (the decryption of Soviet cable communications). Although the dates concerning the individual exercises of VENONA decryption are very murky, most indications would suggest the information that pointed to Fuchs came much later than the autumn of 1946. It should also be pointed out that this period was one where the spectre of Soviet aggression was very much on the mind of MI5 officers; apart from the Gouzenko case, the Joint Intelligence Committee was pressing for plans to go into effect if the Soviets invaded, and intense discussions were taking place about the dangers of Communist penetration in government agencies.[2]

VENONA should thus probably be discounted. It seems highly unlikely that the project would have thrown up any solid clues as early as 1946. True, one of T. A. Robertson's roles was to liaise with the Government Communications Headquarters (GCHQ, renamed in 1943 from its previous title of Government Code and Cypher School), so he would have been one of the first in MI5 to learn of decryption successes. Harvey and Klehr indicated that, in the United States, Meredith Gardner had recovered enough code books and text by mid-1946 to determine that the VENONA messages involved Soviet espionage, but Dick White (who was Assistant Director of 'B' Division of MI5) was reportedly told by the British Embassy only on September 9, 1949 that the spy with the cryptonym CHARLES was Fuchs. Harvey and Klehr, who claimed that the FBI turned over their evidence about Fuchs in late 1948, also wrote that GCHQ personnel started working with the National Security Agency (NSA) only in 1948. On the other hand, Nigel West noted that, at GCHQ, Cecil Phillips and Philip Howse spent six months from June 1946 working at Eastcote on the same 1944 NKVD traffic as Gardner, so it is presumably just possible that they came up with a decryption pointing to Fuchs, and alerted Robertson. Christopher Andrew also wrote that MI5 was first involved with VENONA in 1947 (though the reference is vague), when nine officers had access to the decrypts. Andrew's chronology could be slightly in error.[3] The conclusion, nevertheless, must be that it is very unlikely that GCHQ had enough information (deriving from activities on US soil, of course) to provide MI5 with specific leads to Fuchs and Peierls in the autumn of 1946. The only major reason for supporting VENONA as the trigger is that MI5 would have felt uninhibited in bringing up a more conventional discovery in court, while anything connected with VENONA had to remain concealed.

So what had provoked the suspicions, given that Fuchs had been out of the country? A possible reason to support the first scenario is offered by Robert Williams's study of Fuchs, where he suggests that MI5 may have known that Fuchs was a spy in 1947, was aware of his meetings with Ursula Kuczynski at that time, and may have even tried to turn him.[4] This anecdote came courtesy of the contributions of an ex-MI5 officer, John Saxon, as Costello recorded in a detailed note to his *Mask of Treachery*.[5] Costello even related that the author Nigel West (then an MP with his given name of Rupert Allason) in April 1988 asked in the House of Commons whether the government was planning to take any legal action against Saxon, applying a test to its resolve, and trying to bring the case out into the open.[i] Stories like this can easily become lost in the 'wilderness of mirrors' that brought the US agent James Angleton close to insanity. What is fascinating, however, about this episode is what Costello indicated, hinting that the Fuchs file had been doctored, and that "the real story is even worse". Sources say (he added) "that in 1945 an MI5 officer added a note on the Fuchs file that his case warranted re-examination before he returned to atomic work in England. The recommendation was passed to higher authority – but no such investigation was ever made and Fuchs received routine clearance."[6] The timing of the officers' accusations, however, suggests that they were working on information they possessed before Fuchs resumed any contact with Ursula Kuczynski. Thus the second scenario, generic indications of espionage by Communist sympathisers, merits more attention.

We do know that MI5 officers undertook a careful reassessment of Fuchs when they eventually learned of his posting back to the UK and these accusations surfaced. Indeed, during Fuchs's elongated process of recruitment at Harwell, he underwent a further profound review by MI5. According to Christopher Andrew's official history, 'C' Division, which was responsible for vetting, "concluded that Fuchs was a serious potential security risk who should be immediately removed from atomic research", echoing but also slightly misrepresenting the evidence presented at the beginning of this chapter. What had intensified this reaction? First, it should be noted that the political climate had changed considerably by this time, with Communism in general not so favourably regarded. The Soviet Union was no longer an ally: the Cold War had started. Indeed, since as early as 1944, MI5's sister organisation, SIS (which traditionally was always more anti-communist than MI5) had been made sharply aware that the Soviet Union would rapidly return to its traditional role as the major threat to the British Empire after the war, and SIS was even starting to consider the

---

[i] Nigel West has told this writer that there was no such officer as Saxon. West's intent had been to invite the authorities to denounce him as a fraud, which was in effect what happened.

assistance of Nazis, and Nazi henchmen from intermediate states, as a counterweight to Communist influence in Europe.[ii] In his history of British intelligence, Michael Smith made the startling observation that MI5 had, as early as 1943, learned that the Comintern was already preparing its agents in Western Europe for "the next war".[7] The very same month in which the notes accusing Fuchs were written (October 1946), the Foreign Office delivered a paper titled *Strategic Aspects of British Foreign Office Policy*, which urged military preparation to counter aggressive moves being made by the Soviet Union to control Central European states.[8] Churchill's 'Iron Curtain' speech had been delivered on March 5 of that year, and Fuchs did not return from the United State until the end of June.

What insights had provoked this sudden concern about his reliability, given that MI5 had cleared Fuchs for the Manhattan Project in 1943, are not explicit in the Fuchs archive, but the debate hints at serious conflicts within the Security Service. Andrew commented, without a trace of irony, and without suggesting that there were conflicts among the corps of 'B' Division officers: "Some of the leading officers in 'B' Division (counter-espionage) – among them Dick White, Roger Hollis and Graham Mitchell[iii] – argued that, on the contrary, the evidence against Fuchs was purely circumstantial and was outweighed by outstanding references from two of Britain's leading physicists, Professor (Sir) Neville Mott, a future Nobel Laureate, and Professor Max Born."[9] Yet Andrew did not identify what "the evidence" was, or thus why it should have been discredited. He also presented the debate as one between 'B' and 'C' Divisions, as opposed to one that rent 'B' Division itself. His account does however reinforce the conclusion that there was no unison about the importance or credibility of the evidence, that the disagreement was about the status of Fuchs as a security risk, rather than about what action should be taken (i.e. dismissal or surveillance). That fact constitutes an important dimension of MI5's tribulations.

Why such practised security officers should have taken, in view of the political background and the warnings implicit in Gouzenko's testimony, such a lenient attitude towards a known Communist, why they did not know more about the backgrounds of Mott and Born, and why they had trusted the academic references from two professors more than the product of their own surveillance, is an alarming phenomenon, and indicates a serious professional failure. Liddell decided that a deeper investigation of Fuchs (and Peierls) should be undertaken, but, remarkably, nothing untoward came up, and the evidence that had troubled a number of MI5 officers must have been buried. Nevertheless, the fact that this controversy occurred has serious ramifications for the later cover-up. What is extraordinary – and hitherto unremarked – about this event is the fact that, if the issue went up to arbitration by Liddell, the evidence provided by such 'B'

[ii] A key contributor to alarm in the Western democracies had been the Soviet Union's behaviour when holding back across the Vistula as the Warsaw uprising failed in August 1944. The Mediterranean air commander, Sir John Slessor, wrote: "How, after the fall of Warsaw, any responsible statesman could trust any Russian Communist further than he could kick him, passes the comprehension of ordinary men." [*In These Remain*, p 151.]

[iii] Hollis in fact headed 'F' Division.

Division officers as Robertson, Serpell and Archer (none of whom were mentioned by Andrew) and those in 'C' Division [iv] must have been very substantial (and presumably fresh since the 1943 vetting) if heavyweights such as White, Hollis and Mitchell could not easily counter it, or use their political clout to submerge it. Yet these same seasoned officers, whose main preoccupation should have been to treat such evidence with complete rigour, concluded that it was nonetheless trivial. In addition, for the officers of 'C' Division, with its lowlier status, to have taken such a stance must have meant that they felt they were on very firm ground (with allies in 'B' Division, of course), and that 'B' Division was overall making a major mistake. Finally, the episode must indicate that Liddell, when his arbitrating decision was not to disqualify Fuchs, but simply to conduct surveillance, was convinced, like White, of the correctness of the policy of not disqualifying communists from sensitive positions, and probably motivated by a desire that nothing unpleasant would emerge. That position must have contributed to his failure to be awarded the Director-Generalship of MI5 when Sillitoe retired in 1953.

Liddell showed a high level of cognitive dissonance in his attitude towards the Communist threat. The diaries that he maintained from the outbreak of the war until his rejection as a candidate to replace Sillitoe reveal that he had not forgotten the lessons that Krivitsky imparted to the Service in 1940, and that he understood that the menace of Communist subversion would be one that outlived the temporary alliance to defeat Hitler. Yet he failed to translate this concern into any kind of policy of preventive action, in the apparent hope that the problem would go away, or, of it did surface, responsibility would be laid at the door of the stubborn government managers who had recruited such persons rather than with the Security Service itself. It was a passive and inappropriate stance that must cause the judgment of Nigel West (who edited a portion of the Diaries for publication) of Liddell as "an exceptional intelligence officer in every way" to be revised.[10] For Liddell was himself one of those hiring managers, and his failure to make the linkages between Krivitsky's warnings, the continual detection of Communists in ministries of state and the forces, and the tolerance that he himself showed to 'intellectual communists' is one of the most noteworthy and regrettable aspects of British counter-espionage in this period.

If one analyses the perspectives of White, Hollis, and Mitchell at the time, one might come up with three alternative hypotheses to explain their vigorous defence of Fuchs. One, they simply did not agree that the evidence provided by the other officers was strong enough. Two, they were swayed by the arguments of the others, but erred on the side of inaction, since a decision to remove Fuchs from Harwell for security reasons would immediately shed the spotlight on their earlier incompetence in approving him, and present tough political challenges. Three, they were privately and unanimously convinced that, despite the changing political climate, the communist Fuchs was entitled to share the secrets he was working on with the Soviet Union. An intriguing aspect of the dynamic is shown

---

[iv] The officers of 'C' Division involved have not been identified. In 1941 (and still in 1943) it was led by Brigadier H. I. 'Harry' Allen, but the section was traditionally minimally staffed and short on influence.

in two entries in the Fuchs records at the National Archives.[11] While Hollis had, on November 19, been keen to warn Arnold at Harwell about Fuchs and Peierls, on December 4, he was suddenly pouring water on the whole idea that Fuchs could be involved in espionage, claiming that "excluding Fuchs and Peierls could lead to a purge of highly placed British scientists". Had he been influenced by someone on high, perhaps?

Whichever scenario is correct, it would appear that the three officers did not advance the defence that their vetting procedure in 1941 had been sound, but that they had unfortunately been overruled by the MAP and the DSIR, and that the first opportunity to remedy the mistake should be taken. That choice would suggest that, in 1946, they were satisfied with the procedure of five years before. In addition, of course, was the problem of tradecraft. If they were to recommend having Fuchs removed from Harwell, and survived the political challenge of dealing with his employers by presenting less than conclusive evidence that Fuchs had been spying, they would lose the unique opportunity of catching their target in the act, and detecting his network of contacts, and thus might never know for certain whether he had been as concrete a risk as the evidence suggested. Thus the compromise solution of a period of surveillance met as many needs as possible without harming the reputation of the service.

It appears that the investigation into Fuchs did not complete until August 1948, two years after the actual date of his transfer. On August 14 of that year, a Mr Fadden of the Ministry of Supply wrote to Major Badham of MI5 that "the advantages gained by Harwell through the undoubted ability of Dr Fuchs outweigh the slight security risk, and his establishment is being proceeded with", an ominous echo of Appleton's judgment of 1941.[12] This timing is extraordinary. If Fuchs learned of this protracted but deep decision, it would surely have put him on his guard, and it is therefore not surprising that the further intensive – and expensive – surveillance operation carried out on him at the end of 1949 (when the real evidence was compelling) revealed nothing incriminatory. How MI5 approached the task may have seemed like traditionally sound tradecraft, but it must have been enough to alert Fuchs of a possible problem. Whether it was a coincidence or not, at the end of the month (August 1948) the sceptic T. A. Robertson, who in October 1947 had been appointed head of the Section tackling "Russian and Russian satellite espionage", announced his retirement from the service.[13] John Archer had left the previous year ("a great loss" according to Liddell)[14]: maybe it was no coincidence that these two fine officers left in fairly close succession, as they may well have become disillusioned with the resolve of the Counter-Espionage Division.

More light is shown on the indulgence of White and Hollis by the later investigation that took place while the VENONA leads were being followed up. A note by J. C. Robertson of September 9, 1949, states that "a further report in 1943 suggested that he [Fuchs] might still have Communist tendencies, although these were not considered to be of an extreme nature".[15] (This referred to a second investigation into Fuchs that was carried out before he was despatched to the United States.) The illusion that there were moderate communists and extreme ones, and that MI5 could safely distinguish between them, was now well-established. The "still" betrays that 'B' Division had known of Fuchs's

Communist leanings on previous occasions. Maybe White had forgotten that, as Chapter 8 has shown, in October 1941, 'B' Division had tried to warn the Ministry of Aircraft Production that "there might be a slight risk that information to which FUCHS had access might reach the Russians" (advice given by Jane Archer's husband, John), but they naively tried to emphasise to the Department "the necessity for the minimum disclosure to FUCHS". That was an impossible constraint, and Peierls knew it, and DSIR's Appleton knew it, and ignored the qualification.

Before the full implications of the accusations of 1946 are examined, we return to the first scenario outlined at the beginning of this chapter, namely that Fuchs may have been observed behaving inappropriately. Was it correct? Had real espionage activity by Fuchs prompted the suspicions in the autumn of 1946? And if so, when? Had the officers discovered results of surveillance activity while he was in the USA? If MI5 was indulgent and careless about Communists in general, and Fuchs in particular, and with its policy of dividing the world of Communists into the harmful and the harmless, had the organisation behaved inefficiently when it came to detecting his spying movements, but picked up clues from the time before he moved to the USA in 1943? To consider this question, it is necessary to turn to the person who acted as his 'cut-out', his contact who protected him from direct communication with the Intelligence Service officers at the Soviet Embassy. Without the advantage of evidence gained from such mechanisms as the VENONA decrypts, MI5 had had much less to work on. But should it have been able to do more? The following passage describes the main activities that were going on before their eyes.

Much later (the date is obscure), when more VENONA traffic was decoded, MI5 learned that Fuchs had had contact with Simon [Semyon] Kremer, an official whom Krivitsky had identified during his interrogation in February 1940. From studying Soviet archives, and his acquaintance with a Vladimir Barkovsky, who had worked in the London *rezidentura* between 1941 and 1946, the author Nigel West has determined that Fuchs had been a GRU agent since August 1941, when he had been approached on Jürgen Kuczynski's recommendation through the Soviet Ambassador, Ivan Maisky. "Acccording to the GRU file on Fuchs, Maisky was not on good terms with the NKVD *resident* Ivan Chichayev, so he passed on Kuczynski's information to the GRU *resident* Ivan Sklyarov who ordered his Secretary, Semyon Kremer, to meet Fuchs."[16][v] A meeting between Fuchs and Kremer subsequently took place. Yet it was a dangerous initiative for a known Communist engaged on secret work to have a meeting with a member of the Soviet Embassy, either in the nation's capital, or in its second city, Birmingham.

The decrypted messages strongly suggest that Fuchs had made contact with Soviet Army Intelligence earlier. Chapman Pincher wrote that Fuchs had a meeting with the leading member of the KPD in the UK, Jürgen Kuczynski, as

---

[v] According to VENONA transcripts, Sklyarov replaced Kremer as GRU *resident* in October 1940. West's and Tsarev's *The Crown Jewels* states that "the GRU's Colonel Sklyorov [*sic*] held a meeting with Fuchs on August 8 in Birmingham" (note 3 to Chapter X, p 356). The meeting was actually between Fuchs and Kremer, as the VENONA text makes clear. (See Endnote 7).

early as February 1941, and that Kuczynski introduced Fuchs to Kremer then, but that reference is not directly traceable.[17] Pincher's source, whoever it was, however, may have been reliable. It may have been Soviet archives, since the memoirs of Sudoplatov (head of 'Special Tasks') add an intriguing twist. His editors observed: "Fuchs was recruited through the German Communist Jürgen Kuczynski, who fled to England and also worked for the OSS during the war. Kuczynski, according to Sudoplatov, informed Soviet Ambassador Ivan Maisky of Fuchs's work. Maisky instructed Soviet military attaché Simon Davidovich Kremer, known to Fuchs as Aleksandr, to recruit him."[18] The relevant VENONA cable, written by Colonel Sklyarov of the GRU, pinpoints a definite assignation that took place considerably earlier than the date Fuchs claimed to his interrogators. Skylarov reported, on August 14, 1941, that a meeting between Kremer and Fuchs occurred on August 8, in Birmingham.[19] And in a highly revealing aside, Sklyarov then described Fuchs as a "former acquaintance" of Kremer's, which would bolster the claim that Pincher made about their meeting socially some time earlier in 1941, and might well substantiate Sudoplatov's claim. Indeed, "former acquaintance" suggests a friendship that has lapsed (because of Fuchs's internment?), rather than the idea of a recent previous encounter. This datum reinforces the theory that Fuchs indeed plotted his treachery well before Barbarossa, a timetable that is hinted at by others, although the significance has not up until now been declared so boldly.[20]

Rossiter has added a valuable detail in this regard: he noted that Fuchs made a visit from Glasgow to London as early as April 3, 1941, and stayed there for 12 days, where he almost certainly spent time with Jürgen Kuczynski and other denizens of the Lawn Road Flats Communist haven in Hamspted.[vi] The report of Skardon's first interrogation of Fuchs, written on December 22, 1949, confirms that Fuchs's comrades visited him in Edinburgh, and that Fuchs made a reciprocal visit to London, ostensibly to break contact with his Communist friends rather than to renew them. According to Skardon, when Fuchs obtained Government employment he decided that he must give up his association with Kahle and other people like him. One visit was made by such people to Edinburgh, and one visit was made by Fuchs "to Kahle in London when he was taken by him to a Free German Youth organisation which had a restaurant in the Hampstead area". Skardon's report adds: "There he met a number of refugees and one, whose name he forgets, attempted to renew acquaintance with him when Fuchs was already employed in Birmingham but he shook him off".[21] If Rossiter's fact about an April trip to London is correct, this unmistakably sets Fuchs as knowing about his position with the government before Peierls's formal offer of May 10. Moreover, his acquaintance with Kuczynski was well-established: according to Kuczynski's memoirs, he had known Fuchs since they met in London in August 1936.[22]

This incident also sheds sharp light on how poorly surveillance was being carried out at this time. Fuchs, having been recruited to a sensitive government project, was allowed to roam around the country and consort with known Communist aliens in places already known to harbour such persons. Furthermore,

---

[vi] This writer cannot find any evidence of this information in the National Archives. Rossiter may have obtained it from Russian sources.

how Kremer, a Soviet consular official during wartime, succeeded in gaining permission to cross the three-mile limit from the centre of London that was imposed on consular staff is not explained – if indeed he bothered to seek it. Otherwise, it showed an enormous amount of chutzpah and confidence. The record of such assignations was kept highly confidential, of course. The British government could not reveal the fact that it had decrypted Soviet cable traffic – even decades after the Fuchs trial was over. Moreover MI5 certainly did not want to release the information that Fuchs had slipped through their fingers after internment. Fuchs's error-ridden confession, which at least tidied up the case without any embarrassing revelations, was thus allowed to stand unaltered.

Thus, even though none of this activity was detected at the time, Fuchs lied about the time he started betraying secrets (as Chapter 8 explained). At the August 1941 meeting with Kremer, he told him that the activity he was involved in was work on building the atomic bomb. Later, in his confession to Skardon, he was to suggest that it was only in October 1941, after he was cleared for Top Secret work, that he indicated to a friend that he wanted to pass information to the Russians.[23] By the time he spoke to Perrin, the time had been put back to "early 1942" – corrections that MI5 was only too keen to echo. Moreover, MI5 was also quick to emend Fuchs's testimony. His confession statement, as it appears in the National Archives, dated January 27, 1950, states: "When I learned about the purpose of the work, I decided to inform Russia and I established contact through another [*sic*] member of the Communist Party," thus revealing openly that he was himself a member of the Communist Party at this time.[24] By March 2, the official version had been carefully sanitised to echo the more convenient timetable. "He had begun his career of active espionage on behalf of the Russians at the beginning of 1942 . . . through an alien friend, who was a Communist", the report states, adding: "Fuchs states that his recruitment took place with the help of a Communist friend but there is no evidence to suggest that the Communist Party organisation was involved."[25] The cover-up was well under way, and the official statement was crafted to deny MI5's knowledge of Fuchs's identity as a member of the Communist Party, and to claim that he was not even active until much later.

The Soviets obviously needed a much safer way for Fuchs to deliver confidential information than semi-clandestine trysts in London. On this process, West, who appears to be closest to the inside sources, is very confusing. He indicated that contact between Fuchs and Kremer was lost in the spring of 1942, at which juncture Fuchs approached Jürgen Kuczynski again, and Kuczynski introduced him to his sister Ursula Beurton, who had her first meeting with Fuchs in the summer of 1941. The chronology does not work. Furthermore, West wrote that "according to his file in the NKVD's archive, Fuchs passed information to Ursula Beurton twice in September 1941, and five times in 1943, until his departure for America in November."[26] When in March 1950 Marriott of MI5 was preparing the text that politicians would use to defend their performance in the Fuchs's case, he echoed the NKVD timeline: "From end of 1941 until November 1943, Fuchs's Soviet intelligence contact was a woman whom he met in a country lane near Banbury. Photographs have not enabled Fuchs to identify her."[27] It appears further use of disinformation was being practised here – this time on the Soviets' part, as if they wanted to minimise the contribution of Ursula

Beurton (née Kuczynski), the agent better known as Sonia, whose preparation for subversive work in the UK had been planned long before. Was Sonia really already in touch with Fuchs at the time he met with Kremer?

Ursula Kuczynski's substantial espionage activities have been written up elsewhere.[28] It is important, for the inclusiveness of this analysis, to provide a summary of them, in order to add substance to the rich tapestry of subversive activity that was currently being woven. This section therefore concentrates on a few significant details, derivable mainly from the files held on her and her family at the National Archives, which confirm MI5's inefficiency in surveilling her, as well as from her own memoirs. They concern the timing of Moscow Centre's decisions to send her back to England (from Switzerland), the deceptions over her marriage with Len Beurton, the tracking of her movements by MI5, her activities as a radio-operator in Oxfordshire, and the failure of MI5 to make any linkages with other known Communists throughout this period, but especially when Beurton finally joined her in 1943.

When the GRU decided in 1939 that Ursula was needed in Britain, she faced the expiry of her British passport in May 1940. She was thus ordered to divorce her husband, Rolf Hamburger – a feat she accomplished in October 1939 – and in November she wrote to her sister, Marguerite, advising her of her mission to England. She was then instructed to marry Beurton. The wedding took place on February 23, 1940 – an event that has been described on MI5's files as "bigamous", though this description may have been made in ignorance of her divorce the year before.[29] (Ursula's romantic affairs were very irregular.) As it happened, Len and Ursula had fallen in love the first time they met, and the wedding was no hardship. On the basis of her new marriage, on March 11 Ursula applied in Geneva for a new British passport. At this stage, administrative muddles and delays in MI5 enabled Ursula to re-enter the country. The sequence of events runs as follows: on March 11, the British Consulate in Geneva transmitted Ursula's application for a British passport on the basis of her marriage to Beurton (known as Fenton in MI5 files). The application contained three references. On March 21 1940, J. M. Stafford of the Passport Office wrote to Captain Mars of MI5, asking for any relevant records of Ursula. A week later, Mars replied that MI5 had no record of Ursula Beurton and only a possible trace of her ex-husband [Hamburger?] "with a communistic smell". In May 1940 the dedicated record-keeper Milicent Bagot (see Chapter 8) became involved, pointing out (to Cazalet) that MI5 did indeed possess records on Ursula Kuczynski, and on her father as well, and that the marriage was probably one of convenience. Someone issued a strong opinion that Ursula should not be granted a passport. On May 25 1940 Cazalet recommended to Stafford that Ursula should not be given a passport, but if it could not be refused, it should be for limited validity, and not be valid for travel. Beurton was on the Black List, and was believed to be in Germany. Three days later, Stafford reported that it was too late, as the Passport Office, having grown impatient with the lack of response from MI5, had authorised issuance of the passport on April 24.[30] With this background of bureaucratic inefficiencies did a dangerous Soviet courier gain re-entry into Britain.

It has not been determined exactly how Ursula's mission to the UK had been defined by Moscow at the time. Chapman Pincher promoted very strongly his theory that it was to act as a courier for Roger Hollis, who at the time (March 1940) was completing the process of taking over counter-communist subversion from Jane Archer, and whom Pincher identified as a super-mole who would betray MI5 for years to come. If one rejects that theory (for whatever reason, that no evidence has been found in the Soviet archives to identify Hollis as such, that Hollis was temperamentally incapable of carrying off such a complex schizophrenic existence, or that the relatively lowly Hollis would not have been able to get away with such nefarious activities without the connivance of his bosses), the timing could equally be explained as an attempt by the Soviets to prepare for a deep subversive campaign to steal scientific secrets, based on the threats made to Peierls, Peierls's links with Kapitza, his development of pioneering research with Frisch, and his nurturing of Klaus Fuchs. One highly revealing memorandum, that appears to have been overlooked, was quoted by Rossiter (without his commenting on its potential significance). When Skardon and Serpell of MI5 questioned (unproductively) Ursula Kuczynski at her home in Oxford in 1947, the Security Service was unable to make the link between her and Fuchs. But Moscow did, according to Rossiter. In a sentence that appears to cite a Soviet archive source directly, he wrote: "When they finally received news about her questioning, Feklisov [Modin] in London received a handwritten note. In code it informed him that 'the athlete [agent] who had recruited Charles [Fuchs] had been questioned by the opposition [British intelligence]'".[31] Either this was a careless mistake (i.e. her brother was intended), or a poor translation, or the KGB was indicating that Ursula had played a far more significant role in the exercise immediately she arrived in Britain in January 1941.

In any case, MI5 should have been alarmed by Ursula Kuczynski's move to re-enter the country. The family's name and reputation were known. Moreover, at about the same time that John Strachey had been getting Peierls's naturalisation approved, Strachey was effective (April 1940) in getting the overt Communist and rabble-rouser Jürgen Kuczynski released from internment. Perhaps not coincidentally, Fuchs was told in March 1940 of the outcome of his Edinburgh hearing on internment: he gained the good news that he was exempt from it (before falling to the universal tightening-up on aliens in May). The pro-Soviet forces in British society were marshalling themselves. MI5 should have been on their guard. Yet, when Ursula was freed to travel, she was able to get away with deceitful accounts of why her husband was not with her – inventions about treatment for tuberculosis, for example, which was presented as an explanation as to why he was not able to gain a transit visa out of Switzerland because of his past record, and thus accompany his wife and her children.

Ursula Kuczynski's memoir is not a wholly reliable account of her espionage activity. [vii][32] As with many similar works, it is intended to deceive, but the

---

[vii] This author has come to the conclusion that the memoirs of spies should in principle not be trusted. *Sonjas Rapport* is typical of this genre: her account of her espionage activity in the UK has enormous gaps, for example in her not mentioning Fuchs at all. But some of her other anecdotes (which she presumably felt were less controversial) appear in outline

timetable given of her travels from Geneva to Oxford at the end of 1940 is probably quite dependable. She stated that "in late autumn" Moscow Centre ordered her and her husband to move to Britain. If one can interpret "late autumn" to indicate November, the time is contemporaneous with the news that Fuchs was to be released from internment, Peierls's and Born's discussions concerning Fuchs's job prospects, as well as the return of the NKVD agent Gorsky to Britain. (Gorsky had been recalled to Moscow in February. There are indications of a rivalry between the GRU and the NKVD at this time, concerning the acquisition of atomic secrets.) Indeed, communications between the Passport Office and MI5 suggest that this chronology is correct. On November 29, 1940, Stafford of the Passport Office indicated that he had received a request from the consul in Geneva for Ursula's children to accompany her. (One little known fact in this saga is that the consul in Geneva at that time was one Frederick vanden Heuvel, who was station chief for SIS in Switzerland, having been recruited by Claude Dansey's Z Organisation.)[33] On December 10, Cazalet of MI5 stated that the department had no objection.[34] Len not having acquired the requisite visa to leave Switzerland, she thus set out for Portugal on December 18, accompanied by her two young children, Micheal and Janina (her daughter by her lover in Shanghai, Ernst, being only four-and-a-half at the time). On December 23, they arrived in Madrid, and by the next day reached Lisbon, the main exit point for refugees (and others) from Europe to Britain during the war. Ursula admitted that all three of them were ill. Some time after Christmas, Ursula had a meeting with the British consul, in order to gain approval for the voyage to England, and receive travel slots for her party of three. On January 10, her passport was endorsed.[35]

From a study of her narrative, it seems that it was not until January 17 that she learned from the consul that they had been approved for departure: how she managed to exist in the intervening period with her children in tow is not explained, and, after a voyage lasting three weeks, they arrived on the SS *Androceta* in Liverpool. On her arrival, when questioned by immigration authorities, she was vague about her movements, but again mentioned her husband's tuberculosis as a reason for his not accompanying her. "With difficulty" (understandably), Ursula and her offspring managed to find a hotel in Liverpool (it was during a wartime blackout, of course), and, even more remarkably, succeeded in reaching Oxford by train the next day. Her father had set up a residential address for her to move to temporarily.

What is extraordinary about this highly onerous journey, which surely must have been accomplished with some external support, is that MI5 was fully informed about all its aspects. Ursula was picked up by watchers as soon as she left Liverpool: Milicent Bagot in MI5, who had in May pointed out that Ursula's marriage to Beurton was probably a sham, and had also recommended, on November 23, that Jürgen Kuczynski should be re-interned, informed the Chief Constable of Oxford on January 26 1941, of their father's taking temporary

---

to be reliable, and add useful detail to the chronology, such as in her effort to reach the United Kingdom in 1940, most of which corresponds to information available at the National Archives.

lodgings in Oxford. On February 25 1941, a Mr Ryde wrote to Shillito of MI5, enclosing his report on Ursula. Shillito was of the opinion that no further action was required, but that "an eye should be kept on her".[36] According to her own autobiography, Ursula soon afterwards met with her father (who had not taken up permanent residence in his Oxford address), and eventually made contact with her Soviet Embassy contact, Sergey, in London, in May. She noted Hitler's invasion of the Soviet Union in June, and then stated that she started transmitting messages twice a week by radio, travelling every fortnight or so to visit her father or her brother in London, who supplied her with valuable information to send to Moscow. She also met and befriended her Soviet fellow-courier (and spy), Melita Norwood, as well as Hans Kahle, Fuchs's associate in Canada, now working as a military correspondent for *Time* and *Fortune* magazines. Moscow Central agreed (so she averred) to her suggestion that she meet him regularly as well, as he had access to strategic information. According to Nigel West, she and Fuchs had their first meeting in the summer of 1941, and she ran him until he left for the USA in November 1943, "passing back his material to the *rezidentura* through Nikolai Aptekar, codenamed SERGEI, the military attaché's driver".[37]

Most of the information that Fuchs passed before he left for the USA was no doubt too long and complicated to be sent by radio transmission, but there is no doubt about Ursula's use of clandestine radio, which was strictly forbidden in wartime Britain. Ursula described how, in the autumn of 1942, she moved into a cottage in the grounds of the house of Neville Laski, the brother of the fellow-traveller, Harold Laski.[38] (Harold Laski, it will be recalled, had conspired with such as Strachey, Wilkinson and Cripps either to assist entry into Britain of Comintern agents, or free from internment CP members like Ursula's brother.) Here she strung up her radio: what is even more incredible is that the existence of this apparatus was known to MI5. On January 25, 1943, D. M. Campbell, reporting on behalf of Major J. C. Phipps, wrote that "the Beurtons own a large wireless set".[39] Yet nothing was done about it.[viii]

Len Beurton had now joined his wife, but the string of lies associated with his return to the UK should have alerted MI5 that something was afoot. He had arrived at Poole Airport on July 7 1942, under the false name of Miller, granted to him by some means by the Geneva consul (still the SIS officer, vanden Heuvel), as Switzerland had still refused to give him a transit visa. He denied any knowledge of the tuberculosis that Ursula said he had contracted.[40] The result was that a Mr Vesey in MI5 drew attention to his shady story, wondering why his passport had been issued on such shaky evidence. On December 1, 1942, a warrant for inspection of all postal packets and telegrams addressed to Beurton

---

[viii] Chapman Pincher has written in detail about this aspect of the Kuczynski saga in *Treachery*. Yet his account is directed to show the guilt of Roger Hollis in allowing Ursula to remain untouched by MI5. Hollis, however, would not have been able to perform so casually off his own bat, and would have required the approval of his superiors, Liddell and White. Hollis, moreover, was during the war more stringent than they in demanding that Communists be removed from government positions. The whole saga of Sonia and her radio, and whether her replacement, Alexander Foote, was a double-agent working for the GRU and SIS, merits a separate comprehensive analysis. See http://www.coldspur.com/sonias-radio/

was issued, as he was "thought to have been in touch with agents of a foreign power". A little under three weeks later, Shillito (who had recommended keeping an eye on Ursula) wrote that he thought Beurton was a "Soviet spy".[41] Yet no connections appear to have been made by the officers responsible: if Beurton was a Soviet spy, and he had contracted a bogus marriage to Ursula Kuczynski, née Werner, aka Hamburger, would it not be obvious tradecraft to do more than keep a casual eye on her, and investigate her radio transmission activities more closely? The detection of illicit radio transmission was the responsibility of a unit called RSS, Radio Security Services, then reporting to SIS. While MI5 has been quick to claim that no illegal pro-German transmissions went undetected during the war, Guy Liddell's Diaries catalogue a number of problems with the operation, from faulty detector vans to hints at a deliberate policy of ignoring certain equipment. A year before the Oxford constabulary reported the Beurtons' illegal transmitter, Liddell had noted in his diary that RSS had let MI5 down by eventually tracing an illegal transmission to the Soviet consulate.

The extraordinary conclusion from this analysis, however, is that MI5, despite all the movements and activities engaged upon by a number of linked suspicious characters, had no idea of Fuchs's espionage activity between May 1941 and November 1943, when he left for the USA. Scenario One remains vacant. One has to assume that, had MI5 had anything stronger to go on than the fact that he was a possible Communist, and a potentially dangerous one, they would have shown more resolve in preventing his departure. Yet, while the interlude of Fuchs's time spent in America between 1943 and 1946 is not of direct relevance to the story here, it is worth recording that MI5 similarly fumbled (as it had done in 1941) when it came to the question of his security clearance in 1943 – something demanded by the USA authorities. Again, it was the persistent and sharp Milicent Bagot (not an officer, as Rossiter incorrectly claimed), who showed the most outrage. She, who kept the records, expressed amazement, in November 1943, that Fuchs's naturalisation had been approved.[ix][42] By the time the department got round to investigating the matter of Fuchs's trustworthiness, he was already on his way to the USA. His ship sailed on October 27, but it was not until November 17 that the Department of Science and Industrial Research requested MI5 for his security clearance. Michael Perrin of the Tube Alloys Project valiantly tried to do the right thing (or so he claimed), but communications were badly mishandled, and the hapless MI5 officer Serpell was left to conclude that the opportunity had been missed, and that, since Fuchs was now a British citizen, they could do no more. Such inefficiency would come to haunt the British government later, when the USA found out about Fuchs's treachery and the inability of MI5 to stop his relocation despite what they knew about him. But, in MI5's partial defence, it was an echo of the British government's attitude in 1941 – to approach MI5 only when the horse had bolted.

A few years later, interest in Ursula was indeed renewed. In 1948, when the MI5 officers Skardon and Serpell interviewed her, they failed to gain any

---

[ix] The National Archives do in fact show that MI5 was kept informed of Fuchs's naturalisation application in May 1942, and its opinion was sought before citizenship was granted. (KV 2/1245/1)

admission from her, but by then the atmosphere had changed considerably. The Nazi-Soviet pact was long forgotten; the war had been brought to a successful conclusion through the alliance with the USA and the Soviet Union, but the latter was now a bitter opponent in the Cold War. Williams has suggested that Ursula's "espionage had been against Nazi Germany in an inadvertent cooperation with MI6, which may have known about Fuchs through a turned Soviet agent".[43] Williams pointed to Ursula's membership of the Lucy spy ring, with which MI6 was involved in circumstances that are still not perfectly clear. "Under British law there was no case against her that it could actively pursue", added Williams. Yet the officers still leading MI5 (Liddell and White) had memories of what had happened in the critical period of March 1940 to June 1941, when the Soviet Union was an ally of Nazi Germany, and Krivitsky had warned them of the dangers of the exchange of secret information, and how feebly the two of them had reacted to the threats of the Kuczynskis, and the dubious credentials of Klaus Fuchs. That was not a course of action they could now be proud of.

We thus return to the second scenario, which might explain the grounds for suspicions about Fuchs in 1946, yet the water is again murky. When had the officers first made their accusations? While Tom Bower (Dick White's biographer) is not an altogether reliable source of facts, he provided some interesting commentary. (As an example of his imprecision, he described, having inspected letters exchanged between MI5 and the journalist Alan Moorehead, the officer Jane Archer as contributing opinions about Fuchs's reliability when she was no longer directing the communist counter-espionage section.)[44] Bower wrotes that "Suppell", the 'B' Division officer "had reviewed the Fuchs file some months earlier", implying that this event took place in 1946, when Fuchs was invited to continue his atomic research at Harwell. Bower named the "captured" 1933 Gestapo document and the appearance of Fuchs's name in a diary "seized in Canada following Gouzenko's defection" as the only evidence that Suppell was working on.[x45] He cited Nigel West's *A Matter of Trust*, "confirmed by MI5 sources", as the story's origin, but the well is similarly dry here.[46] At that stage, Serpell [*sic*, not Suppell] recommended an investigation into Fuchs and Peierls, but was essentially overruled, although Liddell, Hollis (his boss) and White, agreed to go ahead with intercepts. What is intriguing about this anecdote is, first, that it reinforces the theory that the suspicions about Fuchs were prompted by an apparently independent source, namely the spur provided by Gouzenko. In addition, it turns the spotlight sharply on Serpell without mentioning the role of Robertson and Archer, whose opinions might have held more weight. Second, the reference to the diary in the context of 1946 is noteworthy, as it is the first indication that White acknowledged such an early appearance of the lead. The diary belonged to a known Communist sympathiser named Israel Halperin, and it contained Fuchs's name and address (in Edinburgh), as well as those of his sister, Kristel Heinemann, who was living in Boston. After conducting an investigation, in which it discovered that Kristel's husband was a well-known communist, and

---

[x] Bower seems to be confusing two items here – the 1933 report from the German consulate in Bristol and a Gestapo report discovered by the US Army (see lower down on this page). Dick White may well have contributed to Bower's confusion.

that Klaus Fuchs was indeed Kristel's brother, the local FBI office compiled a report, which was shared with MI5. As Williams wrote of the time immediately after Fuchs's arrest in 1950:

> "On February 12 columnist Drew Pearson telephoned the FBI and said he had learned that in 1946 Fuchs's name had appeared on a list given to both MI5 and the FBI. Not surprisingly, the FBI had no comment."[47]

Yet it appears that such early references to Halperin were removed from the Fuchs file. The first appearances of Halperin's name occur in September and October 1949, where the record has been edited to make it appear that the FBI had only recently informed MI5 of the discoveries in the Halperin diary.[48] The second of these two records, consisting of a letter from the British Embassy in Washington (in which two paragraphs have been redacted), also refers to the fact that the Nazis knew that the Fuchses were NKVD agents, confirming the rather muddled statement from Bower about the "captured Gestapo document". Again, Williams provides the background:

> "But on June 15, 1945, John Cimperman, the FBI agent in London, forwarded to Washington copies of two captured German documents that had been prepared for the invasion of Russia in 1941. They included a two-volume list of thousands of names of people suspected of communist activity by the counterespionage branch of the Gestapo. The Philadelphia FBI office translated the list, and in Volume 1 appeared: '210. FUCHS, Klaus, student of philosophy, December 29, 1911. Russelsheim, RSHA IVA2, Gestapo Field Office, Kiel.' The list was sent to Hoover as part of a report on 'Soviet Intelligence Activity' on July 31."[49]

The British Embassy letter, dated October 4, 1949, is from a G. T. D. Patterson, addressed to A. S. Martin, Esq., and begins: "With reference to previous correspondence about FUCHS and HEINEMAN I have just received from the FBI some further information about their activities in this country. Much of it you already know, but some is new and I think you will agree of considerable interest."[50] The next paragraph has been redacted: the letter then starts describing (repeating?) the evidence of Halperin's address book when he was arrested in February 1946, and it later cites the captured German document compiled in 1941. Paragraph 18, which appears after Patterson's suggestion that Fuchs and his father are "key GPU and NKVD agents" has also been redacted. The inference is clear: the majority of the information had been given to MI5 some time before. This evidence is conclusive that Archer, Robertson and Serpell were basing their claim on the revelations from Washington in 1946 – intelligence that White and Hollis did not want to accept as valid.

In 1949, all this would come back to haunt those who had defended Fuchs in 1946. There was no disagreement about the reliability of the FBI's identification of Fuchs as the Soviet spy, CHARLES. With this incontrovertible but unusable evidence from VENONA, MI5 set up a further long exercise of surveillance in the hope of trapping Fuchs (which proved fruitless), and then engaged the skills of its lead interrogator, Jim Skardon, to try to gain a confession. Skardon was eventually successful, thus providing the proof that MI5 needed. Yet the conclusiveness of the evidence presented White and Hollis with some acute challenges – facing their internal critics as well as the public backlash that would occur. Thus, when it came to Fuchs's prosecution, trial, and sentencing, MI5 had to prepare for an unpleasant public relations exercise. In addition, as it planned strategies for the trial, the organisation had also to deal with some internal challenges, not least with its new Director-General.

The new man in charge, Percy Sillitoe, had taken up his post in 1946. On the day he joined MI5, the atomic power spy Alan Nunn May had been convicted of espionage, and sentenced to 14 years' hard labour. Sillitoe was thus a leader who knew MI5 only during the Cold War, and looked upon the Soviets as a real threat – indeed as his predecessors in the 1930s had done. His opinions were influenced by the fact that the Soviet Union had recently carried out a successful test of its atomic bomb, in August 1949. As Tom Bower, recording the event of Sillitoe's learning that Fuchs had been under suspicion beforehand, put it: "Sillitoe's fury, at a meeting with White, Liddell, Robertson and Ronald Read, was breathtaking. 'In future,' roared the Director-General incoherently, 'you'll do as you're told!'"[51] But who "told" Liddell and White what to do? The implication by Bower is that it was "White's failure, in the chain of responsibility, to adopt Suppell's [*sic*] suggestion of investigating Fuchs".

Thus what happens next is a desperate attempt by White to preserve his career. Later in life, he would try to protect his legacy before he died, by suggesting to Bower that the failure to uncover any of Fuchs's suspicious activities was due to an oversight, the ignoring of a fellow-officer's advice, at a time when the notion of the Soviet Union as an ally was fresh in White's consciousness. Yet White appears to have been oblivious to the serious intra- and inter-departmental clash in 1946 which Andrew, as authorised historian, recorded, suggesting instead that the whole debacle could be attributable to some minor miscommunication within 'B' Division. White's dewy-eyed explanation even made Bower refer to the officer's self-deceit and sentimentality. "His [Fuchs's] motives were relatively speaking pure. A scientist who got cross at the Anglo-American ploy in withholding vital information from an ally fighting a common enemy", Bower recorded White as telling him.[52] If Bower's account is reliable (echoing the third hypothesis described earlier), here was the only man to lead both MI5 and SIS ascribing a degree of good and honourable intentions to one of Britain's greatest traitors, veiling the facts, distorting the chronology, parroting the conventional leftist cant, and blandly undermining the security role that he should have been professionally committed to. The only part of Bower's titular description of White as *The Perfect English Spy* that was true was that White was indeed English.

White's boss, Guy Liddell, was even more irresolute in dealing with the horrific possibility that Fuchs might be a spy. A careful analysis of his *Diary* entries in the post-war period shows his reactions to a litany of disasters, as, in fairly quick succession, the cases of Nunn May, Fuchs, Pontecorvo, Burgess, Maclean, Philby (and even Blunt) unravelled, and Liddell was left hoping against hope that the stories were not true, trying to convince himself that the evidence pointed towards their innocence. Moreover, he assumed a posture of benevolent uncle, not wanting the truth to become public, hoping that Nunn May and Fuchs could be found some quiet employment at a university somewhere in the country, and that life could continue without any unpleasant court cases or bad publicity. The notion of punishment and deterrence seemed far away: he was very keen that the spy should not have a chance to leave the country, but evidently did not consider a course of confessions and imprisonment as the correct path. One comment encapsulates crisply his lack of backbone:

> "Were he [Fuchs] to do so [*i.e. confess*] he would clearly feel that there was no future for him either here or in the USA; the urge would therefore be to go to the Russians. If, on the other hand, on the basis of his statement about his father to Arnold, it were pointed out to him with the deepest regrets that it would be embarrassing both for us and for him if he remained any longer in atomic energy, but that we would do our utmost to find him other suitable employment. This might possibly be the better course.[53]

The Chief of Counter-Espionage as therapist and Father-Confessor: it is not an edifying spectacle, and, as suggested on page 7 of this Chapter, such attitudes and behaviour no doubt contributed to Liddell's being rejected for the post of replacing Percy Sillitoe in May 1953, thus ending his career in MI5.

In a fascinating coda, when the Soviet spy working for SIS, George Blake, was sentenced to 42 years' imprisonment, in 1961, Dick White and Roger Hollis, sitting in the public gallery, "nodded in quiet satisfaction".[54] Maybe this was expiation for their past leniencies: of course, while White was head of SIS at the time (and had convinced Prime Minister Macmillan that a trial was necessary), they were both MI5 men at heart, and this was an SIS trial. Christopher Andrew gave further evidence of White's and Hollis's collusion and deception: shortly before Kim Philby defected, they co-signed a letter to the FBI's Hoover claiming that any espionage undertaken by Philby had ceased at the end of World War II.[55]

Sillitoe prepared a report for Prime Minister Attlee on February 7, 1950, between Fuchs's arrest and his trial, which minimised MI5's awareness of Fuchs's communism, and reinforced the value of his contribution to the war effort. With a confession in place before the trial, the prosecution expected a smooth ride to conviction. One noteworthy aspect of the exchanges, however, is that Curtis-Bennett, the defence counsel, shrewdly pointed out to Judge Goddard that Fuchs had made no secret of his membership of the German Communist Party when questioned at his naturalisation hearings in 1942.[56] Sir Hartley Shawcross could counter this statement only by saying that "all the investigations at that time and since have not shown that he had any association whatever with British members of the Communist Party ..."[57] Shawcross had in fact been fed this line by White. A planning meeting had been held just before the trial, the minutes of which run partly as follows: "Shawcross wanted to know why Fuchs had been employed at Harwell 'when he was a known Communist from 1942 onwards'. The Attorney General stated that the fact that he was a Communist was known to the authorities and appeared in Home Office files. D. B. [White] stated that the Security Service had no knowledge that Fuchs had ever been a member of the British Communist Party. All that the Security Service knew was that there was a Gestapo report from Kiel alleging Fuchs to be a Communist. This fact had never been confirmed by Police reports in this country."[58] White was apparently allowed to make this statement uncontested and unchallenged. In one brief clause the confusion and misguided logic of security provisions against Communists had been aired: foreign Communists for some reason constituted no threat unless they had made noticeable contact with CPGB members – an echo of MI5's forlorn late 1930s strategy to switch its attention to the CPGB away from the shady foreigners representing the Comintern. The cycle had been completed. Subterfuge was not a game that MI5 understood.

Now the false flag of the Soviet Alliance was being waved again. During his trial, Fuchs gave the impression to his defence lawyer, Derek Curtis-Bennett, that he was expecting the death sentence. According to Norman Moss, Curtis-Bennett replied: "No, you bloody fool, it's fourteen years . . . You didn't give secrets to an enemy, you gave them to an ally."[59] Whereas Fuchs "did not show any relief" at this disclosure, the statement shows that Curtis-Bennett had been taken in as well. According to Curtis-Bennett's logic, if some scale of seriousness of the crime existed (e.g. dependent on the status of the foreign power to which secrets had been betrayed), the verdict might have been different. Had Chief Justice Goddard been aware of Fuchs's treason to the Soviet Union when it had been an ally of Germany, his sentence might presumably have been more severe. Yet Fuchs's claim that he had not betrayed secrets until well after Germany's invasion of the Soviet Union gave support to the useful fiction that sharing information with an ally, although prohibited by the Official Secrets Act, was by some perverted logic defensible. His crime was diminished, and MI5 had connived in that deceit. Even the prosecuting counsel connived at the claim that Fuchs had not started spying until late 1942. And when Fuchs eventually came to trial, he was arraigned on two charges – that he gave information "useful to an enemy" in 1945 and 1947.[60] This was an extraordinary telescoping of his espionage activity, and a very risky characterisation of the Soviet Union for that period.

Reaction to the trial, with its speedy verdict, was however vigorous and sceptical, which prompted Sillitoe to write a follow-up paper for Attlee, recommending that he make a statement in the House of Commons.[61] This document is even more astonishing, full of inconsistencies, and untruths, and effectively digs MI5's grave more deeply. The undignified narrative now seems to run that a) MI5 had no real indications that Fuchs was a communist; b) if it did have suspicions, it felt he was not a dangerous specimen, as he had had no perceived contacts with the CPGB; and c) even if MI5 did have concerns about the security aspects, it was overruled by the hiring departments. Sillitoe reminded Attlee, however, that, owing to "Press commentary", "the public has been left with the impression that a notorious communist was negligently cleared by the Security Service for work in one of the most secret branches of Defence Research, and that he would have been there today but for the perspicacity of the FBI".' The irony was that the Press was exactly right, and Sillitoe, though trying to refute its case, described accurately what had happened. Two days after Fuchs's trial ended, on March 3, 1950, Sillitoe met with Attlee, and Attlee gave his speech on March 6.

In his address, Attlee thus had two major messages to communicate: that the British government had no indications since the German Consul's report of 1934 that Fuchs had been a communist, and that the British security service had worked diligently to protect the nation. Among the statements in his speech were the following:

> "Not long after this man came into this country – that was in 1933 – it was stated that he was a Communist. The source of that information was the Gestapo. At that time the Gestapo accused everyone of being Communists. When it was looked into there was no support for it whatever. And from that time onwards there was no support. A proper watch was kept at intervals."

> "He came back to Harwell. On all those occasions the proper inquiries were made, and there was nothing to be brought against him. His intimate friends had no suspicion. The universities for which he worked had the highest opinion of his work and of his character."

> "I do not think that there is anything that can cast the slightest slur on the security service; indeed, I think they acted promptly and effectively as soon as there was any line they could follow up."[62]

Several distortions appear here. The Gestapo, by reference to which the German consul in Bristol was perhaps inappropriately demonised, was not the only source indicating Fuchs was a Communist. As has been shown, several incidents pointed to Fuchs's communism, including his own public admission, and his friends were well aware of his affiliations. (A diligent Member of Parliament might have questioned Attlee as to what had prompted multiple further investigative inquiries if Fuchs had once been cleared? Attlee was in a Morton's Fork. Lack of constant investigation would have suggested negligence, but failure to detect anything might have indicated incompetence.) Many of Fuchs's university colleagues were likewise either dubious themselves (e.g. Mott), had come under suspicion (Peierls), or had acted duplicitously (Born). Attlee had clearly not been informed of the contentious debate within 'B' Division and between 'B' and 'C' Divisions in 1946. He gave no hint to the "line" that finally allowed MI5 to pursue Fuchs's trail. Meanwhile, in the House of Lords, the Lord Chancellor, Lord Jowett, went overboard, praising the security service for its "brilliant achievement" in tracking down Fuchs.

Since the release of the Fuchs files to the National Archives in 2003, more analysis has pointed to the craven and disturbingly inaccurate advice that Sillitoe gave to Attlee. In a partially insightful but very uneven Research Note published by *Contemporary British History* in 2005, Michael S. Goodman and Chapman Pincher reproduced the texts of Sillitoe's memoranda, both his original report of February 7, and the follow-up "Top Secret" note that he compiled in order to divert "the uninformed criticism of the Security authorities".[63] In their analysis, however, Goodman and Pincher missed some points in presenting the purpose of MI5's claim that it was trying to impress upon Attlee that it "had warned that leakage to the Russians was possible and had been proved right". Given that they had access to all the Fuchs files, the authors gave a rather superficial account, distorting and collapsing the extended process of Fuchs's recruitment, ignoring

Fuchs's public avowals of Communism and overlooking completely the severe dissension between and within Divisions 'B' and 'C' of which Christopher Andrew wrote (which of course suggested that MI5 had by no means acted in a unified and concerted manner). Moreover, even though they correctly identified the strategic post-dating of Fuchs's vetting from May 1941 to August 1941, they then made the familiar error of misreading the implications, since, when annotating the fact that MI5 had indicated that Fuchs would be more likely to give secrets to the Russians, they declared: "It must be remembered at this point that Germany was the enemy whereas Russia was an ally."[64] That was, of course, irrelevant, but even the chief conspiracy theorists have been bewitched by MI5's propaganda.

As Christopher Moran pointed out, after some vague digging around, the tumult over Fuchs dissipated, and the scandal of Burgess and Maclean soon occupied the attention of journalists.[65] Indeed, one of the first challenges to the government's account came from Rebecca West, who, as has been explained in Chapter 8, wrote in the Press about Fuchs's admission to Communism. An obvious reaction might be that some disgruntled officer in 'C' Division, disturbed by how the truth was being mis-portrayed by the government, leaked to her details from the Fuchs files. An astonishing detail that West brought out is that the fact of the Aliens Tribunal was brought to Lord Chief Justice Goddard's attention at the trial by the *defence counsel*, as if in mitigation of the fact that assisting Russian agents could not be "interpreted as prejudicial to the safety or interests of the state".[66] Since the dates of the espionage offences with which Fuchs was being accused ranged from December 1943 to 1947, the fact that the Soviet Union was an ally of Nazi Germany on the day of the relevant Aliens Tribunal Hearing, November 2, 1939, appears to have been overlooked by the officers in the court, as well as by Rebecca West herself.

Yet this episode conceals below the surface an extraordinary series of misunderstandings. The source of West's claim was almost assuredly the FBI, who had gained its interview with Fuchs in May 1950. As had been previously explained, the FBI was not referring to the 1939 Aliens Tribunal, but had learned from Fuchs of a supposed 1941 hearing, so West may have been careless. Yet she was careless again, as Curtis-Bennett referred to a *1942* hearing, while she assumed it was the same one. Was Fuchs playing a clever game with the FBI as well as with Curtis-Bennett, inventing incidents, and hoping that he would not be found out? Or did the second and third hearings actually take place, but with records ignored or destroyed? We shall probably never know the answer, but we do know that MI5 behaved in a similar careless fashion, going to extreme lengths to disprove West's probably erroneous statement in a misguided belief that the organisation might thus be exonerated – and careers saved – if it could disprove her assertion. The archives indicate that its officers overlooked Curtis-Bennett's extraordinary statement at the trial.

Otherwise West gave a withering account of the narcissistic and naïve Fuchs, and of the way that the Communists themselves were able to exploit his conviction: "It helped the Communists, enabling them to present the scientist Communist spies as starry-eyed scientists who imparted secrets to other powers just because they were scientists and wanted their fellow-scientists to have the benefit of their own discoveries, and were so unworldly that they did not know they were doing any harm, and hardly knew what ideologies were about. That was the picture of Fuchs that was spread about the world after his conviction, and it was as untrue of him as it was of Nunn May."[67]

And who assisted in this presentation of Fuchs as noble victim? MI5 itself. In a move that showed blatant scorn for the Official Secrets Act, towards the end of 1951 it recruited a journalist and historian, Alan Moorehead, to write an account of the Fuchs case that would present the organisation in a more favourable light. In any case, MI5's reputation had by then further deteriorated. On September 21, 1951, Arnold, the security officer at Harwell, reported that the physicist Bruno Pontecorvo had fled, and he was soon determined to be in Moscow. The dominant version of what ensued has come via Dick White himself. With morale in MI5 even worse, he conceived a public relations assault. White suggested, in a personal meeting with Attlee, that Moorehead should write an account of "the enemy within" as a defence of MI5's record. The sole source for the claim that White took the initiative is a conversation supposed to have taken place between Dick White himself and his biographer, in which White said that he gained Prime Minster Attlee's approval for engaging Moorehead. (Strangely, Christopher Moran's *Classified*, which introduced the public to the policy of the 'Denning Formula', by which reliable journalists were invited to help MI5's public relations by writing complimentary histories, makes no mention of Moorehead.) Moorehead had to sign the OSA (somewhat paradoxically, as his task was to reveal secrets, rather than keep them concealed), and he set to work in the Ministry of Defence. His account, *The Traitors*, is unscholarly, without references, and, by the Law of Unintended Consequences, condemns White more than it absolves him. As Bower pointed out, "it would also expose White's mistaken assumptions about Soviet penetration, as MI5 approached its *Götterdämmerung*".[68]

This account is yet another distortion of what actually occurred. The Fuchs archives reveal that Alan Moorehead was, at the time of Fuchs's trial, Public Relations Officer at the Ministry of Defence. In March, 1951, he presented his idea for a book on espionage to a Mr Strauss at the Ministry of Supply, who was enthusiastic. Moorehead expected to leave the Ministry before the book was published. While Moorehead's understanding of what really happened during the Fuchs case seemed awry, Perrin and MI5 both heard about it, and were also keen on publication. At the time, Perrin had also been extremely annoyed by Rebecca West's journalism, as it appeared that she must have had access to restricted information. She was, moreover, then also promoting the embarrassing Aliens Tribunal story. A Public Relations counter-offensive was thus required. Sillitoe agreed to the Moorehead project – also to a proposed film being suggested by Pinnacle Productions, so long as MI5 would be able to vet both items. Then, on April 27, 1951, the Home Office declined the Moorehead opportunity: many bureaucrats were concerned about a precedent being set. Fuchs also declined the prospect of a film based on his life.[69]

But by June 1951, the Rebecca West bogey was not going away. She published her second article – in the June 4 *Evening Standard* – which again criticised MI5's ineffectiveness, and also revealed the fact that Harry Gold,

Fuchs's courier in the United States, had given evidence at the Rosenbergs' trial[xi] that he, Gold, had told his Soviet handler that Fuchs had earlier been very concerned that the British would reach Kiel before them, and might find the highly damaging Gestapo dossier on him. [70] All of this annoyed Sillitoe considerably. Sillitoe had to write another mendacious letter to the Prime Minister's office, where he indicated he was hoping to launch a counter-offensive against the report of the American Joint Committee on Atomic Energy, which was the source West presumably had used. Accusing West of judgments based on information that emerged from Fuchs's trial, of "being wise after the event",[xii] he and White pursued the Moorehead opportunity eagerly, and started giving him information. Moorehead was indeed helped considerably, but selectively, despite what Skardon said to White when describing his meeting with Fuchs on it: "I explained that Moorehead is a reputable journalist and writer who, though not having access to official papers, is being given a certain amount of official encouragement to put the case into the correct perspective from the British point of view." A note of September 24 states that "Mr Alan Moorehead has been authorised to see certain material from our files in connection with the book he is writing on Soviet Atomic Espionage." He was also handed a document to sign (presumably the OSA). He noted differences in Fuchs's confessions, presented to MI5 several questions (including some thorny ones on Israel Halperin) that were answered, and in September 1952 his book was vetted by MI5 and the Ministry of Supply.

One alarming aspect of Moorehead's exercise is that the official history of atomic energy appears to rely almost exclusively on his composition for its facts on the Fuchs case.[71] Margaret Gowing's 1974 analysis of the events reached a conclusion that defends MI5's role in the drama, but how much of the unpublished documents she was allowed to see is not clear. In fact she gave as her primary source MI5's public relations piece *The Traitors*, indicating that Moorehead, although a "non-official" author, had more complete access to official information than she did. [72] Gowing was hazy on some details: she finessed the chronology of Fuchs's recruitment (which implies she was being fed information), and, while reporting that Fuchs "had made contact with the Russians soon after he began work in Birmingham", ignored the implications of the Nazi-Soviet Pact, again emphasising the partial truth that the Soviet Union was an ally in wartime. Occasionally she gave hints of knowledge that Moorehead did not provide (such as the FBI interview with Fuchs in prison), but her sources are not provided.[xiii] Anthony Glees has described this work (while discussing the possibility of Roger Hollis's guilt as a mole) in the following terms:

[xi] Julius (1918-1953) and Ethel (1915-1953) Rosenberg, American Soviet spies, were executed on June 19, 1953. VENONA decrypts had led to their detection and arrest.

[xii] Sillitoe's complaint has some merit. In her newspaper articles, West divulged some new information about Fuchs's student activities as a communist in Leipzig and Kiel, but it is not clear what her sources were, or whether the information should have been available to MI5 before his confession and trial.

[xiii] As was mentioned in Chapter 8, Gowing's work takes the standard position that "in accordance with the practice of the official war histories, references to official papers that are not yet publicly available have been omitted."

"Professor Gowing's extremely careful account (which was based upon the documentary record) shows MI5 (and thus Hollis) in a favourable light."[73] Given our knowledge from archival material released in the past ten years, one would have to suggest that Gowing should have been a bit more pertinacious in her research efforts, and a little less reliant on Moorehead. Glees concluded his analysis of Hollis's role in the Fuchs affair by discussing a document provided by Chapman Pincher – the official record of Hollis's testimony at the Tripartite Talks on Security Standards held in Washington in June 1950. Glees's conclusion was that "if MI5 allowed Fuchs to slip through the net it was despite Hollis's personal actions and not because of them", because Sir Edward Appleton, of Tube Alloys, overruled him. But Hollis's evidence is likewise shaky: he again is one who put back the recognition of Fuchs's potential to "late 1941", and a case can be made for claiming that Hollis would not have been able to act independently, as Christopher Andrew's account reinforced. In any case, MI5 propaganda had worked successfully on the official historian.

Moorehead's book contained multiple factual distortions, probably the most egregious being the collapsing of the process of recruitment of Fuchs by Peierls, and the subsequent approval, via the Ministry of Aircraft Production by MI5, to a matter of days in May 1941, when, as Chapter 8 has shown, it took five months.[74] MI5 knew this account was untrue when the organisation approved it, and the unreliable testimony of Perrin suggests that he and White probably conspired to help fabricate an account that shifted responsibility sharply away from MI5 and the Ministry of Aircraft Production/ICI, represented by Perrin. Moreover, Moorehead stubbornly – and very foolishly – echoed MI5's claims about Fuchs's unknowable Communism, even asserting, in response to Rebecca West's article in 1951: "Now, in point of fact, Fuchs never made any such declaration to that tribunal; he never revealed to any official in Britain or America that he was a Communist until Skardon saw him at Harwell on 21 December 1949."[75] His main thrust, however, was to reinforce the wishy-washy views about Communism that White articulated elsewhere, as if such were a coherent aspect of MI5's counter-espionage policy. After making a lengthy apologia for MI5's inaction (while at the same time hinting that it had been very diligent in checking out Fuchs, but had not discovered anything potentially dangerous), Moorehead wrote:

"However one approaches the problem one always comes back to the point that during the war our policy towards Communists was much more lenient than it is now; and it had every reason to be.

There are people who argue that a man who is once a Communist is always a Communist, but if that fallacious doctrine were acted upon then quite a number of high officials on both sides of the Atlantic would be promptly obliged to resign. The years bring changes in men's politics, and there was every evidence before the authorities that Fuchs, like so many others, had changed from a German refugee to a loyal British subject. The authorities would have had no right whatever to refuse Fuchs employment in 1941 on the grounds that he had been a Communist eight years before, even if they had known this."[76]

Again, several items in these sentences must be parsed and analysed in detail, as they represent the core of the flawed White Doctrine. They distort the different circumstances that prevailed in the first 22 months of the war, when the Soviet Union was not an ally. In that period, there was no reason for "leniency" towards Communists, as Krivitsky had so precisely spelled out. When Barbarossa occurred, and Churchill declared support for the Soviets, it should have been remembered that Communism remained a permanently hostile ideology, as the more shrewd members of the government constantly pointed out. It is true that youthful infatuations with Communism may dissipate, but that was no reason for not excluding from confidential and diplomatic work candidates who had shown enthusiasm for Communist dogma at some time. There was no evidence that Fuchs had changed from his status as a German refugee with loyalty to Soviet Communism to a patriotic British subject: he had been required to sign the OSA, and then be naturalised, because his skills were considered that important. (If Fuchs had a conscience, he could have declined signing the Act.) The authorities had every right to refuse Fuchs employment on any security grounds they considered accurate: they did not owe him a living. The final qualification, however, that "even if they had known this" [*that Fuchs was a Communist*], they would have had no right to refuse him, is the most important.

In that phrase lies the essential cause of the cover-up. For, in reality, MI5 made no material objection to Fuchs even though he was known to be a Communist. Indeed, that part of his profile made him acceptable. After all, White and Liddell had recruited Blunt, who was as publically a communist as Fuchs ever was. If Percy Sillitoe, fresh to his role in the scandals of Nunn May and then Fuchs, had learned that it had been part of MI5's policy to recruit communists (and communist sympathisers) – let alone of the episode with Leo Long – he would probably have turned apoplectic, and have wanted to dismiss White and Liddell on the spot. White was quick, however, to cast the mantle of responsibility for the easing-up on others. According to Bower, White "blamed the refusal to discriminate against suspected communists upon politicians, especially Max Beaverbrook, Churchill's confidant and a minister, who would have [*sic*] 'profoundly discouraged' any investigations into undergraduate political activities."[77] But the lenient policy towards communists had started well before then.

Evidence of a broader cover-up – or at least a desire to protect Civil Service mandarins from digging too deeply into potentially embarrassing aspects of MI5's practices – appears in a report on MI5 that was undertaken at the close of the war.[78] Prompted by Foreign Minister Anthony Eden, and encouraged by Sir David Petrie as a method of making the passage of his successor, Sir Percy Sillitoe, into the job that much easier, Prime Minister Attlee charged Sir Findlater Stewart, a civil servant with expertise in India, and now chairman of the Security Executive, to investigate MI5's mission and organisation. Attlee had chosen Sillitoe over Liddell, and wanted to give him a clear directive that the rights of citizens needed to be protected.[79] Stewart was cautious, largely echoed the findings of Hankey in 1940, and made few fresh recommendations. What is remarkable about his report, however, is the lack of urgency it expresses on the Soviet threat, completely omitting it in the account of the 1930s, and not being alive to the changing climate since the Soviet Union's true intentions were acknowledged in 1944. Stewart's isolation from the prevailing thought in the Foreign Office and SIS – and the lack of integration with the JIC, which never appears in the report – is exemplified by statements such as the following, when the author, completely oblivious to the possibility of clandestine spies working outside the party, is discussing the threat from CP members: "Experience has shown that continued membership may lead to conflicting loyalties, particularly if our major policies diverged from those of Russia."[80] Remarkably, the suggestion that Great Britain and the Soviet Union might have been on convergent paths after the defeat of Fascism appears to have escaped the notice of everyone in the Cabinet, from Attlee down. Stewart had moreover clearly been carefully shepherded around the offices of MI5, not knowing what tough questions to ask.

It was thus Sillitoe who had been misled as much as Attlee or the British public. His appointment in 1946 had not been received well by career MI5 officers, and many (with the exception of White) treated him poorly. He retired as Director-General in 1953, and brought out his own autobiography two years later, *Cloak without Dagger*. It is a semi-loyal memoir of his time with MI5, but shows that he had not gained the confidence of the officers working for him, and had not delved deeply into the institution's records. On the Klaus Fuchs affair, he wrote: "This scientist, who had already started to pass information to the Russians as early as 1942, was finally brought to trial in 1950."[81] That throwaway phrase, "as early as 1942", suggesting that Fuchs's main contributions to espionage had happened primarily in the USA, completely ignores the true time-line, echoing the sanitised version compiled by his subordinates, and contributing further to the MI5 cover-up. Sillitoe took up the theme of 'Fuchs as victim', with a Dick Whittingtonesque account of the spy's arrival in the UK: "Fuchs, aged 21, arrived in England, ragged, pale, and hungry, with all his property in a small canvas bag, on 24th September, 1933, and was registered as an alien."[82] Rossiter countered strongly this sentimental account, relating how it was the KPD in Berlin that had decided that Fuchs should go into exile: "When he landed in Britain Fuchs was not, as several writers have portrayed him, a poor, lonely refugee. He was an active and experienced member of the German Communist Party, doing what the party told him, with connections at high levels of the organisation and a sophisticated awareness of clandestine activity."[83]

Moroever, Sillitoe represented faithfully the prevailing sentiments that White and Hollis gave about the struggles of trying to prevent Communist subversion: "Since the end of the last war MI5 has been constantly aware that in this country it is by no means impossible for men in positions of trust and authority to become enamoured of Communist doctrine to the point where they will spy on behalf of the Russians and feel no shame in doing so."[84] That statement reflects a key misunderstanding of how doctrines become inculcated and loyalties warped. The men who were dangerous were not already established in positions of trust and authority, and then subjected successfully to Communist propaganda. They had gained those positions by deceiving their recruiters about fierce ideological attitudes that they had adopted when young, or had even declared them, and found that it did not matter.

Christopher Moran described the furore that erupted when Sillitoe's book was serialised in the *Times*.[85] Dick White was horrified, in a way betraying his guilty conscience when declaring that he wanted the whole chapter on Fuchs deleted, since it essentially undermined the statement about MI5's competence that Attlee had made in the House of Commons. Sillitoe was adamant and unrepentant, however, complaining about "muzzling". He was of course correct, and no doubt would have liked to have written more about White's and Liddell's reprehensible behaviour. He must have felt a deep sense of disenchantment and personal failure, as well as a crisis of honour, over having compiled such an abject and inconsistent document for his Prime Minister. As his entry in the *Dictionary of National Biography* put it: "Sillitoe, who had immense concern for his public reputation, had to answer for what with hindsight could sometimes be seen as blameworthy mistakes."[86] His publication moreover set a precedent: it was difficult to suppress other accounts of wartime exploits in intelligence when the ex-Director-General of MI5 had gone public with his own memoir.

In summary, the history of the clash between the British government and the Soviet Union, over the latter's attempts to steal confidential information about atomic weapons research, can be told as follows. Stalin's Intelligence Services developed a long-term plan to infiltrate British scientific research, in which Pyotr Kapitza played a leading role. Rudolf Peierls was probably encouraged, by virtue of threats to his wife's family, to lead the British-based team of scientists sympathetic to the Communist cause. The Communist John Strachey was effective in getting Peierls's naturalisation request approved, as well as gaining Jürgen Kuczynski's release from internment. When Peierls was adopted by the Maud Committee, he and Max Born conspired, in the summer of 1940, to have Fuchs and other valuable scientists released from internment to join the project, and the Ministry of Aircraft Production bypassed the safeguards in place in order to have Fuchs working productively for Peierls. It presented its application for approval for Fuchs's employment in a half-hearted fashion, well after he had started work, at a time when MI5 was in an organisational upheaval. In any case, MI5 had by then started to relax and minimise its actions to perform surveillance on Communist suspects: it ignored all further signals of Fuchs's activities and avowal of Communist beliefs. Fuchs, who was a conscious part of the long-term Soviet project, contacted his Soviet masters immediately on recruitment, while the Nazi-Soviet pact was still in effect, and began to reveal vital secrets even before his work permit was granted. By the time the Department of Industrial and Scientific Research gained responsibility for Fuchs, when the Tube Alloys project was instituted, the Soviet Union was an ally, and Fuchs had gained momentum and shown excellence at his job. No doubt dismayed by MI5's inefficiency, the Ministry no longer cared what MI5 thought.

MI5 had not prepared any convincing policy about disqualifying Communists from important war work, and it suppressed or ignored its internal pointers to links and contacts between Fuchs, Kahle, the Kuczynskis, and Beurton. It failed in particular to make the connections between the nefarious and deceitful actions of Jürgen and Ursula Kuczynski, and to detect and curtail the latter's role as a courier in Oxfordshire. At the end of the war, when Fuchs returned to England, senior MI5 officers ignored the warnings of their subordinates that Fuchs was probably a spy. When the Cold War started, MI5's senior officers started to experience a sense of acute embarrassment about their laxity over Communist threats, and concealed such lapses of policy from their own Director-General. VENONA traffic began to help identify Communist agents, both natives and those originally aliens, and provided conclusive evidence that Fuchs was a spy. When it could no longer ignore the facts, MI5 resorted to perform a complex cover-up process to conceal its flawed performance, manifested at first in the unmasking of Nunn May, Fuchs, and Pontecorvo, and then engaged Alan Moorehead to write a mendacious account of what actually happened, a work it acknowledged and approved.

Notes

[1] TNA, KV 2/1245/1.

[2] TNA KV 4/468 (Liddell *Diaries*).

[3] Harvey and Klehr, *Venona: Decoding Soviet Espionage in America*, p 35; S. J. Hamrick, *Deceiving the Deceivers*, p 149; Nigel West, *Venona: The Greatest Secret of the Cold War*, p 27; Christopher Andrew, *The Defence of the Realm*, p 377.

[4] Robert Chadwell Williams, *Klaus Fuchs: Atom Spy*, p 62.

[5] Costello, *Mask of Treachery*, p 709, Note 63.

[6] ibid.

[7] Michael Smith, *The Spying Game*, p 182. Smith referred to the fact that the Radio Security Service had intercepted messages emanating from the network of Oliver Green. Yet this claim must be tested: it is more likely that Smith was referring to boasts that Oliver Green had made at Communist Party Headquarters, intercepted electronically. Apart from the ISCOT traffic between the Comintern and agents *behind Nazi lines* that was picked up in 1943, and which was decrypted from 1944 onwards, no record of traffic between Moscow Centre and agents has been released. Smith appears to have corrected his earlier impression in his 2011 book, *The Bletchley Park Codebreakers*.

[8] Stephen Dorrill, *MI6*, p 258.

[9] Christopher Andrew, *The Defence of the Realm*, p 386.

[10] *The Guy Liddell Diaries, Vol. 1 and Vol. 2*, edited by Nigel West (p 1). This volume is a condensation of the full (but redacted) Diaries available at The National Archives, at KV 4/185, KV 4/186, KV 4/187, KV 4/188, KV 4/189, KV 4/190, KV 4/191, KV 4/192, KV 4/193, KV 4/194, KC 4/195, KV 4/196, KV 4/466, KV 4/467, KV 4/468, KV 4/469, KV 4/470, KV 4/471, KV 4/472, KV 4/473, KV 4/474 and KV 4/475.

[11] TNA, KV 2/1245/1.

[12] TNA, KV 2/1245/2.

[13] Geoffrey Elliott, *Gentleman Spymaster*, pp 302-303.

[14] TNA, KV 4/469.

[15] TNA, KV2/1246/1.

[16] Nigel West, *Mortal Crimes*, p 56.

[17] Chapman Pincher, *Treachery*, p 118.

[18] Pavel Sudoplatov, *Special Tasks*, p 193, Note 19.

[19] Nigel West, *Venona: The Greatest Secret of the Cold War*, p 152.

[20] For example, Anthony Glees, *The Secrets of the Service*, p 348.

[21] TNA, KV 2/1249/1.

[22] Mike Rossiter, *The Spy Who Changed the World*, p 83 and p 58.

[23] TNA, KV 2/1250/2.

[24] ibid.

[25] TNA, KV 2/1253/1.

[26] West, *Mortal Crimes*, p 59.

[27] TNA. KV 2/1253/1.

[28] See especially Chapman Pincher's *Treachery* and John Costello's *Mask of Treachery*.

[29] The files on Alexander Foote, (who was recruited by Sonia as a radio operator), at the National Archives indicate that Foote perjured himself by providing evidence to the Swiss authorities that Sonia's husband, Rolf Hamburger, had committed adultery with Sonia's sister in London. TNA, KV-2-1613-1.

[30] TNA, KV 36/1.

[31] Rossiter, p 228.

[32] Ursula Werner, *Sonjas Rapport* [in German].

[33] Anthony Read and David Fisher, *Colonel Z*, p 238.

[34] TNA, KV 36/1.

[35] ibid.

[36] ibid.

[37] West, *Mortal Crimes*, p 58.

[38] Werner, p 295.

[39] TNA, KV 36/1.

[40] ibid.

[41] ibid.

[42] TNA, KV 2/1245/1.

[43] Williams, p 140.

[44] The claim that Jane Archer had indicated that Fuchs would be "more likely to leak information to the Russians rather than the Germans" has been picked up in multiple places. It was in fact Jane Archer's *husband*, an MI5 officer liaising with the Air Ministry (head of 'D3'), who provided this insight to the Head of Security at the Ministry of Aircraft Production, no doubt advised by his wife. Group Captain Archer was the officer who gave the Ministry final clearance for Fuchs to be given his Aliens War Service permit (see Chapter 8). Archer transferred to 'B' Division at some time during the war: Curry has him still leading 'D3' in 1943.

[45] Williams, p 94.

[46] West's *A Matter of Trust (MI5 Operations 1945-1972)* was published in the USA as *The Circus*. Bower's reference (in *The Perfect English Spy*) to page 106 brings up no mention of Suppell and Fuchs. Suppell has only one unrelated entry in the Index. In fact the officer's name was *Serpell*, who worked for Hollis (but whose name also does not appear in West's or Andrew's history). Rossiter suggested that Serpell was treated badly because of his perseverance on the Fuchs case: hence, perhaps, the distortion of his name. Other evidence suggests that Serpell in fact had more influence, and may even have had Sillitoe's ear. In his 2014 biography of 'Klop' Ustinov, Peter Day reported that Serpell wrote a report on NKVD espionage directly for Director-General Sillitoe (*Klop*, p 213), and Liddell recorded, in his Diaries that Serpell was the officer selected to accompany Sillitoe on a visit to Canada in May, 1950 (TNA KV 4/472, May 7 entry).

[47] Williams, p 145.

[48] TNA, KV 2/1246/1 and KV 2/1247/1.

[49] Williams, p 118.

[50] TNA, KV 2/1247/1.

[51] Bower, p 96.

[52] ibid.

[53] TNA KV 4/471; October 31, 1949.

[54] Thomas Grant, *Jeremy Hutchinson's Case Histories*, p 62.

[55] Andrew, p 436.

[56] TNA, KV 2/1264/1. This comment adds an intriguing new twist to the confusion over 'Hearings' and Tribunals'. Added to the Aliens Tribunal of November 1939, and the FBI claim of a Hearing some time in the spring of 1941, Curtis-Bennett presented another (hitherto unrecorded) hearing taking place in 1942. It is possible Fuchs provided Curtis-Bennett with this statement in a manner similar to that in which he primed the FBI. Fuchs submitted his naturalisation papers to the Home Office on April 30, 1942, and he became a British subject on July 30. This observation must have taken Shawcross by surprise: yet he swiftly picked up the thread that Fuchs was known to be a Communist only at this juncture.

[57] Alan Moorehead, *The Traitors*, p 155.

[58] TNA, KV 2/1263/1.

[59] Norman Moss, *Klaus Fuchs, The Man Who Stole the Atom Bomb*, p 158.

[60] TNA, KV 2/1263/2.

[61] TNA, PREM 8/1279.

[62] Quoted in Moss, pp 166-67, and Moorehead, pp 204-205.

[63] Michael S. Goodman and Chapman Pincher (2005) Research Note: *Clement Attlee, Percy Sillitoe and the Security Aspects of the Fuchs Case*, Contemporary British History, 19:1, 67-77, FOI: 10.1080/1361946042000303864 . Since Chapman Pincher is the co-author, the purpose of the note is primarily to incriminate Hollis. The leading roles of White and Liddell in the cover-up are never mentioned.

[64] ibid., Note 19.

[65] Christopher Moran, *Classified: Secrets and the State in Modern Britain*, p 114.

[66] Rebecca West, *The New Meaning of Treason*, p 189.

[67] ibid., p 190.

[68] Bower, p 101.

[69] TNA, KV 2/1257/1.

[70] ibid.

[71] Margaret Gowing, *Britain and Atomic Energy, 1945-1952*, (Volumes 1 and 2).

[72] ibid., *Volume 2*, p 532, Note 4 to Chapter 16.

[73] Glees, p 348.

[74] Moorehead, pp 81-82.

[75] Moorehead, p 206.

[76] ibid., p 207.

[77] Bower, p 48.

[78] TNA, CAB 301/31.

[79] See Attlee's Foreword to Sillitoe's memoir, *Cloak Without Dagger*.

[80] TNA, CAB 301/31, p 87.

[81] Percy Sillitoe, *Cloak Without Dagger*, p 165.

[82] ibid., p 168.

[83] Rossiter, p 52.

[84] ibid., p 167.

[85] Moran, p 292.

[86] *Dictionary of National Biography, 1961-1970*, edited by E. T. Williams and C. S. Nicholls.

Chapter 10: MI5 and the Defence of Democracy

"There is a perfectly good case for not giving freedom to a way of life (Communism) which is opposed to freedom. It is at least that freedom must be worked for, not just taken for granted." (Stephen Potter)

"There is no honor in relativism when radicals of any faith exploit religion to justify murder.
Revolutions sometimes consume their pluralists and their democrats." (Steve Coll)

"That is why pluralism is not relativism – the multiple values are objective, part of the essence of humanity rather than arbitrary creations of man's subjective fancies." (Isaiah Berlin)

The primary research question posed in the initial chapter of this book was introduced as follows: "Was MI5's apparent accommodation of communists caused by incompetence, by confusion, by lack of expertise, by higher political direction, by internal subversion or conspiracy, or by some combination of these factors?" The research undertaken would suggest that all except the influence of 'higher political direction' were true. While one of Churchill's first initiatives on becoming Premier had been to make overtures to the Soviet Union, he knew that it would be an ally only during hostilities with Germany, and the military establishment remained conscious of the durable Communist threat. It was a lack of organisational focus, an inability to withstand more subtle influences, inadequate political resolve, and an unwillingness to represent strongly what its perennial mission implied, that allowed MI5 to be infected by communist influences. In the critical period of the Nazi-Soviet pact, it made severe misjudgments as to how its charter of protecting the Realm should be interpreted. It set the balance between security and freedom wrong.

On the subsidiary research questions, this book has shown that Krivitsky's message was ignored partly out of distraction, partly out of suspicion of defectors, but also because expertise in Soviet counter-espionage had already been reduced in importance. Academic influences, and the success of Soviet propaganda, had fine-tuned the message of Communism as a viable anti-Fascist movement, and directed it to minds not astute or trained enough to challenge or reject it. Guy Burgess and his cronies – whether true spies or agents of influence – then stealthily undermined any resistance to communist influence by inserting themselves into the intelligence framework. Confused, MI5 lost track of its best instincts and practices, and allowed subversives to work on highly confidential projects, the most notorious of whom was Klaus Fuchs. Leading officers, namely White and Liddell, ignored the warning signals until too late, still believing that natural-born Englishmen could not be traitors. To save their own careers, and the independent existence of MI5 itself, they then indulged in a cover-up that has lain largely undisclosed until this day. Could MI5 have prevented this debacle? And what lessons can be learned?

The perpetual operational challenge for MI5 has been: 'How to prevent potential malefactors from doing harm without stepping on individual liberties?' Yet a failure to act could also end a career, and threaten the reputation, or even the existence, of the service. When Guy Liddell recognised the institutional shortcomings over Fuchs in 1950, he engaged in deception in a vain attempt to save himself, and to avoid MI5's being merged with SIS. In 1956, when the fallout from the 'Buster' Crabb affair led to the demise of SIS's Director-General, Sir John Sinclair, MI5's Dick White was brought in to repair the service, as an alternative to its being subsumed into MI5.[1] According to an unverifiable account, senior officers in SIS did not take kindly to being taken over by a "secret policeman"[2], and many notionally scholarly books have maintained that MI5 is a Secret Police organisation. But MI5 has never been a secret police force, like the Gestapo or the KGB. It has no powers of arrest, can authorise no secret or show trials (or sentencing without trials at all), followed by incarceration, or death via the guillotine or a pistol in the back of the neck. The public continually demands protection and safety, but in its mission of protecting the realm, MI5 has had to deal with all the democratic clutter of flux in political direction by virtue of change of governments, of an independent judiciary, of habeas corpus, of the need for firm evidence or voluntary confessions, of the activism of civil libertarians, and of a vigorous free Press. What has always been required – beyond fair and unexploitative surveillance skills – is political resolve independent of party manifestoes, preparedness for the unexpected, and good communication in promoting ideas.

The journey from 1935, when Jane Archer wrote her report on surveillance, to the cover-up over Fuchs in 1951, had been a long and arduous one, reflecting a steady reduction in resolve in MI5's opposition to the Communist menace. Dick White and his boss Guy Liddell, with the irresolute Roger Hollis at their side, had allowed this policy of leniency to happen, as this book has shown, by a failure to internalise what had prompted the build-up of protective measures to safeguard the nation in the early days of Communism. MI5's failure to deal with the Communist threat had three aspects: cultural, organisational, and personal. It was susceptible to the misguided representation of Communism displayed by intellectuals in the 1930s; it comprised a fragmented and top-heavy organisation, with overlapping duties, and no clear lines of responsibility; and the leading officers in counter-espionage were not temperamentally attuned to executing the firm disciplines that were required for anticipating and reacting to the reality of Soviet subversives in government departments.

In the late 1930s, these senior officers of MI5 had shifted their attention from the thorny presence of illegals and their contacts to the easier task of monitoring the Communist Party. White and Liddell had diminished the need for serious efforts to counter Communist subversion and moved out their most capable and experienced officer, Jane Archer, into a backwater. They had ignored and not followed up on the unique and penetrating information and warnings that

Krivitsky had given them. They allowed themselves to be influenced unduly by the intellectual climate of the 1930s that made Marxism respectable, and thus did not alert government to the perpetual threat of the Comintern and of Soviet Communism. They made sophistical distinctions about different kinds of Communists, thus deluding themselves about the supposed harmlessness of many of them. They overrode the objections of such as Curry and Knight and removed obstacles to the recruitment of persons with an obvious Communist past, in that way bringing a virus of corrosive action in-house and setting a precedent for such activities outside the service. After detecting one Soviet spy in an important intelligence department of government during the war, they neglected to take any punitive action against him, and even re-hired the individual at the end of the war. They allowed another spy to infiltrate vital weapons research, even though he was an avowed subversive, and indications of his treachery were presented to them. Conscious of the mistakes they had made, White encouraged a shoddy act of attempting to write history to protect him and his colleagues, as well as the institution they worked for. In summary, having convinced themselves of the fashionable but erroneous notion that communism contained some moral strengths, these officers allowed the fact of Britain's alliance with the Soviet Union against Nazi Germany to destroy their resolve about the enduring dangers of Communist totalitarianism, and the Soviet Union's global designs, and thus exercised loose and unprofessional tradecraft. In that way they undermined and overruled the best intentions and instincts of those elsewhere in MI5 who remained aware of the primal Communist threat that had energised the service in the 1920s and early 1930s.

While many writers have attempted to analyse why the Cambridge Spies betrayed their native democratic country for the self-righteous but cruel certainties of Communism, much less time has been spent on investigating why the nation's security services neglected part of their traditional mission, let their guard down in their defence against Bolshevism, and even recruited Communists into their ranks. It is a multi-faceted matter, coloured by the shifting ideological battles of the 1930s, but one that points unerringly to the conclusion that the subversion effort represented a singular propaganda success by the Soviet Union. The founding Communist state was able to exploit an intellectual bias that favoured its ideology, abetted by an ignorance of what was really happening within Stalin's prison. Even if the Comintern could not spark revolution in the West, at least it succeeded in populating the offices of democratic governments with persons very favourably disposed towards the Soviet Union's mission, men and women who were prepared to help the country make up for its massive failure in innovation and science by giving it proprietary secrets as well as strategic political intelligence. MI5 was, like any other institution, a creature of its age, and had to adapt to the fluctuating ideas of its political masters. Nevertheless, it was responsible for an enduring mission of 'Defending the Realm', which should have required it to show leadership and firmness in protecting the country's offices and projects from subversion. Why did the Security Service succumb to the propaganda? It is useful to step back and survey the ideological framework.

Capitalism versus Communism?

The primary reason the propaganda war was lost in Britain was that the debate was frequently carried out in terms defined by the Communists themselves. Political discussion ceded the territory to the Marxist-Leninist line that the clash of civilisations was between communism and capitalism, almost as if there were a moral equivalence between the two, a false contrast now as then, but one which can nevertheless still be found in new historical studies in 2017. For example, the deliberations of the Joint Intelligence Committee in the latter 1940s, as it tried to come to grips with the reality of the Communist threat, are dotted with references to the clash between 'the capitalist world' and 'Communism' – a misconception which a leading historian of this period, Percy Cradock, does nothing to dismantle, adopting the former phrase himself.[3] (The influence of Marxist teaching pervades historiography well into the twenty-first century.) Many initiatives at this time that took on the cloak of 'anti-communism' were viewed as necessarily being 'reactionary', 'ultra-conservative', 'right-wing', 'imperialist' – even 'fascist' (and some were indeed so), when a far more suitable stance would have employed a set of terms that would have included the ideas behind 'democratic', 'liberal', 'pluralist', 'constitutional', invoking notions of the rule of law, without arbitrary power, and the existence of fair elections and oppositional political parties – all characteristics markedly absent from Soviet totalitarianism. Centrist defenders of human rights always seem to struggle to express vigorous principles when competing with extremist ideologies, and all too often seem reluctant to frame correctly or defend the 'capitalist' model that drives their economies. On the other hand, one can easily detect an element of hypocrisy in those generic critics of capitalism who consider only its inevitable flaws without recognising the benefits that it has brought to society and to themselves, such as A. J. P. Taylor inspecting his investment statements each night while aiding Soviet propaganda during the day, or John le Carré bewailing 'the capitalist system' because of the behaviour of pharmaceutical multinationals while fighting with his publishers over royalties, or Jenifer Hart taking advantage of her estates and legacies while encouraging the Communist revolution.

Thus the struggle should have been described as one between totalitarianism and some form of liberal democracy. For capitalism is not a system of government: it is an arrangement that allocates resources and investments in a society that encourages free-enterprise. True, Marxists, with their rigid class-based interpretation of history, might point out those in command of the wealth may have an inappropriate influence over the reins of government (*plutocracy*); other critics may suggest that there exists a too tight relationship between industry leaders and those who rule (*crony-capitalism*), but capitalism does not in itself define the mechanisms of government. Totalitarianism, on the other hand, is a system of government in which all aspects of social life (e.g. arts, industry, science, media, politics) are controlled by a one-party state apparatus. Both Nazi Germany and Communist Russia satisfied this model, and had much in common with each other.

The liberal democracies, on the other hand, were more variegated. They displayed different forms of government, as far as their constitutions prescribed (monarchies or republics; rules for suffrage; separation of powers; number of political parties; nature of official opposition; existence of upper and lower houses; terms of office and frequency of elections; etc. etc.), yet had in common the notion of the group in power having to face the ballot-box after a specified time. The political order, whichever party was in power, often had, however, an uneasy relationship with the world of free enterprise and the structures of industry on whose success they relied for taxation revenues. Thus notions of economic laissez-faire were frequently disturbed by attempts at government intervention – a symptom that still exists today, as with too-close relationships between politicians and company boards, or the tolerance of cartels in the cause of stability, protection of 'strategic' industries, or efforts to regulate business behaviour that runs the risk of causing social turbulence. Since growing welfare programmes in the Western democracies relied on the profits of capitalist enterprise, [i] governments constantly sought – and still seek – business and financial 'stability' without understanding that turbulence is an inevitable feature of the free enterprise world. That may refer simply to the competitive nature of business, and the 'laws' of the market, where failure is a fact of life, or it may describe the more dramatic upheaval that the Austrian economist Joseph Schumpeter described as "creative destruction", where whole industries are replaced by new models. One can see such ambitions today in the European Union's attempts to fix the 'banking system', or the US Federal Reserve's objective of achieving 'financial stability', or the Chinese government's efforts to inject artificial confidence into the stock market, or keep unprofitable businesses alive.

Marx, on the other hand, described a predestined view of history that took capitalist/imperialist societies on a self-destructive course that led inevitably to the dictatorship of the proletariat. When the Western liberal economies floundered at the end of the third decade of the twentieth century, many intellectuals interpreted the crisis as a crisis of the capitalist model. First, the perpetual yoking of capitalism and imperialism by Marxist critics served as a reminder that the health of their economies was deemed to be dependent upon their colonies, both as a source of raw materials, and as a market for their manufacturing industries. That was a moral argument. Second, free enterprise had failed to keep gainfully employed a population of citizens who wanted to work. That was a fact of life, of boom and bust. Third, public investment was expensive and risky. Governments might plough money into industries that were bound to fail (e.g. shipbuilding in the UK after World War II), or try to increase dole payments that it found harder to afford. That showed that a traditional democracy could not quickly solve the problem of a free enterprise culture that occasionally struggled.

Yet many thinkers and politicians allowed the symptoms of business boom and bust, and the role of a market for labour, to cloud their opinion of the enduring strengths of a liberal, pluralist society, where some semblance of

---

[i] For example: "Mr Schmidt was named Finance Minister in 1972 and promptly sought to make left-wing Social Democrats understand that West Germany's open-armed social benefits could be financed only by a thriving capitalist economy" (from *New York Times* obituary of Helmut Schmidt, November 11, 2015).

democratic control over the organs of government existed. Instead many for some reason concluded that those political traditions and structures themselves were at fault. They thus looked hopefully to the Communist 'experiment', and, without peering closely enough to see what the costs were, assumed that the Soviet model was somehow better adapted to providing widespread prosperity and private contentedness. If 'capitalism' was seriously flawed, and the choice was between capitalism and communism, the later alternative suddenly looked engaging. What is more, Marxism theory came with the alarming thud of historical inevitability.

Defending 'Capitalism'

While Western democracies thus relied on private enterprise, it presented moral challenges. Capitalism was essentially risky, competitive, and inegalitarian, and thus philosophically dubious. Its mercantile practices had origins in the slave trade. Socialists viewed the balance between capital and labour as unfair, with an expanded 'working class' suffering in times of slump. Few people were prepared to defend the tradition of Adam Smith energetically, and no significant works in that cause came out before the war. Friedrich Hayek (leading the Vienna school of economics), who saw the idea of entrepreneurialism closely tied to the notion of personal liberty, was one of the few who did, but his *Road to Serfdom* was not published until 1944. He was denigrated by many critics – including Isaiah Berlin, who, one might think, should have been sympathetic to Hayek's ideas. Berlin referred to "the awful Hayek", and classified his Vienna colleague, Ludwig von Mises as "just as much of a dodo", a judgment that must cast massive doubts about the seriousness of Berlin's belief in individual freedom.[4] Karl Popper, another Austrian philosopher, and intellectual ally of Hayek, decided to write his criticism of Marxism, *The Open Society and its Enemies*, on the day he heard of Hitler's invasion of Austria in 1938, but the book was not published until 1950.

In England, significant voices heralded the approach of socialism, as if government control of the economy could be productively achieved without the horrors of Communism and revolution. George Orwell, the 'Tory anarchist' (a term he used to describe himself), was one of the first political writers who went against the intellectual tide, identifying the horrors implicit in totalitarian Russia. Yet he struggled to define an alternative political structure that would address what he saw as the failures of liberal democracy, and his instincts led him to advocate centralist measures of socialist control. He unequivocally made his celebrated declaration that capitalism was dead, without clearly indicating what to put in its place: as the German bombs were falling round him, he asserted that "private capitalism does not work. It cannot deliver the goods".[5] It was unlikely that Orwell was referring to moral blessings in this phrase: he was undoubtedly complaining that capitalism did not provide material benefits. But that was exactly what capitalism did provide – goods, even if Orwell was disenchanted with the unfair apportionment of such prosperity, and deplored the ranks of the wasted unemployed. Certainly the Soviet Union was not creating consumer goods in comparable volumes at that time – or any time after: its economy was entirely reliant on the export of raw materials derived largely from slavery, and the stealing of industrial secrets from the West. Orwell wanted a 'planned economy'

– something essential during a time of war, but a construct completely unsuitable in a period of peace. He was undoubtedly a firm opponent of totalitarianism, but, like many intellectuals, did not understand economics. Governments, despite the protestations of politicians, cannot 'create jobs' or determine the correct supply and variety of goods required to meet demand: all they can do is encourage the right climate for entrepreneurialism and industry to thrive.

The gloom of the Great Depression had left a broad sense of failure. Even in the United States of America, the pillar of free enterprise, where the Depression had started, politicians committed to massive government intervention in the economy had taken control. Roosevelt's New Deal, an authoritarian but not totalitarian project, in which cartels and prices were regulated, and where the government engaged in massive public works spending, was viewed by many in Britain with awe. Yet it stuttered: 'full employment' was never possible, guardians of the Constitution resisted Roosevelt's attempts to take even stronger *dirigiste* command, and it actually took the advent of World War II to shift the economy into a higher gear, and lower the unemployment figures. Even middle-of-the-road Conservative politicians like R. A. Butler and Harold Macmillan, the latter deeply moved by the misery he observed in his own constituency, Stockton, were recommending programmes that would not have looked out of place in a Labour Party manifesto. The overwhelming political mood was towards massive reform. During the war, such a mood contributed to the deceptive and dangerous belief that the Soviet Union had much in common with the welfarist instincts of the Western democracies: Maisky's *Diaries*, for instance, are dotted with observations by such as Eden, Butler, Bracken, and even Churchill himself, about the common goals of the totalitarians and British parliamentarians. [6] Even allowing for some diplomatic twisting, and the manipulations of Maisky, there remains enough evidence from other sources to suggest that many British politicians, like Roosevelt, severely misjudged Stalin as a 'man of peace'.

Defending Liberal Democracy

It was not as if constitutional liberal democracy, as it existed in the 1930s, enjoyed vigorous championship, either. Britain's fragmented, pluralist approach to politics was perceived as a hindrance in a time of crisis. In fact the democracy that prevailed in UK during the 1930s could be classed more as a liberal aristocracy, with power based on lineage and privilege. Yes, there was universal suffrage, but the avenues to influential careers in such fields as diplomacy and the armed services were closed to persons lacking the right education or pedigree. While some intellectuals (e.g. the Bloomsbury Group) had regarded their *rentier*-enabled enjoyment of the arts as indications of a cultural vanguard, Harold Nicolson was characteristic of another group who cherished their privileges and opportunities for leisure and enjoying the arts, and then sought out 'socialism' as a war aim, as if to purge themselves of their self-indulgence. No one stood up to declare boldly that progress could be made in developing a fairer society without moving to the extreme nationalisation promoted by the Labour Party – at least not until the Hitler war started, when Nicolson (in the Department of Information), prodded by Lord Halifax, was one of the strongest proponents of defining War

Aims of a decidedly socialist nature. Nicolson had been encouraged by Lord Halifax to create a statement of War Aims for the Cabinet to review, of which 'Federalism in Europe and Socialism at home' were the dominant components, reflecting Nicolson's belief that a lack of 'socialism' was what had allowed Hitler to come to power. Churchill quite wisely rejected them (were they not in fact Peace Aims?), giving the reason that "precise aims would be compromising, whereas vague principles would disappoint".[7] Churchill famously declared that he had not engaged in war to supervise the dismemberment of the British Empire: he might equally have said it was not his purpose to see Socialism installed in Britain.

Overall thinking was thus very blinkered. Imperialism, strangely, died a very slow death, however, with Labour Party politicians such as Ernest Bevin, even, trying to protect the Empire. Yet, apart from Churchill, most Conservative politicians understood that 'Empire' was an outdated tenet of the Tory programme, and that a war fought to protect democracy would necessarily imply the liberation of colonies at its conclusion. Quite simply, maintaining and defending an Empire was too expensive. And, if Britain was a pluralist democracy, it was clearly not very confident of what it was defending. Perhaps citizens took it for granted.

In a pluralist society, opinion is fragmented – for example, in the media, in political parties, in churches (or temples or mosques), and between the legislative and the executive arms of government. The individual rights of citizens and their consciences are considered paramount, and all citizens are considered equal under the law. The ethnic, cultural, religious or philosophical allegiances that they may hold are considered private affairs – unless they are deployed to subvert the freedoms that a liberal society offers them. A pluralist democracy values very highly the rights of the individual (rather than of a sociologically-defined group), and preserves a clear line between the private life and the public sphere. So long as the laws are equally applied to all citizens, individuals can adopt multiple roles. The historian of ideas Sir Isaiah Berlin, who has featured so largely in this book, was a major contributor to this notion of the 'incommensurability of values', although he did not confidently project it into political discourse.[8] Moreover, a highly important distinction needs to be made: pluralism is very distinct from 'multiculturalism', which attempts to reduce the notion of individual identity by grouping citizens into 'communities', giving them stereotyped attributes, and having their (assumed) interests represented outside the normal political structure and processes.

There was (and remains) thus no notion of 'Volk' in the United Kingdom: Britain has historically been a land of immigrants, who assimilate, and intermarry, but keep their beliefs, practices, and cultural choices to themselves. Pluralism implies the coexistence of multiple value systems, so long as none of them tries to destroy the practice of pluralism itself. Admittedly, such principles were not comfortably settled in the 1930s – lacking, for example, were such features as respect for women's rights and tolerance of homosexuality. The established church of Protestantism perhaps loomed larger than was necessary, and a mild form of anti-Semitism was a cultural norm. Yet many Jews (for example) found themselves a home, and, having assimilated, resisted Zionist ambitions that might only serve to marginalise them. While such cultural issues took a back seat to pressing economic matters, and international politics, the structures and traditions of British society were flawed, but both meritorious and enduring, certainly underrated, yet capable of evolution.

When he first came to power, Hitler's energetic steps to address economic problems gained much respect. Before his murderous intentions, and persecution of political opponents and Jews, became well-understood, his moves to address inflationary and unemployment problems (e.g. short-term austerity on benefits, tight regulation of wages and profits, emphasis on agriculture and public works, and national conscription), gained some admirers in Britain, such as with Mosley's New Party – after 1932, the British Union of Fascists. It seemed to many that Germany put Britain's way of 'muddling-through', with multi-party compromises, and negotiations, and accounting for pluralist sensitivities, into the shade. It was as if the horrific goals expressed in *Mein Kampf* were ignored while observers watched Germany's unemployment decrease, and the economy grow. In fact, many leading civil servants and politicians (e.g. Macmillan himself) admitted afterwards that they had not read Hitler's testimony, and thus were ignorant of his aims. A few that had, such as Robert Vansittart, warned of the dangers of Nazism from the Foreign Office (where reading *Mein Kampf* had been made compulsory), but Vansittart became increasingly eccentric and isolated. After all, Germany was a civilised country – one would not expect a rogue like Hitler to last (as many middle-class citizens in both countries assumed), and the members of the Anglo-German Fellowship saw Hitler's ousting of the Communists as a welcome defeat of bolshevism. Thus much 'educated' opinion in Britain in the early 1930s reflected the same bewildered passivity that German democrats themselves expressed as the noose of Nazism gradually tightened. Yet the autocratic methods of Hitler were alien to Britain's democratic traditions, and Mosley and his thugs were soon ridiculed off the scene. The impulses towards appeasement derived more from horror of repeated war and desires for co-existence with Hitler's Germany than from a wish to imitate his regime. As Hitler's imperial ambitions became clearer, and his persecution of Jews more obvious, public opinion in Britain turned rapidly against him.

The struggles of liberal Britain therefore began to be squeezed by the contrasting totalitarian ideologies of Hitler's Nazism and the traditional bogey of Stalin's Communism. Both models abjured multi-party politics, and both claimed their authority from the people's will. Hitler's regime had indeed come to power through a democratic process – something the German people have ever since had to explain – while Stalin's propaganda, extolling a model of democratic centralism, where a clique of CP officers claimed to represent the people's will, even found echo in Western apologists. For not only was Communism on the right side of history (according to the Hegelian/Marxist dialectic), the Soviet Union also was recognised as a 'democratic' power, as Stalin so absurdly boasted when signing the new Soviet constitution in 1938. Such a distasteful oxymoron was later institutionalised by the Israeli historian J. L. Talmon, who published his *Origins of Totalitarian Democracy* in 1952, justifying the totalitarianism of the Left while castigating that of the Right, and implicitly granting Stalin's regime the insignia of democracy.

The last aspect of the clash is one of moral equivalence. Many commentators have suggested that the Communists had an equal right to defend their society as the western democracies had to protect theirs, and that spies who betray their country are all morally guilty, independent of their affiliations (or are even innocent, if they were sincerely working for a superior cause). Such an argument ignores the fact that, while the liberal democracies have gradually evolved their constitutional systems, with the broad approval of their populations, the communist dictatorships came to power with no suffrage, and indeed had to fix elections to ensure their dominance. No apology should be made for the claim that liberal pluralist societies, funded by the profits of private enterprise, were superior to the exploitative and murderous regimes of Communists, and that it should have been a desirable goal to see the latter collapse.

As for the detection of spies, those in the west who were native citizens were quietly retired, and given their pensions, to avoid any embarrassment to the service, while their counterparts in Communist regimes almost inevitably faced a hasty death. Patriotism came in different hues. As Jacques Duclos, General Secretary of the French Communist Party, said in 1949 at a meeting in honour of the 25th anniversary of Lenin's death: "Any man of progress had two homelands, his own and the Soviet Union." The bargain that British traitors made was to replace their own patriotism with that of another country: the Soviet traitors were trying to free their native land from tyranny. While some Soviet defectors (e.g. Krivitsky) still maintained a belief in communism, they recognised that Lenin and Stalin had converted Russia into a monstrous prison-camp. Accordingly, many of these brave individuals thought poorly of the cowardice of their western counterparts. Ismail Akhmedov, who saw at first hand the horrors of Stalin's police state, said of Philby in *In and Out of Stalin's GRU*: "This traitor was never a fighter for the cause. He was, and still is, a sick alcoholic weakling", and Akhmedov contrasted the relatively comfortable choices the Cambridge Five made with the perils the Old Bolsheviks suffered – 'the true champions'. "To completely close the circle he [Philby] will pass into oblivion, into an empty abyss during one of his drunken hours, as did Burgess, and join the company of butchers, henchmen, headhunters – call them what you will – the despised enemies of the unfortunate Soviet people still yearning for their freedom." The causes were not equivalent.

Fascism versus Communism

So why was one variant of totalitarianism seen as superior to the other, and why did British intellectual opinion sympathise with Communism? At one critical stage, in 1937, the Foreign Office, while recognising the immediate danger represented by the military hardware of the Nazis, appeared to accept that Communism was a much more enduring threat than Fascism, as the latter depended upon strong leaders, while with the former such leaders could always be replaced.[9] At a more theoretical and intellectual level, however, the assumed goals of Communism (equality, internationalism, the practical brotherhood of man, an end to 'exploitation', and, of course, 'peace') were perhaps seen as more noble than those of Fascism (national strength, and dominance according to ethnic purity and racial superiority; a 'peace' set on the vanquishing Greater Germany's terms). The creator of fascism, Benito Mussolini, had of course been a socialist beforehand: "We declare war on socialism not because it is socialist but because it had opposed nationalism", he had said.[10] So, while the two doctrines had much in common, Communism seemed more humane, echoing the approved trend towards internationalism as opposed to nationalism. Even though Communism rejected superstition, and claimed to be atheistic, many leading Christians (such as the 'Red Dean', Hewlett Johnson, and the publisher Victor Gollancz) saw parallels between Christ's teaching and the lore of Communism, and brusquely ignored its cruelties and exploitation.

Such a refrain was sometimes echoed by spies as their justification. The Soviet spy George Blake explained his treachery as follows: "The formula, 'From each according to his ability, to each according to his need' defines, to my mind, the only right and just relationship between men, born free and equal into this world. To help build such a society, was this not to help build the Kingdom of God on earth? Was this not the ideal that Christianity for two thousand years had been striving for?"[11] The Communists also won the propaganda war in the universities, with their well-placed moles, and agents of influence like Isaiah Berlin, who helped make the study of Marxism respectable, and gave it a place in the liberal tradition that it did not merit. The Communist 'experiment' was forgiven, or watched with interest: at worst, in the minds of many left-wingers, Lenin and Stalin had distorted and abused the Communist message. Others judged that they had rightfully chosen to dispose of enemies who had challenged their authority. Socialism – now seen as a respectable regimen to be introduced after the war, as if it had been the threat of Nazi invasion that had awakened Britain's conscience – was seen as a humane implementation of Communism's principles.[12] Moreover, politicians in Britain were very concerned about the morale and commitment of those on the factory floor, as well as in the armed forces – especially when the war started – and thus did not want to make any overt moves that might be interpreted as quashing socialist goals, and provoking unrest.

What is noteworthy is that this opinion shift occurred before the Holocaust had begun. In fact, at the time war broke out in September 1939, the volumes of murder by Communism in action were dramatically worse than those of Fascism, with millions of its own citizens killed by the Soviet Union compared to the thousands whom Nazi Germany had exterminated. Between 1933 and 1939, the Nazis killed about 20,000 left-wing opponents, and several hundred Jews were slaughtered at the time of *Kristallnacht*, in November 1938. This was a continuation of the oppression that had started in 1933: 400,000 Jews had fled from Germany by the time war was declared.[13] *Mein Kampf* had crisply communicated Hitler's call for exterminating 'inferior' human beings. On the other hand, since the Bolshevik Revolution the Soviet Union had been responsible for about 20 million deaths, of which nearly 700,000 died in the Great Purge of 1937-1938 alone.[14] As the historian Timothy Snyder has informed us:

"As of the end of 1938, the USSR had killed about a thousand times more people on ethnic grounds than had Nazi Germany. The Soviets had, for that matter, killed far more Jews to that point than had the Nazis. The Jews were targeted in no national action, but they still died in the thousands in the Great Terror – and for that matter during the famine in Soviet Ukraine. They died not because they were Jews, but simply because they were citizens of the most murderous regime of the day."[15]

Both regimes thus murdered groups whom they considered undesirable elements, not fit for the society they were building. The Communists murdered aristocrats, professionals, bourgeois, kulaks, ethnic minorities, dissidents, imaginary counter-revolutionaries - or simply out of sheer terror. The Nazis murdered Jews, mentally defectives, gypsies, Communists, rebels, Slavs, but the *Nacht und Nebel* diktat that precipitated the mass murder of Jews did not happen until December 1941, after the time being discussed by this book. What was highly significant, however, was that the facts of Stalin's famines, purges and executions were not broadly known at the time, whereas the slaughter in Germany was well publicised.

The point to be made is not to minimise the Nazi atrocities, but to attempt an explanation as to why the Soviet Union's barbarity was ignored, or accepted. The main reason is probably one of geographic proximity: Germany was part of Western Europe, and still easily accessible in the 1930s. Many British tourists and travellers of various kinds (e.g. reporters, academics, artists) visited Germany (and Austria, after the annexation), and were able to report first-hand on the oppression and cruelty they witnessed. There was no real language barrier: visitors were able to communicate with ordinary citizens, and learn from such encounters. Moreover, refugees were coming to the United Kingdom in increasing numbers, an estimated 40,000 from Germany, then more from Austria and Czechoslovakia, bringing with them stories of their experiences. Ironically, the Western democracies showed a woeful lack of imagination and justice by accepting the German state's argument that there was a 'Jewish problem' rather than countering that there was, in fact, a serious 'German problem', and in abetting the Jewish exodus they helped to underline the righteousness of the Nazis' campaign to rid their territory of Jews.

The Soviet Union, on the other hand, was remote, closed, enormous, and its horrors largely hidden. Many who witnessed them (such as the famines in Ukraine) suppressed their testimony, or subverted it to the inhuman notion that the Communist 'experiment' required such a process, with lives necessarily sacrificed for some future benefit. Joseph Stalin had written no personal manifesto outlining barbarous goals. The White Russian refugees had left nearly 20 years before. The few tourists who ventured to the Soviet Union had to be approved by the Soviet government: many were Communists die-hards who already had a blinkered idea of the truth. Visits were carefully stage-managed to avoid the obvious signs of hunger and murder. The concentration camps and slave settlements were remote and largely unvisited. Yet it is not true that the casualties of Stalin's programmes were unknown in the West. The Countess of Atholl, for example, in 1931 recorded how, in the campaign to eliminate the kulaks as a class, "out of four or five millions sent to the camps some three million had perished."[16] And many who went there refused the evidence of their eyes (such as the Webbs, G. B. Shaw, and H. G. Wells), and reported falsely on the oppression and poverty. Malcolm Muggeridge was one of the few whose eyes were opened, but others, like Hewlett Johnson and Dennis Pritt, attended the show trials, and applauded them for their fairness and justice. Some returned, conscious of the murder and suffering, but claimed it was all worthwhile in the cause of future happiness and prosperity. Britons had much less empathy with the 'Eurasian' victims of Stalin's Terror, who were by some strange judgment viewed as being criminally responsible in opposing the dictator's plan for a new society.

The final posited argument that supposedly swayed Britain towards Communism was the Comintern's specious claim that Communism was the only effective bulwark against Fascism. Noel Annan wrote that this story developed when David Guest and Humphrey Slater witnessed street fighting provoked by the Nazis in Berlin in 1930, and then spread the news to other intellectuals.[17] Yet the Comintern's claim was manifestly untrue: Hitler had immediately and easily eliminated the Communist Party in Germany when he came to power, and then chased it out of Austria. Stalin then grappled with the issue in his cautious entry into the Spanish Civil War, where he had presented the Soviet Union as the only power to be able to assist the elected Republican government in defeating Franco's variant of nationalism/fascism (assisted by Hitler). But his clumsy methods of using the conflict as a way to enrich the Soviet Union with Spanish gold, as well as to settle old scores against anarchists and Trotskyists, showed his true murderous colours. And of course the Republicans lost. Lastly, Stalin made any claims of wanting to counter Fascism absurd by signing the Nazi-Soviet pact in September 1939, which should have been a clear indication to the liberal democracies that he shared more with Hitler's regime than he did with them, a conclusion that was to be confirmed by the ensuing carve-up of Poland, and Stalin's brutal annexation of the Baltic States in June 1940. It took a high degree of sophistry to sympathise with Stalin in this scenario, but the propaganda machine still worked. The Nazi-Soviet Pact was allowed to take place without any massive ideological campaign against it. Maybe people thought the pact would not last, that Stalin was playing for time, that Hitler would eventually renege on it. Those who should have led public opinion simply did not understand how malevolent Stalin's and the Comintern's objectives were, or simply chose to ignore them. For all the 1930s noise about communism being the spearhead of anti-fascism, it was Great Britain, not the Soviet Union, that eventually declared war on Germany.

Leftist Intellectuals and Tradecraft

This culture of following such fashionable ideas, and ignoring the evidence that their institutional learning should have warned them about, provoked the corrosion that set in. It was not difficult for academics involved with intelligence, like Isaiah Berlin, Hugh Trevor-Roper, and Dick White, to declare, without apology, that they had been leftist sympathisers in the 1930s. The spectrum of leftist opinion-holders ranged from democratic socialists to diehard bolshevists committed to revolution. As with any other spectrum, it was necessary for many reasons to draw the line somewhere. MI5 definitely did not know how to draw such lines. Which members of the Communist Party were committed to the democratic process, and were not seeking a dictatorship of the proletariat unless the CP gained a majority in the House of Commons? Were crypto-Communist politicians (such as Stafford Cripps or Dennis Pritt) outwardly close friends of the Soviet Union, but still patriots dedicated to their own country's security, or were they dangerous and pernicious influences who should be silenced? (When such persons became ministers of the crown, or represented their country abroad as ambassadors, it should have imposed strains on the intelligence officer's equilibrium, and prompted him to remind himself of his mission.) Which 'useful idiots', speaking openly about the virtues of the Communist system, were nothing but irritating windbags, and which were dangerous foreign agents? Should the CP be banned, as its declared goals were contrary to the freedoms implicit in a pluralist democracy? Which ambitious young men and women who had once shown enthusiasm for Communism (perhaps even joining the Party) had succumbed to youthful infatuation but matured out of their revolutionary zeal, and which might be dissembling, and acting traitorously?[18]

Thus the intellectual self-deception was translated into a defective practice of tradecraft. MI5's role was to 'Defend the Realm', to ensure that subversive or hostile elements were not allowed into the corridors of power, or to be employed on projects (such as Tube Alloys) of high sensitivity and confidentiality. This should have demanded a policy, a methodology, a practice that would attempt to exclude potentially dangerous individuals without an undue infringement of personal liberties. Assuredly, every case in principle had to stand on its own merits, but without some framework, some set of guidelines, the task would be not only onerous, but also capricious. Yet MI5 appeared to exercise no consistent policy, the responsibility for execution on the contrary being frequently delegated to whoever happened to be in the role at any particular time, when departmental missions were not clearly defined or differentiated, and communication was apparently lax. Thus individual officers (according to the records that have been made available) made arbitrary decisions, based on their individual experience, and whom else they knew. Information on possible threats was, however, rarely cast-iron: the enemy practised its own tradecraft of deception, and mistakes would obviously be made.

Much of the blame must lie with Guy Liddell, who was temperamentally not strong enough to impose any firm policies upon his organisation. When he applied for the position of replacing Sillitoe as head of MI5 in the summer of 1953, he was rejected in favour of his subordinate, Dick White. According to Christopher Andrew's history, Liddell was rejected because "he is not a good organiser and lacks forcefulness. And doubts have been expressed as to whether he would be successful in dealing with Ministers, with heads of departments and with delegates of other countries."[19] The evidence of Liddell's *Diaries* suggests that the Committee was right. Liddell was very reactive: he did not appear to prepare his team for any eventuality that came along.[20] Thus MI5 was several times wrong-footed, not knowing what to do when unpleasant news came along. Liddell was no doubt intelligent, and sensitive, but he was too absorbed with items of policy far removed from his job of minding the store. Thus he would write at length about activities in the war theatre that were intellectually fascinating, but not really relevant, and the fact that he spent so much time writing his *Diaries* rather than attending to office business is a symptom of that distraction itself. He also did not sell any strong measures outside his department, and while his heart appeared to be in the right place, he was not nearly strict enough about the subversive threat in front of him. He was impressionable, and even gullible. He appeared to lose confidence from some of the sharper minds working for him, such as Serpell and T. A. ('Tar') Robertson, the latter probably resigning in disgust.

It must be said that the problem was not purely MI5's. After the arrest of the spies Dave Springhall (a communist agitator) and Desmond Uren (an officer in the Special Operations Executive) in 1943, Curry tried to defend the organisation in his official history, pointing out that the failure of government departments to frame a consistent reaction to "the threat of the problem caused by the existence of the Communist Party" was the dominant reason why as many as 57 members of the Communist Party were engaged in critical positions in 1942.[21] Yet his claim that "the advice given by the Security Service in such cases was uniform" rings very hollow. He provided no evidence, rather apologetically referring to the "inevitable loopholes" in the vetting system. But a security service is presumably chartered with minimising loopholes, and providing leadership, and, if the evidence from the Fuchs files is representative, it certainly did neither of those things. Curry was very aware, when he produced his work in 1946, of the controversy over Blunt (though of course not aware of his espionage activities), and he himself had persuaded Liddell not to hire Burgess, so he knew that MI5 had not provided a good example to other government departments.

Moreover, MI5 owned a classic dilemma once employment approval had been granted to a potentially risky prospect. If the candidate was turned down, he (or she) might have a grudge, but that particular danger passed. But if a candidate was approved with qualifications ('keep an eye on X'), and became established and productive, some manner of surveillance would have to come into play – an expensive and problematic process. Presumably, after a certain time of innocence, the watch on the target could be dropped – but not for sure. Alternatively, if some evidence that alarmed the watchers arose (as happened with Fuchs), what was the decision to be? Demanding the person be fired, without clear proof of malfeasance, would encounter stern opposition from the employer, probably, and, if the suspect were guilty, immediately send a warning signal to the person's contacts. It was notionally far more attractive to keep a string on the person, in the hope that he (or she) would lead to a network of accomplices, so that a whole group could be dispensed with at the same time. Yet that process required an enormous amount of guile and care not to alert the person being surveilled. That experience should probably have directed MI5 to be more stringent at the time of recruitment.

Yet, as has been shown, the growing leniency towards Communists had started as the 1930s wound down, well before the case of Fuchs, at a time when MI5 seemed to adopt a policy whereby the threat of Communism itself was downgraded. Struggling with the phenomenon of the illegals, MI5 turned its attention to the Communist Party itself, like the proverbial drunkard looking for his keys under the street-lamp, maybe hoping the problem would go away. Even with the warnings of Krivitsky, it could not face the discomforting notion that the

Comintern might already have inserted moles into the offices of state. The reality of war with the Nazis created oversimplified notions of communists as useful allies in the cause against Fascism and towards 'social justice'. Thus, when reputed Communists appeared in the ranks of refugees, MI5 overlooked the fact that they might turn out to be an enduring threat. And as the Cold War took over, MI5 still could not really speak openly about such episodes as the Fuchs case: did MI5 let him through because it never knew he was a dedicated Communist, or did it let him through because it knew he was only a harmless communist?

MI5 (and SIS) struggled with the implications of that last question. It was beyond their capacity for complexity to accept that young men of good breeding like themselves would ever betray their country. Donald Maclean famously told his review board at the Foreign Office that he had not entirely abandoned his leftist beliefs from Cambridge; Vivian Valentine queried Kim Philby's father (before taking him on to head Soviet counter-espionage in SIS) as to his son's juvenile enthusiasm for leftist ideas, and was gratified to hear from St. John Philby that it was all a thing of the past. And the fault extended to the USA even, where the supposed defects of 'class solidarity' that affected the United Kingdom were supposed to have been eradicated. When Roosevelt's economic adviser, Lauchlin Currie, was exposed in 1948 as a Soviet agent by Elizabeth Bentley, her testimony was disbelieved by some. John Rankin, a member of the House UnAmerican Activities Committee, declared that "Currie was a 'Scotchman' and therefore ethnically immune to communism."[22] Thus the belief was spawned, in the late 1930s, that no doubt dangerous communists did exist, but they were all foreigners. Domestic variants of the species must be harmless. Subterfuge was not the practice of gentlemen, as Dick White had pointed out in his scorn for Krivitsky.

Whether it was out of conviction or self-delusion, or simply a desire to delude others, White's statement to the Attorney-General, Sir Hartley Shawcross in 1950, that, since Klaus Fuchs had never been a member of the CPGB, it was unreasonable to have expected MI5 to have identified him as a possible risk, is emblematic of MI5's confusion. At this time, of course, White must have been regretting his wartime indulgences, but his ingenuous claim was allowed to pass by unopposed. Moreover, Prime Minister Clement Attlee, in March 1948, had decided, in light of the communist scares arising from the Gouzenko affair, to initiate a 'Purge Procedure' that would remove all communists (and fascists) from positions in the government where state security was at stake.[23] White and Liddell, with their public record of hiring communists in the Security Service, and approving their recruitment in other government departments, must have been mortified.

It was thus MI5's cardinal error to conclude not just that cultured Britons could not conceivably develop as agents of a foreign power, but also that not all Communists were inherently dangerous. The failure to recognise that a commitment to Communism, however veiled, was effectively a call for a bloodthirsty revolution, in which educated, emancipated persons like themselves would be the first to be eliminated or sent to the death-camps, allowed them to accept as allies a whole brood of undesirable characters who did not have the nation's interests at heart. Communism was not democratic, or pluralist. To deny such persons a role in government, or a job in intelligence, was not censorship or unlawful discrimination, but a valid security policy (as Attlee later articulated). If such characters openly worked against the principles of liberal democracy, there was no reason why their voice or career should be subsidised, and their viewpoints encouraged. Yet MI5 (and SIS) made the calamitous mistake of identifying such persons (most notoriously in MI5, Anthony Blunt) because they had assessed that intellectual Marxists like him posed no threat, and could be used in the war against the Nazis. Moreover, White and Liddell allowed their more congenial nature to dominate in their choice of social companion, resulting in their mixing with characters who were known for having spotty reputations, and dubious pasts. Burgess's highly familiar letters to Liddell over the former's indiscretions in Tangier, and Liddell's' too indulgent response, are a symptom of the officers' lack of discipline and objectivity.[24]

MI5 had for 20 years had a mission of protecting the country against Bolshevik revolution. Yet it did not need a so-called 'super-mole', planted by the Soviets, to undermine this task. It is impossible to pinpoint an exact moment or act that defines when its resolve weakened, but the trend of appeasement seems to coincide with the recruitment of its first graduate, Dick White. Overly influenced by the intellectual climate at Oxford, he was able to change the cultural climate in the Security Service to think differently about the nature of Communism. This was not an act of sabotage, but it evolved to be more than a change in culture: it effectively let MI5's guard down, so that Communism, instead of representing an existential threat, became a movement for social reform to be tolerated and even encouraged. For several calamitous years, MI5 languished with this delusion, until the harsh realities of the Cold War forced its leading officers to reassess their approach.

What should have been done? Overall, MI5 should have displayed a much more steely determination, and a strong voice to other government departments, about the perennial danger, instead of leading by poor example. If it had had the resolve to heed Krivitsky's warnings that Communist agents had been recruited from the universities, and to protect itself from such subversion, how might it have done it? Since Moscow was very particular about the commitment of its spies – and their couriers as well – candidates would have had to show a fierce dedication to Communist principles and rigour before they were recruited. But this did not have to involve membership of the Communist Party: in fact it was preferable if the agents were *never* associated with the CP, as it made them less traceable. It is nevertheless a fact that each agent must have undergone a period when he (or she) – Blunt, Burgess, Philby, Cairncross, Maclean, Long, etc. etc. – *demonstrated openly* strong leftist sympathies before their recruitment was approved by Moscow Centre. Thus even a casual inspection of such characters by MI5 would have alerted the organisation that they were a security risk. In 1935, Conservative Central Office told the BBC that it had rejected Burgess for employment as he had been a Communist, but MI5 either did not hear about this (negligence) or did not think it important (a catastrophic failure of policy.)

Moreover, the spies were not 'lone wolves'. Apart from Cairncross, who was something of an odd man out, they had close social and educational links which might have led from one to the other – a process of investigation that did eventually take place. That MI5 even subverted such a strategy of caution by its infamous decision to recruit Anthony Blunt is testimony to how far it had moved to the Left in this period. This culture of tolerance and encouragement of leftist intellectuals in a domain that demanded more rigorous mental attitudes is what infuriated disciplined intelligence experts like Gubbins, Clarke, Wild and Mure, who called for greater accountability of Intelligence, preferably to the military. For example, the intelligence officer Colonel Noël Wild wrote: "What is required is men of sound character and background. MI5 to my certain knowledge contained at one time policemen, dons, teachers, lawyers and even (admittedly through ill-health) a tea-planter. The latter became Director General. Before aspiring to such distinction he once assured me 'there will never be a threat from Communism in this country'. Brave words from Sir Roger Hollis!"[25] Yet the balancing argument was that the heritage of SOE, after its assimilation by SIS after the war, resulted in a series of rash, adventurous, and militarist intelligence exercises that lost hundreds of lives without making any impact on overthrowing Communism or gaining useful intelligence. Towards Communism MI5 was soft, indulgent, and appeasing; SIS was impulsive, reckless, and provocative. The need for serious and pragmatic intelligence skills in both MI5 and SIS, without either over-conciliatory appeasement or ebullient militarism, and a tight process of oversight over the two organisations by the Joint Intelligence Committee, was never more clear.

The other side of the coin is that many decent public servants might have been excluded from such a process. After all, many such persons did have flirtations with the CP in the 1930s, which turned out to be merely flings, not deep infatuations that had to be concealed later. The Labour politician Dennis Healey was one notorious example whose membership lasted a lot longer than an undergraduate affair. He joined the CP in 1937, but stayed there for a few years, seeing out the Nazi-Soviet pact, and not resigning until after the fall of France in 1940. ('Why then?' one might ask.) He was still orating about 'revolution' after the war, yet turned out to be a respectable middle-of-the-road politician. (Some observers have hinted that Healey was actually employed by MI6 all this time, which might just be plausible, although the cover seems to have been taken a bit too far.) And then, on the other hand, there is the famed Sovietologist, and fierce opponent of Communism, Robert Conquest, whose *Great Terror*, exposing the horrors of Stalin's slave-state, influenced many in the 1970s, including this writer. Conquest joined the CP at Oxford in the 1930s. Was his flirtation just a youthful fling, after which he became disillusioned? Probably so, as he was hired by SIS, and sent to Bulgaria. But how did SIS know it was just a fling? Or had he joined the CP with MI6 guidance? That would appear unlikely, as his cover would then have been blown for any undercover intelligence operation overseas. It all just shows what a careful methodology has to be applied by counter-intelligence officers trying to determine a suspect's – or a potential recruit's – true beliefs and motivations.

Counter-intelligence in a free society comes across all manner of challenges, especially from those protecting individual rights. That is as true in 2017 as it was in 1940. Yet there remain significant differences between the two eras and the two threats: Communist subversion and Islamo-fascist terrorism. While the large-scale threat of Bolshevik revolution was the strategic menace that the security service had to protect against, individual agents (in Britain, at any rate) were not committed to terrorist activity. (The one exception may be Harold Laski, who succeeded in planting an explosive device at Oxted Station in Surrey.) Their goals were to weaken gradually the democratic structures and will of the United Kingdom to remove a class enemy of the Soviet Union, and facilitate world revolution. As atheists, they did not believe that an afterlife would reward them for creating havoc and mayhem, and committing murder. They belonged to a group whose intellectual sympathies were consistent, but, unless they were caught in the act of stealing or passing on secrets, it was difficult to apprehend them, and lock them away. The menace was so insidiously implanting itself that it was hardly noticeable.

Sir Richard Dearlove, former head of SIS, was recently quoted as saying: "During the Cold War we lived reasonably comfortably with communist parties in our midst, who, if you analysed the logic of their position, would be fundamentally opposed to the value of our democratic society. There was the problem of subversion from within, but we didn't treat it as a problem to be legislated against." [26] That is an alarming admission, for it echoes the 1940 policy of MI5 that the main threat was within the official Communist Party, whereas, as we now know, the betrayers of secrets lay *outside* the CP apparatus. Dearlove's main message, however, was to declare that the cure for extremism today can only be found within Britain's Muslim communities, making it a "cultural and social issue more than a legal issue". That again is an abdication of the real problem. In a pluralist society, there should not be separately recognised 'communities' that are outside the reach of the normal democratic and legal mechanisms. What is more, the message of condoning multiculturalism rather than encouraging pluralism sends an erroneous signal to the members of such 'communities' that their practices and traditions are somehow beyond the scope of a society that makes no distinctions as to how private citizens should pursue their own interest, religions, etc., so long as they are not contrary to the law of the land. Such a policy is divisive, and creates false and unnecessary stereotypes.

There was no such entity as 'the communist community' in 1940. Protecting against subversion may have to follow group patterns of behaviour, but it was – and remains – essentially a task of old-fashioned detective work. The graduate who belonged to the university socialist club may have had similar characteristics to the jihadist who searches for like minds on Facebook – a desire to seek others like him, who will help him in his nefarious goals. At some stage, the police force may have to make a decision to apprehend such a person, based on solid intelligence, before any vile deed has been accomplished. The intention may not be provable, and some comparatively innocent citizens may be imprisoned so that they may perform no more harm. In 1940, MI5, however misguided about the nature of Communism, did not face the prospect of mass murder in the streets of the nation's cities. Sadly, the problem in 2017 concerns a terrorist threat that shows scant concern for taking innocent life in a brutal and immediate fashion. There is no Jihadist Party to ban, but relegating the problem to self-appointed 'leaders' of ghettoised 'communities' is not the answer either. Such figures may be the source of the problem, as the government of Tunisia is finding as it attempts to clean up its mosques of violent influences.

In summary, politicians in the 1930s misidentified the ideological clash as 'capitalism versus communism' when it was in effect 'liberal pluralism versus totalitarianism'. MI5 made serious mistakes in not identifying the enemy clearly, and even embracing some of its principles, thus showing intellectual flabbiness and a lack of discipline. Similarly, in 2017 the struggle does not concern 'Christendom versus Islamism', but 'liberal pluralism versus Islamo-fascism': again the putative champions of liberal pluralism do not appear to have the confidence the principle deserves, and have been influenced unduly by the intellectual chorus of 'multiculturalism'. One cannot deny the influence of the 'Judaeo-Christian' heritage on British and other European societies, but that does not mean it has an exclusive ownership of popular sentiment, belief and habit. Several commentators, including T. S. Eliot and Arthur Koestler, have suggested that Protestantism is perhaps the only religious creed that allows a healthy divergence of beliefs within the environment it dominates. Hugh Trevor-Roper offered a similar agnostic thought: "In fact, I support the poor old C of E, of which I am a member (Like Garrod, I am an Anglican, not a Christian), because it does (except where perverted) support civil liberty; it has (if we except some high-church nonsense and some low-church vulgarity) a certain constitutional relation to common sense; and its sound relation to civil power is some guarantee against extravagant pretensions."[27]

By now Britain has developed more universal democratic structures, and has learned how to assimilate immigrants with unfamiliar habits and beliefs. While embracing such persons into full citizenship, it needs to reinforce strongly the notion of a common set of laws that apply to everyone, to make clear distinctions between the private, individual world and the public one, and not to divide society into artificial 'communities' that bypass the traditional mechanisms of political representation and the policy of equality before the law. And in that framework the increasingly difficult domestic task of surveillance, detection and interception must carry on, while the Western democracies grapple with the extremely challenging task of dealing with the evolution of a murderous caliphate abroad, and determining to what extent that threat is an existential one, as were the menaces of the 1930s. While pluralist liberal democracy has evolved in the past 70 years, it is just as worth defending and preserving as it was then: the identity of the threat to it is different, but it bears the same totalitarian characteristics of Fascism and Communism, complemented by a messianic view of religion.

Notes

[1] The challenge of SIS might be described as 'How to gain useful intelligence without causing a diplomatic rumpus'. In a poorly designed and executed mission, Crabb was engaged to inspect the hull of the SS *Ordzhonikidze* during the visit of the Soviet leaders Bulganin and Khrushchev. Crabb's headless body was discovered in Portsmouth Harbour, weeks later.

[2] Paddy Hayes, *Queen of Spies* (a biography of SIS's first female officer, Daphne Park), p 120.

[3] Percy Cradock, *Know Your Enemy*, pp 25-29.

[4] Isaiah Berlin, *Letters 1928-1946*. Letter to Elisabeth Morrow, April 4, 1945.

[5] George Orwell, *The Lion and the Unicorn*, February 19, 1941.

[6] For example: "Eden said, word for word: 'At the present moment, no conflict exists between Great Britain and the USSR anywhere in the world. On the contrary, they have one common and highly important interest – the preservation of peace. You need peace to complete your great experiment, and need it for the development and flourishing of trade. This creates favourable conditions for improving Anglo-Soviet relations'." (*The Maisky Diaries*, edited by Gabriel Gorodetsky, p 17). This statement was made as early as November 1934: it is in keeping with Eden's (and the Foreign Office's) rather benign attitude to the Soviet regime, and reflects an alarming naivety on Eden's part about the real manifestations of Stalin's 'experiment' with human lives.

[7] Harold Nicolson, *The Diaries and Letters of Harold Nicolson*, (Volume II), (entry of January 22, 1941).

[8] see Henry Hardy at http://berlin.wolf.ox.ac.uk/writings_on_ib/hhonib/isaiah_berlin's_key_idea.html.

[9] Lammers, *Fascism, Communism and the Foreign Office, 1937-39*, Journal of Contemporary History, Vol 6, No. 3, (1971), pp 66-86, cited by Purvis and Hulbert in *Guy Burgess, the Spy Who Knew Everyone*, p 85.

[10] Cited by John Whittam in *Mussolini*, from *Telling Lives*, edited by Alistair Horne.

[11] Thomas Grant, *Jeremy Hutchinson's Case Histories*, p 52.

[12] An extraordinary aspect of the justification by intellectuals – mainly in the USA, but also in the UK – of the behaviour of the spies was shown when the VENONA decrypts were released, and the Soviet archives briefly opened. Now no longer able to deny that figures such as Hiss, Currie and Dexter White had been spies, several pro-Communist academics now declared that their sincerity and internationalist commitment to building the workers' paradise eliminated any guilt that should be directed to them. See John Earl Haynes and Harvey Klehr, *In Denial: Historians, Communism & Espionage*, Chapter 10.

[13] Richard J. Evans, *The Third Reich in Power*, p 599.

[14] See, for example, Stéphane Courtois, Introduction to *The Black Book of Communism*.

[15] Timothy Snyder, *Bloodlands*, Chapter 3.

[16] The Countess of Atholl, *The Conscription of a People*, p 72.

[17] Noel Annan's *Our Age*, pp 180-183, contains an analysis of the attractions of Communism for intellectuals in the 1930s. It does not discuss the horrors of Communism in practice.

[18] The political commentator, Edward Lucas recently wrote about recruitment to intelligence services: "For applications from Western Europe, such political activity [*former membership of the Communist Party*], except possibly as a temporary student affectation, would have been an instant bar" (*Deception*, p 293). But he does not explain how a recruiter can determine whether the affiliation was merely an affectation.

[19] Christopher Andrew, *The Defence of the Realm*, p 325.

[20] A story picked up by several commentators is that Liddell's failure to be appointed to the Director-General job was due to the intervention of Ellen Wilkinson, the mistress of the Home Secretary, Herbert Morrison. She allegedly told Morrison that Liddell was a double-agent. The source of this story may be David Mure's *The Last Temptation*, p 100, but, given Wilkinson's track record, one might imagine that she would have welcomed that role for a fellow-traveller who had shown such excellent skills in subterfuge.

[21] John Curry, *The Security Service 1908-1945*, p 355.

[22] John Earl Haynes and Harvey Klehr, *Venona: Decoding Soviet Espionage in America*, p 150.

[23] Andrew, p 383.

[24] Stewart Purvis and Jeff Hulbert, *Guy Burgess: The Spy Who Knew Everyone*, p 214.

[25] Noel Wild, in Foreword to David Mure's *Master of Deception*, p 12.

[26] Interview in *Prospect* magazine, September 2015.

[27] Hugh Trevor-Roper, *Wartime Journals*, May 1944.

Appendix: Affinity Charts

1) Politicians and Society

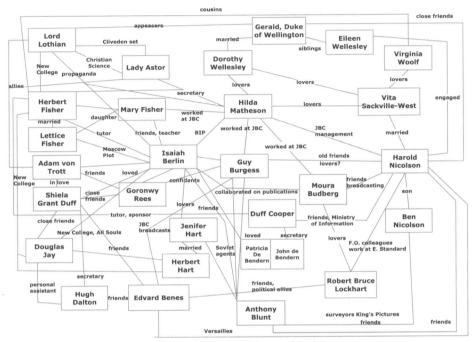

Affinity Chart 1: Politicians and Society

2) Spies, Fellow-travellers and Others

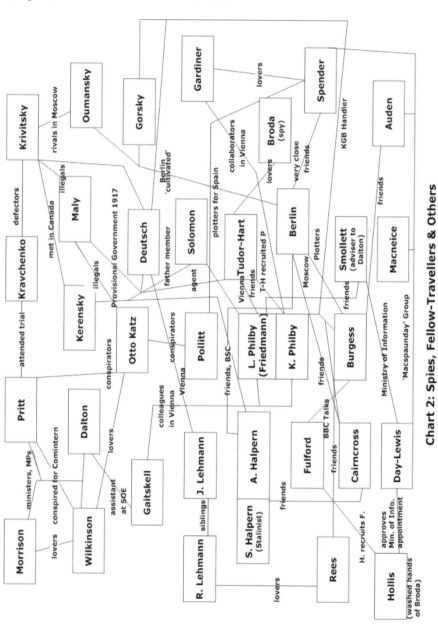

Chart 2: Spies, Fellow-Travellers & Others

3) Physicists and Spies

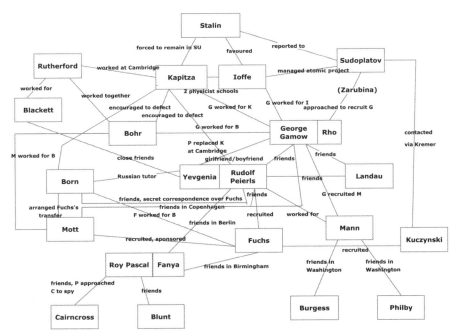

Affinity Chart 3: Physicists and Spies

Biographical Index

This index concentrates on the salient facts of the careers of significant persons appearing in the book, primarily as they relate to the story, i.e. the counter-espionage efforts of MI5 leading up to Barbarossa, and the investigation of Klaus Fuchs in the late 1940s. The full achievements, titles, ranks and awards of individuals are *not* given, unless (as in the case of some UK titles) they resulted in a change of name by which such figures were frequently identified (e.g. Lord Swinton). If no nationality is given, the subject is British by birth. Otherwise, citizenship by birth is stated, although with the fluid concept of nationhood in Central and Eastern Europe in the early part of this century, such identities are often debatable. A distinction is made between 'Soviet' figures (who were part of the government apparatus), and 'Russians' who were either born before the revolution, or who could be classified as 'dissidents', unsupportive of the regime. Members or recruits of the Soviet intelligence organisations who handled spies are classified as 'officers', '*rezidents*', or 'illegals', while their operatives who actually carried out espionage are identified as 'spies'. British intelligence personnel are generally 'officers', while they employed 'agents' to perform domestic spying (within the CPGB, for example). US intelligence officers are identified as 'agents'.

Agabekov, Georges (1896-1937), Soviet OGPU officer and the first major defector. Agabekov fell in love with Isabel Streater, and defected in 1930. He was killed by Soviet agents in 1937.

Akers-Douglas, Aretas, 2nd Viscount Chilston (1879-1947), diplomat. Akers-Douglas was Ambassador to the Soviet Union from 1933 to 1938.

Akhmatova, Anna (1886-1966), Russian poet who engaged Stalin's wrath, especially when Isaiah Berlin visited her in 1945.

Akhmedov, Ismail (1904-?), Soviet military intelligence officer and defector. Akhmedov was interrogated by Philby in Turkey, and excoriated him in his memoir *In and Out of Stalin's GRU*.

Anderson, John, 1st Viscount Waverley (1882-1958), civil servant and politician. Anderson was Home Secretary from the outbreak of WWII until October 1940 (thus during the period of the 'Fifth Column' scare), and then Lord President of the Council and Chancellor of the Exchequer in Churchill's wartime coalition.

Annan, Noel (1916-2000), academic and intelligence officer. Annan was a member of the Apostles while at King's College, Cambridge, and, after working with Leo Long in MI14 during WWII, joined the Joint Intelligence Staff.

Appleton, Edward (1892-1965), physicist. Appleton headed the Department of Scientific and Industrial Research, responsible for atomic energy and weaponry research, from 1939.

Archer, Jane (Kathleen, née Sissmore) (1898-1982: m. 1939 John Archer), MI5 officer. Archer was MI5's leading expert on Soviet subversion and espionage in MI5 when she attended the interrogations of Walter Krivitsky, and wrote a report on the process. Effectively replaced by Roger Hollis, she was abruptly fired for insubordination in 1940, resurfacing in SIS, where she impressed Kim Philby.

Archer, John (1887-1968), MI5 officer. Archer was liaison officer between the Air Ministry and MI5, heading section 'D3'. He married Jane Sissmore in September 1940.

Auden, Wystan Hugh (1907-1973), poet. Auden went through an influential Communist phase in the early 1930s. He left the UK for the USA with Christopher Isherwood, before WWII broke out.

Ayer, Alfred Jules ('Freddie') (1910-1989), philosopher and intelligence officer. Colleague of Isaiah Berlin, and admirer of his book on Karl Marx, Ayer has been named by Nigel West as a member of the 'Oxford Ring' of Soviet spies.

Bagot, Milicent (1907-2006), MI5 officer. Bagot rose from the rank of secretary to senior MI5 officer, and was notable for her knowledge, and doggedness in identifying anomalies in stories of potential Communist threats.

Ball, Joseph (1885-1964), lawyer, politician and intelligence officer. After a shady career as fixer for Chamberlain and the Conservative Party, Ball was in May 1940 appointed Vice-Chairman of the Security Executive, a role that he denied when preparing to sue Goronwy Rees in 1964 over his association with Guy Burgess.

Belfrage, Cedric (1904-1990), intelligence officer and Soviet spy. Educated at Gresham's School, Holt (the alma mater of several communist spies), during WWII Belfrage worked for British Security Coordination in New York.

Ben-Gurion, David (1886-1973), politician and founder of Israel. In 1940, Ben-Gurion, as a Zionist leader, met Isaiah Berlin in New York to discuss Soviet help for the cause.

Beneš, Edvard (1884-1948), Czech politician. Beneš collaborated with Stalin by passing on rumours of Soviet generals' disloyalty originating from the Germans, and during WWII transmitted secrets from London to Moscow.

Bentley, Elizabeth (1908-1963), US Soviet spy. Bentley's defection in 1945, and subsequent confessions to the FBI, helped identify dozens of Soviet spies in the US administration.

Beria, Lavrentiy (1899-1953), Soviet politician and secret policeman. In 1938, Beria took over from Yezhov as Minister of Internal Affairs of the Soviet Union, and was responsible for the Soviet atomic bomb project. He was executed shortly after Stalin's death.

Berlin, Isaiah (1909-1997), Latvian/Russian-born historian of philosophy and intelligence officer. Berlin's friendship with Guy Burgess, and their planned visit to the Soviet Union in 1940, when employed by Section D of SIS, represented an aspect of his double life that he tried to conceal. For a period in the 1940s he was the lover of the Soviet spy, Jenifer Hart.

Bernal, John Desmond (1901-1971), scientist. A dedicated Stalinist, Bernal managed to overcome objections to his recruitment by the Ministry of Home Security in 1939, and contributed substantially to the war effort.

Beurton, Leon Charles (Len) (1914-1997), Soviet agent. A veteran of the International Brigades, Beurton was recruited by Ursula Hamburger in Switzerland, and married her so that she could gain British citizenship, and thus gain re-entry to the United Kingdom, in January 1941. He followed her there, with the assistance of SIS officers in Switzerland, in July 1942.

Bevin, Ernest (1881-1951), politician. Bevin was a left-wing but anti-communist Minister of Labour and National Service in Churchill's coalition government, and Foreign Secretary in Attlee's post-war administration.

Blake (né Behar), George (b. 1922), British intelligence officer and Soviet spy. Blake was a Dutch-Egyptian-Jewish citizen who was recruited by SIS in 1944, but became a double-agent after being captured in Korea. After a posting in Berlin, he confessed to his SIS interrogators in 1961.

Bland, George Nevile Maltby (1886-1972), diplomat. Bland, as Envoy Extraordinary to the Netherlands, had escaped before the Nazi invasion in 1940, and was responsible for an alarmist report on the Fifth Column when he returned to the UK.

Blunt, Anthony (1907-1983), art historian, intelligence agent, and Soviet spy. Blunt used his connections to confirm his appointment to Military Intelligence, and was then recruited, with Victor Rothschild's help, by MI5 in 1940, where he soon became Liddell's personal assistant.

Bohr, Niels (1885-1962), Danish physicist. Bohr was a refugee from the Nazis who in 1943 escaped to London to join the Tube Alloys project, but was wooed by the Soviets to work for them.

Born, Max (1882-1970), German physicist. Born emigrated to the UK in 1933, mentored Klaus Fuchs at Edinburgh University, and with Rudolf Peierls, helped to gain Fuchs's release from internment.

Bracken, Brendan (1901-1958), politician. Bracken was a long-time supporter of Churchill, and took over from Duff Cooper as Minister of Information in July 1941.

Broda, Engelbert (1910-1983), Austrian-born chemist and physicist, and Soviet spy. Broda escaped to the UK in 1938, and worked at the Cavendish Laboratory on radioactivity and nuclear fission from 1941.

Brooman-White, Richard (1912-1964), politician and intelligence officer. Brooman-White joined MI5 in 1940 to deal with Spanish espionage. In 1943, he moved to SIS.

Browder, Earl (1891-1973), US political activist and leader of CPUSA. In 1928, Browder went to China with his girl-friend Kitty Harris: he was convicted of passport fraud at the outbreak of WWII, and later jailed.

Brown, Isabel (1894-1984), teacher and activist. Brown was a founder of the Communist Party of Great Britain, and was active in helping European Communists enter Britain to foment sedition.

Budberg, Moura (1891-1974), Russian-born double-agent for OGPU and British intelligence. Budberg deceptively consorted with Bruce Lockhart, Maxim Gorky, and H. G. Wells, whose marriage offer she turned down.

Burgess, Guy (1911-1963), broadcaster, diplomat and Soviet spy. Burgess was working for SIS's Section D at the onset of WWII, and successfully used his cover of disreputableness, and his connections, to spearhead the successful response to Krivitsky's 1940 warnings about Communist infiltration of Britain's corridors of power. He accompanied Isaiah Berlin on a mission to Moscow in July 1940, but was suddenly recalled.

Burgess, Nigel (1913-?), MI5 officer. Nigel was the brother of Guy, and his wife, Constance, helped him to gain employment working for Roger Hollis in 'F4'.

Butler, Richard Austen (1902-1982), politician. Butler was Under-Secretary of State for Foreign Affairs from February 1938 to July 1941, and had an uncomfortable role in Churchill's deceptions over the appeasers.

Bystrolyotov, Dmitry (1901-1975), Soviet illegal. Bystrolyotov, a colleague of Krivitsky, handled the British spy Ernest Oldham. On his recall to the Soviet Union in 1937, he was fortunate not to be executed, and survived the Gulag.

Cadogan, Alexander (1884-1968), civil servant and diplomat. Cadogan was Permanent Under-Secretary of State for Foreign Affairs from 1938 to 1946, and thus at the centre of political and military debate. He wrote a very revealing and informative diary.

Cairncross, John (1913-1995), civil servant, intelligence officer, and Soviet spy. Cairncross has been named the 'Fifth Man' of the Cambridge Five. He was recruited in April 1937 by the NKVD when working in the Foreign Office. He transferred to the Treasury, and in April 1939 became Maurice Hankey's secretary. He betrayed secrets from both ministerial offices, as well as from the Government Code and Cypher School (Bletchley Park), and SIS.

Cecil, Robert (1913-1994), diplomat and intelligence officer. Cecil was First Secretary at the British Embassy in Washington in 1949, and wrote a biography of Donald Maclean, *A Divided Life*.

Chadwick, James (1891-1974), physicist. Chadwick worked at the University of Liverpool, in 1940 was invited to join the MAUD committee on atomic weaponry, and drafted its final report in the autumn of 1941.

Chamberlain, Neville (1869-1940), politician. Chamberlain was Prime Minister from May 1937 to May 1940, when he was replaced by Churchill after the failure of the Norway adventure. While Chamberlain knew that re-armament would have to take place before Hitler could be seriously challenged, he failed to recognise the true threat in his desire for avoiding war.

Chambers, Whittaker (1901-1961), American writer and Soviet spy. After the Nazi-Soviet pact in 1939, Chambers went with Isaac Don Levine to Assistant Secretary of State Adolf Berle to denounce other spies, but his warnings were ignored.

Churchill, Winston (1874-1965), politician. Churchill was appointed First Lord of The Admiralty when WWII broke out, and his coalition government replaced Chamberlain's administration in May 1940. His challenge was to stave off Hitler until the time when the USSR and the USA could become allies against Nazism.

Clark Kerr, Archibald, 1st Baron Inverchapel (1882-1951), diplomat. Clark Kerr was Ambassador to the Soviet Union from 1942 to 1946, and to the USA from 1946 to 1948. He built a good – but perhaps too close – relationship with Stalin while in Moscow. He assisted in Isaiah Berlin's visa application to the Soviet Union after WWII.

Clarke, Dudley (1899-1974), Army and intelligence officer. Clarke was a key figure in military deception operations, and believed they needed to be tightly integrated with military strategy (unlike the manner in which MI5's Double-Cross system operated).

Cookridge, E. H. (né Philo) (1908-1979), Austrian-born author, broadcaster, and intelligence officer. Cookridge was a journalist in Vienna in 1933-34 when he witnessed Philby's communist activities. He served in British Army intelligence during WWII.

Cooper, Alfred Duff, 1st Viscount Norwich (1890-1954), author, politician and diplomat. The anti-appeaser Cooper was appointed First Lord of the Admiralty in 1937, but resigned after the Munich Agreement. He was made Minister of Information in Churchill's coalition government.

Coplon, Judith (1921-2001), US Soviet spy. Coplon was convicted on counts of espionage (1949) and conspiracy (1950), but her convictions were overturned on procedural grounds.

Cot, Pierre (1895-1977), French politician and Soviet spy. Cot, an overt Communist, was French Air Minister, then Commerce Minister. Known to Krivitsky (but not identified by him), he spied for the Soviet Union in the USA during WWII.

Cripps, Stafford (1889-1952), lawyer and politician. Cripps was a Communist sympathiser whom Churchill appointed as Ambassador to the Soviet Union in May 1940, where he strenuously articulated the interests of Stalin to His Majesty's Government rather than vice versa. He supported the Soviet invasion of Finland in November 1939, and the annexation of Bessarabia in June 1940. He leaked information to the spy Robert Kuczynski.

Crocker, William (1886-1973), lawyer. Personal lawyer to Joseph Ball, Crocker was a member of the 1940 Security Executive, introduced to 'sort out' MI5's 'B' (Counter-Espionage) Division.

Cunliffe-Lister, Philip, 1st Earl of Swinton (1884-1972), politician. Swinton had been Secretary of State for Air from 1935 to 1938. Churchill brought him in as chairman of the Security Executive in May 1940, with the prime mission of addressing the 'Fifth Column' threat.

Currie, Lauchlin (1902-1993), Canadian-born economist, adviser to Roosevelt, and Soviet agent. An adviser to Roosevelt throughout WWII. Currie was named by Chambers and Bentley, and his guilt established by VENONA transcripts.

Curry, John (1887-?), intelligence officer. Curry worked for MI5 and SIS, and wrote an internal history of MI5 after the war, not published until 1999. He was a solid opponent of communists, but lacked the authority and personality to have much influence on policy.

Daladier, Édouard (1884-1970), French politician. Daladier was Prime Minster of France from April 1938 to March 1940. He was a vigorous opponent of Fascism and Communism, but could not orchestrate an effective resistance, being replaced by Paul Reynaud.

Dalton, Hugh (1887-1962), politician. A Labour Party economist, Dalton became Minister of Economic Warfare in Churchill's 1940 administration, and manoeuvred successfully to own and launch the Special Operations Executive, but was replaced by Lord Selborne in February 1942.

Dansey, Claude (1876-1947), Army and intelligence officer. In the mid-1930s, Dansey created the shadow Z organisation, which maintained a group of spies in Europe outside SIS. He may have recruited Alexander Foote as a way of penetrating Soviet spy-rings. During WWII he competed with Vivian Valentine as deputy to Menzies in SIS.

Davies, Joseph (1876-1958), US lawyer and diplomat. Davies had served as US Ambassador to the Soviet Union from 1936 to 1938, and was taken in by Stalin's show trials. He acted as adviser to Secretary of State, Cordell Hull, at the beginning of WWII.

Dawson, Geoffrey (1874-1944), newspaper editor. Dawson was a member of the Anglo-German Fellowship, and a Fellow of All Souls, and promoted a policy of appeasement when editor of the *Times*.

Day-Lewis, Cecil (1904-1972), Anglo-Irish poet. Day-Lewis was a member of the Communist Party from 1936 to 1938, but in April 1940 was employed by the Ministry of Information with MI5's (Roger Hollis's) approval.

Deutsch, Arnold (1903-1942), Austro-Hungarian Soviet illegal. One of the claimants to the recruitment of Kim Philby, Deutsch managed the Cambridge spy ring from 1933 to 1937. He avoided execution on his recall to Moscow, but died in a sinking by a U-boat in 1942.

Dimitrov, Georgi (1882-1949), Bulgarian Communist. Arrested for complicity in the Reichstag fire of 1933, Dimitrov was leader of the Comintern from 1935 to 1943, and carried on after its supposed dismantling thereafter.

Dobb, Maurice (1900-1976), Marxist economist and academic. As a Communist Party member, and lecturer at Trinity College, Cambridge, Dobb exerted a strong influence on undergraduates, and recruited Kim Philby (and others) to the Communist movement.

Driberg, Tom (1905-1976), journalist and politician. Driberg was a close friend of Guy Burgess, and, while acting as an agent for MI5 inside the Communist Party, may also have been a Soviet spy.

Drummond, James Eric, 7th Earl of Perth (1876-1951), politician and diplomat. A fascist sympathiser, Drummond resigned from ambassadorship to Italy in 1939, and was controversially appointed Minister of Information by Chamberlain. He was soon demoted, and fired in July 1940.

Duclos, Jacques, (1896-1975), French Communist politician. The Stalinist Duclos tried to negotiate with the Nazis for the legalisation of the French Communist Party after the fall of France in 1940.

Eden, Anthony, 1st Earl of Avon (1897-1977), politician. Eden resigned as Foreign Secretary in 1938 as a protest against Chamberlain's policy to Italy. Churchill appointed him Secretary of State for War in May 1940, and for Foreign Affairs in December of that year.

Eitingon, Naum (aka Leonid) (1899-1981), Soviet intelligence officer. Eitingon had set up the 'illegals' program' in 1933, and was Guy Burgess's contact in Paris in 1938. He arranged the murder of Leon Trotsky in Mexico in 1940.

Ewer, William (1885-1977), journalist and spy. Ewer was an early recruit of the Comintern, and a friend of Churchill's relative, Diane Sheridan. MI5 decided not to prosecute him in 1929.

Eytan (né Ettinghausen), Walter, (1910-2001), German-born intelligence officer. A contemporary of Isaiah Berlin at St. Paul's School and Oxford, Eytan was recruited by the Government Code and Cypher School. After WWII he emigrated to Israel, and became a diplomat.

Fischer-Williams, Jenifer (see Hart, Jenifer)

Fisher, H. A. L. (1865-1940), historian and politician. Fellow and warden of New College, Oxford, who mentored and influenced Isaiah Berlin. He married the economist Lettice Ilbert.

Fisher, Warren (1979-1948), civil servant. Fisher was head of the Home Civil Service from 1919 to 1939, and had been chairman of the Secret Service Committee.

Fitin, Pavel (1907-1971), Soviet intelligence officer. Fitin became head of Soviet Foreign Intelligence (the NKVD) in 1939, and controlled the network of spies on the Manhattan Project, which he named '*Enormoz*'.

Floud, Bernard (1915-1967), politician and Soviet spy. Educated at Gresham's School, Holt, and Oxford University, Floud was a member of the Oxford spy 'ring', and recruited Jenifer Hart to the cause. He committed suicide after being interrogated by MI5.

Foote, Alexander (1905-1956), Soviet spy and possible SIS agent. Dave Springhall recruited Foote to Soviet Military Intelligence in Spain in 1937. In early 1939, Foote was recruited by Ursula Hamburger (née Kuczynski, aka 'Sonia') into the 'Lucy Ring' as a radio operator, and passed information to Moscow. His enigmatic defection from the Soviets after the war is problematic: his memoir *A Handbook for Spies*, was ghosted by the MI5 officer, Courtenay Young. Some accounts claim he had been recruited by Claude Dansey in 1936.

Footman, David (1895-1983), author and intelligence officer. Footman was a friend of Guy Burgess, and headed the Political Intelligence Section in SIS, even though his Communist leanings were known.

Frankfurter, Felix (1882-1965), Austrian-born US jurist and member of the Supreme Court. Frankfurter had become friends with Isaiah Berlin when at Oxford in 1933-1934. An enthusiastic New Dealer, he recommended several leftist lawyers to Roosevelt's administration, including Alger Hiss. He was elected to the Supreme Court in 1939.

Friedmann (née Kohlmann), Alice (Litzi) (1910-1991), Vienna-born communist, first wife of Kim Philby. Friedmann and Philby collaborated in Vienna in 1934, and they married to enable her to escape to the UK. While they split up soon afterwards, they awkwardly did not divorce until 1946.

Frisch, Otto Robert (1904-1979), Austrian-born physicist. Frisch was stranded in Birmingham at the outset of WWII, and co-authored with Rudolf Peierls the paper that explained how a nuclear explosion could occur, thus prompting the formation of the Tube Alloys project.

Fuchs, Klaus (1911-1988), German-born physicist and Soviet spy. A Communist Party member, Fuchs escaped to the UK, where he was helped by Neville

Mott at Bristol and Max Born at Edinburgh. After internment, he passed on atomic secrets in the UK and the USA, not being detected until VENONA transcripts implicated him. He confessed in 1949.

Fulford, Roger (1902-1938), intelligence officer. Fulford met Roger Hollis at Worcester College in 1934, worked for the BBC with Guy Burgess, and beside Hollis in MI5. He was lenient towards communists.

Furnival-Jones, Martin (1903-1997), solicitor and intelligence officer. Furnival-Jones joined MI5 in 1937, became head of 'C' Branch after the war, and replaced Hollis as Director-General in 1965. He did not want to pursue investigations into the 'Oxford Ring' of spies.

Gaitskell, Hugh (1906-1963), politician and leader of the Labour opposition. Educated at Winchester and New College, Gaitskell knew Philby in Vienna in 1934, but did not disqualify him from employment by SOE in 1940. The KGB has been suspected of foul play in his early death.

Gallagher, William (1881-1965), Communist politician. Once imprisoned for sedition, Gallagher helped found the Communist Party of Great Britain and represented West Fife as a Communist from 1935 to 1950.

Gamow, Georgiy Antonovich (1904-1968), Soviet physicist. Gamow engineered an extraordinary escape from the Soviet Union, accompanied by his wife, in 1934, and moved to Washington. He recruited several scientists to the Soviet espionage cause, probably including Wilfrid Mann.

Gardiner, Muriel (1901-1985), US psychoanalyst. Gardiner moved to Vienna in the early 1930s, met Kim Philby, and became the lover of Stephen Spender. She was the model for the heroine of the Stalinist writer Lillian Hellman's largely fictional 'memoir', titled *Julia*.

Gaster, Jack (1907-2007), lawyer and CPGB member. Gaster married Maire Lynd, another Communist, who was a close friend of Isaiah Berlin. Gaster was the son of the Zionist Moses Gaster, who collaborated with Chaim Weizmann.

Glading, Percy (1893-1970), co-founder of CPGB and spy. Glading worked at the Woolwich Arsenal, and passed secrets to Theodore Maly. He was trapped by the MI5 agent Olga Gray, and sentenced to six years' penal servitude.

Godfrey, John Henry (1888-1970), naval and intelligence officer. Godfrey was Director of Naval Intelligence between 1939 and 1942, failing to be appointed chief of SIS despite Churchill's recommendation. Relations between him and other intelligence departments were strained.

Gollancz, Victor (1893-1967), publisher. Educated at St Paul's School and New College, Oxford, Gollancz was a Stalinist supporter until the Nazi-Soviet pact. He co-founded the Left Book Club in 1936, and married his communism with Christianity.

Gold, Harry (1910-1972), US chemist and Soviet spy. Gold was recruited by Jacob Golos, and worked as a courier for Klaus Fuchs, delivering atomic secrets to the Soviets. He confessed under interrogation: Fuchs identified him from photographs.

Goldmann, Nahum (1895-1982), German-born Zionist. Goldmann co-founded the World Jewish Congress in 1936, and settled in the USA in 1940. He was a friend of Isaiah Berlin, and tried to get Konstantin Oumansky to help him get to the Soviet Union in 1944.

Golos, Jacob (1889-1943), Ukrainian-born Soviet agent. Golos was a founder of the Communist Party of the USA, and secured illegal passports in New York. He managed a spy ring, and became the lover of the courier Elizabeth Bentley, who replaced him when he had a fatal heart attack in 1943.

Goold-Verschoyle, Brian (1912-1942), Irish Communist. Goold-Verschoyle acted as a courier to Bystrolyotov, and was murdered by the NKVD as a 'Trotskyist'.

Gorsky (aka Gromov), Anatoly (1907-1980), Soviet intelligence officer. Gorsky returned to London to handle the Cambridge Five in November 1940. He moved to the USA as *rezident* in 1944, where he was cultivated by Isaiah Berlin, and wanted to kill Elizabeth Bentley when she confessed to the GBI.

Gouzenko, Igor (1919-1982), Soviet cipher clerk and defector. In September 1945, Gouzenko defected from the Soviet Embassy in Ottawa, which led immediately to the identification of Nunn May as a Soviet spy, and the awareness that Canada and the USA were riddled with Soviet agents.

Graham (née Meyer), Katherine (wife of Phillip) (1917-2001), US publisher. Katherine Meyer married Phillip Graham in May 1940, and hosted the dinner party where Donald Maclean and Isaiah Berlin had an apparent argument over political ideals.

Graham, Phillip (husband of Katherine) (1915-1963), US publisher. Graham was a clerk to Felix Frankfurter, married Katherine Meyer in May 1940, and became publisher of the *Washington Post* in 1946. He committed suicide in 1963.

Grand, Laurence (1898-1975), intelligence officer. In March 1938, Major Grand set up Section D within SIS, to pursue sabotage and propaganda. Guy Burgess was reputed to be its 'ideas-man', and he recruited Isaiah Berlin to the organisation. Grand was moved out when SOE was established in August 1940.

Gray, Olga (1906-?), MI5 intelligence agent. Olga Gray was used by Maxwell Knight of 'B5b' as a penetration agent in the Communist Party of Great Britain, and her activities led to the apprehension in 1937 of Percy Glading and three other Soviet spies.

Greene, Graham (1904-1991), novelist and intelligence officer. Greene joined the Communist Party in his youth, and worked for the Ministry of Information and for SIS (under Kim Philby) during WWII. He wrote a sympathetic introduction to Philby's memoir, *My Silent War*.

Groves, Leslie (1896-1970), US Army officer. Groves took over responsibility for the Manhattan project in September 1942, and held it until 1947. He was very disciplined about national security, but could not prevent Soviet theft of secrets.

Gubbins, Colin McVean (1896-1976), military and intelligence officer. A veteran of the Russian Campaign in WWI, Gubbins was invited by Hugh Dalton to join SOE, and was appointed Director of Operations and Training in November 1940, at which point he fired Guy Burgess.

Halban, Hans von (1908-1964), French physicist of Austrian-Jewish descent. Halban escaped to London from Paris with Lew Kowarski and a supply of heavy water, and in 1943 went to Canada to head up local research on the Manhattan project. In 1943 he married Aline Strauss, who would later marry Isaiah Berlin.

Halevy, Ephraim (b. 1934), Israeli lawyer and intelligence officer. Born in London, Halevy, a relative of Isaiah Berlin by marriage, accompanied Berlin to Moscow in 1956. In 1998 he became head of Mossad, Israel's intelligence service.

Halifax, Lord (see Edward Wood)

Halpern, Alexander (1879-1956), Russian lawyer and British intelligence officer. Halpern served as Cabinet Secretary in Kerensky's government of 1917. After emigrating to the UK, he worked for SIS, and then at British Security Coordination in New York in WWII.

Hankey, Maurice (1899-1963), civil servant and politician. Hankey was Cabinet Secretary from 1916 to 1938, and ran the Committee of Imperial Defence from 1912 to 1938. Chamberlain brought him back from retirement in 1939, when he performed an analysis of the intelligence services. The Soviet spy John Cairncross was his personal secretary in 1939-1940.

Harker, Oswald Allen ('Jasper') (1886-1968), intelligence officer. Harker was appointed acting Director-General of MI5 in June 1940, after Vernon Kell's dismissal, but returned to his role as Deputy Director-General when David Petrie was appointed D-G in April 1941.

Harris, Kitty (Katherine) (1899-1966), Soviet agent. London-born Harris started a varied career as a Soviet agent and courier after her Russian-born father moved the family to Canada in 1908. After an affair with Earl Browder, she became courier to Donald Maclean from 1938, having an affair with him in London and Paris that ended when Maclean married Melinda Marling in 1940.

Harris, Tomás (1908-1964), intelligence officer. Harris worked for MI5 in WWII, handling the double-agent GARBO, and entertained intelligence officers at his house in London. He came under suspicion as a Soviet spy after Philby's defection, but was killed in a car accident before any interrogation could take place.

Hart, Herbert (husband of Jenifer) (1907-1992), jurisprudential scholar and intelligence officer. On the recommendation of his girl-friend, the Soviet spy Jenifer Fischer-Williams, Hart was recruited by MI5 in June 1940, and by 1941 headed 'B1b' (Espionage Special Sources). He married Fischer-Williams in November 1941.

Hart (née Fischer-Williams), Jenifer (wife of Herbert) (1913-2005), civil servant, academic, and Soviet spy. Hart joined the Communist Party, was recruited by Bernard Floud as a Soviet spy, and then worked at the Home Office under Alexander Maxwell. At some stage in the 1940s she became Isaiah Berlin's lover.

Henderson, Loy W. (1892-1986), US diplomat and civil servant. Henderson warned of a Soviet-Nazi rapprochement while in Moscow in the 1930s, and he was sought out by Isaac Don Levine when Krivitsky needed a government contact. His antipathy to the Soviets stood him out in Roosevelt's administration, and after.

Hill, Christopher (1912-2003), academic historian and Soviet spy. Hill joined the Communist Party while at Balliol College, Oxford, but was nevertheless recruited by the Intelligence Corps in 1941. He was member of the 'Oxford spy ring', and suggested to Jenifer Hart that she recruit Isaiah Berlin to the CP.

Hiss, Alger (1904-1996), US government official and Soviet spy. Hiss was a protégé of Felix Frankfurter, and joined Roosevelt's administration. He attended the Yalta Conference, was denounced by Whittaker Chambers in 1948, and convicted on charges of perjury in 1950.

Hoare, Samuel, 1st Viscount Templewood (1880-1959), politician. Hoare served under Baldwin and Chamberlain, and was co-responsible for the Hoare-Laval pact. Dismissed by Churchill in his May 1940 coalition, Hoare was soon sent to Spain as Ambassador, charged with keeping Franco out of the war.

Hollis, Roger (1905-1973), journalist and intelligence officer. Hollis joined MI5 in 1938, assumed responsibility for countering Communist subversion and espionage in 1941, and succeeded Dick White as Director-General in 1956. The journalist Chapman Pincher believed that Hollis was the Soviet agent and mole 'ELLI'.

Holt-Wilson, Eric (1875-1950), military and intelligence officer. Holt-Wilson was second-in-command of MI5 from 1931 until 1940, when he resigned at the sacking of his boss, Vernon Kell. He had been an ineffective representative for the service on the Joint Intelligence Committee.

Hoover, J. Edgar (1895-1972), US intelligence officer. Hoover was appointed head of the Bureau of Investigation in 1924, which was renamed the Federal Bureau of Investigation in 1935. In 1938, Hoover tried to have Walter Krivitsky deported.

Ironside, William Edmund (1880-1959), military officer. Ironside was rejected by Chamberlain as possible emissary to Moscow in 1939, because he was too eager for a military agreement. On the outbreak of war, he was appointed Chief of the Imperial General Staff.

Jebb, Gladwyn (1900-1996), civil servant and politician. Jebb acted as liaison between the Foreign Office and MI5, was present at the interrogations of Walter Krivitsky, and assisted Guy Burgess and Isaiah Berlin in preparation for their Section D mission to Moscow.

Johnson, Hewlett (1874-1966), Church of England priest. As ('Red') Dean of Canterbury, and a self-described Christian Marxist, Johnson enthusiastically supported the Soviet Union. He attended Stalin's show trials, in 1937, and pointed to the fairness of the Soviet justice system.

Joliot-Curie, Jean Fréderic (1900-1958), French physicist and communist. A Nobelist in 1935, Joliot-Curie was a colleague of Hans von Halban. He justified Leslie Groves's mistrust in him (and other French scientists) by passing on Manhattan Project secrets to the Soviets in 1944.

Kahle, Hans (1899-1947), German-born journalist and Soviet spy. A Communist Party member and International Brigades fighter in Spain, Kahle was

interned with Klaus Fuchs in 1940, and despite his known history, was
allowed to work as a military correspondent in WWII.

Kamenev, Lev (1883-1936), Russian Bolshevik revolutionary. Kamenev was a
member of the first Politburo, but opposed Stalin in 1925, and was thus
convicted in the 1936 show trials, and executed.

Kannegiesser, Eugenia [see Peierls, Eugenia].

Kapitza, Pyotr (1894-1984), Soviet physicist and Nobelist. Kapitza worked at
Cambridge under Ernest Rutherford from 1924 to 1934, but Stalin forbade
his return. Thereafter he was the driving-force behind the development of the
Soviet atom bomb.

Katz, Otto (1895-1952), Soviet agent. Katz worked for the Comintern in the
1930s as a multi-national activist and hit-man, and was protected by Ellen
Wilkinson in the UK. He was executed (as André Simone) after the Slansky
trial in Prague.

Kell, Vernon (1873-1942), Army and intelligence officer. Kell founded the
precursor to MI5 in 1909, and remained its head until 1940, when Churchill
dismissed him, ostensibly for mismanaging the 'Fifth Column' threat.

Kelly, David Victor (1891-1959), diplomat. Kelly was Ambassador to
Switzerland in June 1940 when the Germans sent von Hohenlohe to make
peace overtures to Churchill via him.

Kennedy, Joseph P. (1888-1969), US businessman and politician. Appointed US
Ambassador to Great Britain in 1938, Kennedy supported appeasement
policies, and undermined resistance to Hitler through isolationist statements,
which forced him to resign in November 1940.

Kent, Tyler (1911-1988), American diplomat. As a cipher clerk in Moscow, Kent
was suspected of spying for the Soviet Union, then moved to London where
he stole documents from the US Embassy. He was detected by MI5 agent
Joan Miller, arrested in May 1940, and convicted in October.

Kerensky, Alexander (1881-1970), Russian lawyer and politician. Kerensky was
Chairman of the 1917 Provisional Government. He escaped to France after
the October Revolution, and met Walter Krivitsky in Montreal, Canada in
January 1940.

Kerr, Phillip Henry, 14th Marquess of Lothian (1882-1940), politician and
diplomat. An appeaser of Germany in the 1930s, Kerr was UK Ambassador
to the United States from June 1939 to December 1940, when he died in
office as a Christian Scientist.

King, John Herbert (1884-?), Foreign Office cipher clerk and spy. King was
recruited as a spy in Geneva by Henri Pieck, and provided documents to the
Soviets between 1935 and 1937. A tip from Walter Krivitsky to Isaac Don
Levine led to his detection and conviction in 1939.

Klugmann, Norman John (James) (1912-1977), writer, intelligence officer, and
Soviet spy. Educated at Gresham's School, Holt, and Trinity College,
Cambridge, Klugmann recruited John Cairncross. Despite his background, he
was posted to Cairo for SOE, and influenced policy in Yugoslavia in favour
of the Communists.

Knight, Maxwell (1900-1968), intelligence officer and broadcaster. Knight rose
to lead 'B5b' in MI5, and patiently ran agents, primarily against the

Communist Party. He warned of Communist infiltration, but may have been blackmailed into keeping silent.

Koestler, Arthur (1905-1993), Hungarian-born author and journalist. Koestler left the Communist Party in 1938, published *Darkness at Noon* in 1941 after escaping from France to Britain, drawing on Walter Krivitsky's experiences, and then worked for the Ministry of Information.

Kollek, Teddy (1911-2007), Hungarian-born Israeli politician. After consorting with Kim Philby in Vienna in 1934, Kollek moved to Palestine, where he became the Jewish Agency's liaison with MI5 in the 1940s. He expressed his surprise at encountering Philby as an intelligence officer in Washington in 1949.

Kravchenko, Victor (1895-1966), Ukrainian-born Soviet engineer and defector. Kravchenko was posted to Washington with the Soviet Purchasing Commission in 1943, but defected in 1944. His life and trials after his defection were recorded in his autobiography *I Chose Freedom*.

Krivitsky, Walter (1899-1941), Soviet intelligence officer and illegal. After the murder of his colleague Ignace Reiss in 1937, Krivitsky escaped to France, Canada and the USA, where he revealed damaging truths about Stalin. He was brought to London in January 1940 for interrogations by MI5 and SIS, but died under mysterious circumstances in Washington in February 1941.

Kuczynski, Jürgen (son of Robert) (1904-1997), German-born economist and Soviet spy. Kuczynski moved to Britain in 1935, and worked openly as a member of the Communist Party. He introduced Klaus Fuchs to his sister, Ursula, and later in WWII worked for US intelligence.

Kuczynski, Robert (1876-1947), German-born economist and demographer. In 1933 Kuczynski moved to Great Britain, where he lectured and advised the Colonial Office. He and his wife had six children, including Jürgen and Ursula.

Kuczynski, Ursula (aka Ruth Werner, 'Sonia') (daughter of Robert) (1907-2000), German-born author and Soviet spy. Kuczynski travelled widely as a Communist agent, and became known as 'Sonia' working with Richard Sorge in China in the 1930s. She recruited Alexander Foote and Len Beurton in Switzerland in 1939, and engineered a marriage to Beurton in 1940 so that she could enter Britain to assume a role of courier for Klaus Fuchs. She fled to East Germany when Fuchs was arrested in 1949.

Kulczar, Ilsa (née Pollak) (1902-1973), Austrian-born journalist. Kulczar worked with Kim Philby in Vienna in 1934. She married the Spanish author and activist Arturo Barea in 1938, and they escaped to the UK in 1939.

Lamphere, Robert J. (1918-2002), US CIA agent. Lamphere assisted Meredith Gardner in decrypting the VENONA cablegrams, and pursued the trail that led to the arrest and prosecution of the atom spies, most notably the Rosenbergs and Klaus Fuchs.

Laski, Harold (1883-1950), economist and writer. A professor at the London School of Economics from 1926 to 1950, Laski was a left-wing socialist who encouraged communists, and preached revolution. When he did so as the chairman of the Labour Party in the 1945 election, it had to disown him.

Laski, Neville (brother of Harold) (1890-1969), judge and leader of Anglo-Jewry. Laski was a non-Zionist. He rented out a cottage by his house in Oxford to Ursula Kuczynski, who fitted up a wireless transmitter there.

Leeper, Reginald (1888-1971), Australian-born civil servant and diplomat. Leeper headed the Political Intelligence Department of the Foreign Office when it was re-formed in 1939. In August 1940, he took over SO1 (propaganda) in Hugh Dalton's SOE.

Lehmann, John (brother of Rosamond) (1907-1987), writer and communist sympathiser. Lehmann was educated at Trinity College, Cambridge, and possibly recruited by the Soviets in Vienna in 1934. At the end of 1939, Guy Liddell of MI5 recommended to the Ministry of Information that it not hire Lehmann.

Lehmann, Rosamond (sister of John) (1901-1990), novelist and communist sympathiser. Lehmann spoke at anti-fascist meetings in 1938, and accompanied Guy Burgess to Paris in March 1940 when she was having an affair with Goronwy Rees.

Levine, Isaac Don (1892-1981), Russian-born US journalist and writer. Levine developed a hostility towards Soviet infiltration of the US in the 1920s and 1930s. He assisted, and collaborated with, Walter Krivitsky, and ghost-wrote the latter's memoirs.

Liddell, Guy (1892-1958), intelligence officer. Liddell joined MI5 from Scotland Yard in 1931, and rose to be appointed Director of Counter-Espionage ('B' Division) in June 1940. His lack of experience in handling agents deploying subterfuge contributed to a disastrous policy of allowing Communists into the machinery of government in the first two years of the war.

Litvinov, Maxim (1876-1951), Russian revolutionary and diplomat. Litvinov was Commissar for Foreign Affairs from 1930 until May 1939, when he was replaced by Molotov, Stalin wanting a non-Jew to start negotiations with Hitler. He served as Ambassador to the US from November 1941 to August 1943.

Lloyd George, David (1863-1945), Liberal politician. Lloyd George had been Prime Minister from 1916 to 1922. In the 1930s, he expressed sympathy for Germany, but became disenchanted with Chamberlain. He played an ambiguous role in Churchill's manoeuvres in the summer of 1940.

Lockhart, Bruce (1887-1970), diplomat and intelligence officer. Lockhart had been an agent for SIS in the Soviet Union, and the lover of Moura Budberg. He was appointed liaison officer to the Czech government-in-exile in July 1940, and head of the Political Warfare Executive in July 1941.

Long, Leo (1916 - ?), civil servant and Soviet spy. A lesser-known 'Cambridge Spy', Long was recruited by Anthony Blunt at Cambridge, and joined Army Intelligence MI14 in 1940. Joan Miller's memoir claims that his spying there was detected, but went unpunished, and Long later worked for the Allied Control Commission in 1945.

Longworth, Alice Roosevelt (1884-1980), US writer and socialite. Longworth was the daughter of Theodore Roosevelt, but an ardent opponent of her cousin Franklin Roosevelt, and thus a potent symbol to Communist sympathisers during WWII.

Lothian, Lord (see Kerr, Phillip)

Lynd, Maire (1912-1990), CPGB member. Daughter of Irish nationalists, Lynd was tutored at Oxford by Isaiah Berlin, with whom she became a close friend. She married Communist lawyer Jack Gaster in 1938.

Maclean, Donald (1913-1983), diplomat and Soviet spy. Educated at Gresham's School, Holt, and Trinity Hall, Cambridge, Maclean was recruited by Soviet intelligence in 1934. He succeeded in gaining entry to the Diplomatic Service, and revealed valuable secrets during his career in London, Paris, Cairo and Washington. After an affair with his courier, Kitty Harris, he married the American Melinda Marling in Paris in July 1940.

Maclean, Fitzroy (1911-1996), soldier, writer and politician. Maclean had witnessed the 1937 Moscow show trials, and thus opposed Stalinism. He was working in the Foreign Office in 1940, and tried to derail the mission by Guy Burgess and Isaiah Berlin to reach Moscow.

Macmillan, Harold, 1st Earl of Stockton (1894-1986), Conservative politician. MacMillan steered an awkward intermediate course during the late 1930s, but was instrumental in bringing down Chamberlain. He was appointed Parliamentary Secretary to the Ministry of Supply in May 1940.

Maisky, Ivan (1884-1975), Soviet diplomat and politician. Maisky was a Menshevik who gained enough of Stalin's confidence to serve as Soviet Ambassador to Britain from 1932 until 1943, using his rich connections to gain information and try to influence policy.

Mallet, Victor (1893-1969), diplomat and author. Mallet was counsellor in the British Embassy in Washington from 1936 to 1939, and shrewdly picked up the importance of Krivitsky's testimony for uncovering espionage in London.

Maly, Teodor (1894-1938), Soviet illegal. Maly came to the UK in 1932 to control the spies John King and Ernest Oldham. He was one of the controllers of the Cambridge Five, and may have recruited Arthur Wynn at Oxford. He returned to the Soviet Union in 1937 to be executed the following year.

Mann, Wilfrid Basil (1908-2001), physicist and Soviet spy. Identified first by Andrew Boyle, Mann denied that he was the 'Fifth Man' of the Cambridge Spies, but almost certainly left the Tube Alloys project for the US to help the Soviet cause. He was probably recruited there by George Gamow.

Masterman, John (1891-1977), academic and intelligence officer. A history don at Christ Church, Oxford, Masterman was recruited into MI5 in December 1940, and thereafter became chairman of the XX ('Double-Cross') Committee that managed German double-agents.

Matheson, Hilda (1888-1940), broadcaster. Matheson resigned from the BBC as Director of Talks. She was director of the clandestine propaganda organisation, the Joint Broadcasting Committee, of which Guy Burgess was a member, until her death.

Maxwell, Alexander (1880-1963), civil servant. Maxwell was Permanent Under-Secretary at the Home Office from 1938 to 1948, and thus responsible for the treatment of aliens in 1940. Jenifer Fischer-Williams (later Hart) was his secretary in 1940.

McNamara, John (1905-1944), military officer and politician. McNamara was an MP, and member of the Anglo-German Fellowship. Guy Burgess was his Parliamentary Secretary from 1935 to 1936.

McNeil, Hector (1907-1955), politician. McNeil was a Labour MP who protected his Private Secretary, Guy Burgess, after he was appointed Minister of State at the Foreign Office in October 1946.

Menzies, Stewart (1890-1968), Army and intelligence officer. Menzies headed SIS from 1939 to 1952. He succeeded in maintaining control of the Government Code and Cypher School when SIS's reputation was poor, and thus was responsible for the distribution of Ultra intelligence.

Miller, Joan (1916-1984), MI5 agent. Miller worked for Maxwell Knight in MI5, and infiltrated the Right Club in order to investigate Tyler Kent. During WWII, she worked for MI14, where she detected Leo Long stealing files. The British Government tried to ban her memoir *One Girl's War* shortly before she died.

Milne, Tim (1912-2010), intelligence officer. Milne was a close friend of Kim Philby at Westminster College. He was recruited by SIS in October 1941, and was one of the coterie that attended Tomás Harris's house. His posthumous memoir describes how MI5 blocked an investigation into Philby.

Milner, Ian (1911-1991), New Zealand-born civil servant, academic and Soviet spy. Milner was a Rhodes Scholar at New College, Oxford. He campaigned against the war, and was revealed by the VENONA transcripts to have been involved in a spy ring at the Australian Department of External Affairs.

Mitchell, Graham (1905-1984), intelligence officer. Mitchell, who had worked for Joseph Ball, was recruited by MI5 on Ball's recommendation. After a period working for Roger Hollis's 'F' Division, he became assistant to Hollis on the latter's appointment to Director-General in 1956.

Modin, Yuri (1922-2007), Soviet intelligence officer. Modin was the controller for the Cambridge Spies from 1948 to 1951, and facilitated the escape of Burgess and Maclean. He helped popularise their identity with his 1994 memoir, although there was some disagreement as to who the Fifth Man was.

Molotov, Vyacheslav (1890-1986), Soviet diplomat and politician. An Old Bolshevik, Molotov was appointed Minister of Foreign Affairs, in May 1939, and engineered the details of the Nazi-Soviet Pact. He fell out of favour in the late 1940s, but escaped Stalin's purges.

Monckton, Walter Turner (1891-1965), lawyer and politician. Monckton was appointed President of the Press and Censorship Bureau in October 1939, and won the post of Deputy Director-General of the Ministry of Information in April 1940, despite sharing some subversive notions with Harold Laski.

Montagu, Ivor (1904-1984), filmmaker, activist and Soviet spy. Montagu, the brother of the SIS officer, Ewen, author of *The Man Who Never Was*, became a Soviet spy in 1940. He was awarded the Lenin Peace Prize in 1959.

Moorehead, Alan (1910-1983), Australian-born journalist. A well-respected frontline correspondent during WWII, Moorehead was in 1951 engaged by MI5 to write as propaganda an account of the atom spies, *The Traitors*, which misrepresents the facts of what happened.

Morrison, Herbert (1888-1965), politician. Morrison was appointed Minister of Supply in Churchill's May 1940 coalition government, and then Home Secretary in October 1940. For some years until 1947, he carried on an affair with Ellen Wilkinson, who had been his wartime Parliamentary Secretary.

Morton, Desmond (1891-1971), politician and intelligence officer. An ex-SIS officer, and a close colleague of Churchill, Morton was appointed Principal Assistant Secretary at the Ministry of Economic Warfare in 1939, and became Churchill's personal assistant after May 1940, responsible for handling Ultra decrypts.

Mosley, Oswald (1896-1980), politician. Mosley was the founder of the British Union of Fascists (renamed the British Union), and the focus of MI5's attention on the 'Fifth Column' in 1940, which led to his internment and imprisonment. He was released in 1943.

Mott, Nevill Francis (1905-1996), physicist. Mott, a Communist sympathiser, was Professor in Theoretical Physics at Bristol University, where he supported Klaus Fuchs, and recommended him to Max Born at Edinburgh. He won the Nobel Prize in 1977.

Muggeridge, Malcolm (1903-1990), author, broadcaster, and intelligence officer. Muggeridge's visits to the Soviet Union in the early 1930s convinced him of the iniquities of communism. After working in the Ministry of Information at the start of WWII, and a spell in Army intelligence, he was recruited by SIS, and posted to Lourenço Marques.

Münzenberg, Willi (1889-1940), communist political activist. Münzenberg was a founding member of the German Communist Party. Banned from Britain, he sent his assistant, Otto Katz, to represent the communist front against Fascism. After speaking out against Stalinism, he was murdered in France in October 1940.

Murdoch, Iris (1919-1999), author, philosopher, and probable Soviet spy. Murdoch was educated at Somerville College, Oxford, joined the Communist Party in 1938, yet was still hired by the Treasury in 1942. Nigel West has named her as one of the 'Oxford Ring' of spies.

Nelson, Frank (1883-1966), civil servant, politician and intelligence officer. In 1931, Nelson resigned his parliamentary seat to work for Claude Dansey's Z Organisation in Basle, Switzerland. In September 1940 he was appointed Executive Director of SOE, but retired in 1942 to move to Air Intelligence.

Newsam, Frank Aubrey (1893-1964), civil servant. Newsam helped draft the 1936 Public Order Act. Soon after WWII broke out, he was appointed Assistant Under-Secretary of State in the Home Office, and in April 1942, Deputy Under-Secretary. He was in charge of internment policies for fascists and enemy aliens in 1940.

Nicolson, Harold (1886-1968), author, politician and journalist. As a National Labour MP, Nicolson alerted his peers to the dangers of fascism in the late 1930s. In May 1940, he was appointed Parliamentary secretary to Duff Cooper in the Ministry of Information, but was dismissed by Churchill in 1941. He was a close friend of Guy Burgess.

Norwood (née Sirnis), Melita (1912-2005), civil servant and Soviet spy. Norwood joined the Communist Party in 1935, and was recommended to the NKVD by

Andrew Rothstein. Transferred to Soviet Military Intelligence, she provided a rich supply of information on atomic weapons research, for whose project director she worked.

Nunn May, Alan (1911-2003), physicist and Soviet spy. Nunn May was educated at Trinity Hall alongside Donald Maclean. He worked on the Tube Alloys Project, was transferred to Canada in 1943, and his spying was revealed by the defection of Igor Gouzenko. He confessed, and was sentenced in 1946.

Oldham, Ernest (1894-1933), civil servant and Soviet spy. Oldham was a cipher clerk, and between 1929 and 1933 provided his handler Dmitry Bystrolyotov with secrets for monetary reasons. His death was probably a suicide: Walter Krivitsky told MI5 his story in 1940.

Orlov, Alexander (1895-1973), Soviet intelligence officer. After a short spell as resident in Britain, Orlov was later posted to Spain in the Civil War, where he supervised the extraction of Spain's gold to the Soviet Union. He successfully convinced Stalin, by threats of revelations, not to touch him when he defected to the US in 1938.

Orwell, George (Eric Blair) (1903-1950), novelist and journalist. Orwell was a Spanish Civil War veteran who became vitally opposed to totalitarianism and Stalin's Russia. Always a man of the Left, he worked for the Ministry of Information, and then the BBC, during WWII, leaving the BBC in 1943 to write *Animal Farm*, the publication of which was obstructed by Peter Smollett.

Oumansky, Konstantin (1902-1945), Soviet journalist, diplomat and intelligence officer. Oumansky was posted to the USA in 1936, and served as Ambassador from June 1939 to November 1941, where Isaiah Berlin sought his help. After being moved to Mexico, he died in a plane crash.

Palmer, Roundell Cecil, 3rd Earl of Selborne (1887-1971), politician and intelligence officer. Selborne moved from Director of Cement at the Ministry of Works to take over as Minister of Economic Warfare from Hugh Dalton in February 1942, and hence assume responsibility for SOE.

Pascal, Roy (1904-1980), academic in German language and literature. Pascal was a close friend of Maurice Dobb, and married a fervent Communist, Fanya Polyanowski, who had known Rudolf Peierls in Berlin. Pascal approached Cairncross in 1937 for espionage purposes. He became chair of German Studies at Birmingham University in 1939.

Peierls (née Kannegiesser), Eugenia (1908-1996), Russian-born physicist. Kannegiesser had been a friend of George Gamow in the Soviet Union. She met Rudolf Peierls in Odessa in 1930, and was allowed to marry him and move to Switzerland in 1931.

Peierls, Rudolf (1907-1995), communist German-born British physicist. Peierls was working in Cambridge at the outbreak of WWII, and co-wrote an important memorandum on fissionable uranium in 1940, which led to the creation of the Maud Committee. He sponsored Klaus Fuchs, and recruited him to the Tube Alloys project.

Perrin, Michael Willcox (1905-1988), scientist. Perrin played a leading role in the Tube Alloys project, and skillfully managed the relationship with the USA.

He applied pressure to recruit Fuchs, and then was the recipient of Fuchs's confession in 1949.

Petrie, David (1879-1961), police and intelligence officer. Petrie was called in to take over as Director-General of MI5 in April 1941. He immediately reorganised counter-espionage (with the creation of 'F' Division) to relegate opposition to communist influences as a domestic subversion issue.

Philby, Harold Adrian Russell (Kim) (1912-1988), intelligence officer and spy. Despite his communist activities in Vienna in 1934, Philby was recruited by SOE in 1940, and later moved to SIS. He rose to lead Section 9 (Communist counter-espionage) in November 1944, but was suspected of aiding the escape of Burgess and Maclean in 1951.

Pieck, Henri (1895-1972), Dutch artist and Soviet agent. Pieck was recruited by Walter Krivitsky (or maybe Ignace Reiss), and handled Ernest Oldham and John King. After WWII, he was interviewed by MI5.

Pollitt, Harry (1890-1960), Stalinist Secretary of the CPGB. Pollitt was General Secretary of the Communist Party of Great Britain from 1929 to 1956 (with one short hiatus during the Nazi-Soviet pact). He failed ever to win a parliamentary election. He persuaded Stephen Spender to perform espionage for the CP.

Pontecorvo, Bruno (1913-1993), Italian-born physicist and Soviet spy. Pontecorvo worked for Joliot-Curie in Paris, and joined the Communist Party the day after the Nazi-Soviet pact was announced. Turned down by the British, he moved to the USA, and spied for the Soviets. He worked at Harwell after WWII, but fled to the Soviet Union in 1950.

Pritt, Dennis (1887-1972), barrister and politician. Pritt was a Labour Party Member of Parliament, who aided communist subversion by helping agents into the country. He attended Stalin's show trials, in 1936, and supported the purges. He was expelled from the Labour Party in 1940 for defending the Soviet invasion of Finland.

Proctor, Philip Dennis (1905-1983), civil servant and spy. A member of the Apostles at Cambridge, Proctor was a friend of Guy Burgess and Anthony Blunt. Proctor joined the Ministry of Health in 1929. He helped Blunt be reinstated in Military Intelligence in 1939, and failed to clear himself when challenged by Peter Wright of MI5.

Proskurov, Ivan (?-1941), Soviet military and intelligence officer. Proskurov was head of military intelligence in 1939-1940, and consistently told Stalin the truth. He opposed the Nazi-Soviet pact, and his reward was to be replaced in July 1940 and executed a year later.

Pyatakov, Georgy (1890-1937), Bolshevik revolutionary. Pyatakov was Chairman of the Provisional Government in 1918-1919. He was later accused of Trotskyism, and became a victim of the purges in January 1937.

Radek, Karl (1885-1939), Marxist theorist and politician. Radek was a close affiliate of Lenin's, and later led the Comintern. He helped write the Soviet Constitution of 1936, but was convicted of Trotskyism in 1937, and killed in a labour camp in 1939.

Rees, Goronwy (1909-1979), journalist, academic, and Soviet spy. Rees was a friend of Burgess whose commitment to Communism was broken by the

Nazi-Soviet pact. Burgess wanted to have him killed as a risk. On 1956, he wrote a series of articles for *The People* newspaper that revealed secrets about Burgess, but the establishment rejected him, and Joseph Ball threatened to sue him.

Reif, Ignaty (né Max Wolisch) (?-1938), Polish-born Soviet *rezident*. Reif may have approved the recruitment of Kim Philby in 1934. Krivitsky described him to MI5 in 1940, but Reif had by then been recalled to Moscow and executed.

Reilly, Patrick (1909-1999), diplomat and civil servant. Reilly joined the Ministry of Economic Warfare in 1939, and in 1942 was appointed Private Secretary to Stewart Menzies, head of SIS. While he claimed to have detected Philby's unreliability, he contributed to the cover-up over Burgess in the 1950s.

Reiss [né Poretsky], Ignace (1899-1937), Soviet illegal. Reiss served in the 1920s in Berlin and Vienna, and then in the 1930s, Paris, and was a close friend of Walter Krivitsky. He chose to challenge Stalin over the show trials in 1937, and was hunted down and shot by NKVD operatives in Switzerland.

Roosevelt, Franklin Delano (1882-1945), US politician. Roosevelt provided moral and material support to Britain after WWII started, but had to remain neutral until the Japanese attacked at Pearl Harbor in December 1941. His failing health, and dislike of Britain's empire, made him an ineffective counterpoint to Stalin's ambitions for eastern Europe as victory approached, especially since his administration was riddled with Soviet spies.

Rosenberg, Ethel (née Greenglass, wife of Julius), (1915-1953), US Soviet spy. Rosenberg met her husband at the Young Communist League: they were married in 1939. Klaus Fuchs's confession led to that of Harry Gold, who identified Rosenberg's brother, David Greenglass, as a member of the spy ring. She and her husband were convicted and executed.

Rosenberg, Julius (husband of Ethel) (1918-1953), US Soviet spy. Rosenberg met his wife at the Young Communist League: they were married in 1939. Rosenberg was recruited by the NKVD in 1942 when working for the Army Signals Corps. Fuchs's confession led to him and his wife, and they were both convicted and executed.

Rothschild, Miriam (1908-2005), zoologist. Rothschild was the sister of Victor Rothschild. When in Washington in 1940, she reportedly tried to prevent the attempt by Guy Burgess and Isaiah Berlin to reach Moscow. Later in WWII, she worked at Bletchley Park.

Rothschild, Tess (née Mayer, second wife of Victor) (1915-1996), MI5 employee. Tess Mayer became Rothschild's secretary in MI5 in 1941, and married him in 1946. The defector Anatoli Golitsin suggested that she and her husband were the DAVID and ROSA mentioned in VENONA transcripts.

Rothschild, Victor (1910-1990), biologist, intelligence officer, and agent of influence. Rothschild joined MI5 in early 1940, and established a counter-sabotage section. He worked to increase sympathy for communists: the defector Anatoli Golitsin suggested that he and his second wife, Tess, were the DAVID and ROSA mentioned in VENONA transcripts. In 1986 he impractically appealed to Margaret Thatcher to offer evidence that he had never been a spy.

Rothstein, Andrew (1898-1994), journalist and CPGB member. A co-founder of the Communist Party of Great Britain, Rothstein recruited Melita Sirnis and Tom Wintringham to the Soviet cause. He worked as press officer for the Soviet news agency TASS during WWII.

Seeds, William (1882-1973), diplomat. Seeds served as Ambassador to the Soviet Union from 1939 to 1940. He was held partly responsible for the failure of negotiations in the summer of 1939, and after criticising the Soviet invasion of Finland in November of that year, was called back 'on leave' in January 1940. An awkward interregnum arose, closed by Cripps's appointment in May 1940.

Selborne, Lord (see Palmer)

Serpell, Michael (?-?), intelligence officer. Serpell was an officer in 'B1c' of MI5, who drew attention to the anomalies and risks inherent in the files of Fuchs and other suspects, but whose cautions were ignored by senior MI5 officers.

Shawcross, Hartley William (1902-2003), politican and barrister. Shawcross was Attorney General from August 1945 until April 1951. He was lead prosecutor at the Nuremberg War Crimes Tribunal, and prosecuted the Soviet spies Allan Nunn May and Klaus Fuchs.

Sillitoe, Percy Joseph (1888-1962), police and intelligence officer. Sillitoe became Director-General of MI5 in 1946, and was not served well by the existing directors. They indulged in a cover-up of failure to detect communist spies, and Sillitoe was obliged to lie to Prime Minister Attlee over the Fuchs case. He retired in 1953.

Simon, John (1873-1954). An ally of Chamberlain, Simon served as Home Secretary under Baldwin from 1935 to 1937, and then as Chancellor of the Exchequer under Chamberlain until May 1940. He was seen as one of the leading appeasers of Hitler. Churchill made him Lord Chancellor, without a seat in the Cabinet, for the remainder of WWII.

Sissmore, Jane (see Archer, Jane)

Skardon, William James (1904-1987), Special Branch investigator and interrogator. Skardon joined MI5 from Special Branch in 1945. He successfully elicited a confession from Klaus Fuchs in 1949, but his reputation in such arts was exaggerated, and he failed with Philby, Blunt and Cairncross.

Smollett, Peter (né Smolka) (1912-1980), Austrian-born journalist and Soviet spy. Smollett was a friend of Litzi Friedmann, and may have been recruited by Kim Philby. He came to the UK in 1933 as a NKVD spy. He befriended Brenda Bracken, gained entry to the Ministry of Information, and rose to head its Soviet relations branch in August 1941.

Solomon, Flora (née Benenson) (1895-1984), Russian-born Zionist. Solomon was a long-time friend of Kim Philby, who tried to recruit her as a spy when in Spain. In 1962 she declared to Victor Rothschild her suspicion that Philby and Tomás Harris had been Soviet spies in the 1930s.

Spender, Stephen (1909-1995), poet and man of letters. A close friend of W. H. Auden and Christopher Isherwood at Oxford, Spender became the lover of Muriel Gardiner in the early 1930s. He joined the Communist Party in 1936, and in 1937, at Harry Pollitt's request, undertook a mission to Spain on behalf of the Soviet Union. He was a close friend of Isaiah Berlin.

Spiegelglass, Sergey (1897-1941), Soviet intelligence officer. After recruiting agents in Europe, Spiegelglass was acting head of the Soviet Foreign Intelligence Service in 1938. He engineered the murder of Georges Agabekov and Ignace Reiss in 1937, but became a victim of Stalin's purges.

Springhall, Frank Douglas (Dave) (1901-1953), activist and Soviet spy. Springhall studied in Moscow from 1928-1931, where he was recruited by Soviet military intelligence. After serving in the International Brigades in Spain, he ensured that the Communist Party of Great Britain supported the Nazi-Soviet Pact. He was convicted of spying in 1943.

Stalin, Iosif (1878-1953), Soviet leader. Stalin carried out extensive purges in the mid-1930s, sometimes preceded by elaborate show trials. After failing to build any alliance with western democratic powers, he forged a pact with Hitler in August 1939, and contributed materiel to Hitler's war effort against the Allies. Hitler's attack on the Soviet Union in June 1941 caused Churchill to embrace his long-standing Communist enemy, and Stalin was able to exploit latent sympathy in Britain via propaganda and spying.

Stark, Freya (1893-1993), explorer. Stark had been an unofficial agent for SIS before WWII, when she joined the Ministry of Information. In 1943, Isaiah Berlin manipulated her by inviting her to Washington to give an Arabist view on the future of Palestine, which in fact aided the Zionist cause.

Stephenson, William (1897-1989), Canadian businessman and intelligence officer. Churchill appointed Stephenson to run British Security Coordination, a propaganda outfit, in New York in June 1940. It eventually represented MI5, SIS, SOE and the Political Warfare Executive in the western hemisphere. Stephenson was a valuable conduit to Roosevelt, but his contribution was overstated by his biographer.

Stewart, Robert J. (Bob) (1877-1971), politician and CPGB member. Stewart was responsible for the London-based spy cell that communicated by radio with Moscow in the 1930s, and he received purloined information from Anthony Blunt during WWII. MI5 arranged for his office at Communist Party Headquarters to be bugged.

Strachey, John (1901-1963), politician and writer. Strachey was a Communist sympathiser in the 1930s, and co-founded with Victor Gollancz the Left Book Club. His support for Stalin weakened after the Nazi-Soviet pact, but he sponsored Rudolf Peierls's request for naturalisation in March 1940.

Straight, Michael (1916-2004), US writer and Soviet spy. Straight was an Apostle and Communist Party member at Cambridge University. He was recruited by Anthony Blunt, and ordered back to the US in 1937, to penetrate government institutions. Guy Burgess sought him out in Washington in July 1940, when he was working for the Department of State. His 1963 confession led to the exposure of Blunt.

Strang, William (1893-1978), diplomat. Strang was head of the Central Department of the Foreign Office in the summer of 1939, when he went to Moscow to discuss a possible British-Soviet pact. He returned in early August as the abortive military mission arrived in the Soviet Union.

Sudoplatov, Pavel (1907-1996), Soviet intelligence officer. Sudoplatov joined OGPU in 1933, and worked as an illegal and assassin in Europe. He escaped Stalin's purges, was put in charge of the project to assassinate Trotsky, and in June 1941 led the 'Special Tasks' group responsible for sabotage and extra-legal murders.

Sweet-Escott, Bickham (1907-1981), banker and intelligence officer. Sweet-Escott joined Laurence Grand's Section D before WWII, and then became a regional director of SOE, and personal assistant to Frank Nelson in July 1941. He recorded in his memoir *Baker Street Irregular* that Guy Burgess and Isaiah Berlin undertook their mission to Moscow on behalf of 'D' Section.

Swinton, Earl of (see Cunliffe-Lister)

Tangye, Derek (1912-1996), author and intelligence officer. Tangye worked as press officer under Liddell in the 1941 re-organisation of MI5. By 1943, he was working under Maxwell Knight, in the Agents and Press Section, which reported to the Director-General, David Petrie. He testified to Knight's insights about Communist infiltration in his memoir *The Way to Minack*.

Taylor, Alan John Percivale ('A. J. P.') (1906-1990), academic historian and suspected Soviet agent of influence. Taylor was recruited into the Communist Party in 1924 by Thomas Wintringham, but left soon after. He visited the Soviet Union twice, and was a sympathiser of Communism thereafter. Nigel West has listed Taylor as one of the 'Oxford Ring' of spies.

Toynbee, Phillip (1916-1981), writer, communist and suspected Soviet spy. Toynbee was the first Communist president of the Oxford Union in 1936, and visited Spain in the Civil War. Nigel West has listed him as a member of the 'Oxford Ring' of spies.

Trevor-Roper, Hugh, Baron Dacre of Glanton (1914-2003), academic historian and intelligence officer. E. W. B. Gill invited Trevor-Roper to join the Radio Security Service in December 1939: they claimed quickly to have deciphered Abwehr codes, but gained resentment from the Government Code and Cypher School thereby. Trevor-Roper had generally low opinions of intelligence officers, but diminished the scope of Kim Philby's influence in a Foreword to the latter's memoir.

Tudor-Hart, Edith (née Suschitsky) (1908-1973), Austrian-born photographer and Soviet spy. Suchitsky married Alex Tudor-Hart and left Vienna for England in 1933. She variously acted as courier and recruiter, being a friend of Kim Philby's first wife, Litzi Friedmann. She may have recruited Arthur Wynn, the head of the 'Oxford Ring' of spies.

Tukhachevsky, Mikhail (1893-1937), Soviet general. Stalin saw Tukhachevsky as a threat to his power, and engineered charges against him. He was arrested in May 1937, and convicted and executed the next month. Walter Krivitsky provided the West with details of the German involvement in providing false evidence.

Uren, Ormond (Desmond) (1919-2015), Australian SOE officer and Soviet spy. Uren joined the Army at the outset of WWII, and was recruited by SOE in 1942. He had joined the Communist Party in 1940. The next year he was arrested after passing SOE plans to Dave Springhall, and sentenced to seven years' penal servitude.

Vansittart, Robert, First Baron (1881-1957), diplomat and writer. Vansittart was Permanent Under-Secretary at the Foreign Office from 1930 to 1938, and an opponent of appeasement to Fascism as well as to Communism. His somewhat eccentric ways led to his being removed to the artificial post of Chief Diplomatic Adviser to the government.

Vivian, Valentine (1886-1969), Army and intelligence officer. Before WWII, Vivian led Section 'V' of SIS, which chiefly monitored the activities of the Comintern. He represented SIS at the interrogations of Walter Krivitsky, and soon afterwards recruited Kim Philby to the group. After 1941, he competed with Claude Dansey as Deputy Chief to Stewart Menzies.

Voroshilov, Kliment (1881-1969), Soviet military officer and politician. Voroshilov abetted Stalin in the purge of the Red Army in the mid-1930s, escaping arrest himself. He was chief negotiator with the British/French military mission in the summer of 1939. As People's Commissar for Defence, he was blamed for the disastrous invasion of Finland in November 1939, and removed from his post in May 1940.

Weizmann, Chaim (1874-1952). Russian-born chemist and Zionist politician. Weizmann became a British citizen in 1910, and led the World Zionist Organisation in 1920. At the outbreak of WWII, he advised the Ministry of Supply, and he became the first President of Israel in 1948. Isaiah Berlin, who admired him greatly, may have sought to go to Moscow in 1940 to discover the fate of Weizmann's brother Schmuel, who had in fact been executed in 1939.

Welles, Benjamin Sumner (1892-1961), US politician and diplomat. Welles was appointed by Franklin Roosevelt to Under-Secretary in the State Department. In July 1940, he issued a policy that condemned the Soviet Union's annexation of the Baltic States, and he tried to drive a wedge between Germany and the Soviet Union during the time of the Nazi-Soviet pact.

West, Rebecca (née Cicely Isabel Fairfield) (1892-1983), writer. West was an opponent of the dual totalitarian systems, Fascism and Communism. Her reporting of the Fuchs trial in 1950 was an important spur to MI5 to engage in a public relations exercise to cover up its mistakes.

White, Dick Goldsmith (1906-1993), intelligence officer. White was the first Oxbridge graduate recruited by MI5, in 1936. After spending time in Germany, White was quickly promoted, and headed 'B1' (Espionage) under Guy Liddell by 1941. He contributed to the cover-up after the Fuchs episode, but went on to be the only person to head MI5 and SIS.

White, Harry Dexter (1892-1948), US economist, government official and Soviet spy. White joined the Treasury in 1934. Whittaker Chambers's 1939 denunciation of White had been ignored: Elizabeth Bentley's accusations of 1945 and 1948 were taken more seriously, and VENONA transcripts later confirmed White's guilt.

Wild, Noël (?-1995), Army officer. Wild was an expert in deception, and helped devise the Bodyguard operation that concealed the real activities of the Allied invasion of Europe. He was very critical of MI5's amateurish efforts with the Double-Cross system, and the overall culture within MI5 and SIS.

Wilkinson, Ellen (1891-1947), politician. Wilkinson joined the Communist Party, but represented Middlesborough East as a Labour Party candidate in 1924. She agitated for Comintern agents to enter Britain, and became the lover of Otto Katz. In WWII, she worked under Herbert Morrison at the Ministry of Home Security, and became his lover.

Winterbotham, Frederick William (1897-1990), Air Force intelligence officer. Winterbotham was a regular visitor to Germany in the 1930s, providing intelligence for SIS. When WWII broke out, he was responsible for ensuring the secure distribution of Ultra material to British forces commanders. His book *The Ultra Secret* was the first comprehensive account of the project.

Wolkoff, Anna Nikolayevna (1902-1973), Russian émigrée and German spy. Wolkoff was Secretary of the Right Club, an organisation sympathetic to Fascism founded by Captain Ramsay. At the beginning of WWII, she was under observation by Joan Miller of MI5, and in April 1940 she was caught in possession of secret documents passed to her by Tyler Kent.

Wood, Edward Frederick Lindley, 1st Earl of Halifax (1881-1959), politician and diplomat. Halifax was Secretary of State for Foreign Affairs from February 1938 to December 1940. He was linked to Chamberlain's appeasement policy, but Churchill kept him in his administration. Halifax played an ambiguous role in Churchill's manoeuvres in the summer of 1940, and was sent to Washington as Ambassador to replace Lord Lothian when Churchill felt his own position was secure without Halifax.

Worsley, Thomas Cuthbert (1907-1977), writer and critic. Worsley was a left-wing writer who, somewhat improbably, was selected to accompany Stephen Spender on the Communist Party-sponsored mission to investigate missing Soviet sailors in Spain in January 1937.

Wright, Peter (1916-1995), scientist and intelligence officer. Wright worked for the Admiralty in WWII, and was recruited by MI5 as Principal Scientific Officer in 1954. From 1964, he chaired the FLUENCY sub-committee that investigated Soviet penetration of MI5, and published his memoirs in *Spycatcher*, which the British government tried to ban.

Wynn, Arthur (1910-2001), civil servant and Soviet spy. A member of the Communist Party at Oxford, Wynn was recruited by Edith Tudor-Hart in 1936, and built the 'Oxford Ring' of spies. He worked on advanced radar projects during WWII.

Yagoda, Genrikh (1891-1938), Soviet secret policeman. Yagoda served as Commissar for Internal Affairs (the NKVD) from July 1934 to September 1936, and supervised the show trials and execution of the Old Bolsheviks before himself falling victim of Stalin's purges.

Yezhov, Nikolai (1895-1940), Soviet secret police officer. Yezhov succeeded Genrikh Yagoda as Commissar for Internal Affairs (the NKVD) from 1936 to 1938, giving his name to the most brutal period of Stalin's purges, the 'Yezhovshchina'. In 1938 he was demoted, replaced by Beria, and in 1940 convicted of anti-Soviet activities, and shot.

Zinoviev, Grigory (1883-1936), Bolshevik revolutionary. Zinoviev is best known for the forged letter under his name that encouraged revolutionary action in

Britain in 1924. He later fell foul of Stalin as an Old Bolshevik, and became a victim, alongside his ally Lev Kamenev, of the 1936 show trials.

Sources and Bibliography

The main archival sources used were:
The National Archives at Kew, Surrey
The Isaiah Berlin Archive held at the Bodleian Library, Oxford
The Harold Nicolson Diaries held at Balliol College, Oxford
The Alexander Cadogan Diaries held at Churchill College, Cambridge
Transcript of Tape 7 of conversations held between Isaiah Berlin and his biographer, Michael Ignatieff

I thank the following for giving me permission to reproduce text from unpublished papers:
Ms Juliet Nicolson, for extracts from her grandfather's *Diaries*;
The Masters and Fellows of Churchill College, Cambridge, for an extract from Alexander Cadogan's *Diaries*;
Ms Jenny Rees, for a quotation from a letter sent by her father to Isaiah Berlin;
Dr Henry Hardy, for permission to quote extracts from transcriptions of dialogue between Isaiah Berlin and his biographer, Michael Ignatieff.

The following books have been used:

General History

Annan, Noel, *Our Age, English Intellectuals between the World Wars: A Group Portrait*, (New York, NY: Random House, 1990)

Antonov-Ovseyenko, Anton, *The Time of Stalin: Portrait of a Tyranny*, (New York, NY: Harper & Row, 1981)

Aster, Sidney, (ed.), *Appeasement and All Souls: A Portrait with Documents, 1937-1939*, (Cambridge: Cambridge University Press, 2004)

Atholl, Duchess of, *The Conscription of a People*, (New York, NY: Columbia University Press, 1931)

Balfour, Michael, *Propaganda in War, 1939-1945: Organisation, Policies and Publics in Britain and Germany*, (London: Routledge and Kegan Paul, 1979)

Barros, James and Gregor, Richard, *Double Deception; Stalin, Hitler and the Invasion of Russia*, (Dekalb, IL: Northern Illinois Press, 1995)

Beevor, Antony, *The Second World War*, (London: Weidenfeld and Nicolson, 2012)

Beevor, Antony, *The Battle for Spain*, (London: Weidenfeld and Nicolson, 2006)

Benda, Julien, (tr. by Richard Aldington), *The Treason of the Intellectuals*, (Boston, MA: Beacon Press, 1955)

Berlin, Isaiah, *The Soviet Mind*, (Washington, D. C.: Brookings Institution Press, 2011)

Boyd, Douglas, *The Kremlin Conspiracy: A Long, Hot and Cold War*, (Hersham, Surrey: Ian Allan Publishing, 2010)

Breitman, Richard and Lichtman, Allan J., *FDR and the Jews*, (New Haven, CT: The Belknap Press of Harvard University Press, 2014)

Briggs, Asa, *The History of Broadcasting in the United Kingdom*, (Oxford: Oxford University Press, 1961)

Bullock, Alan, *Hitler and Stalin: Parallel Lives*, (New York, NY: Alfred A. Knopf, 1992)

Burleigh, Michael, *Moral Combat*, (London: Harper Press, 2010)

Butterfield, Herbert, *The Whig Interpretation of History*, (London: G. Bell and Sons, 1931)

Cannadine, David, *In Churchill's Shadow*, (London: Allen Lane, The Penguin Press, 2002)

Carr, Edward Hallett, *The Soviet Impact on the Western World*, (London: Macmillan, 1947)

'Cato' [Owen, Frank, Foot, Michael and Howard, Peter], *Guilty Men*, (London: Gollancz, 1942)

Caute, David, *The Fellow Travellers: Intellectual Friends of Communism*, (New Haven, CT: Yale University Press, 1988)

Charlton, Michael, *The Eagle and the Small Birds*, (London: British Broadcasting Corporation, 1984)

Churchill, Winston, *The Second World War*, (London: Cassell, 1948-1954)

Cohn, Norman, *The Pursuit of the Millennium*, (London: Secker & Warburg, 1957)

Collingwood, R. G., *The Idea of History*, (Oxford: Oxford University Press, 1994)

Collini, Stefan, *Absent Minds: Intellectuals in Britain*, (Oxford: Oxford University Press, 2006)

Conquest, Robert, *Reflections on a Ravaged Century*, (New York, NY: W. W. Norton, 2000)

Conquest, Robert, *The Great Terror: A Reassessment*, (Oxford: Oxford University Press, 1990)

Costello, John, *Ten Days to Destiny*, (New York, NY: W. Morrow, 1991)

Cull, Nicholas John, *Selling War: the British Propaganda Campaign against American 'Neutrality' in World War II*, (Oxford: Oxford University Press, 1995)

Dallek, Robert, *The Lost Peace: Leadership in a Time of Horror and Hope, 1945-1953*, (New York, NY: Harper, 2010)

Dallin, David and Nicolaevsky, Boris, *Forced Labor in Soviet Russia*, (London: Hollis & Carter, 1948)

Dams, Carsten and Stolle, Michael, *The Gestapo: Power and Terror in the Third Reich*, (Oxford: Oxford University Press, 2014)

De Jong, Louis, *The German Fifth Column in the Second World War*, (Chicago, IL: University of Chicago Press, 1956)

Deakin, F. W., *The Embattled Mountain*, (Oxford: Oxford University Press, 1971)

Eliot, T.S., *Notes Towards the Definition of Culture*, (London: Harcourt Brace, 1949)

Evans, Richard J., *The Third Reich in Power, 1933-39*, (London: Penguin Press, 2005)

Farmelo, Graham, *Churchill's Bomb*, (London: Faber & Faber, 2013)

Farrell, Brian P., (ed.), *Leadership and Responsibility in the Second World War: Essays in Honor of Robert Vogel*, (Montreal: McGill Queens' University Press, 2004)

Fleming, J.V., *The Anti-Communist Manifestos*, (New York, NY: W. W. Norton, 2009)

Gaddis, John Lewis, *The Landscape of History: How Historians Map the Past*, (Oxford: Oxford University Press, 2002)

Gardiner, Juliet, *The Thirties – An Intimate History*, (London: Harper Press, 2010)

Gedye, G. E. R., *Betrayal in Central Europe: Austria and Czechoslovakia; The Fallen Bastions*, (London: Harper and Brothers, 1939)

Gellately, Robert, *Stalin's Curse*, (Oxford: Oxford University Press, 2013)

Geller, Mikhail and Nekrich, Aleksandr, *Utopia in Power*, (New York, NY: Summit Books, 1986)

Goodman, Nahum, *The Jewish Paradox*, (London: Weidenfeld & Nicolson, 1978)

Goldschmidt, Bertrand, *Atomic Rivals*, (New Brunswick, NJ: Rutgers University Press, 1990)

Gorodetsky, Gabriel, *Grand Delusion, Stalin and the German Invasion of Russia*, (New Haven, CT: Yale University Press, 1999)

Gorodetsky, Gabriel, *The Precarious Truce: Anglo-Soviet Relations 1924-27*, (Cambridge: Cambridge University Press, 1977)

Gorodetsky, Gabriel, *Stafford Cripps' Mission to Moscow 1940-42*, (Cambridge: Cambridge University Press, 1984)

Gorodetsky, Gabriel, (ed.), *Soviet Foreign Policy 1917-1991: A Retrospective*, (London: Frank Cass, 1994)

Gowing, Margaret, *Britain and Atomic Energy, 1939-45*, (London: Macmillan, 1964)

Gowing, Margaret, *Britain and Atomic Energy, 1945-52*, (London: Macmillan, 1974)

Graebner, Norman A. and Bennett, Edward M., *The Versailles Treaty and its Legacy: The Failure of the Wilsonian Vision*, (Cambridge: Cambridge University Press, 2011)

Hamby, Alonzo, *For the Survival of Democracy: Franklin Roosevelt and the World Crisis of the 1930s*, (New York, NY: Free Press, 2004)

Harriman, W. Averell and Abel, Elie, *Special Envoy to Churchill and Stalin, 1941-46*, (New York, NY: Random House, 1975)

Hayek, F. A., *The Fatal Conceit*, (Chicago, IL: The University of Chicago Press, 1988)

Hayek, F. A., *The Road to Serfdom*, (Chicago, IL: The University of Chicago Press, 1994)

Hobsbawm, *On History*, (New York, NY: The New Press, 1998)

Holland, James, *The War in the West: Germany Ascendant 1939-1941*, (London: Bantam Press, 2016)

Howson, Gerald, *Arms for Spain: The Untold Story of the Spanish Civil War*, (London: John Murray, 1998)

Hyde, H. Montgomery, *Stalin: The History of a Dictator*, (New York, NY: Farrar, Straus & Giroux, 1971)

Jackson, Julian, *The Fall of France: The Nazi Invasion of 1940*, (Oxford: Oxford University Press, 2003)

Jones, Michael K., *After Hitler: The Last Ten Days of World War II in Europe*, (London: John Murray, 2015)

Kennan, George, *Russia and the West under Lenin and Stalin*, (Boston, MA: Little, Brown, 1961),

Kershaw, Ian, *To Hell and Back: Europe 1914-1949*, (New York, NY: Viking, 2015)

Kilzer, Louis, *Churchill's Deception: The Dark Secret that Destroyed Nazi Germany*, (New York, NY: Simon & Schuster, 1994)

Kitchen, Martin, *British Policy towards the Soviet Union in the Second World War*, (Basingstoke: Macmillan, 1986)

Knight, Amy, *How the Cold War Began*, (New York, NY: Basic Books, 2007)

Kohn, Hans, *Revolutions and Dictatorships: Essays in Contemporary History*, (Cambridge, MA.: Harvard University Press, 1939)

Kostyrchenko, Gennadi, *Out of the Red Shadows: Anti-Semitism in Stalin's Russia*, (New York, NY: Prometheus Books, 1995)

Laqueur, Walter, *Putinism: Russia and its Future with the West*, (New York, NY: Thomas Dunne Books, 2015)

Laqueur, Walter, *Stalin: The Glasnost Revelations*, (London: Unwin, Hyman, 1990)

Laqueur, Walter and Breitman, Richard, *Breaking the Silence*, (New York, NY: Simon & Schuster, 1986)

Large, David Clay, *Between Two Fires: Europe's Path in the 1930s*, (New York, NY: Norton, 1990)

Laski, Harold J., *On the Communist Manifesto*, (London: Allen & Unwin, 1948)

Laski, Harold J., (ed.), *Where Stands Democracy?*, (London: Macmillan, 1940)

Laucht, Christopher, *Elemental Germans: Klaus Fuchs, Rudolf Peierls and the Making of British Nuclear Culture, 1939-59*, (Basingstoke: Palgrave Macmillan, 2012)

Leonhard, Wolfgang, *Betrayal: The Hitler-Stalin Pact of 1939*, (New York, NY: St Martin's Press, 1989)

Lindsay, A. D., *The Essentials of Democracy*, (London: Oxford University Press, 1935)

Lochery, Neill, *Lisbon: War in the Shadows of the City of Light, 1939-1945*, (New York, NY: Public Affairs, 2007)

London, Louise, *Whitehall and the Jews, 1933-1948: British Immigration Policy, Jewish Refugees and the Holocaust*, (Cambridge: Cambridge University Press, 2000)

Lukacs, John, *A Short History of the Twentieth Century*, (Cambridge, MA: Belknap Press, 2013)

Lukacs, John, *The Duel: May 10 – July 31, 1940: The Eighty-Day Struggle between Churchill and Hitler*, (Boston, MA: Ticknor, 1990)

Lukacs, John, *Five Days in London: May 1940*, (New Haven, CT: Yale University Press, 1999)

Lukacs, John, *June 1941: Hitler and Stalin*, (New Haven, CT: Yale University Press, 2006)

Lukacs, John, *The Future of History*, (New Haven, CT: Yale University Press, 2011)

Lukacs, John, *The Last European War*, (Garden City, NY: Anchor Press, 1976)

Lukacs, John, *The Legacy of the Second World War*, (New Haven, CT: Yale University Press, 2010)

Lukes, Igor, *Czechoslovakia between Stalin and Hitler: The Diplomacy of Edvard Benes*, (New York, NY: Oxford University Press, 1996)

Mazower, Mark, *Hitler's Empire*, (London: Allen Lane, 2008)

McLaine, Ian, *Ministry of Morale: Home Front Morale and the Ministry of Information in World War II*, (London: George Allen & Unwin, 1979)

Miner, Steven Merritt, *Between Churchill and Stalin: The Soviet Union, Great Britain and the Origins of the Grand Alliance*, (Chapel Hill, NC: University of North Carolina Press, 1988)

Miner, Steven Merritt, *Stalin's Holy War: Religion, Nationalism and Alliance Politics, 1941-1945*, (Chapel Hill, NC: University of North Carolina Press, 2003)

Moorhouse, Roger, *The Devils' Alliance: Hitler's Pact with Stalin, 1939-1941*, (New York, NY: Basic Books, 2014)

Murphy, David, *What Stalin Knew: The Enigma of Barbarossa*, (New Haven, CT: Yale University Press, 2005)

Nesbit, Roy Conyers and Van Acker, Georges, *The Flight of Rudolf Hess: Myths and Reality*, (Stroud: Sutton, 2007)

Nicholas. H. G., (ed.), *Washington Despatches 1941-45: Weekly Reports from the British Embassy*, (London: Weidenfeld & Nicolson, 1981)

Nicolson, Harold, *Why Britain is at War*, (Harmondsworth: Penguin, 1939)

Oakeshott, Michael, *Rationalism in Politics: And Other Essays*, (London: Methuen, 1974)

Olson, Lynne, *Troublesome Young Men*, (London: Bloomsbury, 2007)

Orlov, Alexander, *The Secret History of Stalin's Crimes*, (London: Jarrolds, 1954)

Overy, Richard, *The Twilight Years: The Paradox of Britain between the Wars*, (New York, NY: Viking, 2009)

Persico, Joseph E., *Roosevelt's Secret War: FDR and World War II Espionage*, (New York, NY: Random House, 2002)

Prior, Robin, *When Britain Saved the West: The Story of 1940*, (New Haven, CT: Yale University Press, 2005)

Ragsdale, Hugh, *The Soviets, the Munich Crisis, and the Coming of World War II*, (New York, NY: Cambridge University Press, 2004)

Rayfield, Donald, *Stalin and His Hangmen: The Tyrant and Those Who Killed for Him*, (New York, NY: Random House, 2004)

Read, Anthony and Fisher, David, *The Deadly Embrace: Hitler, Stalin and the Nazi-Soviet Pact 1939-1941*, (New York, NY: W. W. Norton, 1988)

Reynolds, David, *In Command of History*, (London: Penguin, 2005)

Reynolds, David, *The Long Shadow; The Great War and the Twentieth Century*, (London: Simon & Schuster, 2014)

Roberts, Andrew, *Eminent Churchillians*, (London: Weidenfeld & Nicolson, 1994)

Roberts, Andrew, *Hitler and Churchill: Secrets of Leadership*, (London: Weidenfeld & Nicolson, 2003)

Roberts, Andrew, *A History of the English-Speaking Peoples Since 1900*, (London: Weidenfeld & Nicolson, 2006)

Roberts, Geoffrey, *Stalin's Wars: From World War to Cold War, 1939-1953*, (New Haven, CT: Yale University Press, 2006)

Rose, N. A., *The Gentile Zionists: A Study in Anglo-Zionist Diplomacy, 1929-1939*, (London: Cass, 1973)

Rubenstein, Joshua and Naumov, Vladimir, P., *Stalin's Secret Pogrom: The Postwar Inquisition of the Jewish Anti-Fascist Committee*, (New Haven, CT: Yale University Press, 2001)

Shearer, David R., *Industry State and Society in Stalin's Russia, 1926-1934* (Ithaca, NY: Cornell University Press, 1996)

Smith, Elton Edward, *The Angry Young Men of the Thirties*, (Carbondale, IL: Southern Illinois University Press, 1975)

Snyder, Timothy, *Bloodlands: Europe between Hitler and Stalin*, (New York, NY: Basic Books, 2010)

Stafford, David, *Roosevelt and Churchill: Men of Secrets*, (London: Little & Brown, 1999)

Stafford, David, *Britain and European Resistance 1940-1945: A Survey of the Special Operations Executive*, (London: Macmillan, 1980)

Spender, Stephen, *Forward from Liberalism*, (London: Victor Gollancz, 1937)

Super, Robert H., (ed.) *The Complete Prose Works of Matthew Arnold* (Ann Arbor, MI: The University of Michigan Press, 1960-1977); Volume V: Culture and Anarchy with Friendship's Garland and Some Literary Essays (1965).

Swann, Paul, *The British Documentary Film Movement, 1926-1946*, (Cambridge: Cambridge University Press, 1989)

Tawney, R. H., *The Radical Tradition, Twelve Essays on Politics, Education and Literature*, (London: Allen & Unwin, 1964)

Taylor, A. J. P., *English History 1914-1945*, (Oxford: Oxford University Press, 1965)

Taylor, Philip M., *British Propaganda in the 20th Century: Selling Democracy*, (Edinburgh: Edinburgh University Press, 1999)

Thomas, Hugh, (ed.), *The Establishment*, (London: A. Blond, 1959)

Thompson, Neville, *The Anti-Appeasers: Conservative Opposition to Appeasement in the 1930s*, (Oxford: Clarendon Press, 1971)

Tucker, Robert C., *Stalin in Power: The Revolution from Above, 1928-1941*, (New York, NY: Norton, 1990)

Vital, David, *A People Apart: The Jews in Europe 1789-1939*, (Oxford: Oxford University Press, 1999)

Wapshott, Nicholas, *Keynes-Hayek: the Clash that Defined Modern Economics*, (New York, NY: W. W. Norton, 2012)

Watt, David Cameron, *How War Came*, (New York, NY: Pantheon Books, 1989)

West, Rebecca, *The New Meaning of Treason*, (New York, NY: Viking Press, 1964)

Wheeler-Bennett, John, *Munich: Prologue to Tragedy*, (London: Macmillan, 1963)

Wheeler-Bennett, John, *Special Relationships: America in Peace and War*, (London: Macmillan, 1975)

Wiener, Jan, *The Assassination of Heydrich*, (New York, NY: Grossman Publishers, 1969)

Wilson, Edmund, *The Thirties*, (New York, NY: Farrah, Straus & Giroux, 1980)

Wilson, Edmund, *To the Finland Station: a Study in the Writing and Acting of History*, (London: Collins, 1960)

Wood, Neal, *Communism and British Intellectuals*, (London: Victor Gollancz, 1959)

Espionage and Intelligence History

Akhmedov, Ismail, *In and Out of Stalin's GRU*, (Frederick, MD: University Publications of America, 1984)

Aldrich, Richard, *GCHQ*, (London: Harper Press, 2010)

Aldrich, Richard, *The Hidden Hand: Britain, America and Cold War Secret Intelligence*, (New York, NY: Overlook, 2001)

Andrew, Christopher, *Defend the Realm; The Authorized History of MI5*, (New York, NY: Knopf, 2009)

Andrew, Christopher, *Her Majesty's Secret Service: The Making of the British Intelligence Community*, (New York, NY: Viking Penguin, 1986)

Andrew, Christopher and Gordievsky, Oleg, *KGB: The Inside Story*, (New York, NY: Harper Collins, 1990)

Andrew, Christopher and Mitrokhin, Vasily, *The Mitrokhin Archive and the Secret History of the KGB*, (New York, NY: Basic Books, 1999)

Bagley, Tennent H., *Spymaster*, (New York, NY: Skyhorse Publishing, 2013)

Barron, John, *KGB: The Secret Work of Soviet Secret Agents*, (New York, NY: Dutton, 1974)

Bennett, Gill, *Churchill's Man of Mystery: Desmond Morton and the World of Intelligence*, (London: Routledge, 2007)

Bower, Tom, *The Red Web*, (London: Aurum, 1989)

Boyd, Douglas, *The Kremlin Conspiracy: A Long, Hot and Cold War*, (Hersham, Surrey: Ian Allan Publishing, 2010)

Boyle, Andrew, *The Climate of Treason*, (London: Hutchinson, 1982)

Brinson, Charmaine and Dove, Richard, *A Matter of Intelligence: MI5 and the Surveillance of Anti-Nazi Refugees*, (Manchester: Manchester University Press, 2014)

British Security Coordination, *The Secret History of British Intelligence in the Americas, 1940-45*, (New York, NY: Fromm, 1999)

Brook-Shepherd, Gordon, *The Storm Petrels*, (New York, NY: Ballantine, 1977)

Brook-Shepherd, Gordon, *The Storm Birds*, (London: Collins, 1977)

Bryden, John, *Best-kept Secret: Canadian Secret Intelligence in the Second World War*, (Toronto: Lester Publishing, 1993)

Bryden, John, *Fighting to Lose: How the German Secret Intelligence Service Helped the Allies Win the Second World War*, (Toronto: Dundurn, 2014)

Budiansky, Stephen, *Code Warriors: NSA's Codebreakers and the Secret Intelligence War against the Soviet Union*, (New York, NY: Alfred A. Knopf, 2016)

Bulloch, John, *MI5: The Origin and History of the British Counterespionage Service*, (London: A. Barker, 1963)

Burke, David, *The Lawn Road Flats*, (Woodbridge: The Boydell Press, 2014)

Cave-Brown, *Anthony, Treason in the Blood: H. St. John Philby, Kim Philby and the Spy Case of the Century*, (London: Robert Hale, 1995)

Chester, Lewis, Fay, Stephen and Young, Hugo, *The Zinoviev Letter*, (London: Heinemann, 1967)

Conant, Jennet, *The Irregulars: Roald Dahl and the British Spy Ring in Wartime Washington*, (New York, NY: Schuster, 2009)

Cookridge, E. H., *Soviet Spy Net*, (London: G. Muller, 1955)

Corera, Gordon, *The Art of Betrayal: The Secret History of MI6*, (New York, NY: Pegasus Books, 2013)

Costello, John, *Mask of Treachery: The First Documented Dossier on Blunt, MI5 and Soviet Subversion*, (London: Collins, 1988)

Costello, John and Tsarev, Oleg, *Deadly Illusions*, (London: Century, 1993)

Cradock, Percy, *Know Your Enemy: How the Joint Intelligence Committee Saw the World*, (London: John Murray, 2002)

Curry, John Court, *The Security Service 1908-1945: The Official History*, (Kew: Public Record Office, 1999)

Dallin, David, *Soviet Espionage*, (New Haven, CT: Yale University Press, 1955)

Deacon, Richard, *A History of the British Secret Service*, (London: Grafton, 1991)

Deacon, Richard, *A History of the Russian Secret Service*, (London: Grafton, 1987)

Deacon, Richard, *The British Connection*, (London: Hamish Hamilton, 1979)

Deacon, Richard, *The Greatest Treason: The Bizarre Story of Hollis, Liddell and Mountbatten* (London: Century, 1990)

Deacon, Richard, *With My Little Eye: Memoirs of a Spy Hunter*, (London: Frederick Muller, 1982)

Dear, Ian, *Spy and Counterspy: Secret Agents and Double Agents from the Second World War*, (Stroud: Spellmount, 2013)

Dorril, Stephen, *MI6: Inside the Covert World of Her Majesty's Secret Intelligence Service* (New York, NY: Simon & Schuster, 2000)

Duff, William E., *A Time for Spies: Theodore Stephanovich Mally and the Era of the Great Illegals*, (Nashville, TN: Vanderbilt University Press, 1999)

Elliott, Geoffrey and Shukman, Harold, *Secret Classrooms: A Memoir of the Cold War*, (London: St Ermin's, 2003)

Evans, M. Stanton and Romerstein, Herbert, *Stalin's Secret Agents: The Subversion of Roosevelt's Government*, (New York, NY: Threshold Editions, 2012)

Farago, Ladislas, *Burn after Reading*, (New York, NY: Walker & Co., 1961)

Farago, Ladislas, *The Broken Seal: The Story of Operation Magic and the Pearl Harbor Disaster*, (New York, NY: Random House, 1967)

Firsov, Fridrich Igorevich, Klehr, Harvey and Haynes, John Earl, *Secret Cables of the Comintern 1933-1943*, (New Haven, CT: Yale University Press, 2014)

Foot, M.R.D., *SOE: The Special Operations Executive 1940-1946*, (London: Pimlico, 1999)

Garnett, David, *The Secret History of PWE: The Political Warfare Executive*, (London: St. Ermin's Press, 2002)

Glees, Anthony, *The Secrets of the Service: British Intelligence and Communist Subversion 1939-51*, (London: Cape, 1987)

Hamrick, D. J., *Deceiving the Deceivers: Kim Philby, Donald Maclean and Guy Burgess*, (New Haven, CT: Yale University Press, 2004)

Haslam, Jonathan, *Near and Distant Neighbors: A New History of Soviet Intelligence*, (Oxford: Oxford University Press, 2015)

Hastings, Max, *The Secret War: Spies, Codes and Guerrillas, 1939-1945*, (London: William Collins, 2015)

Haynes, John Earl and Klehr, Harvey, *In Denial: Historians, Communism & Espionage*, (San Francisco, CA: Encounter Books, 2003)

Haynes, John Earl and Klehr, Harvey, *Venona: Decoding Soviet Espionage in America*, (New Haven, CT: Yale University Press, 1999)

Haynes, John Earl, Klehr, Harvey and Vassiliev, Alexander, *Spies: The Rise and Fall of the KGB in America*, (New Haven, CT: Yale University Press, 2009)

Hennessy, Peter, *The Secret State: Whitehall and the Cold War*, (London: Allen Lane The Penguin Press, 2002)

Hingley, Ronald, *The Russian Secret Police: Muscovite, Imperial Russian and Soviet Political Operations, 1565-1970*, (London: Hutchinson, 1970)

Hinsley, F. H., *et al.*, *British Intelligence in the Second World War, Volumes 1 & 4*, (London: Her Majesty's Stationery Office, 1979 & 1990)

Hinsley, F.H. and Stripp, Alan (ed.s), *Codebreakers: The Inside Story of Bletchley Park*, (Oxford: Oxford University Press, 2003)

Irving, David (ed.), *Breach of Security: The German Secret Intelligence File on Events Leading to the Second World War*, (London: William & Kimber, 1968)

Jeffery, Keith, *The Secret History of MI6*, (New York, NY: Penguin, 2011) [in the UK *The History of MI6*]

Jeffreys-Jones, Rhodri, *In Spies We Trust: The Story of Western Intelligence*, (Oxford: Oxford University Press, 2015)

Keegan, John, *Intelligence in War: Knowledge of the Enemy from Napoleon to Al-Qaeda*, (London: Hutchinson, 2003)

Knight, Amy W., *The KGB: Police and Politics in the Soviet Union*, (Boston, MA: Allen & Unwin, 1988)

Lamphere, Robert J. and Tom Shachtman, *The FBI-KGB War: A Special Agent's Story*, (New York, NY: Random House, 1986)

Leigh, David, *The Wilson Plot: The Intelligence Services and the Discrediting of a Prime Minister*, (London: Heinemann, 1988)

Lewin, Ronald, *Ultra Goes to War: The Secret Story*, (London: Hutchinson, 1978)

Lucas, Edward, *Deception: The Untold Story of East-West Espionage Today*, (New York, NY: Walker Publishing, 2012)

Lulushi, Albert, *Operation Valuable Fiend: The CIA's First Paramilitary Strike against the Iron Curtain*, (New York, NY: Arcade, 2014)

Macksey, Kenneth, *The Searchers: Radio Interception in Two World Wars*, (London: Cassell, 2004)

Madeira, Victor, *Britannia and the Bear, The Anglo-Russian Intelligence Wars 1917-1929*, (Woodbridge: Boydell Press, 2014)

Martin, David, *Wilderness of Mirrors*, (New York, NY: Harper & Row, 1980)

Mahl, Thomas E., *Desperate Deception: British Covert Operations in the United States, 1939-44*, (Washington, D.C.: Brassey's, 1998)

Masterman, John, *The Double-Cross System*, (New York, NY: Avon Books, 1972)

McKay, Sinclair, *The Secret World of Bletchley Park*, (London: Aurum, 2011)

McKenzie, William, *The Secret History of SOE: The Special Operations Executive 1940-1945*, (London: St. Ermin's Press, 2000)

McKnight, David, *Espionage and the Roots of the Cold War: The Conspiratorial Heritage*, (London: Frank Cass, 2002)

Moorehead, Alan, *The Traitors: The Double Life of Fuchs, Pontecorvo and Nunn May*, (London: Hamish Hamilton, 1952)

Moran, Christopher, *Classified: Secrecy and the State in Modern Britain*, (Cambridge: Cambridge University Press, 2013)

Mure, David, *Master of Deception: Tangled Webs in London and the Middle East*, (London: W. Kimber, 1980)

Newton, Verne, *The Cambridge Spies: The Untold Story of Maclean, Philby and Burgess in America*, (Lanham, MD: Madison Books, 1991)

Page, Bruce, Leitch, David and Knightley, Phillip, *The Philby Conspiracy*, (Garden City, NY: Doubleday, 1968)

Pincher, Chapman, *Treachery: Betrayals, Blunders and Cover-ups: Six Decades of Espionage against America and Great Britain*, (New York, NY: Random House, 2009)

Pincher, Chapman, *Too Secret Too Long: The Great Betrayal of Britain's Crucial Secrets and the Cover-up*, (London: Sidgwick & Jackson, 1984)

Quinlan, Kevin, *The Secret War between the Wars: MI5 in the 1920s and 1930s*, (Woodbridge: Boydell Press, 2014)

Rositske, Harry A., *The KGB: The Eyes of Russia* (London: Sidgwick & Jackson, 1982)

Schechter, Jerrold and Schechter, Leona, *Sacred Secrets: How Soviet Intelligence Operations Changed American History*, (Washington, D.C.: Potomac Books, 2002)

Scott, L.V., and Jackson, Peter, (ed.s), *Understanding Intelligence in the Twenty-First Century: Journeys in Shadows*, (London: Routledge, 2004)

Shipley, Peter, *Hostile Action: the KGB and Secret Soviet Operations in Britain*, (London: Pinter, 1989)

Shulsky, Abram N. and Schmitt, Gary J., *Silent Warfare: Understanding the World of Intelligence*, (Washington, D.C.: Potomac Books, 2002)

Sinclair, Andrew, *The Red and the Blue: Intelligence, Treason and the Universities*, (London: Coronet Books, 1986)

Smith, James, *British Writers and MI5 Surveillance, 1930-1960*, (Cambridge: Cambridge University Press, 2012)

Smith, Michael, *Six: A History of Britain's Secret Intelligence Service, Part 1: Murder and Mayhem 1909-1939*, (London: Biteback, 2010)

Smith Michael, *The Spying Game: The Secret History of Britain's Espionage*, (London: Politico's, 2003)

Stafford, David, *Churchill & Secret Service*, (London: John Murray, 1997)

Trevor-Roper, Hugh, *The Philby Affair*, (London: William Kimber, 1968)

Turnbull, Malcolm, *The Spycatcher Trial*, (Topsfield, MA: Salem House, 1989)

Twigge, Stephen, Hampshire, Edward and Macklin, Graham, *British Intelligence: Secrets, Spies and Sources*, (Kew: National Archives, 2008)

University Publications of America, *The Rote Kapelle: The CIA's History of Soviet Intelligence and Espionage Networks in Western Europe, 1936-1945*, (Washington, D.C.: University Publications, 1979)

Urbach, Karina, *Go-betweens for Hitler*, (Oxford: Oxford University Press, 2015)

Walton, Calder, *Empire of Secrets: British Intelligence, the Cold War and the Twilight of Empire*, (London: William Collins, 2014)

Weinstein, Allen and Vassiliev, Alexander, *The Haunted Wood: Soviet Espionage in America – the Stalin Era*, (New York, NY: Random House, 1999)

Welchman, Gordon, *The Hut Six Story: Breaking the Enigma Codes*, (New York, NY: McGraw-Hill, 1982)

West, Nigel, *GCHQ: The Secret Wireless War 1900-86*, (London: Weidenfeld & Nicolson, 1986)

West, Nigel, *Mask: MI5's Penetration of the Communist Party in Great Britain*, (London: Routledge, 2005)

West, Nigel, *Molehunt: Searching for Soviet Spies in MI5*, (London: Weidenfeld & Nicolson, 1987)

West, Nigel, *MI5*, (London: Grafton, 1987)

West, Nigel, *MI5. 1945-72: A Matter of Trust*, (London: Coronet Books, 1983)

West, Nigel, *MI6*, (New York, NY: Random House, 1983)

West, Nigel, *Mortal Crimes; The Greatest Theft in History: Soviet Penetration of the Manhattan Project*, (New York, NY: Enigma Books, 2004)

West, Nigel, *The Illegals: The Double Lives of the Cold War's Most Secret Agents*, (London: Coronet Books, 1984)

West, Nigel, *Venona: The Greatest Secret of the Cold War*, (London: Harper Collins, 1989)

West, Nigel and Tsarev, Oleg, *The Crown Jewels: The British Secrets at the Heart of the KGB Archive*, (New Haven, CT: Yale University Press, 1999)

West, Nigel and Tsarev, Oleg, (ed.s), *Triplex: Secrets from the Cambridge Spies*, (New Haven, CT: Yale University Press, 2009)

West, W. J., *The Truth About Hollis*, (London: Duckworth, 1989)

West, W. J., *Truth Betrayed*, (London, Duckworth, 1987)

Williams, Wythe and Van Narvig, William, *Secret Sources*, (Chicago, IL: Ziff Davis, 1943)

Winterbotham, F. W., *The Nazi Connection*, (London: Weidenfeld & Nicolson, 1978)
Winterbotham, F. W., *The Ultra Secret*, (London: Weidenfeld & Nicolson, 1974)
Wright, Peter, *Spycatcher*, (New York, NY: Viking, 1987)

Biography, Memoir, Letters and Diaries

Abraham, Richard, *Alexander Kerensky: The First Love of the Revolution*, (New York, NY: Columbia University Press, 1987)
Albright, Madeleine, *Prague Winter*, (New York, NY: Harper, 2013)
Andrews, Geoff, *The Shadow Man: At the Heart of the Cambridge Spy Circle* (London: I. B. Tauris, 2015)
Annan, Noel, *Changing Enemies: The Defeat and Regeneration of Germany*, (Ithaca, NY: Cornell University Press, 1997)
Balabanoff, Angelica, *My Life as a Rebel*, (London: Hamish Hamilton, 1938)
Bartley, Paula, *Ellen Wilkinson, From Red Suffragist to Government Minister*, (London: Pluto Press, 2014)
Belfrage, Cedric, *The Frightened Giant: My Unfinished Affair with America*, (New York, NY: Secker & Warburg, 1957)
Bennett, Mary, *An Autobiography*, (Oxford: St. Hilda's College, 1997 [private])
Bentley, Elizabeth, *Out of Bondage*, (New York, NY: Devin Adair, 1951)
Berberova, Nina, *Moura: The Dangerous Life of the Baroness Budberg*, (New York, NY: New York Review Books, 2005)
Berlin, Isaiah, *Letters 1930-1946*, (New York, NY: Cambridge University Press, 2004)
Berlin, Isaiah, *Karl Marx*, (Princeton, NJ: Princeton University Press, 2013)
Berlin, Isaiah, *Personal Impressions*, (Princeton, NJ: Princeton University Press, 2001)
Berlin, Isaiah, and Jahanbegloo, Ramin, *Conversations with Isaiah Berlin*, (London: Phoenix, 2000)
Born, Max, *My Life and My Views*, (New York, NY: Scribner, 1968)
Born, Max, *My Life: Recollections of a Nobel Laureate*, (London: Taylor & Francis, 1968)
Borovikh, Genrikh, *The Philby Files: The Secret Life of Master Spy Kim Philby*, (Toronto: Little, Brown, 1994)
Bower, Tom, *The Perfect English Spy: Sir Dick White and the Secret War, 1935-90*, (New York, NY: St. Martin's Press, 1996)
Brivati, Brian, *Hugh Gaitskell*, (London: Politico's, 2006)
Burke, David, *The Spy Who Came in from the Co-Op*, (Woodbridge: Boydell Press, 2013)
Cadogan, Sir Alexander, *The Diaries of Sir Alexander Cadogan O.M., 1938-1945*, (New York, NY: Putnam, 1972)
Cairncross, John, *The Enigma Spy*, (London: Century, 1997)
Carney, Michael, *Stoker, the Life of Hilda Matheson, OBE*, (Llangynog: privately published, 1999)
Carter, Miranda, *Anthony Blunt: His Lives*, (New York, NY: Picador, 2001)
Caute, David, *Isaac and Isaiah: The Covert Punishment of a Cold War Heretic*, (New Haven, CT: Yale University Press, 2013)
Cave-Brown, Anthony, *'C': The Secret Life of Sir Stewart Graham Menzies, Spymaster to Winston Churchill*, (New York, NY: Macmillan, 1997)
Cecil, Robert, *A Divided Life, a Biography of Donald Maclean*, (London: Bodley Head, 1988)
Chambers, Whittaker, *Odyssey of a Friend*, (*New York*, NY: National Review, 1969)
Chambers, Whittaker, *Witness*, (New York, NY: Random House, 1952)
Cookridge, E. H., *The Third Man: The Truth about 'Kim' Philby, Double Agent*, (London: Barker, 1968)
Cooper, Duff, *Old Men Forget*, (London: Hart Davis, 1953)

Dalos, György, *The Guest from the Future: Anna Akhmatova and Isaiah Berlin*, (London: John Murray, 1998)

Dalton, Hugh, *The Fateful Years: Memoirs, 1931-1945*, (London: Muller, 1962)

Damaskin, Igor, with Geoffrey Elliott, *Kitty Harris: The Spy with Seventeen Names*, (London: St. Ermin's Press, 2002)

Davies, Joseph, *Mission to Moscow, a Record of Confidential Despatches to the State Department*, (New York, NY: Simon & Schuster, 1941)

Day, John, *Klop: Britain's Most Ingenious Secret Agent*, (London: Biteback, 2014)

De Lattre, Lucas, *A Spy at the Heart of the Third Reich, the Extraordinary Story of Fritz Kolbe, America's Most Important Spy in World War II*, (New York, NY: Grove Press, 2006)

Draitser, Emil, *Agent Dimitri: The Remarkable Rise and Fall of the KGB's Most Daring Operative*, (London: Duckworth, 2012)

Driberg, Tom, *Guy Burgess: A Portrait with Background*, (London: Weidenfeld & Nicolson, 1956)

Driberg, Tom, *Ruling Passions*, (London: Cape, 1977)

Dubnov, Arie M., *Isaiah Berlin: The Journey of a Jewish Liberal*, (Basingstoke: Palgrave Macmillan, 2012)

Dugdale, Blanche, *The Diaries of Blanche Dugdale, 1936-1947*, (London: Vallentine, Mitchell, 1973)

Elliott, Nicholas, *Never Judge a Man by His Umbrella*, (Wilton: Michael Russell, 1991)

Evans, Trevor, *Bevin of Britain*, (New York, NY: Norton, 1946)

Fest, Joachim, *Not I: Memoirs of a German Childhood*, (New York, NY: Other Press, 2013)

Foote, Andrew, *Handbook for Spies*, (Garden City, NY: Doubleday, 1949)

Freeman, Simon and Penrose, Barry, *Conspiracy of Silence: The Secret Life of Anthony Blunt*, (London: Grafton Books, 1986)

Fry, Helen, *Spymaster: The Secret Life of Kendrick*, (London: CreateSpace Publishing, 2014)

Gamow, George, *My World Line: An Informal Autobiography*, (New York, NY: Viking, 1970)

Gardiner, Muriel, *Code Name 'Mary': Memoirs of an American Woman in the Austrian Underground*, (New Haven, CT: Yale University Press, 1983)

Gazur, Edmund, *Alexander Orlov: The FBI's KGB General*, (New York, NY: Carroll & Graf, 2002)

Gide, André, *Return from the USSR*, (London: Secker & Warburg, 1937)

Gillies, Donald, *Radical Diplomat: The Life of Sir Archibald Clark Kerr, Lord Inverchapel, 1882-1951*, (London: I. B. Tauris, 1998)

Gladwyn, Lord, *The Memoirs of Lord Gladwyn*, (London: Weidenfeld & Nicolson, 1972)

Glover, Gerald, *115 Park Street*, (Kettering: privately published, 1982)

Graham, Katherine, *Personal History*, (New York, NY: Vintage, 1998)

Grant, Thomas, *The Casebook of Jeremy Hutchinson*, (London: John Murray, 2015)

Grant Duff, Shiela, *The Parting of Ways: A Personal Account of the Thirties*, (London: Unwin Paperbacks, 1982)

Halifax, Lord, *Fullness of Days*, (New York, NY: Dodd, Mead & Company, 1957)

Hampshire, Stuart, *Innocence and Experience*, (Cambridge, MA: Harvard University Press, 1989)

Harriman, W. Averell and Abel, Elie, *Special Envoy to Churchill and Stalin, 1941-1946*, (New York, NY: Random House, 1975)

Harris, Kenneth, *Attlee*, (New York, NY: W. W. Norton, 1983)

Harrison, Edward, *The Young Kim Philby*, (Exeter, Devon: The University of Exeter Press, 2012)

Hart, Jenifer, *Ask Me No More*, (London: Peter Halban, 1998)

Hayes, Paddy, *Queen of Spies: Daphne Park, Britain's Cold War Spy Master*, (New York, NY: Duckworth Overlook, 2015)

Hayward, James, *Double Agent Snow: The True Story of Arthur Owens, Hitler's Chief Spy in England*, (London: Simon & Schuster, 2013)

Henderson, Sir Nevile, *Failure of a Mission*, (New York, NY: G. P. Putnam's Sons, 1940)

Heppenstall, Ray, *Four Absentees*, (London: Barrie & Rockcliffe, 1960)

Hingley, Ronald, *Joseph Stalin, Man and Legend*, (New York, NY: Konecky & Konecky, 1974)

Hiss, Alger, *Recollections of a Life*, (New York, NY: Seaver Books, 1988)

Hobsbawm, Eric, *On the Edge of the New Century*, (New York, NY: The New Press, 2000)

Holzman, Michael, *Donald and Melinda Maclean: Idealism and Espionage*, (Briarcliff Manor, NY: Chelmsford Press, 2014)

Holzman, Michael, *Guy Burgess: Revolutionary in an Old School Tie*, (Briarcliff Manor, NY: Chelmsford Press, 2012)

Hyde, H. Montgomery, *Room 3603 [The Quiet Canadian: The Secret Service Story of Sir William Stephenson]*, (New York, NY: Farrar, Strauss, 1962)

Ignatieff, Michael, *Isaiah Berlin: A Life*, (New York, NY: Metropolitan Books, 2008)

Jenkins, Roy, *Churchill: A Biography*, (New York, NY: Farrar, Strauss & Giroux, 2001)

Johnson, R. W., *Look Back in Laughter: Oxford's Postwar Golden Age*, (Newbury: Threshold Press, 2015)

Joll, James, *Three Intellectuals in History*, (New York, NY: Harper & Row, 1962)

Jowitt, the Earl, *Some Were Spies*, (London: Hodder & Stoughton, 1954)

Karski, Jan, *Story of a Secret State: My Report to the World*, (London: Penguin, 2012)

Kennan, George, *Memoirs, 1925-1950*, (Boston: Little, Brown, 1967)

Kern, Gary, *A Death in Washington: Walter G. Krivitsky and the Stalin Terror*, (New York, NY: Enigma, 2003)

Kern, Gary, *The Kravchenko Case: One Man's War on Stalin*, (New York, NY: Enigma, 2007)

Kershaw, Ian, *Hitler: Hubris 1889-1936*, (New York, NY: W. W. Norton, 1999)

Kershaw, Ian, *Hitler: Nemesis 1936-1945*, (New York, NY: W. W. Norton, 2000)

Koch, Eric, *Deemed Suspect: A Wartime Blunder*, (Toronto: Methuen, 1980)

Koestler, Arthur, *Promise and Fulfilment, Palestine 1917-1949*, (New York, NY: Macmillan, 1983)

Koestler, Arthur, *The Yogi and the Commissar, and Other Essays*, (London: Jonathan Cape, 1985)

Koestler, Arthur, *The Invisible Writing: The Second Volume of an Autobiography, 1932-1940*, (London: Hutchinson, 1969)

Kramnick, Isaac and Sheerman, Barry, *Harold Laski, a Life on the Left*, (London: Hamish Hamilton, 1993)

Krivitsky, Walter, *In Stalin's Secret Service*, (New York, NY: Enigma Books, 2000)

Lacey, Nicola, *A Life of H. L. A. Hart: The Nightmare and the Noble Dream*, (Oxford: Oxford University Press, 2004)

Lacouture, Jean, *Léon Blum*, (New York, NY: Holmes & Meier, 1982)

Levine, Isaac, *Eyewitness to History*, (New York, NY: Hawthorne, 1973)

Levine, Isaac, *I Rediscover Russia 1924-1954*, (New York, NY: Duell, Sloan & Pearce, 1964)

Liddell, Guy, (ed.) West, Nigel, *The Guy Liddell Diaries, Volume 1: 1939-1942*, (Abingdon: Routledge, 2005)

Liddell, Guy, (ed.) West, Nigel, *The Guy Liddell Diaries, Volume 2: 1942-1945*, (Abingdon: Routledge, 2005)

Lockhart, Robert Bruce, (ed.) Young, Kenneth, *The Diaries of Sir Robert Bruce Lockhart, 1915-1938*, (New York, NY: St. Martin's Press, 1973)

Lockhart, Robert Bruce, (ed.) Young, Kenneth, *The Diaries of Sir Robert Bruce Lockhart, 1939-1965*, (London: Macmillan, 1980)

Lockhart, Robert Bruce, *Comes the Reckoning*, (London: Putnam, 1947)

Lockhart, Robert Bruce, *Guns or Butter*, (Boston, MA: Little, Brown, 1938)

Lockhart, Robert Bruce, *Retreat from Glory*, (New York, NY: Garden City, 1938)

Lownie, Andrew, *Stalin's Englishman: The Lives of Guy Burgess*, (London: Hodder & Stoughton, 2015)

Maclean, Fitzroy, *Eastern Approaches*, (London: Penguin, 1991)

Macmillan, Harold, *Winds of Change, 1914-1939* (London: Macmillan, 1966)

Maisky, Ivan, *Memoirs of a Soviet Ambassador: The War 1939-1943*, (London: Hutchinson, 1967)

Maisky, Ivan, (ed.) Gabriel Gorodetsky, *The Maisky Diaries: Red Ambassador to the Court of St. James's, 1932-1943*, (New Haven, CT: Yale University Press, 2015)

Manchester, William, and Reid, Paul, *The Last Lion: Winston Spencer Churchill, Defender of the Realm 1940-1965*, (New York, NY: Little, Brown, 2012)

Mann, Wilfrid Basil, *Was There a Fifth Man?: Quintessential Recollections*, (New York, NY: Pergamon Press, 1982)

Marton, Kati, *True Believer: Stalin's Last American Spy*, (New York: NY: Simon & Schuster, 2016)

Masterman, John, *On the Chariot Wheel*, (London: Oxford University Press, 1975)

Masters, Anthony, *The Man Who Was M: The Life of Maxwell Knight*, (Oxford: Basil Blackwell, 1984)

Macintyre, Ben, *A Spy among Friends: Kim Philby and the Great Betrayal*, (New York, NY: Crown, 2014)

McKinnon, Janice and McKinnon, Stephen, *Agnes Smedley: The Life and Times of an American Radical*, (Berkeley, CA: University of California Press, 1988)

Miles, Jonathan, *The Nine Lives of Otto Katz: The Remarkable Story of a Communist Super-Spy*, (London: Bantam, 2010)

Miller, Joan, *One Girl's War: Personal Exploits in MI5's Most Secret Station*, (Dingle, Eire: Brandon, 1986)

Milne, Tim, *Kim Philby: The Unknown Story of KGB's Master Spy*, (London: Biteback, 2014)

Mitchison, Naomi, *Vienna Diary 1934*, (Glasgow: Kennedy & Boyd, 2009)

Modin, Yuri, *My Five Cambridge Friends*, (New York, NY: Farrar, Strauss, Giroux, 1994)

Moravec, Frantisek, *Master of Spies*, (New York, NY: Doubleday, 1975)

Morton, Frederick, *The Rothschilds: A Family Portrait*, (New York, NY: Atheneum, 1962)

Moss, Norman, *Klaus Fuchs: The Man Who Stole the Atom Bomb*, (New York, NY: St. Martin's Press, 1987)

Muggeridge, Malcolm, *Chronicles of Wasted Time*, (London: Collins, 1972)

Mulley, Clare, *The Spy Who Loved: The Secrets and Lives of Christine Granville, Britain's First Female Special Agent of the Second World War*, (London: Macmillan, 2012)

Mure, David, *The Last Temptation: A Novel of Treason*, (London: Buchan & Enright, 1984)

Neville, Peter, *Eduard Beneš and Tomáš Masaryk: Czechoslovakia*, (London: Haus, 2010)

Nicolson, Harold, (ed.) Nicolson, Nigel, *Volume II of the Diaries & Letters of Harold Nicolson: The War Years, 1939-1945*, (New York, NY: Atheneum, 1967)

Peierls, Rudolf, *Bird of Passage: Recollections of a Physicist*, (Princeton, NJ: Princeton University Press, 1985)

Perry, Roland, *Last of the Cold War Spies: The Life of Michael Straight, the Only American in Britain's Cambridge Spy Ring*, (Cambridge, MA: Da Capo Press, 2005)

Perry, Roland, *The Fifth Man*, (London: Sidgwick & Jackson, 1994)

Philby, Kim, *My Silent War*, (New York, NY: Grove Press, 1968)

Philby, Rufina, with Peake, Hayden, and Lyubimov, Mikhail, *The Private Life of Kim Philby: The Moscow Years*, (New York, NY: Fromm International, 2000)

Pincher, Chapman, *Dangerous to Know: A Life*, (London: Biteback, 2014)

Poretsky, Elisabeth K., *Our Own People: A Memoir of 'Ignace Reiss' and his Friends*, (Ann Arbor, MI: University of Michigan Press, 1969)

Purvis, Stewart and Hulbert, Jeff, *Guy Burgess: The Spy Who Knew Everyone*, (London: Biteback, 2016)

Radzinsky, Edward, *Stalin*, (New York, NY: Doubleday, 1996)

Rand, Peter, *Conspiracy of One: Tyler Kent's Secret Plot against FDR, Churchill and the Allied War Effort*, (Guildford, CT: Lyons Press, 2013)

Read, Anthony and Fisher, David, *Colonel Z*, (New York, NY: Viking Penguin, 1985)

Rees, Goronwy, *A Chapter of Accidents*, (New York, NY: The Library Press, 1972)

Rees, Jenny, *Looking for Mr Nobody: The Secret Life of Goronwy Rees*, (New Brunswick, NJ: Transaction Publishers, 2000)

Riley, Morris, *Philby: The Hidden Years*, (Penzance: United Writers, 1990)

Roberts, Andrew, *The Holy Fox: A Life of Lord Halifax*, (London: Head of Zeus, 2014)

Rose, Kenneth, *Elusive Rothschild: The Life of Victor, Third Baron*, (London: Weidenfeld & Nicolson, 2003)

Rose, Norman, *Chaim Weizmann: A Biography*, (London: Weidenfeld & Nicolson, 1986)

Rose, Norman, *Harold Nicolson*, (London: Pimlico, 2006)

Roskill, S. W., *Hankey: Man of Secrets*, (London: Collins, 1974)

Rossiter, Mike, *The Spy Who Changed the World*, (London: Headline, 2004)

Rothschild, Nathaniel Meyer Victor, Baron, *Meditations of a Broomstick*, (London: Collins, 1977)

Schlesinger, Arthur M. Jr., *A Life in the Twentieth Century: Innocent Beginnings, 1917-1950*, (Boston, MA: Houghton Mifflin, 2000)

Schofield, Victoria, *Witness to History*, (New Haven, CT: Yale University Press, 2012)

Seale, Patrick and McConville, Maureen, *Philby, the Long Road to Moscow*, (Harmondsworth: Penguin, 1978)

Serge, Victor, *Memoirs of a Revolutionary, 1901-1941*, (London: Oxford University Press, 1963)

Sillitoe, Sir Percy, *Cloak without Dagger*, (London: Cassell, 1955)

Sisman, Adam, *An Honorable Englishman, the Life of Hugh Trevor-Roper*, (New York, NY: Random House, 2011)

Skidelsky, Robert, *Oswald Mosley*, (London: Macmillan, 1981)

Solomon, Flora, *Baku to Baker Street*, (London: Collins, 1984)

Spender, Matthew, *A House in St. John's Wood*, (New York, NY: Farrar, Strauss & Giroux, 2015)

Spender, Stephen , *Letters to Christopher*, (Santa Barbara, CA: Black Sparrow Press, 1970)

Spender, Stephen, *World within World*, (New York, NY: St. Martin's Press, 1994)

Stallworthy, Jon, *Louis Macneice: A Biography*, (New York, NY: Norton, 1995)

Stanford, Peter, *C. Day Lewis: A Life*, (London: Continuum, 2007)

Straight, Michael Whitney, *After Long Silence*, (New York, NY: W. W. Norton, 1983)

Strauss, Michel, *Pictures, Passions and Eye*, (London: Halban, 2011)

Sudoplatov, Pavel, and Sudoplatov, Anatoli, *Special Tasks*, (Boston: Little, Brown, 1994)

Sutherland, John, *Stephen Spender: A Literary Life*, (New York, NY: Oxford University Press, 2005)

Sweet-Escott, Bickham, *Baker Street Irregular*, (London: Methuen, 1965)

Thomas, Hugh, *John Strachey*, (New York, NY: Harper & Row, 1973)

Toynbee, Philip, *Friends Apart: A Memoir of the Thirties*, (London: McKibbon & Kee, 1954)

Trevor-Roper, H. R., *Historical Essays*, (London: Macmillan, 1957)

Trevor-Roper, Hugh, (ed.) Harrison, Edward, *The Secret World: Behind the Curtain of British Intelligence in World War II and the Cold War*, (New York, NY: I. B. Tauris, 2014)

Trevor-Roper, Hugh, (ed.) Davenport-Hines, Richard, *The Wartime Journals*, (New York, NY: I. B. Tauris, 2015)

Ulam, Adam B., *Stalin, the Man and his Era*, (New York, NY: Viking, 1973)

Ulrich, Volker, *Hitler: Ascent 1889-1939*, (New York, NY: Alfred A. Knopf, 2016)

Valtin, Jan, *Out of the Night*, (London: Fortress, 1988)

Vansittart, Robert Gilbert, Baron, *The Mist Procession*, (London: Hutchinson, 1958)

Volkogonov, Dmitri, *Stalin, Triumph and Tragedy*, (New York, NY: Grove, Weidenfeld, 1991)

Volodarsky, Boris, *Stalin's Agent: The Life and Death of Alexander Orlov*, (Oxford: Oxford University Press, 2015)

Weizmann, Chaim, *The Letters and Papers of Chaim Weizmann*, (London: Oxford University Press, 1980)

Werner, Ruth, *Sonjas Rapport*, (Berlin: Verlag Neues Leben, 1977)

Wheeler-Bennett, John, *Knaves, Fools and Heroes: In Europe between the Wars*, (London: Macmillan, 1974)

Wheen, Francis, *Tom Driberg: His Life and Indiscretions*, (London: Chatto & Windus, 1990)

Whitwell, John, *British Agent*, (London: Kimber, 1966)

Williams, Francis, *A Prime Minister Remembers: The War and Post-war Memoirs of the Rt. Hon. Earl Attlee*, (London: Heinemann, 1961)

Williams, Phillip, *Hugh Gaitskell: A Political Biography*, (Oxford: Oxford University Press, 1982)

Williams, Robert Chadwell, *Klaus Fuchs: Atom Spy*, (Cambridge, MA: Harvard University Press, 1987)

Wilmers, Mary-Kay, *The Eitingons: A Twentieth-Century Story*, (London: Faber, 2010)

Wilson, Jim, *Nazi Princess: Hitler, Lord Rothermere and Princess Stephanie von Hohenlohe*, (Stroud: History Press, 2011)

Index

A

Abwehr, 105, 192
AERE (Atomic Energy Research Establishment, 'Harwell'), 206, 235, 240, 243, 259, 261, 263
Agabekov, Georges, 53
Agents of Influence, 138-165, 177, 271, 281
Air Intelligence, 232
Akhmatova, Anna, 124, 157
Akhmedov, Ismail, 280
Akhmerov, Iskhak, 52
Albright, Madeleine, 187
Aliens, 4, 8, 83, 175, 181, 185, 188, 189, 224, 247, 250, 267
Aliens Review Board (Tribunal), 220, 232-234, 259, 260, 261
Aliens War Service permit, 224, 226, 229, 235
All Souls College, 8, 95, 97, 124, 150, 158
Allen, Walter, 21
Alsop, Joseph, 103
American Joint Committee on Atomic Energy, 262
Anderson, John, 17, 178, 181, 188, 218-219
Androceta, 251
Angleton, James, 242
Anglo-German Fellowship, 43, 84, 93, 106, 108, 137, 139, 163, 279
Anti-Semitism, 173, 278, 279
Annan, Noël, 97, 158, 192, 199, 283
Apostles, 140, 190, 196
Appleton, Edward, 226, 245, 246, 263
Arandora Star, 188
Archer, Jane (née Sissmore)
    alleged 'long inquiry' into Soviet espionage, 181
    appointed to MI5, 3
    attempt with Kell to track Krivitsky, 12, 66, 67
    career in MI5 and expertise on communism, 21-24, 36, 55, 64-65, 75, 133
    congratulated by Vivian, 32
    dismissed from MI5 for insubordination, 67, 119
    doggedness in tracking down Foreign Office spies, 55, 119
    identifies threat of Nazi-Soviet conspiracies, 56-57, 65
    interrogation of Krivitsky, and report, 10-11, 32, 33, 50-51, 53, 56, 60-64, 71, 74, 116, 170
    marriage to John Archer, 10, 29
    paves the way for Bagot, 228
    recruitment by, and dissatisfactions in, SIS, 33
    replaced by Roger Hollis, 56, 121, 222, 224, 250
    & Regional Security Liaison Officers, 64, 183, 204
    report on Communist Party (1935), 3, 272
    report on Glading affair, 31-34
    response to Woolwich Arsenal trial, 33-35
    sidelined by MI5, 43-44, 55, 64-65, 119, 272
    suspicions about Fuchs (attributed), 198, 254
    verdict on Dennis Pritt, 27
Archer, John, 10, 29, 224, 225, 240, 245, 246, 254, 255
Arnold, Henry, 142, 235, 240, 245, 257, 261
ARCOS (All-Russian Cooperative Society), 2, 10, 20, 21, 24, 211
Artuzov, Artur, 170
Atholl, Countess of, 282
Attlee, Clement, 23, 197, 257, 258-259, 261, 264-266
Auden, W. H., 25, 143

Auslands Organisation, 7, 174
Ayer, A. J., 94, 155

B

Bagot, Milicent, 133, 223-227, 248, 250, 252
Baldwin, Stanley, 16, 88
Ball, Joseph, 64, 85, 97, 98-99, 100, 102, 107, 132
Baltic States, 49, 59, 84, 103, 105, 177, 203
Barbarossa, 105-106, 246, 257, 262
Barea, Ilse, 40
Battle of Britain, 227
Beaverbrook, Max, 92, 262
Beneš, Edvard, 54, 101
Ben-Gurion, David, 125
Bentley, Elizabeth, 69, 130-131, 139, 286
Beria, Lavrentiy, 51, 67, 68, 69, 72, 177
Berlin, Isaiah
    alleged plea to Spender not to join CP, 153
    apparent switch in political convictions, 128
    approves of Spender's joining CP, 8, 152-153
    arrival in Washington, 72, 102
    assessment of communism & CPGB, 8, 150, 155
    assists Andrew Boyle, 122-123
    association with Israeli intelligence, 126
    association with intellectuals in Russia, 157
    & 'Casual Sources', 128-129
    conceals secrets, 207
    cultivation of Gorsky, 125-126, 129-132
    dissimulation over acquaintances, 132-133
    evasiveness over (Michael) Straight, 123-124
    exchange with Rees, 97-98
    fabulism, 132-133
    familiarity with Philby, 74
    friendship and relationship with Burgess, 94, 143, 144
    friendship with Frankfurter, 103, 124, 127
    friendship and affair with Jenifer Hart, 113, 121-122, 131, 154-155
    friendship and relationship with (Donald) Maclean, 125-128, 132
    friendship & relationship with Spender, 151-154
    friendship with Rothschild, 86
    gains visa for Moscow in 1945, 132
    & Halevy, 126, 157
    incident at Katherine Graham's party, 126-128
    incurs wrath of Stalin, 157
    informs friends and relatives of Burgess's recall, 104, 123
    intellectual mentor for spies, 149-151
    intelligence-gathering with father, 158
    interpreter for Burgess, 121
    interviewed by MI5, 144
    introduced to Jebb by Nicolson, 146
    introduces Hart to Burgess, 118
    leftist sympathiser, 8, 281
    letter from Trevor-Roper, 43
    & Marxism, 150, 155-157, 160
    meets Ben-Gurion in New York, 125
    meets Weizmann, 125
    member of Section D, 122
    misinterpets Spender's message, 154
    negative influence on Britain's security, 160
    on Churchill's speeches, 86
    opens Pandora's Box, 106
    overall assessment, 159
    plots for mission to Moscow, 81-82, 92-99 *passim*, 104,

107, 119-121, 122-125
passim, 145, 147-148
& pluralism, 276
possible courier for Maclean,
129-130
possible threats by Stalin, 158-
159, 209
possible identity as EDWARD,
132
possible recruit to CP, 154
private plans for Moscow, 124-
5, 132
relationship with Oumansky,
103-104 *passim*, 124-125,
129, 132
reluctance to articulate political
views, 158
reputation, 81, 150, 159
risks in harassing Krivitsky,
133
reports Oumansky's
shortcomings to Laski, 125
SIS insider, 94
study of Marx, 150
torture of Uncle Lev, 157
view of Hayek & von Mises,
274
wants to restore Marxism's
reputation, 153
works for Halifax in
Washington, 86, 94, 125
works with Burgess for Section
D, 81, 122
& Zionism, 83, 124, 125-126,
129, 159
Berlin, Mendel, 158
Bernal, John, 178
Berzin, Jan, 170
Bessarabia, 49, 68, 105
Beurton, Len, 248-249, 251-253,
266
Bevin, Ernest, 187, 278
Birmingham University, 204, 206,
207, 212, 216-217, 220-221,
224-226, 223, 261, 262
Blake, George, 257, 281
Bland, Nevile, 180, 218

Bletchley Park, 73, 105, 106, 192,
195, 199, 232
Bloomsbury Group, 277
Blunt, Anthony,
admits revealing MI5 names to
Russians, 197
alleged confessions, 163, 197,
198
Annan's judgment, 199
appointed Liddell's personal
assistant, 189, 196
as known communist in MI5,
183, 228, 285, 287
at Tomás Harris's house, 73
& Apostles, 196
& (Jane) Archer's Woolwich
Arsenal report, 34
attempts to infiltrate Burgess
into MI5, 107, 185
background known to Curry,
283
Burgess as courier, 74
charms Maxwell Knight, 196
communism as intellectual pose,
150, 160, 179
convinces Liddell of Burgess's
harmlessness, 137
death, 193, 214
discovers Driberg spying, 35
escapes from France, 183, 196
exposed, 184, 256
expresses astonishment when
Burgess & Maclean defect,
143
friend of Pascal, 221
friendship with Burgess &
Philby, 136, 140
& Gorsky, 73, 179, 213
hints to Rosamond Lehmann,
120-121
& Intelligence Corps, 114, 115,
136-137, 178-179, 217
intermediary for Long, 191, 193,
195
& Liddell's weakness, 255
Mure's disdain, 160-161

on fringe of leftist cultural
networks, 25
& Nazi-Soviet pact, 106, 117
passes information to Moscow,
32, 34, 72, 73, 214
receives information on
Krivitsky, 115
recommends Long for MI5,
196-197
recruited by Liddell, 107, 183,
204, 219, 264, 288
recruits Cairncross, 213
recruits Long, 190-193,
recruits Straight, 69, 102, 142
& Rothschild, 99, 142, 183
treachery acknowledged, 63
Boddington, Herbert, 19-20
Bohr, Niels, 210-212
Born, Max, 174, 206, 210, 212,
217-221, 229-230, 243, 251,
259, 266
Bracken, Brendan, 174, 277
Brandes, Willy & Mary, 32-34
Brickendonbury Hall, 121
British Information Services, 125
British Press Office, 124
British Security Coordination, 125
British-Soviet Treaty, 66
British Union (of Fascists) (BUF), 4,
6, 9, 16, 17, 18, 180, 188, 279
Brookhaven National Laboratory,
208
Brooman-White, Dick, 73
Broda, Engelbert, 174, 177
Browder, Earl, 62
Brown, Isabel, 27-28
Bryan, Derek, 178
Bukharin, Nikolai, 104
Burgess, Constance, 185
Burgess, Guy
abscondence with Maclean, 82,
114, 128, 139, 143, 149,
197, 260
acquaintance with Gamow and
Mann, 209
admits being communist agent,
145, 159

Akhmedov's opinion of, 280
& Apostles, 196
arrival in Washington, 72
assumes handling of Long from
Blunt, 215
at Tomás Harris's house, 73
collaboration with Blunt, 142,
185
collaboration with Philby, 41
& Comintern, 93, 102, 108
communicates British policy to
Moscow, 101
& Cairncross, 72, 115, 212-216
courier for Long, 114, 217
crony of Ball, 85, 98-99
death, 213
demonstrated leftist sympathies,
136, 139, 285
dines with Straight, 102-104
passim
& Eitingon, 67, 120, 216
engineers entry of Rothschild &
Blunt into MI5, 107
fired on return from
Washington, 93, 101, 148,
164
friendship with Berlin, 74, 94,
113, 119, 121-122, 132
friendship with Driberg, 94
friendship with Jebb, 148
friendship with Maclean, 148
friendship with Pascal, 215
& Gorsky, 213
& Jenifer Hart, 117-118
& Wilfrid Mann, 210
hoodwinks political elite, 106,
107, 108, 144, 145
influential figure, 101-102
intermediary between
Chamberlain & Daladier,
101
interviews Churchill, 101-102
introduced to Menzies *et al.* by
Rothschild, 100
introduces Philby to SIS, 41
leading the Joint Broadcasting
Company, 99

leaves Cairncross's notes in his flat, 213-214, 215

& Liddell's weakness, 198, 255

lover Peter Pollock interviewed, 143

meeting with Deutsch, 31

member of Apostles, 196

& Nazi sympathies (Anglo-German Fellowship), 93, 102, 106, 108, 139, 163

nurtures Cairncross, 215

offered asylum through Gorsky, 130

plots for mission to Moscow, 71, 81-82, 92, 93-100 *passim*, 106-108 *passim,* 119-123 *passim*

poor tradecraft, 133

on fringe of leftist cultural networks, 25

organiser of Cambridge ring, 74, 94

& 'Oxford Ring', 118

plots to counter Krivitsky, 72, 113, 116

protected by government officials, 139-140, 146, 149, 164

recalled from Washington, 104, 145

& Goronwy Rees, 97-99, 106, 118, 133, 136, 144

rejected by MI5, 106, 185, 285

replaces Blunt as Long's contact, 97, 196

reputation and allies, 100-102 *passim*

responds to Krivitsky's revelations, 113-121 *passim,* 133, 141

& Rothschild, 86, 119, 140-144

& Section D, 73, 81, 83, 94-95, 107, 121

& Spender, 152-153

transferred to SOE, 42

treachery known, 63

view of Berlin's book on Marx, 156

visit to Paris, 116, 120-121

volunteers to kill Rees, 106

Burgess, Nigel, 185

Burt, Commander, 20, 217, 232

Butler, R. A., 87, 89-90, 277

Bystrolyotov, Dimitry, 61

C

Cadogan, Alexander, 54, 55, 62, 74, 75, 95, 99, 101, 139, 146, 147, 180, 195

Cairncross, John,
access to Hankey's reports, 116, 181, 212

access to Ultra secrets, 106

confession to MI5, 215-216

contacts with Burgess, 74, 115, 211-212, 215

contacts with Gorsky, 115, 172, 213, 214

contact with Philby, 74

demonstrated leftist sympathies, 287

fiction in *The Enigma Spy*, 212-215

file retained by Home Office, 215

first in Civil Service examination, 118

in France, 121

friend of Pascals, 216

interrogated by MI5, 212-213

Krivitsky's attitude to, 52, 60

leads from Krivitsky, 11, 60, 73-74, 94, 114-115, 118

meeting with Arnold Deutsch, 31, 172, 212

member of Apostles, 196

mole in Foreign Office, 71

odd man out, 285

passes atomic secrets to Burgess, 212, 215

primary source on Krivitsky, 72, 74, 115

recruited by Maly via Klugmann, 115, 172
wasted without channel to Moscow, 119
Canaris, Wilhelm, 76
Capitalism, 274-276, 290
Carew-Hunt, Robert, 94
Carter, Colonel, 17, 20
'Casual Sources', 128, 130
Cavendish Laboratory, 174, 210
Cecil, Robert, 130, 148, 149
Chadwick, James, 204, 221
Chamberlain, Neville,
　accommodation of Fascism, 5, 83, 89
　appeasement of Hitler, 5, 7, 8, 9, 16, 83, 89, 91, 101
　appeasement of Stalin, 33
　appoints Monckton, 96
　cabinet's recognition of Hitler's villainy, 85
　charters Hankey to investigate intelligence services, 116, 181
　Churchill joins his cabinet, 7, 176
　& Daladier, 101
　disdain for intelligence matters, 181
　dithers, 8
　enemy of Comintern, 177
　Hankey joins cabinet, 115
　learns of Maisky's indiscretions, 92
　little respect for Stalin, 48
　maintains control of Tory majority, 8
　negotiates with German generals, 180
　opposition to Communism, 9, 33, 106
　overestimates German power, 8
　replaced by Churchill, 6, 58, 113, 121, 161, 186
　sets up JIC, 121
　sets up Maud committee, 212
　Stalin's attitude towards, 48, 84

struggles to respond to communists, 33, 177
threat to Churchill, 88, 161
Chapman, Oscar, 103, 129
Chilston, Viscount, 58
Christianity, 25, 281
Churchill, Randolph, 90
Churchill, Winston
　acknowledgment of fifth column exaggeration, 188, 218, 219
　alliance with Soviet Union, 85
　appoints Dalton to head SOE, 42
　appoints Nicolson to Ministry of Information, 146
　as appeaser, 86-87, 186
　cited by Maisky, 272
　coalition government, 186
　communicating resolve to Stalin, 92, 269
　convinced that Hitler will attack Soviet Union, 189
　deception plan with Halifax against Hitler, 87-92
　demands internment of Fifth Columnists, 216
　desire that Germany would attack Soviet Union, 105
　dismisses Kell, 12, 186
　exchanges with Halifax & Clark Kerr, 131
　excited response to internment, 188
　faces Chamberlainite majority, 161
　facing Nazi military machine, 83-85
　& Halifax's peace-feelers, 86
　hatred of Bolshevism, 85
　imperialism & socialism, 276-277
　interviewed by Burgess, 101-102
　intrigues from Maisky, 92, 161
　introduces Security Executive, 62, 95, 182, 186

'Iron Curtain' speech, 243
joins Chamberlain's Cabinet, 7
keen to keep Stalin's goodwill, 186
leaking of exchanges with Roosevelt, 190
memory of German espionage, 7
offers Lloyd George appointments, 90-91
opinion of Jebb, 101, 147
opposition to totalitarianism, 4
overcomes suspicions of Roosevelt, 240
presses for detention of aliens, 218, 219
rejects 'War Aims', 278
replaces Chamberlain, 121, 161, 169, 185, 219
security risks with secretary, 59
sends Cripps to Moscow, 85, 186-187
speaks in support of Soviet Union, 106, 176, 177, 264, 271
support for intelligence, 186
tells Smuts of German intentions, 105
turns to Burgess and Berlin, 92, 100
uses Cripps to warn Stalin, 105
warns Roosevelt, 88-89
Cimperman, John, 255
Clark Kerr, Archibald, 131-132
Clarke, Dudley, 76, 161, 288
Cliveden set, 4
Collective security, 5, 8, 16
Cohen, Andrew, 74
Cohen, Benjamin, 103, 129
Cold War, 70, 138, 197, 242, 254, 256, 267, 286, 287, 289
Collier, Laurence, 57-58, 75
Comintern, 1-4, 9, 18, 20-26, 28, 29, 34, 35-36, 40-42, 50, 56, 65, 66, 69, 81-82, 93, 102, 106-108, 117, 120-121, 133, 136-137, 142, 147, 151, 153, 154, 160, 161, 163, 170, 172, 174, 176, 177, 181, 219, 225, 227, 243, 252, 258, 273, 283, 286
Committee for the Relief of Victims of German Fascism, 27
Committee of Imperial Defence, 2, 115, 118, 182, 183
Communist Party of Great Britain (CPGB), 2-3, 6, 9, 11, 16-20, 22, 25, 26, 27, 30, 49, 55, 59, 75, 117, 122, 124, 137, 138, 139, 140, 151-154, 164, 170, 178, 184, 185, 189, 196, 232, 233, 248, 257, 272, 282, 283, 285, 287, 289
Communist Party of USA, 62
Conquest, Robert, 70, 288
Contemporary British History, 259-260
Cookridge, E. H., 37, 41, 95
Cooper, Duff, 102, 142
Corson, Edward, 220
Cot, Pierre, 52, 59
Council of the Association of Atomic Scientists, 207
Cowgill, Felix, 42, 67
Crabb, 'Buster', 193, 272
Cradock, Percy, 274
Cripps, Stafford,
assists in Peierls's naturalisation, 222-223
appointment as ambassador to Moscow, 83, 85, 93, 96, 176, 186
& Berlin's role in Moscow, 94, 97, 103-104, 122, 123, 129
communicates revolutionary aspirations, 97
conspires to let in Comintern agents, 252
crony of Monckton, 97, 176
election to Labour Party executive, 37
expelled from Labour Party, 187
friend of Pritt, 27
intermediary with Maisky, 177

justifies Soviet actions in Eastern Europe, 176, 180, 186

& Monckton's lobbying to replace Churchill, 97

pro-Stalinist opinions, 16, 139, 160, 176, 180, 187, 282, 284

Stalin passes his conversations to Germans, 105, 107

used by Churchill as messenger to Stalin, 105, 106

Crocker, William, 64-65, 99

Currie, Lauchlin, 131, 138, 286

Curry, John, 17-19, 20, 21-23, 36, 56, 65-66, 107, 175, 179, 181, 185, 224-227, 273, 285

Curtis, Lionel, 96

Curtis-Bennett, Derek, 257-258, 260

D

Daily Herald, 184

Daily Sketch, 180

Daily Worker, 92, 151-152, 176, 232

Dalton, Hugh, 41, 42, 92, 96, 100-101, 146

Dansey, Claude, 251

Davies, Joseph, 58

Davison, Boris, 209

Dawson, Geoffrey, 4

Day-Lewis, Cecil, 25, 189

Deacon, Richard (McCormick, Donald), 38, 40, 69, 71, 164, 207-208

Dearlove, Richard, 289

Department of Scientific and Industrial Research (DSIR), 224, 226, 245, 246, 253, 266

De Ropp, William, 89

Deutsch, Arnold, 24, 31, 37-40, 43, 60, 62, 117-120, 144, 171, 172, 212

Deutscher, Isaac, 70

Dimitrov, Georgi ,60

Dobb, Maurice, 24, 160, 211

Double-Cross System, 76, 89, 163, 198, 240

Driberg, Tom, 35, 93, 94, 99, 117, 123, 148, 149, 190

Duclos, Jacques, 280

Duke of Windsor, 88

Dzerzhinsky, Felix, 220

E

Eden, Anthony, 57, 58, 90, 96, 147, 264, 277

Edinburgh University, 174, 206, 217-220, 227, 230, 231, 234

Edward VIII, 6

Einstein, Albert, 210

Eisenhower, Dwight, 76

Eitingon, Naum, 67, 120-121, 170, 216

Eliot, T.S., 290

Elliott, Nicholas, 38, 40

Emergency Powers Act, 175

Enigma machines, 59, 105, 106, 195

Enormoz Project, 212

Ettrick, 218, 231

European Union, 275

Evening Standard, 261

Ewer, William, 2, 6, 20

Eytan, Walter, 126

F

Facebook, 289

Fascism, 4, 5, 7, 15, 16, 27, 48, 52, 65, 137, 151, 204, 219, 229, 232, 265, 280-283, 286, 290

Federal Bureau of Investigation (FBI), 51, 52, 56, 62, 69, 114, 126, 130-131, 208, 222-223, 232, 234, 241, 255, 257-8, 260, 262

Federal Reserve, 275

Fifth Column,

anxiety subsides, 204

appeasement of communists, 186

Archer signs off, 225

Bagot's inquiry, 225

causes confusion, 64-65, 108, 180, 182, 186-188, 206
Churchill backtracks, 219
Churchill's demand for internment, 218, 219
distortion of term, 9, 175, 188, 218, 219
distraction to Krivitsky investigation, 11
MI5's investigation, 11
provokes RSLO set-up, 64
rarity of, 186
replaced by communist threat, 189, 217-218
Security Executive's campaign against, 85, 187
threat magnified, 83, 169, 189
use by Nazi Germany, 6-7, 188, 218
Fisher, H. A. L., 96, 104, 150
Fisher, Lettice, 96, 104, 124
Fisher, Mary, 104, 121-122
Fisher, Warren, 17
Fitin, Pavel, 212
Fletcher, Rex, 23
Floud, Bernard, 117, 178
Foote, Alexander, 35
Foreign Office, 5, 7, 10, 49, 50, 51, 54, 57, 58, 60-75 *passim*, 82, 89, 90, 92, 93-95, 97, 98, 99, 101-108 *passim*, 114, 128, 129, 132, 133, 139-140, 145-149, 160, 161, 163, 164, 171, 174, 176, 182, 195, 216, 243, 265, 279, 280, 286
Fortune, 232, 252
Foster, John, 100
Frankfurter, Felix, 103, 124, 127
Friedman, Litzi, 37-38, 42
Frisch, Otto, 204, 205, 211
Fuchs, Gerhard, 209
Fuchs, Klaus
accompanies Peierls to Cambridge, 217-218
acquaintance with Peierls, 207, 208, 217, 218, 250

& Aliens Review Board, 220, 232-234
& Aliens War Service permit, 223, 226-227, 230-231, 235
arrest, trial, and sentencing, 205, 209, 253, 255-258, 267
association with Kahle, 206, 230-232, 234, 247, 252
betrayal of nuclear secrets, 205-216 *passim*
career, 205
conceals CP affiliation, 174, 231, 263
concern about Gestapo dossier, 261
confession, 143, 205-206, 247
contact with Kremer, 245
correspondence with Ministries, 228
& courier Gold, 261-262
delayed permission to work on atomic weaponry, 223
espionage misrepresented by MI5, 221-222, 235, 257-259, 264-266
evidence of treachery, 204, 205, 246
friendship with Jürgen Kuczynski, 246-247
guilt confirmed by VENONA, 206, 241, 247-248, 254-256, 267
& Hollis, 263
internment and reasons for release, 207, 218, 221, 250, 251
interviewed by FBI, 232, 260
investigation by FBI, 126
joins AERE, 206, 235
known as Communist to Gestapo, 254, 258
leads from Krivitsky, 11
leaks to *Washington Post*, 126
lies over timetable of betrayal, 205, 248
links ignored by MI5, 217, 250, 253, 266

meetings with Ursula Kuczynski, 207, 224, 248, 252

member of Birmingham University's 70 Club, 221

Moorehead's account, 228-229, 262-264

motivations described by White, 255

naturalisation process, 229, 253, 262

not followed up after Serpell's recommendations, 197-198

open beliefs, 42, 174, 207, 219-220, 229-230, 232, 266

Pincher's & Goodman's superficial account, 259-260

profile of harmless communist, 42, 229

recommended to and by Max Born, 174, 218, 220, 229

recruited by Peierls, 205, 217, 221, 248, 250, 262

recruited to Maud Committee, 212, 221, 223, 226

recruitment as GRU agent, 245-246

rejects film based on his life, 261

reputation and history as communist, 219-220, 229-230, 231, 233, 254, 256, 258

returns to UK to work at Harwell, 221, 233, 240-241, 258

security risks overridden, 224-225, 228-229, 242-245, 252, 265, 269

significance of timing of treason, 257, 259

signs OSA, 205, 223, 224, 228, 230, 264

story misrepresented by Gowing, 223-224, 262-263

suspected by MI5 officers of espionage, 240-241, 242, 254

tumult replaced by Burgess & Maclean, 259

West's (Rebecca) account, 233-234, 260-261, 262, 263

White's excuses, 255

works on Manhattan project, 205, 233, 240

Fulford, Roger, 224

G

Gaitskell, Hugh, 40-42

Gamow, George, 210

Gardiner, Muriel, 41, 151

Gardner, Meredith, 240

Gaster, Jack, 124

Gaytor, George, 186

Gestapo, 192, 223, 254, 255, 257, 259, 262, 272

Glading, Percy, 6, 24, 26, 30-35, 172

Glees, Anthony, 74, 17, 262-263

Goddard, Lord, 257, 258, 260

Godfrey, John, 96, 182

Goebbels, Joseph, 84, 88, 89

Goering, Hermann, 85, 89, 178

Gold, Harry, 261-262

Goldmann, Nahum, 129

Gollancz, Victor, 28, 152, 281

Goodman, Michael, 259

Goold-Verschoyle, Brian, 61

Gorsky, Anatoly, 72-73, 103, 106, 114, 115, 116, 118, 120, 125, 126, 129-132 *passim*, 136, 139, 172, 179, 212-216 *passim*, 251

Gouzenko, Igor, 196, 241, 242, 254, 286

Government Code & Cypher School (GCCS, later GCHQ), 2, 22, 73, 131, 192, 241, 242

Gowing, Margaret, 262-263

Graham, Katherine, 126-128, 132

Graham, Philip, 126

Grand, Laurence, 72, 82-83, 95, 123

Gray, Olga, 30-33, 35, 172

Great Depression, 277
Great Terror, 172, 282, 288
Greene, Benjamin, 35, 198
Greene, Graham, 95
Greene, Hugh, 95
Groves, General, 240
GRU (Soviet Military Intelligence), 3, 6, 10, 39, 50, 52, 61, 72, 170, 213, 217, 221, 246, 247, 249, 251, 280
Gubbins, Colin, 100, 101, 164, 288
Guest, David, 283
Gunn, Jessie, 206
Gunn, Ronald, 206

H

Halban, Hans, 142, 217
Haldane, J.B.S. (John), 231-232
Halder, Franz, 84
Halevy, Efraim, 126, 157
Halifax, Lord, 58, 71, 81-82, 85-97 *passim*, 99, 101, 102, 104, 105, 106, 124, 131, 145, 177, 277-278
Halperin, Israel, 254-255, 262
Halpern, Alexander, 132
Hamburger, Rolf, 249
Hankey, Maurice, 17, 72, 115, 116, 141, 146, 181-182, 212, 264
Harker, Jasper
    agrees to take on Rothschild, 141
    alleged expert on Communism, 65
    approaches Jenifer Hart for candidates, 184
    approves new B Branch mission, 21
    concern about protecting industry & military, 22
    confused by Agabekov's defection, 53
    disrespect from Jane Archer, 34-35, 67
    distributes Archer's report, 64
    incompetence, 36, 184, 186
    head of B Division with Liddell, 19, 20
    insensitivity to 'illegals' programme, 24
    insensitivity to Communist threat, 36
    interviews Krivitsky, 51, 52, 55
    & observation section, 20
    required to report to Swinton, 186
    respect for Maxwell Knight, 20, 34, 198
    retires, 198
    signs off on Sissmore's report, 3
Harris, Kitty (Katherine Harrison), 62, 67, 114, 121
Harris, Tomás, 73, 95, 162
Harrison, H. D., 95
Hart, Herbert, 122, 141, 150, 184
Hart, Jenifer,
    approached by Harker, 184-185
    Berlin's *Letters* dedicated to, 131
    career in espionage, 117-119 *passim*
    & Christopher Hill, 154
    friendship and affair with Berlin, 121-122, 129, 154
    hypocrisy, 155, 274
    informs spies of Krivitsky report, 74, 117
    introduced to Burgess, 118
    joins the CPGB, 116, 154
    member of 'Oxford Ring', 117
    memoir, 118, 154, 156
    not asked about Communist past, 150
    possible link between Gorsky & Berlin, 118, 124
    reads Krivitsky report, 11, 63, 117
    recruited by Bernard Floud, 117
    secretary to Maxwell, 117, 186
    spies for Comintern, 74, 117, 154
Hayek, Friedrich, 41, 276

Healey, Denis, 288
Heinemann, Kristel, 254
Hill, Christopher, 117, 154
Hingley, Ronald, 70, 220
Hitler, Adolf,
    addressing economic problems, 279
    admired by Stalin, 60
    appeased by Chamberlain & Halifax, 6, 8-9, 33, 86, 187
    assumption of power, 3, 278, 279
    attack on Soviet Union, 105-106, 169, 189, 232, 234, 252
    attitude towards Britain, 4, 6, 7, 15, 60, 84-85, 88-89, 105, 205
    bulwark against Bolshevism, 277
    deception by Churchill, 87-92
    elimination of Communist Party, 283
    expulsion of Jews and anti-semitism, 4, 7, 173, 279, 281
    gavotte with Churchill & Stalin, 60, 83
    Halifax's peace-feelers, 86
    invasion of Austria, 276
    message in 'Mein Kampf', 4, 7, 8, 84, 279, 281
    & nuclear weapons, 204, 221
    pact with Stalin, 9, 13, 42, 52, 55, 56, 58-59, 71, 83-84
    rape of Czechoslovakia, 85
    rape of Poland, 104
    refugees from, 28, 83, 165, 169-176 *passim,* 206
    risk of seeing through Churchill's deception, 91
    threat to Europe's stability, 15
    totalitarianism, 4, 279, 283
    use of intelligence, 5-6, 8, 59, 107
Hoare, Samuel, 16, 17, 88
Hobsbawm, Eric, 132

Hollis, Roger,
    agrees to intercepts on Fuchs & Peierls, 254
    amazed at indulgence towards communism, 189
    approves recruitment of Day-Lewis, 189
    as alleged 'ELLI', 72, 194, 222, 248, 250, 262-263
    attitude towards Fuchs, 22, 222, 240, 243, 244, 245, 255, 263
    challenged by evidence on Fuchs, 255-256
    chastised by Martin over Long, 194
    deception to FBI over Philby, 256
    deputises for Jane Archer, 29, 55, 64
    discusses leakage through CP members, 196
    dismisses evidence against Fuchs, 242
    distances himself from Krivitsky's opinions, 56
    expertise on communism, 66, 176, 185, 189, 196, 222, 265
    friendship with Fulford, 225
    friendship with White, 66
    gesture in removing agents, 63
    heads F2 under Curry, 185, 224, 226
    passes on CPGB's support for war, 176
    promoted prematurely, 44
    reaction to Blake's trial, 266
    recruitment and training, 29
    rejects Maxwell Knight's report, 35
    replaces Jane Archer, 75, 121, 222, 224, 248
    replaces Curry as head of F Division, 185, 227
    scorned by Wild, 288

shown in favourable light by Gowing, 263
suspected of being a Soviet agent, 163, 194
testifies to Tripartite Talks, 263
Ursula Kuczynski as alleged courier, 250
Holt-Wilson, Eric, 182
Home Office, 4, 5, 6, 9-12, 21, 26, 27, 28, 29, 32, 63-64, 108, 117, 119, 121, 171, 174, 175, 179-182, 184, 185, 186, 207, 215, 218, 219, 221, 234
Hoover, J. Edgar, 51-52, 114, 255
House Committee on UnAmerican Activities, 56, 70, 114, 286
House of Commons, 8, 83, 88, 90, 121, 140, 157, 161, 181, 184, 192, 241, 257
Hoyer Millar, Derek, 100
Hutchings, Stephen, 21

I
ICI Mond, 223, 226, 263
Ilk, Berthold, 170
'Illegals', 6, 10, 24, 31, 61, 113, 115, 118, 119, 139, 144, 169-172, 180, 272, 285
Imperialism, 1, 219, 275, 278
INO (OGPU's Foreign Intelligence Service), 39, 170
Invergordon Mutiny, 3, 20, 21
Ironside, General, 176
Ismay, Hastings, 121, 161
Ivanov, Yevgeny, 28
Izvestia, 95

J
Jane, Charles, 20
Jay, Douglas, 184
Jebb, Gladwyn
    Churchill's and Cadogan's scathing opinions, 101
    death, 99
    eased out of SOE, 101
    expressed sympathy for communists, 146-147
    friendship with Burgess, 101, 102, 123, 144, 148, 9
    friendship with Nicolson, 146
    liaison with intelligence services, 51, 99, 101, 146
    meeting with Berlin, 99, 122, 123, 146, 147, 149
    & Moscow Plot, 146-148
    opinion of Burgess, 100, 102, 144
    & sacking of Burgess, 100-101
    recommends Oumansky, 103
    receives copy of Archer's report, 64
    role in protecting Burgess & co., 139-140, 145-149, 160
    supervises interrogation of Krivitsky, 51, 55, 62, 146
    undermined by Dalton, 100-101, 146
    work for SIS, 146
    & 1955 report, 140
'Jewish Problem', 173, 282
Johnson, Hewlett, 281, 283
Joint Broadcasting Company (JBC), 99, 101, 104
Joint Intelligence (Sub-) Committee, 58, 107, 121, 133, 161, 176, 182, 241, 274, 288
Jowett, Lord, 259

K
Kahle, Hans, 28, 206, 207, 231-232, 234, 240, 247, 252, 266
Kapitza, Pyotr, 209-212, 220, 250, 266
Katz, Joseph, 69, 130
Katz, Otto, 26-29, 171
Katz, Rudolph, 144
Keeler, Christine, 28
Kell, Vernon, 7, 8, 12, 17, 21, 27, 29, 32, 35, 36, 54, 60, 66, 75, 174, 179, 180, 182, 183, 186
Kelly, David, 88
Kennedy, Joseph, 191, 219
Kent, Tyler, 6, 35, 91, 190-191, 219
Kerensky, Alexander, 51, 173

Kesselring, Albert, 89
KGB, 36, 37, 69, 100, 131, 141, 147, 157, 194, 196, 213, 215, 250, 272
King, John Herbert, 10, 33, 49-50, 52, 54, 55, 59, 60, 62, 73
Klugmann, James, 115, 137, 143, 178, 212, 213, 216
Knight, Maxwell, 17-20, 22-24, 30, 31-32, 35-36, 163, 190-193, 196, 198-199, 273
Knox, Dillwyn, 192, 195
Koestler, Arthur, 25, 52, 290
Kollek, Teddy, 41
KPD (German Communist Party), 174, 199, 208, 231, 246, 265
Kravchenko, Victor, 53
Kremer, Simon, 37, 213, 246-249
Kristallnacht, 281
Krivitsky, Walter
    activities in the USA, 114
    adversary of Oumansky, 51, 68, 103
    advises of OGPU takeover of GRU, 170
    alarms Guy Burgess, 94, 188
    alleged invention of events, 61
    also *ex nostris*, 130
    Cadogan's role, 54-55, 62, 114
    Cairncross's role, 72-73
    Cot as agent of, 59
    death of, 11, 67-70, 120
    declines to murder Reiss, 32, 67
    draws attention to Stalin's slave colony, 50
    follow-up by Kell & Archer, 66-67
    Hankey's awareness, 116, 181-182
    history, defection and interrogation of, 10-12, 34, 44, 50-56, 146, 180
    identifies 'illegals', 31, 113, 119, 169-172
    identifies Kremer, 246
    imprecise identification of agents, 31, 60-62, 118, 169

    influence on Koestler, 52
    informs French police about Maly, 31
    & inserting 'illegals', 6
    & Laqueur, 71
    leaves for Canada, 141, 182
    maintains belief in communism, 280
    Moscow's alleged awareness of his interrogation, 73
    ordered to ease off subversion in Germany, 71
    ordered to murder Reiss, 32, 51, 67
    overlooked by historians, 70
    pointers to Soviet spies, 36, 54, 62, 75, 94, 118, 162, 195, 243
    potential wake-up call, 180
    publication of memoirs, 50, 51, 52, 57, 67, 69, 114
    refers to Committee of Imperial Defence, 72
    report by Archer, 55, 61, 63-64, 71, 73, 116-117, 146
    response of MI5 to, 12, 53, 55, 56, 60, 62, 65, 69, 74-75, 113, 133, 136, 163, 180-182, 188-189, 205, 244, 271-272, 285-287
    response of spies to, 94, 104, 113-116, 119, 156
    reveals Stalin's plans to ally with Hitler, 56-57, 65, 71, 84, 254
    watched by Straight, 103
Kuczynski family, 27, 31, 43, 121, 206, 232, 246, 249, 254, 266
Kuczynski, Hilde, 28
Kuczynski, Jürgen, 28, 121, 174, 207, 217, 231, 246-247, 248, 250, 251, 266
Kuczynski, Marguerite, 248
Kuczynski, Robert, 121, 245, 250
Kuczynski (Beurton), Ursula ('Sonia'), 185, 206, 232, 240, 242, 247-253, 266

L

Labarthe, Jerome, 59
Lamphere, Robert, 82, 126, 232-233
Landau, Jacob, 129
Laqueur, Walter, 67, 71
Laski, Harold,
    aids citizenship request of Peierls, 222
    Communist sympathiser, 139
    conspires to aid entry of Comintern agents, 252
    declines to write book on Marx, 150
    election to Labour Party Executive, 27
    helps members of KPD, 174
    not pleased with Spender's textual changes, 152
    plants explosive device, 289
    supporter of Otto Katz's entry, 171
    sways MI5, 12
    works with Oumansky & Ben-Gurion, 125
Laski, Neville, 252
Lawn Road Flats, 247
League Against Imperialism, 26, 30
League of Nations, 5, 16
Le Carré, John, 227, 274
Lecoutre, Alta, 59
Leeper, Rex, 100
Lehmann, John, 40, 120, 180
Lehmann, Rosamund, 120, 133
Lenin, Vladimir, 1, 42, 52, 160, 278, 280, 281
Levine, Isaac Don, 49-51, 54-56, 58. 61, 114
Liberal Democracy, 160, 274-280 *passim,* 287, 290
Liddell, Guy
    agrees to intercepts on Fuchs & Peierls, 254
    anti-communist team in Special Branch, 20
    & Archer's clandestine work for MI5, 34

    & Archer's demotion/dismissal, 21-22, 64, 67, 119, 245
    at Harris's house, 73
    attitude towards Knight, 30, 34
    awareness of communist espionage, 75, 143, 195, 254
    bypassed in planning for Krivitsky, 55, 65-67
    cognitive dissonance over communists, 57, 137, 176, 177, 185, 189, 244
    concentration on CPGB, 20
    considers communists as ally against Nazis, 177
    decides on investigation of Peierls & Fuchs, 242
    desires to interrogate Krivitsky, 50
    desires to recruit Burgess, 107, 185
    dismisses evidence against Fuchs, 243, 266
    encounters and recruits Rothschild, 182-183
    excluded from ARCOS case, 20
    failed custody lawsuit, 65
    failings as officer, 75, 137, 142, 165, 244, 284-285
    failure to be appointed Director-General, 244, 257, 264, 284
    & Fifth Column neurosis, 188
    forestalls merger with SIS, 272
    ignorance of Moscow Plot, 106
    indulgence towards Burgess, 143, 145, 185, 285, 287
    influenced by Rothschild and friends, 73, 138, 140-142, 145, 182-183, 287
    insensitivity to Communist threat, 36, 57, 62, 75, 185, 186, 269, 272
    irresoluteness over Fuchs *et al.*, 184, 256-257, 271-272
    & *Last Temptation*, 161-163, 198

lunches with Blunt and Long, 196

notes increased communist espionage, 180

passive reaction to Krivitsky, 52, 253

& possible cover-up over Long, 190, 194, 197-198

reaction to counter-espionage disasters, 256

recruits Blunt, 183, 196, 264

reports problems with illicit radio detection, 253

sees through Cairncross's deception, 213

sets up RSLOs, 64-65

signs off on Sissmore's report, 3

speaks out against Lehmann, 180

transfer to B branch, 19-20

unwilling to remove communists, 195, 243

views on Krivitsky's information, 52-53, 59

wants to tighten screws on communists, 185

Litvinov, Maxim, 9, 57, 58, 71

Lloyd George, David, 90-92

London School of Economics, 232

Long, Leo,
  Blunt's attempt to recruit to MI5, 196-197
  Burgess replaces Blunt as courier, 114, 217
  connection with Blunt's confession, 163
  cryptonym 'RALPH', 192
  delivers information to secret CP contacts, 118
  demonstrated leftist sympathies, 287
  detected in espionage (*'One Girl's War'*), 190-199
  espionage known to Annan, 192, 199
  implications for Sillitoe, 264
  installed in MI14, 59, 192
  member of Apostles, 196
  recruited by Blunt, 190
  treachery acknowledged, 63
  underestimated espionage, 59, 119

Longworth, Alice, 127

Lothian, Lord, 49, 54, 88, 94, 96, 99, 104, 114, 123, 125

'Lucy' spy ring, 254

Lynd, Maire, 122, 124

M

Macartney, William, 21

Maclean, Donald,
  abscondence with Burgess, 81, 82, 120, 139, 143, 149, 197, 213, 215, 260
  accusation to Rees, 127
  admitted leftist beliefs, 137, 150, 286
  alleged receipt of Jane Archer's report, 71
  & *Casual Sources*, 128-129, 130
  confesses to wife (Melinda), 148
  death, 214
  demonstrated leftist sympathies, 287
  friendship with Kim Philby, 74-75
  handled by Deutsch, 31, 172
  handled by Gorsky, 126, 130, 139
  identity revealed by VENONA decrypts, 131
  intervenes with 'Casual Sources', 128
  Jebb's *faux pas*, 149
  & leads from Krivitsky, 11, 54, 60, 72, 75, 94, 115, 146
  leaks CID minutes, 73
  leaks NATO secrets, 149
  & Liddell's weakness, 256
  lover of Katherine Harrison, 62
  Maly reports on, 31

offered asylum through Gorsky, 130
promoted to First Secretary, 130
recruited by Reif, 171-172
Reilly's dissimulation, 140
relationship with Berlin, 125, 128, 129, 130, 131, 132, 140, 159
relationship with Jebb, 148
spat with Berlin, 126-128
Third Secretary in Paris, 71, 114
treachery known, 63
Maclean, Fitzroy, 82, 92, 99, 102, 104, 107, 161
Macmillan, Harold, 28, 90, 257, 277, 279
Macmillan, Lord, 178
Maisky, Ivan, 92, 97, 101, 147, 161, 177, 211, 246, 247, 277
Mallet, Victor, 55,56, 61
Maly, Teodor, 31-34, 43, 60, 61, 62, 119, 170, 171-172
Manhattan Project, 206, 207, 240, 243
Mann, Wilfrid, 210
Martin, Kevin, 179
Marxism & Marxists, 1, 41, 75, 94, 137, 144, 153, 155-160, 164, 178, 179, 184, 221, 273, 274-274-281 *passim*, 287
MASK, 22-23
Masterman, John, 76, 163
Maud Committee, 205, 212, 218, 223, 226, 266
Maxwell, Alexander, 117, 186
McCarthyism, 128
Mein Kampf, 3, 5, 7, 84, 90, 279, 281
Meitner, Lisa, 205
Melland, Brian, 192
Menzies, Stewart, 54, 96, 100, 196
Mercader, Ramon, 67-68
Metropolitan Police, 2, 17
MI14, 59, 190-192, 194, 195
Miller, General, 67

Miller, Joan, 163, 190-194, 196, 198-199
Milne, Tim, 73
Milner, Ian, 117
Ministry of Aircraft Production (MAP), 222, 223-226, 230-231, 246, 263, 266
Ministry of Defence, 261
Ministry of Economic Warfare, 41, 140
Ministry of Information, 72, 82, 96, 101, 113, 122, 132, 147, 175-176, 178, 180, 188, 189, 204, 218
Ministry of Labour and Supply, 184, 187, 206, 218, 224, 229, 245, 261, 262
Mitchell, Graham, 226, 243, 244
Modin, Yuri, 39, 95, 100, 250
Molotov, Vyacheslav, 9, 48, 60, 71, 101, 105, 132
Monckton, Walter, 96-97, 139, 176
Mond Laboratory, 210
Montagu, Ivor, 27
Moorehead, Alan, 223, 228-229, 254, 261-263, 267
Morrison, Herbert, 28, 74, 187
Morton, Desmond, 17, 20, 35, 85, 198
Moscow Centre, 11, 24, 31, 69, 72, 113, 114, 115, 118, 120, 136, 170, 192, 216, 249, 251, 287
Moscow show trials, 4, 8, 27, 52, 117, 118, 152, 153, 154, 272, 283
Mosley, Oswald
  admiration for Hitler, 279
  arms cache, 188
  founds British Union of Fascists, 4, 279
  internment, 7
  tirades,16
Mott, Neville, 206, 219-220, 230, 243, 259
Muggeridge, Malcolm, 103, 145, 179, 283
Multiculturalism, 278, 289, 290

Munday, Charles, 32
Murdoch, Iris, 117
Mure, David, 76, 161-165, 198, 288
Münzenberg, Willi, 26
Mussolini, Benito, 158, 281
Mynatt, Margaret, 186

N
Nation, 114
National Security Agency (NSA), 131, 241
Nazi-Soviet (Ribbentrop-Molotov) Pact, 9, 36, 42, 48-50, 51, 52, 55, 56, 57, 59, 60, 70, 81, 83, 92, 94, 101, 106, 117, 118, 136, 169, 176, 177, 195, 204-205, 214, 219, 223, 230, 232, 233, 254, 262, 266, 271, 281, 283, 288
Nelson, Frank, 95
New British Broadcasting Station, 187
New Deal & Newdealerism, 126, 127, 277
Newsam, Frank, 117, 185
New York Times, 51, 67, 114, 158, 233
Nicolson, Harold, 82, 93-95, 96-97, 99, 101, 102, 122, 146-147, 151, 277-278
Night of the Long Knives, 52
NKVD, 3, 6, 24, 38, 39, 50-52, 54, 59, 61, 62, 65-71 *passim*, 72-74, 94, 105, 114, 116, 119, 120, 121, 124, 125, 126, 129, 130, 133, 140, 152, 158, 170, 171, 172, 177, 207, 212, 216, 223, 241, 246, 248, 251, 255
Norwood, Melita, 25, 31, 32, 33, 252
Nunn May, Alan, 208, 241, 256, 261, 264, 267

O
Observer, 191
Official Secrets Act (OSA), 29, 32, 62, 99, 159, 161, 163, 184, 190, 194, 205, 206, 208, 222, 223, 224, 228, 230, 257, 258, 261, 262, 264
OGPU, 3, 29, 50, 51, 52, 53, 61, 68, 70, 97, 103, 157, 170, 209
Oldham, Ernest, 33, 61
Orlov, Alexander, 6, 31, 37, 39, 40, 61, 69, 115-116, 171, 172, 193
Orwell, George, 25, 276
Oshima, Hiroshi, 59
Ottaway, John, 20
Oumansky, Konstantin, 51, 59, 68, 72, 97, 103-104, 106, 124-125, 129, 132, 147
Oxford 'Ring', 117-118

P
Palestine, 125-126
Pascal, Fanya, 216, 221
Pascal, Roy, 216, 221
Passport Office, 249, 251
Peace Ballot, 16
Peace Pledge Union, 9, 180, 224
Peel Commission, 125
Peierls, Eugenia, 209-211, 220
Peierls, Rudolf,
    acquaintance with Pascals, 216, 221
    appeals to reduce Nunn May's sentence, 207
    appointed to Mond Laboratory, 209
    autobiography, 208, 209, 217, 221
    awarded knighthood, 208-209
    becomes British citizen, 222-223
    collaboration with Bohr, 211
    correspondence & collaboration with Born, 212, 218, 220, 221, 265
    cryptonym of VOGEL, 217
    disqualified from radar work, 212, 223
    errs over Fuchs's clearance, 222
    & General Groves, 240
    investigated by FBI, 208

joins MAUD committee, 206, 212, 266

knowledge of Fuchs's beliefs, 230

misrepresents relationship with Fuchs, 217, 218, 223

misrepresents visit to Soviet Union, 210-21

naturalisation approved, 216, 250, 266

overcomes objections to work on atomic weaponry, 222

paper with Frisch, 204, 212, 216

recruits Fuchs at Birmingham, 206, 207, 218, 221, 223-224, 226, 228, 234, 247, 251, 263

reference and support for Fuchs, 222, 228-229, 246, 250

relationship with Kapitza, 209-210, 248

resigns from AERE Harwell, 208

role in Soviet espionage, 266

rude to customs officials, 211

surveilled by MI5, 208

suspected of espionage, 208, 240, 242, 243, 245, 254, 259

sympathy for Soviet Union, 211

takes Fuchs to see Halban, 217-218

takes legal action against Deacon, 207-208

threats from Soviet Union, 209-210, 250

works on Manhattan project, 206, 207, 235

People, 97-99

Perrin, Michael, 206-207, 222, 228, 229, 248, 253, 261, 263

Perth, Lord, 122

Petrie, David, 142, 196, 198, 224-225, 227, 228, 264

Philby, H.A.R. ('Kim'),

activities in Vienna, 37-40, 42, 95, 120, 137, 150

alleged knowledge of Krivitsky, 71

& Anglo-German Fellowship, 43

argues for Ultra to be given to Russians, 142

arrival from Vienna, 171

at (Tomás) Harris's house, 73

Bagot's doubts, 227

beliefs questioned by Vivian, 286

Burgess as courier, 148

career and mythology, 36-43 *passim*

courier with Lehmann, 120

death, 214

discloses nothing on Moscow Plot, 107

discloses information on espionage to Soviets, 194-195

encounter with Muriel Gardiner, 151

escapes vetting, 11, 26

expresses disgust with Burgess, 143

friendship with Berlin, 74, 132

friendship with Burgess & Blunt, 136

friendship with (Donald) Maclean, 74

friendship with Rothschiild, 140

friendship with Smolka, 174

handled by Gorsky, 214

in Section D, 95, 107, 133

introduced to Orlov, 31, 172

introduces Maclean to Reif, 171

joins British Expeditionary Force, 114

judgment by Akhmedov, 280

Krivitsky's attitude to, 52

& leads from Krivitsky, 11, 54, 60, 75, 94, 115, 118

& Liddell's weakness, 256

meets (Kitty) Harris in Paris, 121
Mure's scathing opinion, 161-162
& Nazi-Soviet pact, 106
ordered to assassinate Franco, 172
treachery known, 63
tutored by Dobb, 24, 211
White's & Hollis's dissimulation, 257
White's suspicions, 197
Wild's opinion, 76
Pieck, Henri, 33, 50, 60
Pincher, Chapman, 38, 66, 72, 144, 194, 196, 197, 215, 222, 246, 247, 250, 259-260, 263
Pluralism, 150, 278, 289, 290
Poland, 6, 8, 9, 10, 49, 58, 60, 104, 115, 131, 138, 176, 178, 187, 213, 283
Politburo, 170
Pollitt, Harry, 30, 152, 153, 154, 158, 176
Pontecorvo, Bruce, 256, 261, 267
Popper, Karl, 276
Popular Front, 4, 23
Portal, Lord, 240
Pravda, 95
Pravdin, Vladimir, 130
Prichard, Edward, 127
Pritt, Dennis
  advises Woolwich Arsenal spies, 32
  approves of Moscow show trials, 27, 283
  banishment from Labour Party, 27
  crypto-communist, 160, 284
  elected to Parliament, 137
  election to Labour Party Executive, 27
  frustrates MI5's efforts, 43, 63, 121, 171
  helps members of KPD, 121, 174
  MI5's files, 26-27

mounts defence for Glading & co., 32
in Paris with Burgess?, 121
possible backlash from, 63
role in Brandes affair, 33
serves with Katz & Wilkinson on anti-Fascist Committee, 27
supporter of Otto Katz, 26, 171
sways MI5, 12
underestimated by MI5, 43
Proctor, Dennis, 74, 115, 179
Profumo Affair, 28
Profumo, John, 28
Proskurov, Ivan, 105-106
Prytz, Bjørn, 89-90
Purge Procedure, 286
Pyatnitsky, Iosif, 170

Q
Quebec Agreement, 240

R
Radio Security Service (RSS), 37, 105, 253
Radomysler, Asik, 232
Radziwill, Janusz, 178
Raeder, Erich, 88, 105
Rankin, John, 286
Reade, Arthur, 24
Rees, Goronwy, 97-99, 106, 118, 120, 127, 132, 133, 136, 143, 144
Refugees, 4, 28, 169, 173-174, 176, 179-181, 188, 223, 225, 247, 251, 282, 286
Regional Security Liaison Officers (RSLO), 64-66, 119, 188, 204
Reif, Ignaty, 38, 40, 119, 171-172
Reilly, Patrick, 43, 140, 210
Reiss, Ignace, 10, 31-32, 51-52, 67, 69, 70, 171
Ribbentrop, Joachim, 48, 71, 88, 90, 101
Ridley, Cressida, 128
Right Club, 190
Robertson, J. C., 19, 221-222

Robertson, T. A. ('Tar'), 197, 233, 240, 241, 244, 245, 253-256 *passim*, 285
Roosevelt, Franklin Delano, 83, 87, 88, 91, 103, 104, 127, 131, 147, 190, 240, 277, 286
Rosenberg, Alfred, 89
Rosenberg, Ethel, 130, 262
Rosenberg, Julius, 130, 262
Rothermere, Harold, 6, 84
Rothschild, Miriam, 99-100
Rothschild, Tess, 141, 143
Rothschild, Victor,
    'agent of influence', 142, 149, 161
    aided by Burgess, 197
    alleged cryptonym of DAVID, 141
    at Tomás Harris's house, 73
    avoids interrogation, 144
    conceals secrets, 207
    confidence in Burgess, 102
    Costello's accusation, 141
    death, 99
    demands exoneration, 141-142
    distances himself from Burgess, 143
    effect on Liddell, 138, 183, 198
    enables Hart's recruitment, 184
    engineers Burgess's recall, 145
    exerts pro-Communist influence, 100, 142, 186
    friendship with Straight, 123-124
    guilty secret, 208
    head of B1c in MI5, 141, 183, 204
    helps in Blunt's success at MI5, 183
    impresses Wright, 143
    informed of Philby's past, 41
    introduces Blunt to Liddell, 183, 196
    joins MI5, 72, 85-86, 100, 107, 141, 144, 182-183, 204, 219
    & KGB, 142
    mission to Paris, 121, 183
    & mission to Moscow, 85, 99-101, 140, 145
    patron to Burgess, 100-102, 119, 140-141, 144
    performs damage control for spies, 144, 161
    possible head of MI5, 142
    protected by MI5, 143, 144
    ruthless about MI5's weaknesses, 182
    secret project at War Office, 141
    snooping, 142
    socializing at Bentinckt St., 73, 145
    wheedles information from Liddell, 142
    wields influence, 139, 141, 143, 186
    & Zionism, 144
Rothstein, Andrew, 24-25, 31, 211
Royal Canadian Mounted Police, 66
Rutherford, Ernest, 210

S
Saturday Evening Post, 50-52, 69, 114
'Saxon, John', 242
Schapiro, Leonard, 94
Schlesinger, Artur, 124
Schmidt, Helmut, 275
Secret Intelligence Service (SIS, or MI6)
    Archer works for, 34-35
    authorised history, 82-83
    aware of renewed threat of Soviet Union, 241
    Casuals, 17, 18, 30
    'Central Register', 95
    competition with MI5, 2, 17
    contrast with MI5, 286
    control of intelligence machinery, 2
    dealing with defectors, 53
    discussions with MI5 on crypto-communists, 196

dismissal of Liddell's role in 1931, 201
excluded from JISC, 176
& 'illegals' strategy, 24
involvement with 'Lucy' spy ring, 252
Hankey's review, 141, 146, 181
intelligence on Reiss, 32
Jebb's role, 147
Menzies's appointment, 96
mission, 3, 17, 60, 163
& Moscow Plot, 95
& Nazi-Soviet pact, 49
opportunity from Krivitsky, 11, 50-51, 55, 58, 63, 74, 181
organisational turmoil, 108
passes information on Fuchs to MI5, 229
passes MASK traffic to MI5, 22-23
& Passport Control Office, 104
& 'Peace Party', 89
Philby's role, 36, 41, 42, 43, 74, 113
poor intelligence-sharing, 133, 176
Radio Intelligence Service, 37
Section D (*see separate entry*)
SIME, 161
tampers with evidence on Crabb, 193-194
White as Director-General, 100, 257, 272
Secret Service Committee, 2-3, 17
Section D, 29, 36, 41, 73, 81, 93, 94-96, 99, 101, 104, 107, 121-123, 133, 146, 161, 185
Security Executive, 35, 63, 64, 85, 99, 107, 182, 186, 187, 189, 264
Seeds, William, 58, 180
Selborne, Lord, 101
Serpell, Christopher, 197, 232, 240, 244, 250, 253-255, 285
SHAEF (Supreme Headquarters Allied Expeditionary Force), 198

Shaw, George Bernard, 180, 282
Shawcross, Hartley, 257
Sheridan, Diana, 85
Shillito, Hugh, 252-253
Sicherheitsdienst (German Security Service), 192
Signal Security Agency (SSA), 131
Sillitoe, Percy, 197, 198, 233, 244, 256-262, 264-266
Simon, John, 17
Sissmore, Jane (see Archer, Jane)
Skardon, William (Jim), 126, 143, 144, 206, 214, 240, 247-248, 250, 253, 255, 262, 263
Sklyarov, Ivan, 246-247
Slater, Humphrey, 283
Smollet (Smolka), Peter, 174-175
Smith, Adam, 276
Smuts, Jan, 105
Solomon, Flora, 41, 133
Soviet Union
ally of GB, 91, 66
& anti-fascism, 5, 15, 283
as democracy, 25, 277, 279
deaths responsible, 281-282
defectors, 52-53, 63
economy, 274-5
encipherment procedures, 10
espionage objectives & rules, 6, 13, 24, 38, 39, 40, 176-177, 180, 271, 288
fortunes and reputation, 2
interest in nuclear secrets, 203
invades Finland, 27, 49, 180
& League of Nations, 16
occupies Baltic States, 49, 103, 105, 177, 187, 204, 282
occupies Bessarabia, 49, 105
overtures with Britain, 9, 84, 85, 107, 161
plans for Kapitza & Fuchs, 205, 266
perspective from the UK, 7-8, 63, 113, 121, 163, 189, 277
propaganda, 13, 22, 25, 29, 54, 61, 63, 70, 271, 273, 274, 276

relationship with Germany (*see* 'Nazi-Soviet Pact')
'second homeland', 280
subversion, 6, 11
threatening exiles, 209
totalitarianism, 273, 274, 277
treaty with Britain (1942), 66, 239
Spanish Civil War, 4, 25, 61, 65, 187, 231, 283
Special Branch, 2-3, 6, 17, 20, 25, 26, 33, 50, 121, 143, 144, 164, 171, 172, 192, 193, 211, 228
Special Operations Executive (SOE), 36, 42, 83, 95, 96, 100-101, 107, 115, 146-148, 160, 164, 185, 288
'Special Tasks' Force, 52-53, 119, 210, 247
Spender, Stephen
    attempts to distance himself from Burgess, 152
    & CPGB, 8, 138, 151-154
    death, 154
    declares Burgess's open communism, 145
    friendship with Berlin, 140, 144, 151, 153
    & Hyndman, 151
    lover of Muriel Gardiner, 41, 151
    misleads on CP membership, 152, 153
    performs mission for CPGB, 138, 151, 153
    questioned by MI5, 144-145
    tracked by Special Branch, 25
    under pressure from Politt, 154
    witness to Churchill's inscription to Burgess, 102
    writings in support of Communism, 151-152
Spiegelglass, Sergey, 67, 120
Springhall, Dave, 285
Spycatcher trial, 142, 163, 191
Stalin, Joseph
    appeasement of, 6
    attitude towards Chamberlain, 33, 48, 84
    biographies, 70-71
    Britain as adversary, 60, 83, 91
    & collective security, 8
    considers joining Axis Powers, 60
    demands interference in foreign powers, 177
    devours intelligence, 8
    distorts the communist message, 279
    distrust of Red Army, 50
    furious at Gamow, 210
    & Great Terror, 8, 83, 104, 172, 282, 288
    ignores intelligence warnings, 105
    & Krivitsky, 51-52, 69
    lack of manifesto, 280
    leaks conversations with Cripps to Germans, 105, 107
    'man of peace' , 272
    & Nazi-Soviet pact, 9, 57, 83
    needs time to rebuild army, 83
    opposition to Franco, 283
    orders hunting down of defectors, 10, 67
    purges agents, 8, 10, 51, 52
    reality of his prison-camp, 5, 10, 50, 280
    receives 'Casual Sources' information, 128
    risk of gaining idea that Churchill could be ousted, 92
    scorn for democratic socialists, 15
    threatens (Isaiah) Berlin, 157-159, 209
Stark, Freya, 95
Stephenson, Bill, 95
Stewart, Findlater, 264
Stewart, Robert ('Bob'), 178, 192
Strachey, John, 152, 217, 222, 250, 252, 266
Straight, Daphne, 124

Straight, Michael, 69, 71-72, 102-104, 106, 108, 121, 123-124, 132, 140-142
Strang, William, 59
Streater, Isabel, 53
Stuart, Campbell, 96
Sudoplatov, Pavel, 54, 67, 69, 70, 116, 119, 120, 177-178, 209, 247
Sweet-Escott, Bickham, 82, 95
Swinton, Lord , 64, 186-187, 189
Szilard, Leo, 221

T
Talmon, J.T., 279
Tangye, Derek, 35
Taylor, A. J. P., 16, 117, 274
Thatcher, Margaret, 129, 163, 184, 192, 193, 195
Thomsen, Hans, 59
Thompson, Derwent, 221
Thomson, Basil, 24
Thomson, George, 212
Time, 252
Tito, Josip, 178
Tizard, Henry, 212
Tomlinson, J. N., 104
TORCH (Operation), 195
Totalitarianism, 272-280 *passim*, 290
Toynbee, Philip, 117
Tradecraft, 63, 73, 133, 136, 170, 235, 245, 253, 273, 283-284, 286-288
Treaty of Rapallo, 9
Trevor-Roper, Hugh, 37, 42-43, 138, 283, 290
Tribune, 176
Trilliser, Mikhail, 170
Trinity College, Cambridge, 164, 211
Tripartite Pact, 60
Tripartite Talks on Security Standards, 263
Trotsky, Leon, 51-52, 67-68, 70, 119, 120, 121, 129
Troyanovsky, Alexander, 68

Tube Alloys, 174, 206, 207, 212, 218, 222, 226, 234, 240, 253, 263, 266, 284
Tucker, Robert, 70
Tudor-Hart, Edith, 38-39, 40, 120, 172, 186
Tukhachevsky, Mikhail, 58, 67, 70, 71

U
Ultra, 106, 142, 195, 199
Uren, Desmond, 285

V
vanden Heuvel, Frederick, 251, 252
Van Ginhoven, Hubertus, 20
Van Narvig, William, 68
Vansittart, Robert, 5, 7, 17, 23, 57, 92, 100, 161, 174, 279
Vasilevsky, Lev 121
VENONA, 58, 130-132, 138, 140, 141, 197, 206, 217, 241-247 *passim*, 255, 267
Versailles Treaty, 5
Vesey, Desmond, 252
Vivian, Valentine,
    confused by Agabekov's defection, 53
    contacted by White over communist refugees, 181
    convinced of Burgess's suitability for Moscow, 95
    convinced of Philby's reliability, 41, 286
    co-operation with Jane Archer, 21, 24, 32, 33, 55
    failure to press Foreign Office, 60
    & 'illegals' programme, 24
    insouciance over communist infiltration, 194-195
    interviews Krivitsky, 51-52
    questions MI5 on Otto Katz, 29
    receives report on Krivitsky, 63
von Hohenlohe, Max, 88
von Mises, Ludwig, 276
Voroshilov, Marshall, 9, 48

W

Wallace, Henry, 127
Walpole, Hugh, 84
War Cabinet, 90, 91, 115, 116, 176, 180, 181, 218
War Office, 56-60, 62, 141, 143, 178-180, 184, 190, 194-195, 206
Washington Post, 126
Weizmann, Chaim, 125
Weizmann, Schmuel, 125
Webbs (Beatrice & Sidney), 180, 282
Welles, Sumner, 59, 104
Wells, H.G., 282
West, Rebecca, 233-234, 259, 260-261, 263
West, Nigel, 18, 20, 39, 50, 54, 59, 63, 73, 74, 117, 131, 162, 163, 164, 173, 190, 208, 212, 213-216, 222, 230, 232, 234, 241, 242, 244, 246, 252, 254
Wheatley, Dennis, 187
White, Dick,
  acknowledges lead on Fuchs, 253
  agrees to intercepts on Fuchs & Peierls, 253
  appointed Director-General of MI5, 284
  appointed Director-General of SIS, 272
  approves Trevor-Roper's assessment of Philby, 42
  assumes responsibility for Krivitsky, 66-67
  blames Beaverbrook, 264
  Burgess introduced to, 100
  claims ignorance of Fuchs's communism, 257-258
  concealment of evidence from FBI, 257
  conspires with Perrin, 228
  contacts Vivian over communist refugees, 180
  death, 213
  deception to FBI over Philby, 256
  'doctrine' on communists, 263
  dismisses evidence against Fuchs, 242, 243, 255, 266
  & Double-Cross System, 76
  encourages & handholds Moorehead's 'research', 229, 261, 262, 272
  feeds Shawcross for Fuchs trial, 254, 282
  first intellectual recruit to MI5, 75, 287
  friendship with Hollis, 66
  gesture in removing agents, 63
  horrified by Sillitoe's memoir, 265-266
  inappropriate coverage of Comintern, 28
  indulgence towards Fuchs, 245, 256
  informed by NSA of Fuchs's espionage, 240
  ingenuousness, 271, 286
  insensitivity to Communist threat, 36, 56, 197, 269
  interviews Philby on Moscow Plot, 106
  lack of counter-intelligence expertise, 64
  leftist sympathiser, 283
  manipulation via *The Last Temptation*?, 198
  mistrust of Krivitsky, 53
  note on Ellen Wilkinson, 28
  passive reaction to Krivitsky, 254
  possible cover-up over Long, 194
  promotion to Assistant Director, 29
  reaction to Blake's trial, 256
  rebuked by Sillitoe, 197, 256
  recruitment and rise, 19
  scorns subterfuge, 286
  sophistry over recruiting Blunt, 183, 263

supports Long, 197
suspects Philby is 'Third Man', 197
tries to preserve career, 256, 273
unwilling to dismiss communists, 243
Whomack, George, 32, 64
Wild, Noël, 76, 288
Wilkinson, Ellen,
    appointed PPS to Morrison, 187
    elected as MP, 137
    enables entry of Czech communists, 174, 180
    frustrates MI5, 12, 43
    helps members of KPD, 174, 252
    lover of Herbert Morrison, 28
    lover of Otto Katz, 27-28
    possible backlash from, 63
    supporter of Otto Katz, 26, 28, 171
    underestimated by MI5, 28
Wilson, Horace, 102
Wilson, Peter, 73
Winterbotham, F. W., 84, 89
Wolkoff, Anna, 190-191
Woolwich Arsenal, 6, 10, 26, 30, 32, 35, 36
Wright, Peter, 141, 143-144, 162, 191, 193, 197, 215
Wynn, Arthur, 117

Y
Yalta Agreements, 131, 138
Yezhov, Nikolai, 52, 67, 71, 152

Z
Z Organisation, 251
Zionism, 95, 124-126, 129, 142, 144, 159, 278

June 23rd, 1941.

ML LAD   MAR   2019